STUDY GUIDE

for

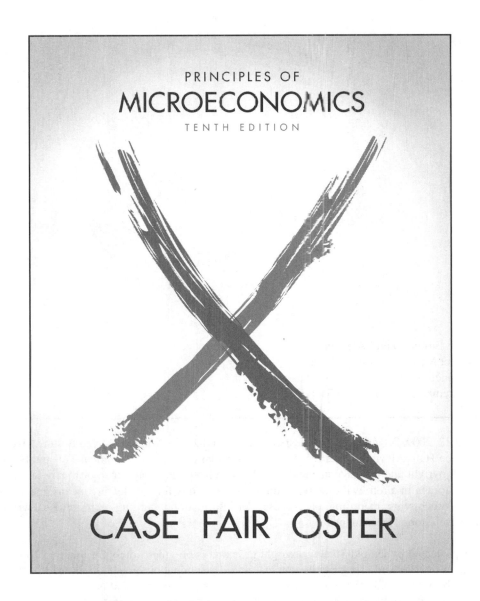

PRINCIPLES OF
MICROECONOMICS
TENTH EDITION

CASE FAIR OSTER

THOMAS M. BEVERIDGE
DURHAM TECHNICAL COMMUNITY COLLEGE

Pearson Prentice Hall

Boston San Francisco New York
London Toronto Sydney Tokyo Singapore Madrid
Mexico City Munich Paris Cape Town Hong Kong Montreal

AVP/Executive Editor: David Alexander
Editorial Project Manager: Lindsey Sloan
Associate Production Project Manager: Alison Eusden
Senior Manufacturing Buyer: Carol Melville

Pearson Prentice Hall™ is a trademark of Pearson Education, Inc.

Prentice Hall
is an imprint of

www.pearsonhighered.com

1 2 3 4 5 6 EB 15 14 13 12 11

ISBN-13: 978-0-13-138890-1
ISBN-10: 0-13-138890-8

Contents

Preface

This Study Guide has been developed to accompany *Principles of Microeconomics* by Karl Case, Ray Fair and Sharon Oster. For students using Case, Fair and Oster's *Principles of Economics* (Chapters 1–36), the corresponding chapter and page numbers appear in brackets. When referring to specific pages, the *Microeconomics* reference is given first. I have devised this Guide to help you as you learn the concepts that are presented in the text; if used consistently throughout your course, this Guide can enable you to master the material in what is likely to be your first economics course. In addition, you'll be given opportunities to learn how to apply these concepts in a variety of situations. Most economists stress the need to develop competence in three major areas—the application of economic concepts to real-world situations, the interpretation of graphs, and the analysis of numerical problems. This Guide gives you practice in developing these important skills.

I believe that learning how to apply concepts to our world creates a better and more long-lasting understanding of the material than mere memorization of those concepts. A reasonable goal for a noneconomics major is to have absorbed enough insight to understand the economic content of an article in a publication like the *Wall Street Journal*.

STUDY GUIDE CONTENTS

The Study Guide contains one chapter for each corresponding chapter in the textbook. In general, each chapter has two large sections and an Answers and Solutions section.

- The *Objectives* section tells you what you should be able to accomplish after you've studied the material.

  It gives a summary of the chapter's important ideas. Each point is followed by some multiple-choice questions so that you can monitor how well you're understanding the concepts. You'll find some applications and examples, along with specific learning tips, comments, and "helpful hints." Concepts that may prove particularly troublesome are covered in the Objectives section. Many of the "tricks" and memory aids have been suggested to me by students. In most chapters I've also included a *Brain Teaser* related to the concepts to be covered in that chapter—an issue for you to chew over while learning the concepts. Also included are *Economics in Practice* features, extending the practice features presented in the textbook.

- The *Practice Test* section contains *Multiple-Choice Questions* and *Application Questions*.

  These questions provide opportunities to practice the skills—graphing, numerical analysis, and application of concepts—presented in the text. Go through this section thoroughly.
  These exercises give you an opportunity to try your hand at using economic principles and practices—often in fairly complex situations. Complete the problem sets in the textbook as well. Many of the *Multiple-Choice Questions* are quite tough. Think of each multiple-choice question as four true-false statements; don't just decide on the one "right" answer—determine why the other three options are wrong.

- The *Answers and Solutions* feature numerical and graphical solutions. Be aware, though, that real-world analysis is much more difficult to condense into such simple forms.

The textbook is divided into several parts. I've provided a Comprehensive Review Test for each part of the textbook. If you have problems with any of the questions on the review test, treat it as a red light; go back and review that material before proceeding.

STUDY RECOMMENDATIONS

I recommend the following procedure for using this Guide to improve your effective understanding and use of both the key principles and practices from the text.

1. Read the textbook chapter. There is no substitute for this step! Ideally, you should do this *before* the material is presented in class; in any case, *don't* wait until the day before your professor has scheduled a test! Use the *Objectives* section of the Guide to both identify the key issues and to test your knowledge.

2. Attend class regularly! In study after study, researchers have shown that regularity of class attendance is the single best predictor of performance.

3. Now that you're acquainted with the material, use the *Learning Tips* to polish your understanding.

4. Complete the practice sections to test your ability to utilize key concepts. If you fail to complete an exercise correctly, even after having seen the answers, reread the text. If you're still stuck, ask your professor for clarification.

5. Before a scheduled examination, read the *Objectives* sections for review.

6. Before a scheduled examination, do the relevant Comprehensive Review Test.

With a conscientious and consistent use of this Guide, you can improve both your understanding of economics and your ability to use and apply the concepts contained in this field of study. Learning can be interesting, as well as enjoyable.

This Guide has been written with the hope that, after the final exam, it will have helped you to gain a better understanding of both economic issues and analysis, and the exciting and challenging concerns that we must address in our contemporary world.

Best wishes to you with your study of economics. I hope that you will find it to be a rewarding and worthwhile experience, and that this Guide will stimulate you in your endeavors.

Please send any comments, brain teasers, or suggestions about this study guide to my e-mail address: scotecon@mindspring.com.

Thomas Beveridge
Hillsborough, North Carolina

Acknowledgments

I am grateful to the many students whose questions through the years have given me a better insight into the difficulties that arise when approaching microeconomics for the first time. The practice material included in this Guide springs largely from such "after class" discussions.

The efforts of reviewers and other correspondents have added much to the quality of the final product. Lindsey Sloan and Melissa Pellerano of Prentice Hall deserve credit for keeping things moving smoothly. Needless to say, any remaining *lapsi calami* are my responsibility.

This Guide is dedicated to the memory of my parents, Pam (my long-suffering wife of over 30 years who drew the diagrams and orchestrated the formatting), Andrew (our own "micro" economist, who did much to disrupt its production), and to the dogs and cats, for whom all lunches are free.

1
The Scope and Method of Economics

Chapter Objectives

1. Define economics.
2. State four reasons for studying economics.
3. Distinguish between the concepts of opportunity cost and marginal cost.
4. Define market efficiency in terms of profit opportunities.
5. Make clear the difference between microeconomic and macroeconomic concerns.
6. Distinguish between positive economics and normative economics.
7. Explain the value of the *ceteris paribus* assumption within the context of economic modeling.
8. State the fallacies discussed in the text, give examples, and explain *why* such statements are fallacious.
9. State and explain the four criteria used to assess the outcomes of economic policy.
10. Construct and interpret both graphs and linear equations.

Much of this chapter is devoted to setting out the framework of economics. Don't be overwhelmed and don't try to remember it all. Chapter 1 is simply a good place to *gather together* this information, which will be dealt with more fully as the chapters go by.

BRAIN TEASER: An increasing number of basketball players move directly to the NBA draft without graduating from college. Some players even go to the NBA straight from high school. LeBron James, the first pick in the NBA draft of 2003, was one of the first to make such a move, signing a three-year, $12.96 million contract with the Cleveland Cavaliers. He also signed a $90 million endorsement deal with Nike. For LeBron James, what was the opportunity cost of choosing to go directly to the NBA, given that he was eligible for college?

SOLUTION: The answer to this and subsequent brain teasers will be found after our discussion of the learning objectives, and before the Practice Tests.

Objective 1

Define Economics.

Because of conditions imposed by nature and the choices previously made by society, resources are scarce. Economics studies how we choose to use these resources to best satisfy society's unlimited wants. In a sense, economics is the "scientific study of rational choice." (page 1)

Practice

1. Which one of the following best describes the study of economics? Economics studies
    (a) how businesses can make profits.
    (b) how the government controls the economy and how people earn a living.
    (c) how society uses its scarce resources to satisfy its unlimited desires.
    (d) the allocation of income among different sectors of the economy.

    ANSWER: (c) All of the options represent aspects of the study of economics. However, the most general statement is given in Option (c)—economics is the study of choice. ■

Objective 2

State four reasons for studying economics.

A study of economics helps one to learn a way of thinking, to understand society, to understand global affairs, and to be an informed citizen. Essential to the economic way of thinking is the concept of "opportunity cost"—choices involve forgoing some options. Accordingly, the applicability of the economic way of thinking is very extensive. (page 2)

Objective 3

Distinguish between the concepts of opportunity cost and marginal cost.

"Marginal" is a frequently used term in economics that is important to understand right away. "Marginal" means "additional" or "extra." "Marginal cost," then, means "additional cost."

Suppose you buy a nonreturnable, nontransferable ticket to the zoo for $10. This is not an additional cost. You've paid whether or not you visit the zoo.

Let's change the example a little. Suppose you win a free admission to the zoo and decide to go this Saturday. The trip is not entirely free, however. You still have to bear some costs—travel, for example. There is certainly an additional cost (caused by the trip to the zoo). It is a *marginal cost*. Suppose you always buy lunch on Saturdays. The cost of lunch is not a marginal cost since you'd have bought lunch on Saturday, whether or not you went to the zoo. The cost of lunch is not contingent on the trip to the zoo— it's not an extra cost.

If wants exceed the resources to satisfy those wants, choices must be made and some alternatives must be forgone. If you choose to visit the zoo this Saturday, the *opportunity cost* is the value of the activity you would have undertaken instead—that is, the next most-preferred activity. Perhaps it might be playing a round of golf or studying for a big economics test. The opportunity cost of the trip to the zoo is the value you attach to that *one* activity you would otherwise have chosen. (page 2)

Opportunity Cost and Marginalism: The "big concept" in this chapter is *opportunity cost*, with *marginalism* and *efficiency* running a close second and third. You'll see all three of these concepts repeatedly throughout the textbook. For practice on the concept of opportunity cost, try Application Questions 4 and 6 below in this chapter. For practice on marginal thinking, look at Application Question 7.

LEARNING TIP: Any time you make a choice where one alternative is chosen over others, remember that an opportunity cost is involved.◀

Practice

2. Your opportunity cost of attending college does not include
   (a) the money you spend on meals while at college.
   (b) your tuition.
   (c) the money you spend on traveling between home and college.
   (d) the income you could have earned if you'd been employed full-time.

   ANSWER: (a) You would have bought food whether or not you were at college. All the other expenses occur solely because of attending college.

3. _____ may be defined as the extra cost associated with an action.
   (a) Marginal cost
   (b) Operational cost
   (c) Opportunity cost
   (d) Action cost

   ANSWER: (a) Refer to page 3. Marginalism is a fundamental tool of economic analysis.

4. Jean owns a French restaurant—*La Crème*. Simply to operate this week, he must pay rent, taxes, wages, food costs, and so on. These operating costs amount to $1,000 per week. This evening, a diner arrives and orders a bottle of Château Neuf du Pape wine to go with her meal. Jean has none on hand and sends out to Wine World for a bottle. It costs $20, and Jean in turn charges his guest $30. Which of the following is true for Jean?
   (a) The marginal cost of the wine is $20.
   (b) The marginal cost of the wine is $30.
   (c) The efficiency cost of the meal is $1,020.
   (d) The efficiency cost of the meal is $1,030.

   ANSWER: (a) The up-front expense is $1,000. The extra cost that Jean bears for buying the wine is $20. "Efficiency cost" is not a real term. ■

ECONOMICS IN PRACTICE: Your textbook offers (page 6), as an example of "economics in practice" for this chapter, the case of Apple's iPod. Where is it manufactured? This is a more difficult question to answer than it might at first appear. Our northern neighbor and most important trading partner, Canada, imports 34 percent of its merchandise. Although the United States imports only 15 percent of its overall production, most of the goods that you buy contain "foreign content." Can you think of any goods that are produced purely domestically? Of course, we don't buy only tangible goods. What else do we buy? Are those other items more likely to be domestically produced and, if so, why?

ANSWER: Agricultural produce, perhaps bought at a farmers' market, is (almost by definition) "home-grown." The labor used to harvest the crop domestically may be foreign, as may other factors used in production, such as oil or fertilizer. Goods frequently have high levels of foreign content, but this is less true of services. Although your computer support may originate in India, your hairdresser, car mechanic, or accountant offer services with a high domestic content. Services are more likely to have a relatively high domestic content because it's usually more difficult to transport services than goods.

Objective 4

Define market efficiency in terms of profit opportunities.

The rapid elimination of profit opportunities is a signal that a market is operating efficiently. The stock market is a good example of this. If a firm's stock is priced "too low," increased bidding will drive the price higher, eliminating the excess profits. At a farmers' market, Farmer Brown may charge $1.20 for a dozen eggs, although the going rate is $1.00. She might make excess profits for a while, but this will not persist in an efficient market. Sustained high profits indicate the presence of an inefficient market. (page 3)

Objective 5

Make clear the difference between microeconomic and macroeconomic concerns.

Economics is divided into two broad parts. *Microeconomics* focuses on the operation of individual markets and the choices of individual economic units (firms and households). *Macroeconomics* deals with broad economic variables such as national production, total consumer spending, and overall price movements. Economics also contains a number of subfields, such as international economics, labor economics, and industrial organization. (page 8)

Practice

5. **Macroeconomics** approaches the study of economics from the viewpoint of
    (a)   individual consumers.
    (b)   the government.
    (c)   the entire economy.
    (d)   the operation of specific markets.

    ANSWER: (c) Macroeconomics looks at the big picture—the entire economy.

6. **Microeconomics** approaches the study of economics from the viewpoint of the
    (a)   entire economy.
    (b)   government.
    (c)   operation of specific markets.
    (d)   stock market.

    ANSWER: (c) Microeconomics examines what is happening with individual economic units (households and firms) and how they interact in specific markets.

7. Which of the following is most appropriately a microeconomic issue?
    (a)   The study of the relationship between the unemployment rate and the inflation rate
    (b)   The forces determining the price level in an individual market
    (c)   The determination of total output in the economy
    (d)   The aggregate behavior of all decision-making units in the economy

    ANSWER: (b) Microeconomics examines what is happening with individual economic units (households and firms) and how they interact in specific markets. ∎

Objective 6

Distinguish between positive economics and normative economics.

Economists classify issues as either positive or normative. Positive questions explore the behavior of the economy and its participants without judging whether the behavior is good or bad. *Positive economics* collects data that describe economic phenomena (descriptive economics) and constructs testable (cause-and-effect) theories to explain those phenomena (economic theory). *Normative economic questions* evaluate the results of personal behavior and explore whether the outcomes might be improved. (page 9)

Practice

8.   A difference between positive statements and normative statements is that
     (a)   positive statements are true by definition.
     (b)   only positive statements are subject to empirical verification.
     (c)   economists use positive statements while politicians use normative statements when discussing economic matters.
     (d)   positive statements require value judgments.

     ANSWER: (b)   A positive statement is not necessarily true by definition and can be disproved by empirical verification. ■

Objective 7

Explain the value of the *ceteris paribus* assumption within the context of economic modeling.

Economists (and other scientists) construct models—formal statements of relationships between variables of interest—that simplify and abstract from reality. Graphs, words, or equations can be used to express a model. In testing the relationships between variables within a model, it is convenient to assume *ceteris paribus*, that all other variables have been held constant. (page 11)

   Models focus on the most essential elements under examination. Distracting real-world details are set aside. Many factors may have affected your decision to buy Case, Fair and Oster's textbook for example—theory attempts to isolate the *key* factors.

Practice

9.   "An increase in the price of shampoo will cause less shampoo to be demanded, *ceteris paribus*." *Ceteris paribus* means that
     (a)   there is a negative relationship between the price and quantity demanded of shampoo.
     (b)   the price of shampoo is the only factor that can affect the amount of shampoo demanded.
     (c)   other factors may affect the amount of shampoo demanded, but they are assumed to be constant in this analysis.
     (d)   the price of shampoo is equal for all buyers.

     ANSWER: (c)   The price of shampoo is equal for all buyers, and there may be a negative relationship between the price and quantity of shampoo demanded, but *ceteris paribus* means that any other factors that may affect the amount of shampoo demanded are assumed to be constant. ■

ECONOMICS IN PRACTICE: One of the newer areas of economic research involves experiments concerning transactions and trust, as discussed in your textbook (page 9). A further aspect of transactions and trust is rationality (or its lack). A recent experiment looked at responses to requests for assistance. Consider the following situation—what would be your response? A friend asks you to help with a task, such as changing a tire. Suppose, because you have the time and the skill to help, you are willing to oblige. Now suppose your friend asked you for the same favor but offered you $5 as a payment! Would you still be as willing to help out?

ANSWER: Research suggests that the offer of payment makes us less willing to help out a friend in need. In fact, many individuals feel insulted, even though the "reward" for helping would seem to be greater in the second case. Clearly, there's more going on in interpersonal transactions than meets the eye!

A further study, published in 2010, offers additional insight by suggesting that people at opposite ends of the financial scale respond differently to requests for charity. Poorer people tend to empathize with those in need more than the well-heeled , displaying more generosity and helpfulness. The researchers suggest that this behavior, which promotes increased trust and cooperation, bestows essential survival benefits during hard times.

Objective 8

State the fallacies discussed in the text, give examples of each, and explain *why* such statements are fallacious.

Beware false logic! The *fallacy of composition* involves the claim that what is good for one individual remains good when it happens for many. If one farmer gains by having a bumper harvest it *doesn't* mean that all farmers will gain if each has a bumper crop. The *post hoc, ergo propter hoc* fallacy occurs when we assume that an event that happens after another is caused by the first event. (page 12)

Two examples of the fallacy of composition: One person at a football game who stands up to see a good play derives a benefit, therefore all will benefit similarly if the entire crowd stands up. Running to the exit when there is a fire in a theater will increase your chances of survival, therefore, in a fire, we should all run for the exit.

Practice

10.   Which of the following is **not** an example of the fallacy of composition?
   (a)   Jane leaves work at 4:00 each day and avoids the rush-hour traffic at 5:00. Therefore, if businesses regularly closed at 4:00, all commuters would avoid the rush-hour traffic.
   (b)   John stands up so that he can see an exciting football play. Therefore, if the entire crowd stands up when there is an exciting play, all spectators will get a better view.
   (c)   Because society benefits from the operation of efficient markets, IBM will benefit if markets become more efficient.
   (d)   Because Mary, on her own, can escape from a burning building by running outside, individuals in a crowded movie theater are advised to run outside when there is a fire.

   ANSWER: (c) This example is arguing from the general to the specific. The fallacy of composition argues from the specific to the general. ∎

Objective 9

State and explain the four criteria used to assess the outcomes of economic policy.

Economists construct and test models to aid policy making. Policy makers generally judge proposals in terms of efficiency, equity (fairness), growth, and stability. (page 13)

Practice

11.   The nation of Arboc claims to have achieved an equitable distribution of income among its citizens. On visiting Arboc, we would expect to find that
   (a)   each citizen receives the same amount of income.
   (b)   Arbocali residents believe that the distribution of income is fair.
   (c)   Arbocali residents believe that the distribution of income is equal.
   (d)   each citizen receives the amount of income justified by the value of his or her contribution to production.

   ANSWER: (b) Whether or not the distribution of income is equitable depends on what Arbocali citizens believe to be fair.

Use the following information to answer the next two questions. Nicola and Alexander each have some dollars and some apples. Nicola values a pound of apples at $3 whereas Alexander values a pound of apples at S1.

12.   In which of the following cases has an allocatively efficient trade taken place?
    (a)   The market price of apples is $3 per pound. Nicola sells apples to Alexander.
    (b)   The market price of apples is $1 per pound. Nicola sells apples to Alexander.
    (c)   The market price of apples is $2 per pound. Nicola sells apples to Alexander.
    (d)   The market price of apples is $2 per pound. Alexander sells apples to Nicola.

    ANSWER: (d) When the market price of apples is $2 per pound and Alexander is the seller, he gains $1. Nicola also gains because she receives goods she values at $3, for a payment of only $2.

13.   In which of the following cases has an allocatively efficient trade **not** taken place?
    (a)   The market price of apples is $3 per pound. Alexander sells apples to Nicola.
    (b)   The market price of apples is $1.50 per pound. Alexander sells apples to Nicola.
    (c)   The market price of apples is $1.50 per pound. Nicola sells apples to Alexander.
    (d)   The market price of apples is $2 per pound. Alexander sells apples to Nicola.

    ANSWER: (c) An efficient trade can occur only when some participant is better off and no participant is worse off (or if the gainer can adequately compensate the loser). In Option (a), Alexander gains $2 and Nicola does not lose. In Option (b), Nicola and Alexander both gain. In Option (d), Alexander and Nicola both gain. In Option (c), Alexander gains 50¢ but Nicola loses $1.50. ■

Objective 10 (Appendix)

Construct and interpret graphs and linear equations.

Economic graphs depict the relationship between variables. A curve with a "rising" (positive) slope indicates that as one variable increases, so does the other. A curve with a "falling" (negative) slope indicates that as one variable increases in value, the other decreases in value. Slope is easily measured by the "rise over run" formula—the extent of vertical change divided by the extent of horizontal change. (page 17)

LEARNING TIP: It is a natural tendency to shy away from graphs—they may seem threatening—but this is a mistake. To work with economic concepts, you must master all the tools in the economist's tool kit. Economists almost automatically begin to scribble diagrams when asked to explain ideas, and you'll need to learn how to use this tool of the trade. In economics, graphs often feature financial variables like "price," "the interest rate," or "income." Usually the dependent variable is placed on the vertical axis and the independent variable on the horizontal axis. When graphing economic variables, it's a pretty safe bet that the *financial* variable will go on the vertical axis every time. Application Questions 9 and 10 and the Graphing Tutorial that follow offer some graphing practice. ◀

LEARNING TIP: Examine the graphs you see in the daily newspaper or news magazines that accompany economics-based articles. It's common to find examples of deceptive graphs, especially when variables are being compared over time. A graph comparing, say, the difference between government spending and tax revenues can be quite misleading if the vertical axis does not start at zero. ◀

Practice

Use the following diagram to answer the next four questions.

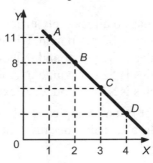

14.   In the diagram, the slope of the line is
    (a)   positive and variable.
    (b)   positive and constant.
    (c)   negative and variable.
    (d)   negative and constant.

    ANSWER: (d) The diagram shows a straight line, and straight lines have a constant slope. Visually, or by using the "rise over run" formula, the relationship is negative because as one variable increases in value the other decreases in value.

15.   The slope of line between Point *A* and Point *B* is
    (a)   3.
    (b)   1/3.
    (c)   −3.
    (d)   −1/3.

    ANSWER: (c) Use the "rise over run" formula. The rise is −3 (from 11 to 8) and the run is +1 (from 1 to 2).

16.   At Point *D*, the value of *Y* is
    (a)   −3.
    (b)   3.
    (c)   5.
    (d)   2.

    ANSWER: (d) As *X* "steps up" in value by 1, *Y* "steps down" in value by 3. At Point *B*, *X* has a value of 2 and *Y* has a value of 8. Moving to Point *D*, *X* increases by 2 and *Y* decreases by 6, from 8 to 2.

17.   In the diagram, when the line reaches the vertical (*Y*) axis the value of *Y* will be
    (a)   3.
    (b)   8.
    (c)   11.
    (d)   14.

    ANSWER: (d) As *X* "steps down" in value by 1, *Y* "steps up" in value by 3. At Point *A*, *X* has a value of 1 and *Y* has a value of 11. *X* decreases by 1 and *Y* increases by 3, from 11 to 14. ■

BRAIN TEASER SOLUTION: James's opportunity cost was the value of the next most-preferred alternative to going to the NBA. We might assume that that choice would be college. Was it a sensible choice for him? In fact, it's a no-brainer. Taking only the three-year contract amount of $12.96 million, and dividing by 40 (earning years), James would have to have averaged $324,000 per year from his college degree to match his earnings. You should note that the present discounted value of those earnings decades into the future will be significantly less than $324,000. Also, we are ignoring any earnings James might have made in addition to his player's contract, such as the Nike endorsement or income from future contracts. So, not only is LeBron James a talented basketball player, he has a solid grasp of economics!

PRACTICE TEST

I. MULTIPLE-CHOICE QUESTIONS

Select the option that provides the single best answer.

_____ 1. Local farmers reduce the price of their tomatoes at the farmers' market. The price of corn is 30¢ per ear. A passing economist theorizes that, *ceteris paribus*, buyers will purchase more tomatoes than before. Which of the following is TRUE? The economist is
    (a) implying that the price of tomatoes will fall even further.
    (b) assuming that the price of corn will remain at 30¢ per ear.
    (c) assuming that tomatoes are of a better quality than before.
    (d) implying that corn is of a poorer quality than before.

_____ 2. Which of the following is **not** given in the textbook as a criterion for judging the results of economic policy?
    (a) Economic stability
    (b) Employment
    (c) Efficiency
    (d) Equity

_____ 3. Economic growth may occur if
    (a) more machines become available.
    (b) more workers become available.
    (c) workers become more efficient.
    (d) All of the above are correct.

_____ 4. Economics is the study of how
    (a) scarce resources are used to satisfy unlimited wants.
    (b) we choose to use unlimited resources.
    (c) limitless resources are used to satisfy scarce wants.
    (d) society has no choices.

_____ 5. The opportunity cost of Choice X can be defined as the
    (a) cheapest alternative to Choice X.
    (b) most highly valued alternative to Choice X.
    (c) price paid to obtain X.
    (d) most highly priced alternative to Choice X.

_____ 6. In economics, efficiency means that
(a) income is distributed equally among all citizens.
(b) there is a low level of inflation and full unemployment of economic resources.
(c) total productivity is increasing at a constant and equal rate within each sector of the economy.
(d) the economy is producing those goods and services that citizens desire and is doing so at the least possible cost.

_____ 7. Which of the following statements is true?
(a) Microeconomics studies consumer behavior, whereas macroeconomics studies producer behavior.
(b) Microeconomics studies producer behavior, whereas macroeconomics studies consumer behavior.
(c) Microeconomics studies behavior of individual households and firms, whereas macroeconomics studies national aggregates.
(d) Microeconomics studies inflation and opportunity costs, whereas macro-economics studies unemployment and marginal costs.

_____ 8. Which of the following statements is true?
(a) There is a positive relationship between the price of a product and the quantity demanded.
(b) There is a positive relationship between the number of umbrellas bought and the amount of rainfall.
(c) There is a negative relationship between height and weight.
(d) There is a negative relationship between sales of ice cream and noonday temperatures.

_____ 9. Oliver Sudden discovers that if he cuts the price of his tomatoes at the farmers' market, his sales revenue increases. Expecting similar results, all the other tomato sellers follow his example. They are guilty of committing
(a) the fallacy of composition.
(b) the fallacy of *post hoc, ergo propter hoc*.
(c) the fallacy of correlation.
(d) *ceteris paribus*.

_____ 10. The quantity of six-packs of Quite Lite beer demanded per week (Q_d) in Hometown is described by the following equation:

$$Q_d = 400 - 100P,$$

where P (in dollars) is the price of a six-pack. This equation predicts that
(a) 300 six-packs will be bought this week.
(b) a $1 rise in price will cause 100 more six-packs to be bought this week.
(c) 300 six-packs will be bought per $100 this week.
(d) a 50¢ rise in price will cause 50 fewer six-packs to be bought this week.

_____ 11.   The *ceteris paribus* assumption is used to
  (a) make economic theory more realistic.
  (b) make economic analysis more realistic.
  (c) avoid the fallacy of composition.
  (d) focus analysis on the effect of a single factor.

Use the following diagram below to answer the next four questions.

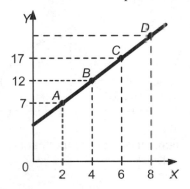

_____ 12.   In the preceding diagram, the slope of the line is
  (a) positive and variable.
  (b) positive and constant.
  (c) negative and variable.
  (d) negative and constant.

_____ 13.   In the preceding diagram, the slope of the line between Point A and Point B is
  (a) 5/2.
  (b) 2/5.
  (c) −2/5.
  (d) −5/2.

_____ 14.   In the preceding diagram, at Point D, the value of Y is
  (a) 5.
  (b) 8.
  (c) 19.5.
  (d) 22.

_____ 15.   In the preceding diagram, when the line reaches the vertical (Y) axis the value of Y will be
  (a) 2.
  (b) 5/2.
  (c) 7.
  (d) 12.

Use the following diagrams to answer the next four questions.

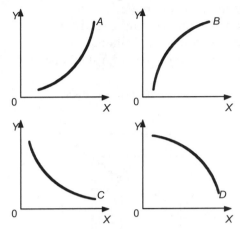

_____ 16. Of the four curves, which curve has a slope that is negative and decreasing?
(a) A
(b) B
(c) C
(d) D

_____ 17. Of the four curves, which curve has a slope that is positive and increasing?
(a) A
(b) B
(c) C
(d) D

_____ 18. Of the four curves, which curve has a slope that is positive and decreasing?
(a) A
(b) B
(c) C
(d) D

_____ 19. Of the four curves, which curve appears to be described by the equation $y = x^2$?
(a) A
(b) B
(c) C
(d) D

_____ 20. During the debate about balancing the federal government's budget, it was proposed that Medicaid benefits be reduced. This proposal was criticized because low-income families (who receive Medicaid) would spend a higher percentage of their income on medical services than high-income families would spend. This argument was based on concerns about
(a) economic growth.
(b) efficiency.
(c) economic stability.
(d) equity.

_____ 21.   The Channel Tunnel, linking the United Kingdom and France, was originally planned to cost $100 million. After work had begun and the two excavators were under the English Channel, with $70 million already spent, the estimate of the total bill was revised to $150 million. At this point the marginal cost of completion was best estimated as
   (a) $30 million.
   (b) $50 million.
   (c) $70 million.
   (d) $80 million.

II. APPLICATION QUESTIONS

1.   The small nation of Smogland is unhappily situated in a valley surrounded by mountains. Smogland's Secretary of the Environment has determined that there are 4,000 cars in operation, each of which pollutes the air. In fact, Smogland's air is so unhealthy that it is rated as "hazardous." If emission controls costing $50 per car are introduced, the air quality will improve to a rating of "fair." A survey has revealed that of the 40,000 inhabitants, 10,000 would value the air quality improvement at $5 each and the other 30,000 would value it at $7 each. The Secretary of the Environment has asked you to analyze the issue and make a recommendation. Should emission controls be introduced?

2.   Refer to the following diagram, which plots the inflation rate and unemployment rate.

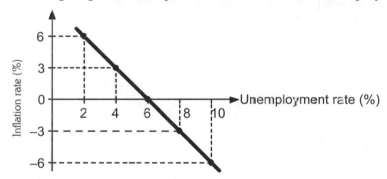

   (a)   Construct a table from the data presented in the diagram.

   (b)   Calculate the slope of the line.

   (c)   What is the inflation rate when the unemployment rate is 9 percent?

   (d)   What is the inflation rate when the unemployment rate is 5 percent?

3.   What are some elements of the opportunity cost of "clean" air? In total, the "cost" of cleaner air increases as we remove more and more pollution. Does the extra (marginal) cost of cleaner air increases as we progressively remove pollution? Graph the behavior of "extra cost" (vertical axis) and "cleanness of air" (horizontal axis).

4.   Suppose that the opportunity cost of attending today's economics class is study time for a math test. By not studying you will lose 15 points on that test. Attending the economics class will increase your future economics test score by no more than three points. Was your choice—to attend the economics class—rational?

5.   Just before your senior year, you have a summer internship in a bank.. You are "noticed" and are offered a full-time position, with a salary of $35,000 a year. A rival bank, keen to attract you, offers you $37,000 for a similar position. After much thought, you decide to return to college to complete your economics degree. Based on the information given, what was the opportunity cost of your decision?

   If you had chosen one of the banking jobs instead of resuming your studies, how could you have explained your decision to your parents, who would have pointed out that you would have "wasted" three years of college?

6.   Choose a local natural resource with which you are familiar, e.g., an acre of farmland or a nearby lake.
   (a)   List three alternative uses for your chosen raw material.
   (b)   Choose one of the three uses. What is the opportunity cost of this use? Should you include the cost of clean-up (if this is appropriate) following use?
   (c)   Is the resource renewable or not? If not, should this be factored into your calculations?
   (d)   Describe how your community has chosen to use the resource so far, if at all. Who and what have determined that choice?

7.   You're offered three deals, each of which will give you $11 in return for $8. Your profit will be $3 in each case. *Deal A* is a straight swap—$11 for $8.

   Deal B involves four steps and you can quit at any point.
   Step 1. $5 in exchange for $2
   Step 2. $3 for $2
   Step 3. $2 for $2
   Step 4. $1 for $2
   What would you do? Go all the way through the four steps and collect a total of $3 profit? A better solution, stopping after two steps, would yield $4.

   Deal C also involves four steps.
   Step 1. $4 in exchange for $1
   Step 2. $4 for $2
   Step 3. $2 for $2
   Step 4. $1 for $3
   Would you collect your $3 profit or stop after two steps and gain $5?

   Moral: If you assess the effects of extra (marginal) steps, you can raise your profits above $3. Without examining each step, the chance of greater profits would have been missed.

8.   Using your intuition, graph each of the following relationships in the space below.

   (a)   Height and weight of adult females.

   (b)   Height and weight of adult males (on the same graph).

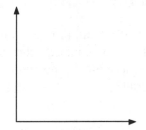

   (c)   Do these lines have a positive slope or negative slope?

(d)   Have you drawn the relationships differently? If so, why? By referring to your own observations, you have constructed a model!

(e)   Which factors have you "held constant"?

(f)   (i)   In the space following, sketch the relationship between the price of California wine and the consumption of California wine. Use your intuition.

        (ii)   According to your theory and your diagram, is there any point, even if wine is free, at which consumers will not wish to buy any more wine?

        (iii)   Will the total number of dollars spent on wine remain the same at every price level?

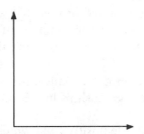

(g)   (i)   In the space following, sketch the relationship between the interest rate and house purchases. Use your intuition.

        (ii)   According to your theory and your graph, is there any interest rate that will completely deter house purchases?

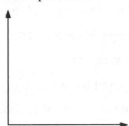

9.   Suppose there is a relationship between two variables, X (on the horizontal axis) and Y (on the vertical axis), and that you have collected the following data.

X	2	4	6	8	10
Y	5	6	7	8	9

(a)   Do we have a positive or a negative relationship?

(b)   Describe (in words) what these data would look like graphically.

(c)   Calculate the slope (rise over run) of the line.

(d)   Graph the relationship here.

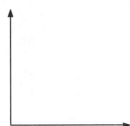

10. You have a new brand of low-alcohol, reduced-calorie beer, "Quite Lite," that you intend to market. What variables do you think will be important in determining the amount of Quite Lite that people will want to buy? You should be able to develop a fairly long list of variables. You have begun to construct an economic model of consumption behavior. Now prune down your list to include, say, the five most important variables.

    Now work out in which way each variable will impact the consumption of Quite Lite. You should be able to work out a specific cause-and-effect pattern in each case. A higher price for Quite Lite should cause less to be bought. A price hike for competing beers should increase the demand for Quite Lite. Note that not all variables have been included in the model; an all-inclusive list would (1) be cumbersome, and (2) distract from the major elements in the model. You have wielded Ockham's razor!

    The variables that you have compiled in your list will be continually changing their values. To isolate the effect of any one on the consumption of Quite Lite, you must invoke the *ceteris paribus* assumption. You might think of this as being the economic equivalent of the "standard temperature and pressure" conditions applied in the natural sciences.

    Use the model that you developed for Quite Lite beer. Putting "quantity demanded" on the horizontal axis, graph each of the relationships in the model.

11. Which of the following statements are positive and which are normative?

    (a) The moon is made of green cheese.

    (b) States to the west of the Mississippi have lower state income tax rates than states to the east have.

    (c) The federal government should be required to balance its budget.

    (d) The most serious economic problem confronting the nation is unemployment.

    (e) We should abolish the minimum wage.

    (f) We should index-link the minimum wage to the rate of price inflation.

    (g) If the federal budget deficit is reduced, then interest rates will decrease.

12. Which of the following—your campus bookstore or Amazon.com—is more likely to be efficient and why?

13. Opportunity cost may well be the biggest concept in all of economics—it's everywhere. Any time you make a choice, you choose to get something and you necessarily choose to give up the next-best alternative. Consider your Economics course. What is the opportunity cost of your course?

14. Some time ago, you bought a ticket for a concert by a local group, Saxon Violins, for $40. However, more recently, a friend invited you to a party that you'd much prefer to attend. All your efforts to sell your concert ticket have been unsuccessful. Should you go to the concert, which you've paid for, or to the party?

Practice Test SOLUTIONS

I. SOLUTIONS TO MULTIPLE-CHOICE QUESTIONS

1.   (b)   If the price of corn fell, perhaps very sharply, buyers might buy more corn and fewer tomatoes. Therefore, the economist is assuming that the price of corn is not going to change. That's what *ceteris paribus* implies.

2.   (b)   Unemployment is certainly an important economic variable, but it is not one of the criteria for evaluating the results of economic policy. Refer to page 13.

3.   (d)   Growth will occur if resources become more plentiful or more productive.

4.   (a)   Economics is about choice—how we ration scarce resources to meet limitless wants.

5.   (b)   Price is not necessarily a reliable guide to value for a particular individual. Opportunity cost is the measure of the value placed on the next most-preferred item forgone as a result of Choice *X*.

6.   (d)   Efficiency means that producers are using the least costly method of production to supply those goods that are desired by consumers.

7.   (c)   To review the micro/macro distinction, refer to page 6.

8.   (b)   There is a *negative* relationship between price and quantity demanded, so A is incorrect. The greater the rainfall, the larger the number of umbrellas bought.

9.   (a)   Just because an action taken by one individual produces a given outcome, the same action taken by many need not.

10.   (d)   Put in numbers. If $P = \$2$, then Qd will equal $400 - 100(2)$, or 200. If the price rises by 50¢, then Qd will equal $400 - 100(2.5)$, or 150—a fall of 50.

11.   (d)   The *ceteris paribus* assumption freezes the effect of all but one change so that the effects of that change may be examined.

12.   (b)   The diagram shows a straight line—straight lines have a constant slope. Visually, or by using the "rise over run" formula, the relationship is positive because, as one variable increases in value, the other also increases in value.

13.   (a)   Use the "rise over run" formula. The rise is +5 (*Y* goes from 7 to 12) and the run is +2 (*X* goes from 2 to 4).

14.   (d)   As *X* "steps up" in value by 2, *Y* "steps up" in value by 5. At Point *C*, *X* has a value of 6 and *Y* has a value of 17. Moving to Point *D*, *X* rises by 2 and *Y* rises by 5, from 17 to 22.

15.   (a)   As *X* "steps down" in value by 2, *Y* "steps down" in value by 5. At Point *A*, *X* has a value of 2 and *Y* has a value of 7. *X* decreases by 2 and *Y* decreases by 5, from 7 to 2.

16.   (c)   The relationship shows that as X increases in value, Y decreases in value—a negative relationship. The slope is decreasing because, as X increases in value, the decrease in the value of Y becomes smaller and smaller.

17.   (a)   The relationship shows that as X increases in value, Y also increases in value—a positive relationship. The slope is increasing because, as X increases in value, the increase in the value of Y becomes larger and larger.

18.   (b)   The relationship shows that as X increases in value, Y also increases in value—a positive relationship. The slope is decreasing because, as X increases in value, the increase in the value of Y becomes smaller and smaller.

19.   (a)   As X assumes higher values, the values of Y will increase more rapidly.

20.   (d)   For equity, read "fairness." Critics of the proposal argue that it is unfair to make poor families spend a larger part of their lower income on medical services.

21.   (d)   To complete the project would cost $80 million more than had already been spent.

II. SOLUTIONS TO APPLICATION QUESTIONS

1.   The (marginal) cost of the air quality improvement is valued at $50 \times 4,000$, or $200,000. The benefit derived from the improvement is valued at ($5 \times 10,000$) + ($7 \times 30,000$), or $260,000. Smogland should proceed with the implementation of emission controls.

2.   (a)

Unemployment Rate (%)	Inflation Rate (%)
2.0	6.0
4.0	3.0
6.0	0.0
8.0	−3.0
10.0	−6.0

(b)   Slope is −1.5.

(c)   −4.5 percent.

(d)   1.5 percent.

3.   To have cleaner (if not clean) air, we might wish to reduce emissions of cars, homes, and factories. The next most-preferred use of the resources to achieve this would be included in the opportunity cost. An initial 5 percent improvement in the quality of the air might be accomplished quite simply—perhaps by requiring more frequent car tune-ups—but progressively, the "cost" of achieving more stringent air cleanliness standards will rise. The marginal cost will increase. This will graph as an upward-sloping line that rises progressively more steeply.

4.   The answer cannot be determined given the information. This choice may well have been rational. Perhaps the three extra points will save you from flunking the economics course, whereas in the math class you are confident of making an easy "A."

5. The opportunity cost is the salary forgone—$37,000 if you had chosen the first bank. Presumably, the offer of the job at the bank was based on your abilities—some of which would have been developed while at college. That time, then, was not wasted. You could have taken the bank job and explained that the three years of college got you the internship and sufficient skills to be noticed in the first place. Also, the three college years cannot be relived—decisions should be based on the future, not the past.

6. This is an open question. The natural resource might be a river, a seam of coal, deer, a piece of waste land used as a dump, prime agricultural land, or downtown lots. The main point is that using the resource one way means that it is not available for other uses. The final part of the question may lead you into a consideration of private property rights, social pressure, and the role of the government.

7. The answer to Question 7 is included in the question.

8. (a, b)   Refer to the diagram below.

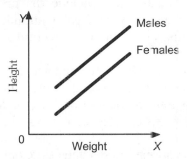

(c)   Both positive—as height increases, so does weight.

(d)   Probably the lines will be different. Perhaps, at any given height, males may weigh more than females, for example.

(e)   Race, geographical location, and age are factors that have been ignored.

(f)   (i)   Refer to the following diagram.

(ii)   Even if wine is free, consumers are likely to reach a point of satiation. This is shown on the diagram as the quantity at which the line reaches the horizontal axis.

(iii)   It depends on your demand for wine, of course, but probably not. We take up this issue in Chapter 5 of *Principles of Microeconomics*, when we consider elasticity of demand. In general, we'll find that total spending declines at high prices.

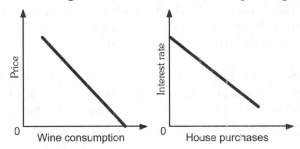

(g)   (i)   Refer to the preceding diagram.

(ii)   It depends on the demand for houses, of course, and is shown as the point at which the line reaches the vertical axis.

9.   (a)   It's a positive relationship.

(b)   The line would be "rising" to the right.

(c)   Rise over run: *Y* rises by one unit every time *X* rises by two units, so the slope is +1/2.

(d)   Refer to the following diagram.

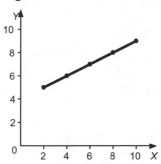

10.   Your short list of variables probably will include the price of Quite Lite, the prices of its competitors, advertising, the time of year, health attitudes, the income of potential buyers (launching a new product during an economic downturn might be difficult, for instance), and so on.

   The negative relationship you will have modeled (if not, why not?) between price and quantity demanded is called the demand curve. A movement along this curve indicates that price has changed, causing a change in the amount of beer demanded, while all other variables are held constant (*ceteris paribus*). (Keep this conclusion in mind when you read Chapter 3.)

11.   Positive statements are testable; normative statements are opinions.

(a)   Positive. A statement need not be correct to be positive.

(b)   Positive. Data can be gathered and analysis undertaken.

(c)   Normative, as signaled by the use of *should*.

(d)   Normative. This is an opinion, even during the Great Depression.

(e)   Normative. This is an opinion, as signaled by the use of *should*.

(f)   Normative. This is an opinion, as signaled by the use of *should*.

(g)   Positive. This statement can be tested.

12.   With all due respect to your campus bookstore, it is less likely to be as efficient than Amazon. Amazon is open to competition from other internet firms and it's fairly easy to make comparisons between offers from different sellers. High prices at Amazon will be penalized as customers go elsewhere. Your campus bookstore, on the other hand, may have no local competition and, with "captive" customers, it can afford to sustain high prices.

13.   Your opportunity cost is the value of the next most-preferred alternative you gave up in order to take the course. Perhaps you would have taken another course in the same time slot. Or worked. Or used the time to study. Whatever. The most-valued alternative you couldn't pursue is the opportunity cost of your Economics course.

14.   Go to the party! The $40 you paid should be irrelevant to your decision. In either case, the $40 has been spent.

Appendix

Introduction: Why a Special Section on Graphing?

You may be surprised by the amount of mathematics—geometry in particular—that you encounter in economics. Your professor introduces a new concept and quickly draws a graph to illustrate the idea—economic theory and graphs are inseparable. This union of social science and mathematical techniques can baffle some students. You may even struggle so much with the techniques that you miss the powerful insights that economics has to offer. This section is designed to help you gain both a working understanding of graphing techniques and to help you apply this knowledge to economics.

Why Are Graphs Important?

Graphs are important for several reasons. First, graphs are a compact way of conveying a large amount of information. An old adage says that "a picture is worth a thousand words." This is particularly true in economics as the movement of an economic variable over time, or the relationship between two economic variables can be quickly grasped through the use of graphs. Second, as Case, Fair and Oster mention in the Appendix to Chapter 1, economics uses quantitative (mathematical) techniques more than any other social science. Every academic discipline possesses its own "tool kit" which must be mastered in order to truly appreciate the content of the course. In an economic principles class, the primary "tool" is graphs. Third, there is a clear relationship between student success in economics, and their skill with graphs. Research on student performance indicates that of the skills that lead to success (verbal, quantitative reasoning, graphing) graphing ability is vital. Fourth, an important component of a vibrant democratic society is *economic literacy*: a basic understanding of certain central economic concepts. Both print and television journalists use the visual medium to communicate with their audience; citizens who follow current events will constantly encounter graphs. .

Why Graphs Trouble Many Students

Several factors may cause you to have difficulty with graphs. Several years may have elapsed since you completed a high school geometry course. Consequently, many graphing skills that you developed may have been forgotten. More fundamentally, while you read every day, you do not practice math every day. Therefore, most students enter an economic principles class with a stronger reading ability than a mathematical ability. Because of this, you must remember that the graphs in your textbook are not photographs worthy of only a glance, but *graphs that must be studied.*

General Tips for Studying Graphs

Here are some general tips that should assist you in developing graphing skills:

1. *Relax!* Remember that math is simply another language; graphs are just a specific form of communication.
2. When studying a graph, first identify the labels that are on the graph axes and curves. These labels are like road signs, which inform the reader.
3. Once the labels are recognized, try to understand what economic intuition lies behind the curve (e.g., the demand curve indicates that as the product price falls, the amount that consumers wish to buy increases).
4. Get into the habit of tracing the graphs that are in the text and copying the graphs into your notes.
5. *Draw, draw, draw!!!* The process of learning economics must be an active process. Graphing skills can be enhanced only by repeated attempts to graph economic concepts.

What Are Graphs?

Graphs are visual expressions of quantitative information. Economic theory attempts to establish relationships between important concepts. If the value of a concept changes, the concept is considered a *variable*. Graphs illustrate the relationship between two variables. If two variables have a *direct* (positive) relationship the value of one variable increases as the value of the other variable increases. If two variables have an *inverse* (negative) relationship, the value of one variable decreases as the value of the other variable increases.

EXAMPLE 1

As children get older, they grow taller. There exists a direct relationship between a child's age and its height.

Age	6	7	8	9	10
Height	48"	50"	52"	54"	56"

This relationship can be graphed:

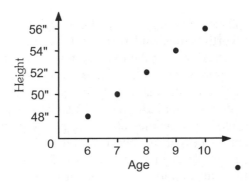

EXAMPLE 2

After attending class, sleeping, eating, and working at a part-time job, a student has seven hours that can be used for either studying or socializing. There exists an inverse relationship between time spent studying and time spent socializing.

Studying	7	5	3	1	0
Socializing	0	2	4	6	7

A graph of this relationship is shown below:

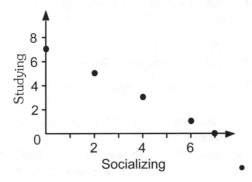

Types of Graphs

There are two types of graphs. *Descriptive* graphs relate the observed association of two variables. The graphs in Examples 1 and 2 are descriptive graphs. Newspapers often express monthly unemployment data in descriptive graphs. *Analytical* graphs convey the hypothetical relationship between two variables. The existence of association is derived from economic theory, and its accuracy is the object of economic research.

EXAMPLE 3

An understanding of both a firm's goals and constraints leads to the development of a hypothesis, which states that as wages rise, a firm would hire fewer workers. Graphically, this relationship is expressed as:

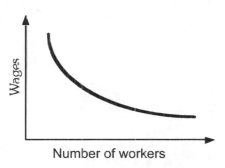

Often, the value of one variable determines the value of the other variable. In these cases, the former variable is called the *independent* variable; the latter variable is called the *dependent* variable. The independent variable is the *cause*; the dependent variable is the *effect* Normally (but not always), the independent variable is placed on the horizontal axis and the dependent variable is placed on the vertical axis.●

Drawing Graphs

Earlier, we examined the direct relationship between a child's age and its height. One would expect a direct relationship between a child's age and its weight.

EXAMPLE 4

Age	6	7	8	9	10
Weight	70 lbs	75 lbs	80 lbs	85 lbs	90 lbs

Graph this relationship on the axes below.

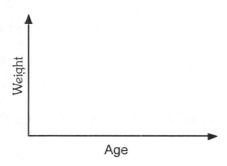

Combining the two series of data yields the following table:

Age	6	7	8	9	10
Height	48"	50"	52"	54"	56"
Weight	70 lbs	75 lbs	80 lbs	85 lbs	90 lbs

●

EXAMPLE 5

Graph the height-weight combination for each age on the axes below.

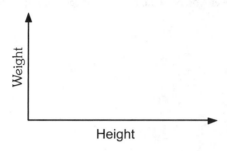

Is the relationship between height and weight direct or inverse? _____ •

EXAMPLE 6

Graph the relationship between the annual U.S. unemployment rate (*U*%) over time.

Year	1986	1987	1988	1989	1990	1991	1992	1993	1994	1995	1996	1997	1998	1999
U%	7.0	6.2	5.4	5.3	5.5	6.7	7.4	6.8	6.1	5.6	5.4	4.9	4.5	4.2

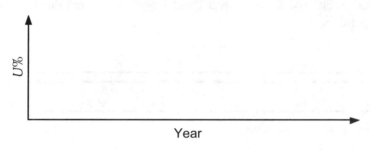

This graph, depicting the movement of one variable over time, is called a *time-series* graph. Between which years is there a direct relationship?

Between which years is there an inverse relationship? _____ •

Reading Graphs

In addition to graphing economic relationships, students must develop the skill of reading graphs.

EXAMPLE 7

Following are a time-series graph of the movement of the poverty rates for U.S. families between 1986 and 1998, and a scatter diagram indicating the association between the poverty and unemployment rates. Study both graphs and answer the following questions:

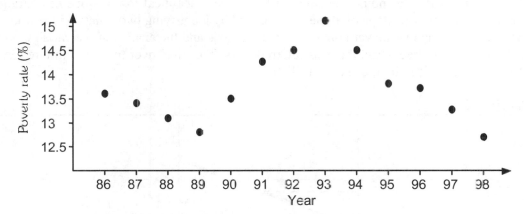

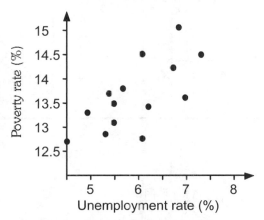

Year	1986	1987	1988	1989	1990	1991	1992	1993	1994	1995	1996	1997	1998
U%	7.0	6.2	5.5	5.3	5.5	6.7	7.4	6.8	6.1	5.6	5.4	4.9	4.5
Poverty Rate %	13.6	13.4	13.1	12.8	13.5	14.2	14.5	15.1	14.5	13.8	13.7	13.3	12.7

1. What is the poverty rate in:

(a) 1987 _____

(b) 1990 _____

(c) 1995 _____

2. What are the poverty rate/unemployment rate combinations in:

(a) 1988 _____ _____

(b) 1992 _____ _____

(c) 1996 _____ _____

3. When is there a direct relationship between the poverty rate and unemployment rate?

4. Is there ever an inverse relationship between the poverty rate and unemployment rate?●

Understanding and Calculating Slopes

The *slope* of a curve is one measure of the relationship between two variables. It indicates both the type of relationship (direct or inverse) and the rate of change of one variable as the other variable changes. For a straight line, the slope is constant. For a curve, the slope changes from one point along the curve to another. At any particular point, the slope of the curve is identical to the slope of a straight line that is tangent to that point. The slope of a line is calculated by identifying two points on the line and computing the ratio of the change in the variable on the vertical axis and the change in the variable on the horizontal axis. (In high school geometry, this was referred to as "the 'rise' over the 'run'"; more formally, slope is the "change in Y divided by the change in X.")

EXAMPLE 8

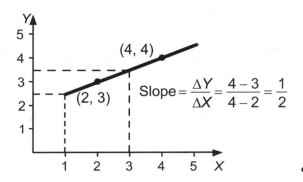

EXAMPLE 9

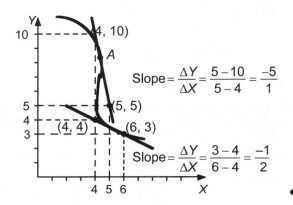

In Example 8, any two points along that line will show a slope of 1/2. In Example 9, the slope varies: at point A, the slope is $-5/1$; at point B the slope is $-(1/2)$. These slope numbers can be interpreted as indicating the unit change in the value of Y in response to a one-unit change in X. For Example 8, Y will increase by 1/2 in response to a one-unit change in X. At Point A in Example 9, Y decreases by 1 and at Point B Y decreases by 1/2. The fact that the slope is positive in Example 8 means that there is a direct relationship between Y and X. The negative slope in Example 9 illustrates an inverse relationship between Y and X.

Solving Equations

Often, the economic relationship between two concepts can be expressed algebraically as an equation. The advantage of this approach is that we can calculate the specific impact that a change in one variable has upon another variable.

EXAMPLE 10

It is a reasonable assumption that as the price of a good rises, more of that good will be supplied. This positive relationship can be expressed with an equation. Let P represent price and Qs represent quantity supplied. For our purposes, let $Q_S = -10 + 80P$. Thus, if $P = 1$, then $Q_S = 70$. The table below captures this relationship:

Price	1	2	3	4	5
Quantity supplied	70	150	230	310	390

1   What is Qs if $P = 7$?

2   What is Qs if $P = 10$?

The table can be graphed. The line is a supply curve, as you will see in Chapter 3—it is usually labeled "S."

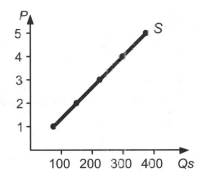

3.   What is the slope of the line?

If the equation is $Qs = -10 + 50P$, the slope of the line will change. Below is the new table.

Price	1	2	3	4	5
Quantity supplied	40	90	140	190	240

4.   Draw this new line on the graph below. Label it S_1.

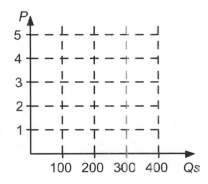

5.   What is the slope of this line?

If the equation for the supply curve is $Qs = -20 + 75P$, answer the following question.

6.   Complete the following table.

Price	1	2	3	4	5
Quantity supplied					

7. Graph the line shown in the table on the following graph. Label it S_2.

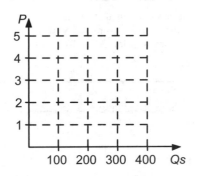

8. What is the slope of the line?

9. What is Qs if $P = 8$?

10. What is Qs if $P = 20$? _____ •

Solutions to Appendix Problems

Example 4
Refer to the following diagram.

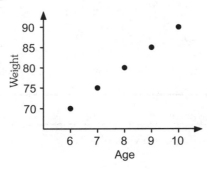

Example 5
Refer to the following diagram.

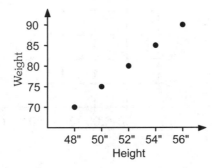

The relationship between height and weight is direct (positive).

Example 6
Refer to the following diagram.

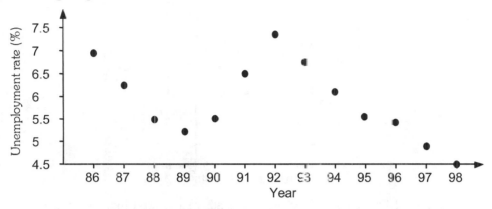

Between 1989 and 1992, there is a direct (positive) relationship.
Between 1986 and 1989, there is an inverse (negative) relationship. There is also an inverse relationship between 1992 and 1999.

Example 7

1. (a) 13.4 percent

    (b) 13.5 percent

    (c) 13.8 percent

2. (a) 1988 5.5 percent 13.1 percent

    (b) 1992 7.4 percent 14.5 percent

    (c) 1996 5.4 percent 13.7 percent

3. There is a direct relationship between the poverty rate and unemployment rate in all years except 1993.

4. There is an inverse relationship between the poverty rate and unemployment rate only in 1993.

Example 10

1. $Qs = -10 + 80P = -10 + 80(7) = 550.$

2. $Qs = -10 + 80P = -10 + 80(10) = 790.$

3. Slope = rise/run = 1/80. A 1-unit increase in P leads to an 80-unit increase in Qs.

4. Refer to the following diagram.

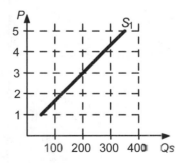

5. Slope = rise/run = 1/50. A 1-unit increase in P leads to a 50-unit increase in Qs.

6.	Price	1	2	3	4	5
	Quantity supplied	55	130	205	280	355

7.   Refer to the following diagram.

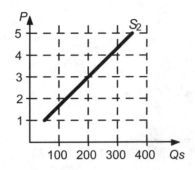

8.   Slope = rise/run = 1/75. A 1-unit increase in P leads to a 75-unit increase in Qs.

9. $Qs = -20 + 75P = -20 + 75(8) = 580$.

10. $Qs = -20 + 75P = -20 + 75(20) = 1480$.

2

The Economic Problem: Scarcity and Choice

Chapter Objectives

1. Identify the three basic economic questions.
2. Distinguish between absolute advantage and comparative advantage. Relate comparative advantage to the theory that individuals can gain from specialization and exchange.
3. Explain why a production possibility frontier has a negative slope and why the slope depicts the concept of opportunity cost.
4. Interpret what is depicted by a production possibility frontier.
5. Explain why increasing opportunity costs occur and how this is shown in the production possibility frontier diagram.
6. Identify ways in which economic growth may occur.
7. Identify and distinguish how economic systems differ in their use of government to solve the three basic questions. State the "mistakes" to which an unregulated market system is prone.

BRAIN TEASER: You graduate from college and are offered three jobs (Job A, Job B, and Job C). Assume that they are identical in all respects (duties, benefits, promotion prospects, and so on) except that the salaries differ, as shown below:

Job A	$150,000
Job B	$120,000
Job C	$100,000

First, which of the three jobs would you choose? (No, you can't have all three!) Because you have made a choice, you have incurred an opportunity cost. What is the opportunity cost of your job choice? Comparing benefits and costs, have you made a rational choice? Why or why not?

Suppose, that you select Job B. What is the cost of that choice? Comparing benefits and costs, have you made a rational choice? Why or why not?

Now suppose that you select Job C. What is the cost of that choice? Again, is Job C a rational choice? Why or why not?

SOLUTION: The answer to this and subsequent brain teasers will be found after our discussion of the learning objectives, and before the Practice Tests.

ECONOMICS IN PRACTICE: In the textbook, this chapter's first example of economics in action in the real world centers on opportunity costs, in particular, the value we place on our time. Refer to page 28 in the textbook. First, think about the costs of preparing a meal. To be sure, the price of the ingredients is one factor, but time is another. The textbook makes the point that we are often willing to trade dollars (and perhaps taste) for convenience. Can you think of two or three other examples of the same sort of trade-off in your own life? What do you consider in your decision-making process?

ANSWER: Answers will vary of course, but fast food is an obvious example. How much more convenient it is to go through the drive-through than spend the time shopping and cooking? If you use paper plates on a picnic, you're making the same sort of calculation. A trip to a (typically high-price) convenience store is another example. Many students who sign up for online classes cite "convenience" as the main reason for preferring this form of learning experience. Finally, how much more convenient is it to "google" a subject rather than visit your campus library's book stacks?

Objective 1

Identify the three basic economic questions.

Economics studies the production and consumption choices that are made by society and the outcomes that result from those choices. Solutions must be found to three "basic questions": What goods should be produced? How should the goods be produced? and Who gets what is produced? Every economy must transform its scarce natural, capital, and human resources into usable production. In a complex society, the opportunity to cooperate and specialize offers great scope for increased production—but decisions must be made regarding the extent of cooperation, who specializes in what, and how goods are distributed. Even Robinson Crusoe and Friday on their hypothetical island must come up with answers to these questions. Wants are limitless, but resources are scarce. We are compelled to make choices. (page 26)

Opportunity Cost: Economics has to do with making choices when constraints (scarcity) are present. Constrained choice occurs, for example, when you go to the grocery store with only a $20 bill in your pocket—you have to make choices based on this limitation. Unconstrained choice would be if you were allowed to take as many groceries home as you wanted, free of charge. Sadly, though, we know there's "no such thing as a free lunch."

Practical examples of the consequences and costs of choice include: present vs. future benefits (do you study hard now so that at exam time reviewing is easier, or do you take it easy now and sweat it before the exam?), and capital vs. consumer production (should we produce taxicabs or sports cars?).

LEARNING TIP: Everyone has been confronted with some version of the following scene: A favorite grandmother lets you choose one item from two or more items (ice cream sundaes, for example) on a menu. From your viewpoint, is your chosen ice cream sundae free, or is there an opportunity cost? If you have a range of sundaes from which to choose, what is the cost? Is that cost the dollar amount of the chosen sundae, or all the other sundaes you could have had? The opportunity cost is the value you place on the next most-favorite sundae. ◀

LEARNING TIP: To calculate opportunity cost, use the "give up to get" approach. If you can determine what (next-best) choice was forgone to get your preferred selection, you have determined opportunity cost. This is most clearly seen as a movement along a production possibility frontier. ◀

Practice

1. Which of the following statements about the operation of an economy is **false**? Each economy has a mechanism to determine
    (a) what is produced.
    (b) how to satisfy all of the desires of its citizens.
    (c) how much is produced.
    (d) how goods and services are distributed among its citizens.

    ANSWER: (b) Because resources are limited, the economy cannot satisfy all the desires of its citizens. ■

Objective 2

Distinguish between absolute advantage and comparative advantage. Relate comparative advantage to the theory that individuals can gain from specialization and exchange.

A producer has an *absolute advantage* in the production of Good A if, compared with another producer, she can produce Good A more efficiently. A producer has a *comparative advantage* in the production of Good A if, compared with another producer, she can produce Good A at a lower opportunity cost.

The *theory of comparative advantage* provides the rationale for free trade. In a two-country, two-good world, Ricardo showed that trading partners can benefit from specialization in the production of the good in which they have a comparative advantage. (page 28)

Specialization and trade based on comparative advantage lets each participant achieve a higher consumption level than would otherwise be possible. As shown graphically, each participant can live outside the constraints of his own production opportunities. (page 31)

LEARNING TIP: If you're like most individuals, you'll need several numerical examples to strengthen your grasp of comparative advantage. The following end-of-chapter questions take you through all the steps included in the text. Problems 4 and 6 in the textbook are recommended. ◀

Comparative advantage hinges on the concept of opportunity cost. The producer (person, firm, or country) with the lowest opportunity cost holds the comparative advantage in that product. Don't be misled—it is irrelevant to comparative advantage whether or not the producer can produce *more* of the good. The issue revolves around the relative opportunity costs. The increased production could be traded. In terms of a *production possibility* diagram, trade will be advantageous if the diagrams have differing slopes because differing slopes indicate differing opportunity costs.

ECONOMICS IN PRACTICE: Think back to when you used to trade baseball or Pokemon cards in the schoolyard. Why did you trade? Did you and your trading partner necessarily benefit equally? Should that matter?
ANSWER: Presumably, if you entered into a trade voluntarily, you did so because you thought it would be beneficial for you. Perhaps you traded a duplicate card for one you didn't have. Likewise, your partner approached the deal in the same way. Just because you got a good deal didn't necessarily mean that s/he got a bad deal—both traders could gain, although there's no requirement that the traders will gain equally.

Practice

Use the following information to answer the next seven questions. Barack and Michelle live on an island in the Caribbean. Their diet is fish and biscuits. Barack can bake 20 biscuits or spear 10 fish each day, while Michelle can bake 48 biscuits or spear 12 fish each day. For each person, costs remain constant.

2.   Which of the following statements is **false**?
    (a)   For Barack, the opportunity cost of 1 fish is 2 biscuits forgone.
    (b)   For Michelle, the opportunity cost of 1 fish is 4 biscuits forgone.
    (c)   The opportunity cost of 1 fish is greater for Michelle than for Barack.
    (d)   An increase in Barack's production of fish requires a decrease in Michelle's production of biscuits.

    ANSWER: (d) An increase in Barack's production of fish requires a decrease in *Barack's* production of biscuits. In fact, both Barack and Michelle might choose independently to increase fish production.

3.   Which of the following statements is true?
    (a)   For Barack, the opportunity cost of 1 biscuit is 2 fish forgone.
    (b)   For Michelle, the opportunity cost of 1 biscuit is 4 fish forgone.
    (c)   The opportunity cost of 1 biscuit is greater for Michelle than for Barack.
    (d)   The opportunity cost of 1 biscuit is greater for Barack than for Michelle.

    ANSWER: (d) For Barack, the opportunity cost of a biscuit is 1/2 of a fish forgone, and for Michelle, the opportunity cost of a biscuit is 1/4 of a fish forgone.

4.   For _____ , the opportunity cost of 1 fish is _____ biscuits forgone, which is less than the opportunity cost of 1 fish for _____ .
    (a)   Barack; 1/2; Michelle
    (b)   Barack; 2; Michelle
    (c)   Michelle; 4; Barack
    (d)   Michelle; 1/4; Barack

    ANSWER: (b) For Barack, each fish "costs" 2 biscuits forgone. For Michelle, each fish "costs" 4 biscuits forgone. Fish cost less for Barack to produce.

5.   For _____ , the opportunity cost of 1 biscuit is _____ fish forgone, which is less than the opportunity cost of 1 biscuit for _____ .
    (a)   Barack; 1/2; Michelle
    (b)   Barack; 2; Michelle
    (c)   Michelle; 4; Barack
    (d)   Michelle; 1/4; Barack

    ANSWER: (d) For Barack, each biscuit "costs" 1/2 of a fish forgone. For Michelle, each biscuit "costs" 1/4 of a fish forgone. Biscuits cost less for Michelle to produce.

6.   According to the preceding information,
    (a)   Barack has a comparative advantage in the production of both goods.
    (b)   Barack has a comparative advantage in producing fish, and Michelle has a comparative advantage in producing biscuits.
    (c)   Barack has a comparative advantage in producing biscuits, and Michelle has a comparative advantage in producing fish.
    (d)   Michelle has a comparative advantage in the production of both goods.

    ANSWER: (b) Barack has a comparative advantage in the production of fish (1 fish costs 2 biscuits forgone), and Michelle has a comparative advantage in the production of biscuits (1 biscuit costs 1/4 of a fish forgone). Note: neither person can be relatively better at producing both goods!

7.   Which of the following statements is **false**?
   (a)   If Barack spent half his time fishing and the other half baking, he could produce 10 biscuits and 5 fish each day.
   (b)   If Michelle spent half her time fishing and the other half baking, she could produce 24 biscuits and 6 fish each day.
   (c)   If Barack and Michelle specialized according to comparative advantage, they could produce 34 biscuits and 11 fish each day.
   (d)   If Barack and Michelle specialized according to comparative advantage, they could produce 48 biscuits and 10 fish each day.

   ANSWER: (c)   Barack should produce fish, and he can spear 10 each day. Michelle should produce biscuits, and she can bake 48 each day. Option (c) is incorrect because it fails to take account of the effects of comparative advantage.

8.   Barack and Michelle specialize according to comparative advantage and trade at a rate of 1 fish for 3 biscuits. Barack sells Michelle 5 fish. Which of the following statements is true?
   (a)   Barack gains from trade but Michelle does not, because Barack's opportunity cost for producing fish is greater than 3 biscuits per fish.
   (b)   Barack gains from trade but Michelle does not, because Barack's opportunity cost for producing fish is less than 3 biscuits per fish.
   (c)   Both Barack and Michelle gain from trade, because each attains a consumption level impossible without trade.
   (d)   Both Barack and Michelle gain from trade, because each is able to maximize their resources.

   ANSWER: (c)   Barack's opportunity cost for producing fish is less than 3 biscuits per fish, so he gains from trade. However, Michelle also gains because her opportunity cost of producing biscuits is less than 1/3 of a fish. Barack ends up with 5 fish and 15 biscuits, and Michelle ends up with 5 fish and 33 biscuits. ∎

Objective 3

Explain why a production possibility frontier has a negative slope and why the slope depicts the concept of opportunity cost.

A production possibility frontier depicts the boundary between possible and impossible (unattainable) levels of production. Employing resources for one use prevents them from being employed for other uses—there is an *opportunity cost* involved in the choice. The *production possibility frontier* graphically portrays the opportunity cost of transferring resources from one activity to another in a two-good environment. If all resources are fully employed, as more of Good A is produced, fewer resources are available to produce Good B. (page 33)

Why Does the Production Possibility Frontier Slope Downward? The production possibility frontier is the key piece of economic analysis in this chapter. It's always presented as having only two goods or bundles of goods. It slopes downward because "the more you get of one thing the less you get of the other." The more you study economics, the less time you have for other activities. The opportunity cost of an extra hour of studying economics is the value of an hour of other activities.

Graphing Pointer: Draw a graph with "study time per day" on the horizontal (X) axis and "time for all other activities per day" on the vertical (Y) axis. As you increase "study time" you must reduce "other time." Graphically, the cost of one hour of study time (the lost time for other activities) is the (negative) change in Y divided by the (positive) change in X. The slope of the PPF is the geometric representation of the opportunity cost of transferring resources from one productive activity to another.

Graphing Pointer: When drawing a production possibility frontier, remember that the frontier extends all the way from the vertical axis to the horizontal axis. It is a mistake to leave the frontier unconnected to the axes. If the frontier is not connected, it implies that an infinitely large quantity of either good could be produced, which is the exact opposite message that the diagram is intended to give.

Practice

9.   Along the production possibility frontier, trade-offs exist because
   (a)   buyers will want to buy less when price goes up, but producers will want to sell more.
   (b)   even on the frontier itself, not all production levels are efficient.
   (c)   at some levels, unemployment or inefficiency exists.
   (d)   the economy has only a limited quantity of resources to allocate between competing uses.

   ANSWER: (d) Along the production possibility frontier, resources are fully and efficiently employed. However, because resources are scarce, an increase in the production of Good A requires that resources be taken from the production of Good B. ■

Objective 4

Interpret what is depicted by a production possibility frontier.

The production possibility frontier shows all the combinations of two goods that can be produced when all resources are employed efficiently. Points inside the production possibility frontier represent unemployment and/or inefficiency whereas points outside are currently unattainable. An outward movement of the production possibility frontier represents growth. Growth occurs if more resources become available or if existing resources become more productive (e.g., through better education, more efficient techniques of production, or technological innovations). (page 34)

Production Efficiency and Output Efficiency: The vision of a great volume of production with all resources employed is attractive. For this reason, it's often difficult to understand that, in serving the needs of consumers, producing the *right* goods is more important than mere quantity. This distinction lies at the heart of most confusion about production and output efficiency. Consider a remote Inuit economy that is fully employed producing refrigerators. Would it be "better" (more efficient) for the Inuits to have some unemployment but be producing warm clothing? Turning out (unwanted) refrigerators is productively efficient, whereas making warm clothing is efficient (in terms of output). Ideally, you'd want to be on the production possibility frontier (output efficiency) and also producing the most desired mix of output.

LEARNING TIP: Think of the production possibility frontier as a way to depict opportunity cost and constrained choice. In general, you want to be somewhere on the curve because otherwise you're losing production, which is inefficient. Production on the curve means that resources are being used to the maximum (no unemployment). However, the inefficiency of a mismatch between an "efficient" production mix and society's needs is easily explained—just because we're producing "on the line" doesn't mean we're meeting society's needs as effectively as possible. Employing all our resources to produce taxicabs, for example, is unlikely to be desirable!◀

LEARNING TIP: Suppose that, at one point on the production possibility frontier, we can produce 16 cars and 5 pickups, and at another point, we can produce 12 cars and 7 pickups. Note that the opportunity cost is calculated by looking at the change in production levels—2 extra trucks cost 4 cars.◀

LEARNING TIP: Reducing unemployment does not shift the production possibility frontier. Remember the underlying assumptions! The production possibility frontier is drawn *given* a set of resources (whether or not those resources are being used). Unemployment represents a situation where the resources are not fully utilized. If unemployment is reduced, the economy moves closer to the production possibility frontier.◀

Practice

10. Which of the following is **not** an assumption underlying the production possibility frontier?
    - (a) Technological knowledge is fixed.
    - (b) Resources are fully employed.
    - (c) Resources are efficiently employed.
    - (d) The quantity of labor resources is variable.

    ANSWER: (d) When drawing a PPF, all resources are assumed to be fixed in quantity.

11. The production possibility frontier represents
    - (a) the maximum amount of goods and services that can be produced with a given quantity of resources and technology.
    - (b) those combinations of goods and services that will be demanded as price changes.
    - (c) the maximum amount of resources that are available as the wage level changes.
    - (d) those combinations of goods and services that will be produced as the price level changes.

    ANSWER: (a) The production possibility frontier represents what it is "possible to produce" given the available resources and technology.

12. The Arbezani economy is operating at a point inside its production possibility frontier. This may be because
    - (a) the economy has very poor technological know-how.
    - (b) Arbez is a very small nation and can't produce much.
    - (c) poor management practices have led to an inefficient use of resources.
    - (d) Arbez has only a small resource base.

    ANSWER: (c) Very poor technological know-how or a small resource base will result in a production possibility frontier that is close to the origin. Fully and efficiently employed resources would still be on the production possibility frontier. ■

Objective 5

Explain why increasing opportunity costs occur and how this is shown in the production possibility frontier diagram.

Increasing opportunity costs are present when the production possibility frontier bulges outwards from the origin. Increasing costs occur if resources are not equally well suited to the production of Good A and Good B. (page 35)

> **LEARNING TIP:** Why is the production possibility frontier bowed out? The geometry of the production possibility frontier flows from its economics. A bowed-out production possibility frontier indicates that the opportunity cost (marginal rate of transformation) is increasing as resources become more heavily allocated to the production of one good. That bowed-out shape occurs because of the imperfect adaptability of resources to different uses. A farmer wishing to produce dairy products, for example, will select the best-suited resources first, and production will increase sharply. Further increases will be less easy to achieve and more expensive in terms of lost production of other goods, as resources more suited to other endeavors are pressed into dairy service. If all resources were identical in their productive abilities, the opportunity cost of reallocation would be constant, and the production possibility frontier would be a straight line (a constant slope). ◀

Practice

13.   There are increasing costs in the economy of Arbez. To portray this fact in a production possibility diagram, we should
      (a)   move the production possibility frontier outwards (up and to the right).
      (b)   draw the production possibility frontier bulging outwards.
      (c)   shift the production possibility frontier's endpoint on the horizontal axis to the right.
      (d)   shift the production possibility frontier's endpoint on the vertical axis upwards.
      ANSWER: (b)   The slope of the production possibility frontier represents the behavior of opportunity cost as production level changes. A straight-line (constant slope) production possibility frontier represents constant costs. To show increasing costs, the production possibility frontier is bowed outwards from the origin. ■

Objective 6

Identify ways in which economic growth may occur.

If an economy increases the quantity or quality of its resources, or if technological change or innovation increase productivity, economic growth can occur—the production possibility frontier shifts outward. (page 36)

Investment and Capital: "Investment" and "capital" are two terms with very specific meanings in economics. Beware! Investing doesn't just mean buying something. To an economist, investing means only the creation of capital. What, then, is capital? Capital refers to tangible or intangible resources usable in the production of other goods and services. A hammer is capital; a share of GM stock is not. A carpenter's skill is capital; a dollar bill is not. Buying a hammer or training to be a carpenter is capital investment; buying GM stock is not!

   If this capital/noncapital distinction gives you problems, ask yourself if the purchase of the item in question increases the economy's ability to produce. If it does, then it's an investment in capital.

Practice

14.   France experiences an improvement in productivity due to the introduction of improved technology. In terms of France's production possibility frontier, we would show this change as a
      (a)   movement along the frontier.
      (b)   shift from a point inside the frontier to a point on the frontier.
      (c)   shift from a point on the frontier to a point outside the frontier.
      (d)   shift outwards by the entire frontier.
      ANSWER: (d)   France's resource base has improved in quality, so it is possible for it to produce more than it could previously. ■

ECONOMICS IN PRACTICE: On page 39, your textbook considers limited resources and the differences in trade offs between rich and poor countries. It has been observed that, in the poorest countries, consumers spend a high proportion of their income on food, and typically food that is both processed and high in sugar. This is also true for the United States, where poverty rates and obesity tend to move together because the poor can't afford the more nutritious diet options.

In poor economies, which are frequently starved of both capital and natural resources, what else might families do in order to increase their ability to produce and survive? How might governments promote increased birth rates?

ANSWER: If capital and natural resources are constrained, it may be a rational choice to increase labor resources by having large families. Certainly, this has been a strategy in agricultural societies in the past. Similarly, in the present, some countries have become concerned at their declining populations. Estonia, for example, which was described in 2001 as "one of the fastest-shrinking nations on earth," launched an initiative to boost it's sagging fertility rate by paying mothers a "baby bounty" of up to $1,560 per month. (The average Estonian salary is about $650 per month.) There is evidence that the incentive is working as Estonia's fertility rate has climbed from a low of 1.28 children per woman in 1998 to 1.65 children per woman in 2008. Other countries, such as France and Russia, have adopted similar schemes.

Objective 7

Identify and distinguish how economic systems differ in their use of government to solve the three basic questions. State the "mistakes" to which an unregulated market system is prone.

The two "pure" types of economic systems are the command economy and the laissez-faire economy. A *command (planned) economy* has a central government agency that sets production targets, income, and prices, and finds answers for the three basic questions. In a *laissez-faire (market) economy*, the three basic questions are answered through the operation of individual buyers and sellers following their own self-interest in markets. In an unregulated (free enterprise) market, profit-seeking producers respond to the preferences of consumers, while the distribution of output, income, and wealth is dictated by competitive forces.

All economies are driven by a mixture of market forces, government intervention, and regulation. More or less government intervention is felt to be necessary to correct laissez-faire "mistakes" such as an excessive inequality in the distribution of income, and periodic spells of unemployment or inflation. (page 39)

Practice

15.   The basic mechanism that coordinates activities in a laissez-faire economy is
      (a)   how much customers wish to buy.
      (b)   how much producers wish to sell.
      (c)   price.
      (d)   how much producers are able to sell.

      ANSWER: (c) Price regulates market activities, reflecting the desires of both buyers and sellers.

16.   Advocates comparing the performance of a pure laissez-faire system with that of a command economy would claim that a pure laissez-faire system would do all of the following EXCEPT
      (a)   promote efficiency.
      (b)   stimulate innovation.
      (c)   achieve an equal income distribution.
      (d)   be directed by the decisions of individual buyers and sellers.

      ANSWER: (c) A pure laissez-faire system, which rewards those who contribute most, would have an unequal income distribution. ■

BRAIN TEASER SOLUTION: Presumably, you would choose Job A. The opportunity cost is the next-best alternative given up (Job B), which is valued at $120,000. You have made a rational choice because the benefits ($150,000) outweigh the costs ($120,000).

If you select Job B, the opportunity cost is the next-best alternative given up (Job A), which is valued at $150,000. This isn't a rational choice, because you receive a benefit of $120,000 at a cost of $150,000.

If you select Job C, once again the opportunity cost is the value of Job A, which you could have chosen instead. Job C isn't a rational choice, because you receive a benefit of $100,000 at a cost of $150,000.

PRACTICE TEST

I. MULTIPLE-CHOICE QUESTIONS

Select the option that provides the single best answer.

_____ 1. Because the nation of Arboc is operating at a point inside its production possibility frontier, it
   (a)   has full employment.
   (b)   has unemployed or inefficiently employed resources.
   (c)   must cut output of one good to increase production of another.
   (d)   will be unable to experience economic growth.

_____ 2. Arboc commits more of its resources to capital production than does Arbez. _____ should experience a(n) _____ rapid rate of economic growth.
   (a)   Arboc; more
   (b)   Arbez; more
   (c)   Arboc; less
   (d)   Both; equally

_____ 3. Which of the following does not count as a productive resource?
   (a)   Capital resources, such as a tractor
   (b)   Natural resources, such as a piece of farmland
   (c)   Financial resources, such as a $20 bill
   (d)   Human resources, such as a hairdresser

Use the following diagram to answer the next four questions.

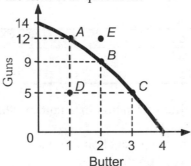

_____ 4.   Point *E* might become attainable if this economy
(a)   reduces prices.
(b)   reduces wages.
(c)   improves the quality of its workforce.
(d)   encourages emigration.

_____ 5.   A movement from *A* to *B* and then to *C* indicates that the
(a)   cost of additional butter is decreasing.
(b)   cost of additional guns is increasing.
(c)   economy is becoming more efficient.
(d)   cost of additional butter is increasing.

_____ 6.   To move from *D* to *A* indicates that
(a)   the opportunity cost would be zero.
(b)   some butter would have to be given up.
(c)   there would have to be an increase in the quantity of resources.
(d)   the opportunity cost would be 7 guns forgone.

_____ 7.   The opportunity cost of producing another unit of butter is
(a)   higher at *B* than at *C*.
(b)   lower at *D* than at *C*.
(c)   higher at *A* than at *B*.
(d)   equal at *D* and at *C*.

_____ 8.   A production possibility frontier diagram illustrates all of the following concepts EXCEPT
(a)   scarcity.
(b)   unlimited wants.
(c)   constrained choice.
(d)   the marginal rate of transformation.

_____ 9.   Of the following, the least serious problem for laissez-faire economies is
(a)   unemployment.
(b)   income inequality.
(c)   inflation.
(d)   satisfaction of consumer sovereignty.

Use the following production possibility table to answer the next three questions. Suppose that wheat is on the *y*-axis.

Alternative	A	B	C	D	E	F
Wheat	0	1	2	3	4	5
Tobacco	15	14	12	9	5	0

_____ 10. The marginal rate of transformation of a unit of wheat as the economy moves from *C* to *D* is
(a) 1/3 unit of tobacco production forgone.
(b) 3 units of tobacco production forgone.
(c) 9 units of tobacco production forgone.
(d) 12 units of tobacco production forgone.

_____ 11. The marginal rate of transformation of a unit of tobacco as the economy moves from *C* to *B* is
(a) 1/2 unit of wheat production forgone.
(b) 1 unit of wheat production forgone.
(c) 2 units of wheat production forgone.
(d) 12 units of wheat production forgone.

_____ 12. An output of 3 units of wheat and 7 units of tobacco indicates that
(a) this economy has poor technology.
(b) resources are being used inefficiently.
(c) tobacco is preferred to wheat.
(d) it is not possible for this economy to produce at a point on the production possibility frontier.

_____ 13. Which of the following is most likely to shift the production possibility frontier outward?
(a) A sudden expansion in the labor force
(b) An increase in stock prices
(c) A shift of productive resources from capital goods to consumer goods
(d) A general increase in the public's demand for goods

_____ 14. Which of the following is not one of the basic economic questions?
(a) What will be produced?
(b) How will it be priced?
(c) How will it be produced?
(d) Who will get what is produced?

_____ 15. Private markets work best when
(a) they are competitive.
(b) they are regulated by a government agency.
(c) a monopolist is present.
(d) consumer sovereignty is restricted.

_____ 16. Arboc has an increasing-cost production possibility frontier. Its slope must be
(a) positive and increasing.
(b) positive and decreasing.
(c) negative and increasing.
(d) negative and decreasing.

_____ 17.   For Jill to have a comparative advantage in the production of pins means that with the same resources and relative to Jack,
(a)   Jill is relatively better at producing pins than at producing needles.
(b)   Jill is relatively better at producing both pins and needles.
(c)   Jill can produce fewer needles than Jack can produce.
(d)   Jill can produce more pins than Jack can produce.

_____ 18.   Each of the following is a basic concern of any economic system EXCEPT the
(a)   allocation of scarce resources among producers.
(b)   mix of different types of output.
(c)   distribution of output among consumers.
(d)   quality of resources allocated among consumers.

The following table shows the maximum output of each good in each country, e.g. maximum Arbezani production of goat milk is 6 units.

	Arboc	Arbez
Goat milk	3	6
Bananas	5	2

_____ 19.   According to the preceding table,
(a)   Arboc has a comparative advantage in producing both goods.
(b)   Arboc has a comparative advantage in the production of bananas, and Arbez has a comparative advantage in the production of goat milk.
(c)   Arboc has a comparative advantage in the production of goat milk, and Arbez has a comparative advantage in the production of bananas.
(d)   Arbez has a comparative advantage in the production of both goods.

_____ 20.   The nation of Regit has a bowed-out production possibility frontier with potatoes on the vertical axis and steel on the horizontal axis. A movement down along the PPF will incur _____ opportunity costs in the production of steel; a movement up along the PPF will incur _____ opportunity costs in the production of potatoes.
(a)   increasing; increasing
(b)   increasing; decreasing
(c)   decreasing; increasing
(d)   decreasing; decreasing

II. APPLICATION QUESTIONS

1.   Farmer Brown has four fields that can produce either corn or tobacco. Assume that the marginal rate of transformation between corn and tobacco _within_ each field is constant. The maximum yields for each field are given in the following table. Field A, for instance, can produce 40 units of corn and no tobacco or, as another alternative, no corn and 10 units of tobacco.

Field	A	B	C	D
Corn	40	30	20	10
Tobacco	10	20	30	40

(a)   Draw Farmer Brown's production possibility frontier.
(b)   To be on the production possibility frontier, what conditions must hold true?

(c)   Brown is currently producing only corn: If he wants to produce some tobacco, in what order would he switch his fields from corn to tobacco production?

(d)   Explain your answer to (c).

2.   Two countries, Arboc and Arbez, produce wine and cheese, and each has constant costs of production. The maximum amounts of the two goods for each country are given in the following table.

Arboc	Arbez	Goods
40	120	Wine
20	30	Cheese

(a)   Draw the production possibility frontier for each country.

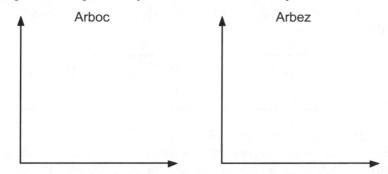

(b)   Calculate the opportunity cost of wine in Arboc and in Arbez.

(c)   In which country, then, is wine production cheaper?

(d)   Answer questions (b) and (c) for cheese production—remember that the opportunity costs are reciprocals of one another.

        Note that Arbez has an advantage in both goods in terms of total production, but a comparative advantage only in wine production.

        Now assume that Arboc becomes more efficient and can double its output of both wine and cheese.

(e)   Graph the new production possibility frontier on the preceding diagram.

(f)   Which good should Arboc now produce?

        Suppose instead, that Arbez has a specific technological advance that permits it to increase cheese production to a maximum of 90.

(g)   Now which nation should produce wine?

3.   In a national contest, the first prize is a town. The winner receives a furnished house, a general store and gasoline station, a pick-up truck, and 100 acres of land. The store comes fully stocked with everything you might find in a country general store. The town is located 100 miles from a small city. It is the shopping center for about a thousand families who live in the countryside. In addition, the road through the town is fairly well traveled. Suppose you win the contest and decide to try running the town as a business for at least a year.

(a)   Describe the resources available to the economy of your town. What is the potential labor force? What are the natural resources?

(b)   Describe the capital stock of your town.

(c)   List some of the factors beyond your control that will affect your income.

(d) List some of the decisions you must make that could affect your income, and explain what their effects might be.

(e) At the end of the year, you must decide whether to stay or go back to college. How will you decide? What factors will you weigh in making your decision? What role do your expectations play?

4. The following data give the production possibilities of an economy that produces two types of goods, guns (horizontal axis) and butter (vertical axis).

Production Possibilities	Guns	Butter
A	0	105
B	10	100
C	20	90
D	30	75
E	40	55
F	50	30
G	60	0

(a) Graph the production possibility frontier.

(b) Explain why Point D is efficient, but Point H (30 guns and 45 units of butter) is not.

(c) Calculate the per-unit opportunity cost of an increase in the production of guns in each of the following cases.
(i) From Point A to Point B?
(ii) From Point B to Point C?
(iii) From Point E to Point F?
(iv) From Point F to Point G?

(d) Calculate the per-unit opportunity cost of an increase in the production of butter in each of the following cases.
(i) From Point G to Point F?
(ii) From Point D to Point C?
(iii) From Point C to Point B?
(iv) From Point B to Point A?

(e) Using the production possibility frontier concept, explain what will happen if this nation declares war on one of its neighbors.

5.   Draw a production possibility frontier with farm goods (*X*-axis) and manufacturing goods (*Y*-axis) on the axes. In each of the following cases, explain what will happen to the production possibility frontier.

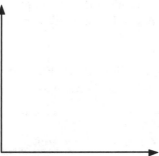

(a)   There is an increase in the unemployment rate.

(b)   There is an improvement in farming techniques.

(c)   There is a decrease in quantity of physical capital.

(d)   The productivity of workers doubles.

(e)   The government requires farmers to slaughter a portion of their dairy herds.

6.   Consider the following production possibility frontier diagram.

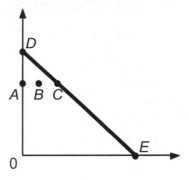

(a)   Which point is "best" and which is "worst"?

(b)   Now suppose that you're told that the axes measure food (horizontal) and moonshine whisky (vertical). Would your answer be different?

(c)   Point *B* may be preferable to Point *D*, although in terms of production Point *B* is less efficient. Why might it be preferable?

7.   The nation of Arbez can produce two goods—corn and steel. The table shows some points on the Arbezani production possibility frontier.

Alternative	A	B	C	D	E	F
Corn	0	1	2	3	4	5
Steel	20	16	12	8	4	0

(a)   Draw the production possibility frontier in the space below.

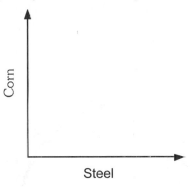

(b)   Moving from Alternative A to B, B to C, and so on, calculate the opportunity cost of each additional unit of corn. Going from F to E, E to D, and so on, calculate the opportunity cost *per unit* of steel. Confirm that the pairs of values are reciprocals of each other. (This must always be true.)

Production Alternative	Opportunity Cost of 1 Unit of:	
	Corn	Steel
$A - B$	_____	_____
$B - C$	_____	_____
$C - D$	_____	_____
$D - E$	_____	_____
$E - F$	_____	_____

(c)   Consider each of the following situations.
Situation X: Arbez is producing 4 units of corn and no steel. What is the opportunity cost of the next unit of corn? The next unit of steel?
Situation Y: Arbez is producing 4 units of corn and 4 units of steel. What is the opportunity cost of the next unit of corn? The next unit of steel?

(d)   Why do you find a different set of answers in Situation X and Situation Y?

(e)   Now consider a new situation, Situation Z: Arbez is producing 3 units of corn and 5 units of steel. What is the opportunity cost of the next unit of corn? The next unit of steel?

(f)   Which situation (X, Y, or Z) is the most productively efficient and which is the least productively efficient?

(g)   On the Arbezani production possibility frontier, what is the cost of each unit of corn and what is the cost of each unit of steel?
The nation of Arboc also produces corn and steel. The following table shows some points on the Arbocali production possibility frontier.

Alternative	A	B	C	D	E	F
Corn	0	1	2	3	4	5
Steel	10	8	6	4	2	0

(h)   On the Arbocali production possibility frontier, what is the cost of each unit of corn and what is the cost of each unit of steel?

(i)   Point to ponder: Because steel is relatively cheaper to produce in one country (which?) and corn is relatively cheaper to produce in the other country (which?), might mutually beneficial trade be possible?

8.   Refer to the following diagram.

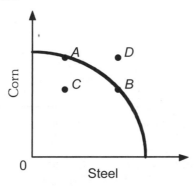

(a)   Which point is unattainable?

(b)   To achieve this currently unattainable production combination, what must happen (two possible answers)?

(c)   Which point represents unemployment or inefficiency?

(d)   Will a movement from B to A increase corn production or steel production?

(e)   What is the opportunity cost of moving from C to B?

9.   Draw the axes of a production possibility frontier. Use corn (on the vertical axis) and steel (on the horizontal axis) as the two goods.

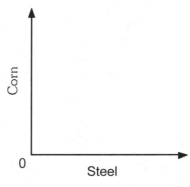

Choose a point, A, that represents some corn and some steel production. Suppose that this point is on the PPF—it's a maximum point. Split the diagram up into quarters, with Point A in the center.

(a)   Is a production mix to the southwest possible?

(b)   Would such a mix be efficient in terms of production efficiency?

(c)   Would such a mix be efficient in terms of output efficiency?

(d)   Is a move to the northeast quadrant possible? What do you know about it? Only the northwest and southeast quadrants are possible locations in which productively efficient output alternatives can occur.

(e)   What would happen if the present level of corn production (at Point *A*) was reduced?

If steel production does not change, unemployment occurs. The unemployed resources can be absorbed by the steel industry and more steel can be produced. A parallel case can be made given cutbacks in steel production. Can you see how the production possibility frontier *must* have a negative slope and that it portrays the concept of opportunity cost?

10.   Use the diagrams below to answer this question.

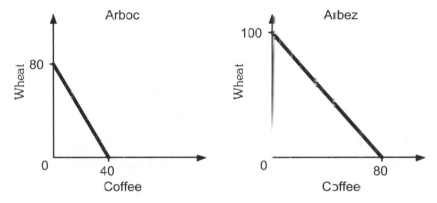

(a)   What is the opportunity cost of one unit of coffee in Arboc?

(b)   What is the opportunity cost of one unit of coffee in Arbez?

(c)   Which country has a comparative advantage in the production of coffee?

(d)   What is the opportunity cost of one unit of wheat in Arboc?

(e)   What is the opportunity cost of one unit of wheat in Arbez?

(f)   Which country has a comparative advantage in the production of wheat?

(g)   *Ceteris paribus*, ignoring other issues, which good should Arboc produce and which good should Arbez produce?

11.   Draw a production possibility curve. Put guns on the vertical axis and butter on the horizontal axis. Suppose that the technology for producing butter improves but the technology for producing guns does not. Describe how your diagram would change. In general, how will this technological advance affect the opportunity cost of producing guns?

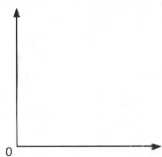

12.   Kara has a total of 12 hours to work on two projects. She must study for an economics test and "polish" an English composition paper. She believes that, with no studying at all, she would score

30 points on the economics test whereas, if she turned in her English paper with no extra work, it would earn 40 points. Suppose that, for each hour studying economics, she can raise her economics score by 10 points, and that, for each hour of work on her composition, she can raise her English score by 6 points.

(a)   Draw a production possibility frontier graph, showing all the points (combinations of time) that are feasible if Kara has 12 hours to allocate between economics and English. Put "hours of study for economics" on the vertical axis and "hours of study for English" on the horizontal axis.

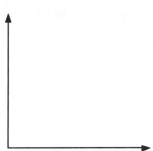

(b)   Show Point *A*, where Kara is studying 6 hours for economics and 6 hours for English.

(c)   Show Point *B*, where Kara is studying 12 hours for economics and 0 hours for English.

(d)   True or false? It is possible for Kara to score 100 on the economics test and at least 70 on the English paper.

(e)   True or false? It is possible for Kara to score 80 on the economics test and at least 80 on the English paper.

(f)   Kara decides to spend 4 hours studying for the economics test. What's the highest score she can expect to get on the English paper?

(g)   If Kara is satisfied with 70 in both subjects, how many hours would she need to study in total this weekend?

(h)   True or false? If Kara scored 70 on the economics test, she could have made at least 90 on the English paper.

(i)   The opportunity cost of scoring 6 points higher on the English paper is a score of _____ points LOWER/HIGHER on the economics test.

(j)   Draw a line (labeled EE) showing all the points that have exactly 2 hours of study time for the English paper.

13.   (a)   Consider the three fundamental economic questions in the context of a restaurant you're planning to open. Someone (you!) must decide what will be on the menu. Will it be Chinese, Mexican, or Italian cuisine? This is the "what to produce" question. You must also determine how your meals will be prepared and served. Will it be fast food or cordon bleu? The "for whom" question involves determining who your clientele will be. How do you advertise? Which demographic is important for you?

(b)   Now consider the case of Jonah Staw. Jonah, a 29-year old advertising executive earning $140,000 annually, quit his job to found Little Miss Matched, a company that produces "mismatched" gloves and socks for children. What was his opportunity cost? Now do some research—you can Google Staw's name. How did he answer the three economic questions?

Practice Test SOLUTIONS

I. SOLUTIONS TO MULTIPLE-CHOICE QUESTIONS

1. (b) To be on the production possibility frontier, Arboc must have all of its resources fully and efficiently employed. Because it is operating inside the production possibility frontier, at least one of these conditions must have been violated.

2. (a) If Arboc produces relatively more capital, then it is expanding its resource base more rapidly and, *ceteris paribus*, it will grow more rapidly.

3. (c) Financial resources may be used to purchase real productive resources, but are not themselves productive. Note that, to an economist, "investment" is the creation of real productive capacity, not merely the purchase of stock in a company.

4. (c) To reach Point *E* the economy must grow, shifting out its production possibility frontier. This could occur if the labor force became more efficient.

5. (d) This is an increasing-cost production possibility frontier. As we increase the production of one good (butter), the cost in terms of the other good increases. In this case, a one-unit increase in butter (*A* to *B*) costs 3 guns; the move from *B* to *C* costs more (4 guns).

6. (a) Opportunity cost is defined (loosely) as the quantity of Good *B* given up to increase production of Good *A*. The quantity of butter remains at 1 unit, and gun production is increased.

7. (b) Refer to the answer to Question 6. Opportunity cost of one unit of butter is 0 at Point *D*. The opportunity cost of one unit of butter at Point *C* is 5 guns.

8. (b) The production possibility frontier depicts what it is possible to produce but nothing about what is wanted.

9. (d) Laissez-faire economies generally respond well to the needs of private consumers.

10. (b) A one-unit increase in wheat results in a three-unit decrease in tobacco production.

11. (a) A two-unit increase in tobacco results in a one-unit decrease in wheat.

12. (b) This point is inside the production possibility frontier. (We could be producing two more units of tobacco with the same amount of wheat production, for example.) This indicates that our resources are unemployed and/or inefficiently employed.

13. (a) The labor-force expansion represents an increase in productive resources. Note that the production possibility frontier depicts what can be supplied—demand is not reflected in the diagram.

14. (b) Refer to page 26 for a discussion of the three basic questions.

15. (a) A general theme in economics is that private competition is highly efficient in providing most goods.

16. (c) With scarce resources, the production possibility frontier will *always* have a negative slope. With an increasing-cost production possibility frontier, the cost of producing one good in terms of the other accelerates as production level increases.

17. (a) Comparative advantage is a relative concept. If, relative to Jack, Jill is better at producing pins, then she has a comparative advantage in this.

18. (d) The first three answers are statements of the three "basic" questions. In any case, resources are allocated among producers, not consumers.

19. (b) The cost of one unit of goat milk in Arboc is 5/3 units of bananas whereas the cost of one unit of goat milk in Arbez is 1/3 unit of bananas. Arbez has the advantage in goat milk. One unit of bananas in Arboc costs 3/5 unit of goat milk whereas one unit of bananas in Arbez costs 3 units of goat milk. Arboc has the advantage in bananas.

20. (a) A bowed-out production possibility frontier indicates increasing costs; the costs increase whether the movement is down along the PPF or up along the PPF.

II. SOLUTIONS TO APPLICATION QUESTIONS

1. (a) Your production possibility frontier should include the following points:

Corn	100	90	70	40	0
Tobacco	0	40	70	90	100

There will be a straight line between each of the points.

   (b) Resources are fully employed and employed in the more efficient activity. For example, Field *A* may be producing its maximum output of tobacco, but (because the opportunity cost of tobacco production in that field is high) it should be used to produce tobacco only after the other fields have been switched over to tobacco production. If it is switched before Field *B*, for instance, Brown will be producing inefficiently and inside his PPF.

   (c) *D, C, B, A.*

   (d) Refer to the explanation for (b).

2. (a) Refer to the following diagrams.

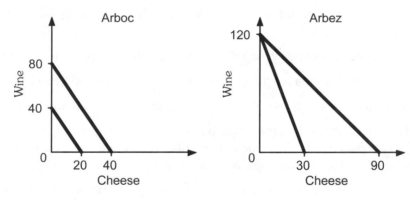

   (b) 1 wine = 1/2 cheese, 1 wine = 1/4 cheese.

   (c) Arbez

   (d) 1 cheese = 2 wine (Arboc), 1 cheese = 4 wine (Arbez). Arboc can produce cheese more cheaply than Arbez can.

   (e) Refer to the diagrams above.

   (f) Arboc should still produce cheese, as the comparative costs have not changed.

   (g) Arboc. Recompute the opportunity costs. Note that, relatively, the steepness of the production possibility frontiers has changed.

3. (a, b) This question is intended to get you to think about all of the decisions that must be made in an economic system. The owner has land, labor, and capital at his/her disposal. The capital stock includes the store, the gas station, inventories, trucks, the house, and so

forth. The road is also capital even though it was produced by the government. We are not told much about the natural resources of the town. These would include the fertility of the land. The potential labor force includes some fraction of those who live nearby.

(c)   The people who travel the road, the general economic circumstances of the people who live nearby, the weather, gasoline prices, the potential for competition from other stores, and so forth.

(d)   What to sell, whether to advertise, what prices to change, whether to fix up the town, how many people to hire, and so forth.

(e)   I will add up all the future income I will earn, net of costs. I must consider all the alternatives and my expectations about them. How much will I earn here? How much will college cost? What am I likely to earn when I have graduated from college? I also need to consider carefully the personal pleasure I will derive from the two situations.

4.   (a)   Refer to the following diagram.

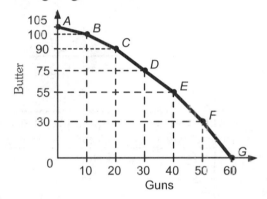

(b)   Point D is on the PPF, indicating full employment of resources whereas Point H is inside the curve, indicating underproduction and an underutilization of scarce resources.

(c)   (i)   1/2 unit of butter
       (ii)   1 unit of butter
       (iii)   2 1/2 units of butter
       (iv)   3 units of butter

(d)   (i)   1/3 of a gun
       (ii)   2/3 of a gun
       (iii)   1 gun
       (iv)   2 guns

(e)   The PPF will not shift position! We would expect the balance of production to shift in favor of guns. If unemployment exists, indicated by a bundle of goods inside the PPF, war production will shift the economy towards the production possibility frontier.

5.   (a)   No change in the position of the production possibility frontier.

(b)   The end of the PPF on the X-axis will shift out. The end on the Y-axis will not move.

(c)   The production possibility frontier would shift inwards.

(d)   The production possibility frontier would shift outwards.

(e)   The end of the PPF on the X-axis will shift in. The end on the Y-axis will not move.

6. (a) You might think *C* and *A* are "best" and "worst," respectively—but the question is a trap! What do we mean by "best"? Perhaps a particular point inside the PPF is better than a particular point on it. There's not enough information to give a complete answer.

    (b) Clearly, all points on the production possibility frontier are not created equal, and Point *E* might be the "best" choice of those depicted.

    (c) The "best" output mix depends on what best meets society's wants. If you think about it, what society *wants* isn't shown on a PPF diagram—only what can be *produced*.

7. (a) Refer to the following diagram.

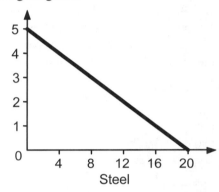

    (b)

Production	Opportunity Cost of 1 Unit of:	
Alternative	Corn	Steel
A – B	4 steel	1/4 corn
B – C	4 steel	1/4 corn
C – D	4 steel	1/4 corn
D – E	4 steel	1/4 corn
E – F	4 steel	1/4 corn

    (c) Situation *X*: 0 steel; 0 corn
    Situation *Y*: 4 steel; 1/4 corn

    (d) In Situation *X* there are still some unemployed (inefficiently used) resources. In Situation *Y*, Arbez is already utilizing all of its resources, and a trade-off is necessary. (Plot the points on the diagram to see the difference.)

    (e) Situation *Z*: 1 steel; 0 corn

    (f) Situation *Y* is the most productively efficient. Either *X* or *Z* is the least productively efficient—we don't have enough information.

    (g) Each unit of corn costs 4 units of steel; each unit of steel costs 1/4 unit of corn.

    (h) Each unit of corn costs 2 units of steel. Each unit of steel costs 1/2 unit of corn.

    (i) Arbez; Arboc. Yes, trade can be mutually beneficial.

8. (a) *D*

    (b) The economy must either grow (more resources) or experience a technological improvement.

    (c) *C*

    (d) Corn

(e) There is no opportunity cost; more steel is produced without any reduction in corn production. Note that there are "free lunches" if the economy is operating at an inefficient point.

9. (a) Yes

(b) No, because it is possible to produce more of each good. Also some resources are unemployed.

(c) No, not relative to Point *A*, where consumers would have more of each good available to them.

(d) It is beyond the maximum level of production, given current resources and technology.

(e) Resources would be released and transferred to steel production.

10. (a) 2 units of wheat

(b) 5/4 units of wheat

(c) Arbez

(d) 1/2 unit of coffee

(e) 8/10 unit of coffee

(f) Arboc

(g) Arboc should specialize in wheat production, and Arbez should specialize in coffee production.

11. The production possibility frontier would pivot at its "guns" endpoint and become flatter, which indicates that it is possible to produce a greater maximum quantity of butter than before, while still producing the same maximum quantity of guns. The slope of the PPF represents opportunity cost. Producing only guns means that we surrender a larger quantity of butter than before—the opportunity cost of guns has increased (and the opportunity cost of butter has decreased).

12. (a) Refer to the following diagram.

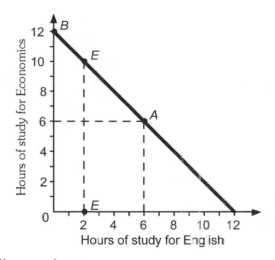

(b) Refer to the diagram above.

(c) Refer to the diagram above.

(d) True. Economics: $30 + (10 \times 7) = 100$. English: $40 + (6 \times 5) = 70$.

(e) True. Economics: $30 + (10 \times 5) = 80$. English: $40 + (6 \times 7) = 82$. If she gets 80 on the economics test, 82 is the maximum she can get on the English paper.

(f) She has 8 hours for the English paper. English: $40 + (6 \times 8) = 88$.

(g) Economics: $30 + (10 \times 4) = 70$. English: $40 + (6 \times 5) = 70$. This totals 9 hours.

(h) False. Economics: $30 + (10 \times 4) = 70$. English: $40 + (6 \times 8) = 88$.

(i) Ten points lower—an extra hour of work on the English paper will cut Kara's economics score by 10 points.

(j) Refer to the preceding diagram.

13. (a) Clearly, there are no definitive answers for the restaurant—that's why entrepreneurs are an unusual breed.

(b) Staw's opportunity cost of founding his company would include the salary he gave up (and his promotion prospects). He opted to produce deliberately mismatched products, made to his specifications by overseas textiles producers. He set up marketing deals with large retail chains such as Sears.

3

Demand, Supply, and Market Equilibrium

Chapter Objectives

1. Define and apply quantity demanded and quantity supplied, and state the law of demand and the law of supply.
2. Draw and interpret demand and supply graphs.
3. Identify the determinants of demand and supply and incicate how each must change for demand and supply to increase or decrease.
4. Derive market demand and market supply curves from individual demand and supply schedules.
5. Differentiate between a shift of a demand curve or supply curve and a movement along a curve, and depict these cases correctly on a graph.
6. Provide explanations for the slope of a typical demand curve.
7. Distinguish the relationship that exists between two goods that are substitutes and the relationship that exists between two goods that are complements.
8. Distinguish between a good that is normal and a good that is inferior.
9. Determine equilibrium price and quantity, and detail the process by which the market moves from one equilibrium situation to another when demand or supply shifts.
10. Define excess demand (shortage) and excess supply (surplus) and predict their effects on the existing price level.

The single best piece of advice, particularly for this essential chapter is "practice, practice, practice." A second piece of advice must be "draw, draw, draw." Don't be put off by the graphs—develop a solid intuitive feel for demand and supply by talking your way through how the market should behave.

In most of the multiple-choice questions in this chapter, the *first* thing to do is to sketch a demand and supply picture. Graphs are an effective and timesaving tool for organizing your analysis.

Cultivate the habit of asking "What should happen to demand?" and "Will this make supply increase or decrease?" Predict whether price should rise or fall in a given circumstance (common sense should carry you a long way here). Don't try to avoid graphs—they'll make your course a lot easier *and* more rewarding. If you have some initial problems, check the Appendix to Chapter 1 and the "Learning Tips" in this Guide.

BRAIN TEASER I: During the past ten years, the price of cell phones has fallen, while the numbers sold have increased. Is this a contradiction of the law of supply? How could you best explain this phenomenon, both in words and graphically?

SOLUTION: The answer to this and subsequent brain teasers will be found after our discussion of the learning objectives and before the Practice Tests.

BRAIN TEASER II: Many large firms (McDonald's, for example) perform research in order to determine where best to locate new branches. Suppose you're responsible for choosing your burger company's next location. Which factors would be important in your deliberations?

Objective 1

Define and apply quantity demanded and quantity supplied, and state the law of demand and the law of supply.

Quantity demanded is the amount of a product that a household would buy, in a given period, if it could buy all it wanted at the current price. *Quantity supplied* is the amount of a product that a firm would be willing and able to offer for sale at a particular price during a given time period. The *law of demand* states that there is a negative relationship between the price and the quantity demanded of a product. When the price of McDonald's fries increases, we buy less. The *law of supply* states that there is a positive relationship between the price and the quantity supplied of a product. When McDonald's raises its hourly wage, it attracts more job applicants. (pages 50, 60)

Objective 2

Draw and interpret demand and supply graphs.

A *demand schedule* is a table showing how much of a given product households would be willing and able to buy at different prices in a given time period; a *demand curve* shows this relationship graphically. Demand curves slope downward. (page 51)

   A *supply schedule* is a table listing how much of a product a firm will supply at alternative prices in a given time period; a *supply curve*, shows this relationship graphically. Supply curves slope upward. (page 61)

Note: Demand and supply graphs *always* have price on the vertical axis and quantity (demanded or supplied, as appropriate) on the horizontal axis. It is a bad (though common) mistake to reverse the variables. Learn to draw the demand and supply graphs quickly! A demand curve slopes down to the right; a supply curve slopes up to the right. Practice to increase your speed. Label each curve as you go. In diagrams where there are several curves, clear, consistent labeling is critical.

Practice

1.   At each price shown, estimate how many apples per month you might demand.

Price per Apple	Quantity Demanded
60¢	1
50¢	2
40¢	3
30¢	4
20¢	5
10¢	6

   You have constructed a demand schedule. Now draw vertical (price) and horizontal (quantity) axes. Plot your monthly demand curve for apples. Label the curve D_1.

ANSWER: Although this line is unlikely to be smooth like those in the textbook, it should have a general downward slope—the lower the price, the more apples you're likely to buy. You should have the horizontal axis labeled "quantity demanded per month" and the vertical axis labeled "price."

2. In the following diagrams, match each of the numbers with the appropriate term to produce a correct demand or supply diagram for apples.

 (a) Price of apples
 (b) Price of apples
 (c) Quantity of apples supplied per month
 (d) Quantity of apples demanded per month
 (e) Demand curve
 (f) Supply curve

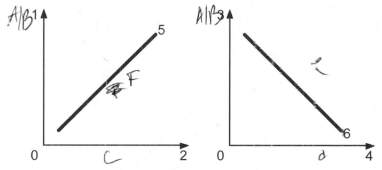

ANSWER: 1 = (a) and (b); 2 = (c); 3 = (a) and (b); 4 = (d); 5 = (f); 6 = (e) ■

Objective 3

Identify the determinants of demand and supply and indicate how each must change for demand and supply to increase or decrease.

The willingness and ability of a household to buy units of a good during a given time period (quantity demanded) are likely to depend principally on the price of the good itself. Other factors—including the household's income and wealth, the prices of other products, tastes and preferences, and expectations about price, income, and wealth—will influence demand.

Comment: This section of the textbook may be your most frustrating section. Be patient—time spent understanding demand/supply analysis will serve you well in future chapters.

LEARNING TIP: When analyzing the impact of change in a determinant on demand and supply curves, a golden rule to remember is that each curve shifts no more than once for any such change. The market price is changed by shifts in the demand and supply curves, but the demand and supply curves are not changed by shifts in the market price. ◀

 Again: a change in price does not cause the demand curve or the supply curve to shift position! Analyze the following sequence of events for errors. "Demand goes up. That makes price go up, which encourages sellers to supply more. But, when more is supplied, price goes down. When price goes down, demand goes up again, and so on."

Answer: A demand increase from D_1 to D_2 will make price rise from P_1 to P_2. Sellers will supply more from Q_1 to Q_2—an increase in *quantity supplied*, not an increase in supply, as the statement claims. Price, therefore, will *not* go back down. The remainder of the statement is incorrect. Draw this example.

When you constructed your demand schedule and demand curve with varying price levels in Practice Question 1, you made assumptions about your income level, wealth, prices of other goods, and so on. Change the assumptions and you will change the diagram. The curve shifts position—a *change in demand*.

Factors that can cause a change in demand are:
(a)   Income
(b)   Wealth
(c)   Prices of related products
(d)   Tastes or preferences of the household
(e)   Expectations (page 54)

Increases in income and wealth, improved preferences, or expectations of a higher price, income, or wealth will increase demand for normal goods. An increase in the price of a substitute product or a decrease in the price of a complementary product will also increase demand, i.e., the entire demand curve shifts to the right. Graphically, an increase in demand (D_1 to D_2) appears as shown in the following diagram:

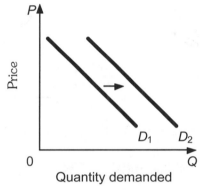

LEARNING TIP: When shifting the demand curve, you might naturally associate "rise" and "fall" with a vertical shift. This causes no problems in the case of demand, and you'd expect to be correct in using the same approach in the case of supply—but you'd be wrong! A vertical shift up in supply is a *decrease* in supply. When shifting the demand or supply curve, think in terms of the curve sliding *left* for a decrease (demand less or supply less) and *right* for an increase (demand more or supply more), *not* up and down.◀

The decision to supply is affected by the ability to earn profits (the difference between revenues and costs). The willingness and ability of a firm to offer units of a good for sale during a given time period (quantity supplied) are likely to depend mainly on the price of the good itself. If other factors important to producers change, then the supply curve diagram will change. The supply curve shifts position—a *change in supply*.

Factors that can cause a change in supply are:
(a)   Changes in costs of production (input prices)
(b)   New costs and market opportunities
(c)   Changes in prices of related products (page 63)

Improvements in technology, decreases in the costs of inputs and other costs of production, or increases in the price of complementary products, will increase supply. Decreases in the price of substitute products will also increase supply, i.e., the entire supply curve will shift to the right. Graphically, an increase in supply (S_1 to S_2) appears as shown in the following diagram:

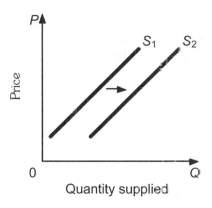

Demand: Do "thought experiments." Pick a good that you buy frequently (preferably a name brand), such as Exxon gasoline. How would you react if Exxon hiked the price of its gas? If your income fell? If the price of engine oil (a complement) increased? If the price of Chevron gas (a substitute) decreased?

Supply: Perhaps you have a part-time job—you supply labor. Which factors affect how many hours you would work per week? The wage (price) you earn affects the quantity of labor you supply. What other factors would make you more or less willing and able to work?

Supply is analyzed in greater detail in Chapters 7, 8, and 9 of *Principles of Economics*. Note the reference to the *short run* and the *long run* on page 62. These are important economic concepts that you'll meet later on. Essentially, suppliers will be more responsive to demand-side changes in a longer time period than they will be in a shorter time period.

Practice

3.   A decrease in the supply of American cars might be caused by
        (a)   an increase in the price of imported Japanese cars.
        (b)   an increase in the wages of U.S. car workers.
        (c)   an increase in demand that causes car prices to rise.
        (d)   a reduction in the cost of steel.

        ANSWER: (b) The supply of American cars will decrease if input prices, such as the wages of
                    U.S. car workers, increase. Refer to p. 63.

4.   Energizer batteries and Duracell's Coppertop batteries are substitutes. The Energizer Bunny cuts supply and increases the price of its batteries. Equilibrium price will _____ and quantity exchanged will _____ in the market for Duracell.
     (a)   rise; rise
     (b)   fall; rise
     (c)   fall; fall
     (d)   rise; fall

     ANSWER: (a)   If Energizer increases the price of its batteries, consumers will switch over to substitutes such as Duracell, increasing the demand for Duracell. This will raise both equilibrium price and quantity.

5.   Barney's Bowling Balls and Fred's Bowling Shoes are complements. Fred notices a decrease in the quantity demanded of bowling shoes (a movement along his demand curve). This could have been caused by
     (a)   a decrease in the income of Fred's customers.
     (b)   an increase in the price of Fred's Bowling Shoes.
     (c)   an increase in the price of Barney's Bowling Balls.
     (d)   an increased expectation that Fred will reduce the price of his bowling balls in the near future.

     ANSWER: (b)   This is a change in quantity demanded, not a change in demand! The only thing that can cause a change in quantity demanded is a change in price. Refer to page 56.

6.   As the price of oranges increases, orange growers will
     (a)   use more-expensive methods of growing oranges.
     (b)   use less-expensive methods of growing oranges.
     (c)   increase the supply of oranges.
     (d)   decrease the supply of oranges.

     ANSWER: (a)   An increase in price results in an increase in quantity supplied. Suppliers are able to produce more because at the higher price they can afford to hire more-expensive resources. Refer to page 63.

7.   The supply of oranges to households will shift to the right if
     (a)   the price of oranges increases.
     (b)   oranges are rumored to have been treated with an insecticide that causes heart disease.
     (c)   the Florida government requires that all orange workers be given more substantial health benefits by employers.
     (d)   citrus growers see the price of grapefruits decreasing permanently.

     ANSWER: (d)   As the price of grapefruits falls, citrus farmers will switch over to another production option—oranges. Refer to page 63. ■

Objective 4

Derive market demand and market supply curves from individual demand and supply schedules.

Market demand is the sum of all the quantities of a good or service demanded per period by all the households buying in the market for that good or service. The *market demand curve* is a summing of all the individual demand curves. At a given price level, the quantity demanded by each household is determined and the total quantity demanded is calculated. (pages 58/65)

   The *market supply curve* is a horizontal summing of all the supply curves for the product.

Practice

---

8. If the firms producing fuzzy dice for cars must obtain a higher price than they did previously to produce the same level of output as before, then we can say that there has been
   (a) an increase in quantity supplied.
   (b) an increase in supply.
   (c) a decrease in supply.
   (d) a decrease in quantity supplied.

   ANSWER: (c) Draw the supply curve. At the same output level and at a higher price, the supply curve has shifted to the left—a decrease in supply. Refer to page 63.

9. The market supply curve for wheat depends on each of the following EXCEPT
   (a) the price of wheat-producing land.
   (b) the price of production alternatives for wheat.
   (c) the tastes and preferences of wheat consumers.
   (d) the number of wheat farmers in the market.

   ANSWER: (c) Tastes and preferences are determinants of demand, not supply. Refer to page 63.
   ■

Objective 5

Differentiate between a shift of a demand curve or supply curve and a movement along a curve, and depict these cases correctly on a graph.

When important factors other than the price of the product change, such as tastes or income, the entire demand curve shifts position. This is called a *change in demand* to distinguish it from a movement along the demand curve, which represents a *change in quantity demanded* and can be caused *only* by a change in the price of the commodity. (page 56)

Similarly, when important factors other than price change for a producer, the amount of a given product offered for sale will change, even if the price level is unchanged. This is a *change in supply*. If *only* the price of the product itself changes, there will be a movement along the original supply curve—a *change in quantity supplied*. (page 63)

Graphing Pointer: Changes in Quantity Demanded (Supplied) vs. Changes in Demand (Supply). Most students experience confusion regarding the distinction between a "change in quantity demanded" and a "change in demand." The distinction is rather artificial; the six factors (listed on page 50) that affect demand include the price of the product. However, we regard the price-quantity demanded relationship as the most important and draw the demand curve with these two variables on the axes, assuming that all other factors are fixed at a "given" level. This is the *ceteris paribus* assumption.

Look at a demand curve; price and quantity demanded can have a range of values whereas all other factors (income, other prices, etc.) are fixed at a particular level. If price changes, we move along the curve; if another factor changes, our *ceteris paribus* assumption is broken, and we must redraw the price-quantity demanded relationship.

The *only* thing that can cause a "change in the quantity demanded" of Pepsi is a change in the price of Pepsi—a movement from one point on the demand curve to another point on the same demand curve.

If any other factor on the list changes, we will have to redraw the entire diagram—a "change in demand"—because the "all else being equal" assumption has been broken.

Similarly, a "change in the quantity supplied" of chicken can only be caused by a change in the price of chicken. A change in any other factor on the list on page 63 of the text causes a "change in supply."

LEARNING TIP: Here is an example that points up the difference between a "change in quantity demanded" and a "change in demand." In the following diagram, we have a demand curve for Ford Rangers on the left and a demand curve for Dodge Rams on the right.

Initially, the price of the Ranger is $27,000, and 2,000 are demanded per week. The Ram sells for $26,000 and has 2,500 demanders at that price. (Note: It's irrelevant whether the Ram's price is above, below, or equal to that of the Ranger—at any realistic price, each truck will have some enthusiasts.)

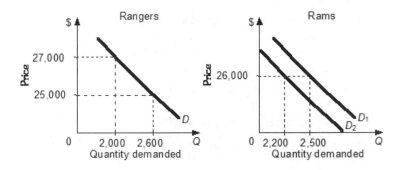

Suppose that the price of Rangers decreases to $25,000. More truck buyers will order Rangers—an increase in quantity demanded, as there is a movement along the demand curve. Some of those new Ford customers would have bought the Dodge Ram, but now will not. At the same price ($26,000) as before, demand for Rams has decreased, perhaps to 2,200. The entire demand curve for Rams has shifted. ◀

Practice

10.   Return to Practice Question 1. Suppose that the prices of other fruits you might buy increase. What would happen to the number of apples you demand per month? Sketch this change on your diagram. Label the demand curve D_2. What is likely to happen to the price of apples?

ANSWER: Refer to your diagram for Practice Question 1. Presumably you'd demand more apples at each price. The demand curve shifts right, to D_2. Because apples are more popular now, the price of apples will likely rise.

11.   A "change in demand" means
(a)   the quantity demanded changes as price changes.
(b)   a movement along a given demand curve or schedule.
(c)   a shift in the position of the demand curve.
(d)   a change in the shape of a demand curve.

ANSWER: (c) A "change in demand" means that, at every price level, more or less is being demanded. This is represented as a shift in the position of the demand curve. Refer to page 56.

12.   Which of the following will cause a decrease in the demand for tennis racquets?
(a)   A rise in the price of squash racquets
(b)   A rise in the price of tennis racquets
(c)   A rise in the price of tennis balls
(d)   A fall in the price of tennis shoes

ANSWER: (c) A decrease in the demand for tennis racquets will occur if a complement (tennis balls) increases in price because fewer tennis balls will be bought. ■

Objective 6

Provide explanations for the slope of a typical demand curve.

Demand curves slope down—as price rises, quantity demanded falls. We know this intuitively, but economists have explored this important "social law" more analytically. The higher the price of a good, lowfat milk, for instance, the higher the opportunity cost of buying it (i.e., the more of other goods we will give up, and the less willing we are to buy lowfat milk).

Utility is a conceptual measure of satisfaction. Successive units of a good bestow satisfaction, but typically at a decreasing rate—the second cup of coffee may be less enjoyable than the first. Accordingly, the price we are willing to pay will decrease. (page 53)

Practice

13.   The demand curve diagram has "price" on the
   (a)   vertical axis, "quantity demanded per time period" on the horizontal axis, and an upward-sloping demand curve.
   (b)   horizontal axis, "quantity demanded per time period" on the vertical axis, and an upward-sloping demand curve.
   (c)   vertical axis, "quantity demanded per time period" on the horizontal axis, and a downward-sloping demand curve.
   (d)   horizontal axis, "quantity demanded per time period" on the vertical axis, and a downward-sloping demand curve.

   ANSWER: (c) Refer to p. 52.

14.   We are trying to explain the law of demand. When the price of pretzels rises,
   (a)   the opportunity cost of pretzels increases along the demand curve.
   (b)   sellers switch production and increase the quantity supplied of pretzels.
   (c)   income rises for producers of pretzels.
   (d)   the opportunity cost of other goods increases.

   ANSWER: (a) Refer to p. 53 for a full explanation of the negative relationship between price and quantity demanded. ■

Objective 7

Distinguish the relationship that exists between two goods that are substitutes and the relationship that exists between two goods that are complements.

If, when the price of Good *A* rises, the demand for Good *B* also rises, then *A* and *B* are *substitutes*. However, if the demand for *B* falls when the price of *A* rises, then *A* and *B* are *complements*. Substitutes are used in place of each other, complements are used together. (page 54)

LEARNING TIP: Think of several ready-made examples of substitute goods and complementary goods from your own life. Using your own examples (during an exam) makes it easier to do the analysis correctly. Here are a few examples.

Substitutes: Coke and Pepsi, Exxon gasoline and BP gasoline, phone calls and e-mail.

Complements: peanut butter and jelly, CDs and CD players, cars and gasoline, cameras and film, left and right shoes.◀

Practice

15. The demand for JIF peanut butter will decrease if there is an increase in the
    (a)   price of JIF peanut butter.
    (b)   price of Peter Pan peanut butter (a substitute).
    (c)   demand for jelly (a complement).
    (d)   price of bread (a complement).

    ANSWER: (d) Bread and peanut butter are complements. An increase in the price of bread will result in less bread being bought, and a lower demand for JIF to spread on it. Refer to page 54.

16. Good *A* and Good *B* are substitutes for one another. An increase in the price of *A* will
    (a)   increase the demand for *B*.
    (b)   reduce the quantity demanded of *B*.
    (c)   increase the quantity demanded of *B*.
    (d)   reduce the demand for *B*.

    ANSWER: (a) Suppose *A* is Coke and *B* is Pepsi. If Coke rises in price, we would buy less Coke (a fall in quantity demanded of Coke) and more of Pepsi (an increase in the demand for Pepsi). Refer to page 54. ∎

ECONOMICS IN PRACTICE: Your textbook (page 55) refers to electronic books and Amazon's Kindle as an example of complements. The cheaper e-books become, the greater will be the consumer demand for Kindles. It is sensible for Amazon to market e-books cheaply in order to attract customers to its own product. Think about complements in the video game market. Can you come up with examples of the same marketing technique?

ANSWER: In the video game arena, the strategy is in some sense reversed, as it is the new consoles (PlayStation, Xbox 360, Wii) that companies market cheaply enough to cause initial shortages (and great publicity!) Having purchased the console, consumers then have an interest in buying games that go with the system. Guitar Hero and its accessories is another good example of complementarity.

Objective 8

Distinguish between a good that is normal and a good that is inferior.

When income increases, demand increases for *normal* goods. If demand for a good decreases when income increases, then the good is *inferior*. (page 54)

LEARNING TIP: Think of several ready-made examples of both normal goods and inferior goods from your own life. Slotting in your own examples (during an exam) makes it easier to do the analysis correctly. Here are some examples:

Normal goods: movie tickets, steak, restaurant meals, imported beers.

Inferior goods: second-hand clothes, store-brand (versus name-brand) foods, generic medicines, rice, beans, bus rides. ◀

Practice

17. If the economy's income rises by 10 percent, *ceteris paribus*, we would predict
    (a)   a decrease in demand for a normal good.
    (b)   an increase in quantity demanded for a normal good.
    (c)   an increase in quantity demanded for an inferior good.
    (d)   a decrease in demand for an inferior good.

ANSWER: (d) Refer to page 54. Remember that a change in "quantity demanded" can only be due to a change in the price of the good.

13.   The demand for Good *A* has been increasing over the past year. Having examined the following facts, you conclude that Good *A* is an inferior good. Which fact led you to that conclusion?

(a)   The price of Good *A* has been increasing over the past year.

(b)   An economic slowdown has reduced the income of the traditional buyers of Good *A*.

(c)   Good *B*, a substitute for Good *A*, has cut its price over the last 12 months.

(d)   Household wealth has increased among the traditional buyers of Good *A*.

ANSWER: (b) Inferior goods experience increasing popularity as income levels fall. Refer to page 54.

19.   Turnips are available in both the United States and in Mexico. During the past year, incomes have grown by 10 percent in each country. The demand for turnips has grown by 12 percent in the United States and by 3 percent in Mexico. We can conclude that turnips are

(a)   normal goods in the United States and normal goods in Mexico.

(b)   normal goods in the United States and inferior goods in Mexico.

(c)   inferior goods in the United States and normal goods in Mexico.

(d)   inferior goods in the United States and inferior goods in Mexico.

ANSWER: (a) In each case, demand has increased as income has increased. Refer to p. 54. ∎

Objective 9

Determine equilibrium price and quantity, and detail the process by which the market moves from one equilibrium situation to another when either demand or supply shifts.

In the market for a particular good or service, quantity demanded may be greater than, less than, or equal to quantity supplied. *Equilibrium* occurs when quantity demanded equals quantity supplied. There is no tendency for the price to change because, at that price, there is a perfect match between the quantity of the good demanded and the quantity supplied. (page 66)

LEARNING TIP: Equilibrium. The notion of equilibrium is important throughout the remainder of the course. The simple, less analytical, way to think about this concept is as "the point where the lines cross." It will help your understanding if you remember that equilibrium is the "balance" situation in which there is no tendency for change—unless some outside factor intervenes.

Changes in Equilibrium Price and Quantity. Demand and supply may change position simultaneously. If the magnitudes of the shifts are unknown, then the effect either on equilibrium price or on equilibrium quantity *must* be uncertain. It's easy to forget this important fact. If demand and supply change position simultaneously, break down the situation into two separate graphs, one for the "demand shift" and the other for the "supply shift." In each case, decide the direction of change in price and quantity, and then add them together. ◀

Example: Demand decreases and supply increases.

	Price Change	Quantity Change
Demand-side effect	Decrease	Decrease
Supply-side effect	Decrease	Increase
Total effect	Decrease	Uncertain

In this case, where demand decreases and supply increases, we predict a certain decrease in price and an uncertain change in equilibrium quantity.

ECONOMICS IN PRACTICE: On page 70, the textbook looks at the effects of demand and supply on the market for tomatoes. What about other markets? Following a severe drought, Australian wool production slumped to record low levels. Wool prices surged to a 15-year peak. What do you think was the effect of the price surge of wool on the market for cotton, a substitute fiber?
ANSWER: Initially, cotton prices had been languishing at a 30-year low. However, as garment producers switched from wool to cotton, they caused the demand for cotton to increase, resulting in a 50 percent boost in the price of cotton. For "extra credit," can you draw a demand and supply diagram (one for wool and another for cotton) depicting what happened?

ECONOMICS IN PRACTICE (CONTINUED): During the spring and summer of 2008, the corn-growing states of the Midwest suffered from extreme wet weather. Corn planting declined by 10 percent while the use of corn for ethanol was increasing. The Chicago Board of Trade has a futures market where dealers can bid for future deliveries of corn and other goods, such as soybeans. This market is driven largely by predictions about future market conditions. What do you think happened to the price of corn and soybeans on the futures market as a result of the storms?
ANSWER: The price of corn tripled to about $7.00 per bushel. Soybeans, (a production substitute of corn) also experienced price increases.

ECONOMICS IN PRACTICE: On page 73, your textbook examines the opinions on the cause of rising newspaper prices of three analysts . Essentially, the issue of rising prices boils down to whether it is triggered by changes in demand or rather changes in supply. The market for corn offers another example. During the first few months of 2008, corn prices rose throughout the world. Was this caused by cutbacks in supply or increases in demand? Background: Over the two previous years, major corn-growing regions had experienced poor weather conditions, the Chinese economy was experiencing increased affluence, and there had been a push by environmentally conscious governments to produce more ethanol (an oil substitute that uses corn). Given these facts, how would you analyze the changes in the corn market?
ANSWER: There were changes in both supply and demand. The poor growing conditions reduced supply while increasing affluence expanded the demand for corn (a normal good). At the same time, the demand for corn used to produce ethanol increased, which reduced the amount available for food production.

ECONOMICS IN PRACTICE (CONTINUED): In the summer of 2008, gas prices were hovering around $4.00 per gallon and President Bush appealed to Saudi Arabia to increase the supply of oil in order to reduce pressure on gas prices at the pumps. His point was that restricted supply had forces up prices. The Saudi response, in summary, was "There is no shortage of oil. World oil prices are responding as they should to the increase in demand." However, the Law of Demand states that rising prices should reduce the amount of a good demanded. First, is there some inconsistency here in the Law of Demand?

Following this, can you analyze who was correct about the oil market in 2008, President Bush or the Saudi Oil Ministry?

ANSWER: There's no contradiction of the Law of Demand. In fact, as prices rose in the United States, oil consumption fell, as we should expect. On the second point, both parties are correct. An increase in supply would have slowed or, perhaps, reversed the rise in oil prices, as President Bush argued. However, the main cause of rising oil prices was the worldwide increase in demand. The Saudis were correct—the market was seeking to "compete away" excess demand by raising prices. If a market is in equilibrium there is no shortage.

Practice

20.   Equilibrium quantity will certainly decrease if demand
    (a)   and supply both increase.
    (b)   and supply both decrease.
    (c)   decreases and supply increases.
    (d)   increases and supply decreases.

    ANSWER: (b) A decrease in demand will decrease equilibrium quantity. Similarly, a decrease in supply will decrease equilibrium quantity.

21.   The market for canned dog food is in equilibrium when
    (a)   the quantity demanded is less than the quantity supplied.
    (b)   the demand curve is downward sloping and the supply curve is upward sloping.
    (c)   the quantity demanded and the quantity supplied are equal.
    (d)   all inputs producing canned dog food are employed.

    ANSWER: (c) A market is in equilibrium when price has adjusted to make the quantity demanded and the quantity supplied equal. Refer to page 66.

22.   In the market for broccoli, the price of broccoli will certainly increase if the supply of broccoli
    (a)   increases and the demand for broccoli increases.
    (b)   increases and the demand for broccoli decreases.
    (c)   decreases and the demand for broccoli increases.
    (d)   decreases and the demand for broccoli decreases.

    ANSWER: (c) An increase in demand will increase equilibrium price. Similarly, a decrease in supply will increase equilibrium price.

23.   In the market for mushrooms, the price of mushrooms will certainly increase if the supply curve shifts
    (a)   right and the demand curve shifts right.
    (b)   right and the demand curve shifts left.
    (c)   left and the demand curve shifts right.
    (d)   left and the demand curve shifts left.

    ANSWER (c) When demand increases and supply decreases, both shifts are prompting a price increase.

24.   In the market for broccoli, the equilibrium quantity of broccoli will certainly increase if the supply of broccoli _____ and the demand for broccoli _____ .
    (a)   increases; increases
    (b)   increases; decreases
    (c)   decreases; increases
    (d)   decreases; decreases

    ANSWER: (a) An increase in supply will increase the quantity traded; similarly, an increase in demand will increase the quantity traded. ∎

Objective 10

Define excess demand (shortage) and excess supply (surplus) and predict their effects on the existing price level.

If the quantity demanded of a good is greater than the quantity supplied, there is *excess demand* (shortage). We would expect the price of the good to rise. If quantity supplied is greater than the quantity demanded of a good, there is an *excess supply* (surplus), and we would expect the price of the good to fall. (page 66)

Practice

25.   When there is a surplus, quantity supplied _____ quantity demanded. Price will _____ .
        (a)   exceeds; rise
        (b)   is less than; fall
        (c)   is less than; rise
        (d)   exceeds; fall

        ANSWER: (d) A surplus (excess supply) occurs when quantity supplied exceeds quantity demanded. This surplus will force price down. Refer to page 67.

26.   The equilibrium price of a gallon of unleaded gas is $4.50. At a price of $3.00 quantity supplied will be
        (a)   less than quantity demanded, causing a shortage of unleaded gas.
        (b)   greater than quantity demanded, causing a surplus of unleaded gas.
        (c)   greater than quantity demanded, causing a shortage of unleaded gas.
        (d)   less than quantity demanded, causing a surplus of unleaded gas.

        ANSWER: (a) If the current price is less than the equilibrium price, a shortage will occur (quantity supplied will be less than quantity demanded). This shortage will force price to increase. ∎

BRAIN TEASER I SOLUTION: Behavior in the cell phone market did not contradict the law of supply. Market behavior depends on both supply and demand. Demand increased (the demand curve shifted to the right from D_1 to D_2) as more consumers were attracted to the benefits of cell phones—particularly their convenience, and supply increased (the supply curve shifted to the right from S_1 to S_2) due to technological improvements. Increasing supply and vigorous competition drove down the price (from P_1 to P_2) even as the market grew (from Q_1 to Q_2).

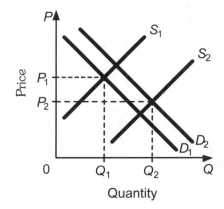

BRAIN TEASER II SOLUTION: The presence of competitors, income and wealth of the neighborhood, the percentage of families with young children, expected growth, and volume of traffic should all be important considerations. It is rumored that McDonald's also figures in the direction of after-work traffic.

PRACTICE TEST

I. MULTIPLE-CHOICE QUESTIONS

Select the option that provides the single best answer.

_____ 1. Households are
   (a) suppliers in the input market.
   (b) demanders in the labor market.
   (c) suppliers in the product market.
   (d) demanders in the input market.

_____ 2. Following a decrease in supply, Good C increases its price. The demand for Good D increases. The goods are
   (a) complements.
   (b) substitutes.
   (c) normal.
   (d) inferior.

_____ 3. The demand for prerecorded CDs is downward sloping. Suddenly the price of CDs rises from $12 to $20. This will cause
   (a) demand to shift to the left.
   (b) demand to shift to the right.
   (c) quantity demanded to increase.
   (d) quantity demanded to decrease.

_____ 4. All of the following will shift the supply curve of yo-yos to the right EXCEPT
   (a) an increase in price of yo-yos.
   (b) an improvement in the production processes used to manufacture yo-yos.
   (c) a reduction in the price of plastic from which yo-yos are made.
   (d) an improvement in storage resulting in fewer defective yo-yos.

_____ 5. Along a given supply curve for eggs,
   (a) supply increases as price increases.
   (b) supply increases as technology improves.
   (c) quantity supplied increases as price increases.
   (d) quantity supplied increases as technology improves.

_____ 6. Price is currently below equilibrium. There is a situation of excess _____ . We would expect price to _____ .
   (a) demand; rise
   (b) demand; fall
   (c) supply; rise
   (d) supply; fall

_____ 7. Consumers expect their income to rise. For a normal good, this would result in an increase in
   (a) quantity demanded, and a fall in price.
   (b) demand, and a fall in price.
   (c) quantity demanded, and a rise in price.
   (d) demand, and a rise in price.

_____ 8.   The price of Frisbees (a normal good) will definitely increase if
     (a)   there is an improvement in the technology of making Frisbees and Frisbees become more popular.
     (b)   the cost of plastic used to produce Frisbees increases and people have more leisure time to throw Frisbees.
     (c)   Frisbee workers negotiate a wage increase and boomerangs (a Frisbee substitute) decrease in price.
     (d)   a sales tax is imposed on Frisbees and (because of widespread unemployment) incomes fall.

_____ 9.   A rightward shift in the supply of U.S. cars might be due to
     (a)   an increase in the price of steel.
     (b)   a reduction in foreign competition.
     (c)   the introduction of cost-saving robots.
     (d)   increased popularity of foreign cars.

_____ 10.   If the market is initially in equilibrium, a technological improvement will cause price _____to _____ and quantity demanded _____to _____.
     (a)   fall; fall
     (b)   rise; rise
     (c)   fall; rise
     (d)   rise; fall

_____ 11.   The price of beans rises sharply. Which of the following cannot be true?
     (a)   The supply of beans may have decreased with no change in the demand for beans.
     (b)   The demand for beans may have increased with no change in the supply of beans.
     (c)   The demand for beans may have increased with an increase in the quantity supplied of beans.
     (d)   The supply of beans may have increased with an increase in the quantity demanded of beans.

_____ 12.   The market for peas is experiencing a surplus. You should predict that price will
     (a)   increase, quantity demanded will fall, and the quantity supplied will rise.
     (b)   increase, quantity demanded will rise, and the quantity supplied will fall.
     (c)   decrease, quantity demanded will rise, and the quantity supplied will fall.
     (d)   decrease, quantity demanded will fall, and the quantity supplied will rise.

_____ 13.   Today, you change your expectations about your future income. In fact, you now believe that your future income will be significantly higher than you had previously expected. For a normal good, this would result in an increase in
     (a)   quantity demanded today.
     (b)   demand today.
     (c)   quantity demanded but only in the future.
     (d)   demand, but only in the future.

_____ 14.   If less is demanded of a product at each possible price, then there has been
     (a)   a decrease in the quantity demanded.
     (b)   a decrease in demand.
     (c)   an increase in demand.
     (d)   an increase in the quantity demanded.

_____ 15. Chuck's Chips and Debi's Dip are complements. Costs of chip production fall. At the same time, a government health report alleges that dip consumption causes bone cancer. For Debi's Dip, the equilibrium price _____ will _____ and the equilibrium quantity _____ will _____.
   (a) fall; be indeterminate
   (b) be indeterminate; rise
   (c) be indeterminate; fall
   (d) be indeterminate; be indeterminate

_____ 16. The market for legal secretaries is in equilibrium. Suddenly there is a simultaneous increase in the demand for legal secretaries and a decrease in the supply of legal secretaries. If there is no change in the wage paid to legal secretaries,
   (a) there will be a shortage of legal secretaries.
   (b) there will be a surplus of legal secretaries.
   (c) law firms will have no difficulty in hiring the desired number of legal secretaries at the current wage.
   (d) the supply of legal secretaries will decrease even more.

Use the following diagram to answer the next six questions. The diagram refers to the demand for and supply of hot dogs. The hot dog market is initially in equilibrium at Point A. Assume that hot dogs are a normal good.

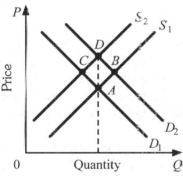

_____ 17. The hot dog market moves from Point A to a new equilibrium at Point B. There has been an increase in
   (a) demand and an increase in supply.
   (b) demand and an increase in quantity supplied.
   (c) quantity demanded and an increase in quantity supplied.
   (d) quantity demanded and an increase in supply.

_____ 18. The movement from Point A to Point B might have been caused by
   (a) an increase in the price of hamburgers (a substitute for hot dogs).
   (b) an increase in the price of fries (a complement for hot dogs).
   (c) a new widespread belief that meat products are bad for the heart.
   (d) a decrease in the price of ketchup (an ingredient used in making hot dogs).

_____ 19. The hot dog market moves from Point A to a new equilibrium at Point C. There has been a decrease in
   (a) demand and a decrease in supply.
   (b) demand and a decrease in quantity supplied.
   (c) quantity demanded and a decrease in quantity supplied.
   (d) quantity demanded and a decrease in supply.

_____ 20. The movement from Point *A* to Point *C* might have been caused by a
    (a) decrease in the price of hamburgers (a substitute for hot dogs).
    (b) tightening of sanitary regulations required for the preparation of hot dogs.
    (c) decrease in the wages of workers in the hot dog industry.
    (d) decrease in the price of hot dog buns.

_____ 21. The hot dog market moves from Point *A* to a new equilibrium at Point *D*. There has been a(n)
    (a) increase in demand and an increase in supply.
    (b) increase in demand and a decrease in supply.
    (c) decrease in demand and an increase in supply.
    (d) decrease in demand and a decrease in supply.

_____ 22. The movement from Point *A* to Point *D* might have been caused by a(n)
    (a) increase in the price of hot dogs and no change in the equilibrium quantity of hot dogs.
    (b) expected increase in the income of hot dog consumers and a hike in the wages of hot dog preparers.
    (c) expected decrease in the price of hot dogs and an increase in the cost of making hot dogs.
    (d) decrease in the income of hot dog consumers and a reduction in the cost of making hot dogs.

_____ 23. Generic aspirin is an inferior good. As Jorge's income decreases we would expect a(n)
    (a) decrease in Jorge's demand for generic aspirin.
    (b) increase in Jorge's quantity demanded of generic aspirin.
    (c) increase in Jorge's demand for generic aspirin.
    (d) decrease in Jorge's quantity demanded of generic aspirin.

_____ 24. The supply of computer software packages increases. As a result, the demand for personal computers rises. These two goods are _____ . The price of microchips, used to produce personal computers, will _____ .
    (a) substitutes; increase
    (b) substitutes; decrease
    (c) complements; increase
    (d) complements; decrease

_____ 25. Along a given demand curve for corn, which of the following is not held constant?
    (a) The price of corn
    (b) The income of corn farmers
    (c) The income of corn demanders
    (d) The price of wheat

_____ 26. The law of demand is best illustrated by
    (a) the price of Pepsi rising, leading consumers to buy more Coke.
    (b) increased purchases of Coke, as the price of Coke decreases.
    (c) an increase in income, which results in reduced purchases of store-brand soft drinks.
    (d) an increase in income, which results in increased purchases of Coke.

Use the following table to answer the next three questions. The table refers to the demand for and supply of cans of tuna.

Price of Tuna	Quantity Demanded	Quantity Supplied
90¢	30	80
80¢	45	70
70¢	60	60
60¢	75	50
50¢	90	40
40¢	105	30

_____ 27. The equilibrium price is _____ and the equilibrium quantity is _____ cans.
(a) 70¢; 60
(b) 60¢; 75
(c) 60¢; 50
(d) 70¢; 70

_____ 28. There would be an excess demand for tuna if the price were at
(a) 90¢.
(b) 80¢.
(c) 70¢.
(d) 60¢.

_____ 29. If the price were 80¢, there would be an excess
(a) demand of 70 cans.
(b) demand of 25 cans.
(c) supply of 25 cans.
(d) supply of 70 cans.

_____ 30. New costly regulations to protect workers are introduced in the production of tuna. We would expect the equilibrium price of tuna to _____ and the equilibrium quantity of tuna to _____ .
(a) increase; increase
(b) increase; decrease
(c) decrease; increase
(d) decrease; decrease

II. APPLICATION QUESTIONS

1. Consider the following information regarding the quantity of corn demanded and supplied per month at a number of prices.

Price per Bushel	Quantity Demanded	Quantity Supplied
80¢	39,000	83,000
70¢	48,000	78,000
60¢	58,000	74,000
50¢	67,000	67,000
40¢	75,000	62,000
30¢	81,000	59,000

(a)   What is the equilibrium price? What is the equilibrium quantity?

(b)   Describe the situation when the price is at 80¢ per bushel and predict what will happen.

(c)   Describe the situation when the price is at 30¢ per bushel and predict what will happen.

(d)   Explain what would happen if a serious transport strike reduced corn output (at each price) by 30,000 bushels.

2.   DoughCrust Bread is a normal good produced by the DoughCrust Bakery. What will happen to the equilibrium price and quantity of DoughCrust Bread in each of the following situations?

(a)   Due to a recession, households that buy DoughCrust experience a decrease in income.

(b)   The cost of wheat used in DoughCrust increases significantly.

(c)   DoughCrust buys improved ovens that reduce the costs of DoughCrust bread.

(d)   Luvly Loaf, a rival, cuts the price of its bread.

(e)   Consumers become health conscious and switch to low-calorie breads.

3.   How will each of the following changes affect the supply of hamburgers?

(a)   There is an increase in the price of hamburger buns (used in the production of burgers).

(b)   There is an increase in the price of hamburgers.

(c)   Producers discover that the price of cheeseburgers is increasing.

4.   Pietro Cavalini sells ice cream at the beach. He is in competition with numerous other vendors. How will each of the following changes affect the demand for Pietro's ice cream?

(a)   Hot dog vendors reduce the price of hot dogs. Hot dogs are consumption substitutes for ice cream.

(b)   The cost of refrigeration decreases.

(c)   Fine weather attracts record crowds to the beach.

5.   The market for DVDs has demand and supply curves given by $Qd = 60 - 2P$ and $Qs = 3P$, respectively. DVDs are a normal good.

(a)   Complete the following table.

Price	Quantity Demanded	Quantity Supplied
$30		
$25		
$20		
$15		
$10		
$5		
$0		

(b)   Calculate the equilibrium price and quantity. You can do this either by graphing the curves or algebraically.

(c)   Suppose that the current market price of a DVD is $20. Calculate the number of units that will be traded.

(d)   Suppose that the demand equation changed to $Qd = 80 - 2P$. Is this an increase or a decrease in demand? Suggest what might have caused such a change.

(e)   Calculate the new equilibrium price and quantity.

6.   Here is a demand and supply schedule for loaves of bread in East Yeastville, Colorado.

Price ($)	Quantity Demanded	Quantity Supplied
5.00	1,000	6,000
4.50	1,300	4,500
4.00	1,600	4,000
3.50	2,000	3,500
3.00	3,000	3,000
2.50	3,200	2,700
2.00	4,000	2,200
1.50	4,500	1,800
1.00	5,400	1,400
0.50	7,000	1,200

(a)   Find equilibrium price and equilibrium quantity.

(b)   Graph the demand (D_1) and supply (S_1) schedules in the space below and confirm the equilibrium values.

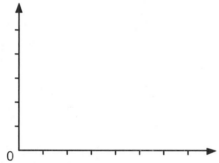

(c)   At a price of $1, is there an excess demand or supply? How great is the excess?

Suppose supply increases by 1,800 loaves at each price level.

(d)   Draw the new supply curve (S_2) on the graph in (b).

(e)   At the original equilibrium price level, is there an excess demand or an excess supply?

(f)   What will now happen to price, quantity demanded, and quantity supplied?

7.   The diagram following shows the labor market. D is the demand for labor and S is the supply. The minimum wage is $6.00 and unemployment is 150 workers. Can you verify that 150 workers are unemployed?

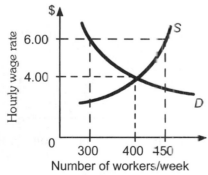

If the minimum wage law was revoked, the wage would fall to an equilibrium level of $4.00, and there would be no unemployment because quantity demanded would be equal to quantity supplied. However, the number of workers demanded would rise by only 100, not 150. Reconcile this apparent contradiction.

8.   Here are the demand schedules for orange juice for three buyers in the orange juice market, and the supply schedules for three sellers in the orange juice market.

Price/Gallon	Quantity Demanded By:			Quantity Supplied By:		
	Blue	**Black**	**Brown**	**Gray**	**Green**	**Scarlett**
$5	1	0	0	5	10	14
$4	3	2	0	4	7	9
$3	7	5	4	3	6	7
$2	9	9	5	0	4	5
$1	11	12	7	0	0	1

(a)   Graph market demand (D_1) and market supply (S_1).

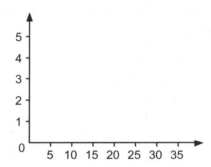

(b)   Show equilibrium price (P^*) and quantity (Q^*).

(c)   Now suppose the farm workers who pick oranges are given a higher wage rate. Show on your graph the changes that will occur in the orange juice market. Label any new demand curve D_2 and supply curve S_2. Discuss why curves shift, why price changes, and the significance of any shortage or surplus. Note that you don't have the data to draw precise curves.

(d)   Suppose now that, in addition to the orange pickers' higher wage rate, All-Cola, a substitute for orange juice, reduces its price. Sketch the new demand curve for orange juice (D_3), and explain the reason why you moved the curve as you did.

9.   (a)   Draw a demand and supply graph for milk, and establish the equilibrium price (P^*).

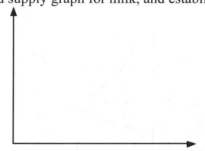

(b)   There is an increase in the demand for milk (from D_1 to D_2). How will this change affect the equilibrium price?

(c)   In terms of the diagram you just sketched, what is the only way that the equilibrium price can increase, if the supply curve doesn't shift?

(d)   Draw in the new demand curve. Now trace through the process by which a new equilibrium is established.

10.   Mooville is a small town in Texas. Assume that beef is a normal good. What happens to the amount of beef demanded or supplied in each of the following cases? Draw a separate demand and supply graph for each part of this question, label the axes, and show how the change will shift the demand and/or the supply curve. Explain any curve shifts in each case. Show initial and final equilibrium price (P^* and P^{**}) and initial and final equilibrium quantity (Q^* and Q^{**}) for beef.

(a)   A subsidy that reduces production costs for beef producers.

(b)   A reduced supply of fish (consumers view beef and fish as substitutes).

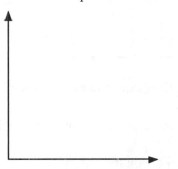
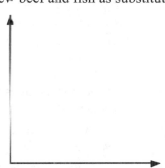

(c)   A rise in the wage rate in the beef industry.

(d)   A rise in income.

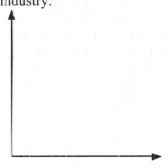
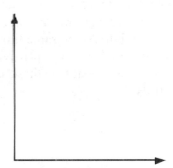

(e)   An improvement in the productivity of producing beef.

(f)   A bad tomato crop (beef and ketchup are complements and tomatoes are used to produce ketchup).

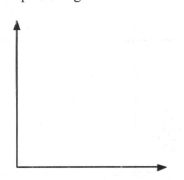
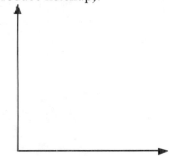

11. Think of some commodity that you like. Try to avoid "lumpy" things, like cars or houses, and pick something like coffee, movies, CDs, or long-distance phone calls.

    (a) Sketch your demand curve for this good. Does it intersect the price axis? Where? How much of this commodity would you buy at a zero price?

    (b) Are there substitutes for this commodity? How does the availability of substitutes affect the shape of your curve?

    (c) How would your demand curve change in response to an increase in the price of a substitute?

    (d) How would your demand curve change if you won the lottery and were to receive $2,000 per week for life?

12. During the last few years, home prices in the northeastern United States have soared. The result was a significant increase in new home construction and a large increase in the demand for labor in the region. At the same time, though, high home prices caused a drop in the supply of labor, as people found it too expensive to live in the region. Draw a diagram of the labor market and discuss the impact of these events on wages and thus on the costs of doing business in the Northeast.

13.   In London, cabbies must be able to demonstrate "the knowledge" of at least 400 streets in order to obtain a license. This is quite difficult, so the number of cabbies is rather limited.
    (a)   Draw a demand and supply diagram for taxi service in London. How has this diagram been affected by the presence of the test?

    (b)   How has the presence of the test affected usage of other forms of public transport—for example, the red buses and the "tube" (subway)? How have these prices responded?

    (c)   If the effect of restricting the numbers of cabbies is to reduce the number of customers, why might cabdrivers favor the restriction?

14.   Indicate in each case whether demand for steak (a normal good) will increase (I), decrease (D), or remain unchanged (U) in the following cases.
    (a) ____   Pork, a substitute for steak, decreases in price.
    (b) ____   High levels of unemployment sweep the nation.
    (c) ____   The price of steak falls.
    (d) ____   The price of steak sauce increases dramatically.
    (e) ____   A government report establishes a conclusive link between the consumption of steak and cancer.
    (f) ____   New refrigeration techniques reduce spoilage of steaks before they reach the market.
    (g) ____   It is expected that the price of steak will skyrocket within two months.

15.   Indicate in each case whether the supply of beer will increase (I), decrease (D), or remain unchanged (U) in the following cases.
    (a) ____   Wine coolers become more popular with consumers.
    (b) ____   Beer decreases in price.
    (c) ____   States impose a new tax on beer producers.
    (d) ____   Beer workers' wages increase.
    (e) ____   The price of hops, an important ingredient in brewing, decreases.
    (f) ____   Costs of transportation decrease.
    (g) ____   Improved technology results in less waste of beer.
    (h) ____   The economy enters a downturn, and many beer drinkers become unemployed.
    (i) ____   Fuel costs rise at the brewery.

16. Indicate in each case whether the market price and quantity of popcorn will increase (I), decrease (D), or be uncertain (U) in the following cases. Assume that popcorn and lemonade are normal goods.

	Price	*Quantity*	
(a)	____	____	The price of lemonade, a complement of popcorn, rises while the harvest of popcorn is unusually poor this year.
(b)	____	____	Consumers' income falls; low-cost migrant workers cause the cost of popcorn to decline.

	Price	*Quantity*	
(c)	____	____	Oil, used in popcorn production, falls in price; consumers expect an imminent rise in the price of popcorn.
(d)	____	____	Eating popcorn is shown to be healthy; new hybrid corn is less expensive to produce and provides higher yields.

17. Kornville is a small town in rural Virginia. Work out what will happen to the amount of corn supplied in each of the following cases and explain your answer.

    Result *A* = increase in the supply of corn
    Result *B* = decrease in the supply of corn
    Result *C* = increase in the quantity supplied of corn
    Result *D* = decrease in the quantity supplied of corn

    (a) ____ A new government tax is imposed on corn.

    (b) ____ Landlords raise the rent on land used for growing corn.

    (c) ____ A new spray, effective in controlling insects harmful to corn plants, is made available.

    (d) ____ The local senator campaigns effectively for an increase in the price of corn, which can be grown in Kornville.

    (e) ____ The local senator campaigns effectively for a rise in the price of tobacco.

    (f) ____ Many corn-growing farmers suffer bankruptcy.

    (g) ____ The cost of diesel fuel, used in farm machinery, falls.

    (h) ____ Red McPinkie unionizes agricultural workers and raises their wages.

    (i) ____ Tougher laws stop foreign workers from working at harvest time.

    (j) ____ Cornflakes (which are made from corn) become much more popular. (Careful!)

Practice Test SOLUTIONS

I. SOLUTIONS TO MULTIPLE-CHOICE QUESTIONS

1. (a) In the input market, firms demand inputs and household supply inputs.

2. (b) To check your answer, put in a pair of substitutes, such as Pepsi and Coke. If Pepsi increases in price, we will buy less Pepsi and the demand for Coke will increase.

3. (d) A change in price leads to a movement along the demand curve. This is a "change in quantity demanded." An increase in price causes a decrease in quantity demanded.

4. (a) A change in price leads to a movement along the supply curve. Refer to page 63.

5. (c) A movement along a supply curve (a change in quantity supplied) can only be caused by a change in the price of the good itself. Refer to page 63.

6. (a) Draw the demand and supply diagram. In equilibrium, quantity demanded equals quantity supplied. At lower prices, quantity demanded exceeds quantity supplied.

7. (d) For a normal good, higher income will stimulate additional demand. Higher demand will cause the equilibrium price to increase. Refer to page 54.

8. (b) If the cost of plastic increases, supply will decrease. If buyers have more leisure time, demand for leisure goods (like Frisbees) will increase. A decrease in supply, coupled with an increase in demand, will push up the price.

9. (c) A rightward shift—an increase in supply—will occur if costs are reduced.

10. (c) A technological improvement will increase supply. This will drive down the equilibrium price. As the price decreases, quantity demanded will increase.

11. (d) If the price of beans rises, then it cannot have been caused by an increase in the supply of beans.

12. (c) A surplus means that quantity supplied is greater than the quantity demanded. To reduce the surplus, sellers will accept lower prices. As price falls, quantity demanded will increase and quantity supplied will decrease.

13. (b) For a normal good, expected higher income will increase demand now and in the future.

14. (b) Try drawing this. At each price level the demand curve will be further to the left.

15. (d) Chip supply increases because costs have fallen. Consumers will buy more chips (and the demand for dip will increase). The health report will reduce demand for dip. Because we don't know which has the stronger effect on the demand for dip, the change in both equilibrium price and quantity is indeterminate.

16. (a) Higher demand and less supply will lead to a shortage if the wage level doesn't increase.

17.   (b)   The demand curve has shifted right from D_1 to D_2. As the price increased, quantity supplied increased.

18.   (a)   There has been an increase in demand. This could have been due to an increase in the price of hamburgers because consumers would wish to buy fewer hamburgers and would instead demand more hot dogs.

19.   (d)   The supply curve has shifted left, from S_1 to S_2. As the price increased, quantity demanded decreased.

20.   (b)   There has been a decrease in supply. This could have been due to a tightening of the sanitary regulations required for the preparation of hot dogs (which would have increased costs and/or reduced the number of sellers).

21.   (b)   The demand curve has shifted right, from D_1 to D_2, and the supply curve has shifted left, from S_1 to S_2.

22.   (b)   An expected increase in the income of hot dog consumers will increase demand for a normal good, and a hike in the wages of hot dog preparers will increase costs and reduce supply. Option *A* is incorrect—it describes the effect rather than the cause.

23.   (c)   As income changes, it changes the *demand* for a good. A decrease in income results in a decrease in the demand for a normal good. A decrease in income results in an increase in the demand for an inferior good.

24.   (c)   If the supply of software increases, the price will fall. As one might expect, software and computers are complements—the evidence in the question bears this out. As the quantity of computers traded increases, the demand for microchips will increase, which pushes up their price. Refer to p. 54.

25.   (a)   A movement along a demand curve is a change in quantity demanded. The only factor that can cause such a change is a change in the price of the good. Refer to page 56.

26.   (b)   The law of demand relates the relationship between the price of a good and the quantity demanded. Refer to page 52.

27.   (a)   Equilibrium occurs where quantity demanded equals quantity supplied. Refer to page 66.

28.   (d)   At 60¢, quantity demanded is 25 units greater than quantity supplied.

29.   (c)   At 80¢, quantity supplied is 25 units greater than quantity demanded.

30.   (b)   The new regulations will decrease the supply of tuna which, in turn, will increase the equilibrium price and decrease the equilibrium quantity.

II.   SOLUTIONS TO APPLICATION QUESTIONS

1.   (a)   50¢. 67,000 bushels.

   (b)   There is a surplus of 44,000 bushels at a price of 80¢ per bushel. Pressure is present to force price down.

(c)   There is a shortage of 22,000 bushels at a price of 30¢ per bushel. Pressure is present to force price up.

(d)   Supply would shift to the left by 30,000 bushels. Equilibrium price would increase to 70¢ per bushel, and the equilibrium quantity would be 48,000 bushels.

2.   (a)   A decrease in income will reduce demand. Equilibrium price will fall and equilibrium quantity will fall.

    (b)   An increase in the cost of wheat will decrease supply. Equilibrium price will rise and equilibrium quantity will fall.

    (c)   A decrease in the cost of wheat will increase supply. Equilibrium price will fall and equilibrium quantity will rise.

    (d)   A fall in the price of a substitute will reduce the demand for DoughCrust. Equilibrium price will fall and equilibrium quantity will fall.

    (e)   There will be a decrease in demand. Equilibrium price will fall and equilibrium quantity will fall.

3.   (a)   Supply will decrease—cost of inputs has increased.

    (b)   Supply will not change. A change in the price of a good results in a change in quantity supplied.

    (c)   Supply of hamburgers will decrease—producers will switch resources to cheeseburger production.

4.   (a)   Hot dogs are substitutes for ice cream. Demand for ice cream will decrease.

    (b)   No effect on demand. Changes in the cost of refrigeration will affect supply.

    (c)   Demand will increase as the number of buyers increases.

5.   (a)

Price	Quantity Demanded	Quantity Supplied
$30	0	90
$25	10	75
$20	20	60
$15	30	45
$10	40	30
$5	50	15
$0	60	0

    (b)   Equilibrium price is $12 and equilibrium quantity is 36. In equilibrium, $Qd = Qs$, therefore,

$$60 - 2P = 3P$$
$$60 = 5P \text{ and } P = 12$$

If $P = 12$, then $Q = 60 - 2(12) = 36$.

    (c)   At $20, there is an excess supply of 40 units. It's a buyers market—only 20 units will be traded.

    (d)   This is an increase in demand. Tastes might have changed, consumer incomes may have risen (if DVDs are a normal good), and so on.

(e)   Equilibrium price is $16 and equilibrium quantity is 48. In equilibrium, $Qd = Qs$, therefore,

$$80 - 2P = 3P$$
$$80 = 5P \text{ and } P = 16$$

If $P = 16$, then $Q = 80 - 2(16) = 48$.

6.   (a) $3; 3,000 loaves

   (b)   Refer to the following diagram.

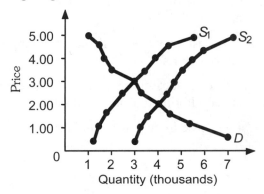

   (c)   There is an excess demand (shortage) equal to 4,000 units (5,400 – 1,400).

   (d)   Refer to the diagram above ($2, 4,000).

   (e)   There will be an excess supply (surplus) of 1,800 loaves.

   (f)   Price will fall to $2; quantity demanded and supplied will move to 4,000 loaves.

7.   The unemployment was removed because 100 extra jobs were created (increase in quantity demanded), and because the wage had become too low, 50 workers decided to cease offering themselves for employment (decrease in quantity supplied).

8.   (a)   Refer to the following diagram.

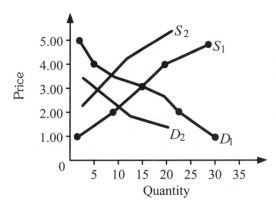

   (b) $P^* = \$3; Q^* = 16$.

   (c)   Refer to the preceding diagram. There will be no change in demand! Costs have risen, reducing profits, so supply will shift to the left (although we can't say how far). At $3, a shortage now exists, which will push prices higher.

(d)   Refer to the preceding diagram. Demand for orange juice will fall (although we can't say by how much). Consumption of All-Cola will rise, and some consumers of orange juice will substitute the relatively cheap All-Cola.

9.   (a)   Refer to the following diagram.

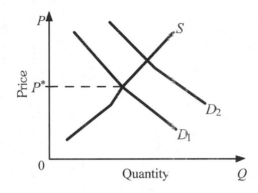

(b)   Increase

(c)   The demand curve must shift to the right.

(d)   Excess demand, leading to pressure for price to rise, will cause a reduction in the quantity demanded and an increase in the quantity supplied. This will continue until a new equilibrium is established.

10.   (a)   The subsidy will increase supply. Price will fall and output will rise.

        (b)   The price of fish will increase and consumers will switch to beef. The demand for beef will increase. Price will rise and output will rise.

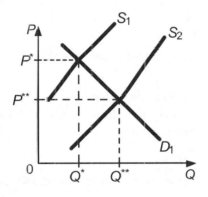

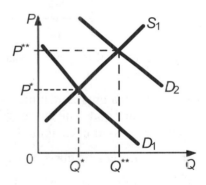

(c)   Costs of production have risen. This will decrease supply. Price will rise and output will fall.

(d)   Beef is a normal good. Higher incomes will cause the demand curve to shift right. Price will rise and output will rise.

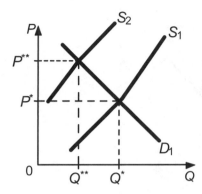

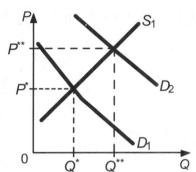

(e)   Costs of production will fall. Supply will shift to the right. Price will fall and output will rise.

(f)   A poor tomato crop will drive up the price of tomatoes (and ketchup). Less ketchup will be used, so less beef will be demanded. Price and output will fall.

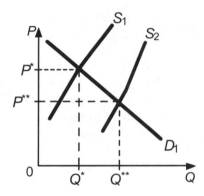

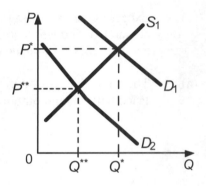

11.   (a)   Presumably, your demand curve is downward sloping and intersects the price axis at some point.

        (b)   With a greater number of substitutes, you will be more sensitive to changes in the price of your good. The curve will tend to be flatter. This refers to elasticity of demand, which is discussed in Chapter 5 of *Principles of Microeconomics*.

        (c)   The demand curve would shift to the right.

        (d)   If this is a normal good, demand would increase. If it is an inferior good, demand would decrease.

12.   Demand for labor would increase and, as workers moved away from the region, supply of labor would decrease. Wages, then, would increase, and the costs of doing business in the Northeast would rise.

13.   (a)   The test has reduced the supply of cabbies. This has forced up the price of taxi rides in London.

        (b)   Given the raised price of cab rides, the demand for substitutes will have increased. Other forms of public transportation will have been able to increase their prices.

(c)   Cabbies who have passed the test and earned their license like the scheme because it reduces competition. This is especially true if the degree of substitutability with other types of public transportation is slight.

14.	(a)	D	(b)	D	(c)	U	(d)	D
	(e)	D	(f)	I or U	(g)	I		

15.	(a)	U	(b)	U	(c)	D	(d)	D
	(e)	I	(f)	I	(g)	I	(h)	U
	(i)	D						

16.	(a)	U and D	(b)	D and U	(c)	U and I	(d)	U and I
17.	(a)	*B*	(b)	*B*	(c)	*A*	(d)	*C*
	(e)	*B*	(f)	*B*	(g)	*A*	(h)	*B*
	(i)	*B*	(j)	*C*				

Demand and Supply Applications

1. Explain and demonstrate how the market uses the price-rationing mechanism to allocate resources and distribute output.
2. List nonprice rationing policies designed to supplant the price rationing mechanism, identify the rationale behind these, and analyze their effects.
3. Explain, using words and/or diagrams, how an oil import fee would affect the domestic production and total consumption of oil.
4. Define consumer surplus and producer surplus and explain how these concepts relate to market efficiency.

BRAIN TEASER I: The textbook discusses the effects of a price floor such as the minimum wage in this chapter.

First, draw a demand and supply diagram to depict the effect of an effective price floor in the labor market.

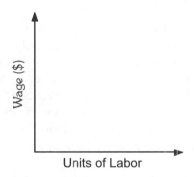

Why might economists oppose the minimum wage? Based on your diagram, what will happen to the number of jobs available if there is a minimum wage increase?

Suppose you own a fast-food restaurant—with many of your staff being paid minimum wage. Why might you oppose a hike in the minimum wage?

BRAIN TEASER II: Over the years, the U.S. government has developed two distinct strategies regarding illegal drugs. One strategy ("the war on drugs") has been to cooperate with the governments of countries where drugs are grown in order to destroy the supply at its source. The other strategy (the "Just say no" campaign) has been aimed at discouraging drug consumption. Assume the two strategies have the same effect on the equilibrium quantity of drugs traded. Which strategy would you prefer, if you were a drug dealer?

Objective 1

Explain and demonstrate how the market uses the price-rationing mechanism to allocate resources and distribute output.

The price system has two important functions—it allocates productive resources and rations scarce output. Because of scarcity, rationing always occurs. Price rationing distinguishes those who are "willing and able" to buy from those who are only able but no longer willing, i.e., it allocates according to the willingness and ability of consumers to pay—those who are willing and able to pay as the price increases will continue to get the good. Demand is constrained by income and wealth but, within those limits, individual preferences will prevail. If demand increases, price rises, signaling producers that profits may be made. More of the good will be produced, with resources being switched from other lines of production. (page 79)

LEARNING TIP: Note the lobster example in the textbook which describes the allocative and rationing roles that prices play in the marketplace.

Note, too, that the profit motive is highly durable. Limitations (such as price ceilings or rationing) placed on the operation of the market can lead to black markets so that demand can continue to be serviced.◀

ECONOMICS IN PRACTICE: In fact, the lobster market in Maine is changing. In recent years, catches of lobsters and the average size of the lobsters caught have been increasing. This may be due to global warming—lobsters may be moving away from the warmer waters in the south—or because of overfishing of lobster predators, such as cod. What effect will this change in supply have on the Maine market for lobsters?

ANSWER: With larger catches, the supply of lobsters will shift to the right. More resources will be allocated to the lobster industry and the price of lobsters will decrease. In fact, the dockside price of lobsters reached an eleven-year low in 2009.

ECONOMICS IN PRACTICE (CONTINUED): It's a common error to confuse "price" with "total expenditure" (or "total revenue"), which is "price times quantity." As the textbook's lobster example demonstrates (page 81), a change in the price of a good is not a reliable predictor of the effect on total spending. If your school wishes to increase its overall revenue, it may choose to increase its tuition, but the same tactic, employed by a local business, may cause revenue to decline. Total expenditures might be increased by cutting prices—think about Walmart! The Law of Demand tells us that a decrease in price will increase quantity demanded, but the law doesn't claim that such a price change will necessarily increase total spending. Given your knowledge of the market for Maine lobsters, what actions might lobstermen take to boost their incomes?

ANSWER: If an increase in the supply of lobsters reduces income (total revenue), then a decrease in supply should have the opposite effect. In fact, Maine has imposed limitations on the numbers of lobster traps that may be used. Additionally, lobstermen report that rivals have been deliberately cutting the lines of their lobster pots.

ECONOMICS IN PRACTICE: Given the behavior of the dockside price of lobsters, predict the effect on the restaurant price of lobster.

ANSWER: With a decrease in the price of lobster, restaurant prices should also decrease. However, this does not seem to be the case because restaurant owners have resisted the pressure to reduce the price in order to retain lobster's image as an exclusive "luxury" food.

Practice

1. In a market, either price must increase or nonprice rationing must occur when a _____ exists.
    (a)   shortage
    (b)   surplus
    (c)   horizontal demand curve
    (d)   vertical supply curve

    ANSWER: (a) Given a shortage, either price will increase (price rationing) or nonprice rationing must be enforced.

2. In a free market, the rationing mechanism is
    (a)   price.
    (b)   quantity.
    (c)   demand.
    (d)   supply.

    ANSWER: (a) Given an imbalance between quantity demanded and quantity supplied, a free market will adjust price to achieve equilibrium.

Use the following diagram to answer the next five questions. Assume that the demand curve and the supply curve each must be in one of the three possible positions shown. The initial market demand and market supply curves for Sam's Supreme Submarine Sandwiches are D_1 and S_1.

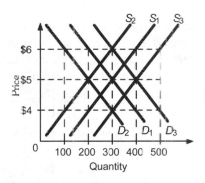

3. There is an increase in the cost of ingredients. If the price is held at the initial equilibrium level, there will be an excess
    (a)   demand of 100 units.
    (b)   demand of 200 units.
    (c)   supply of 100 units.
    (d)   supply of 200 units.

    ANSWER: (a) Supply has fallen to S_2. Demand is unchanged. At a price of $5, quantity demanded is 300 units and quantity supplied is 200 units.

4. There is both a simultaneous increase in demand and decrease in supply. At the initial equilibrium price, there will be an excess
    (a)   demand of 200 units.
    (b)   demand of 400 units.
    (c)   supply of 200 units.
    (d)   supply of 400 units.

    ANSWER: (a) Supply has decreased to S_2. Demand has increased to D_3. At a price of $5, quantity demanded is 400 units and quantity supplied is 200 units.

5. There is a simultaneous decrease in demand and decrease in supply. At the initial equilibrium price there will be
    (a)   an excess demand of 200 units.
    (b)   an excess demand of 100 units.
    (c)   an excess supply of 200 units.
    (d)   equilibrium.

    ANSWER: (d) Supply has decreased to S_2. Demand has decreased to D_2. At a price of $5, quantity demanded is 200 units and quantity supplied is 200 units. Equilibrium prevails.

6. Herman reduces the price of his Humongous Hoagie (a substitute for the Supreme Submarine). At the Supreme Submarine's initial equilibrium price, there will be an excess
    (a)   demand of 100 units.
    (b)   demand of 200 units.
    (c)   supply of 100 units.
    (d)   supply of 200 units.

    ANSWER: (c) Demand has decreased to D_2. Supply has not changed. At a price of $5, quantity demanded is 200 units and quantity supplied is 300 units.

7. Herman reduces the price of his Humongous Hoagie (a substitute for the Supreme Submarine). *Following* any shifts in the curves, we would expect a(n) _____ in the Supreme Submarine market.
    (a)   increase in quantity demanded and an increase in quantity supplied.
    (b)   increase in quantity demanded and a decrease in quantity supplied.
    (c)   decrease in quantity demanded and an increase in quantity supplied.
    (d)   decrease in quantity demanded and a decrease in quantity supplied.

    ANSWER: (b) Demand has decreased to D_2. Supply has not changed. There is an excess supply which will cause Sam's price to fall. A fall in price will increase quantity demanded and decrease quantity supplied. ∎

Objective 2

List nonprice rationing policies designed to supplant the price rationing mechanism, identify the rationale behind these, and analyze their effects.

Rationing by price may be considered "unfair"—poor people might be priced out of the market for some essentials—so other nonprice rationing methods, including queuing, ration coupons, favored customers, and lotteries, are applied. Such schemes usually involve hidden costs (queuing costs time, for example) that may make them inefficient. Note that different types of rationing benefit different groups of people. (page 82)

At many colleges, basketball tickets are distributed on a first-come, first-served basis—meaning that students must queue, perhaps for days, to get tickets to the big game. Not-so-hidden costs include the inconvenience, loss of study time, and possible negative health effects. As an example of a lottery, colleges may allocate dorm rooms, not by price or need, but by random number selection.

> **LEARNING TIP:** It may seem confusing to have a ceiling below the equilibrium price. Remember that a price ceiling stops the price going higher (just like a ceiling in a room), whereas a price floor is a lower limit. To have an effect on equilibrium price, a ceiling must be set *below* the equilibrium price and a floor must be set *above* the equilibrium price.◀

A price ceiling sets a maximum price; a price floor sets a minimum price. The minimum wage is a price floor. An effective price ceiling creates a shortage; an effective price floor creates a surplus.

A price ceiling need not be established below the equilibrium price, although a ceiling set *above* the equilibrium has no effect. Similarly, the imposition of a minimum wage of $2.00 per hour will have no effect on the labor market. Verify that this is true. If demand and/or supply conditions change however, a price ceiling or floor may become effective. For instance, adjustable rate mortgages have "caps" on how high the interest rate can move in response to market conditions—this is a price ceiling.

ECONOMICS IN PRACTICE: There's an old saying that "time is money." Have you noticed how many of the textbook examples of "economics in practice" in this and previous chapters hinge on the trade-off between time and money? The same applies to the Shakespeare example in this chapter on page 87. Typically, those for whom time is less valuable are more inclined to queue to get lower prices. But what about situations where price is not explicitly involved? Duke University's Cameron Indoor Stadium (at a pinch) can accommodate 11,000 spectators for basketball games. Students receive tickets for these popular games on a "first-come, first-served" basis. Students set up "Krzyzewskiville," a tent village, in order to get tickets. Can you think of other similar examples where time and money are traded off?

ANSWER: There are numerous examples. If you've ever clipped coupons or sent off for a rebate, used the services of a ticket scalper, or queued to sign up for a popular class, you've traveled beyond the conventional pricing system.

ECONOMICS IN PRACTICE (CONTINUED): In 2009, the minimum wage was increased to $7.25 per hour. Who gains and who loses from an increase in the minimum wage? How do teenagers fit into your answer?

ANSWER: There is a transfer of income from employers to minimum-wage employees with jobs. There is a reduction in the quantity of labor demanded—fewer workers are hired. Workers who cannot find jobs (or who lose jobs) as a result of the wage floor are losers. The level of unemployment increases amongst the poor and unskilled—those least able to afford a reduction in job opportunities. Teenagers are amongst the least experienced workers, and evidence suggests that they suffer as a result of the minimum wage. Indeed, to redress the balance, an "opportunity wage" (a sub-minimum wage) was proposed for teenagers in the 1990s.

Practice

8. A price ceiling is set below the equilibrium price. We can predict that
    (a)   quantity demanded will decrease.
    (b)   quantity supplied will be greater than quantity demanded.
    (c)   demand will be less than supply.
    (d)   quantity supplied will decrease.

    ANSWER: (d) Price will be reduced by the price ceiling. A decrease in price causes quantity supplied to decrease (not a shift in the supply curve).

9. A price ceiling is set below the equilibrium price. We can predict that
    (a)   there will be a leftward shift in the demand curve.
    (b)   there will be a leftward shift in the supply curve.
    (c)   quantity demanded will be greater than quantity supplied.
    (d)   quantity supplied will be reduced to equal quantity demanded.

    ANSWER: (c) A change in price does not cause the demand and/or supply curve to shift position! If price is "too low," a shortage (quantity demanded greater than quantity supplied) will occur.

10.   A price floor is set below the current equilibrium price. If supply increases, price would
        (a)   increase.
        (b)   decrease.
        (c)   not change.
        (d)   be indeterminate.
        ANSWER: (b) Initially, the price floor will have no effect. As supply increases, there will be a pressure for the market price to fall. If the price falls enough, then the price floor will become effective.

11.   Ticket scalping will be successful if the
        (a)   demand curve is fairly steep.
        (b)   demand curve is fairly flat.
        (c)   official price is below the equilibrium price.
        (d)   official price is above the equilibrium price.
        ANSWER: (c) The slope of the demand curve is irrelevant in this case. The important issue is that a shortage of tickets exists because the official price has been set too low. ∎

Objective 3

Explain, using words and/or diagrams, how an oil import fee would affect the domestic production and total consumption of oil.

The text offers the imposition of a tax on imported oil (an oil import fee) as an example of the usefulness of demand and supply analysis. A new tax will raise the domestic price of oil, cutting quantity demanded and encouraging domestic production. The size of these changes depends on the slopes of the demand and supply curves or, more accurately, the *responsiveness* of demand and supply. Although the imposition of this tax would raise government revenues, reduce dependence on foreign oil, and stimulate domestic production of oil, inefficient domestic producers may be sheltered from lower priced foreign competition. (page 87)

Which consumers are most likely to be penalized by an oil import fee? Within the market, some buyers will have a demand that is relatively unresponsive to price changes, whereas others will be more able to trim demand if price rises. Would a price hike discriminate more against the poor (who may have little choice in their fuel consumption) than against those who are better off (who can afford to buy other kinds of heating)?

Practice

Refer to the following diagram for the next four questions. The world price of oil is $160 per barrel.

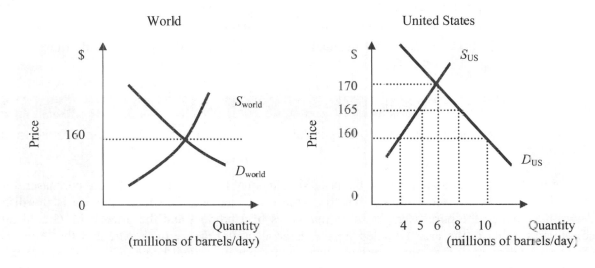

World   United States

12.   If the world price is the market price in the United States, then there will be a _____ million barrels per day.
       (a)   surplus of 10
       (b)   surplus of 6
       (c)   shortage of 10
       (d)   shortage of 6

ANSWER: (d) At $160 per barrel, quantity supplied is 4 million and quantity demanded is 10 million.

13.   Suppose that the United States imposes a $5 per barrel import fee. This will result in each of the following EXCEPT
       (a)   a decrease in imports to 3 million barrels per day.
       (b)   an increase in the quantity supplied of oil in the United States to 5 million barrels per day.
       (c)   a decrease in the quantity demanded of oil in the United States to 8 million barrels per day.
       (d)   a decrease in U.S. imports of oil by 2 million barrels per day.

ANSWER: (d) Oil imports had been 6 million barrels per day. After the imposition of the fee, oil imports are 3 million barrels per day. Imports decreased by 3 million barrels per day.

14.   Suppose that the United States imposes a $5 per barrel import fee. This will generate a tax revenue of
       (a) $3 million per day.
       (b) $5 million per day.
       (c) $8 million per day.
       (d) $15 million per day.

ANSWER: (d) Imports are 3 million barrels per day. Each barrel yields a tax revenue of $5.

15. Suppose that the United States wishes to become self-sufficient in oil. This could be done by
    (a) establishing a price ceiling (maximum price) of $15 per barrel of oil.
    (b) establishing a price ceiling (maximum price) of $30 per barrel of oil.
    (c) imposing a fee of $10 per barrel on foreign oil.
    (d) imposing a fee of $30 per barrel on foreign oil.

    ANSWER: (c) A fee of $10 per barrel on foreign oil will result in equilibrium in the U.S. market. ■

Objective 4

Define consumer surplus and producer surplus and explain how these concepts relate to market efficiency.

For the final unit of a good purchased, the price should equal the value derived by the purchaser. Previous units should be valued more highly, but the same price charged. *Consumer surplus* is the difference between the value the purchaser places on purchases of a product and the price paid. Graphically, the consumer surplus is the area bounded by the demand curve, the vertical axis, and the product price. Changes in the size of the area reflect changes in consumer well-being. Can you see that, if the consumer's demand for steak increases, *ceteris paribus*, then the consumer surplus will increase if price is unchanged? (page 89)

> **LEARNING TIP:** Put simply, consumer surplus is "the difference between the price you do pay and the price you would pay." If you win an eBay auction at a lower price than you would have paid, the difference is your consumer surplus.◀

Producer surplus is a similar concept but from the point of view of the seller. The difference between the market price and the lowest price a seller would accept is the producer surplus. If you auction a CD on eBay and would take $5 for it but you end up selling it for $12, your producer surplus is $7. (page 90)

> **LEARNING TIP:** Graphically, consumer surplus is the triangular area between the demand curve and the market price; producer surplus is the triangular area between the supply curve and the market price.◀

By driving buyers and sellers to the intersection of demand and supply, market forces maximize the total surplus derived by participants. Any action that moves production away from the equilibrium level will reduce society's surplus and will result in a deadweight loss to society. (page 91)

Practice

16. Given your demand curve for bananas, as the price of bananas decreases, your consumer surplus will
    (a) increase, because the gap between the price you would pay and the price you do pay is greater than before.
    (b) decrease, because marginal utility diminishes as more of a good is bought.
    (c) remain constant, because the demand curve has not changed position.
    (d) remain constant, because the maximum price you would pay has not changed.

    ANSWER: (a) Refer to the definition of consumer surplus on page 89.

Use the following diagram to answer the following question.

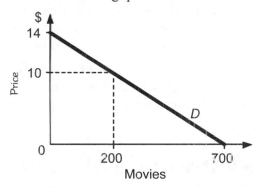

17.   When the price of a movie is $10, the consumer surplus is
       (a) $4.
       (b) $200.
       (c) $400.
       (d) $300.
       [Hint: the area of a triangle is 1/2(base × height).]
       ANSWER: (c) Consumer surplus is the area between the demand curve and the price. With a straight-line demand curve it is $1/2(P_{max} - P) Q_d$. In this case, consumer surplus is $1/2(\$14 - \$10)200$, or $400.

18.   The market for baseballs is in equilibrium. Suddenly there is a decrease in the supply of baseballs. Assuming normally sloped curves, consumer surplus will _____ and producer surplus will _____.

       (a)   increase; increase
       (b)   increase; decrease
       (c)   decrease; increase
       (d)   decrease; decrease

       ANSWER: (d) As the supply curve shifts to the left the area above the supply curve and below the demand curve becomes smaller. ∎

BRAIN TEASER I SOLUTION:

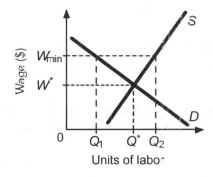

The minimum wage is an effective price floor. Both price floors and price ceilings restrict the free operation of the market. With an effective price floor, quantity supplied of labor will exceed quantity demanded, creating a surplus of job seekers—unemployment. There may be job loss, too, resulting in lower production. With rising labor costs, the economy's ability to compete with low-wage foreign imports is reduced, although this is not a strong argument—minimum wage earners (only about 5 percent of the labor force) tend to cluster in service industries, and services are not exported or imported.

As the owner of a fast-food restaurant, your bottom line will be hurt. Workers earning above the minimum wage (perhaps with more experience) would expect wage increases (the "ripple effect"). Small businesses on thin profit margins might have to trim back on employment through firing or by reducing hours. Alternatively, prices might have to rise, again reducing business.

BRAIN TEASER II SOLUTION: The first ("the war on drugs") strategy reduces supply and will increase the price. The second ("Just say no") strategy reduces demand and will decrease the price. As a dealer, you should prefer the first strategy because the price you can charge, and the revenue you can earn, would be greater.

PRACTICE TEST

I. MULTIPLE-CHOICE QUESTIONS

Select the option that provides the single best answer.

_____ 1. The government has decided that the free-market price for baby formula is "too high." Which of the following rationing proposals will result in the **least** misallocation of baby formula resources?
  (a) Proposal A: establish an official price ceiling, then let sellers decide how to allocate baby formula among customers.
  (b) Proposal B: issue coupons for baby formula that cannot be resold.
  (c) Proposal C: issue coupons for baby formula that can be resold.
  (d) Proposal D: establish a price ceiling and require purchasers to queue.

_____ 2. A government-imposed **ceiling** on apartment rents, if set above the equilibrium rent level, would
  (a) have no effect on the housing market.
  (b) lead to a persistent shortage of apartments.
  (c) lead to a persistent surplus of apartments.
  (d) shift the supply curve for apartments to the right.

_____ 3. A ticket to a concert by the Skreeming Habdabs costs you $35. However, your roommate offers you the "scalping" rate of $100 for your ticket. Your opportunity cost of refusing the offer and attending the concert is
  (a) $35.
  (b) $65.
  (c) $100.
  (d) $135.

_____ 4. Joe would pay $2.00 for his first cup of soda during the NCAA basketball championship game. He would pay $1.20 for his second, $1.00 for his third, and 80¢ for his fourth. If the price is
  (a) $1.00 per cup, Joe will buy 3 cups and have a consumer surplus of $4.20.
  (b) $1.00 per cup, Joe will buy 3 cups and have a consumer surplus of $3.20.
  (c) $1.10 per cup, Joe will buy 2 cups and have a consumer surplus of $1.00.
  (d) $1.10 per cup, Joe will buy 2 cups and have a consumer surplus of $2.10.

_____ 5. The market demand curve for pizza is given by $Q_d = 400 - 25P$ where P is the price of pizza in dollars. If the price of pizza is $10, the consumer surplus is
(a) $150.
(b) $225.
(c) $450.
(d) $800.
[Hint: the area of a triangle is 1/2(base × height).]

Use the following graph to answer the next question.

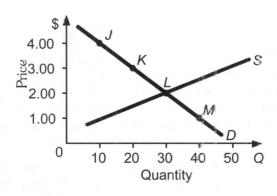

_____ 6. Suppose a price ceiling of $1.00 is set. This will cause a
(a) surplus of 50 units.
(b) shortage of 50 units.
(c) shortage of 30 units.
(d) surplus of 30 units.

Use the following diagram showing the oil market in the United States to answer the next two questions. The world price for gasoline is $4.50 per gallon. The equilibrium price in the U.S. market is $5.50 per gallon. Units on the horizontal axis are millions of gallons.

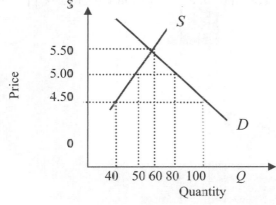

_____ 7. Assume that the United States neither imports nor exports gasoline. At the world price for gasoline, there is a _____ of gas in the U.S. market of _____ units.
(a) surplus; 60
(b) surplus; 100
(c) shortage; 60
(d) shortage; 100

_____ 8. The government imposes an import tax that raises the domestic price of gas to $5.00 per gallon. If, because of discoveries of new oilfields, the domestic supply of gas increases by 30 million gallons per day
(a) the domestic shortage of gas would be eliminated.
(b) government tax revenues would be 30 million times 50¢.
(c) quantity demanded would increase.
(d) the equilibrium price would remain at $5.50.

_____ 9. In a market economy the rationing mechanism operates through adjustments in
(a) price
(b) quantity
(c) expectations
(d) queuing

_____ 10. Jill's consumer surplus for Good *A* will
(a) increase if the price of *A* increases.
(b) increase if the price of *B*, a substitute for *A*, decreases.
(c) decrease if Jill's income decreases and *A* is a normal good.
(d) decrease if the price of *C*, a complement for *A*, decreases.

_____ 11. The supply curve of bottled water on an island is completely vertical. The market for bottled water is in equilibrium. A ferry load of thirsty holidaymakers arrives and the demand for bottled water increases. Which of the following statements is true?
(a) Price will serve as a rationing device.
(b) Price will not serve as a rationing device because the quantity supplied cannot change.
(c) Price will not serve as a rationing device because the equilibrium quantity demanded cannot change.
(d) Price will not serve as a rationing device because neither the equilibrium quantity demanded nor the equilibrium quantity supplied can change.

_____ 12. A price ceiling is set above current equilibrium price. If supply decreases, price would
(a) increase.
(b) decrease.
(c) not change.
(d) be indeterminate.

Use the following graph to answer the next three questions. Suppose a price ceiling of $1.00 is set in this market.

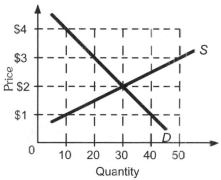

_____ 13.   The price ceiling will cause a
(a)   surplus of 50 units.
(b)   shortage of 50 units.
(c)   shortage of 30 units.
(d)   surplus of 30 units.

_____ 14.   If the price ceiling is left in place, we would predict that, eventually,
(a)   demand would decrease until quantity demanded and quantity supplied were equal at a price of $1.
(b)   supply would increase until quantity demanded and quantity supplied were equal at a price of $1.
(c)   the market participants will be convinced that $1 is the equilibrium price.
(d)   a persistent excess demand would lead to the emergence of nonprice rationing practices such as queuing.

_____ 15.   Relative to equilibrium, what is the value of the deadweight loss if the price ceiling is left in place?
(a) $30
(b) $40
(c) $45
(d) $60
[Hint: the area of a triangle is 1/2(base × height).]

_____ 16.   An effective minimum wage is imposed. In the market for unskilled labor we would expect
(a)   a surplus and an increase in employment.
(b)   a surplus and a decrease in employment.
(c)   a shortage and an increase in employment.
(d)   a shortage and a decrease in employment.

Use the following diagram to answer the next five questions.

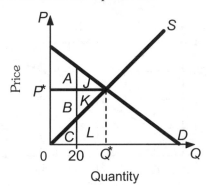

_____ 17.   When the market is in equilibrium, area(s) _____ represent consumer surplus.
         (a)   J and K
         (b)   A and B
         (c)   A and J
         (d)   B and K

_____ 18.   When the market is in equilibrium, area(s) _____ represent producer surplus.
         (a)   J and K
         (b)   A and B
         (c)   A and J
         (d)   B and K

_____ 19.   When the market is in equilibrium, area(s) _____ represent deadweight loss.
         (a)   J and K
         (b)   C and L
         (c)   J, K and L
         (d)   None of the above are correct.

_____ 20.   If output is restricted to 20 units, area(s) _____ represent consumer surplus and area(s) _____ represents producer surplus.
         (a)   B and K; A and J
         (b)   A and J; B and K
         (c)   B; A
         (d)   A; B

_____ 21.   If output is restricted to 20 units, area(s) _____ represent the deadweight loss.
         (a)   J and K
         (b)   C and L
         (c)   J, K and L
         (d)   A, B and C

II. APPLICATION QUESTIONS

1. Consider the following diagram, which shows the market for fluid milk. Quantity is in thousands of gallons.

    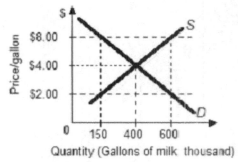

    (a) Calculate total income for dairy farmers.

    (b) Suppose that this income level is felt to be inadequate and that a political decision is made to boost farm income to $3,600,000. The government establishes a price floor at $6.00, with the government buying the surplus. How much milk will be supplied?

    (c) Who gets the milk?

    (d) The plan achieves the income objective, but what else has it done? There are costs involved with tampering with the price mechanism. What are they?

    Now suppose the government establishes a price ceiling of $2.00 per gallon.

    (e) How much milk do consumers actually receive?

    (f) Which plan is better for a milk consumer who pays no state tax? Why?

    (g) Calculate the deadweight loss if a price ceiling of $2.00 is imposed.

2. In Application Question 5 of Chapter 3, we examined the market for DVDs where the supply and demand curves are given by $Q_s = 3P$ and $Q_d = 60 - 2P$, respectively. Refer to the following diagram.

    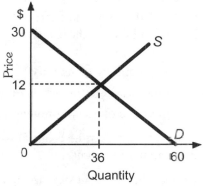

    (a) If the government imposes a price ceiling of $5 in this market, what will happen to the positions of the demand and supply curves?

    (b) Calculate the consumer surplus at the equilibrium price.

    (c) Calculate the producer surplus at the equilibrium price.

Now suppose that a $6 per unit maximum price is imposed in this market. The diagram shows the impact on quantity demanded and quantity supplied.

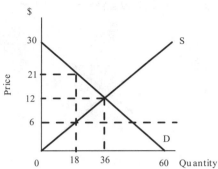

(d)   Calculate the consumer surplus. (Careful!)

(e)   Calculate the producer surplus.

(f)   Calculate the deadweight loss.

3.   In many Eastern European cities, there is a thriving market in farm produce.
   (a)   Draw a demand and supply diagram below for the Warsaw egg market. Label the curves D_1 and S_1 respectively. Show the equilibrium price (P_1) and quantity (Q_1).

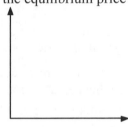

   (b)   In August, the price of eggs triples because of a decrease in supply caused by very hot weather. Show how the market changed in August. Label the new supply curve S_2. Show the new equilibrium price (P_2) and quantity (Q_2).

   (c)   Is the Warsaw egg market operating efficiently?

   (d)   Suppose the government decided to maintain the initial price (P_1). Should it impose a price ceiling or a price floor? Explain whether an excess demand or an excess supply will result.

   (e)   Is the Warsaw egg market now operating efficiently?

   (f)   How do you think suppliers might react to the price ceiling?

   (g)   Which nonprice methods might develop to circumvent the imbalance in this market?

4.   A freeze destroys much of the South American coffee crop. This causes an increase in the price of tea. Explain why, using supply and demand diagrams.

5.   Use the following demand and supply schedule to answer the questions.

Price	Quantity Demanded	Quantity Supplied
$6	10	70
$5	20	60
$4	30	50
$3	40	40
$2	50	30
$1	60	20

    (a)   Calculate the equilibrium price and the equilibrium quantity.

    (b)   Suddenly the government establishes a price ceiling of $2. Will this cause an excess supply or an excess demand? An excess of how many units?

6.   Several members of a college faculty were standing in a rather long line at the campus cafeteria. One was heard to remark that she wished the cafeteria would increase prices. Can you explain why?

7.   Who gained and who lost from government intervention in the market in the following case? In 1993, Congress scrapped a long-standing subsidy for honey producers. Until 1988, a price floor was in place, with the government purchasing surpluses of honey. From 1980 to 1988, $525 million was spent on the program. The "honey subsidy" was reinstated in 2002. What arguments were made in its favor?

8.   The auction site, eBay, offers an opportunity to observe both consumer surplus and the demand curve. Choose an auction where many bidders have participated. Presumably, each bidder has bid up to the maximum value he or she places on the good for sale. These maximum bids (with the exception of the winner's) are revealed after the auction ends. Can you construct the demand curve for your chosen auction? Suppose the actual price was lower than the winning price—determine the extent of the consumer surplus.

Practice Test SOLUTIONS

I.   SOLUTIONS TO MULTIPLE-CHOICE QUESTIONS

1.   (c)   Issuing coupons that can be resold will lead to a market for coupons, with those willing and able to pay the most receiving the right to buy baby formula.

2.   (a)   To be effective, a price ceiling must be set below the equilibrium price.

3.   (c)   The opportunity cost is the value of the next best alternative given up, i.e., in monetary terms, whatever the $100 offered price would buy. The $35 has already been spent—it is a sunk cost.

4.   (c)   Consumer surplus is the difference between the price and the demand curve. Joe would buy two sodas because the value of the third and subsequent sodas is less than the price. His consumer surplus is ($2.00 – $1.10) + ($1.20 – $1.10).

5.   (b)   Given $Q_d = 400 - 25P$, the maximum value for P is $16 (i.e., 400/25). When P = $10, Q_d = 150. Consumer surplus is $1/2(P_{max} - P)Q_d$. so 1/2($16 – $10)150 = $450.   Refer to page 89.

6.   (c)   An effective price ceiling (set below the equilibrium price) will create a shortage. Quantity demanded is 40, but quantity supplied is only 10.

7.   (c)   The price is below the equilibrium price, with quantity demanded being 100 and quantity supplied being only 40. A shortage of 60 exists.

8.   (a)   The increase in supply would eliminate the shortage and eliminate government tax revenues. Recall that an "increase in supply" will shift the position of the supply curve to the right.

9.   (a)   When there is a market imbalance, price adjusts to allocate production.

10.   (c)   A decrease in income will reduce the demand for a normal good and, given the market price, consumer surplus will decrease.

11.   (a)   Demand has increased causing an excess demand. Price will rise to remove the imbalance.

12.   (a)   A price ceiling above the equilibrium price will have no effect. A decrease in supply, therefore, will result in a higher price.

13.   (c)   An effective price ceiling (set below the equilibrium price) will create a shortage. Quantity demanded is 40, but quantity supplied is only 10, so a shortage of 30 exists.

14.   (d)   Demand and supply curves do not shift in response to changes in price!

15.   (a)   The deadweight loss is the area between the demand curve and the supply curve from the restricted output level (10) to the equilibrium output level (30). 1/2($4 – $1)(30 – 10) = $30.

16.   (b)   The minimum wage is a price floor. To be effective it is set above the equilibrium wage. As the wage increases, more workers will seek jobs but employers will demand fewer workers (a decrease in employment).

17.   (c)   Consumer surplus is the area between the price and the demand curve.

18.   (d)   Producer surplus is the area between the price and the supply curve.

19.   (d)   There is no deadweight loss when the market is in equilibrium.

20.   (d)   Consumer surplus is the area between the price and the demand curve from zero to 20 units of output. Similarly, producer surplus is the area between the price and the supply curve from zero to 20 units of output.

21.   (a)   The deadweight loss is the area between the demand curve and the supply curve from the restricted output level to the equilibrium output level.

II. SOLUTIONS TO APPLICATION QUESTIONS

1.   (a) $1,600,000

      (b)   600,000 gallons

      (c)   150,000 gallons are bought by consumers, and the rest (450,000 gallons) is taken by the government.

      (d)   Milk is now more expensive and less plentiful for consumers. Taxpayers—who needn't be milk consumers—will have to pick up the subsidy tab. There will be storage and administrative costs, too. Also, there is an overallocation of resources toward milk production.

      (e)   At $2.00 per gallon, consumers receive 150,000 gallons. In this case there is a shortage of 450,000 gallons.

      (f)   The second plan is better in that the price of milk is lower for milk consumers.

      (g)   Deadweight loss equals $1/2(\$6 - \$2)(400 - 150)$, or $500,000

2.   (a)   Nothing! A change in price leads to movements along the given demand and supply curves.

      (b)   The consumer surplus equals $(\$30 - \$12)(36)/2$, or $324.

      (c)   The producer surplus equals $(\$12 - 0)(36)/2$ or $216.

      (d)   The consumer surplus equals $(\$30 - \$21)(18)/2 + (\$21 - \$6)(18)$ or $351.

      (e)   The producer surplus equals $(\$6 - 0)(18)/2$, or $54.

      (f)   The deadweight loss equals $(\$21 - \$6)(36 - 18)/2$ or $135.

3.   (a)   Refer to the following diagram.

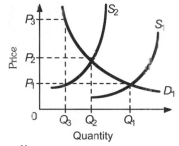

      (b)   Refer to the preceding diagram.

(c) The market is efficient in that it is reflecting the change in supply and equalizing quantity demanded and quantity supplied.

(d) The government should impose a price ceiling to place an upper limit on price. Quantity demanded will exceed quantity supplied—there will be an excess demand.

(e) This is now a seller's market. Output is restricted to Q_3. At that output, an excess demand exists.

(f) Suppliers may withdraw eggs from the controlled Warsaw market—selling them either outside Warsaw or on the black market within the city. Substandard (small or damaged) eggs may be offered for sale. Egg quality may be sacrificed.

(g) Other rationing methods, such as queuing or preferred customers, might be used. Black markets with higher prices are likely to develop. Eggs may be sold as part of a "package" of commodities.

4. Higher coffee prices increased the demand for tea (a substitute). Refer to the following diagrams.

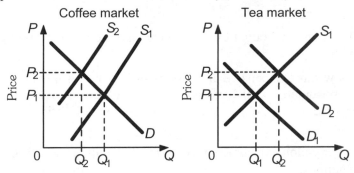

5. (a) $3; 40

   (b) Excess demand; 20

6. Higher prices would reduce quantity demanded and cut down on waiting time. If you value your time highly, you would probably be willing to pay higher prices to avoid waiting in line.

7. There was a transfer of wealth from taxpayers in general to the nation's 2,000 commercial beekeepers. Honey consumers also lost because the market price was kept higher than it should have been. There was an overallocation of resources to honey production. Note that honey consumption was less than its most efficient level despite the excess supply. The subsidy was reinstated because honey producers, it was argued, provide pollination services for other agriculturalists.

8. Answers, of course, will vary with the auction chosen. Consumer surplus will be the value of total differences between your supposed actual price and the maximum bid of each participant.

5
Elasticity

Chapter Objectives

1. Define the concept of elasticity.
2. Define price elasticity of demand. Interpret the terms elastic, inelastic, and unitary elasticity in the context of price elasticity of demand. Use the "percentage change" formula to measure price elasticity of demand.
3. Use the midpoint formula to measure price elasticity of demand.
4. Predict the effect on total revenue of a price change, given the elasticity of demand. Apply the total revenue test.
5. List the three determinants of price elasticity of demand and explain their effects.
6. Distinguish between and calculate cross-price elasticity of demand and income elasticity of demand.
7. Calculate and interpret elasticity values for the price elasticity of supply.

BRAIN TEASER I: The textbook discusses the effects of a price floor such as the minimum wage in Chapter 4. If there is a minimum wage hike, do you think the income of minimum wage workers will increase or decrease? What does this tell you about the wage elasticity of labor demand for minimum wage workers?

BRAIN TEASER II: Here are real-world price (i.e., salary) elasticities of supply for some occupations. First, can you decide which occupation goes with which salary? (Hint: Try ranking them.)

Child-care labor	−0.30
Young female physicians	0.00
Young male physicians	0.20
Primary-care physicians	0.50
Medical specialists	2.00

Objective 1

Define the concept of elasticity.

For "elasticity" read "responsiveness." The elasticity measures that are developed in this chapter are intended to quantify relationships you first met in Chapter 3. We know that quantity demanded decreases as price increases—that's the law of demand. *Price elasticity of demand* allows us to measure *how much* quantity demanded changes (how responsive we are) when price changes. We know that, as income increases, the demand for a good will increase or decrease (depending on whether it's normal or inferior). *Income elasticity of demand* allows us to measure *how much* demand will change and in which direction. We know that a change in the price of one good will increase or decrease the demand for a related good (depending on whether they are substitutes or complements). *Cross-price elasticity of demand* quantifies the relationship.

Boiled down, elasticity quantifies the response of one variable to a change on another variable. The concept is not limited to demand; it is a general concept.

LEARNING TIP: The best way to understand "elasticity" is to equate the term with "responsiveness." Select a good for which demand is fairly insensitive to price changes (prescription drugs, gasoline, college tuition) and one for which demand is quite sensitive (a particular brand of gasoline or soft drink). When you need to think through an elasticity problem (during an exam), plug in your chosen example. ◀

Practice

1.   Intuitively, which purchasers of which good will be least responsive to an increase in its price?
    (a)   Gasoline
    (b)   Exxon gasoline
    (c)   Shell gasoline
    (d)   BP gasoline

    ANSWER: (a) For each of the other options, close substitutes are present. For most drivers, there are few close substitutes for gasoline in general. When price increases, quantity demanded will decrease only slightly.

2.   The formula for "the elasticity of *A* with respect to *B*" is
    (a)   change in *A* divided by change in *B*.
    (b)   change in *B* divided by change in *A*.
    (c)   percentage change in *A* divided by percentage change in *B*.
    (d)   percentage change in *B* divided by percentage change in *A*.

    ANSWER: (c) Elasticity is a relative concept. It measures the relative change in one variable with respect to the relative change in the other variable. ■

Objective 2

Define price elasticity of demand. Interpret the terms elastic, inelastic, and unitary elasticity in the context of price elasticity of demand. Use the "percentage change" formula to measure price elasticity of demand.

Price elasticity of demand is the most frequently used measurement and sets a pattern for all the formulas—it is the "percentage change in quantity demanded divided by the percentage change in price." (page 98)

Demand responsiveness may be classified as:
(a)   Perfectly elastic. The absolute price elasticity measure is infinity.
(b)   Elastic. The absolute price elasticity measure is > 1.
(c)   Unitarily elastic. The absolute price elasticity measure is 1.
(d)   Inelastic. The absolute price elasticity measure is < 1.
(e)   Perfectly inelastic. The absolute price elasticity measure is 0.
    Recall that elasticity measures responsiveness. The more responsive a buyer is to a price change, the more elastic is demand and (in absolute terms) the larger is the price elasticity of demand.

LEARNING TIP: Here is a simple memory aid for elasticity graphs. The demand curve is vertical (|) for perfectly (**I**)nelastic demand, but horizontal (—) for perfectly (**E**)lastic demand. Exactly the same relationship is true when we consider supply. ◀

Comment: Elasticity changes continuously all the way along a straight-line curve, so using the slope of a demand or supply curve as a measure of elasticity is a bad idea.

Practice

3.   A 10 percent fall in the price of shampoo results in a 5 percent increase in the quantity of shampoo demanded. Demand is
  (a)   inelastic.
  (b)   elastic.
  (c)   unitarily elastic.
  (d)   perfectly elastic.
  ANSWER: (a) "Inelastic" means "unresponsive." In this example, a 10 percent change in price provokes a relatively modest 5 percent response in quantity demanded.

4.   The price elasticity of demand can be calculated by
  (a)   multiplying the percentage change in quantity demanded by the percentage change in price.
  (b)   dividing the percentage change in quantity demanded by the percentage change in price.
  (c)   dividing the percentage change in price by the percentage change in quantity demanded.
  (d)   multiplying the percentage change in price by the percentage change in quantity demanded.
  ANSWER: (b) Refer to p. 99 for the price elasticity of demand formula.

5.   The supply of flapdoodles increases. There is no effect on the equilibrium quantity. Demand is
  (a)   perfectly inelastic.
  (b)   elastic.
  (c)   inelastic.
  (d)   perfectly elastic.
  ANSWER: (a) If demand is completely unresponsive to a price change, it is perfectly inelastic—a vertical demand curve.

6.   The demand for potato chips has a downward-sloping, straight-line demand curve. As the price of chips increases, the price elasticity of demand
  (a)   becomes more elastic.
  (b)   becomes less elastic.
  (c)   remains constant—the slope of a straight line is constant.
  (d)   remains constant—each price increase causes an equal decrease in quantity demanded.
  ANSWER: (a) Slope does not give a good guide to elasticity. A general rule, though, for a straight-line demand curve is that as price rises demand becomes more elastic.

7.   A 10 percent increase in the price of video games results in a 5 percent decrease in the quantity of video games demanded. The price elasticity of demand is _____ and demand is _____ .
  (a)   –0.5; elastic
  (b)   –2.0; elastic
  (c)   –0.5; inelastic
  (d)   –2.0; inelastic
  ANSWER: (c) Options (a) and (d) must be wrong—an "elastic" value must have an absolute value of more than 1 whereas an "inelastic" value must have an absolute value of less than 1. The relatively large price change prompts a relatively small quantity change—that's inelastic. ∎

Objective 3

Use the midpoint formula to measure price elasticity of demand.

Elasticity requires a comparison of the percentage change in quantity to the percentage change in price. In the midpoint formula, the "price" value is calculated by taking the average of both prices $(P_2 + P_1)/2$. Similarly, the "quantity" value is calculated by taking the average of both quantities $(Q_2 + Q_1)/2$. The "change in price" is determined by the difference between the final price (P_2) and the initial price (P_1), or $(P_2 - P_1)$. Similarly, the "change in quantity" is determined by the difference between the final quantity (Q_2) and the initial quantity (Q_1), or $(Q_2 - Q_1)$.

> **LEARNING TIP:** The midpoint formula, for all its complexity, is an essential part of elasticity. Even if you're averse to formulas in general, you should practice this one. Be aware, though, that if all you need is to find whether demand is "elastic" or inelastic", the total revenue test (in the following section) will be sufficient.◀
>
> **LEARNING TIP:** By canceling the 2's in the textbook formula, the midpoint elasticity formula can be simplified to:
>
> $$\frac{(Q_2 - Q_1)/(Q_2 + Q_1)}{(P_2 - P_1)/(P_2 + P_1)}$$
>
> Make sure you have the "quantity" terms in the numerator and the "price" terms in the denominator—we're measuring how much *quantity* (top) responds to a change in the *dollar* amount (bottom).◀

Practice

Use the following information to answer the next three questions: Stellio's Pizzeria has been experimenting with the price of its Supreme Pizza. At a price of $12, quantity demanded is 100. At $10, quantity demanded increases to 120 pizzas. When the price is $8, quantity demanded increases to 140 pizzas.

8. Using the midpoint formula, the price elasticity of demand between $12 and $10 is
    (a) elastic with an elasticity value of –2.
    (b) unitarily elastic with an elasticity value of –1.
    (c) elastic with an elasticity value of –10.
    (d) inelastic with an elasticity value of –0.1.

    ANSWER: (b) P_1 is 12; P_2 is 10; Q_1 is 100; Q_2 is 120. Plug the values into the formula. Note: Confirm your result using the total revenue test. Refer to Objective 4 following.

9. Using the midpoint formula, the price elasticity of demand between $10 and $8 is
    (a) elastic with an elasticity value of –13/9.
    (b) elastic with an elasticity value of –9/13.
    (c) inelastic with an elasticity value of –13/9.
    (d) inelastic with an elasticity value of –9/13.

    ANSWER: (d) P_1 is 10; P_2 is 8; Q_1 is 120; Q_2 is 140. Options (b) and (c) must be incorrect—an elastic demand cannot have an elasticity of –9/13. Note: Confirm your "inelastic" result using the total revenue test. Refer to Objective 4 following.

10. Using the midpoint formula, the price elasticity of demand between $12 and $8 is
    (a) elastic with an elasticity value of –6/5.
    (b) elastic with an elasticity value of –5/6.
    (c) inelastic with an elasticity value of –6/5.
    (d) inelastic with an elasticity value of –5/6.

ANSWER: (d) P_1 is 12; P_2 is 8; Q_1 is 100; Q_2 is 140. Options (b) and (c) must be incorrect—an elastic demand cannot have an elasticity of –5/6 and an inelastic demand cannot have an elasticity of –6/5. Note: Confirm your "inelastic" result using the total revenue test. Refer to Objective 4 following. ■

Objective 4

Predict the effect on total revenue of a price change, given the elasticity of demand. Apply the total revenue test.

Total revenue is "price × quantity." The relationship between elasticity and total revenue as price increases may be classified as:
(a) Elastic if total revenue decreases
(b) Unitarily elastic if total revenue remains constant
(c) Inelastic if total revenue increases

Given with a good with an elastic demand (Pepsi), a small increase in the price of will trigger a relatively large decrease in the quantity demanded as consumers switch over to Coke and other close substitutes. Total spending on Pepsi will decrease.

Given a good with an inelastic demand (gasoline), even a large price hike will result in only a small decrease in the quantity demanded, because consumers have few close substitutes for the product. Total spending on gas will increase. (page 105)

The *total revenue test* shows whether demand is elastic or inelastic when price changes. The following table summarizes the results of the test.

Price	Quantity	Elasticity	Total Revenue
increase	decrease	perfectly elastic	falling to zero
increase	decrease	elastic	falling
increase	decrease	unitarily elastic	constant
increase	decrease	inelastic	rising
increase	no change	perfectly inelastic	rising

If you don't know (or don't want to calculate) exact elasticity values, checking how total revenue is changing is an effective way to discover if the good has an elastic demand or not.

ECONOMICS IN PRACTICE (SUPPLEMENTAL): During the twelve months from June 2007 to May 2008, the average price of gasoline rose by 40 percent. It was reported that the number of miles driven during that period fell by 4 percent. What do we learn about the price elasticity of demand for gasoline? According to this information, did the revenues received by oil corporations increase or decrease?
ANSWER: Demand is inelastic, with a value of –0.1. With rising prices at the pump, the gas companies received increasing revenues. In fact, Exxon Mobil's earnings surged by 42.6 percent and the company displaced Walmart as the nation's biggest corporation.

Practice

11. The price of canned salmon increases; total spending on canned salmon remains unchanged. Canned salmon has a(n) _____ demand.
  (a) perfectly inelastic
  (b) perfectly elastic
  (c) unitarily elastic
  (d) inelastic

ANSWER: (c)   Total revenue will increase if salmon has an inelastic demand, and will decrease if salmon has an elastic demand. This is the middle case where the price change results in no change in total spending.

12.   Total revenue will decrease if price _____ and demand is _____ .
(a)   increases; inelastic
(b)   increases; unitarily elastic
(c)   decreases; inelastic
(d)   decreases; elastic

ANSWER: (c)   College tuition has an inelastic demand. Total revenue on tuition will increase if college administrators declare a price increase. By the same argument, if tuition rates are reduced, total revenue will decrease.

13.   An excellent harvest causes apples to fall in price by 10 percent. Consumers buy 5 percent more apples. The price decrease has caused consumers to
(a)   spend less on apples.
(b)   spend more on apples.
(c)   reduce the quantity of apples bought. We can't tell what has happened to spending.
(d)   increase the quantity of apples bought. We can't tell what has happened to spending.

ANSWER: (a)   The price elasticity of demand is –0.5—inelastic. A decrease in price will reduce the number of dollars spent. ∎

Objective 5

List the three determinants of price elasticity of demand and explain their effects.

The responsiveness of demand to changes in price is affected by the availability of substitutes, the fraction of total spending that a good absorbs, and the time factor. The elasticity of demand will *increase* if more substitutes become available, if the good commands a greater portion of the household's budget, or if the response time is longer rather than shorter. (page 107)

LEARNING TIP: To remember how price elasticity is influenced by its determinants (the availability of substitutes, the fraction of total spending that a good absorbs, and time), make up a few intuitive examples.

Substitutes: Exxon gas has an elastic demand because there are many substitutes (BP, Texaco, etc.); gasoline, in general, has few substitutes—elasticity will be lower. Pepsi has many substitutes, electricity has few.

As more substitutes become available, demand becomes more elastic. The first drug to combat AIDS, AZT, had no substitutes—inelastic demand. The producer was attacked for setting the price too high and reaping substantial revenues. The emergence of substitutes made AZT's demand more elastic.

Fraction of total spending: Suppose Bazooka Joe bubblegum (or salt, or pepper) doubled in price. It's such a small portion of expenditures for most people that the price increase would pass almost unnoticed and quantity demanded would respond only slightly—inelastic demand. In contrast, a doubling in the price of a good that is important in one's budget (gasoline, perhaps) will provoke a greater response.

Time: The longer the consumer has to "shop around" following a price increase, the more responsive he or she can be. In the late 1970s, for instance, gas prices rose rapidly. Initially, drivers planned trips more carefully, then came carpooling. Eventually, as cars aged, newer, more fuel-efficient models were bought. Progressively, fuel consumption was reduced. As gas prices subsided, drivers moved on to SUVs and Hummers and forgot the lessons that they'd learned. With the recent upsurge in oil prices, some of those old strategies have been rediscovered.

In each example, remember to apply the total revenue test. If gasoline increases in price, your gas bill will increase (inelastic demand). If Pepsi increases in price, your spending on Pepsi will decrease (elastic demand). ◀

ECONOMICS IN PRACTICE: This chapter's first "economics in practice" example examines the responsiveness of cigarette smokers to price changes. First, how sensitive do you think the typical smoker is to price changes? Will demand be elastic or inelastic? Second, do you think that teenage smokers are more or less sensitive to cigarette price changes than the typical smoker?

Now, do you think that marijuana is more or less addictive than cigarettes for teenagers? Based on your answer, predict what should happen to the spending of teenage marijuana users if the price of the substance increased.

Finally, what about crack cocaine? Do you think the elasticity (responsiveness) will be greater or less than for marijuana?

ANSWER: Nicotine is now accepted as addictive. Seasoned smokers find it difficult to quit smoking, so we should predict that the demand for cigarettes is inelastic. Researchers report a price elasticity value of –0.4, in fact. Younger smokers, perhaps because they are less addicted, or perhaps because they earn less income, are somewhat more price sensitive, with an elasticity value of –0.7.

A study showed that the price elasticity of demand for marijuana was –0.4 (less elastic) indicating that many users were likely to keep on buying even if the price increased. We should predict increased expenditures if the price was raised.

A further study reports that crack has a price elasticity of –1.0 (unitarily elastic). This implies that crack users are more responsive to price changes than marijuana users! This may appear counterintuitive until you consider the implications of the total revenue test.

ECONOMICS IN PRACTICE (CONTINUED): In Chapter 4 we considered the U.S. government's two strategies to restrict drug use ("Just say no" and "war on drugs"). Let's consider the latter strategy, which attempts to curtail supply. The available evidence suggests that drugs (even marijuana) have a fairly inelastic demand. First, if the government's strategy is successful, what will happen to the supply of drugs and to their price? Given your answer, what will happen to the revenue received by drug dealers? Assuming that much of the money that users spend on illegal drugs is "earned" from illegal activities—some studies estimate that as much as 60 percent of crime is drug related—what is the policy's likely impact on crime in our communities?

ANSWER: If the "war on drugs" strategy is successful, drug supplies will be reduced and prices will increase. If demand is inelastic, then revenues received by drug dealers will increase—this is an application of the total revenue test. In order to finance their habit, drug purchasers are likely to increase their illegal activities—mugging, car theft, pilfering, prostitution, and so on.

Practice

14. Nita is a senior at East Dakota University. Probably, she will have the most elastic demand for
    (a) East Dakota University tuition.
    (b) the textbook for her economics course.
    (c) Exxon gasoline for her car.
    (d) required prescription drugs.

    ANSWER: (c) There should be many substitutes (other companies' gasoline), and Nita may consider gas an important part of her budget. Tuition may be important in Nita's budget, but few substitutes are likely to be available. ■

Objective 6

Distinguish between and calculate both cross-price elasticity of demand and income elasticity of demand.

Income elasticity of demand—which measures how much demand for Good *A* shifts when income level changes—shows whether goods are inferior (negative elasticity) or normal (positive elasticity). (page 110)

    Cross-price elasticity of demand—which measures how the demand for Good *A* shifts when the price of Good *B* changes—shows whether goods are substitutes (positive elasticity) or complements (negative elasticity). (page 110)

    The main point is the sign (positive or negative) of the relationship rather than the magnitude. However, the larger (in absolute terms) the elasticity value, the more related are the two goods. For instance, a small decrease in the price of Pepsi may trigger a sizable decrease in the demand for Coke (close substitutes) but a smaller decrease in the demand for Yoo-Hoo Chocolate Drink.

LEARNING TIP: Check these results by "plugging in" your own examples from Chapter 3.

Substitutes. An increase in the price of Pepsi will lead to a decrease in the quantity demanded of Pepsi and an increase in the demand for Coke (positive sign).

Complements. An increase in the price of CDs will lead to a decrease in the demand for CD players (negative sign).

Inferior Goods. Rice, beans, and generic aspirin are good examples of inferior goods. As your income increases, you will probably decrease your spending on such goods (negative sign).

Normal Goods. As your income increases, you will probably increase your spending on soft drinks, books, clothes, CDs, etc. (positive sign).

Remember: put the "**n**umber" term (quantity) in the **n**umerator and the "**d**ollar" term (price or income) in the **d**enominator. ◖

Practice

15.   The cross-price elasticity of demand between Exxon gas and Havoline motor oil is –0.7. Exxon gas and Havoline motor oil are _____ . The cross-price elasticity of demand between Exxon gas and Chevron gas will be_____ .
    (a)   substitutes; positive
    (b)   substitutes; negative
    (c)   complements; positive
    (d)   complements; negative

    ANSWER: (c) A negative cross-price elasticity indicates that goods are complements. Because Exxon and Chevron are substitutes, the cross-price elasticity will be positive.

16.   The income elasticity of demand for Havoline oil is +0.6. We can conclude that Havoline oil
    (a)   is an inferior good.
    (b)   is a normal good.
    (c)   is a substitute.
    (d)   has a demand that is not very sensitive to changes in its price.

    ANSWER: (b) An increase in income will raise demand for Havoline. The elasticity is positive. Options C and D do not refer to income elasticity. ∎

Objective 7

Calculate and interpret elasticity values for the price elasticity of supply.

Price elasticity of supply looks at the responsiveness of suppliers to changes in price whereas price elasticity of labor supply does the same thing for the labor supply curve. The labor supply curve can be backward bending (if price elasticity of supply is negative). (page 111)

ECONOMICS IN PRACTICE: As time passes, price elasticity of demand (or supply) becomes *more* elastic, as we see from the delicatessen example on p. 109. Here are two values (−0.38, −1.00) for price elasticity of demand for dental services. Which is the long-run value and which is the short-run value? Can you give some rationale for this result?
ANSWER: The short-run elasticity is −0.38 and the long-run elasticity is −1.00. In the short run, clients are not particularly concerned with the price charged by the dentist—they wish to have their dental problems fixed! In the longer term, with rising prices, clients will avail themselves more rigorously of preventative practices.

ECONOMICS IN PRACTICE (CONTINUED): Here are two values (+0.36, +0.51) for price elasticity of supply of milk. Which is the long-run value and which is the short-run value in this case? Again, why would you expect this sort of result?
ANSWER: The short-run elasticity is +0.36 and the long-run elasticity is +0.51. In the short run, an increase in the price of milk will provoke an increase in quantity supplied, but there are limited dairy facilities. In the longer term, herds can be expanded more substantially.

Practice

17. The price elasticity of labor supply is 0.7. Labor supply is _____ and _____ .
    (a)   elastic; upward sloping
    (b)   elastic; downward sloping
    (c)   inelastic; upward sloping
    (d)   inelastic; downward sloping

    ANSWER: (c)   The elasticity is positive—a rise in the wage results in an increase in the quantity of labor supplied. Because the elasticity has a value of less than one, a given percentage increase in wage will result in a smaller percentage increase in quantity of labor supplied—an inelastic response. ∎

BRAIN TEASER I SOLUTION: A wage hike is likely to increase the income of recipients. This implies that the wage elasticity of labor demand for minimum wage workers is strongly inelastic. Relate this to the total revenue test as covered in this chapter.

BRAIN TEASER II SOLUTION: The order is simply reversed. Child-care workers have a quite high price elasticity of supply (2.00) while that of medical specialists is negative (−0.3). For extra credit, what does this final value tell you about the slope of the supply curve for medical specialists? To find a more complete explanation for this unusual phenomenon, refer to the discussion in Chapter 6 (pp. 135-135) on the interplay between the income effect and the substitution effect.

PRACTICE TEST

I. MULTIPLE-CHOICE QUESTIONS

Select the option that provides the single best answer.

_____ 1.   Price elasticity of demand is –0.50. Price increases by 10 percent. We would predict a
     (a)   50 percent increase in quantity demanded.
     (b)   20 percent decrease in quantity demanded.
     (c)   5 percent increase in quantity demanded.
     (d)   5 percent decrease in quantity demanded.

_____ 2.   Sellers of yo-yos want to raise their revenues. They should _____ price by 30¢ if they believe demand to be _____ in that price range.
     (a)   lower; elastic
     (b)   lower; inelastic
     (c)   raise; elastic
     (d)   Two of the above are feasible scenarios.

_____ 3.   A 10 percent fall in the price of apples results in a 20 percent increase in the quantity of apples demanded. Demand is
     (a)   inelastic.
     (b)   elastic.
     (c)   unitarily elastic.
     (d)   perfectly elastic.

_____ 4.   Which of the following is NOT a determinant of price elasticity of demand for gasoline?
     (a)   The quantity of gasoline produced
     (b)   The amount of time given to adjust to a price change
     (c)   The availability of close substitutes
     (d)   The importance of gasoline in one's budget

_____ 5.   Price elasticity of demand is a measure of the
     (a)   extent of competition in the market.
     (b)   percentage change in quantity times the percentage change in price.
     (c)   slope of the demand curve.
     (d)   degree of consumer responsiveness to changes in price.

_____ 6.   The price elasticity of demand for Chevron gas will tend to be
     (a)   less elastic, the lower the price of substitutes.
     (b)   less elastic, the smaller the share of consumers' income spent on Chevron gas.
     (c)   less elastic, the greater the availability of close substitutes for Chevron gas.
     (d)   more elastic, the more urgently gas is needed.

_____ 7. Two goods are complements. Their cross-price elasticity of demand will be
(a) a negative number.
(b) a positive number.
(c) a positive number greater than one.
(d) one.

Use the following graph to answer the next question.

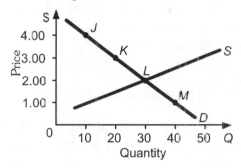

_____ 8. Which statement is false? "Demand for this product is _____ in the range _____."
(a) elastic; J to K
(b) elastic; J to L
(c) inelastic; L to M
(d) elastic; K to L

_____ 9. The cross-price elasticity between Wendy's Biggie Fries and Wendy's Frostie is _____.
The cross-price elasticity between Burger King's Whopper and McDonald's Big Mac is

_____ .

(a) positive; positive
(b) positive; negative
(c) negative; positive
(d) negative; negative

_____ 10. The income elasticity of Good A is positive, and the cross-price elasticity between Good A and Good B is negative. Good A is a(n)
(a) normal good and a substitute for Good B.
(b) inferior good and a substitute for Good B.
(c) normal good and a complement for Good B.
(d) inferior good and a complement for Good B.

_____ 11. The price of a yo-yo rises from $5 to $6. Total revenue falls from $400 to $360. We can conclude that price elasticity of demand is (roughly) _____ , which means that demand is _____ .
(a) −0.579, inelastic
(b) −1.571, elastic
(c) −0.579, elastic
(d) −1.571, inelastic

_____ 12. Good *C* has a *negative* income elasticity. Which of the following goods is most likely to be Good *C*?
  (a)   Alfa Romeo sports car
  (b)   A vacation in Europe
  (c)   A compact disc
  (d)   A can of generic beer

_____ 13. An increase in the labor costs of the sellers of a product, combined with a relatively inelastic demand curve, will result in a
  (a)   relatively small reduction in output.
  (b)   relatively small increase in equilibrium price.
  (c)   rightward shift in the supply curve.
  (d)   leftward shift in the demand curve.

_____ 14. A leftward shift in the supply curve of buttermilk beer causes its price to rise by 10 percent. Harry Potter thereafter buys 20 percent fewer buttermilk beers. The price rise has caused Harry to
  (a)   spend less on buttermilk beers.
  (b)   spend more on buttermilk beers.
  (c)   reduce the quantity bought. We can't tell what has happened to how much he spends.
  (d)   increase the quantity bought. We can't tell what has happened to how much he spends.

_____ 15. Moo U. radio station reports that, because the college eatery, *The Five Beans*, raised the price of hot dogs, fewer hot dogs have been bought and *The Five Beans's* total revenue on hot dogs has been halved. This indicates that
  (a)   the demand schedule for hot dogs at *The Five Beans* is horizontal.
  (b)   at present, prices are in the elastic section of the demand schedule.
  (c)   hot dogs are an inferior good.
  (d)   the price elasticity of demand for hot dogs is –0.5.

_____ 16. The closer substitutes two goods are, the _____ will be their cross-price elasticity.
  (a)   more positive
  (b)   more negative
  (c)   less positive
  (d)   less negative

_____ 17. Basil's restaurant sells its Waldorf salad for $10 and 30 are demanded each day. If the price is increased to $12, quantity demanded decreases to 20 each day. Using the midpoint formula, Basil finds that the price elasticity of demand is
  (a)   –0.4545, meaning that demand is elastic.
  (b)   –2.20, meaning that demand is elastic.
  (c)   –0.4545, meaning that demand is inelastic.
  (d)   –2.20, meaning that demand is inelastic.

_____ 18.   The price elasticity of demand for Colby cheese is –2.1 in Wisconsin and –0.9 in Arizona. Demand is _____ in Wisconsin and _____ in Arizona.
(a)   elastic; elastic
(b)   elastic; inelastic
(c)   inelastic; elastic
(d)   inelastic; inelastic

_____ 19.   Roach and Beetall discover that the price elasticity of demand of their patent insecticide is –2.0. They wish to increase the quantity of insecticide demanded by 5.0 percent. They should
(a)   increase price by 10.0 percent.
(b)   increase price by 2.5 percent.
(c)   decrease price by 10.0 percent.
(d)   decrease price by 2.5 percent.

_____ 20.   The cross-price elasticity of demand between beans and rice is – 4.0 percent. A 2 percent decrease in the price of beans will lead to
(a)   an 8 percent increase in the demand for rice.
(b)   a 0.5 percent increase in the demand for rice.
(c)   an 8 percent decrease in the demand for rice.
(d)   a 0.5 percent decrease in the demand for rice.

II. APPLICATION QUESTIONS

1.   You've just bought a company that publishes cookbooks. You consult your in-house economist. The conversation goes like this:
    He tells you that the price elasticity of demand for your cookbooks is –2.4.
    Then you tell him that you want to maximize sales revenue.
    He tells you that you should raise the price of the cookbooks.
    Then you tell him that he is a useless collection of carbon-based molecules.
    Explain your reaction.

2.   The price of Good A and of Good B is $10, and both goods have a quantity demanded of 100 units/week. When the price of Good A falls to $9, the quantity demanded rises to 200 units/week. However, the price of Good B must fall to $8 in order to achieve sales of 200.
(a)   In the price ranges given, which good has the more **elastic** demand?
(b)   Use the total revenue test to confirm that both goods face elastic demand curves.
(c)   Verify your answer by calculating the price elasticity for Good A and Good B. Use the midpoint formula.

3.   The cross-price elasticity for Good X (to a change in Good Y's price) is –0.7. The cross-price elasticity for Good X (to a change in Good Z's price) is +0.7. Good X's income elasticity is –0.7.
    If Good X's producer wishes its demand to increase, which of the following scenarios is the most preferred?
(a)   The economy experiences unexpected prosperity; the price of Good Y increases.
(b)   The economy experiences an unexpected recession; the price of Good Y increases.
(c)   The economy experiences unexpected prosperity; the price of Good Y decreases.
(d)   The economy experiences an unexpected recession; the price of Good Z increases.
(e)   The price of Good Y increases; the price of Good Z increases.
    Explain your answer.

4.   In Application Question 5 of Chapter 3, we examined the market for DVDs where the supply and demand curves are given by $Q_s = 3P$ and $Q_d = 60 - 2P$, respectively. Refer to the following diagram.

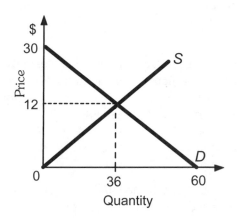

(a)   Considering the demand curve in isolation, calculate the total revenue when price is $5 and when price is $10.

(b)   Considering the demand curve in isolation, calculate the total revenue when price is $20 and when price is $25.

(c)   Use the total revenue test to estimate the price elasticity of demand between $5 and $10 and between $20 and $25.

(d)   Using the midpoint formula, calculate the price elasticity of demand between $5 and $10 and between $20 and $25.

5.   (a)   Use the following demand schedule to complete the table for the final (TR) column, put in "rises," "falls," or "is constant."

Price	Quantity Demanded	Total Revenue	Elasticity (in words)	Elasticity Measure	As Price Rises, TR
$6	10	$60			
$5	20	$100			
$4	30	$120			
$3	40	$120			
$2	50	$100			
$1	60	$60			

(b)   Work out a rule, based on your results in the last two columns, linking the change in total revenue and elasticity.

6.   Use the information in the table to answer the following questions.

Month	Income per Month	Quantity Demanded of Chicken per Month	Quantity Demanded of Steak per Month
1	$400	5 pounds	3 pounds
2	$800	3 pounds	5 pounds
3	$800	5 pounds	3 pounds

(a)   Using Months 1 and 2, is the income elasticity of chicken positive, negative, or zero? What kind of a good is chicken?

(b)   Using Months 1 and 2, estimate the income elasticity of steak. Is steak a normal good?

(c)   Intuitively, what sort of demand relationship do you think will exist between chicken and steak?

(d)   In Month 3 the price of steak rose from $2/pound to $3/pound. Estimate the cross-price elasticity to check your intuition regarding your answer to part c.

7.   On January 1, 2011, the Board of Aldermen of Dukeham, VT, doubled the rate it charged residents for water in order to pay for a new sewage-treatment plant. The table shows the town manager's predictions of revenues and the actual revenues collected. (Assume a straight-line demand curve throughout.)

Year	Price (/1,000 gal)	Revenue Predicted	Actual Quantity Used	Actual Revenue
2010	$0.60	_____	300,000	$180,000
2011	$1.20	$300,000	200,000	$240,000

(a)   What price elasticity of demand (elastic/inelastic/unitarily elastic) did the town manager assume in her predicted revenue estimate?

(b)   How can you tell that this was her assumption without first calculating the elasticity of demand?

(c)   Using the midpoint formula, calculate the "predicted" price elasticity of demand.

(d)   Using the midpoint formula, calculate the "actual" price elasticity of demand.

Based on what happened, Alderman Phil E. Buster claims that water rate hikes are an easy way to increase town funds. He proposes that the water rate be raised to $5.00 per 1,000 gallons.

(e)   What do you think will happen to the position of the demand for water curve?

(f)   Do you think the elasticity will be the same?

(g)   Explain your answer to Part (f).

8.   Here is some information about the daily demand for milk in Collegeville.

Price/gallon	Quantity Demanded
$6.00	8,000
$5.00	12,000

Now, suppose the price of a gallon of milk rises from $5.00 to $6.00.

(a)   Using the midpoint formula, calculate the elasticity of demand using the prices and quantities above.

(b)   Calculate the change in the buyers' total expenditure.

(c)   On the basis of your calculations, is demand elastic, inelastic, or neither, in this price range?

(d)   Is your answer in part (c) consistent with your calculations in part (a)?

Practice Test SOLUTIONS

I.   SOLUTIONS TO MULTIPLE-CHOICE QUESTIONS

1.   (d)   Price elasticity looks at the percentage change in quantity demanded divided by the percentage change in price. If $X/Y = -0.5$ and Y equals 10 percent, then X equals 5 percent.

2.   (a)   Check the total revenue test. If price is raised on a good with an elastic demand, many customers will stop buying it and revenue will fall. Therefore, cutting the price on a good with an elastic demand will increase total revenue. Refer to page 105.

3.   (b)   Price elasticity measures the percentage change in quantity demanded divided by the percentage change in price. Here, elasticity is –2.0, which is elastic.

4.   (a)   A change in the quantity of gasoline produced is shown by a supply curve shift.

5.   (d)   For "elasticity" read "responsiveness."

6.   (b)   The elasticity of demand tends to be greater when an item represents a large part of our budget. An increase in its price hurts! If an item is insignificant, changes in its price are insignificant, too, and we are less sensitive to such changes. Refer to page 107.

7.   (a)   Price of Good A rises, and quantity demanded falls. The other partner in the pair, Good B, experiences a decrease in demand. Cross-price elasticity measures the percentage change in quantity demanded of Good B divided by the percentage change in price of Good A—a negative divided by a positive.

8.   (d)   Apply the total revenue test. When price is $2.00, total revenue is $60. When price is $3.00, total revenue is $60. Demand is unitarily elastic in this price range.

9.   (c)   Wendy's products "go together"—a cut in the price of fries, for example, will encourage more customers to buy Frosties, too. The Whopper and Big Mac are substitutes—a lower price for the Whopper will reduce demand for the Big Mac.

10.   (c)   A positive income elasticity indicates that Good A is normal. A negative cross-price elasticity indicates that Good A is a complement of Good B. Refer to page 110.

11. (b) If price rises and total revenue falls, we have a good with an elastic demand. Elasticity must be more negative than –1. (In fact, if you work out the value, it is –1.571, but this is not necessary to answer the question.)

12. (d) A negative income elasticity indicates that Good C is inferior. For most people, the inferior good on the list would be the can of generic beer. Refer to page 110.

13. (a) The increase in labor costs will make supply shift left. Price will rise and quantity demanded will fall. If demand is relatively inelastic, the increase in price will be relatively large and the decrease in quantity demanded relatively small.

14. (a) Harry's price elasticity is –2.0—elastic. An increase in price will reduce the number of dollars he spends. Refer to page 105.

15. (b) Price has risen and total revenue has fallen. Demand is elastic.

16. (a) Substitutes have a positive cross-price elasticity. The closer they are, the more responsive buyers are to changes in price and the higher the elasticity will be. Refer to page 110.

17. (b) Options (a) and (d) are both internally inconsistent. Refer to the midpoint formula on p. 102. Also, check your elasticity conclusion by considering the change in total revenue—a higher price reduces total revenue, so demand must be elastic.

18. (b) An elasticity value of –2.1 is elastic; an elasticity value of –0.9 is inelastic.

19. (d) To increase quantity demanded, Roach and Beetall must decrease price. An elasticity value of –2.0 tells us that demand is elastic. Numerically, +10 percent/–2.5 percent = –5.0 percent.

20. (a) A positive cross-price elasticity of demand indicates complements. A decrease in the price of beans will increase the demand for rice. Numerically, +8.0 percent/–2.0 percent = –4.0 percent.

II. SOLUTIONS TO APPLICATION QUESTIONS

1. An elasticity of demand of –2.4 indicates that demand is elastic. When demand is elastic, an increase in price will cause total revenue to decrease.

2. Good A has the more elastic demand. The same "change in quantity" response is elicited with a lesser change in price.

    The total revenue test shows an elastic demand in each case. For Good A, a decrease in price, from $10 to $9, leads to an increase in total revenue from $1,000 to $1,800. For Good B, a decrease in price, from $10 to $8, leads to an increase in total revenue from $1,000 to $1,600.

    More formally, the midpoint formula for Good A is:

$$\frac{(100-200)/\left[(100+200)/2\right]}{(10-9)/\left[(10+9)/2\right]}$$

The price elasticity for Good A is –6.333.

The midpoint formula for Good B is:

$$\frac{(100-200)/\left[(100+200)/2\right]}{(10-8)/\left[(10+8)/2\right]}$$

The price elasticity for Good B is –3.000.

3.   Option (d) is best. Good *X* and Good *Y* are complements. Good *X* and Good *Z* are substitutes. Good *X* is an inferior good. A recession will increase the demand for Good *X*; prosperity will not. An increase in the price of Good *Z* will reduce the quantity demanded of *Y* and increase the demand for substitute Good *X*. An increase in the price of *Y* will reduce the quantity demanded of *Y* and reduce the demand for complementary Good *X*.

4.   (a)   When the price is $5, quantity is 50 units. Total revenue is $250. When the price is $10, quantity is 40 units. Total revenue is $400.

      (b)   When the price is $20, quantity is 20 units. Total revenue is $400. When the price is $25, quantity is 10 units. Total revenue is $250.

      (c)   As price increases from $5 to $10, total revenue increases from $250 to $400. Demand is inelastic. As price increases from $20 to $25, total revenue decreases from $400 to $250. Demand is elastic.

      (d)   The midpoint formula when price lies between $5 to $10 is:

$$\frac{(50-40)/\left[(50+40)/2\right]}{(5-10)/\left[(5+10)/2\right]}$$

The price elasticity in this price range is –0.333.
The midpoint formula when price lies between $20 to $25 is:

$$\frac{(20-10)/\left[(20+10)/2\right]}{(20-25)/\left[(20+25)/2\right]}$$

The price elasticity in this price range is –3.000.

5.   (a)   Refer to the following table.

Price	Quantity Demanded	Total Revenue	Elasticity (in words)	Elasticity Measure	As Price Rises, TR
$6	10	$60			
			elastic	–3.667	falls
$5	20	$100			
			elastic	–1.800	falls
$4	30	$120			
			unit elastic	–1.000	is constant
$3	40	$120			
			inelastic	–0.556	rises
$2	50	$100			
			inelastic	–0.273	rises
$1	60	$60			

      (b)   As price rises, total revenue rises when demand is inelastic. Given a price increase, total revenue will decrease when demand is elastic.

6.   (a)   As income rises, quantity demanded falls. Income elasticity is negative—chicken is an inferior good.

      (b)   As income doubles, quantity demanded rises but doesn't double. Steak's income elasticity is positive but less than one—steak is a normal good.

      (c)   They are likely to be substitutes.

      (d)   Quantity demanded of chicken rose as the price of steak rose. Cross-price elasticity is positive—chicken and steak are substitutes.

7. (a)   Inelastic

    (b)   An increase in price led to a (predicted) increase in total revenue.

    (c)   –3/11, or –0.2727

    (d)   –3/5, or –0.60

    (e)   The position of the curve will remain unchanged. A change in price causes a change in quantity demanded!

    (f)   No, given that we have assumed a straight-line demand curve.

    (g)   With a straight-line demand curve, movements along the curve to higher price levels lead to less inelastic (more elastic) regions.

8. (a)   –11/5 or –2.20

    (b)   A fall of $3,000, from $15,000 to $12,000

    (c)   Elastic. When price rises, total revenue falls.

    (d)   Both results indicate an elastic demand.

Comprehensive Review Test

The following questions provide a wide-ranging review of the material covered in Part I (Chapters 1–5) of the textbook. Each question deals with a topic or technique important for your understanding of economic principles. If you miss a question you should return to the relevant section of the chapter in the textbook and fine-tune your understanding.

I. MULTIPLE-CHOICE QUESTIONS

Select the option that provides the single best answer.

_____ 1. The Arbezani economy is operating at a point inside its production possibility frontier. This may be because
  (a) the economy has very poor technological know-how.
  (b) Arbez is a very small nation and can't produce much.
  (c) Arbez has specialized in producing a good in which it has a comparative disadvantage.
  (d) Arbez has some unemployment.

_____ 2. Movements along the production possibility frontier illustrate
  (a) the concept of opportunity cost.
  (b) the operation of market forces.
  (c) improvements in technology.
  (d) changes in the resource mix.

_____ 3. The Arbezani economy can produce consumer goods and capital goods. There is a technological improvement in the production of consumer goods. Along the production possibility frontier, the opportunity cost of consumer goods will
  (a) increase.
  (b) decrease.
  (c) remain unchanged.
  (d) be indeterminate.

Use the diagram for the next five questions. It illustrates the production possibility frontier for Arbez.

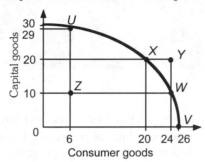

_____ 4. Which point implies the existence of unemployment?
(a) U
(b) V
(c) Y
(d) Z

_____ 5. Of those shown, with which combination of goods would the Arbezani economy grow most rapidly?
(a) U
(b) V
(c) Y
(d) Z

_____ 6. Which statement is true? Along the production possibility frontier
(a) the opportunity cost of capital goods is decreasing.
(b) the opportunity cost of consumer goods is constant.
(c) producing at Point V can never be economically efficient.
(d) the opportunity cost of consumer goods is increasing.

_____ 7. Arbez is at Point W. The opportunity cost of increasing capital goods production by 10 is
(a) 24 consumer goods given up.
(b) 20 consumer goods given up.
(c) 14 consumer goods given up.
(d) 4 consumer goods given up.

_____ 8. Arbez is at Point Z. The opportunity cost of increasing capital goods production by 20 is
(a) 24 consumer goods given up.
(b) 14 consumer goods given up.
(c) 6 consumer goods given up.
(d) 0 consumer goods given up.

_____ 9. Coke and Pepsi are consumption substitutes. The supply of Pepsi increases. This will cause
(a) an increase in the demand for Pepsi.
(b) an increase in the demand for Coke.
(c) a decrease in the demand for Pepsi.
(d) a decrease in the demand for Coke.

Each week, Jack and Jill can each produce vinegar and brown paper in the quantities shown in the following table. Constant costs apply for each individual.

	Jack	Jill
Vinegar	8	12
Brown paper	10	24

_____ 10. According to the table,
 (a) Jack has a comparative advantage in the production of both goods.
 (b) Jack has a comparative advantage in the production of vinegar, and Jill has a comparative advantage in the production of brown paper.
 (c) Jack has a comparative advantage in the production of brown paper, and Jill has a comparative advantage in the production of vinegar.
 (d) Jill has a comparative advantage in the production of both goods.

_____ 11. If producers must obtain a higher price than they did previously in order to produce the same level of output as before, we can say that there has been
 (a) an increase in quantity supplied.
 (b) an increase in supply.
 (c) a decrease in supply.
 (d) a decrease in quantity supplied.

_____ 12. The widget market is in equilibrium at a price where
 (a) there is no shortage of the good.
 (b) the demand curve is downward sloping and the supply curve is upward sloping.
 (c) the quantity demanded and the quantity supplied are equal.
 (d) there is no surplus of the good.

_____ 13. The market for peas is experiencing a shortage. You should predict that
 (a) quantity demanded will decrease and quantity supplied will increase.
 (b) demand will increase and supply will decrease.
 (c) quantity demanded will increase and quantity supplied will decrease.
 (d) demand will decrease and supply will increase.

_____ 14. Californian wine and Italian wine are consumption substitutes. The Italian wine industry decreases wine production following a drought. The equilibrium price will _____ and quantity traded will _____ for Californian wine.
 (a) increase; increase
 (b) decrease; increase
 (c) decrease; decrease
 (d) increase; decrease

_____ 15. Initially, the market for peas is in equilibrium. Suddenly, at the same price level, there is a surplus. This might have been caused by an increase in
 (a) quantity demanded.
 (b) quantity supplied.
 (c) demand.
 (d) supply.

_____ 16. Greaseboro's local coffeehouse, *The Daily Grind*, cut the price of coffee and doughnuts by 6 percent and boosted the number of servings sold. *The Daily Grind's* total revenue on coffee and doughnuts has risen by 3 percent. This information shows that
  (a) the demand curve for coffee and doughnuts at *The Daily Grind* is horizontal.
  (b) at present, prices are in the elastic section of the demand schedule.
  (c) coffee and doughnuts are a normal good.
  (d) the price elasticity of demand for coffee and doughnuts is –2.0.

_____ 17. The income elasticity of Good *A* is –0.7, and the cross-price elasticity between Good *A* and Good *B* is –0.7. Good *A* is a(n)
  (a) normal good and a substitute for Good *B*.
  (b) inferior good and a substitute for Good *B*.
  (c) normal good and a complement for Good *B*.
  (d) inferior good and a complement for Good *B*.

_____ 18. Costs of production decrease for Debi's Dip. At the same time a government health report alleges that dip consumption causes bone cancer. For Debi's Dip, the equilibrium price will _____ and the equilibrium quantity will _____ .
  (a) increase; be indeterminate
  (b) decrease; be indeterminate
  (c) be indeterminate; increase
  (d) be indeterminate; decrease

_____ 19. The Board of Aldermen of Polka, West Virginia, implement rent control—a ceiling on the maximum rent that can be charged for an apartment. As a result we would expect to see
  (a) an increase in the number of apartments supplied in order to meet the increased demand.
  (b) higher prices for single-family homes, which will become more popular.
  (c) renters renting more expensive or poorer quality apartments outside Polka.
  (d) renters now able to find an adequate number of low-rent apartments.

_____ 20. An oil spill reduces lobster fishing off the Maine coast and a recession simultaneously reduces consumers' incomes. Compared to the equilibrium price and quantity in the market for lobsters (a normal good) before these events, in the new equilibrium, the
  (a) price will be lower and the quantity will be lower.
  (b) price will be higher and the quantity will be lower.
  (c) price will be lower; the effect of the events on quantity cannot be determined without further information.
  (d) effect of the events on price cannot be determined without further information; the quantity will be lower.

_____ 21. The law of demand is best illustrated by
  (a) the fact that as the price of Pepsi rises consumers buy more Coke.
  (b) increased purchases of Coke as the price of Coke decreases.
  (c) an increase in income that results in reduced purchases of store-brand soft drinks.
  (d) an increase in income that results in increased purchases of Coke.

_____ 22. Sam's demand curve for kiwi fruit is given by the equation $Q_d = 50 - 2P$. Suddenly her demand changes to $Q_d = 100 - 2P$. Assuming that the market price is unchanged, this

implies that her price elasticity of demand for kiwi fruit will become _____ elastic and her consumer surplus will _____ .
    (a)   more, increase
    (b)   more, decrease
    (c)   less, increase
    (d)   less, decrease

_____ 23.   Each of the following will cause an increase in the demand for tennis racquets (a normal good) EXCEPT
    (a)   a decrease in the price of tennis racquets.
    (b)   an increase in income.
    (c)   a decrease in the price of tennis balls.
    (d)   an increase in the number of persons playing tennis.

_____ 24.   In the lettuce industry, an increase in the wage of lettuce harvesters will
    (a)   increase the supply of lettuce, as workers will work harder than before.
    (b)   increase the supply of lettuce, as more workers will be employed.
    (c)   decrease the supply of lettuce, as workers will not need to work as hard as before.
    (d)   decrease the supply of lettuce, as fewer workers will be employed.

_____ 25.   The demand for Good A has been decreasing over the past year. Having examined the following facts, you conclude that Good A is a normal good. Which fact led you to that conclusion?
    (a)   The price of Good A has been decreasing over the past year.
    (b)   An economic slowdown has reduced the income of the traditional buyers of Good A.
    (c)   Good B, a substitute for Good A, has increased its price over the last twelve months.
    (d)   Household wealth has decreased among the traditional buyers of Good A.

Use the following diagram to answer the next five questions. The diagram refers to the market for Vito's Vitamins (a good with a positive income elasticity of demand). Vito's Vitamins has a positive cross-price elasticity of demand with Vinnie's Vitamins. On demand curve D_1, at a price of $5.00, price elasticity of demand is −2.0.

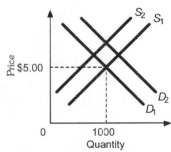

_____ 26.   Given demand curve D_1, if supply moves from S_1 to S_2,
    (a)   supply has increased.
    (b)   demand has decreased.
    (c)   price has decreased.
    (d)   quantity demanded has decreased.

_____ 27.   Given demand curve D_1, if supply moves from S_1 to S_2, we would expect Vito's total revenue to
(a)   increase because demand is elastic.
(b)   increase because demand is inelastic.
(c)   decrease because demand is elastic.
(d)   decrease because demand is inelastic.

_____ 28.   A change in supply from S_1 to S_2 might have been caused by an
(a)   increase in the price of Vinnie's Vitamins.
(b)   increase in the demand for Vito's Vitamins.
(c)   improvement in the technology of manufacturing Vito's Vitamins.
(d)   increase in the production costs of Vito's Vitamins.

_____ 29.   A change in demand from D_2 to D_1 might have been caused by
(a)   an increase in the price of Vito's Vitamins.
(b)   an increase in the consumption of Vito's Vitamins.
(c)   a decrease in the price of Vinnie's Vitamins.
(d)   an increase in the income of Vito's customers.

_____ 30.   Demand moves from D_1 to D_2 whereas supply moves from S_1 to S_2. At the initial price level of $5.00 a _____ exists. Price will _____ .
(a)   shortage; increase
(b)   shortage; decrease
(c)   surplus; increase
(d)   surplus; decrease

Use the following diagram to answer the next two questions. The world price for gasoline is $4.00 per gallon. The equilibrium price for domestically produced gasoline in the U.S. market is $5.00 per gallon. Quantity is millions of gallons.

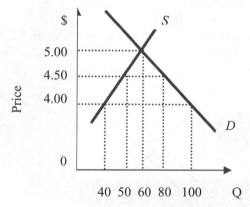

_____ 31.   Assume that the United States imports gasoline. The government imposes an import tax that raises the domestic price of gasoline to $4.50 per gallon. Based on the diagram, we can infer that
(a)   demand is elastic between $4.00 and $4.50.
(b)   demand is inelastic between $4.00 and $4.50.
(c)   the market is now in equilibrium.
(d)   demand is unitarily elastic between $4.00 and $4.50.

_____ 32.   Assume that the United States imports gasoline. The government imposes a tax that raises the domestic price of gas from $4.50 per gallon to $5.00 per gallon. Based on the diagram, which of the following is true?
  (a)   Supply is price-elastic between $4.50 and $5.00.
  (b)   Government tax revenues will be 50¢ times 50 million.
  (c)   Demand is price-elastic between $4.50 and $5.00.
  (d)   Equilibrium price is now $4.50.

_____ 33.   In a free market, the government feels that health care costs are too high. Accordingly, the government sets a maximum price per unit of health care that is below the equilibrium price. *Ceteris paribus,*
  (a)   the quantity of health care services received will increase.
  (b)   the quantity of health care services received will decrease.
  (c)   total spending on health care will increase if the demand curve is elastic.
  (d)   the health of the population will improve if the demand curve is elastic.

II. APPLICATION QUESTIONS

The market for fish oil has supply and demand curves given by $Q_s = -4 + P$ and $Q_d = 28 - P$, respectively. Units are millions of barrels of fish oil per day.

1.   Complete the following table.

Price (P)	Quantity Demanded (Qd)	Quantity Supplied (Qs)
$20	_____	_____
$18	_____	_____
$16	_____	_____
$14	_____	_____
$12	_____	_____
$10	_____	_____
$8	_____	_____
$6	_____	_____

2.   Determine the equilibrium price and quantity traded.

3.   If the government imposes a price ceiling of $12 in this market, what will happen to the positions of the demand and supply curves?

4.   If the government imposes a price ceiling of $12 in this market, what effect will this have on the market?

5.   Considering the demand curve in isolation, calculate the total revenue when price is $8 _____ and when price is $10 _____ .

6.   Use your knowledge of the relationship between price and total revenue to estimate the price elasticity of demand between $8 and $10.

7.   Considering the demand curve in isolation, calculate the total revenue when price is $16 _____ and when price is $18 _____ .

8.   Use your knowledge of the relationship between price and total revenue to estimate the price elasticity of demand between $16 and $18.

9.   Use the midpoint formula to calculate the price elasticity of demand between $8 and $10 _____ and between $16 and $18 _____ .

10.   If the world price of fish oil is $10 per barrel, how many barrels will the United States import each day?

11.   If the United States imposed a $4 per barrel tax on imported fish oil, how many barrels will the United States import each day?

12.   If the United States imposed a $4 per barrel tax on imported fish oil, calculate the tax revenue that would be generated.

Review Test SOLUTIONS

I. SOLUTIONS TO MULTIPLE-CHOICE QUESTIONS

1. (d) If the economy is producing inside its frontier, there is an underuse of available resources.

2. (a) At full capacity, an increase in the production of one good requires a reallocation of resources and a reduction in the production of the second good.

3. (b) One way to look at this is to note that it now takes fewer resources to produce a given quantity of consumer goods—the amount of capital goods forgone is less than before. Recall that the slope of the production possibility frontier (which has changed) depicts opportunity cost.

4. (d) Refer to the answer to Question 1.

5. (a) The more heavily Arbez indulges in capital formation (rather than consumption), the more quickly will its resource base expand.

6. (d) This production possibility frontier is bowed outwards: it is an increasing-cost production possibility frontier. As more of a good is produced, the cost in terms of the other good forgone, will increase.

7. (d) Currently the economy is producing 10 capital goods and 24 consumer goods. To increase capital goods production by 10, the economy would have to be at Point X, where 20 consumer goods are produced—a loss of 4 consumer goods.

8. (c) Currently the economy is producing 10 capital goods and 6 consumer goods. To increase capital goods production by 20, the economy would have to be on the vertical axis, where no consumer goods are produced—a loss of 6 consumer goods.

9. (d) If the price of Pepsi decreases, the quantity demanded of Pepsi will increase and the demand for the substitute good will decrease.

10. (b) For Jack, the opportunity cost of a unit of vinegar is 1.25 units of brown paper. For Jill, the opportunity cost of a unit of vinegar is 2 units of brown paper. Jack has the comparative advantage in vinegar. For Jack, the opportunity cost of a unit of brown paper is 0.8 of a unit of vinegar. For Jill, the opportunity cost of a unit of brown paper is 0.5 of a unit of vinegar. Jill has the comparative advantage in brown paper.

11. (c) Draw this if you got it wrong! Begin with a supply curve. At any given output the price will be higher than before. The entire price/quantity relationship has shifted.

12. (c) Equilibrium occurs only at the price level at which all active buyers and sellers can have their needs satisfied.

13. (a) To restore equilibrium, price must increase. As price increases, quantity demanded decreases (movement along the demand curve) and quantity supplied increases (movement along the supply curve).

14.   (a)   The decrease in the supply of Italian wine will force up its price. Quantity demanded will fall. The demand for the substitute will increase.

15.   (d)   Draw the diagram if you missed this one! Remember the distinction between a change in supply (the supply curve shifts) and a change in quantity supplied (there is a movement along a given supply curve).

16.   (b)   Price has decreased and total revenue has risen. This is enough to confirm that demand is elastic.

17.   (d)   A negative income elasticity indicates an inferior good. A negative cross-price elasticity occurs when the two goods are complements.

18.   (b)   The decrease in production costs will increase profitability and increase supply. The report will reduce demand. Each factor decreases price but, whereas the increase in supply increases output, the decrease in demand will reduce output. The net effect on output is uncertain.

19.   (c)   The rent control is a price ceiling. Assuming that it is set below the equilibrium price, a shortage of rent-controlled housing will occur, forcing renters to take apartments that are not subject to rent control.

20.   (d)   The oil spill will decrease supply (it is now more costly to catch lobsters). The recession will reduce demand for a normal good. Each factor decreases output but, whereas the decrease in supply increases price, the decrease in demand will decrease price. The net effect on price is uncertain.

21.   (b)   Each of the other answers will shift the demand curve for Coke. Recall that the law of demand is depicted as a movement along a given demand curve.

22.   (c)   Demand has increased. At any given price level, demand becomes less elastic as the curve shifts to the right. Given the price level, the consumer surplus (the area between the price and the demand curve) increases.

23.   (a)   A decrease in the price of tennis racquets will cause a movement along the demand curve.

24.   (d)   Higher costs reduce profitability and reduce supply.

25.   (b)   If a good is a normal good, a decrease in income will reduce demand.

26.   (d)   As supply decreases, price rises and there is a movement along the demand curve.

27.   (c)   Price elasticity of demand is –2.0 (elastic). A good with an elastic demand will see total revenue fall as price increases.

28.   (d)   If production costs increase, profitability will decrease, prompting a decrease in supply.

29.   (c)   Vinnie's Vitamins is a substitute (positive cross-price elasticity). Vito's decrease in demand could have been prompted by a decrease in Vinnie's price.

30.   (a)   Quantity demanded exceeds quantity supplied. Price will increase in this seller's market.

31. (a) Apply the total revenue test. As price rises from $4.00 to $4.50, total revenue would fall from $400 million to $360 million.

32. (c) As price increases from $4.50 to $5.00, total spending would decrease from $360 million to $300 million. Demand is elastic if, when price rises, total spending falls. Tax revenues would be $30 million (50¢ times 60 million).

33. (b) A price ceiling is in effect and a shortage of health care has been created. Assuming an upward sloping supply curve, fewer health care services will be offered.

II. SOLUTIONS TO APPLICATION QUESTIONS

1. Refer to the following table.

Price (P)	Quantity Demanded (Qd)	Quantity Supplied (Qs)
$20	8	16
$18	10	14
$16	12	12
$14	14	10
$12	16	8
$10	18	6
$8	20	4
$6	22	2

2. Equilibrium price is $16 and equilibrium quantity is 12. You can derive this by inspecting the demand and supply schedules, careful graphing, or algebra. In equilibrium, $Q_d = Q_s$, therefore, $28 - P = -4 + P$. Given that, $32 = 2P$ and $P = 16$. If $P = 16$, then $Q = 28 - 1(16) = 12$.

3. The curves will not change position. A change in price leads to movements along the given demand and supply curves. If you missed this, return to Chapter 3 and review the distinction between a "change in demand" and a "change in quantity demanded."

4. Quantity demanded will increase to 16, and quantity supplied will shrink to 8. There will be a shortage. Black markets may occur. Queuing is likely.

5. When the price is $8, quantity is 20 units. Total revenue is $160. When the price is $10, quantity is 18 units. Total revenue is $180.

6. As price increases from $8 to $10, total revenue increases from $160 to $180. Demand is inelastic.

7. When the price is $16, quantity is 12 units. Total revenue is $192. When the price is $18, quantity is 10 units. Total revenue is $180.

8. As price increases from $16 to $18, total revenue decreases from $192 to $180. Demand is elastic.

9.   The midpoint formula when price lies between $8 and $10 is:

$$\frac{(20-18)/[20+18)/2]}{(8-10)/[8+10)/2]}$$

The price elasticity of demand in this price range is –0.4737.
The midpoint formula when price lies between $16 and $18 is:

$$\frac{(12-10)/[(12+10)/2]}{(16-18)/[16+18)/2]}$$

The price elasticity of demand in this price range is –1.5455.

10.   If the price is $10, U.S. suppliers will offer 6 (million) barrels, but buyers will demand 18 (million) barrels. 12 (million) barrels will be imported.

11.   If the price is $14, U.S. suppliers will offer 10 (million) barrels, but buyers will demand 14 (million) barrels. 4 (million) barrels will be imported.

12. $16 million—4 (million) barrels will be imported, yielding $4 each.

6

Household Behavior and Consumer Choice

Chapter Objectives

1. Draw and explain the meaning of a budget constraint diagram, given price and income data. Indicate the constraints on a household's consumption choices and relate these to the concept of the opportunity set.
2. Distinguish between total utility and marginal utility. State the law of diminishing marginal utility.
3. State the utility-maximizing rule both in words and mathematically, and analyze how the consumer would respond to disequilibrium situations.
4. Relate the utility-maximizing rule to the diamond/water paradox.
5. Explain why the concept of utility is useful in demand analysis.
6. Distinguish between the income effect and the substitution effect and explain their role in the theory of household behavior.
7. Analyze the shape of the labor-supply curve using the income and substitution effects.
8. Explain why indifference curves are negatively sloped and cannot intersect.
9. Derive a demand curve using indifference curve analysis.

BRAIN TEASER: Your brain teaser in this chapter is to explain a classic economics puzzle—the diamond/water paradox. Why is it that diamonds, which, for most of us, have little practical use, are valued much more highly than water, which is essential for life? The solution is offered in the textbook—see if you can puzzle it out before the textbook covers it on page 129.

Objective 1

Draw and explain the meaning of a budget constraint diagram, given price and income data. Indicate the constraints on a household's consumption choices and relate these to the concept of the opportunity set.

Each household operates within constraints (income, wealth, and the prices of goods "real income") and, therefore, must make three choices:

(a) Which combination of goods to buy
(b) How many hours of work to provide
(c) How much money to save rather than to spend

The analysis of household choice assumes that there is perfect competition in all (input and output) markets, that price is governed by demand and supply, and that households are "informed"—that they have perfect knowledge about the price, availability, and quality of goods; about wage rates; and (later) about interest rates. (page 121)

Each semester, you must weigh your own situation. How much money will the semester cost? What is essential (tuition, housing, food, textbooks, aspirin, coffee, leisure) and what is, perhaps, optional (movies, phone calls home)? How much do these items cost? How much spending power have you set aside from your summer job (wealth)? What income will you have during the semester, perhaps from a part-time job? In simplified form, the *budget constraint diagram* illustrates the limited set of opportunities available to you.

The *budget constraint* defines the maximum amount of goods possible that can be bought and is determined by the household's income, wealth, and prices. In a two-good situation, this constraint looks rather like a production possibility frontier—think of it as a "consumption" possibility frontier, if you will. The real cost of buying more of one good is the value of the other good that must be forgone. Points on and inside the constraint are combinations of goods that can be bought; they comprise the *opportunity (choice) set*. Points outside cannot be bought. The budget constraint will shift to the right if income or wealth increases, or if prices fall there is an increase in possible consumption levels. The slope is determined by the relative prices of the two goods. If the price of one good falls, the budget constraint *swivels* and the slope of the constraint changes. Given the constraints, decisions depend on the preferences of the household.

Formally, the budget constraint for two goods (*X* and *Y*) can be written as:

$$P_X X + P_Y Y = I$$

where P_X is the price of Good *X*, P_Y is the price of Good *Y*, and *I* is household income.

LEARNING TIP: Don't skip over the introductory material on pp. 117-119. This easily-missed little section sets the scene and establishes the assumptions (perfect knowledge, perfect competition, homogeneous products) for the analysis contained in Chapters 6-12. Figure II.1 will be referenced throughout. ◀

LEARNING TIP: The extended "Ann and Tom" example in the textbook is particularly effective in making the points you need to know. Be sure to cover it thoroughly. ◀

Practice

1.   The budget constraint is the limit imposed on household choices by the household's
      (a)   expectations about future income, wealth, and prices.
      (b)   budget.
      (c)   income, wealth, and prices.
      (d)   preferences and monthly spending plan.

      ANSWER: (c) Refer to page 122. The basic analysis provided to this point has not yet incorporated expectations about future income, wealth, or prices.

2.   Gretchen's opportunity set can be increased by
      (a)   a decrease in prices.
      (b)   a decrease in income.
      (c)   an increase in quantity demanded.
      (d)   a decrease in quantity demanded.

      ANSWER: (a) The opportunity set defines what is available—rather than what is demanded. A price decrease permits Gretchen to stretch her dollars further.

3.   Jenny the Junior buys only two goods: meals and movies. This semester she has $500 in a savings account that she plans to spend, but no income. Meals cost $5 each and movies cost $10 each. Jenny's maximum spending on meals is _____ and her maximum spending on movies is _____.

      (a) $500; $0
      (b) $0; $500
      (c) $250; $250
      (d) $500; $500

ANSWER: (d) At one extreme, Jenny could spend all of her resources on meals or, at the other, all of her resources on movies.

4. Jenny the Junior buys only two goods: meals and movies. This semester she has $500 in a savings account that she plans to spend, but no income. Meals cost $5 each and movies cost $10 each. Jenny can buy a maximum of _____ meals and a maximum of _____ movies.
   (a) 100; 0
   (b) 100; 100
   (c) 0; 50
   (d) 100; 50

   ANSWER: (d) With $500 and facing a meal price of $5, Jenny could buy as many as 100 meals. With $500 and facing a movie price of $10, Jenny could buy as many as 50 movies.

5. Draw Jenny's budget constraint in the space below. Place "meals" on the horizontal axis and "movies" on the vertical axis. Write in the maximum value for meals and for movies at the appropriate places.

   ANSWER: The budget constraint should be a downward-sloping straight line. The "meals" and "movies" endpoints should be 100 and 50, respectively.

6. The slope of Jenny's budget constraint is
   (a) −2.
   (b) −1/2.
   (c) 1/2.
   (d) 2.

   ANSWER: (b) "Rise over run" is the formula for the slope of a straight line. If you are uncertain about this, review the textbook's Appendix to Chapter 1 now.

7. Refer to your diagram. Along the budget constraint, the opportunity cost of one movie is
   (a) zero, as the goods have already been bought.
   (b) 1/2 a meal.
   (c) 1 meal.
   (d) 2 meals.

   ANSWER: (d) The $10 could have bought two meals.

8. Refer to your diagram. If _____ , Jenny's new budget constraint will _____ .
   (a) the price of movies increases; shift out and be parallel to the initial budget constraint
   (b) her income increases; swivel inwards
   (c) her income decreases; swivel inwards
   (d) the price of movies decreases; swivel outwards

   ANSWER: (d) Income (or wealth) changes cause a parallel shift in the budget constraint. A lower price of movies increases the maximum number of movies it is possible for

Jenny to attend, but leaves unaffected the maximum number of meals she may consume.

9.   Your real income may increase in each of the following cases EXCEPT if your income _____ , and prices _____ .
(a)   increases; increase
(b)   increases; decrease
(c)   decreases; increase
(d)   decreases; decrease
ANSWER: (c)   Only if income decreases and prices increase is there certain to be a decrease in your real spending power. For instance, if your income rose and prices rose (but by less), then your real income would have risen. ■

Objective 2

Distinguish between total utility and marginal utility. State the law of diminishing marginal utility.

Utility (satisfaction) is derived from goods and services, including leisure. The *marginal utility* you derive from a good (potato chips, for example) is the additional satisfaction you get from each additional portion. The *total utility* is the sum of these additional contributions to your level of satisfaction. The *law of diminishing marginal utility* states that extra units of a good yield less and less extra satisfaction. Although the first few potato chips may provide quite significant increases in utility, subsequent chips are likely to provide progressively less additional utility (as your hunger decreases and your guilt increases). (page 126)

ECONOMICS IN PRACTICE (SUPPLEMENTAL): Use your knowledge of diminishing marginal utility to analyze the frequently reported phenomenon that lottery winners do not seem to be much happier after winning than they were before winning.
ANSWER: We tend to be surprised when we hear that although the winner's income level has risen, his satisfaction has not. Apparently money doesn't buy happiness. This is only true in part, though. An extra $1,000 received by someone in poverty can make a significant difference; an extra $1,000,000 for a lottery winner is unlikely to contribute much. In the latter case, the marginal utility of the extra dollars is insignificant.

Practice

10.   The law of diminishing marginal utility indicates that, after some point, marginal utility
(a)   decreases at a constant rate.
(b)   decreases at an increasing rate.
(c)   decreases at a decreasing rate.
(d)   decreases.
ANSWER: (d)   The rate at which marginal utility diminishes will vary from person to person and from good to good. All we can claim is that marginal utility will decrease after some point.

11.   Mario plays video games. Although he is experiencing diminishing marginal utility, his marginal utility remains positive. We can say that Mario's total utility is
(a)   increasing at an increasing rate.
(b)   increasing at a decreasing rate.
(c)   decreasing at an increasing rate.
(d)   decreasing at a decreasing rate.

ANSWER: (b) Because Mario's marginal utility is positive, each new game increases his total satisfaction, but at a decreasing rate of increase.

12.   Candy has eaten 10 Hershey's Kisses and admits that each additional Kiss has been less enjoyable than the previous one. We can deduce that, for Candy, the
(a)   marginal utility of Kisses is positive but decreasing.
(b)   marginal utility of Kisses is negative.
(c)   total utility of Kisses is diminishing.
(d)   total utility of Kisses has peaked.

ANSWER: (a) This is an example of the law of diminishing marginal utility. Because Candy is still eating Kisses, she must still be deriving some (positive) marginal utility from them. So the total utility is increasing, but at a decreasing rate.

Use the following table to answer the next three questions. Susan visits the state fair and rides the Ferris wheel several times.

Number of Rides	Total Utility	Marginal Utility
1	10	_____
2	24	_____
3	34	_____
4	_____	7
5	46	_____

13.   The marginal utility of the first ride on the Ferris wheel is
(a)   5.
(b)   10.
(c)   12.
(d)   14.

ANSWER: (b) The total utility derived from no rides must be zero. One ride added 10 units of utility.

14.   The total utility of the fourth ride is
(a)   6.
(b)   7.
(c)   12.
(d)   41.

ANSWER: (d) The total utility derived from three rides is 34. The fourth ride added an additional 7 units of utility for a total utility of 41.

15.   Diminishing marginal utility sets in after the _____ ride.
(a)   first
(b)   second
(c)   third
(d)   fourth

ANSWER: (b) The first ride adds 10 units of utility; the second, 14; the third, 10, so diminishing marginal utility sets in after the second ride. ■

Objective 3

State the utility-maximizing rule both in words and mathematically, and analyze how the consumer would respond to disequilibrium situations.

Assuming that households try to maximize their utility, they should select those goods that give the largest marginal utility per dollar. Utility will be maximized when the per-dollar marginal utility of the last unit of each good bought is equal. Formally it is stated:

$$MU_X/P_X = MU_Y/P_Y$$

All this means is that, to get the most satisfaction from one's money, the "extra benefit per dollar" must be equalized for all goods purchased.

An *imbalance* in the utility-maximizing condition, for example,

$$MU_X/P_X > MU_Y/P_Y$$

means that you could shuffle your income around—buying more of the good giving the greater marginal utility per dollar (X) and less of the other (Y)—and get a better deal. Buying more of X reduces its marginal utility and buying less of Y increases its marginal utility. So the imbalance is removed. (page 129)

LEARNING TIP: The idea of maximizing utility—despite the graphs and algebra—is fairly intuitive. If you want to get the most satisfaction for your dollar ("bang for your buck"), you should choose the good that gives you the most extra satisfaction per dollar (*MU/P*). Remember, in economics choices are made at the margin. (If you've forgotten this important point, review Chapter 1.) In the final analysis, with perfectly divisible goods, this becomes the utility-maximizing rule:

$$MU_X/P_X = MU_Y/P_Y$$

where the marginal utilities per dollar are balanced. ◀

Practice

16. Arthur Dent is buying shirts and shoes such that the marginal utility of shirts is 12 and the marginal utility of shoes is 3. Shirts and shoes are priced at $8 and $2 respectively. It can be concluded that Arthur is
     (a)   spending too much on shirts and not enough on shoes.
     (b)   spending too much on shoes and not enough on shirts.
     (c)   spending his income on shirts and shoes in such a way as to maximize his satisfaction.
     (d)   failing to maximize his satisfaction.

     ANSWER: (c) Arthur is complying with the utility-maximizing rule. The marginal utility per dollar of shirts (12/8) equals the marginal utility per dollar of shoes (3/2).

17. My $MU_{coffee}/P_{coffee} > MU_{tea}/P_{tea}$. This implies that
     (a)   switching some funds from coffee to tea will increase my utility.
     (b)   switching some funds from tea to coffee will increase my utility.
     (c)   coffee is more expensive than tea.
     (d)   tea is more expensive than coffee.

     ANSWER: (b) The per-dollar satisfaction from an extra cup of coffee is greater than the per-dollar satisfaction from an extra cup of tea. I should spend less on tea and use the saved dollars to buy more coffee.

18. $MU_{Snickers}/MU_{Mars\ Bar} > P_{Snickers}/P_{Mars\ Bar}$. Given my income, to increase my utility, I should spend
   (a)   more on Snickers and more on Mars Bars.
   (b)   more on Snickers and less on Mars Bars.
   (c)   less on Snickers and more on Mars Bars.
   (d)   less on Snickers and less on Mars Bars.

   ANSWER: (b) Given my income, I cannot buy more of both goods. Because the marginal utility
   per dollar of Snickers is relatively high, I should spend less on Mars Bars and use
   the saved dollars to buy more Snickers. ∎

Objective 4

Relate the utility-maximizing rule to the diamond/water paradox.

One of the most important ideas in economics is introduced on page 129. It is the notion that the true cost
of an item is the value of the other things that you give up when you buy it. Underlying consumer choice
is opportunity cost. This insight gives us the key to the diamond/water paradox. Water is abundant while
diamonds are not. The marginal value of water is low but the consumer surplus it bestows is substantial;
while the marginal value of diamonds is high but, in some sense, diamonds have little practical value.
(page 129)

Practice

19.   The diamond-water paradox is resolved by recognizing that the price of a product tends to reflect
   its
   (a)   use value.
   (b)   total value.
   (c)   consumer surplus.
   (d)   marginal value.

   ANSWER: (d) Refer to page 129 for more on this issue.

20.   Diamonds are more expensive than water because the price of each product tends to reflect its
   (a)   total value.
   (b)   consumer surplus.
   (c)   marginal value.
   (d)   revealed preference.

   ANSWER: (c) The consumer assesses whether or not to buy by comparing the price with the
   marginal utility. If the marginal utility is low, the price will need to be low to
   encourage purchase. ∎

Objective 5

Explain why the concept of utility is useful in demand analysis.

Utility analysis explains the downward slope of the demand curve. Because marginal satisfaction falls
with each additional unit bought, price must fall to "encourage" additional purchases of a good.
(page 129)
   It is quite easy to see this "diminishing marginal utility" explanation in operation when one finds
examples of "Buy the first, and get the second for half price."

Practice

21. Angela will buy additional units of a good (apples) if the value of the good's
    (a) total utility exceeds the price.
    (b) total utility is less than the price.
    (c) marginal utility exceeds the price.
    (d) marginal utility is less than the price.

    ANSWER: (c) If Angela's extra benefit is greater than the cost of the apple, then the purchase will be worthwhile.

22. Consider Good X. The law of diminishing marginal utility indicates that
    (a) the individual's quantity demanded for Good X will increase as the price of Good X decreases.
    (b) the individual's budget constraint is downward sloping.
    (c) total utility decreases as an individual consumes more of a product.
    (d) Good X is an inferior good.

    ANSWER: (a) Option (b) is true, but not related to the law of diminishing marginal utility. ∎

Objective 6

Distinguish between the income effect and the substitution effect and explain their role in the theory of household behavior.

The income effect and the substitution effect provide a second explanation for the downward slope of the demand curve. Most goods are *normal goods*. As the price of a normal good (lowfat milk, for instance) rises, you become poorer because your food dollar can't stretch as far as it did before (*income effect*), and you seek substitutes such as regular milk (*substitution effect*). Both effects result in a decrease in the quantity demanded of lowfat milk as its price increases.

Although the demand curve for *inferior goods* (Spam, perhaps), still slopes down, the income effect is reversed. As before, a rise in price of the good (Spam) makes you seek substitutes, such as other meats (substitution effect). But you're poorer because of the higher price—your food dollar can't stretch as far. In the case of an inferior good, however, the income effect results in more of the good being bought. Because you're poorer after a price rise, you may no longer be able to afford that steak you were going to buy—Spam is the best you can manage. In general, the substitution effect (price higher—buy less) is stronger than the income effect (price higher—buy more), so on balance quantity demanded falls when price rises. (page 130)

ECONOMICS IN PRACTICE: On page 133, the textbook examines the false basis for a grocery store's advertisement. Harry's Food claims that its customer's food choices cost more when bought at its competitor's store. First, why is this a false comparison, and more pointedly, why is it very likely to favor Harry's Food?
ANSWER: Harry's Food required that its customer replicate the basket of goods that she had selected. Consider two colas—Cola A and Cola B—between which Ms. Smith is indifferent. She may have selected Cola A over Cola B because Cola A was relatively lower in price at Harry's Food. But Cola B might be the better buy in the rival store. Her choice wasn't based on utility but on price. By restricting Ms. Smith's ability to shop for low-priced substitutes, the basis for comparison is undermined.

Practice

23. The substitution effect occurs when
    (a) a decrease in the price of Good *A* makes the good relatively cheaper and encourages consumers to buy more.
    (b) a decrease in the price of Good *A* encourages consumers to buy more of substitute Good *B*.
    (c) a decrease in the price of Good *A* makes consumers better off so that they can buy more of the good.
    (d) an increase in the price of Good *A* encourages consumers to buy less of substitute Good *B*.

    ANSWER: (a) The substitution effect refers to the behavior of consumers of Good *A* when the price of that Good *A* itself changes.

24. The income effect helps to explain why
    (a) the demand curve for a normal good shifts to the right when income increases.
    (b) the quantity demanded of a good increases when the price of that good decreases.
    (c) the demand curve of an inferior good shifts to the left when income decreases.
    (d) normal goods have higher prices than inferior goods do.

    ANSWER: (b) The income effect provides part of the explanation for the slope of the demand curve as the price of the good changes.

25. The substitution effect helps to explain why _____ when the price of Good *A* rises.
    (a) sellers switch production and increase quantity supplied of Good *A*
    (b) the demand curve for Good *A* is sloped as it is
    (c) demand for another Good *B*, rises
    (d) price elasticity increases along the curve

    ANSWER: (b) Together, the income effect and the substitution effect offer an alternative explanation of the negative relationship between price and quantity demanded.

26. The price of Froot Loops cereal falls. Consumers switch over from other cereals to Froot Loops because its price is relatively lower. This is the _____ effect in operation.
    (a) income
    (b) substitution
    (c) *ceteris paribus*
    (d) quantity demanded

    ANSWER: (b) The lower price is causing buyers to substitute Froot Loops for other cereals.

27. The price of Froot Loops cereal falls. Wanda finds that she has some extra money left over after buying her usual quantity of Froot Loops. She spends some of that money on more Froot Loops. This is the
    (a) income effect in operation.
    (b) substitution effect in operation.
    (c) normal effect in operation.
    (d) inferior effect in operation.

    ANSWER: (a) The reduced price has increased Wanda's spending power—her income, in this sense, has increased. We can see that this good is a normal good for Wanda because she buys more. ∎

Objective 7

Analyze the shape of the labor-supply curve using the income and substitution effects.

A household chooses how much labor to supply (and how much leisure and unpaid work time to relinquish). The opportunity cost of paid work is the value of leisure and unpaid work time given up. Think of the wage rate as the "price" of unpaid work or leisure. If the wage rate rises, the substitution effect encourages supplying additional labor (the opportunity cost of leisure is now higher), but the income effect discourages additional work (higher income makes the worker want to increase consumption of normal goods, including leisure). When the income effect overwhelms the substitution effect, the labor-supply curve bends backwards. (page 132)

> **LEARNING TIP:** Throughout the textbook, Case, Fair, and Oster stress the links between the input and output markets. For you to make sense of the remainder of the book, you must develop a good understanding of the material on household behavior in the labor market.
>
> There is an interesting example of a strong income effect in operation in the Algerian labor market. To attract workers, U.S. companies in Algeria paid wages that were about four times the local norm. To their dismay they found that, after a short time on the payroll, workers would not show up for work. The workers, who had earned a year's worth of income in a few months, simply chose to take the leisure time to enjoy their prosperity!
>
> A good way to understand the section on labor supply is to turn the concept around and consider the amount of leisure demanded. As the "price" of leisure (the wage rate) increases, the quantity demanded of leisure will decrease (substitution effect). If higher wage rates increase income and if leisure is a normal good, the quantity demanded of leisure will increase (income effect). So two conflicting forces are in operation.◀

ECONOMICS IN PRACTICE: On page 136, the textbook examines how an unpaid internship becomes more attractive during periods of unemployment. This can be understood in terms of opportunity cost. When jobs are plentiful, the opportunity cost of an unpaid internship is high and few new labor market entrants will be tempted. But how might a job applicant respond if, when jobs are readily available, the salary range is quite narrow for most jobs? Denmark has been identified as the "happiest country in the world," despite bad weather and incredibly high taxes. Can you use the income and substitution effects to analyze why the Danes seem so contented? (Hint: income tax rates in Denmark are extraordinarily high, but the government has an extensive "cradle to grave" welfare state. As a consequence, in practical terms, income levels are similar across most occupations.)

ANSWER: With a very strong welfare state (offering, for example, free health care and education, child care and elder care), the Danes don't need much income to sustain a reasonable standard of living. Also, because additional earnings are taxed highly—average taxes are about 50 percent of income—there is little incentive to substitute labor for leisure in order to achieve a higher standard of living. The average Dane works 37 hours a week at a job he likes (rather than a job that pays well) and has six weeks of paid vacation. Clearly, the substitution effect of increased wages plays a relatively weak role in Danish decision making.

ECONOMICS IN PRACTICE (CONTINUED): Extending the "internship" example, can you see how returning to college for additional classes becomes more attractive during an economic slowdown than when employers are keen to hire?

ANSWER: The opportunity cost of attending college is high if you must give up a job in order to take classes. The opportunity cost is much lower if lucrative job offers are not presently available. Typically, college enrollment spikes when the job market falters.

ECONOMICS IN PRACTICE (CONTINUED): Many workers lost their jobs for an extended period of time during the "Great Recession" of 2009–2010. As a consequence, Congress extended the period during which laid-off workers could receive unemployment benefits, in some cases up to 99 weeks. Do you think that the extended unemployment benefits discouraged workers from accepting jobs when they became available?

ANSWER: Certainly, there would be some substitution effect—a worker with no job is more likely to accept any employment than one who is receiving some income. There is evidence on both sides of this debate, with the conservative Heritage Foundation concluding that, for every thirteen-week extension of benefits, workers might remain unemployed for two additional weeks, whereas Nobel prize winner Paul Krugman asserted that the substitution effect is minimal.

Practice

28. In Crantown, an increase in the wage of deckhands results in an increase in the number of deckhands making themselves available for work. This indicates that the
    (a) income effect is stronger than the substitution effect.
    (b) substitution effect is stronger than the income effect.
    (c) income effect is positive.
    (d) substitution effect is negative.

    ANSWER: (b) The supply of deckhands is upward sloping. This indicates that, although deckhands may wish to work less and enjoy leisure at higher wage rates (income effect), the substitution effect predominates.

29. Assume that leisure is a normal good. The income effect of an increase in the wage rate will cause a(n) _____ in the demand for leisure and a _____ quantity of labor supplied.
    (a) increase; greater
    (b) increase; lesser
    (c) decrease; greater
    (d) decrease; lesser

    ANSWER: (b) Higher wages will encourage workers to take more leisure time, reducing the quantity of labor supplied.

30. The interest rate increases. The substitution effect will cause a(n) _____ in saving and the income effect will cause a(n) _____ in saving.
    (a) increase; increase
    (b) increase; decrease
    (c) decrease; increase
    (d) decrease; decrease

    ANSWER: (b) A higher interest rate increases the opportunity cost of current consumption but reduces the need to save to achieve a given future level of savings.

Use the following diagram, which depicts Kevin's supply of labor mowing lawns during the summer, to answer the following question.

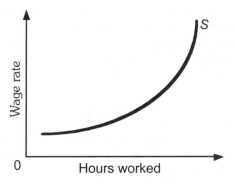

31.   Along Kevin's labor supply curve, the
        (a)   income effect dominates the substitution effect as the wage rate increases.
        (b)   substitution effect dominates the income effect as the wage rate increases.
        (c)   substitution effect of a wage increase is zero.
        (d)   income effect of a wage increase is zero.

        ANSWER: (b) When the labor supply curve has its typical positive slope, the attractiveness of substituting labor for leisure outweighs the ability to take time off and enjoy the extra income. ∎

Objective 8 (Appendix)

Explain why indifference curves are negatively sloped and cannot intersect.

Indifference curves plot bundles of goods giving equal satisfaction. If there is less of one good, the individual must be compensated by having more of the other good—a negative relationship. Indifference curves cannot intersect because this would imply that the same bundle of goods could give more than one level of satisfaction. (page 141)

Graphing Pointer: It's easier to draw an indifference curve tangential to a given budget constraint rather than to draw the indifference curve first.

    Be careful when there is a price change: a price increase swivels the budget constraint inwards, and a price decrease swivels it outwards. This may be counterintuitive. For extra practice on this topic, draw the diagram but have the budget constraint swivel from the horizontal rather than the vertical axis. Theoretically, the analysis is identical—visually, it becomes more challenging.

Practice

32.   An indifference curve plots all the combinations of Good *X* and Good *Y* that
        (a)   may be bought with a given income level and given prices for Good *X* and Good *Y*.
        (b)   give maximum satisfaction as income level changes.
        (c)   give the same marginal utility.
        (d)   give the same total utility.

        ANSWER: (d) A movement along an indifference curve shows that the individual is gaining more of one good but losing some of the other. The gain in satisfaction from the former exactly equals the loss in satisfaction from the latter.

33.   An indifference curve is downward sloping because
    (a)   more is preferred to less.
    (b)   preferences remain constant as income level increases.
    (c)   the marginal rate of substitution increases as one moves along the indifference curve.
    (d)   the marginal rate of substitution decreases as one moves along the indifference curve.

    ANSWER: (a) Because more is preferred to less, an increase in the quantity of Good X consumed must be balanced by a decrease in the quantity of Good Y consumed. Option C refers to the curvature of an indifference curve, not to its slope. ∎

Objective 9 (Appendix)

Derive a demand curve using indifference curve analysis.

The budget constraint diagram is combined with indifference curves to depict the utility-maximizing mix of purchases. Four assumptions are made, the main one being that the marginal rate of substitution is diminishing. An indifference curve maps all the combinations of goods that provide a particular level of utility. Indifference curves bend inwards because we assume that the rate of marginal substitution is diminishing. Higher (further right) indifference curves indicate higher levels of utility. (page 141)

The *marginal rate of substitution* (MRS) is a ratio, the rate at which an individual is willing to surrender units of one good for units of the other good. Put differently, it's the ratio of the marginal utility of one good to the marginal utility of the other. Formally this ratio is stated:

$$MRS = MU_X/MU_Y$$

In equilibrium, this ratio is equal to the price ratio, so that

$$MU_X/MU_Y = P_X/P_Y$$

for all pairs of goods.

The analysis makes two important points. First, utility is maximized where the budget constraint is tangent to the highest possible indifference curve—this is where the price ratio equals the marginal rate of substitution. Second, by decreasing the price of one good, the quantity demanded of it can be shown to rise—another explanation of the downward-sloping demand curve.

Practice

34.   My marginal rate of substitution between a round of golf and a game of tennis is 6. This implies that
    (a)   a round of golf is 6 times more valuable to me than a game of tennis.
    (b)   a game of tennis is 6 times more valuable to me than a round of golf.
    (c)   tennis is 6 times as expensive as golf.
    (d)   golf is 6 times as expensive as tennis.

    ANSWER: (a) The marginal rate of substitution represents the rate at which I am willing to substitute one good for another.

35.   In a two-good world, Jason is in equilibrium when
    (a) $MU_x / MU_y = P_x / P_y$.
    (b) $MU_x / MU_y = P_y (P_x)$.
    (c) $MU_x / MU_y = P_y / P_x$.
    (d) $MU_x / MU_y = - P_y / P_x$.

    ANSWER: (a) Refer to page 143. ∎

BRAIN TEASER SOLUTION: The textbook offers the solution to the diamond/water paradox on page 129. Briefly, how much we pay depends on the value we place on the final unit consumed. Because water is readily available, its marginal utility (and its price) is low. Because diamonds are in short supply, the marginal utility gained from receiving one (and the price) is high. If "you never miss the water till the well runs dry," the diamond/water paradox may be in the process of reversal for townships in desert areas of Arizona. Here, water is difficult to find. One (expensive) option is to truck it in; another is to drill wells as much as 2,000 feet deep to reach the aquifer. Citizens assume the duty of checking that community pumps are operating correctly. Clearly, the price of water consumption is high in such circumstances.

PRACTICE TEST

I. MULTIPLE-CHOICE QUESTIONS

Select the option that provides the single best answer.

_____ 1. Good A and Good B cost $3 and $4, respectively. Jo, spending all of her income, buys 4 units of Good A and 3 units of Good B. The final unit of each good gives her 12 units of utility.
(a) Jo is maximizing her utility.
(b) Jo should buy more of Good A and less of Good B to maximize utility.
(c) Jo should buy less of Good A and more of Good B to maximize utility.
(d) Jo should buy less of both goods to maximize utility.

_____ 2. P_X is $12 and P_Y is $6. These prices indicate that the individual can
(a) trade 12 units of Good X for 6 of Good Y.
(b) trade 1 unit of Good X for 2 of Good Y.
(c) increase his utility by buying more units of the cheaper Good Y.
(d) increase his utility by buying more of the more highly valued Good X.

_____ 3. A given budget constraint will swivel
(a) out if the price of one of the goods increases.
(b) in if household income falls.
(c) out if household income falls.
(d) in if the price of one of the goods increases.

_____ 4. If prices double and income doubles, the budget constraint will
(a) double.
(b) move inward.
(c) move outward by 50 percent.
(d) not shift position.

_____ 5. An increase in the wage rate will _____ the quantity of labor supplied, according to the substitution effect, and will _____ the quantity of labor supplied, according to the income effect.
(a) increase; increase
(b) increase; decrease
(c) decrease; increase
(d) decrease; decrease

_____ 6. The wage rate rises. If the quantity of labor supplied falls, the most likely explanation is that the substitution effect
  (a)   and the income effect are both positive.
  (b)   is negative and the income effect is positive.
  (c)   and the income effect are both negative.
  (d)   is positive and the income effect is negative.

_____ 7. Higher interest rates cause
  (a)   future consumption to increase.
  (b)   current consumption to increase.
  (c)   current borrowing to increase.
  (d)   current saving to decrease.

_____ 8. Jill is maximizing her utility. The price of Good _A_ falls. Jill will buy
  (a)   more of Good _A_ because it is relatively cheaper—the substitution effect.
  (b)   less of Good _A_ because her marginal utility is diminishing.
  (c)   more of Good _A_ because her marginal utility is increasing.
  (d)   more of Good _B_—the substitution effect.

_____ 9. Fred has had 4 hamburgers and 2 hot dogs this week and is now indifferent between them. Hamburgers cost $2 and hot dogs cost $1. Currently
  (a)   Fred's marginal utility per unit of hamburgers is twice that of hot dogs.
  (b)   Fred's total utility of hamburgers equals that of hot dogs.
  (c)   Fred's total utility of hamburgers is twice that of hot dogs.
  (d)   Fred's marginal utility per unit of hamburgers equals that of hot dogs.

_____ 10. In a two-good analysis, the slope of the budget constraint is determined by the
  (a)   prices of the two goods.
  (b)   income and wealth of the household.
  (c)   income but not the wealth of the household.
  (d)   income, wealth of the household, and the prices of the two goods.

_____ 11. The wage rate can be seen as a measure of the opportunity cost of
  (a)   work.
  (b)   saving.
  (c)   leisure.
  (d)   future consumption.

_____ 12. The utility-maximizing combination of two goods (cakes and ale) occurs when the MRS of cakes for ale equals
  (a)   the MRS of ale for cakes.
  (b)   the ratio of MU_{cakes} / MU_{ale}.
  (c)   the ratio of the price of cakes to the price of ale.
  (d)   the ratio of the price of ale to the price of cakes.

_____ 13. A price decrease
  (a)   increases the choice set.
  (b)   decreases the opportunity set.
  (c)   makes utility-maximizers worse off.
  (d)   decreases the choice set.

_____ 14.   "Utility"
(a)   involves the subjective weighing of the satisfaction individuals receive from goods and services.
(b)   is measurable.
(c)   can be used to compare the likes and dislikes of different individuals.
(d)   All of the above are correct.

_____ 15.   Lesley can buy two goods, Good X and Good Y. Good X is represented on the horizontal axis. Which of the following will cause the budget constraint to increase its slope?
(a)   An increase in the price of Good X
(b)   An equal increase in the price of both goods
(c)   An increase in Lesley's income
(d)   An increase in the price of Good Y

_____ 16.   When the price of pretzels rises, the "income effect" helps to explain why
(a)   opportunity cost increases along the demand curve.
(b)   sellers switch production and increase the quantity supplied of pretzels.
(c)   income rises for producers of pretzels.
(d)   the demand curve for pretzels is sloped as it is.

Use the following information for the next two questions. Currently, Zack is using his income to consume two goods, X and Y, in such a way that $MU_X/MU_Y < P_X/P_Y$.

_____ 17.   To maximize his satisfaction, Zack should
(a)   increase consumption of Good X and increase consumption of Good Y.
(b)   increase consumption of Good X and decrease consumption of Good Y.
(c)   decrease consumption of Good X and increase consumption of Good Y.
(d)   decrease consumption of Good X and decrease consumption of Good Y.

_____ 18.   As Zack moves towards equilibrium,
(a)   he will move along the same indifference curve.
(b)   he will move along the same budget constraint.
(c)   the marginal utility of Good X will decrease.
(d)   the marginal rate of substitution will decrease.

Use the following information for the next two questions. Kaori's income is $100; the price of apples is $5 per unit; the price of oranges is $10 per unit. Assume a consumer choice diagram with apples on the vertical axis and oranges on the horizontal axis.

_____ 19.   If Kaori's income falls to $75, but the prices of apples and oranges remain unchanged, there will be a
(a)   parallel shift inwards of the indifference curves.
(b)   parallel shift outwards of the budget line.
(c)   parallel shift inwards of the budget line.
(d)   decrease in Kaori's consumption of both apples and oranges.

_____ 20.   If the price of apples increases to $10 per unit,
(a)   the budget line will rotate clockwise around the intersection of the budget line and the vertical axis.
(b)   the budget line will rotate counterclockwise around the intersection of the budget line and the horizontal axis.
(c)   Kaori will be on the same indifference curve, but fewer apples will be consumed.
(d)   Kaori's consumption of apples will decrease.

II. APPLICATION QUESTIONS

1. The following indifference curve diagram shows Jenny's utility-maximizing goods combinations (*K* and *L*) given two different prices of Good *B*. The vertical axis represents spending on all other goods.

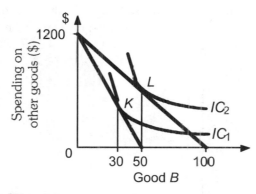

(a) What is Jenny's income?

(b) What is the price of Good *B* at point *K*?

(c) What is the price of Good *B* at point *L*?

(d) When in equilibrium at Point *K*, how much will she spend on Good *B*?

(e) When in equilibrium at Point *L*, how much will she spend on Good *B*?

(f) If Jenny has a straight, downward-sloping demand curve for Good *B*, plot the two points on her demand curve that you know, showing price and quantity information. Sketch in the straight-line demand curve through these points.

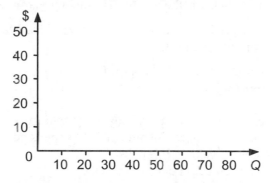

(g) Calculate her price elasticity of demand coefficient for Good *B* as the price changes from $12 to $24. Use the midpoint formula. (Hint: Refer to Chapter 5 if you are unsure of how to do this.)

(h) In this price range, classify Jenny's elasticity of demand for Good *B* as "elastic," "inelastic," or "unit elastic."

(i) Use the total revenue test to confirm your answer to part h.

(j) Jenny's curve for Good *B* is given by $Qd = 70 - (5/3)P$, where *P* is the price of Good *B* in dollars. On the diagram you used in part (f) draw in Jenny's complete demand curve to both axes. Calculate the endpoints.

(k) Calculate Jenny's consumer surplus when the price of Good *B* is $12. (Hint: Refer to Chapter 4 if you are unsure of how to do this.)

(l)   Calculate Jenny's consumer surplus when the price of Good B is $24. (Hint: Refer to Chapter 4 if you are unsure of how to do this.)

2.   Suppose that we are told that the price of Good X and Good Y are $1 and $6, respectively, and that Marina's income is $300.

(a)   Draw Marina's budget constraint (BB), clearly showing the maximum values of X and Y that can be purchased. Plot Y on the vertical axis and X on the horizontal axis.

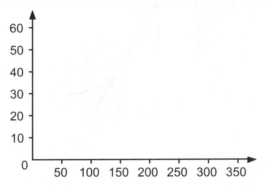

(b)   For Marina to maximize utility, what must be the marginal rate of substitution?

(c)   If the price of Good X were to rise to $3 and the price of good Y were to rise to $10, what would happen to the marginal rate of substitution when Marina is maximizing her utility? What has happened to her opportunity set?

(d)   If Marina's income had doubled simultaneously with the price changes, what would have happened to her opportunity set, relative to the situation in (c) above?

(e)   Suppose, instead, that the price of Good X had become $4 whereas that of Good Y had remained at $6. What is the utility-maximizing marginal rate of substitution now?

(f)   Given the new prices and an income of $300, draw Marina's new budget constraint (B'B') on the diagram in (a) above.

(g)   Make up a rule relating the slope of the budget constraint, the ratio of prices, and the utility-maximizing marginal rate of substitution.

3.   Assume that consumers in Megropolis buy only two goods: bread (a necessity) and cake (a luxury). Lucretia Bourgeois has an income of 1,000 opeks per year. The price of a loaf of bread is 5 opeks, and the price of a cake is 10 opeks.

(a)   Sketch Lucretia's budget constraint (AA).

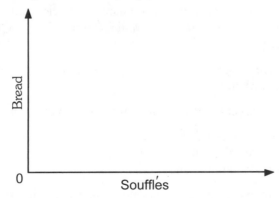

(b)   On the diagram, what is Lucretia's opportunity set?

Chapter 6 Household Behavior and Consumer Choice **161**

(c)   If Lucretia were relatively poor in Megropolis, where on the budget constraint might you expect her choice to lie?

(d)   Suppose that the price of a cake were to fall from 10 opeks to 5 opeks. Sketch Lucretia's new budget constraint (*AB*). What happens to the size and position of Lucretia's opportunity set on the diagram in (a) above?

(e)   Suppose that prior to the price decrease, a tax of 20 percent had been placed on luxury goods. Assume that the tax is paid by the consumer. Sketch the new budget constraint (*AC*) facing Lucretia.

(f)   Suppose that Lucretia's income increases from 1,000 opeks to 2,000 opeks. Sketch the new budget constraint (*DD*).

4.   The following diagram depicts Bill's budget constraint. Bill has $12 to spend on candy and cigarettes. Each candy bar costs $1 whereas each pack of cigarettes costs $4.

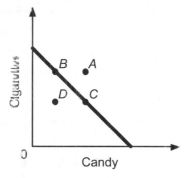

(a)   How many candy bars could Bill buy? How many packs of cigarettes?

(b)   Is the combination of goods represented by Point *A* attainable? Why?

(c)   Is Point D attainable? What is the implication of choosing Point *D*?

(d)   Which is better—the combination at Point *B* or that at Point *C*?

(e)   What would happen to the maximum levels of consumption if Bill's income rose to $20?

(f)   What would happen if cigarettes then increased in price to $10?

5.   Linda spends all of her income on loaves of bread and two-liter bottles of Coke at prices of $2.00 and $1.50, respectively. At the moment, she is buying these two products in amounts such that the marginal utilities from the final units bought are 100 and 80 utils, respectively.

(a)   Is Linda maximizing her utility? Explain your answer.

(b)   If you feel that Linda could increase her total utility, given the conditions, explain how she should adjust her expenditures.

©2012 Pearson Education, Inc. Publishing as Prentice Hall

6. Sally derives utility from pizza slices and hot dogs according to the following weekly schedule. A slice of pizza costs $1.00 and a hot dog costs 50¢.

Pizza Slices			Hot Dogs			
TU	MU	MU/$	⟨-units consumed-⟩	TU	MU	MU/$
20	_____	_____	1	12	_____	_____
36	_____	_____	2	22	_____	_____
50	_____	_____	3	31	_____	_____
62	_____	_____	4	39	_____	_____
72	_____	_____	5	45	_____	_____
80	_____	_____	6	49	_____	_____
86	_____	_____	7	52	_____	_____
90	_____	_____	8	54	_____	_____
91	_____	_____	9	55	_____	_____

(a) Complete the "marginal utility" and "marginal utility per dollar" columns for each good.

(b) Sally's income is $8.00. Assuming that no half units may be bought, how many slices of pizza and how many hot dogs should she consume to maximize her utility?

(c) What would be Sally's total utility?

(d) Sally would not maximize her utility by buying 4 slices of pizza and 5 hot dogs. Why not?

(e) She wouldn't buy 5 slices of pizza and 7 hot dogs. Why not?

(f) It would be possible for Sally's total utility to increase if conditions changed. Give three examples of ways in which conditions could change so that Sally's utility would be greater than before.

(g) Derive "MU/$" values for pizza slices when the price/slice is 50¢, $1.00, $1.50, and $2.00. At each price level, work out the utility-maximizing combination of the two goods. Compare the "marginal utility/dollar" results with the formula in the textbook. Observe that the equality present in the utility-maximizing formula is an *ideal*—in the real world goods are "lumpy." Use the utility-maximizing numbers derived for pizza slices to complete the demand schedule in the following table. Changing prices, combined with utility-maximizing behavior, give us a demand curve.

	Pizza Slices
Price	Quantity Demanded/Week
50¢	_____
$1.00	_____
$1.50	_____
$2.00	_____

(h) Return to the original situation where the price of pizza slices and hot dogs are $1.00 and 50¢, respectively. Sally's income rises from $8.00 to $10.50. Calculate the utility-maximizing combination of goods.

(i) Are pizza slices "normal" goods for Sally?

7. Soon Woo has the following indifference curve map. Her income is 60 yuan. Cotton costs 5 yuan per unit and rice costs 10 yuan per unit.

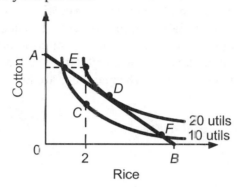

(a) Calculate the maximum amount of cotton and the maximum amount of rice.

(b) Soon would prefer to be at which point?

(c) Suppose she buys 6 units of cotton at Point D. How many units of rice would she buy?

(d) If Soon were at Point F, is she buying too much cotton or too much rice?

(e) Suppose the government requires each individual to buy no more than 2 units of rice. Soon will buy _____ units of cotton and _____ units of rice. Describe where on the diagram her new combination of purchases will be. What has happened to her utility?

(f) Given the government requirement, to restore her original level of utility and be in equilibrium at that level, what would have to happen? (Careful!)

8. Suppose that two gourmet ice cream stores sell ice cream cones in your town. Tom and Jerry's cones sell for $2.50 and Johnson Howard's cones sell for $2.00. Suppose you love ice cream and have decided to budget $100 per month for ice cream cones.

(a) Sketch your budget constraint and the opportunity set of combinations of Tom and Jerry's cones and Johnson Howard's cones available for $50.

(b) Suppose that Tom and Jerry's cones and Johnson Howard's cones are perfect substitutes in your mind—you are indifferent between cones from either store. What point on your budget constraint will you choose?

(c) Suppose that the total demand for Johnson Howard's cones is given by the equation $Q_j = 50 - 2P_j$. At $P_j = 2.00, calculate consumer surplus. Now suppose that Johnson Howard raises the price to $2.50. Find the new consumer surplus. What happens to the loss in surplus?

9. First, draw Georgia's indifference map for the two goods "leisure" and "goods." Maximum leisure time is 24 hours, the wage rate is $6/hour, and "goods" cost $12/unit. Now draw the budget constraint. What is the endpoint value for "goods"? Identify the equilibrium combination of leisure and "goods" as Point A. Why is this the equilibrium?

Now suppose the wage rate increases to $8/hour. Draw in Georgia's new budget constraint. Why is the combination at Point A no longer the equilibrium? Identify the new equilibrium as Point B. What has happened to the amount of leisure time consumed? Is your answer affected by the position of your indifference curve? Experiment with the indifference curve "map" to see if you can produce a different result. Based on this example, discuss how the indifference curve diagram—and the income and substitution effects—might be used to explain the slope of the labor-supply curve.

10.   When Congress passed the Economic Recovery Tax Act, this legislation included, among other provisions, a major reduction in individual income tax rates. Proponents of the bill argued that the reduction in taxes would significantly increase the incentive to work, and they predicted that the result would be an increase in the labor supply. In fact, evidence suggests that, for some groups, labor supply actually declined. Using income and substitution effects, explain how this could be possible. (Hint: A decrease in taxes means that after-tax wages increase.) What determines whether or not labor supply will increase when tax rates are lower?

Practice Test SOLUTIONS

I. SOLUTIONS TO MULTIPLE-CHOICE QUESTIONS

1. (b) To maximize utility, the marginal utility per dollar of the last unit of each good bought should be equal. Currently Jo is receiving greater marginal utility per dollar from Good A. She should increase consumption of A and reduce consumption of B.

2. (b) Good X is worth twice as much as Good Y.

3. (d) The budget constraint swivels with a price change. A price increase will make the budget constraint swivel in.

4. (d) The doubling in prices will not affect the slope of the budget constraint. By doubling income, too, the budget constraint will not shift.

5. (b) The substitution effect indicates that the wage rate increase will cause the opportunity cost of leisure to increase, discouraging leisure time—labor supplied increases—but the income effect indicates that the increase in the wage rate increases income, encouraging workers to consume more normal goods (including leisure).

6. (d) A higher wage rate will both encourage increased labor supply through the substitution effect, and discourage labor supply through the income effect. In this case, the income effect dominates.

7. (a) Higher interest rates encourage more current saving and less current consumption.

8. (a) Marginal utility decreases with additional consumption. More will be bought because Good A is a better buy now, relative to other products—the substitution effect.

9. (a) If Fred is indifferent between the two goods, then the marginal utility per dollar must be equal. Because the price of hamburgers is twice as great as the price of hot dogs, the marginal utility of hamburgers must be twice as great as that of hot dogs.

10. (a) Refer to page 122 for more on the budget constraint.

11. (c) Choosing not to work means that one surrenders the wage that could have been earned.

12. (c) The utility-maximizing condition is $MU_c/MU_a = P_c/P_a$.

13. (a) The price decrease will cause the budget constraint to swivel outwards.

14. (a) Utility is subjective—comparison between individuals is not possible.

15. (a) Lesley will be able to buy less of Good A if its price increases. The endpoint of the budget constraint will move inwards, making the constraint steeper.

16. (d) The income effect and the substitution effect both help to explain the slope of the relationship between the price of pretzels and the quantity demanded of pretzels.

17. (c) Refer to the following diagram. Zack is currently at Point *A*. To maximize satisfaction, he needs to be at Point *B*.

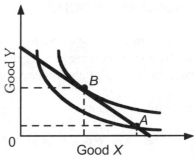

18. (b) The marginal rate of substitution is less at Point *A* (a flatter indifference curve) than at Point *B*. It increases as we move to Point *B* (along the budget line and to a new indifference curve).

19. (c) Kaori can buy less of both goods—her opportunity set has been reduced.

20. (b) When the price of a good increases, there is a decrease in the maximum quantity that can be bought.

II. SOLUTIONS TO APPLICATION QUESTIONS

1. (a) $1,200

   (b) $1,200/50 = $24

   (c) $1,200/100 = $12

   (d) Spending on Good B = price × quantity = $24 × 30 = $720

   (e) Spending on Good B = price × quantity = $12 × 50 = $600

   (f) Refer to the following diagram.

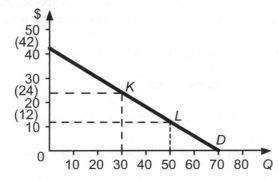

   (g) [(50 − 30) / (50 + 30) / 2] / [(11–24) / 12+24) / 2] = –0.75.

   (h) An elasticity value with an absolute value of less than 1.00 indicates an inelastic demand.

   (i) As the price increases from $12 to $24, total revenue (spending) increases from $600 to $720. This indicates an inelastic demand.

   (j) Refer to the diagram above. When *Q* is zero, *P* is 42. When *P* is zero, *Q* is 70.

(k)   Consumer surplus is the area between the demand curve and the price. With a straight line demand curve it is $1/2(P_{max} - P)Qd$. Jenny's consumer surplus is $1/2(42 - 12)50$, or $750.

(l)   Jenny's consumer surplus is $1/2(42 - 24)30$, or $270.

2.   (a)   Refer to the following diagram.

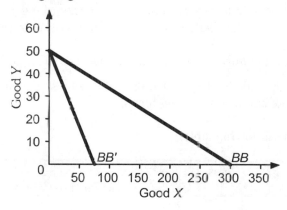

(b)   –1/6

(c)   MRS would change to –3/10 and Marina's opportunity set would shrink.

(d)   Marina's opportunity set would increase, the endpoints of the budget constraint being 200 (X) and 60 (Y).

(e)   –2/3

(f)   Refer to the preceding diagram.

(g)   The slope of the budget constraint is determined by the ratio of the prices. When maximizing utility, the MRS will also equal this ratio.

3.   (a)   Refer to the following diagram.

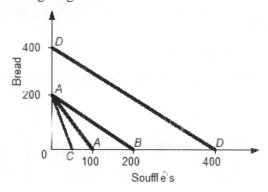

(b)   Lucretia's opportunity set is the area on and under *AA*.

(c)   Presumably, Lucretia would mainly consume bread.

(d–f)   Refer to the preceding diagram.

4.   (a)   12; 3

(b)   The combination at Point *A* is not attainable because Bill doesn't have enough money, given current prices.

(c)   The combination at Point *D* is attainable. Choosing *D* would imply that Bill is not spending all of his income.

(d)   Without knowing Bill's preferences (smoker or sweet-tooth) we can't say which combination (*B* or *C*) is preferable.

(e)   Bill could buy as many as 5 packs of cigarettes or 20 candy bars.

(f)   Bill would be able to buy no more than 2 packs of cigarettes; he could still buy as many as 20 candy bars. His budget constraint would swivel inwards.

5.   (a)   Linda is not maximizing her total utility because $MU_{bread}/P_{bread} \neq MU_{Coke}/P_{Coke}$.

(b)   Because 100 utils/$2.00 < 80 utils/$1.50, she should allocate more of her income to buying Coke and less to buying bread.

6.   (a)   Refer to the following table.

Pizza Slices				Hot Dogs		
TU	*MU*	*MU/$*	<-units consumed->	*TU*	*MU*	*MU/$*
20	20	20	1	12	12	24
36	16	16	2	22	10	20
50	14	14	3	31	9	18
62	12	12	4	39	8	16
72	10	10	5	45	6	12
80	8	8	6	49	4	8
86	6	6	7	52	3	6
90	4	4	8	54	2	4
91	1	1	9	55	1	2

(b)   5 slices of pizza and 6 hot dogs

(c)   121 utils (72 + 49)

(d)   The "marginal utility per dollar" values are the same, but Sally would not be spending all of her income.

(e)   She doesn't have enough money.

(f)   Sally's total utility would increase if her income rose, or if the price of either pizza or hot dogs fell.

(g)   Refer to the following table.

	Pizza Slices
Price	Quantity Demanded/Week
50¢	8
$1.00	5
$1.50	3
$2.00	2

(h)   7 slices of pizza and 7 hot dogs

(i)   Pizza slices are normal goods—demand increases as income increases.

7.   (a)   12 units of cotton; 6 units of rice

(b)   *D*

(c)   3

(d)   Too much rice

(e)   8: 2. This combination will be on the budget constraint between Point *E* and Point *D*. Her utility has been reduced.

(f)   Cotton would have to fall in price and rice increase in price in such a way that the budget constraint would tilt to be tangent to the indifference curve.

8.   (a, b)   You would choose 50 of Johnson Howard's cones because you are indifferent. If the two ice creams are perfect substitutes and we assume that more is better than less, then it's better to buy the brand that is cheaper. Refer to Point *A* the following diagram.

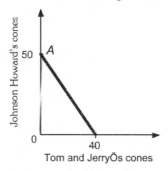

(c)   At $P = \$2$, the consumer surplus will be \$529; at $P = \$2.50$, consumer surplus will be \$506.25. Approximately \$22.75 is lost. Howard's Johnson has taken the lost consumer surplus.

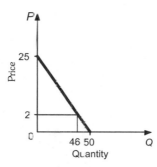

9.   Refer to the following diagram. Working 24 hours will earn Georgia \$144. She would be able to buy 12 goods. Point *A* is the equilibrium because at that point the "price" ratio is equal to the marginal rate of substitution between goods and leisure.

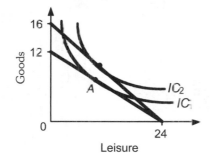

As the wage rate increases, the budget constraint swivels around with the goods endpoint being 16, or ($8 × 24)/$12. Point *A* is no longer the equilibrium because the "price" ratio is no longer equal to the marginal rate of substitution between goods and leisure.

The amount of leisure time consumed may increase or decrease—it depends on the interplay between the income effect and the substitution effect. Shifting IC_2 to the left will decrease the amount of leisure and shifting it to the right will increase leisure time.

10.   The lower tax rate increases the after-tax wage rate. The substitution effect: Leisure is more expensive relative to other goods. Each hour of leisure requires a bigger sacrifice of other goods. Thus, you would expect people to consume less leisure and work more. The income effect: Because the after-tax wage rate has increased, people have more income—they are better off. Assuming that leisure is a normal good, you would expect people to both consume more of it along with the other things that their income can buy, and to work less. The two effects operate against each other.

7

The Production Process: The Behavior of Profit-Maximizing Firms

1. Define economic cost and economic profit, distinguish economic profit from accounting profit, and discuss the meaning of positive, zero, and negative economic profit.
2. Distinguish the short run from the long run.
3. Explain how the production function relates inputs to outputs.
4. State the law of diminishing returns and explain why this phenomenon occurs only in the short run. Explain the relationships between marginal, total, and average product and, given a production function graph, interpret the behavior of marginal and average product.
5. Explain and, given a numerical example with prices, select the least-cost production technology for a firm.
6. Use the isoquant-isocost diagram to identify the optimal capital-labor mix for a given production level.

This chapter moves from the decisions of utility-maximizing households to examine the behavior of profit-maximizing producers. It's a transition chapter that introduces many central topics—including productivity, costs, and economic profits—that will be reused in several subsequent chapters.

BRAIN TEASER: At some time you've probably heard someone say that they've reached "the point of diminishing returns." The implication is that it's not productive to continue. Is that true, however?

Objective 1

Define economic cost and economic profit, distinguish economic profit from accounting profit, and discuss the meaning of positive, zero, and negative economic profit.

Some basic assumptions, which are set out in the introduction to Part II, are used for the *perfectly competitive model* that underlie this and the next five chapters. These assumptions are: many small firms produce a homogeneous (standardized) product, and that those firms have free entry into, and exit from, the market in the long run. (page 119)

Any firm in any industry must make three basic decisions to maximize profits—how much output to supply, how to produce that output (technique/technology), and how much of each input to demand. The principles established in this chapter apply to any profit-maximizing firm.

LEARNING TIP: Take a few minutes to review the introductory material on pp. 117-119. Both the underlying structure of Part II and the ongoing assumptions (perfect knowledge, perfect competition, homogeneous products) for this and subsequent chapters are set out there very clearly. ◀

Normal and Economic Profits: Note that economic costs include out-of-pocket costs and the opportunity costs of *all* factors of production—there is an allowance made for normal profits. A producer who is "breaking even" in an economic sense (total revenue equals total economic cost) will be quite well satisfied. Obviously, (s)he would prefer even more profits, but the normal rate of return is adequate to cover opportunity costs and to ensure continued production.

Profit equals total revenue minus total (economic) cost. Note that economists distinguish between explicit (out-of-pocket or accounting) costs and implicit (economic) costs. *Economic cost* includes both the explicit costs and the implicit costs of all the factors of production (including a normal rate of return for the owners of the firm). In this sense, cost includes a profit component. A normal rate of return is a reward sufficient to compensate the owners for the risk and effort they have undertaken. When total revenue just covers total cost, owners are receiving an adequate reward (i.e., zero economic profit). (page 148)

If you provide your (car repair) services to a friend and charge just enough to cover out-of-pocket expenses, an accountant would claim that you broke even. Given that your time had some value (you might have serviced another customer, perhaps), an economist would say that you did not meet all your costs—you made a negative economic profit.

Positive economic profits (or excess profits) are a higher-than-normal reward. New firms are attracted to an industry by positive economic profits. In the long run, given negative economic profits (i.e., losses), firms will leave the industry.

Nicki can earn $500 a week (after accounting costs) from Activity *A*. This $500 per week is the opportunity cost (the value of the next-best alternative, Activity *B*) for Nicki of Activity *A*. If, after accounting costs are paid, Nicki can clear more than $500 in Activity *B*, she should shift over to Activity *B*. If she stays in Activity *A*, she will be making negative economic profits.

LEARNING TIP: Many students, particularly accounting majors, fumble the distinction between economic costs and accounting costs and the related distinction between economic profits and accounting profits. Here is a simple example that should clarify the issue.

Suppose you have a factory job earning $50,000 a year which you quit to open a small Internet business. Business is brisk and you bring in $200,000 in revenues with accounting expenses of $170,000. Are you earning a profit? Your accountant would say yes—$30,000. An economist would say no—you lost $20,000. Your significant other would perhaps side with the economist and advise you to go back to the factory!◀

Practice

Use the following information for the next three questions. Jason has a plot of land that has three alternative uses: *R*, *S*, and *T*. The revenue from each use is $5, $6, and $8, respectively. The accounting cost of each use is zero.

1.   The opportunity cost of using the land for Use *S* is
        (a) $5, the value in Use *R*.
        (b) $8, the value in Use *T*.
        (c) $1, the difference in value between Use *R* and Use *S*.
        (d) $2, the difference in value between Use *T* and Use *S*.

        ANSWER: (b) Opportunity cost is the value of the next-best alternative, Use *T*.

2.   The economic profit of using the land for Use *S* is
   (a)   −$8, the value in Use *T*.
   (b) $8, the value in Use *T*.
   (c)   −$2, the difference in value between Use *T* and Use *S*.
   (d) $2, the difference in value between Use *T* and Use *S*.

   ANSWER: (c)   Economic profit is total revenue (which for Use *S* is $6) minus total costs. Accounting costs are zero, but economic (opportunity) costs are $8 (the revenue from Use *T*).

3.   To maximize profits, Jason should utilize the land for_____ . If Jason is a typical producer in this industry, we would expect firms to_____ this industry.
   (a)   Use *S*; enter
   (b)   Use *S*; leave
   (c)   Use *T*; enter
   (d)   Use *T*; leave

   ANSWER: (c)   Use *T* offers the highest profit ($2). In the long run, firms will be attracted to the industry by the positive economic profits.

Use the following information for the next two questions. Amos can sell as many cantaloupes as he wishes at the market price of $2.00 each. Total cost to Amos of carrying each cantaloupe to market is 50¢. He chooses to sell 10 cantaloupes.

4.   His total revenue is
   (a) $1.50.
   (b) $2.00.
   (c) $15.00.
   (d) $20.00.

   ANSWER: (d)   Total revenue is price × quantity.

5.   Amos is making a
   (a)   total economic profit of $15.00.
   (b)   total economic profit of $20.00.
   (c)   normal rate of return of 10 percent.
   (d)   total economic profit of $1.50.

   ANSWER: (a)   Total economic profit is total revenue less total cost. For Amos, total revenue is $20.00 and total cost is $5.00.

6.   Jocelyn Willetts starts a VCR repair service. She invests $60,000 in the business. The normal rate of return in the VCR repair trade is 12 percent. At the end of the first year, Jocelyn's economic profit is $5,000. She should
   (a)   leave this industry. A normal profit is $60,000 × 0.12, i.e., $7,200, and she is earning less than this.
   (b)   probably leave this industry. She has ignored other costs of production.
   (c)   stay in the industry. She is earning more than the normal rate of return.
   (d)   probably stay in the industry. 8.33 percent rate of return is below average, but it might take more time to establish customer loyalty.

   ANSWER: (c)   If Jocelyn has an economic profit, she must be earning more than the normal rate of return, i.e., she is earning more than enough to keep her interested. ∎

Objective 2

Distinguish the short run from the long run.

The *long run* is a time period long enough for the firm to alter any and all of its factors of production. The *short run* is the time period less than that—the period in which each firm has a fixed scale of production with at least one resource fixed in quantity. In the long run, new firms can enter or leave the market. In the short run, they can't. (page 150)

LEARNING TIP: Perhaps the best way to remember the difference between the short run and the long run is to understand the long run first. In the long run, the firm has enough time to alter all of its factors of production. Simply put, the short run is anything less.

In the long run, firms can enter or leave an industry. In the short run, a firm that wants to leave an industry can reduce production to zero, but can't leave. (Because it still has some fixed resources, it still has bills to pay. In effect, the closed-down firm is still in existence.) In the short run, a firm that wants to enter an industry hasn't enough time to assemble all of its factors of production—maybe the machines and workers are ready but the factory hasn't been built.

Remember: The short run and long run are **conceptual** time periods—not a specific number of days or weeks. It will be quicker to reach the long run in some industries than in others—think of all the years of training it takes to enter the market as a dentist!◀

Practice

7.   In the short run
      (a)   firms may leave the industry.
      (b)   firms may enter the industry.
      (c)   there are no fixed resources.
      (d)   at least one resource is fixed.

      ANSWER: (d) Refer to page 151. In the long run, all resources (and costs) can be altered.

8.   In the long run
      (a)   the majority of resources are not fixed.
      (b)   all firms will make positive economic profits.
      (c)   a firm can vary all of its inputs, but can't change its mix of inputs.
      (d)   the firm can leave the industry if it so chooses.

      ANSWER: (d) In the long run, a firm can vary all of its inputs and its mix of inputs. It can, indeed, vary the level of its inputs all the way to zero—that is, leave the industry.

9.   In the short run, a firm
      (a)   can shut down and leave the industry.
      (b)   can shut down but cannot leave the industry.
      (c)   cannot shut down.
      (d)   cannot vary its output level.

      ANSWER: (b) The firm can vary its output level (perhaps by laying off workers or working overtime) and can reduce output to zero but, in the short run, the firm does not have enough time to sell off all its assets and, therefore, it remains within the industry. ■

Objective 3

Explain how the production function relates inputs to outputs.

A *production function* is a mathematical or numerical representation of the relationship between inputs and outputs. If more of a variable input causes total production to increase, marginal product is positive. *Marginal product* is the change in total product due to the addition of a unit of an input. (page 152)

Most students are concerned with grades—Ivan Aplus certainly is. For an upcoming economics test, Ivan has some fixed resources (his textbook and lecture notes) and some variable resources (particularly study time for economics). By increasing the study time for his economics test hour by hour, Ivan seeks to increase "production" (his score on the test). In some sense, Ivan has a production function (although it isn't explicit or mathematically precise). An extra hour of study should increase his score by some number of points—this is his marginal product. Ivan may choose to adopt a relatively labor-intensive approach (himself and his notes) or a more capital-intensive approach (viewing videos, getting help from MyEconLab, hiring "human capital" in the form of a tutor).

Practice

10.   The specific mix of resources and technology chosen by a firm depends on the
       (a)   demand for the product.
       (b)   supply of the product.
       (c)   price of the product.
       (d)   prices of inputs.

       ANSWER: (d) Regardless of the good's price, the producer will base his decision on *how* to produce based on the relative prices of inputs. ∎

Objective 4

State the law of diminishing returns and explain why this phenomenon occurs only in the short run. Explain the relationships between marginal, total, and average product and, given a production function graph, interpret the behavior of marginal and average product.

The *law of diminishing returns* states that, when extra units of a variable input are combined with fixed inputs, marginal product will eventually decline. This is a short-run concept—in the long run there are no fixed inputs. (page 154)

   Comment: When marginal product is increasing, the slope of the production function is positive and increasing (rising at an increasing rate). When diminishing marginal returns set in, the slope of the production function is positive but decreasing.

   Comment: It is tempting to assume that marginal productivity declines because the employer hires the "best" resources (workers, for example) first and that subsequent workers are inferior. This may be true in the real world—the boss chooses the most able applicant first—but is not required. Even if all workers are equally capable, diminishing returns will still set in just as, in Chapter 6, when we consume equal additional cans of Coke, diminishing marginal utility will occur.

A frequently used illustration of the validity of the law of diminishing returns is a flowerpot. Space, in this case, is a fixed resource. If the law of diminishing returns did *not* hold, we could add larger and larger quantities of resources such as light and fertilizer, better hybrids, and more effective insecticides and feed everyone in the world from the product of the one flowerpot. Clearly, the law of diminishing returns *does* hold.

LEARNING TIP: **Diminishing Returns:** The law of diminishing returns is easier to understand if you remember the "specialization effect" and the "congestion effect." (These are just made-up names; it's the idea that's important.)

Imagine the inefficient use of resources if one worker had to undertake all the steps necessary to provide you with a Big Mac at your local McDonald's. Add a second worker and a third and allow them to split up the task of producing hamburgers. See how total production increases vigorously? The underemployment of machines is reduced by specialization. The extra (marginal) product and production level per worker will rise. Call this situation where marginal product is increasing the *specialization effect*.

Carry the story further. Imagine the serving area swarming with workers. What has happened? The machines are being worked up to capacity, but workers are having to wait idly to use equipment. Average product and marginal product of workers must be falling. An extra worker will make little contribution to production. Call this the *congestion effect*.

The specialization and congestion effects coexist at all levels of factor usage. At first the benefits from the specialization effect are stronger, but as overcrowding intensifies, the congestion effect begins to prevail. Diminishing returns have set in!◀

ECONOMICS IN PRACTICE (SUPPLEMENTAL): "Speed dating" has been gaining popularity in recent years. Singles assemble to meet each other over short time periods (3 to 8 minutes), making notes afterwards about which participants "follow up" after the event. Can you see how speed dating is related to the law of diminishing returns?

ANSWER: The theory behind speed dating is that you can quite quickly determine whether an individual is worthy of "following up." In theory, on a traditional date the time spent after the first few minutes yields sharply diminishing returns in terms of information gained, and may be mutually embarrassing. Speed dating, therefore, maximizes the exchange of important information in the minimum amount of time. A more recent development is "speed networking" for business connections.

The *average product* (of labor, for example) is the total product divided by the number of units (of labor), and it is related to marginal product. If marginal product exceeds average product, average product increases; if the marginal value is less than average value, the average value decreases. (page 154)

The Average-Marginal Rule: The relationship between marginal and average values is ruled by the laws of arithmetic. If your GPA is 3.0 and you get an "A" in this course, your average will rise. If you pick up a "D," your average will fall. If the extra (marginal) value is more than the average, the average rises; if the marginal value is less than the average, the average falls. This rule, you will discover, pops up throughout your microeconomics course.

ECONOMICS IN PRACTICE (SUPPLEMENTAL): Sometimes (not very often, thank goodness!), a student or advisee will drop by my office and attempt to do some special pleading on grades. The usual pitch is "I need a B rather than a C (or a C rather than a D, etc.) because I need my GPA to be high enough to get into grad school/get a job/qualify for a scholarship." This argument never works. For one thing, grades are grades and aren't subject to negotiation but also because the student is confusing marginal and average. The typical pleader is a senior approaching graduation. The effect of a higher grade in one course (marginal value) on cumulative GPA (average value) will be slight. Can you find other, real-world examples of the same flawed logic?

ANSWER: Switching lanes in heavy traffic may earn you a slight advantage but research has shown that the advantage is slight. On the academic front, cramming for a final, speed-reading textbooks, or last-minute paper production may all feel highly productive, but the effects on grades are unimpressive.

Practice

Use the following table to answer the next five questions.

Labor (Workers)	Total Product	Marginal Product	Average Product
0	0	—	—
1	15		
2	32		
3	48		
4	60		
5		10	
6			13

11. Total product, if six workers are employed, is
    (a) 70 units of output.
    (b) 73 units of output.
    (c) 78 units of output.
    (d) 86 units of output.

    ANSWER: (c) Total product is average product times the number of workers (13 × 6).

12. Average product, if five workers are employed, is
    (a) 10 units of output.
    (b) 12 units of output.
    (c) 14 units of output.
    (d) 15 units of output.

    ANSWER: (c) With four workers, total product is 60 units. The fifth worker adds 10 more units to make a total of 70. Average product is total product divided by the number of workers (70/5).

13. Diminishing returns set in with the_____ worker.
    (a) first
    (b) second
    (c) third
    (d) fourth

    ANSWER: (c) The marginal products of the first, second, and third workers, respectively, are 15, 17, and 16. The decline begins with the third worker.

14. Average product begins to decrease with the_____ worker.
    (a) first
    (b) second
    (c) third
    (d) fourth

    ANSWER: (d) The average products of the first, second, third, and fourth workers, respectively, are 15, 16, 16, and 15. The decline begins with the fourth worker.

15.   The marginal product of the sixth worker is
       (a)   8 units of output.
       (b)   13 units of output.
       (c)   14 units of output.
       (d)   78 units of output.

       ANSWER: (a)   Total product of five workers is 70. Total product of six workers is 78. The sixth
                    worker adds 8 units of output.

16.   When marginal product is decreasing, average product is
       (a)   decreasing.
       (b)   increasing.
       (c)   negative.
       (d)   None of the above are correct.

       ANSWER: (d)   Average product may be increasing or decreasing but, without additional
                    information, we can't say for certain. ■

Objective 5

Explain and, given a numerical example with prices, select the least-cost production technology for a firm.

For a given output level, the producer should attempt to employ the least-cost method of production. The least-cost (profit-maximizing) method of production depends on the available techniques of production and the prices of the factors of production. One gets the best "value for money" by hiring resources to equalize the marginal product per dollar of each resource. (page 156)

LEARNING TIP: The logic here is the same as we saw in Chapter 6 where consumers attempt to maximize utility by equating the marginal utility per dollar of each good purchased. Go back and review that discussion, if the similarity is unclear to you. ◀

ECONOMICS IN PRACTICE: On page 156, the textbook looks at agricultural developments intended to enhance the production of pineapples in Ghana (a relatively new crop for the region). Social learning was an essential element in the adoption of innovative practices—agricultural extension departments offer similar services in this country and for the same reason. The manager of any business faces a similar task as new technologies emerge or the pattern of resource costs change. And so do you, as a student interested in generating good grades. Can you think of ways that today's college student can be more productive than an equivalent student in the 1980s (perhaps your parents)?

ANSWER: The 1980s student had no Wikipedia—in fact, no Internet access at all as we recognize it today. Google didn't exist. Email was rudimentary. Word processors were dominated by typewriters and spell-checkers were unknown. Graphing calculators were uncommon. Campus library resources would have to be searched through a card catalog instead of online. Online classes were non-existent. There were no Andriods or iPhones. All of these innovations (and many more) offer learning advantages to the student of today in his or her quest for a quality education.

ECONOMICS IN PRACTICE: On page 157, the textbook examines how truckers balance labor costs and fuel costs. Once again, time is money. In July 2008, diesel prices were approaching $5 and there were worldwide protests by truckers, but this issue is present whenever there is a change in the structure of resource costs. The same debate was present during the oil price hikes of the 1970s and it led to fuel-saving innovations in the trucking industry. Today, almost all trucks have air-foils (those wedge-shaped structures that sit above the cab and made the vehicle more streamlined). They were adopted as a response to high fuel costs. Can you think of other, similar, innovations driven by changing patterns of costs?

ANSWER: Here are some other examples of the trade-off between time and money. Previously, casinos used to hire workers to move among slot-machine customers and make change for them. Rising labor costs and improved technology have done away with this occupation. Today the slot machines accept notes of different denominations. Self-checkout lines at stores such as Walmart, and the use of robots in car factories or dairies have the same cost-saving impetus. Self-service gas stations and ATMs reduce both the time needed for a transaction and the need for employees.

ECONOMICS IN PRACTICE (CONTINUED): Our textbook suggests that there is a negative relationship between fuel costs and traffic accidents—as fuel costs increase, traffic accidents decrease. But is this true for all classes of road users? What about pedestrians? Cyclists? And those who ride motorcycles?
ANSWER: With rising fuel costs, car drivers seek other forms of transportation. Instead of driving, more persons will be trudging along the verges of highways to the nearby convenience store. Bicycles will become a more attractive, if more dangerous, option. A report published in North Carolina in 2008, when gas prices were unusually high, found that motorcycle accidents had recently increased, especially among inexperienced and infrequent riders.

Practice

Use the following information for the next four questions. Each technology produces the same amount of output.

Technology	Units of Capital	Units of Labor
A	2	15
B	5	8
C	9	3
D	14	1

17. The price of both labor and capital is $1 per unit. Which is the optimal production technique?
    (a) A
    (b) B
    (c) C
    (d) D
    ANSWER: (c) Technique C is best (least-cost). The total cost is $12.

18. If the price of labor remains at $1 per unit and the price of capital rises to $10 per unit, which is the optimal production technique?
    (a) A
    (b) B
    (c) C
    (d) D
    ANSWER: (a) The total cost is $35. The next best is B with a total cost of $58.

19. If the price of capital is $1 per unit and the price of labor is $5 per unit, which is the optimal production technique?
    (a) A
    (b) B
    (c) C
    (d) D
    ANSWER: (d) The total cost is $19. The next best is C with a total cost of $24.

20. Which production technique is the most labor intensive?
    (a)   A
    (b)   B
    (c)   C
    (d)   D
    ANSWER: (a) Technique A uses more units of labor than any of the others. ■

Objective 6 (Appendix)

Use the isoquant-isocost diagram to identify the optimal capital-labor mix for a given production level.

The Appendix to Chapter 7 develops two new graphical tools—the isoquant and the isocost line—with which it becomes possible to work out the least costly (and profit-maximizing) combination of two inputs, given a particular output level. (page 162)

An *isoquant* plots all the combinations of two inputs that will produce a given output level. In general, isoquants are downward sloping—the more labor we use, the less capital we need. The isoquant's slope is the *marginal rate of technical substitution* (MRTS), the rate at which we can surrender workers and hire new machines while holding production constant. Higher levels of production are shown by isoquants that are further from the origin. (page 162)

An *isocost line* plots all the combinations of labor and capital that can be hired for a given amount of money. In general, isocost lines are downward sloping—the more labor we hire, the less money there is left to hire capital. The slope of the line is determined by the relative costs of labor and capital. A higher level of expenditure is shown by an isocost line that is further from the origin. (page 163)

Given the trade-off between labor and capital and the relative prices of the two inputs, the producer's goal is to find the lowest possible cost for producing a chosen level of production. This must also represent the *profit-maximizing input mix*. Equilibrium occurs when the lowest possible isocost line is just tangential to the given isoquant. Formally, the equilibrium condition is stated:

$$MP_L / P_L = MP_K / P_K$$

LEARNING TIP: You should see the relationship between the material in the Appendix of this chapter and in that of Chapter 6. Economists lack imagination and tend to use the same ideas over and over again! For "isoquant," read "indifference curve." For "isocost line," read "budget line." And, of course, the marginal rate of technical substitution is the production-side version of the marginal rate of substitution. If you're a little confused by the Appendix to Chapter 7, go back now and review the Appendix to Chapter 6.◀

Practice

21. A graph showing all the combinations of labor and capital that can be used to produce a given level of output is called
    (a)   an isocost line.
    (b)   an isoquant.
    (c)   an isotech line.
    (d)   a production function.

    ANSWER: (b) There's no such thing as an isotech line. Refer to page 162 for the discussion of isoquants.

Use the following information to answer the next five questions. EBD is the isoquant for 100 units of output.

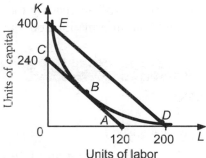

22.   If the price of labor is $12 per unit, the total cost along isocost line *AC*
        (a)   is $10.
        (b)   is $12.
        (c)   is $1440.
        (d)   depends on the price of capital too.

        ANSWER: (c) Each unit of labor costs $12, and 120 can be bought.

23.   If the price of labor is $12 per unit, then the price of a unit of capital is
        (a) $2.
        (b) $6.
        (c) $12.
        (d) $1440.

        ANSWER: (b) Labor costs $12 per unit, and twice as many units of capital can be bought.

24.   If the firm chooses to produce 100 units of output, its least-cost mix of labor and capital is represented by Point
        (a)   *B.*
        (b)   *D.*
        (c)   *E.*
        (d)   *A.*

        ANSWER: (a) Point *B* is the least-cost mix because it is on the lowest possible isocost line that can achieve 100 units of output.

25.   The slope of the isoquant in the diagram above is given by
        (a) $-TP_L / TP_K$.
        (b) $- TP_K / TP_L$.
        (c) $- AP_L / AP_K$.
        (d) $- MP_L / MP_K$.

        ANSWER: (d) Slope is "rise over run." Refer to page 162. The slope of the isoquant is determined by the influence of marginal productivity.

26.   Considering the isocost line that passes through Point *D*: if the price of labor is still $12, the total cost must be_____ and the price of capital must be_____ .
        (a) $2,400; $6
        (b) $4,800; $6
        (c) $2,400; $12
        (d) $4,800; $12

        ANSWER: (a) Twice as much capital can be bought as labor, so capital must be half the price of labor. Total cost is $12 × 200. ∎

BRAIN TEASER SOLUTION: The implication that it's not productive to continue after reaching the point of diminishing returns is false. Once you reach the point of diminishing returns, the marginal productivity of the variable input decreases, but that input is still increasing total production. Those less-productive units may increase profits. You can't tell without information about marginal cost and marginal revenue.

PRACTICE TEST

I. MULTIPLE-CHOICE QUESTIONS

Select the option that provides the single best answer.

_____ 1. Four workers produce 160 units of output and five workers produce 180. The marginal product of the fifth worker is
    (a) 32 units of output.
    (b) 4 units of output.
    (c) 20 units of output.
    (d) 36 units of output.

_____ 2. The return on investment that is just sufficient to satisfy the owners of a business is called
    (a) normal profit.
    (b) marginal profit.
    (c) economic profit.
    (d) excess profit.

_____ 3. The law of diminishing returns
    (a) applies in the short run but not in the long run.
    (b) requires that all factors of production must diminish in equal proportions.
    (c) requires that all factors of production must diminish in unequal proportions.
    (d) states that marginal product must always be less than average product.

_____ 4. Ms. Prudence Juris decides to open a law office. She quits her job as an assistant district attorney (annual salary: $25,000), borrows $50,000 at 10 percent annual interest, hires a secretary at $20,000 per year, and rents office space at $55,000 per year. During her first year, she receives revenues of $100,000. Assuming costs and revenues as represented, what is her **economic profit** for the year?
    (a) $20,000
    (b) Zero, but she does earn a normal profit
    (c) –$5,000
    (d) –$50,000

_____ 5. The short run is a period of time during which
    (a) all resources are fixed.
    (b) all resources are variable.
    (c) the scale of production is fixed.
    (d) the scale of production is variable.

_____ 6.   If diminishing returns have set in, a firm that doubles the number of workers will see total production
(a)   decrease.
(b)   less than double.
(c)   more than double.
(d)   decrease by 50 percent.

_____ 7.   Andy increases the amount of capital his workers use. The average product of labor will_____ and the marginal product of labor will_____ .
(a)   increase; increase
(b)   decrease; decrease
(c)   increase; decrease
(d)   decrease; increase

_____ 8.   Which of the following is most likely to reach the long run soonest?
(a)   An ice cream vendor
(b)   An aircraft manufacturer
(c)   A private college
(d)   A state university

Use the following table to answer the next two questions.

Number of Workers	Marginal Product
1	19
2	26
3	24
4	20
5	18

_____ 9.   Total product, if four workers are employed, is
(a)   20 units of output.
(b)   69 units of output.
(c)   89 units of output.
(d)   107 units of output.

_____ 10.   Average product, if three workers are employed, is
(a)   24 units of output.
(b)   23 units of output.
(c)   26 units of output.
(d)   8 units of output.

_____ 11.   Because of the law of diminishing returns, the general appearance of the production function graph is that it
(a)   increases at an increasing rate.
(b)   increases at a decreasing rate.
(c)   decreases at an increasing rate.
(d)   decreases at a decreasing rate.

_____ 12.   In the short run which of the following is incorrect?
(a)   Existing firms cannot leave the industry.
(b)   New firms cannot enter the industry.
(c)   The firm is operating under a fixed scale of production.
(d)   Firms have no variable factors of production.

_____ 13.   The cost-minimizing combination of labor and capital occurs when the MRTS of capital for labor equals the
(a)   MRTS of labor for capital.
(b)   ratio of MP_L / MP_K.
(c)   ratio of the price of labor to the price of capital.
(d)   ratio of the price of capital to the price of labor.

_____ 14.   On a given isoquant a firm is hiring too much capital (and not enough labor).
(a)   The firm is failing to minimize costs.
(b)   The marginal product of capital is greater than the marginal product of labor.
(c)   The price of capital will fall.
(d)   The marginal product of capital is less than the marginal product of labor.
Note: Try drawing this one!

Use the following diagram to answer the next four questions.

_____ 15.   Based on the diagram, the marginal product of labor for the fifth worker is
(a)   22 units of output.
(b)   19 units of output.
(c)   13 units of output.
(d)   5 units of output.

_____ 16.   Based on the diagram, the total product of labor when there are two workers is
(a)   22 units of output.
(b)   38 units of output.
(c)   41 units of output.
(d)   44 units of output.

_____ 17.   Based on the diagram, the average product of labor when there are four workers is
(a)   5.5 units of output.
(b)   6 units of output.
(c)   21.75 units of output.
(d)   87 units of output.

_____ 18. Based on the diagram above, diminishing returns set in with the
(a)   first worker.
(b)   second worker.
(c)   third worker.
(d)   fourth worker.

_____ 19. The cost-minimizing equilibrium condition is
(a) $MP_L / P_L = MP_K / P_K$.
(b) $-MP_L / MP_K = -P_L / P_K$.
(c) $-MP_L / P_L = MP_K / P_K$.
(d) $P_K / P_L = -MP_L / MP_K$.

_____ 20. When marginal product is zero, total product is_____ and average product is_____ .
(a)   maximized; maximized
(b)   maximized; decreasing
(c)   decreasing; maximized
(d)   decreasing; decreasing

Use the following information for the next two questions. Russell is making plans to open a car wash. His research has isolated four distinct methods of production, each of which will produce the same number of gleaming clean cars.

Technology	Units of Capital	Units of Labor
A	2	20
B	4	15
C	6	11
D	8	8

_____ 21. If the hourly price of a unit of capital is $60 and the hourly wage is $6, which production technology should Russell choose in order to minimize costs?
(a)   A
(b)   B
(c)   C
(d)   D

_____ 22. Which is the most labor-intensive method of production?
(a)   A
(b)   B
(c)   C
(d)   D

II. APPLICATION QUESTIONS

1.   Here are three different mixes of capital and labor, and how they change as output level increases.

Output	Mix 1		Mix 2		Mix 3	
	K	*L*	*K*	*L*	*K*	*L*
11	6	1	4	4	2	7
12	7	3	6	6	3	10
13	9	5	8	8	4	14
14	12	7	10	10	5	20
15	15	9	12	12	6	26
16	21	11	14	14	7	32

(a)   In general, which input mix is the most desirable?

(b)   Which input mix will be chosen if the firm wishes to produce 11 units of output, the price of capital is $4 per unit, and the price of labor is $2 per unit?

(c)   Will this still be cheapest if the input prices change to $3 and $3, respectively?

(d)   Or $2 and $4, respectively?

(e)   For each of the three sets of prices in (b), (c), and (d) above, establish which input mix is cheapest at each output level. To do this, you will have to calculate total costs. Note that no one technology—capital or labor-intensive or intermediate—is always cheapest.

2.   Total cost is $200. The price of a unit of labor is $10 and the price of a unit of capital is $20. Refer to the following diagram.

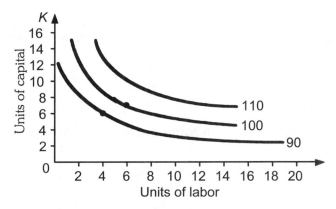

(a)   Draw the isocost line. Call the point of tangency Point *A*.

(b)   What is the maximum output level attainable?

(c)   How many units of labor and capital are used?

(d)   Check that this solution complies with the total cost of $200.

(e)   At Point *A*, is the marginal product of the last unit of labor greater than, less than, or equal to, the marginal product of the last unit of capital?

(f)   Graph the effect of an increase of $20 in the price of labor.

(g)   Calculate the new cost-minimizing combination of inputs. This is Point *B*.

3. Billy-Bob, a "highly paid" economics professor, earns $50,000 per year. He thinks that there must be a better way to make a living and decides to go into hog farming. Billy-Bob resigns his academic job, rents 200 acres of land at $200 per acre, and hires an agricultural college graduate to help him around the farm, drive the tractor, and slop the hogs. In addition, Billy-Bob spends start-up capital of $260,000 for a farrowing barn, finishing barn, feed complex and other requirements. This sum could have been deposited in his bank account at an interest rate of 5 percent.

    At the end of the year, Billy-Bob has incurred the following explicit (out-of-pocket) costs:

Labor	$30,000
Rent	$40,000
Fuel, feed for piglets	$53,000

    Billy-Bob raises 2,400 hogs during the year for an average revenue of $80 each. How much *economic* profit did the farm earn? Assuming that teaching is his only option, should he continue in the hog business?

4. Following is the production function for Wilma's Wicker Baskets.

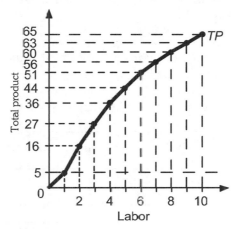

    (a) Compute the marginal product and average product values in the following table.

Labor	Total Product	Marginal Product	Average Product
1			
2			
3			
4			
5			
6			
7			
8			
9			
10			

    (b) With which worker do diminishing returns occur?

5.   Consider the following diagram, which shows isoquants and an isocost constraint. The price of a unit of capital is $20 and the price of a unit of labor is $10.

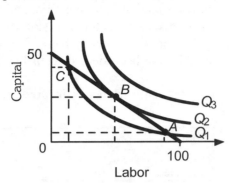

(a)   Calculate the lowest total cost of producing Q_2 units of output.

(b)   Calculate the slope of the isocost line.

(c)   Describe what is happening to output if output changes from Q_2 to Q_1.

(d)   At Point A, compare the marginal rate of technical substitution to the input price ratio. If this information was all that the producer had, how should he adjust his input mix while maintaining the output level? Why?

(e)   Consider the movement from Point C to Point A. Can this move take place in the short run, or can it only occur in the long run?

6.   A firm can sell as much as it wants at the going market price which is $10 per unit.

Quantity	Total Revenue	Marginal Revenue
1		
2		
3		
4		
5		

(a)   Fill in the total revenue column.

(b)   If you graphed these numbers, what sort of slope would total revenue have?

Marginal revenue is the extra revenue brought in by selling one more unit of production (coming up in Chapter 8).

(c)   Use this information to fill in the marginal revenue column.

(d)   If you were to graph the marginal revenue numbers, how would the graph look?

7.   Use the following table for this question.

Number of Workers	Marginal Product	Total Product	Average Product
1	12		
2	16		
3	14		
4	13		
5	10		

(a)   Complete the total product and average product columns.

(b)   With which worker do diminishing returns occur?

(c)   Graph the marginal and average product curves.

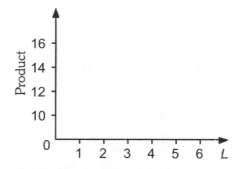

8.   The following diagram is a typical short-run production function.

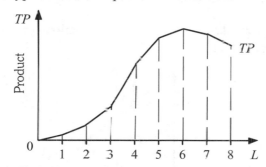

(a)   There exists a unique quantity of labor that no rational, profit-maximizing firm will exceed. Find and label that quantity of labor.

(b)   Explain why a firm would never use more than that amount.

(c)   What must be happening to the marginal product of labor beyond this point?

9.   The following diagram is a marginal product of labor diagram, showing its three distinct phases, with increasing, decreasing/positive, and decreasing/negative marginal product. These are labeled Phases 1, 2, and 3, respectively.

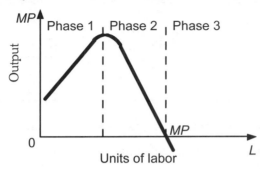

(a)   In which phase(s) are increasing returns occurring?

(b)   Explain why increasing returns are occurring.

(c)   What is happening to total product and to average product in Phase 1?

(d)   In which phase(s) are marginal returns diminishing?

(e)   Go to Phase 3. What is happening to marginal product?

(f)   In Phase 3, what must be happening to total product?

(g)   In Phase 3, what must be happening to average product?

(h)   What is happening to marginal product, average product, and total product in Phase 2?

(i)   Why does average product show this behavior in Phase 2?

10.   The following diagram shows the various combinations of capital and labor that can be used to produce 100 units of output.

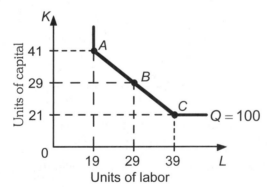

(a)   Consider the techniques represented by Points *A*, *B*, and *C*. If the price of labor and capital were $2 each and the firm decided to produce 100 units of output, which technique would the firm employ?

(b)   If a payroll tax were imposed that pushed the price of labor up to $3 but left the price of capital at $2, which technique would the firm choose?

(c)   If a profits tax pushed the price of capital up to $3 but left the price of labor at $2, which technique would the firm choose?

11.   Assume that wooden chairs can be produced using two different techniques, A and B. The following table provides data on the total input requirement of each at four different output levels.

| | Q = 1 | | Q = 2 | | Q = 3 | | Q = 4 | |
Technique	K	L	K	L	K	L	K	L
A	5	2	8	4	11	5	15	5
B	3	3	6	5	8	7	11	10

(a)   If labor costs $2 per unit and capital costs $3 per unit, what is the minimum cost of producing:
one chair?
two chairs?
three chairs?
four chairs?

(b)   Graph total cost of production as a function of output. (Put output on the X-axis and cost on the Y-axis.)

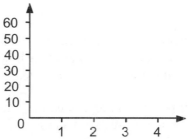

(c)   How much does it cost a profit-maximizing firm to go from an output of:
one chair to two chairs?
two chairs to three chairs?
three chairs to four chairs?

12.   The following example gives some practice in working out which input mix is the most desirable.

| Output | Mix 1 | | Mix 2 | | Mix 3 | |
	K	L	K	L	K	L
11	7	2	4	4	2	7
12	8	4	6	6	3	8
13	9	6	8	8	4	13
14	12	8	10	10	5	19
15	15	10	12	12	6	25
16	21	12	14	14	7	31

(a)   Which input mix will be chosen if the firm wishes to produce 11 units of output, the price of capital is $4 per unit, and the price of labor is $2 per unit?

(b)   Will this mix still be cheapest if the per-unit input prices change to $3 for capital and $3 for labor?

(c)   Will this mix still be cheapest if the per-unit input prices change to $2 for capital and $4 for labor?

No one technology—capital- or labor-intensive or intermediate—is always the cheapest.

Practice Test SOLUTIONS

I. SOLUTIONS TO MULTIPLE-CHOICE QUESTIONS

1.   (c)   Marginal product is the change in total product that occurs when an additional unit of a resource is added.

2.   (a)   Refer to page 149 for a discussion of this point. A normal rate of return is included in the costs of production.

3.   (a)   This law requires that a variable resource is added to a given quantity of a fixed resource. Fixed resources can occur only in the short run.

4.   (c)   Prudence makes an economic loss of $5,000.
Her costs are $(25,000 + 5,000 + 20,000 + 55,000).

5.   (c)   In the short run, at least one factor must be fixed, thus locking the firm into a given scale of production.

6.   (b)   Unless marginal product is negative (which is unlikely), an increase in resources will result in an increase in output. Because each new worker is producing less than previous workers, output will increase but not double.

7.   (a)   Each worker will become more productive, causing marginal product to increase. If each worker produces more, average product will also increase.

8.   (a)   The ice cream vendor has few resource requirements and those (s)he does have can be adjusted rapidly, as opposed to, say, a college, which may have severe limitations on land availability.

9.   (c)   Total product is the sum of the preceding marginal products: $19 + 26 + 24 + 20 = 89$.

10.   (b)   Average product is total product divided by the number of workers: $(19 + 26 + 24)/3 = 23$.

11.   (b)   Although initially the production function may increase at an increasing rate, because of the law of diminishing returns it increases at a decreasing rate.

12.   (d)   In the short run, firms can neither enter nor leave an industry, nor can they adjust their scale of production. However, not all resources are fixed.

13.   (c)   The MRTS equals $- MP_L / MP_K$. Refer to page 162 for more on this.

14.   (a)   We don't know anything about the marginal product of capital relative to the marginal product of labor. However, the marginal product per dollar for capital is less than the marginal product per dollar of labor. The firm could achieve the same level of output by reducing capital and increasing labor.

15.   (b)   The diagram graphs marginal product. Read off the value for the fifth worker, which is 19.

16.   (c)   Add the contributions of the first two workers $(19 + 22)$.

17. (c) Total product is 87 (19 + 22 + 24 + 22). Average product is 87/4.

18. (c) The third worker contributes 24 extra units of output; the fourth worker's contribution is only 22.

19. (a) Refer to page 164.

20. (b) When marginal product becomes negative, total product passes its peak and begins to fall. Given that average product has been positive, an extra (nonproductive) worker will drag down the average.

21. (a) The total cost is (2 × $60) + (20 × $6), or $240.

22. (a) Refer to page 152 for a discussion of this point.

II. SOLUTIONS TO APPLICATION QUESTIONS

1. (a) You can't tell which is the "best" (cheapest) mix without input price information, and even then there may not be a single correct answer.

    (b) Mix 3 is cheapest at $22.

    (c) Mix 1 is cheapest at $21.

    (d) Mix 1 is cheapest at $16.

    (e) Refer to the following tables.

	Capital at $4 and labor at $2		
Output	Mix 1	Mix 2	Mix 3
11	26	24	**22**
12	34	36	**32**
13	46	48	**44**
14	62	**60**	60
15	78	**72**	76
16	106	**84**	92

	Capital at $3 and labor at $3		
Output	Mix 1	Mix 2	Mix 3
11	**21**	24	27
12	**30**	36	39
13	**42**	48	54
14	**57**	60	75
15	72	72	96
16	96	**84**	117

	Capital at $2 and labor at $4		
Output	**Mix 1**	**Mix 2**	**Mix 3**
11	**16**	24	32
12	**26**	36	46
13	**38**	48	64
14	**52**	60	90
15	**66**	72	116
16	86	**84**	142

2.   (a)   Refer to the following diagram.

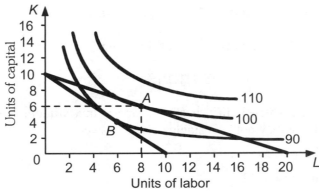

(b)   100 units

(c)   8 labor; 6 capital

(d) $(8 \times \$10) + (6 \times \$20) = \$200$

(e)   Less than. $MP_L / P_L = MP_K / P_K$ are in equilibrium. Because the price of labor is less than the price of capital, the marginal product of labor is less than the marginal product of capital.

(f)   Refer to the diagram in part (a) above.

(g)   6 units of labor and 4 units of capital

3.   Billy-Bob's revenue is $192,000. His explicit (out-of-pocket) cost is $123,000, as indicated by the table. However, he has implicit (opportunity) costs too—the $50,000 he could have made as a professor and the 5 percent interest forgone on the $260,000 spent on improvements ($13,000). His total (economic) cost is $186,000. Because his total revenue is less than his total economic cost, he should stay in farming. He is earning an economic profit of $6,000. Note that the $260,000 investment is not, in itself, included as a cost.

4.   (a)   Refer to the following table. Marginal product of labor is "change in total product divided by change in labor." For worker 5, for instance, change in total product is (44 – 36) and the change in labor is one. Average product of labor is "total product divided by number of workers." For five workers, for instance, total product is 44 and the number of workers is five.

Labor	Total Product	Marginal Product	Average Product
1	5	5	5.0
2	16	11	8.0
3	27	11	9.0
4	36	9	9.0
5	44	8	8.8
6	51	7	8.5
7	56	5	8.0
8	60	4	7.5
9	63	3	7.0
10	65	2	6.5

      (b)   Diminishing returns set in with the fourth worker.

5.   (a)   Total cost is $1,000.

      (b)   –1/2

      (c)   A movement from Q_2 to Q_1 is a decrease in output.

      (d)   At Point A, the marginal rate of technical substitution is less than the price ratio. The firm should reduce its labor input and increase its capital input because the final dollar spent on labor provides a lower marginal product than the final dollar spent on capital will.

      (e)   The movement from Point C to Point A requires that the quantities of both labor and capital change. In the short run, at least one input must be fixed. Only in the long run can the quantities of all inputs vary.

6.   The price is $10 per unit.

Quantity	Total Revenue	Marginal Revenue
1	$10	$10
2	$20	$10
3	$30	$10
4	$40	$10
5	$50	$10

      (a)   Refer to the preceding table.

      (b)   Total revenue would graph as a straight, upward-sloping line.

      (c)   Refer to the preceding table.

      (d)   Marginal revenue would graph as a horizontal line, equal to price.

7.   (a)   Refer to the following table.

Number of Workers	Marginal Product	Total Product	Average Product
1	12	12	12
2	16	28	14
3	14	42	14
4	13	55	13.75
5	10	65	13

   (b)   Diminishing returns set in with the third worker.

   (c)   Refer to the following diagram. [Note that marginal curves are drawn halfway between the quantity values.]

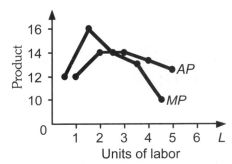

8.   (a)   Six workers

   (b)   Hiring more than six workers will cause total production to fall.

   (c)   Marginal product of labor not only is diminishing, it is *negative*.

9.   (a)   Phase 1

   (b)   The "specialization effect" is stronger than the "congestion effect."

   (c)   Average product is rising, but is less than marginal product. Total product is rising rapidly.

   (d)   Over the remainder of the diagram—Phases 2 and 3

   (e)   Marginal product has become negative.

   (f)   Total product must be falling.

   (g)   Average product must be falling.

   (h)   Marginal product is falling because the congestion effect has prevailed; total product is rising; average product is rising and then falling.

   (i)   This is an example of the "average-marginal rule."

10.   (a)   If the price of capital (P_K) and the price of labor (P_L) are both $2, Technique B is the least expensive. 100 units cost $116, whereas costs are $120 for both Technique A and Technique C.

   (b)   When $P_L = \$3$, Technique A wins with a cost of $139.

   (c)   When $P_K = \$3$, Technique C wins with a cost of $141.

11. (a)   In each case, Technique B is the less expensive.

Technique	$Q = 1$	$Q = 2$	$Q = 3$	$Q = 4$
A:	$19	$32	$43	$55
B:	$15	$28	$38	$53

(b)   Refer to the following diagram.

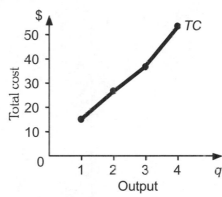

(c)   The marginal cost of increasing production from 1 chair to 2 chairs is $13; from 2 to 3 it is $10; from 3 to 4 it is $15.

12. (a)   Mix 3, with a total cost of $(2 \times \$4) + (7 \times \$2) = \$22$

(b)   Mix 2, with a total cost of $(4 \times \$3) + (4 \times \$3) = \$24$

(c)   Mix 1, with a total cost of $(7 \times \$2) + (2 \times \$4) = \$22$

8

Short-Run Costs and Output Decisions

1. Define, distinguish, and explain the relationships among total cost, total fixed cost, and total variable cost; and among average total cost, average fixed cost, and average variable cost. Interpret cost diagrams.
2. Define and graph marginal cost. Explain the shape of the marginal cost curve, using your knowledge of marginal product. Relate marginal cost to total variable cost and total cost.
3. State the assumptions underlying the perfect competition model and relate these to the firm's role as a "price taker."
4. Define marginal revenue and explain why it is constant in perfect competition.
5. State how firms determine the profit-maximizing level of output and explain why profit is maximized at that production level.
6. Explain why the marginal cost curve above the *AVC* curve is the firm's short-run supply curve.

This chapter deals only with the short run. Fixed resources have costs—and, because those costs don't change, they're irrelevant to the decision of whether or not to produce. In that sense, variable costs (and marginal costs) matter, fixed costs don't.

There are many definitions and a lot of graphical relationships to learn in this chapter. However, the cost relationships will be recycled through the next several chapters, so your "time investment" will be worthwhile. Your ultimate goal is to master Figures 8.8, 8.9, and 8.10—these are the diagrams that you will be using most. Remember that if you know the "average" values and quantity produced, you can work back to the "total" cost values.

BRAIN TEASER: To start you off in this chapter, here is a brain teaser that you should be able to resolve after reading the text. If not, you can find the answer at the end of this section.

By the end of this chapter, you will know that the profit-maximizing output level is where price (or marginal revenue) equals marginal cost. Is that always true? Consider the following example. The price (and marginal revenue) of this product (widgets) is $15 per unit.

Begin by completing the following table. Confirm that there are two output levels where marginal cost and marginal revenue are equal. In terms of profitability, are these output levels equally desirable?

q	TC	TR	MC	MR	Total Profit
0	$30	0	_____	_____	_____
1	$50	_____	_____	_____	_____
2	$65	_____	_____	_____	_____
3	$75	_____	_____	_____	_____
4	$83	_____	_____	_____	_____
5	$90	_____	_____	_____	_____
6	$98	_____	_____	_____	_____
7	$107	_____	_____	_____	_____
8	$117	_____	_____	_____	_____
9	$132	_____	_____	_____	_____
10	$152	_____	_____	_____	_____

In fact, at one of these two production levels, it would be more advantageous to shut down production entirely and, if fixed costs were higher, perhaps neither would be worthwhile. Clearly the "*MR* = *MC*" rule requires modification.

Can you explain why the earlier of the two intersection points can never be the profit-maximizing choice?

Finally, can you explain why we shouldn't set production at eight units of output?

Objective 1

Define, distinguish, and explain the relationships among total cost, total fixed cost, and total variable cost; and among average total cost, average fixed cost, and average variable cost. Interpret cost diagrams.

In the short run, the costs of fixed resources are called *fixed costs* and those of variable resources are called *variable costs*. Added together they are *total costs*. In the short run, total fixed costs (*TFC*) are unavoidable and must be paid—even if the firm has ceased production. In the long run, however, all resources and all costs are variable. Total variable cost (*TVC*) is the cost associated with the cheapest combination of inputs at each level of production. (page 168)

Average fixed cost ($AFC = TFC/q$) graphs as a downward-sloping line—as output increases the overheads are spread over more units. *Average variable cost* ($AVC = TVC/q$) is U-shaped and is influenced by the marginal cost curve because of the "average-marginal" rule. *Average total cost* (*ATC*) is TC/q or $AFC + AVC$. (page 169)

LEARNING TIP: To establish the distinction between fixed and variable costs, consider your own situation in college. Your output is knowledge (measured by GPA, perhaps). Fixed costs are the costs you must pay even if nothing is produced. Tuition, dorm room rent, living expenses, and perhaps a PC are examples of fixed costs. Variable costs are those incurred while increasing

---

knowledge. Books, pencils, notepads, library fines, some traveling expenses, and perhaps floppy disks, black coffee, and aspirins are examples. Because to an economist costs, need not be financial outlays, the opportunity cost of the time spent studying and in class should be included too.◀

Practice

1. Which of the following statements about fixed costs is true?
   (a) Fixed costs increase as time goes by.
   (b) Average fixed cost graphs as a U-shaped curve.
   (c) Fixed costs are zero in the long run.
   (d) Fixed costs are zero when the firm decides to produce no output.

   ANSWER: (c) All resources (and all costs) are variable in the long run.

2. As output increases, total fixed costs
   (a) increase.
   (b) remain constant.
   (c) decrease.
   (d) decrease and then increase.

   ANSWER: (b) Because fixed resources are a given quantity, the costs of those resources are a given quantity too.

3. The _____ curve decreases continuously as output increases.
   (a) average fixed cost
   (b) average variable cost
   (c) total fixed cost
   (d) total variable cost

   ANSWER: (a) Total fixed cost remains constant as output increases. $AFC = TFC/q$ is reduced as quantity increases.

4. Of the following, the _____ is the most likely to be a variable cost.
   (a) wage of a security guard
   (b) firm's rent on its factory building
   (c) firm's electricity bill
   (d) firm's interest payment on a bank loan

   ANSWER: (c) In the other three cases, as output level changes, the cost is unlikely to change.

5. As output level increases, the difference between average total cost and average variable cost
   (a) increases, because total cost includes fixed costs.
   (b) decreases, because additional units of output spread fixed cost over a larger number of units and reduce its importance.
   (c) remains constant, because total fixed cost (which is included in total cost) is a constant.
   (d) decreases and then increases, because they are U-shaped curves.

   ANSWER: (b) Refer to the reason given. $ATC = AVC + AFC$. AFC decreases as output level increases.

6. If labor is a variable resource and the wage rate increases, then the total variable cost curve will _____ and the total cost curve will _____ .
   (a) shift upwards at all levels of output; shift upwards at all levels of output
   (b) shift upwards at all levels of output; pivot upwards
   (c) pivot upwards; shift upwards at all levels of output
   (d) pivot upwards; pivot upwards

ANSWER: (d) When output is zero, variable cost is zero. Both curves will pivot upwards from their point of intersection with the vertical axis.

7.   Complete the following table. Total fixed cost is $10.

q	TC	TFC	TVC	ATC	AFC	AVC
0	$10			—	—	—
1	$18					
2	$24					
3	$30					
4	$36					
5	$40					
6	$54					
7	$70					

ANSWER: Refer to the following table.

q	TC	TFC	TVC	ATC	AFC	AVC
0	$10	$10	$0	—	—	—
1	$18	$10	$8	$18.00	$10.00	$8.00
2	$24	$10	$14	$12.00	$5.00	$7.00
3	$30	$10	$20	$10.00	$3.33	$6.67
4	$36	$10	$26	$9.00	$2.50	$6.50
5	$40	$10	$30	$8.00	$2.00	$6.00
6	$54	$10	$44	$9.00	$1.67	$7.33
7	$70	$10	$60	$10.00	$1.43	$8.57

8.   Eva and ZsaZsa own small factories producing decorative boxes. Eva uses a production process that has high fixed costs and low variable costs, and ZsaZsa uses a process that has low fixed costs and high variable costs. Each factory is producing 100 boxes per week, and the total costs are equal. If each firm increases output by 10 boxes per week
(a)   Eva's total cost will increase more than ZsaZsa's.
(b)   Eva's total cost will increase less than ZsaZsa's.
(c)   Eva's total fixed cost will increase more than ZsaZsa's.
(d)   Eva's total fixed cost will increase less than ZsaZsa's.

ANSWER: (b) An increase in output will increase variable costs, and ZsaZsa's variable costs, which are higher, will increase more. Total fixed costs do not change as output changes. ■

Objective 2

Define and graph marginal cost. Explain the shape of the marginal cost curve, using your knowledge of marginal product. Relate marginal cost to total variable cost and total cost.

Marginal cost (*MC*) is the increase in total cost (and total variable cost) of hiring resources that occurs when an extra unit of output is produced. In the short run, because the firm is constrained by fixed resources, eventually the law of diminishing returns will apply, marginal productivity will decrease, and marginal cost will increase. (page 171)

The marginal cost curve intersects both the average variable cost curve and average total cost curve at the lowest point of each. This is an application of the "average-marginal" rule.

LEARNING TIP: As in Chapter 7, the "average-marginal rule" applies to the relationship between the marginal (extra) value and the average value. Remember: marginal cost shows how total cost changes as output changes. Because total fixed cost doesn't change, it has no effect at all on marginal cost. ◀

LEARNING TIP: The cost diagram represented by AVC, ATC, and MC is important in this and subsequent chapters, and it's crucial that you learn to draw it correctly. Your note taking and understanding will improve if you can draw and interpret the diagram quickly and accurately. ◀

LEARNING TIP: Practice drawing the diagram! It's not merely a collection of randomly positioned U-shaped curves. The marginal cost curve must cut through the other two curves at their minimum value. Always draw the ATC curve above the AVC curve—total cost must be larger than any single component of costs. The vertical gap between ATC and AVC represents the level of AFC. ◀

LEARNING TIP: The easiest way to draw the diagram correctly is to draw the MC curve first, then the ATC curve. Be sure that the ATC curve bottoms out just as it meets the MC curve (because of the "average-marginal rule"). Finally, draw in the AVC curve—it also bottoms out when it reaches the MC curve. Be careful that you draw the AVC curve so that it gets closer to the ATC curve as output increases—the difference between ATC and AVC (that is, AFC) decreases as AFC decreases.

Caution: Be careful of misinterpreting the formula on page 173! It is true that $MC = \Delta TVC$, but *only* when $\Delta q = 1$. As is stated, more generally, $MC = \Delta TVC/\Delta q$. ◀

LEARNING TIP: Clearly, it is wise to become fully familiar with the definitions and formulas included in Table 8.5. Application Questions 5, 6, and 10, in particular, are designed to quiz you on your ability to link and apply these concepts—a good place to begin! ◀

ECONOMICS IN PRACTICE: On page 178, the textbook examines how average costs and marginal costs interact in a college setting. The main point is that, because the extra cost involved in adding additional students is quite small—lower, in fact, than the average costs—average costs continue to decline as the student body increases. We would expect fixed costs to be a relatively large component of expenses and the overhead being spread more thinly. Clearly, it is in the interests of an organization with such a cost profile to attract additional customers. What strategies do colleges use to attract additional students? Can you think of organizations other than colleges with similarly high overheads? What sorts of strategies do they use to attract customers?

ANSWER: Colleges attract students with packages of scholarships, work-study offers, and/or low-cost loans. Other organizations facing similar cost issues would include museums and zoos. Zoos, for example, usually occupy a large amount of land (which may be expensive) and must maintain their animals whether or not there are customers. If the number of visitors declines, some exhibits may be lost, making the zoo less attractive in the future. Museums and zoos often offer memberships and seek charitable donations and volunteers to help defray expenses. Other strategies include season tickets (to encourage return visits), and reduced rates for groups and school trips. This may seem counter-intuitive but zoos can earn a lot of revenue from merchandising and catering once customers have paid their entrance fee! Group trips may encourage attendance by those who would not visit on their own.

ECONOMICS IN PRACTICE (SUPPLEMENTAL): Each NASCAR driver has a pit crew that services his car when he stops during a race. What an extra crew member produces, in effect, is "seconds of time saved." If Jeff Gordon had no pit crew (and had to do all servicing himself) the gain from hiring a helper would be quite significant. Assume each additional crewman can be hired at the same rate. What happens to the marginal cost of hiring additional members for the pit crew?

ANSWER: From Chapter 7 (diminishing returns), we know that additional crew members might exhibit increasing marginal productivity initially but after some point the contribution to "time saved" by extra workers would decrease. The addition to total cost is the same each time an extra worker is hired, but that worker's addition to total product is less than those who have already been hired. Because of diminishing returns, the marginal cost of additional "time saved" increases.

Practice

---

9. Marginal cost can be defined as the
    (a) value of total cost divided by the value of quantity produced.
    (b) change in total variable cost divided by the change in quantity produced.
    (c) change in average total cost divided by the change in quantity produced.
    (d) change in average variable cost divided by the change in quantity produced.

    ANSWER: (b) Marginal cost reports how much total cost (or total variable cost) changes as output level changes.

10. When average cost is greater than marginal cost,
    (a) average cost is rising.
    (b) average cost is falling.
    (c) marginal cost is rising.
    (d) marginal cost is falling.

    ANSWER: (b) This is an application of the "average-marginal rule." If the extra value is less than the average value, the average is pulled down. Option (c) is quite good, but *MC* does decrease before it increases.

11. As marginal product decreases,
    (a) marginal cost increases.
    (b) marginal cost decreases.
    (c) average cost increases.
    (d) average cost decreases.

    ANSWER: (a) As productivity falls, the cost of making extra units rises.

12. Refer to the table you completed earlier in Practice Question 7. The marginal cost of the fourth unit of output is
    (a) $6.
    (b) $10.
    (c) $26.
    (d) $36.

    ANSWER: (a) Total (variable) cost changes by $6 ($36 − $30) whereas quantity changes by 1. ■

Objective 3

State the assumptions underlying the perfect competition model and relate these to the firm's role as a "price taker."

Some basic assumptions that underlie this and the next five chapters, which are set out in the introduction to Part II, are used for the *perfectly competitive model*. These assumptions are: many small firms producing a homogeneous (standardized) product with free entry into, and exit from, the market in the long run. These assumptions lead to two important implications. Each firm faces a perfectly elastic (horizontal) demand curve, and each firm is a price taker. (page 119)

LEARNING TIP: Perfect competition is the yardstick against which subsequent models will be developed and compared. Learn the criteria that identify perfect competition. ◀

Examples of Perfect Competition: The material in this chapter might put you off because of the lack of plausible examples of perfect competition—it may seem rather artificial. A farmers' market is a reasonable example of a perfectly competitive market—tomatoes are a quite homogeneous product. No single farmer sets his/her price independently and any seller who prices above the going rate will make no sales. Traditional examples come from the farming sector (wheat, apples, eggs), but financial markets offer close approximations. In Chapter 9 (page 205) the textbook authors offer the example of hot dog vendors in New York. In the schoolyard, trading in baseball cards fits the criteria quite well. By definition, any seller who claims product differentiation ("We're better than the other firms!") cannot be perfectly competitive.

ECONOMICS IN PRACTICE (SUPPLEMENTAL): Clear-cut examples of perfect competition are hard to find in the real world—it is, after all, a theoretical construct. Around many college campuses, a fairly recent major candidate as a perfectly competitive market is the provision of word processing services. Check by going over each of the criteria for perfect competition and see how well this service fits.

ANSWER: For many, entry into and exit from this market are virtually free—providers already have both skills and computers, and may not even have to surrender a regular job. In college towns, (free) bulletin boards reveal large numbers of advertisers competing to produce term papers and resumes that must be executed according to established conventions (homogeneous products), thus allowing little in the way of product differentiation or control over the "going" market price. Can you find other examples of goods or services that approximate perfect competition? How about the markets for part-time wait staff or babysitters? Except for the free entry condition, even ticket scalpers at big events resemble perfectly competitive sellers.

Practice

13. In a perfectly competitive industry, the market demand curve is
    (a) vertical.
    (b) horizontal.
    (c) downward sloping.
    (d) upward sloping.

    ANSWER: (c) The market demand curve is downward sloping, although for each individual producer the demand curve is horizontal.

14. Elmo sells in a perfectly competitive market. A perfectly elastic demand curve implies that Elmo
    (a) can attract more customers by pricing below the market price.
    (b) will lose all of his customers if he prices above the market price.
    (c) can increase his total revenue by pricing above the market price.
    (d) can increase his total revenue by decreasing his price below the market price.

    ANSWER: (b) By raising his price Elmo will lose all of his customers and all of his revenue. Elmo can attract as many customers as he wishes at the going price—he doesn't need to cut his price. Recall that a perfectly elastic demand curve is horizontal.

15. In a perfectly competitive industry all of the following are true EXCEPT that
    (a) each firm faces a horizontal demand curve.
    (b) there is free entry into the industry.
    (c) to survive in such a competitive environment, firms must advertise.
    (d) firms sell identical products.

    ANSWER: (c) Advertising is unnecessary. Because firms sell identical products, no firm can advertise its good as special.

16. Elmo's firm will find it difficult to make an excess profit in its perfectly competitive industry because
    (a) his firm faces a perfectly elastic demand curve.
    (b) his firm, and all other firms in the industry, are price takers.
    (c) his firm, and all other firms in the industry, sell identical products.
    (d) firms can enter and leave this industry easily.

    ANSWER: (d) The key factor that squeezes out excess profits is the assumption that firms can enter and leave the industry easily. This affects market supply, price, and profits.

17. Which of the following statements about the perfectly competitive firm is not true?
    (a) The firm's demand curve is perfectly elastic.
    (b) There is free entry into, and exit from, the market.
    (c) The firm advertises in order to distinguish its product from those of its competitors.
    (d) The firm is one of many competing firms, each of which is a price taker.

    ANSWER: (c) Firms produce homogeneous (identical) products. There is no point in advertising. ■

Objective 4

Define marginal revenue and explain why it is constant in perfect competition.

The demand curve faced by the perfectly competitive firm is perfectly elastic (horizontal) and is identical to the marginal revenue curve. Total revenue is price × quantity sold, whereas *marginal revenue* is how much total revenue changes as each extra unit is sold. In perfect competition, marginal revenue equals price (because each extra unit sold increases total revenue by the amount of the price). (page 180)

LEARNING TIP: Mathematically, *marginal revenue* is change in total revenue (*TR*) divided by change in quantity. Boiled down, "change in total revenue" is "change in price × change in quantity." However, in perfect competition, price remains constant as the firm's output level changes. The only way that total revenue can change, then, is through a change in quantity. The marginal revenue formula becomes

$$MR = (\text{Price} \times \text{change in quantity})/\text{change in quantity}$$

Because the "change in quantity" terms cancel, we can see that *MR* equals price (and demand) and, therefore, is constant. ◀

Practice

18. Marginal revenue is defined as
    (a) total revenue divided by quantity.
    (b) total revenue divided by change in quantity.
    (c) change in total revenue divided by quantity.
    (d) change in total revenue divided by change in quantity.

    ANSWER: (d) "Marginal" concepts refer to changes. Refer to page 180. ■

Objective 5

State how firms determine the profit-maximizing level of output and explain why profit is maximized at that production level.

To maximize profits, the firm should produce at the level of production where price (or marginal revenue) is equal to marginal cost. The profit-maximizing condition, then, is *MR* = *MC*. (page 180)

LEARNING TIP: To simplify your study, you can immediately adopt the "*MR* = *MC*" profit-maximizing formula, instead of the "*P* = *MC*" formula used in this chapter. Either formula is correct for perfect competition, but the "*MR* = *MC*" formula applies in *all* the cases you will encounter (e.g., monopoly, monopolistic competition). Knowing how to find the profit-maximizing level of output is one of your most powerful tools in microeconomics.

When *MR* exceeds *MC*, output should be increased—the marginal unit brings in more revenue than it costs. When *MR* is less than *MC*, output should be decreased—the marginal unit costs more than it earns in revenue.

In general, the firm first locates the profit-maximizing level of production—*quantity* is decided first. In perfect competition, the firm is a price taker. In other market structures, you will discover, the price is specified *following* the selection of the level of production.

To see the profit-maximization process in a way you've seen before, reread Application 7 (Deal B) in Chapter 1 of this Guide.

ECONOMICS IN PRACTICE: On pages 182-183, Case, Fair, and Oster present an extended example concerning an ice cream parlor. Let's retain most of the values as they appear. However, minimum wage is increased to $7.25 which makes the gross cost of labor $7.80 per hour (instead of $5.84). Also, the parlor's average purchase is now $1.80. Can you determine the firm's *economic* profit or loss? Should the firm stay in business?

ANSWER: Total revenue is $11,232.00 ($1.80 × 240 × 26). Total fixed cost is unchanged at $3,435.00. Total variable cost has risen to $5,257.20 [($65.400 + $12.00 + $124.80) × 26]. Total costs, therefore, are $8,692.20. Total profit is $2,539.80. Taking into account the owner's implicit wage of $2,500, the ice cream parlor is making an economic profit of $39.80 each month and should continue to operate.

ECONOMICS IN PRACTICE (CONTINUED): Suppose that the monthly rent is hiked by $1,000. Should the firm stay in business now?

ANSWER: In terms of decision-making *in the short run*, nothing has changed, even though the economic profit has been turned into an economic loss. If the firm was at its most desirable output level initially, then it still is. Fixed costs do not enter into consideration. Output decisions depend on the interplay between marginal revenue (which has not changed) and marginal cost (which is not affected by changes in fixed costs). Note that, on page 171, Case, Fair, and Oster point out that "marginal costs reflect changes in variable costs." In the long run, however, it's a different situation. No firm will endure perpetual economic losses, and the firm, once freed of its fixed costs, will shut down.

Practice

19. Complete the following table based on the information given. The price of this product is $10 per unit.

q	TC	TR	MC	MR
0	$10			
1	$18			
2	$24			
3	$30			
4	$36			
5	$40			

| 6 | $54 | _____ | _____ | _____ |
| 7 | $70 | _____ | _____ | _____ |

ANSWER: Refer to the following table.

q	TC	TR	MC	MR
0	$10	$0		
1	$18	$10	$8	$10
2	$24	$20	$6	$10
3	$30	$30	$6	$10
4	$36	$40	$6	$10
5	$40	$50	$4	$10
6	$54	$60	$14	$10
7	$70	$70	$16	$10

20. Referring to the table above, what is the profit-maximizing output level?
    (a) 3 units
    (b) 5 units
    (c) 6 units
    (d) 7 units

    ANSWER: (b) Five units is the last output level at which marginal revenue exceeds marginal cost.

21. Referring to the preceding table, the maximum total profit is
    (a) zero.
    (b) $6.
    (c) $10.
    (d) $50.

    ANSWER: (c) At 5 units, total revenue is $50 and total cost is $40.

22. Jill and John Pantera produce earthenware mugs. They can sell their mugs at $2 each. They find that the marginal cost of production for the first, second, third, fourth, and fifth mug is 50¢, $1.00, $1.50, $2.00, and $2.50, respectively. Assuming that Jill and John do produce some mugs, which of the following statements is true?
    (a) The profit-maximizing output level is three mugs.
    (b) Jill and John can make a positive profit from selling their mugs.
    (c) Jill and John should produce the fourth mug.
    (d) Because marginal cost is increasing by 50¢ per mug, there is a constant rate of increase in total cost.

    ANSWER: (c) The fourth mug allows the Panteras to maximize profits (assuming that profits are made). Option (b) is wrong because we have no information about total cost, only how it's changing. Option (d) is incorrect—refer to the information in the next question.

Use the following information about the Panteras' enterprise, Mugs-R-Us, for the next four questions. Total fixed cost is $4.00. Mugs sell for S2.50 each.

q	TC	TR	MC	MR
0	S4.00			
1	_____	_____	$.50	_____
2	_____	_____	$1.00	_____
3	_____	_____	$1.50	_____
4	_____	_____	$2.00	_____
5	_____	_____	$2.50	_____
6	_____	_____	$3.00	_____

23. Total revenue for 4 mugs is _____ and total cost is _____ .
    (a) $2.50; $4.00
    (b) $10; $9.00
    (c) $2.50; $9.00
    (d) $10; $4.00

    ANSWER: (b) $TR = \$2.50 \times 4 = \$10.00$. $TC = \$4.00 + \$0.50 + \$1.00 + \$1.50 + \$2.00 = \$9.00$. Refer to the following table.

q	TC	TR	MC	MR
0	$4.00	$0.00		
1	$4.50	$2.50	$0.50	$2.50
2	$5.50	$5.00	$1.00	$2.50
3	$7.00	$7.50	$1.50	$2.50
4	$9.00	$10.00	$2.00	$2.50
5	$11.50	$12.50	$2.50	$2.50
6	$14.50	$15.00	$3.00	$2.50

24. At three units of output, marginal revenue _____ marginal cost. To maximize profits, Mugs-R-Us should _____ production.
    (a) exceeds; increase
    (b) exceeds; decrease
    (c) is less than; increase
    (d) is less than; decrease

ANSWER: (a) *MR* = *P* = $2.50. *MC* = $1.50. They should increase production. Refer to Question 23 for the completed table.

25.   To maximize profits, Mugs-R-Us should produce _____ mugs. Jill and John Pantera will make a total economic profit of _____ .
(a)   four; $1.00
(b)   four; –$1.00
(c)   five; $1.00
(d)   five; –$1.00

ANSWER: (c) *MR* = *MC* at five units of output. *TR* = $12.50 and *TC* = $11.50. Refer to Question 23 for the completed table.

26.   If the total fixed cost of production increased to $6.00, Mugs-R-Us should produce _____ mugs. Jill and John Pantera will make a total economic profit of _____ .
(a)   four; $1.00
(b)   four; –$1.00
(c)   five; $1.00
(d)   five; –$1.00

ANSWER: (d) *MC* will not be affected by the change in fixed cost, so the profit-maximizing output level will remain at five units. *TR* will still be $12.50, but *TC* will now be $13.50. Refer to Question 23 for the completed table. ■

Objective 6

Explain why the marginal cost curve above the *AVC* curve is the firm's short-run supply curve.

Marginal cost is identified with the firm's short-run supply curve. As price (and marginal revenue) increase, the firm will increase production. The determining factor is the behavior of marginal cost.

Note that for a portion of its length—the portion where *MC* lies below *AVC*—the marginal cost curve is not the firm's short-run supply curve. In the case where the price is so low that the firm is unable to cover its variable costs, it will close down. The *MC* curve is therefore the short-run supply curve above the *AVC* curve. (page 184)

In the Mugs-R-Us example, if the price of mugs was $1.00, Jill and John would sell only two mugs to maximize profits (or, in this case, to minimize losses). If the price was $1.50, they would sell three. If the price was $2.00, four mugs would be sold.

LEARNING TIP: Table 8.5 (p. 177) in the text offers a convenient summary of many of the points made in the chapter.

The Supply Curve and Marginal Cost: Think back to Chapter 3 and the factors that determine the position of the supply curve—revenues and *costs*. Read pages 63-65 again, keeping the definition of marginal cost in mind. The decision to produce (supply) is based on price (marginal revenue) and the extra cost of production (marginal cost).◀

Practice

Refer to the following table used for the next four questions.

q	TC	MC
0	$3.00	
		$1.50
1	$4.50	
		$1.00
2	$5.50	
		$1.50
3	$7.00	
		$2.00
4	$9.00	
		$2.50
5	$11.50	
		$3.00
6	$14.00	
		$3.50
7	$17.50	
		$4.00
8	$21.50	

27. Given the cost information in the table, if the market price is $1.00, the profit-maximizing quantity produced is _____ , and the economic profit is _____ .
    (a) 0; −$3.00
    (b) 0; −$2.00
    (c) 2; −$3.50
    (d) 2; −$4.50

    ANSWER: (a) Producing any quantity will result in a greater economic loss than not producing at all. When the firm closes down, its loss will equal its fixed costs.

28. Given the cost information in the table, if the market price is $1.50, the profit-maximizing quantity produced is _____ , and the economic profit is _____ .
    (a) 0; −$3.00
    (b) 2; −$2.50
    (c) 3; −$2.50
    (d) 3; −$5.50

    ANSWER: (c) If the firm closes down, it will lose $3.00. Producing 3 units will generate $4.50 in total revenue, which will partly offset the total cost of $7.00.

29. Given the cost information in the table, if the market price is $3.00, the profit-maximizing quantity produced is _____ , and the economic profit is _____ .
    (a) 5; $3.50
    (b) 6; $4.00
    (c) 7; $4.00
    (d) 8; $2.50

    ANSWER: (b) Total revenue is $3.00 × 6 = $18.00. Total cost is $14.00.

30.   Based on your preceding calculations, fill in the following table.

Price	Output
$1.00	_____
$1.50	_____
$2.00	_____
$2.50	_____
$3.00	_____
$3.50	_____
$4.00	_____

ANSWER: Refer to the following completed table.

Price	Output
$1.00	0
$1.50	3
$2.00	4
$2.50	5
$3.00	6
$3.50	7
$4.00	8

BRAIN TEASER SOLUTION: *MR* and *MC* are equal at an output level of two widgets and at an output level of nine widgets. If we produce two widgets, we lose $35. If we produce nine widgets, there is an economic profit of $3.

q	TC	TR	MC	MR	Total Profit
0	$30	0			
1	$50	$15	$20	$15	−$30
2	$65	$30	$15	$15	−$35
3	$75	$45	$10	$15	−$35
4	$83	$60	$8	$15	−$30
5	$90	$75	$7	$15	−$23
6	$98	$90	$8	$15	−$15
7	$107	$105	$9	$15	−$8
8	$117	$120	$10	$15	−$2
9	$132	$135	$15	$15	+$3
10	$152	$150	$20	$15	+$3

The earlier of the two intersection points can never be the profit-maximizing choice because, at all output levels until then, the extra cost of production exceeds the extra revenue earned. Each of these units makes a loss.

We shouldn't set production at eight widgets. Recall that cost includes a normal profit component that is sufficient reward for the entrepreneur. She has enough incentive to produce nine widgets, even though economic profit is unchanged.

PRACTICE TEST

I. MULTIPLE-CHOICE QUESTIONS

Select the option that provides the single best answer.

_____ 1. The *TVC* of 11 units is $100. The *TVC* of 12 units is $120. Marginal cost of the twelfth unit is
 (a) $60.
 (b) $10.
 (c) $120.
 (d) $20.

_____ 2. The short-run supply curve for a perfectly competitive firm is upward sloping because, as production increases,
 (a) the firm must pay higher hourly wages to its workers.
 (b) total fixed costs increase.
 (c) the firm is able to assign its workforce to specialized tasks.
 (d) the marginal productivity of additional workers decreases.

_____ 3. In the short run, which of the following is possible?
 (a) *AFC* may be greater than *ATC*.
 (b) *MC* may intersect *ATC* when *ATC* is decreasing.
 (c) *AFC* may be greater than *AVC*.
 (d) *TFC* falls as output rises.

_____ 4. ABC Corporation and XYZ Corporation have identical total variable costs. ABC's total fixed costs are $10,000/month higher than XYZ's are. ABC's *MC* curve
 (a) is identical to that of XYZ.
 (b) has the same shape, but is higher than that of XYZ.
 (c) has the same shape, but is lower than that of XYZ.
 (d) is higher than that of XYZ, and need not have the same shape.

_____ 5. The firm is at the output level where marginal cost intersects average variable cost. We can infer that average
 (a) variable cost is rising.
 (b) variable cost is falling.
 (c) total cost is falling.
 (d) total cost is rising.

_____ 6. The firm's total cost curve is a straight line sloping up to the right. The marginal cost curve is
 (a) upward sloping as output increases.
 (b) downward sloping as output increases.
 (c) horizontal.
 (d) horizontal and equal to zero.

_____ 7.   In the short run, profits will be maximized at the output level where
      (a)   price is equal to marginal revenue.
      (b)   marginal cost is equal to average variable cost (which is when AVC is minimized).
      (c)   average total cost is minimized (and is equal to marginal cost).
      (d)   marginal cost is equal to price (which is equal to marginal revenue).

_____ 8.   At the current production level, ATC is increasing. Of the following situations, we should consider increasing production if price
      (a)   is less than average total cost.
      (b)   is greater than average total cost.
      (c)   exceeds average variable cost, but less than average total cost.
      (d)   is equal to average total cost.

_____ 9.   In the short run, profits will be maximized at that output level where
      (a)   total revenues are maximized.
      (b)   total costs are minimized.
      (c)   marginal costs and marginal revenues are equalized.
      (d)   variable costs are minimized.

_____ 10.   HAL Corporation, a perfectly competitive firm, is currently producing 20 units. The price is $10 per unit, total fixed costs are $10, and average variable costs are $3. The firm is
      (a)   making a total profit of $130.
      (b)   maximizing profit.
      (c)   making a loss of $3 per unit.
      (d)   making a profit of $7 per unit.

Use the following information for the next four questions. Notebooks sell for $4 apiece. Write On Inc. can produce one notebook for a total cost of $3, two notebooks for a total cost of $6, three for $10, four for S15, and five for $21. Total fixed cost is $1.

_____ 11.   The marginal revenue of the fourth unit is
      (a) $2.
      (b) $3.
      (c) $4.
      (d) $5.

_____ 12.   The marginal cost of the second unit is
      (a) $2.
      (b) $3.
      (c) $4.
      (d) $6.

_____ 13.   To maximize profits, Write On will produce
      (a)   two units.
      (b)   three units.
      (c)   four units.
      (d)   five units.

_____ 14.   The average variable cost of five units is
      (a) $20.
      (b) $4.
      (c) $21.
      (d) $6.

Use the following information for the next two questions. Total fixed cost is $20.

Output	ATC
2	$20
3	$15
4	$14
5	$16

_____ 15.   Which of the following statements is false?
(a)   The total cost of producing four units is $56.
(b)   The marginal cost of the fifth unit is $2.
(c)   The average variable cost of the fifth unit is $12.
(d)   The marginal cost of the third unit is $5.

_____ 16.   If the price of this product was $10, _____ units should be produced. _____ profit would be made.
(a)   three; $15
(b)   three; –$15
(c)   four; $16
(d)   four; –$16

Use the following diagram, which refers to Jill and John's Jugs, to answer the next six questions.

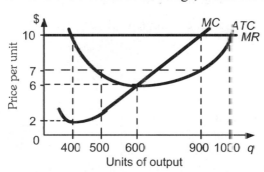

_____ 17.   In the preceding diagram, the profit-maximizing output level is
(a)   400 jugs.
(b)   600 jugs.
(c)   900 jugs.
(d)   1,000 jugs.

_____ 18.   In the preceding diagram, if the firm produces 600 jugs, its profit will be
(a)   zero.
(b) $2,400.
(c) $3,600.
(d) $6,300.

_____ 19.   In the preceding diagram, if the firm produces 400 jugs, its total cost will be
(a) $10.
(b) $400.
(c) $800.
(d) $4,000.

_____ 20. In the preceding diagram, if the firm is producing 600 jugs it should _____ to maximize profits.
(a) increase output to 900 jugs
(b) increase output to 1,000 jugs
(c) maintain its current output level
(d) increase price to $20 and increase output to 1,000 jugs

_____ 21. In the preceding diagram, if the firm produces 900 jugs, total revenue is
(a) $2,700.
(b) $5,600.
(c) $6,300.
(d) $9,000.

_____ 22. In the preceding diagram, if the firm expands production from 600 jugs to 900 jugs, profit will
(a) increase from zero to $2,700.
(b) decrease from $2,400 to zero.
(c) decrease from $2,400 to $1,800.
(d) increase from $2,400 to $2,700.

Use the following information to answer the next three questions. Freda's Flip-Flops, a perfectly competitive firm, is producing 10 units of output (pairs of flip-flops). The market price is $6.00 per pair, average variable costs are $3.50, and total fixed costs are $10.00.

_____ 23. The firm will make a total economic profit of
(a) $15.00.
(b) $1.50.
(c) –$7.50.
(d) –$75.00.

_____ 24. To maximize profits, this firm should
(a) increase output.
(b) decrease output.
(c) maintain its current level of production.
(d) Additional information is needed to answer the question.

_____ 25. Freda now tells you that she is considering increasing production to 11 pairs of flip-flops. *AVC* will increase to $4.00 per pair. Should she expand output?
(a) Yes, because Freda will make an economic profit of $22.00.
(b) Yes, because the marginal cost of the 11th pair of flip-flops is less than the marginal revenue.
(c) No, because the marginal cost of the 11th pair of flip-flops exceeds the marginal revenue.
(d) No, because Freda's average profit will decrease.

_____ 26. The demand curve faced by a perfectly competitive firm is
(a) always downward sloping.
(b) horizontal.
(c) perfectly inelastic.
(d) downward sloping if the law of demand applies.

_____ 27. Each of the following is a decision that must be made by a perfectly competitive firm EXCEPT
   (a) which price level to set for its output.
   (b) how much of each input to demand.
   (c) how to produce its output.
   (d) how much output to supply.

_____ 28. The perfectly competitive firm has no choice regarding
   (a) the price that may be charged.
   (b) how much output to produce.
   (c) the choice of technology.
   (d) how much of each input to hire.

II. APPLICATION QUESTIONS

1. Here is a production function for XYZ Incorporated.

Number of Workers	Output	TVC	TFC	TC	AVC	AFC	ATC	MC
0	0	___	___	___	—	—	—	—
1	12	___	___	___	___	___	___	___
2	31	___	___	___	___	___	___	___
3	41	___	___	___	___	___	___	___
4	50	___	___	___	___	___	___	___
5	58	___	___	___	___	___	___	___
6	64	___	___	___	___	___	___	___
7	67	___	___	___	___	___	___	___

The firm's overheads/day are:

Taxes	$ 15
Rent	$ 50
Machines	$45
Total/day	$110

The variable costs/day are the $30 wage for each worker hired.
   (a) The firm is operating in the short run. How can you tell?

   (b) What is happening to marginal product? Why? (Refer to Chapter 7 if you're uncertain.) At which output level is marginal product greatest?

   (c) Use the figures given to derive the cost information for the table.

(d)   Use the figures to sketch diagrams of the average cost curves and marginal cost. (Remember that the "average-marginal rule" guarantees that *MC* will intersect *AVC* and *ATC* at their minimum points!)

(e)   Compare the output level where *MP* peaks with the output level where *MC* bottoms out. Why are they the same?

2.   You are hired as a consultant by Ken's Cuddly Critters, a manufacturer of soft toy animals. Ken has the most modern equipment and a well-motivated workforce, but he is not sure whether he is maximizing his profits. You are given the following information about Ken's costs and the market he faces. Ken informs you that production comes in "batches" of 100 animals.

Note: The "Other Costs" category includes items like rent, interest on bank loans incurred by Ken, and an allowance for capital depreciation.

Animals per Week	Labor Costs per Week	Material Costs per Week	Other Costs per Week	Sales Revenue per Week
0	$200	$0	$300	$0
100	$250	$150	$300	$430
200	$350	$320	$300	$860
300	$470	$510	$300	$1,290
400	$610	$720	$300	$1,720
500	$770	$950	$300	$2,150
600	$950	$1,200	$300	$2,580
700	$1,150	$1,470	$300	$3,010

(a)   What is the price per stuffed animal?

(b)   Calculate Ken's total fixed cost.

(c)   Calculate Ken's marginal cost per animal and complete the following table.

Animals per Week	Marginal Cost per Week
0–100	
101–200	
201–300	
301–400	
401–500	
501–600	
601–700	

(d)   Having compiled your information, you ask Ken for his present output level and are told that output is 200 animals per week. Ken asks if this is the profit-maximizing output level and, if not, how he should adjust his production. How should you respond?

(e)   Before he makes his decision to accept your recommendation, Ken asks what the maximum economic profit will be.

(f)   Ken now tells you that his landlord is proposing a rent increase to $200 per week, effective next week. How does this change in Ken's costs affect your recommendations?

3.   Examine the following data:

$q = 50$ units $TVC = \$750$ $AVC = \$15$
$TC = \$1,000$ $TFC = \$250$ $AFC = \$5$

The cost of producing the 51st unit is $25. Sketch the *AFC, AVC, ATC,* and *MC* curves as they would be at an output level of 50 units.

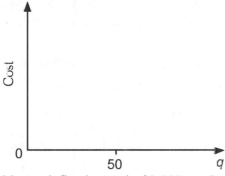

4.   Average total cost is $300, total fixed cost is $2,000, and total cost is $6,000. Calculate the average variable cost.

5.   Total fixed cost is $20, average variable cost is $10, and average total cost is $11. Calculate total variable cost, total cost, and the output level.

         TVC _____   *TC* _____   *q* _____

Extra practice: In each case, sketch the cost curves and indicate the given level of production.

6.   Following is the Average Total Cost schedule for the Watergate Tape-Erase Corporation.

Quantity	ATC
100	$100
101	$101
102	$102

      The firm is currently maximizing profits by selling 101 tape erasers. The president of the corporation, Silas S. Golden, is approached by the White House with an urgent request for an additional tape eraser. He is offered $200.
      Assume that the additional sale will not influence present market sales. If his only criterion is maximizing profits, should he fill the order? Why?

7. Examine the following information about two methods of producing basketballs.

	Method 1		Method 2		Costs	
Output	Capital	Labor	Capital	Labor	TVC	TC
11	7	2	2	6	_____	_____
12	8	4	3	9	_____	_____
13	10	6	4	13	_____	_____
14	12	9	7	18	_____	_____
15	15	11	10	25	_____	_____
16	19	14	13	31	_____	_____

Overheads are $40. Machines and workers cost $4 and $2, respectively.

(a) Work out the total costs and total variable costs of production. Which method of production is cheaper?

(b) Which method is cheaper at low levels of production?

(c) When should the firm switch to the other method?

Note that if input prices for capital and labor were $2 and $4, respectively, different conclusions about the methods of production would be drawn.

(d) If the price of a basketball is $13, how many should the firm produce to maximize profits? _____

(e) Given your answer in Part (d), how much profit is made? _____

8. Suppose that the total costs of a purely competitive firm are as follows:

Output	TFC	MC	TVC	TC	TR	P(MR)	Profit
0	$20	$0	_____	_____	_____	_____	_____
1	_____	$10	_____	_____	_____	_____	_____
2	_____	$20	_____	_____	_____	_____	_____
3	_____	$30	_____	_____	_____	_____	_____
4	_____	$40	_____	_____	_____	_____	_____
5	_____	$50	_____	_____	_____	_____	_____
6	_____	$60	_____	_____	_____	_____	_____

(a) Complete the *TVC* and *TC* columns.

(b) The price of the product is $30. Fill in the *TR* column.

(c) Compare the *TC* and *TR* columns to fill in the profit column.

(d) To maximize profits, what output should the firm choose? _____

What will be the firm's total profit? _____

(e) Fill in the *P(MR)* column. Using the *MR* = *MC* (profit maximization) rule, what output should the firm choose? _____

(f) What do you predict will happen to the number of firms in this industry? In that case, what will happen to supply and to the market price?

(g) Now work out the profit-maximizing output levels when price is
$20 $40 $50 $60

(h)   Graph these points on the following diagram. It's a marginal cost curve, and—because it shows how much will be supplied at each price level—a supply curve, too.

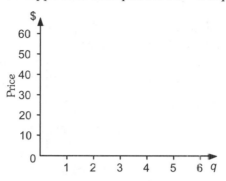

9.   ABC Baseball Corporation checks its production costs. Its overheads are $200 daily, and three workers (the only variable resource) are hired daily, each for $25. Production is running at 500 units per day. If a fourth worker is employed, production would rise to 550 units per day.

(a)   Calculate the marginal product of the fourth worker and the (approximate) marginal cost of the 550th unit.

(b)   Sketch the MC, AVC, and ATC curves for the firm, based on your knowledge and the information given.

(c)   If the price of baseballs is $1 each, is this firm at its profit-maximizing output level? If not, why not? Should the firm increase or decrease its level of production? Explain. Calculate total profit at output levels of 500 and 550.

10.   The table includes information about a perfectly competitive firm.

Output	Total Cost
0	$10
1	$40
2	$60
3	$90
4	$130

Use the table to find the following values.

(a)   Marginal cost of the third unit _____

(b)   Total fixed cost _____

(c)   AVC if four units are produced _____

(d)   The number of units the firm should produce if the price is $30 each _____

(e)   The firm's maximum profit _____

11.   (a)   If average total costs are $500, total fixed costs are $4,000, and total costs are $10,000, calculate the AVC.

(b)   If total fixed costs are $30, average variable costs are $28, and average costs are $31, calculate TVC _____ and the output level.

(c)   If average total costs are $300, total fixed costs are $2,000, and total costs are $6,000, calculate the AVC.

(d)   If total fixed costs are $20, average variable costs are $10, and average total costs are $11, calculate *TVC* _____ and the output level.

12.   ABC Baseball Corporation checks its costs of production. Total fixed costs are $100 daily, and three workers (the only variable resource) are hired daily, each for $20. Production is running at 400 units per day. If a fourth worker is employed, production would rise to 440 units per day.

(a)   Calculate the marginal product of the fourth worker.

(b)   Calculate the marginal cost of the 440th unit.

(c)   If the price of baseballs is $2 each, is this firm at its profit-maximizing output level? If not, why not?

(d)   Should the firm increase or decrease its level of production? Explain.

(e)   Calculate total profit at output levels of 400 and 440.

13.   In Chapter 7 we visited Wilma's Wicker Baskets and found the following production information. Now suppose that each worker costs $24 to hire. In addition, Wilma's Wicker Baskets has total fixed costs of $30.

(a)   Insert the total fixed cost, total variable cost, and total cost values in the following table.

Labor	Total Product	Total Fixed Cost	Total Variable Cost	Total Cost
0	0			
1	5			
2	16			
3	27			
4	36			
5	44			
6	51			
7	56			
8	60			
9	63			
10	65			

(b) Insert the average fixed cost, average variable cost, average total cost, and marginal cost values in the following table.

Labor	Total Product	Average Fixed Cost	Average Variable Cost	Average Total Cost	Marginal Cost
0	0				
1	5				
2	16				
3	27				
4	36				
5	44				
6	51				
7	56				
8	60				
9	63				
10	65				

(c) At a price of $3.00, how many baskets of output will Wilma produce to maximize profits?

(d) At a price of $3.00, determine how much of an economic profit or loss the firm will make in the short run.

(e) At a price of $4.80, how many baskets of output will Wilma produce to maximize profits?

(f) At a price of $4.80, determine how much of an economic profit or loss the firm will make in the short run.

Practice Test SOLUTIONS

I. SOLUTIONS TO MULTIPLE-CHOICE QUESTIONS

1. (d) Marginal cost is the change in total cost ($20) divided by the change in quantity produced (1).

2. (d) The shape of the marginal cost curve is affected by marginal productivity. The upward-sloping section of the *MC* curve is related to diminishing returns as additional units of variable inputs (workers) are added.

3. (c) When low levels of output are produced, few variable resources are hired and fixed costs can exceed variable costs.

4. (a) Fixed costs (which do not change as output level changes) have no effect on the value of marginal cost.

5. (c) *AVC* will be at its minimum value and neither rising nor falling. Because marginal cost is lower than *ATC*, *ATC* will be decreasing.

6.   (c)   *MC* is the change in total cost divided by the change in quantity produced, i.e., the slope of the *TC* curve. With a straight-line *TC* curve, *MC* is constant.

7.   (d)   In perfect competition, price and marginal revenue have the same value. To maximize profits, the firm should produce at the level of output where $MR = MC$.

8.   (b)   If *ATC* is rising, *MC* must be above it. In perfect competition, price equals *MR*. The profit-maximizing firm should increase production only if *MR* exceeds *MC*. This *may* be the case only if price (*MR*) exceeds *ATC*. In all other cases, *MR* is less than *MC* and output should be reduced. Draw the diagram to verify this.

9.   (c)   The profit-maximizing condition is that *MR* should equal *MC*.

10.   (a) $TR = P \times q = \$10 \times 20 = \$200$.
$TVC = AVC \times q = \$3 \times 20 = \$60$.
$TC = TFC + TVC = \$10 + \$60 = \$70$.
Total economic profit $= TR - TC = \$200 - \$70 = \$130$.

The following table applies to the next four questions.

q	0	1	2	3	4	5
TC	$1	$3	$6	$10	$15	$21
MC	—	$2	$3	$4	$5	$6
MR	—	$4	$4	$4	$4	$4

11.   (c)   Marginal revenue is a change in total revenue divided by the change in quantity and is constant for all output levels.

12.   (b)   Refer to the preceding table.

13.   (b)   Write On should produce at the level of output where $MR = MC$.

14.   (b) $TVC = TC - TFC = \$21 - \$1 = \$20$. $AVC = TVC/q = \$20/5 = \$4$.

15.   (b)   *TC* at 4 units of output is $56 ($14 × 4). *TC* at 5 units of output is $80 ($16 × 5). $MC = \$24/1 = \$24$.

16.   (b)   At 3 units, $MR = \$10$ and $MC = \$5$. At 4 units, $MR = \$10$ and $MC = \$11$. At 3 units, $TR = \$30$ and $TC = \$45$.

17.   (c) $MR = MC$ when the output level is 900.

18.   (b) $TR = \$10 \times 600 = \$6,000$. $TC = \$6 \times 600 = \$3,600$.

19.   (d) $TC = ATC \times q = \$10 \times 400 = \$4,000$.

20.   (a) $MR = MC$ at 900 units of output. Note: The perfectly competitive firm is a price taker and cannot increase its price.

21.   (d) $TR = P \times q = \$10 \times 900 = \$9,000$.

22. (d) At 600, $TR - TC = \$6,000 - \$3,600 = \$2,400$.
         At 900, $TR - TC = \$9,000 - \$6,300 = \$2,700$.

23. (a) Total economic profit is total revenue minus total cost. Total revenue is $\$6.00 \times 10 = \$60.00$. Total cost is TVC plus TFC. TVC is $AVC \times$ quantity, or $\$35.00$ ($\$3.50 \times 10$). TFC is $\$10.00$.

24. (d) Surprisingly, none of the other options is certainly true. To maximize profits, this firm needs to know the relationship between marginal revenue, which is $\$6.00$, and marginal cost, which is unknown. Because the firm is making an economic profit, the "shutdown" case (refer to Chapter 9) is ruled out.

25. (c) Freda's average profit will decrease (Option D), but this is not relevant to her decision—total profit may increase even when average profit is decreasing. Freda must compare marginal revenue and marginal cost. Total variable cost of 10 units is $\$35.00$; total variable cost of 11 units is $\$44.00$. MC is $\$9.00$. MR is $\$6.00$. Because MR is less than MC, the 11th unit should not be produced.

26. (b) Each firm is a price taker facing a perfectly elastic (horizontal) demand curve.

27. (a) The perfectly competitive firm is, by definition, a price taker and cannot set the price for its output.

28. (a) The perfectly competitive firm is a price taker.

II. SOLUTIONS TO APPLICATION QUESTIONS

1. (a) There are some fixed costs. That can happen only in the short run.

    (b) Marginal product is decreasing as production increases. This is happening because of diminishing marginal productivity. Marginal productivity is greatest with the second worker (19 units).

    (c) Refer to the following table.

Number of Workers	Output	TVC	TFC	TC	AVC	AFC	ATC	MC
0	0	$0	$110	$110	—	—	—	—
1	12	$30	$110	$140	$2.50	$9.16	$11.67	$2.50
2	31	$60	$110	$170	$1.94	$3.55	$5.48	$1.58
3	41	$90	$110	$200	$2.20	$2.68	$4.88	$3.00
4	50	$120	$110	$230	$2.40	$2.20	$4.60	$3.33
5	58	$150	$110	$260	$2.59	$1.90	$4.48	$3.75
6	64	$180	$110	$290	$2.81	$1.72	$4.53	$5.00
7	67	$210	$110	$320	$3.13	$1.64	$4.78	$10.00

    (d) Refer to the following diagram. Note that marginal curves are drawn halfway between the quantity values.

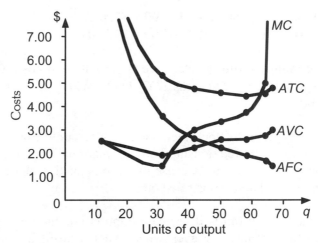

(e) The two levels are the same. At that output level, the extra worker is the most productive of all, so the extra hiring cost is spread over the largest number of extra units.

2. (a) $4.30

(b) Ken's total fixed cost includes any costs that are present when output is zero, therefore, total fixed cost equals $500.

(c) Refer to the following table.

Animals per Week	Marginal Cost per Week
0–100	$2.00
101–200	$2.70
201–300	$3.10
301–400	$3.50
401–500	$3.90
501–600	$4.30
601–700	$4.70

(d) If output is 200, marginal cost is $2.70. Because the price is $4.30, the marginal revenue is also $4.30. Because marginal cost is less than marginal revenue, Ken should increase output. In fact, the profit-maximizing output level is 600.

(e) Ken's maximum profit is $TR - TC = \$2,580 - \$2,450 = \$130$.

(f) This change in Ken's costs will not affect the profit-maximizing output level. Rent is a fixed cost, which, therefore, does not influence marginal cost.

3. Refer to the following diagram.

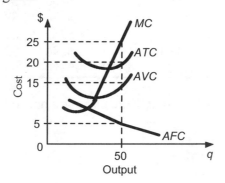

4. $TVC = TC - TFC = 6,000 - 2,000 = 4,000.$ $q = TC/ATC = 6,000/300 = 20.$
     So, $AVC = 4,000/20 = 200.$

5. $AFC = ATC - AVC = \$11 - \$10 = \$1.$ $q = TFC/AFC = \$20/\$1 = 20.$
     $TVC = AVC \times q = \$10 \times 20 = \$200.$ $TC = TVC + TFC = \$200 + \$20 = \$220.$

6.   Silas should not produce the extra tape eraser. To determine this, we need to know marginal revenue and marginal cost information. The marginal revenue is $200. The marginal cost is $203.

Quantity	ATC	TC	MC
100	$100	$10,000	
101	$101	$10,201	$201
102	$102	$10,404	$203

Because the marginal cost of the extra unit exceeds $200, Silas's total economic profit would be reduced by filling the order.

7.   (a)   Refer to the following table. Neither method is always cheaper.

     (b)   Method 2 is cheaper up to and including 14 units of output.

     (c)   After producing the 14th unit of output, Method 1 is cheaper.

	Method 1		Method 2		Costs	
Output	Capital	Labor	Capital	Labor	TVC	TC
11	7	2	2	6	$20	$60
12	8	4	3	9	$30	$70
13	10	6	4	13	$42	$82
14	12	9	7	18	$64	$104
15	15	11	10	25	$82	$122
16	19	14	13	31	$104	$144

     (d)   Produce 13 units.

     (e)   Total profit would be ($13 × 13) – $82 = $87.

8.   (a)   Refer to the following table.

Output	TFC	MC	TVC	TC	TR	P(MR)	Profit
0	$20	—	$0	$20	$0	$30	–$20
1	$20	$10	$10	$30	$30	$30	$0
2	$20	$20	$30	$50	$60	$30	$10
3	$20	$30	$60	$80	$90	$30	$10
4	$20	$40	$100	$120	$120	$30	$0
5	$20	$50	$150	$170	$150	$30	–$20
6	$20	$60	$210	$230	$180	$30	–$50

     (b)   Refer to the preceding table.

     (c)   Refer to the preceding table.

     (d)   The firm should produce three units for a total profit of $10.

(e)   Refer to the table. The firm will choose to produce three units.

(f)   There should be an increase in the number of firms in the long run. Supply will shift to the right, making the market price fall.

(g)   When price is $20, the profit-maximizing output level is two units; at $40, it's four; at $50, it's five; and at $60, it's six.

(h)   Refer to the following diagram.

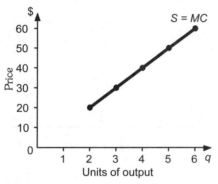

9.   (a)   Marginal product of the fourth worker is 50 units (550 − 500). The approximate marginal cost of the 550th unit is 50¢. $25 wage ÷ 50.

     (b)   Refer to the following diagram. Note that this diagram shows only the parts of the curves about which we have information—some guesswork is involved. *ATC* is falling, from 55¢ (275/500) to 54.54¢ (300/550), indicating that *MC* is below *ATC*. *AVC* is rising, from 15¢ (75/500) to 18.2¢ (100/550), indicating that *MC* is above *AVC*.

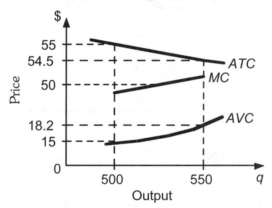

     (c)   Price (marginal revenue) is greater than marginal cost. To maximize profit it should increase production until $P = MC$. At 500 units the firm's profit is $225, and at 550 units its profit is $250.

10.   (a)   Marginal cost is change in total cost ($90 − $60) divided by change in quantity (1). $MC = $30.

     (b)   When no output is produced, no variable resources are hired and all costs are fixed. *TFC* = $10.

     (c) $TVC = TC − TFC$. At four units, $TVC = $130 − $10 = 120.
$AVC = TVC/q = $120/4 = 30.

     (d)   If the price is $30, then *MR* is also $30. The firm should produce up to the output level where *MC* is $30—that is, three units.

(e) $TR = P \times q$. At three units, $TR = \$30 \times 3 = \$90$. $TC = \$90$. The firm is earning a normal profit.

11. (a) $TC = ATC \times q = \$10,000 = \$500 \times q \quad q = 20$
$TVC = TC - \text{TFC} = \$10,000 - \$4,000 = \$6,000$
$AVC = TVC/q = \$6,000/20 = \$300$.

(b) $AFC = ATC - AVC = \$31 - \$28 = \$3$
$TFC = AFC \times q = \$3 \times q = 30 \quad q = 10$
$TVC = AVC \times q = \$28 \times 10 = \$280$

(c) $TC = ATC \times q = \$6,000 = \$300 \times q \quad q = 20$
$TVC = TC - \text{TFC} = \$6,000 - \$2,000 = \$4,000$.
$AVC = TVC/q = \$4,000/20 = \$200$.

(d) $AFC = ATC - AVC = \$11 - \$10 = \$1$
$TFC = AFC \times q = \$1 \times q = 20 \quad q = 20$.
$TVC = AVC \times q = \$10 \times 20 = \$200$.

12. (a) $MP =$ change in total product (40) divided by change in quantity of input (1) = 40.

(b) $MC =$ change in total cost ($20) divided by change in quantity of output (40) = 50¢.

(c) The firm is not at its profit-maximizing output level because marginal revenue ($2.00) is not equal to marginal cost (50¢).

(d) The firm should increase production. The 441st baseball, for instance, will increase profits by $1.50.

(e) Total profit = total revenue – total cost.
At 400 units of output:
$$TR = P \times q = \$2 \times 400 = \$800$$
$$TC = TFC + TVC = \$100 + \$60 = \$160$$
Total Profit = $800 – $160 = $640
At 440 units of output:
$$TR = P \times q = \$2 \times 440 = \$880$$
$$TC = TFC + TVC = \$100 + \$80 = \$180$$
Total Profit = $880 – $180 = $700

13. (a) Refer to the following table.

Labor	Total Product	Total Fixed Cost	Total Variable Cost	Total Cost
0	0	$30	$0	$30
1	5	$30	$24	$54
2	16	$30	$48	$78
3	27	$30	$72	$102
4	36	$30	$96	$126
5	44	$30	$120	$150
6	51	$30	$144	$174
7	56	$30	$168	$198
8	60	$30	$192	$222
9	63	$30	$216	$246
10	65	$30	$240	$270

(b)   Refer to the following table.

Labor	Total Product	Average Fixed Cost	Average Variable Cost	Average Total Cost	Marginal Cost
0	0	—	—	—	—
1	5	$6.00	$4.80	$10.80	$4.80
2	16	$1.88	$3.00	$4.88	$2.18
3	27	$1.11	$2.67	$3.78	$2.18
4	36	$0.83	$2.67	$3.50	$2.67
5	44	$0.68	$2.73	$3.41	$3.00
6	51	$0.59	$2.82	$3.41	$3.43
7	56	$0.54	$3.00	$3.54	$4.80
8	60	$0.50	$3.20	$3.70	$6.00
9	63	$0.48	$3.43	$3.91	$8.00
10	65	$0.46	$3.69	$4.15	$12.00

(c)   At a price of $3.00, Wilma will produce 44 baskets. This output is where her marginal revenue and marginal cost are equal.

(d)   At a price of $3.00, Wilma will earn an economic loss of $18, because total revenue is only $132, whereas total cost is $150.

(e)   At a price of $4.80, Wilma will produce 56 baskets.

(f)   At a price of $4.80, Wilma will earn an economic profit of $70.80 because total revenue is $268.80, whereas total cost is $198.

Long-Run Costs and Output Decisions

1. Graph a firm in short-run equilibrium that is making profits (losses) and identify those profits (losses). Explain the rationale behind the decision to shut down or not shut down when short-run losses occur.
2. Explain why the firm's short-run supply curve is the section of the MC curve above AVC. Derive the industry supply curve and explain the factors that shift the industry supply curve in the long run.
3. Explain why the long-run average cost curve is U-shaped. Distinguish between, and outline, both the short-run explanation and the long-run explanation of U-shaped average cost curves. Provide examples of factors that would cause internal economies or diseconomies of scale. Indicate the long-run profit-maximizing level of production.
4. State the conditions that hold for the firm in long-run competitive equilibrium.
5. Explain the factors that cause increasing-cost, constant-cost, and decreasing-cost industries. Distinguish external from internal economies and diseconomies of scale and explain their role in determining average costs in an industry. List and explain the factors that influence the long-run industry supply curve.

BRAIN TEASER: In 1986, the Reagan administration announced trade sanctions against South Africa's apartheid regime—the importation of ostrich meat was banned. Simultaneously, health-conscious consumers were looking for alternatives to beef—ostrich meat looks and tastes like beef but is low in cholesterol, calories, and fat. Some American farmers moved from traditional livestock and began to raise ostriches. A proven breeding pair could cost up to $70,000, but, in principle at least, they offered a generous return, because an ostrich can provide meat, eggs, leather, and feathers. The initial investment for an ostrich farmer was about $100,000, and this might be recouped within the first year or two.

The ostrich market has many of the hallmarks of perfect competition. Can you identify them? Might ostrich ranching "save the family farm?"

From the late 1980s, there was increasing demand and a very restricted supply of ostrich meat and other products. Predict what happened in this industry in both the short run and long run.

Graph a firm in short-run equilibrium that is making profits (losses) and identify those profits (losses). Explain the rationale behind the decision to shut down or not shut down when short-run losses occur.

In the short run, the firm must be
(1)   making an economic profit;
(2)   breaking even, i.e., making a normal profit; or
(3)   making an economic loss. If the firm can cover its operating expenses, it will continue to produce, otherwise, it will shut down. (page 190)

In the long run, each of the cases above produces a different response.

(1)   The firm making an economic profit will try to expand; new firms, attracted by the extra profits, will enter the industry.

(2)   The firm making a normal profit will maintain its production level; no incentive exists for firms to enter or leave the industry.

(3)   The firm making a loss will leave the industry. (page 194)

LEARNING TIP: The diagrams in this chapter are especially detailed—drawing practice is essential! Redraw each of the four short-run cases—(1) making economic profits, (2) breaking even, (3) making a loss but producing, and (4) making a loss and closing down.

Here is an extended graphical example giving each of the possible short-run cases.

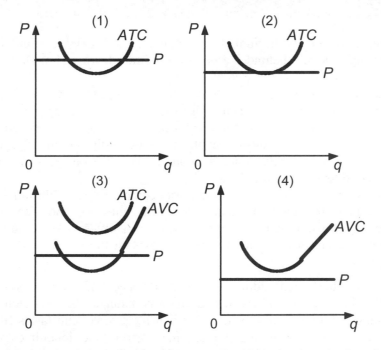

Initially, you're interested only in the "average" curves. For (1), make the price line slice through the *ATC* curve. For (2), the price line just grazes the *ATC* curve at its minimum point. For (3), the price line slices through *AVC* but "misses" *ATC*. For (4), the price line "misses" *AVC* entirely.

Having drawn the price line, draw in the *MC* curve and seek out the profit-maximizing (loss-minimizing) $P = MC$ intersection point. The profit-maximizing quantity (q^*) is where these curves intersect.

Next, work out the total economic profit (Case 1) or loss (Case 3). Find the difference between price and *ATC* at q^*, then multiply by the number of units produced. That gives total profit (or loss). Case 2 gives normal profit. Case 4 gives a loss equal to total fixed costs.◀

Graphing Pointer: When drawing the complete diagram, always start with the "short-run cost diagram" comprised of *AVC*, *ATC*, and *MC*, because this is the most difficult part to draw correctly. The trick then is to position the horizontal price (marginal revenue) line to get the particular result you want.

Practice

Use the following diagram, which describes cost and revenue information for Jill and John Pantera's Mugs-R-Us pitchers, for the next fifteen questions.

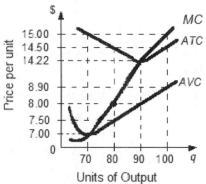

1. If the market price of pitchers is $14.22, Mugs-R-Us should produce _____ pitchers in the short run.
    (a)   70
    (b)   80
    (c)   90
    (d)   100

    ANSWER: (c) The profit-maximizing $MR = MC$ point would be at this output level.

2. If the market price of pitchers is $15.00, Mugs-R-Us should produce _____ pitchers in the short run.
    (a)   70
    (b)   80
    (c)   90
    (d)   100

    ANSWER: (d) The profit-maximizing $MR = MC$ point would be at this output level.

3. If the market price of pitchers is $8.00, Mugs-R-Us should produce _____ pitchers in the short run.
    (a)   70
    (b)   80
    (c)   90
    (d)   100

    ANSWER: (b) The profit-maximizing $MR = MC$ point would be at this output level.

4. If the market price of pitchers is $7.00, Mugs-R-Us should produce _____ pitchers in the short run.
    (a)   70
    (b)   80
    (c)   90
    (d)   100

    ANSWER: (a) The profit-maximizing $MR = MC$ point would be at this output level.

5.   If the market price of pitchers is $6.00, Mugs-R-Us should produce _____ pitchers in the short run.
        (a)   70
        (b)   80
        (c)   90
        (d)   None of the above are correct.
        ANSWER: (d) In fact, Mugs-R-Us should cease operations in the short run because it is not covering its *AVC*.

6.   If the market price of pitchers is $15.00, Mugs-R-Us can earn a _____ economic profit of _____ .
        (a)   positive; $50
        (b)   positive; $1,500
        (c)   negative; $50
        (d)   negative; $1,450
        ANSWER: (a) $TR = \$15 \times 100 = \$1,500$. $TC = \$14.50 \times 100 = \$1,450$. Also, you can use price and *ATC*. At 100 pitchers, P exceeds *ATC* by 50¢ per unit. This is the "per-unit profit." With 100 units, total profit is $50.

7.   If the market price of pitchers is $14.22, Mugs-R-Us can earn an economic profit of _____ .
        (a)   zero
        (b)   −$90
        (c)   −$560
        (d)   −$540
        ANSWER: (a) $P = ATC = MC = \$14.22$.

8.   If the market price of pitchers is $8.00, Mugs-R-Us can earn a _____ economic profit of _____ .
        (a)   positive; $639.80
        (b)   positive; $150
        (c)   negative; $520
        (d)   negative; $640
        ANSWER: (c) $TR = \$8.00 \times 80 = \$640$. $TC = \$14.50 \times 80 = \$1,160$.

9.   At an output level of 70 pitchers, total variable cost is _____ and total fixed cost is _____ .
        (a) $490; $560
        (b) $490; $1050
        (c) $560; $490
        (d) $560; $1050
        ANSWER: (c) $TC = TVC + TFC \rightarrow ATC \times q = (AVC \times q) + (ATC - AVC) \times q = \$15 \times 70 = (\$7 \times 70) + (\$15 - \$7)70 = \$490 + \$560$.

10.   At an output level of 70 pitchers, with a price of $7, Mugs-R-Us makes an economic loss of _____ . If it closes down, Mugs-R-Us will make an economic loss of _____ .
        (a) $490; $490
        (b) $490; $560
        (c) $560; $490
        (d) $560; $560
        ANSWER: (d) If Mugs-R-Us chooses to produce, *TR* will be $7 × 70 = $490. *TC* will be $15 × 70 = $1050. Mugs-R-Us will lose $560. If it closes down, *TR* will be zero, and it will have to pay its fixed costs ($560). Note: At any price less than $7 it is better off closing down. ■

Objective 2

Explain why the firm's short-run supply curve is the section of the MC curve above AVC. Derive the industry supply curve and explain the factors that shift the industry supply curve in the long run.

In the short run, the border between producing at a loss and shutting down occurs where average variable cost is at its minimum (and where marginal cost intersects it). If the price per unit isn't high enough to cover even these minimum average operating expenses, the firm should shut down. Any price above the minimum AVC value will lead to "profit-maximizing" behavior, producing where $P = MC$. Therefore, the portion of the MC curve above its intersection with the AVC curve is the firm's short-run supply curve. (page 193)

The industry supply curve is derived by aggregation. In the short run anything that affects marginal cost, and in the long run alters the number of firms in the industry, can shift the industry supply curve. (page 194)

> **LEARNING TIP:** Table 9.2 (p. 195) in the text is an excellent summary. Refer to it often throughout this chapter.◀

Practice

11. Use the answers to Practice Questions 1–5 to construct a short-run supply schedule for Mugs-R-Us pitchers.

Price	Output
$15.00	____
$14.22	____
$8.90	____
$7.00	____
$6.00	

ANSWER: Refer to the following table.

Price	Output
$15.00	100
$14.22	90
$8.90	80
$7.00	70
$6.00	0

12. A firm makes an operating loss if price is less than average
    (a) total cost.
    (b) total cost but greater than average variable cost.
    (c) variable cost.
    (d) fixed cost.

    ANSWER: (c) Variable costs are the ones that are actively incurred during the firm's operation.

13. If Mugs-R-Us shuts down in the short run, then total
    (a) revenue will be zero and total cost will be zero.
    (b) revenue will be zero but total fixed costs will still have to be paid.
    (c) revenue will be zero but total variable costs will still have to be paid.
    (d) profit will be zero and total costs will be positive.

    ANSWER: (b) In the short run there are some fixed resources (and some fixed costs).

14. If Mugs-R-Us faces a price of $8.90, it will experience an operating
    (a) profit of $112.
    (b) profit of $448.
    (c) loss of $112.
    (d) loss of $448.

    ANSWER: (a) Operating profit or loss depends on price and AVC (times quantity). Refer to page 193.

15. In the short run, Mugs-R-Us will earn a positive economic profit as long as the price is greater than _____ and will produce as long as the price is greater than _____ .
    (a) $7.00; $7.00
    (b) $7.00; $14.22
    (c) $14.22; $7.00
    (d) $14.22; $14.22

    ANSWER: (c) Economic profit occurs as long as price is greater than the minimum ATC value. The firm will continue in operation as long as operating profits can be made (as long as price is greater than the minimum AVC value). ∎

Objective 3

Explain why the long-run average cost curve is U-shaped. Distinguish between, and outline, the short-run explanation and the long-run explanation of U-shaped average cost curves. Provide examples of factors that would cause internal economies or diseconomies of scale. Indicate the long-run profit-maximizing level of production.

In the long run there are no fixed resources—the firm can select any scale of production. The U-shape of the firm's long-run average cost curve can't be due to diminishing returns—the concept of diminishing returns is purely short run. The long-run average cost curve is U-shaped because of internal economies and diseconomies of scale. (The effects of *external* economies and diseconomies are covered in the Appendix.) In the presence of economies of scale, average costs decrease as output rises; in the presence of diseconomies of scale, average costs increase as output rises.

Internal economies of scale (increasing returns to scale) are revealed when the firm's long-run average costs fall as its production increases. If a firm doubles all inputs, output will more than double. Such cost-reducing improvements might be due to standardization or bulk buying. *Internal diseconomies of scale* (decreasing returns to scale) occur when the firm's long-run average costs increase as its production expands. Diseconomies are most frequently blamed on managerial inefficiency as a business becomes too large and unwieldy to operate effectively. Also, regulations (such as fire, health or safety regulations) may only apply to larger firms. Constant returns to scale are a third possibility. (page 195)

Economies and Diseconomies of Scale: Learn the "other names" for internal economies and diseconomies of scale—increasing returns and decreasing returns, respectively. The material in this section explains both the downward- and the upward-sloping long-run average cost curve—why it is U-shaped. As with diminishing returns in the short run (refer to the Learning Tip in Objective 4 of Chapter 7), economies and diseconomies fight for dominance as the firm increases output. Initially, economies of scale represent the stronger effect and push average costs down, but as output rises diseconomies begin to prevail and costs start to rise. The minimum efficient scale is the lowest level of operations at which long-run average costs are minimized.

LEARNING TIP: Keep this material separate from *external* economies and diseconomies of scale (which appear in the Appendix). External economies and diseconomies of scale explain why the firm's *LRAC* curve might shift position (falling in the presence of external economies and rising in the presence of external diseconomies) as output rises. A quick example: As an industry expands, the skilled workers it needs will be able to command higher wages, pushing costs up for all firms, even for those firms that are not expanding production. ◄

Graphing Pointer: As with the short-run diagrams, it's important to draw the long-run diagrams and work though the adjustment process for the firm and industry. This is fairly complicated, as your depiction depends on the assumptions you make about internal and external returns to scale. To start, the simplest assumption is to suppose that the firm faces a U-shaped, long-run average cost curve and constant external returns to scale. Refer to Application Question 9 for some guided practice.

ECONOMICS IN PRACTICE: On page 197, the textbook reports on the presence of economies of scale in Dongguan. Many have argued that China's expansion in manufacturing is due simply to cheap labor or weak regulation. Do Dongguan's successful factories offer an alternative explanation for China's thriving manufacturing sector?
ANSWER: Although cheap labor may have been a factor in firms deciding to establish facilities in Dongguan, the evidence suggests that it's economies of scale and low transportation costs that allow them to retain their competitive edge.

ECONOMICS IN PRACTICE: On page 198, the textbook looks at the economies of scale that may result from the manufacture of solar power generators. A single large system is simply cheaper to set up than multiple medium-sized projects. Often, proposed mergers which would increase the new company's scale of operations are promoted as good for consumers—lower costs, improved service, and so on. In 2008, the buyout of XM by Sirius Satellite Radio was presented as giving subscribers access to both services on one interoperable radio. Can you think of other areas of the economy where mergers are a prominent feature? What might be causing these consolidations?
ANSWER: How about the banking sector, where the number of banks has been halved over the past 20 years? Bookstores, where Borders, Barnes and Noble, and Amazon flourish and small local stores languish? Pet stores? Cell phones? Undoubtedly, in many cases the larger companies gain through bulk-buying and bargaining power, with Wal-Mart being an obvious example. Larger companies also may have the clout to negotiate preferential deals with state or local governments. In some cases (cell phones, Amazon, for instance) a technological innovation may be the main factor driving change. Changes in government regulations may also have an impact. Historically, small banks have been given preferential treatment by regulators. Reductions in those benefits would favor larger banks.

Practice

16.   If a firm experiences constant returns to scale, its long-run average cost curve will be
   (a)   horizontal.
   (b)   U-shaped.
   (c)   upward sloping.
   (d)   downward sloping.

   ANSWER: (a)   Refer to page 199. Increasing returns reduce average costs; decreasing returns increase average costs.

17.   Each point on the long-run average cost curve indicates, at that given output level, the
      (a)   minimum possible average cost when the scale of production can be changed.
      (b)   minimum possible average cost when the scale of production is fixed.
      (c)   average cost due to economies of scale.
      (d)   average cost due to diseconomies of scale.

      ANSWER: (a)   Refer to page 197. In the long run (when all inputs can be adjusted), the firm can vary inputs to minimize costs at any given output level. The long-run average cost curve depicts the lowest cost per unit in these circumstances.

18.   Vigor Vitamins discovers the following long-run information. When it produces 100 units, its total cost is $50; when it produces 200 units, its total cost is $76; and when it produces 300 units, its total cost is $99. Vigor is exhibiting _____ between 100 and 200 units of output and _____ between 200 and 300 units of output.
      (a)   economies of scale; economies of scale
      (b)   economies of scale; diseconomies of scale
      (c)   diseconomies of scale; economies of scale
      (d)   diseconomies of scale; diseconomies of scale

      ANSWER: (a)   At 100 units, *LRAC* is 50¢; at 200 units, *LRAC* is 38¢; at 300 units, *LRAC* is 33¢. *LRAC* is decreasing.

In the following diagram, cost and revenue information is presented for Vigor Vitamins, a typical firm in the vitamin industry. In the short run, Vigor's total fixed costs are $10. Assume that Vigor is currently producing 200 units. Initially the market price is 38¢ per unit. Use the following diagram to answer the next three questions. Assume no external economies or diseconomies of scale.

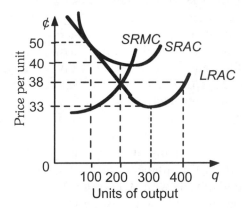

19.   The market price per unit is 38¢ per unit. If the firm is producing 200 units, we can say that in the short run the firm
      (a)   is earning a normal profit.
      (b)   is earning a positive economic profit.
      (c)   is earning a negative economic profit.
      (d)   should close down.

      ANSWER: (c)   The *SRAC* of 40¢ is greater than 38¢ at 200 units of output. This firm is not maximizing profits in the short run because *MR* (38¢) does not equal *SRMC*.

20. The market price per unit is 38¢ per unit. In the short run, at 200 units of output, Vigor is making an operating _____ ; in the long run, market price will _____ .
    (a) profit; increase
    (b) profit; decrease
    (c) loss; increase
    (d) loss; decrease

    ANSWER: (b) Vigor's total cost is $80 (40¢ × 200) and total fixed cost is $10. *TVC* is $70 whereas *TR* is $76. At long-run equilibrium, price will be driven down to the lowest point on the *LRAC*.

21. In the long run, Vigor will _____ its scale of operations and price will _____ .
    (a) increase; increase
    (b) increase; decrease
    (c) decrease; increase
    (d) decrease; decrease

    ANSWER: (b) To survive in this industry, Vigor must become more efficient by adjusting its scale of production. As Vigor and others become more efficient, price will decrease (to 33¢). ■

Objective 4

State the conditions that hold for the firm in long-run competitive equilibrium.

In the short run, firms may enjoy economic profits or suffer economic losses. In either case, the industry is not in long-run equilibrium because firms will adjust their behavior. Given short-run economic profits, new firms will be attracted to the industry. If all economies of scale have not been fully realized, existing firms have an incentive to expand. The entry of new firms and the expansion of existing firms cause the industry's short-run supply curve to shift to the right, reducing price and eroding profits. In the face of short-run economic losses, firms will quit the industry, causing the industry supply curve to shift left. This raises price and eventually eliminates losses for the surviving firms.

In long-run equilibrium, firms maximize profits ($MR = LRMC$) and make zero economic profit ($P^* = LRAC$). However, profit maximizing occurs in the short run too, where $MR = SRMC$. If the firm is in long-run equilibrium, earning normal profit, then this condition also applies in the short run ($P^* = SRAC$). In perfect competition, where price always equals marginal revenue, the complete long-run equilibrium condition holds: $P^* = SRMC = SRAC = LRAC$. (page 203)

Long-Run Competitive Equilibrium: $P^* = SRMC = SRAC = LRAC$. This is an important result that will be used in later chapters, and it may be dissected to advantage. You know the first three elements from Chapter 8. Check your understanding of each of the following statements.

The firm maximizes profits where P^* (or MR) = $SRMC$. $MC = SRAC$ reveals that unit costs are minimized and that average productivity is maximized—inputs are being allocated efficiently. (Recall that the $SRMC$ and $SRAC$ curves intersect at the minimum point on the average cost curve.)

Competition requires that only normal profits be made in long-run equilibrium, so $P^* = LRAC$. A similar logic holds in the short run, so $P^* = SRAC$. You may question this—can't economic profits occur in the short run? Yes, but to achieve long-run equilibrium, they must have been competed away in a perfectly competitive industry. Notice that in equilibrium the typical firm produces at the lowest possible cost per unit, both in the short run and in the long run. This result occurs because of free entry into and exit from the market, forcing each firm to the most cost-efficient output level.

Why is this an equilibrium? Because there's no incentive to change. No new firms want into the industry (forcing price down); no existing firms are dissatisfied with their normal profits and seeking to leave (forcing price up).

ECONOMICS IN PRACTICE: On page 201, the textbook considers the rather technical issue of the shape of the long-run average cost curve. Is it flat or is it U-shaped? In essence, why might a firm not merely continue to expand its plant indefinitely? Choose a market with which you're familiar, and produce evidence that there is some minimum efficient scale of operations.

ANSWER: Answers will vary, depending on the industry chosen. Sometimes, big is not better and small is not beautiful. If we see an industry containing many successful firms with different scales of operation, this would imply that the long-run average cost curve is fairly flat—there's no advantage to being either big or small. If, on the other hand, most firms are of similar size, or if they have multiple plants, this is evidence that this industry does have some optimal scale of operation—tanning salons, pizzerias, or the hot dog vendors mentioned on page 205 might be examples of this case. The image of small family farms grimly enduring in the face of competition from huge agri-firms also suggests that there is an optimal scale of operation (in this case, large). Over the past 70 years, average farm size has tripled and the number of farms has shrunk by two-thirds. eBay might be a case apart—clearly, if it is technologically feasible, it makes sense to spread costs over one large organization.

ECONOMICS IN PRACTICE (CONTINUED): On a related issue, although the figures in this chapter of the textbook feature a long-run average cost curve, no long-run marginal cost curve is shown. Despite this, can you figure out what the long-run marginal cost curve looks like when the long-run average cost curve is U-shaped and when it is flat? [Hint: Think about the average-marginal rule from Chapter 7.]

ANSWER: When the long-run average cost curve is U-shaped, the long-run marginal cost curve is also U-shaped and intersects it at the average curves minimum point. When the long-run average cost curve is horizontal, the long-run marginal cost curve is horizontal and equal to it. It must be—if the marginal value were not equal to the average then the average wouldn't remain constant.

ECONOMICS IN PRACTICE: The article on page 204 looks at the return of General Motors to profitability following its bail-out by the government. First, what was happening to GM in 2008 as the recession started to bite?

ANSWER: During a recession, consumers typically cut back vigorously on purchases of durable goods such as cars. (One study reports that the income elasticity of demand for cars is +2.4.) On top of this, GM's market share was being eroded, particularly by Toyota and Honda. Given significant economies of scale, the decrease in demand was driving up the average cost of a GM vehicle at precisely the time when prices could not be raised safely. Furthermore, GM had substantial "legacy" costs, such as pension payments to retired workers and required interest payments on debts. (At the time of bankruptcy, GM's debt amounted to $53 billion.)

ECONOMICS IN PRACTICE (CONTINUED): By mid-2010, GM had been restored to profit. How did this occur? Consider both the revenue and cost sides of the situation.

ANSWER: Domestic and international demand expanded following the recession, and due to the "cash for clunkers" program, buyers found GM's newer models more attractive than before. GM's sales for the first quarter of 2010 were 17 percent higher than the year before, with revenues expanding by 40%. Additionally, GM produced more high-margin trucks, and major competitor Toyota suffered some bad publicity. On the supply side, as operations expanded, greater capacity utilization and economies of scale allowed average costs to be reduced.

ECONOMICS IN PRACTICE: On page 205, the textbook discusses the phenomenon of differing prices for hot dogs in New York. Similar results occur throughout the world in tourist traps. Souvenir t-shirts and mugs cost more outside the Tower of London, *barbe de papa* (cotton candy) costs more beside the Eiffel Tower in Paris, *matrushka* dolls cost more at Domodedovo airport in Moscow, and a cold soft drink is more expensive near the Mall in Washington. Why? Are there supply-side issues at play?

ANSWER: Higher prices may be due, in part, to the relative affluence of tourists. Convenience and impulse-buying may be other important demand-side factors. Also, a souvenir bought in Cancun on Spring break may mean more to the purchaser than the same item bought cheaper on eBay after returning home. Given those demand-side aspects, other issues may affect price. Sellers may have to work longer hours or endure uncomfortable heat or cold. In addition, they may need a license or pay higher rents for the use of prime locations.

Practice

In the following diagram, cost and revenue information is presented for Pastry Pie Bakery, a typical firm in the pastry industry. In the short run, Pastry Pie's total fixed costs are $1,000. Assume that there are no external economies or diseconomies of scale. Use the diagram to answer the next five questions.

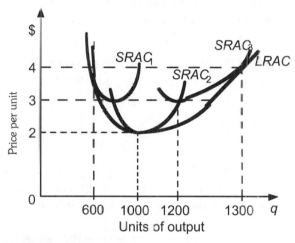

22.   Diseconomies of scale set in after
        (a)   600 units.
        (b)   1,000 units.
        (c)   1,200 units.
        (d)   1,300 units.

        ANSWER: (b) Diseconomies make the *LRAC* curve slope upwards.

23.   In long-run equilibrium, the equilibrium price will be _____ and the equilibrium output level will be _____ .
        (a) $2; 1,300 units
        (b) $2; 1,000 units
        (c) $3; 1,200 units
        (d) $4; 1,300 units

        ANSWER: (b) In long-run equilibrium, the equilibrium price and equilibrium output level depend on the minimum point of the *LRAC* curve.

24.   Suppose that Pastry Pie's *SRAC* curve is $SRAC_3$. The market price is $3.00. In the long run,
        (a)   firms will enter the industry and price will rise because each firm is experiencing internal diseconomies of scale.
        (b)   Pastry Pie will increase its scale of production because it is earning excess profits.
        (c)   Pastry Pie will decrease its scale of production to increase its economic profits.
        (d)   Pastry Pie will reduce its output and the industry will increase output.

        ANSWER: (d) Pastry Pie will be forced to earn normal profits at the minimum *LRAC* point. Because more firms enter the industry, production will increase. Pastry Pie can't earn economic profits in long-run equilibrium. The scale of production will decrease (Option (c)) but economic profit will be zero in long-run equilibrium.

25.   Suppose that Pastry Pie's *SRAC* curve is $SRAC_2$. Demand decreases and the market price falls to $1.50.
      (a)   In the short run, Pastry Pie should shut down.
      (b)   In the long run, the industry supply curve will shift left.
      (c)   In the long run, market demand will increase because the market price has fallen.
      (d)   In the long run, the industry supply curve will not change position.

      ANSWER: (b) The industry supply curve will shift left because firms are leaving the industry. Note: Because Pastry Pie has fixed costs of $1,000, it is worth its while to remain in business in the short run. At an output of 1,000, *TC* is $2,000, $1,000 of which is *TVC*. Because Pastry Pie can earn $1,500, it can cover its operating costs.

26.   Suppose that Pastry Pie's *SRAC* curve is $SRAC_3$. The market price is $3.00. Also suppose that this is an increasing-cost industry. In the long run, the equilibrium price will certainly be
      (a) $3.00.
      (b)   more than $2.00.
      (c)   more than $3.00.
      (d)   between $3.00 and $4.00.

      ANSWER: (b) More than $2.00 is the best answer. If there were constant costs, the equilibrium price would be $2.00. Because of profits, the industry will grow, pushing up the *LRAC* curve. Equilibrium price will certainly be greater than $2.00. ∎

Objective 5 (Appendix)

Explain the factors that cause increasing-cost, constant-cost, and decreasing-cost industries. Distinguish external from internal economies and diseconomies of scale and explain their role in determining average costs in an industry. List and explain the factors that influence the long-run industry supply curve.

An industry may have decreasing costs (which means that it benefits from external economies of scale and has a downward-sloping long-run industry supply curve), increasing costs (which means that it suffers from external diseconomies of scale and has an upward-sloping long-run industry supply curve), or constant costs (where the long-run industry supply curve is horizontal). (page 210)

  External economies of scale are caused by growth in the entire industry and result in decreases in the firm's long-run average costs. If industry growth results in increases in long-run average costs, an *external diseconomy of scale* is present. The *long-run industry supply curve*, which shows how price and total output change as an industry expands in response to an increase in demand, depends on whether external economies or external diseconomies are present. (page 212)

Practice

27.   The typical firm in a perfectly competitive, increasing-cost industry is making economic profits. Predict what will happen in this industry in the long run.
      (a)   Firms will enter this industry. The industry supply curve will shift to the right and the *LRAC* curve will shift down.
      (b)   Firms will enter this industry. The industry supply curve will shift to the right and the *LRAC* curve will shift up.
      (c)   Firms will leave this industry. The industry supply curve will shift to the right and the *LRAC* curve will shift down.
      (d)   Firms will leave this industry. The industry supply curve will shift to the right and the *LRAC* curve will shift up.

ANSWER: (b) Profits attract firms to the industry and supply will increase. Extra competition for scarce resources will make long-run average costs increase.

28.	At all points along the long-run industry supply curve
(a)	industry price level is constant.
(b)	all firms earn a normal profit.
(c)	all firms earn an economic profit.
(d)	industry output level is constant.

ANSWER: (b) In long-run equilibrium, firms can only earn a normal profit.

29.	Refer to the diagram for Vigor Vitamins (in Practice Question 19). Between output levels 300 and 400 the firm is experiencing
(a)	internal economies of scale.
(b)	internal diseconomies of scale.
(c)	external economies of scale.
(d)	external diseconomies of scale.

ANSWER: (b) *LRAC* is increasing. This indicates diseconomies of scale within the firm. Refer to page 200.

30.	Vigor is currently producing 300 units and is in long-run equilibrium. Suddenly demand increases. In the long run, the industry's new equilibrium price stabilizes at 35¢ per unit. This indicates that the industry has experienced external _____ . The long-run industry supply curve is _____ .
(a)	economies of scale; upward sloping
(b)	economies of scale; downward sloping
(c)	diseconomies of scale; upward sloping
(d)	diseconomies of scale; downward sloping

ANSWER: (c) The long-run equilibrium price was 33¢ (minimum *LRAC*). As the industry grew, price increased. This must be due to external diseconomies. ∎

BRAIN TEASER SOLUTION: Perfect competition has many producers (which is potentially correct), selling a homogeneous product in a market with low barriers to entry. Farmers should be price takers. Ostrich farming seems to fit the bill. Small "family" farmers may be squeezed out, however. It depends on economies of scale. If large "agribusinesses" can enter the market, gain economies of scale, and drive down the price, small operators face economic losses. If no such economies of scale exist, small operators should earn long-run normal profits.

There were high short-run profits. Long-run entry into the market was relatively cheap, so early entrants also did well in the long run. However, the market supply curve shifted to the right, driving down the price. On the demand side, meat consumers remained health conscious and advertising campaigns have familiarized consumers with the meat but, by the late 1990s, the price of birds had tumbled. An 18-month-old hen ostrich could be bought for $1,500, and a proven breeding trio of birds could be bought for a total of $5,500. Blown eggs were on sale for $6.50 each. Furthermore, on the supply side, the removal of trade restrictions of South African products and the increase in the number of ostrich ranchers increased foreign supply. As our textbook would predict, only normal profits were being earned in the long run.

PRACTICE TEST

I.   MULTIPLE-CHOICE QUESTIONS

Select the option that provides the single best answer.

_____   1.   ABC Corporation cuts usage of all inputs by 50 percent. Production falls by more than 50 percent. This firm is experiencing
(a)   external economies of scale.
(b)   external diseconomies of scale.
(c)   increasing returns to scale.
(d)   decreasing returns to scale.

_____   2.   In the short run, a perfectly competitive firm incurring losses should still produce if it can cover its
(a)   average costs.
(b)   variable costs.
(c)   fixed costs.
(d)   economic costs.

_____   3.   An industry has external economies of scale. In the long run, an increase in demand will
(a)   decrease price.
(b)   increase price.
(c)   not change price.
(d)   cause an indeterminate change in price.

_____   4.   Suddenly there is an increase in the demand for Frisbees. The most likely result would be
(a)   higher prices in the short run, followed by an increase in production in the long run that would cause prices to decline somewhat.
(b)   higher prices in the short run, followed by larger long-run price increases as the stock of Frisbees is depleted.
(c)   higher prices in the short run because of greater sales volume, and even higher prices later on as plant sizes are increased.
(d)   lower prices in the short run because of higher sales, but higher prices in the long run as the stock of Frisbees is depleted.

_____   5.   In the long-run, perfectly competitive equilibrium, each of the following conditions will hold, EXCEPT
(a) $P = MR$.
(b) $P = SRMC$.
(c) $LRAC$ is minimized.
(d) $SRMC$ is minimized.

_____   6.   An increasing-cost industry experiences external _____ of scale and has a(n) _____ long-run industry supply curve.
(a)   economies; upward-sloping
(b)   economies; downward-sloping
(c)   diseconomies; upward-sloping
(d)   diseconomies; downward-sloping

Use the following table to answer the next seven questions. The data refer to a perfectly competitive firm.

Output	Marginal Cost	AVC	ATC
1	$6.00	$6.00	$24.00
2	$4.00	$5.00	$14.00
3	$2.00	$4.00	$10.00
4	$4.00	$4.00	$8.50
5	$6.00	$4.40	$8.00
6	$8.00	$5.00	$8.00
7	$10.00	$5.72	$8.30

_____ 7. The total fixed cost at six units of output is
- (a) $24.00.
- (b) $8.00.
- (c) $18.00.
- (d) $3.00.

_____ 8. The firm will shut down in the short run if the price falls below
- (a) $8.00.
- (b) $4.00.
- (c) $2.00.
- (d) $6.00.

_____ 9. The price is currently $7.70. To maximize profits in the short run, the firm should
- (a) produce six units.
- (b) produce seven units.
- (c) produce five units.
- (d) shut down.

_____ 10. At this price ($7.70), the firm will make a short-run
- (a) profit of $1.50.
- (b) profit of $2.00.
- (c) loss of $1.50.
- (d) loss of $2.00.

_____ 11. At this price ($7.70), the firm will make a short-run operating
- (a) profit of $1.50.
- (b) profit of $16.50.
- (c) loss of $1.50.
- (d) loss of $16.50.

_____ 12. At this price ($7.70), in the long run firms will _____ this industry. The price will probably _____ .
- (a) enter; increase
- (b) enter; decrease
- (c) leave; increase
- (d) leave; decrease

_____ 13. If this is an industry that is experiencing external diseconomies of scale, the long-run price could be
(a) $7.70.
(b) $8.00.
(c) $8.30.
(d) $9.00.

_____ 14. A perfectly competitive, decreasing-cost industry in long-run equilibrium experiences a permanent decrease in market demand. When the industry reaches its new long-run equilibrium, the equilibrium price of its good will be _____ than before and the equilibrium industry output will be _____ than before.
(a) higher; higher
(b) higher; lower
(c) lower; higher
(d) lower; lower

_____ 15. A firm will not produce where *MR* = *MC* when it is
(a) earning positive economic profits.
(b) making an operating loss.
(c) earning negative economic profits.
(d) making an operating profit.

_____ 16. Jenny's Gemstones is making an operating loss. It should _____ in the short run and _____ in the long run.
(a) shut down; leave the industry
(b) leave the industry; shut down
(c) increase its price; leave the industry
(d) increase its price; reduce production

_____ 17. Jenny's Gemstones is making an operating loss. The industry supply curve will shift _____ in the _____ .
(a) right; short run
(b) right; long run
(c) left; short run
(d) left; long run

_____ 18. Lambert's Lamps finds that when it increases its inputs by 20 percent, its output increases by 25 percent. It can conclude that it is operating in
(a) an increasing-cost industry.
(b) a decreasing-cost industry.
(c) a constant-cost industry.
(d) None of the above are correct.

_____ 19. A perfectly competitive firm sells its output for $40 per unit. Its current output is 1,000 units. At that level, its marginal cost is $50 and increasing, average variable cost is $35, and average total cost is $60. To maximize short-run profits, the firm should
(a) increase production.
(b) increase price.
(c) decrease production.
(d) shut down.

Use the following information to answer the next three questions. Johnny's T-shirts, a perfectly competitive firm, is in long-run equilibrium producing 500 T-shirts per week and operating in an industry that is experiencing external diseconomies of scale . Suddenly, the price of all variable factors of production falls. Also, market demand for T-shirts increases.

_____ 20. In the short run, Johnny's T-shirts will
    (a)   produce more T-shirts, but the effect on profits is uncertain.
    (b)   produce fewer T-shirts and possibly close down.
    (c)   earn positive (economic) profits, but the effect on output is uncertain.
    (d)   produce more T-shirts and earn positive (economic) profits.

_____ 21. In long-run equilibrium, Johnny's T-shirts will
    (a)   produce more than 500 T-shirts per week, but the effect on profits is uncertain.
    (b)   produce fewer than 500 T-shirts per week and earn normal profits.
    (c)   earn normal profits, but the effect on output is uncertain.
    (d)   earn positive (economic) profits, but the effect on output is uncertain.

_____ 22. The short-run industry supply curve will have shifted to the _____ and the long-run industry supply curve is _____ .
    (a)   right; upward sloping
    (b)   right; downward sloping
    (c)   left; upward sloping
    (d)   left; downward sloping

_____ 23. When $P < LRAC$, we would expect _____ and _____ firms in this industry.
    (a)   investment; more
    (b)   investment; fewer
    (c)   disinvestment, more
    (d)   disinvestment; fewer

Use the following diagram, which refers to Jill and John's Jugs, to answer the next two questions. $LRAC$ is minimized at 600 units of output.

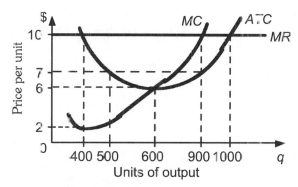

_____ 24. Assume that this firm is maximizing profit in an industry that is experiencing neither external economies nor diseconomies of scale. In the long run, each existing firm will
    (a)   expand production and new firms will enter the industry.
    (b)   expand production and new firms will leave the industry.
    (c)   reduce production and firms will enter this industry.
    (d)   reduce production and firms will leave this industry.

_____ 25.   Assume that this firm is operating in an industry that is experiencing external economies of scale. In the long run, price will be
(a) $6 per unit.
(b)   between $10 per unit and $6 per unit.
(c)   less than $6 per unit.
(d) $10 per unit.

II. APPLICATION QUESTIONS

1.   Review: Check your understanding of the short-run relationships among costs, revenue, and the behavior of the firm in the following table.

Treat each of the examples as a *separate* case.

Assume that *MC* is increasing as output is increasing. The asterisk (*) indicates that the value given is the *minimum ATC or AVC*.

Fill in the spaces and enter in the "Response" column one of the responses provided.

Firm	P	q	TR	TC	TFC	TVC	ATC	AVC	MC	Response
Firm A	10	___	500	___	___		12*	9	___	___
Firm B	10	200	___	___	300			8*	___	___
Firm C	10	___	1,000	___	200			4	10	___
Firm D	___	___	2,000	___	1,500	1,400		7	4	___
Firm E	10	___	700	___	___		8	6	7	___
Firm F	10	___	1,000	___	___		12*	11	___	___
Firm G	10	100	___	___	300			9*	___	___
Firm H	10	___	700	___	140			12	8	___

Response	Meaning
1	The firm is now at the profit-maximizing output level
2	The firm should increase output to maximize profits
3	The firm should decrease output to maximize profits
4	The firm should close down operations

Sketch the diagram for Case A.

2.   Suppose you are a consultant for ABC Inc., a firm in a perfectly competitive industry. Your research reveals two facts: (1) that the cost of producing the final unit of output is just equal to the market price, and (2) that the firm's total revenue is greater than its total variable cost and less than its total fixed cost. What would you recommend ABC do in the short run and in the long run?

     Now XYZ, a firm in the same industry, requests your advice. Your research reveals that: (1) the cost of producing the final unit of output is just equal to the market price, and (2) the firm's total revenue is both greater than its total fixed cost and less than its total variable cost. What would you recommend XYZ do in the short run and in the long run?

3. Currently your firm is losing $2,000 per month. Variable costs are running at $1,200 per month. Your economist advises you to shut down. Why or why not should you accept her advice? The economist adds that your firm is experiencing diminishing marginal product but increasing returns to scale. Isn't there an inconsistency here? Should you fire her?

4. You have been hired as a consultant for DEF, Inc., a firm in a perfectly competitive industry with no external economies or diseconomies of scale. You have developed the following total cost information, based on three feasible plant sizes ("small," "medium," and "large").

q	TC_{small}	TC_{medium}	TC_{large}
0	$1.00	$3.40	$5.00
1	$5.00	$7.40	$12.00
2	$8.00	$10.40	$18.00
3	$9.60	$12.90	$21.00
4	$12.00	$15.00	$23.60
5	$16.00	$16.00	$25.00
6	$20.40	$16.80	$25.80
7	$28.00	$17.50	$26.67
8	$44.80	$18.00	$27.60
9	$68.40	$22.50	$28.71
10	$96.00	$30.00	$30.00
11	$127.60	$41.25	$31.35
12	$163.20	$57.00	$33.00
13	$202.80	$78.00	$36.40
14	$252.00	$112.00	$42.00

(a) Calculate the average total cost information and complete the following table.

q	ATC_{small}	ATC_{mecium}	ATC_{large}
1	_____	_____	_____
2	_____	_____	_____
3	_____	_____	_____
4	_____	_____	_____
5	_____	_____	_____
6	_____	_____	_____
7	_____	_____	_____
8	_____	_____	_____
9	_____	_____	_____
10	_____	_____	_____
11	_____	_____	_____
12	_____	_____	_____
13	_____	_____	_____
14	_____	_____	_____

(b)   Calculate the marginal cost information and complete the following table.

q	MC_{small}	MC_{medium}	MC_{large}
1			
2			
3			
4			
5			
6			
7			
8			
9			
10			
11			
12			
13			
14			

(c)   The market price is $2.40. Based on the information you have and knowing that DEF is intending to produce four units of output, in which plant size, if any, would you advise the firm to invest?

(d)   The market price is $2.40. If DEF wishes to maximize profits, which is the optimal plant size, in your opinion? How many units should be produced? Calculate the firm's economic profit.

(e)   Draw DEF's short-run average cost curves first, and then the long-run average cost curve.

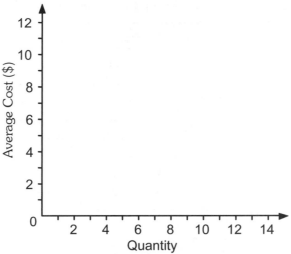

(f)   Over what range of output is DEF experiencing internal economies of scale? Internal diseconomies?

(g)   Consider your answer to Part (d). Is this the end of the adjustments that DEF will face? Describe any further changes that will occur in this industry. Draw a diagram with both market demand and supply curves, and the long-run industry supply curve.

5.   In the following diagram, draw the firm's demand curve.

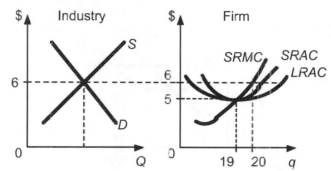

Determine the market price. The firm will make a short-run _____ (profit/loss) of $S_____.
Determine the short-run, profit-maximizing output level. We would expect firms to _____
(enter/leave) this industry.

6.   Draw the "short-run cost diagram" comprised of AVC, ATC, and MC.

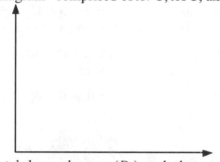

(a)   Draw in a horizontal demand curve (D_a) such that economic profits can be earned. Pick
      out the profit-maximizing output level (q_a).

(b)   Repeat the process, drawing the demand curve (D_b) so that only normal profits occur (q_b).

(c)   Repeat the process, drawing the demand curve (D_c) so that a loss is made but the firm
      continues to produce (q_c).

(d)   Draw in the demand curve (D_d) that would just permit the firm to cover its operating
      expenses (q_d).

(e)   Lastly, present the "shutdown" case (D_e).

(f)   Highlight all the points on the MC curve where production will occur. Confirm that it's
      the short-run supply curve.

7.   Examine the following diagram.

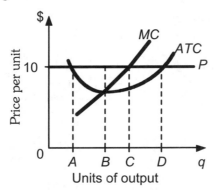

(a)   What can you tell from it? Is it short run or long run? Can profits be made or are losses inevitable? Should the firm shut down? At which output level would profits be maximized?

(b)   At Point *A*, price is equal to average total cost. How much profit is being made here? Is this a long-run equilibrium? If not, how about Point *D*?

(c)   Suppose this is a constant-cost industry. Can you say anything definite about the price level? The number of firms in the market?

8.   Interpret the following diagram, and predict what will happen in this industry.

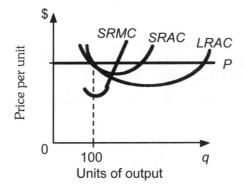

(a)   In the short run, at 100, are any profits being made?

(b)   In the long run, what will happen in this industry?

9.   Study the following diagram. Assume constant costs for the industry. The firm's long-run average cost curve is $LRAC_1$.

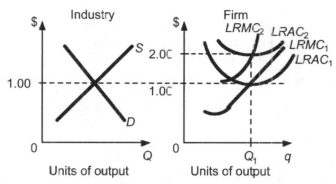

(a)   Verify that the firm is making normal profits and that it is in long-run equilibrium at a price of $1.

Suppose that there is an increase in average costs to $LRAC_2$.

(b)   What will happen to the average and marginal cost curves?

(c)   What will happen to the short-run profits of the typical firm in this industry?

(d)   What will happen to output in the short run, and why?

(e)   What will happen to industry supply in the long run, and why?

(f)   If this had been an increasing-cost industry, would average cost be experiencing a pressure to rise or fall?

10.   In the following diagram, which is for a firm operating in a constant-cost industry, the initial curves have the notation "1"—e.g., demand curve D_1. The firm is at q_1.

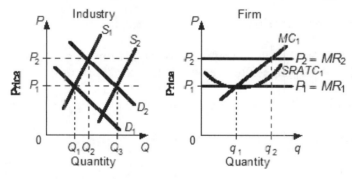

(a)   What will this typical firm will do in the short run?

(b)   Now suppose demand rises to D_2. What are the immediate effects on both the industry and the firm?

(c)   In the short run the firm will produce _____ units and the industry will produce _____ units.

(d)   Examine the graph. Does your answer in Part (c) represent an equilibrium?

(e)   Depict the firm's short-run profits on your diagram.

(f)   Explain your answer to Part (d).

(g)   What will happen to this industry in the long run? How far will price fall?

Note that although more is being supplied by more firms, the size of the typical firm has not changed because of the assumption of a constant-cost industry.

11.   You can display the relationship between *SRAC* curves and the *LRAC* quite simply. Consider the following information about the average costs of three short-run methods of production. In each case one resource is fixed; others are variable.

Output	Method 1	Average Cost Method 2	Method 3
100	10.00	13.00	17.00
200	9.00	11.50	14.30
300	8.50	9.75	12.50
400	8.30	8.40	10.80
500	8.40	8.10	9.60
600	8.90	7.50	8.60
700	9.60	7.30	8.10
800	11.70	7.60	7.80
900	14.80	8.10	8.00
1,000	17.00	8.90	8.30
1,100	23.00	10.20	9.00

(a)   Is each curve a "typical" short-run *ATC* curve?

(b)   Which method should be used if an output of 100 is desired?

(c)   Which method should be used if an output of 500 is desired?

(d)   Which method should be used if an output of 1,000 is desired?

(e)   Plot each of the curves on a single piece of graph paper.

(f)   You're using Method 1. If you want to move from an output level of 100 units to 1,000 units, what would happen to average cost, in the short run?

(g)   In the long run, what would be your lowest-cost strategy?

(h)   What does this firm's *LRAC* curve look like?

(i)   Why is this the *long-run* AC curve?

(j)   When output was doubled from, say, 300 to 600, average costs fell in the long run. What does this information tell you about returns to scale in this part of the firm's *LRAC* curve?

12. There are 100 firms in the perfectly competitive "beanie bear" industry. Each firm has identical costs. The total costs of one such perfectly competitive firm (Barney's Beanie Bears) are as follows:

Output	Total Cost	Total Variable Cost	Average Total Cost	Average Variable Cost	Marginal Cost
0	$10		—	—	—
1	$22				
2	$28				
3	$38				
4	$50				
5	$64				
6	$80				
7	$100				
8	$126				

(a)   Complete the *TVC*, *AVC*, *ATC*, and *MC* columns.

(b)   If the price of the product is $12, what output should the firm choose?

(c)   At a price of $12, how much will be the firm's total economic profit?

(d)   Calculate the firm's total economic profit if the price is $6, $10, $16, or $10, respectively.

Output	Profit when Price = $6	Profit when Price = $10	Profit when Price = $16	Profit when Price = $20
0				
1				
2				
3				
4				
5				
6				
7				
8				

(e)   Collect your answers from the previous question in the following table. At each price level, indicate which case is present, e.g., loss-minimization, shutdown.

Price	Quantity Supplied	Case
S6		
$10		
$12		
$16		
$20		

(f)   Based on your answers to the previous questions, derive values for the "beanie bear" industry supply curve.

Price	Quantity Supplied
$6	
$10	
$12	
$16	
$20	

(g)   Based on your previous analysis, if the price level is currently $12, predict what will happen to the industry supply curve and to the price level in the long run.

13.   In Chapters 7 and 8 we examined the production and cost conditions facing Wilma's Wicker Baskets. The production information is summarized in the following table. Each worker costs $24 to hire, and Wilma has total fixed costs of $30.

Labor	Total Product	Total Cost	Average Variable Cost	Average Total Cost	Marginal Cost
0	0	$30	—	—	—
1	5	$54	$4.80	$10.80	$4.80
2	16	$78	$3.00	$4.88	$1.60
3	27	$102	$2.67	$3.78	$2.18
4	36	$126	$2.67	$3.50	$2.67
5	44	$150	$2.73	$3.41	$3.00
6	51	$174	$2.82	$3.41	$3.43
7	56	$198	$3.00	$3.54	$4.80
8	60	$222	$3.20	$3.70	$6.00
9	63	$246	$3.43	$3.91	$8.00
10	65	$270	$3.69	$4.15	$12.00

(a)   If the price is $1.60, how many baskets should Wilma produce in the short run? What will her economic profit be ?

(b)   What is the lowest price at which Wilma will produce in the short run?

(c)   If the price is $3.43, how many baskets should Wilma produce in the short run? What will her economic profit be ?

(d)   At a price of $3.00, predict what will happen to the number of firms in this industry in the long run. Explain your prediction.

(e)   Wilma operates in an industry with no external economies or diseconomies. At a price of $3.00, predict what will happen to market price in this industry in the long run. Explain your prediction.

(f)   At a price of $6.00, determine how many units Wilma will produce in the short run.

Practice Test SOLUTIONS

I. SOLUTIONS TO MULTIPLE-CHOICE QUESTIONS

1. (c) External (dis)economies of scale refer to industry-wide changes. Refer to page 210.

2. (b) If a firm can earn an operating profit it will minimize losses by producing.

3. (a) Refer to page 211. The long-run industry supply curve is downward sloping.

4. (a) Initially, existing firms will increase production as higher prices earn them greater profits. In the long run, new firms will enter the industry, increasing supply and decreasing the price level.

5. (d) In long-run equilibrium, price will equal the minimum value of average cost. Refer to Figure 9.8 on page 203.

6. (c) As the number of firms increases, costs increase. This pushes up the price charged by the industry.

7. (c) At one unit of output, $TC = ATC \times q = \$24.00$ and $TVC = AVC \times q = \$6.00$. $TFC = TC - TVC$.

8. (b) If price is less than the minimum AVC ($\$4.00$), then the firm should shut down.

9. (c) $P = MR = \$7.70$. To maximize profits, increase production where MR is equal to or exceeds MC.

10. (c) When the output is set at 5 units, $TR = \$7.70 \times 5 = \$38.50$. $TC = ATC \times q = \$8.00 \times 5 = \$40.00$. The firm will make a negative economic profit of $\$1.50$.

11. (b) $TR = \$7.70 \times 5 = \$38.50$. $TVC = \$4.40 \times 5 = \$22.00$.

12. (c) Because losses are being experienced, firms will leave the industry. Market supply will decrease, causing the price to increase (unless there are external economies of scale resulting in a downward-sloping industry supply curve).

13. (a) At a price of $\$7.70$, firms will leave this industry in the long run. In an industry experiencing external diseconomies of scale, this reduction in output will reduce average cost from $\$8.00$ and reduce equilibrium price.

14. (b) In a decreasing-cost industry, costs decrease as output increases, and they increase as output decreases.

15. (b) A firm that is making an operating loss will close down. Note: Making a negative economic profit is not an adequate answer because the firm could still be making an operating profit.

16. (a) Perfectly competitive firms can't change the price they face—they are price takers. Because Jenny can't cover her variable costs, she should shut down in the short run and leave the industry in the long run.

17. (d) Firms will leave the industry in the long run.

18. (d) The behavior of costs for an individual firm (its internal economies of scale) are no guide to the behavior of costs for the entire industry (its external economies of scale).

19. (c) If price is $40, then marginal revenue is also $40. *MR* is less than *MC*—the firm's output level is too high. It should not shut down as it can cover its variable costs.

20. (d) Marginal cost is affected by the behavior of variable costs. A decrease in variable costs will decrease marginal cost. An increase in price will increase marginal revenue. Together, these effects will increase the profit-maximizing output level. In long-run equilibrium, Johnny's T-shirts was earning a normal profit. With higher prices and lower costs, the firm will earn an economic profit.

21. (c) In long-run equilibrium, the competitive firm always earns normal profits. As the industry expands, external diseconomies (increasing costs) are experienced, reducing the firm's profit-maximizing output level. Without extra information we cannot say whether the final output level will be greater than, equal to, or less than 500 T-shirts.

22. (a) New firms have entered this industry, shifting the short-run supply curve to the right. The long-run industry supply curve is upward sloping because of the external diseconomies of scale.

23. (d) If price is less than long-run average cost, disinvestment will occur, and firms will leave the industry in search of normal profits in other activities.

24. (c) New firms will enter, attracted by the economic profits, pushing down the price. As price falls, existing firms will cut back production.

25. (c) As firms enter the industry, external economies of scale will reduce costs. The minimum average cost will be less than $6. In equilibrium, price equals average cost.

II. SOLUTIONS TO APPLICATION QUESTIONS

1. Refer to the following table.

Firm	*P*	*q*	*TR*	*TC*	*TFC*	*TVC*	*ATC*	*AVC*	*MC*	Response
Firm A	10	50	500	600	150	450	12*	9	12	3
Firm B	10	200	2,000	1,900	300	1,600	9.5	8*	8	2
Firm C	10	100	1,000	600	200	400	6	4	10	1
Firm D	10	200	2,000	2,900	1,500	1,400	14.5	7	4	2
Firm E	10	70	700	560	140	420	8	6	7	2
Firm F	10	100	1,000	1,200	100	1,100	12*	11	12	3 or 4
Firm G	10	100	1,000	1,200	300	900	12	9*	9	2
Firm H	10	100	700	1,400	140	1,200	14	12	8	2 or 4

A (fairly complex) sketch that would describe the situation for Firm A is presented next. (For more practice, try to do the other cases—without first peeking at the following sketches!)

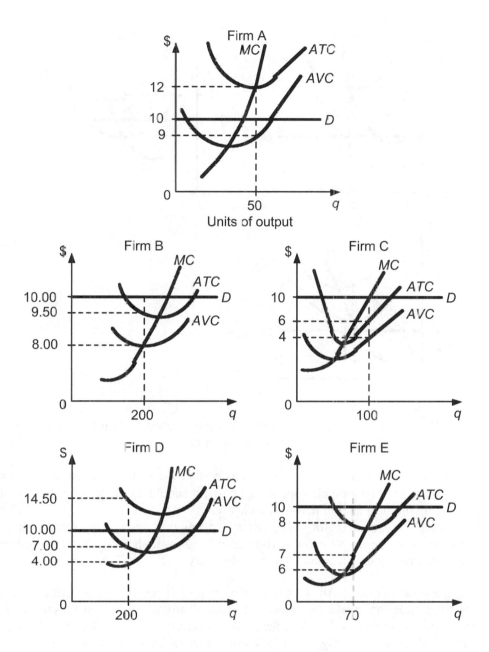

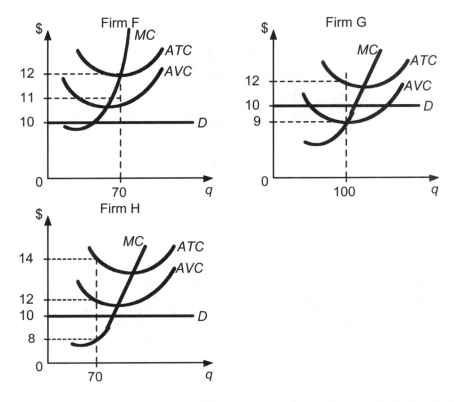

Note: Firm F and Firm H have two possible outcomes, depending on the behavior of *AVC*. Again, try sketching these cases and try to get the different results.

2. ABC. Fact 1 means that $MR = MC$. Fact 2 means that the firm is making an economic loss, but because it is covering its variable (operating) costs, it should continue to produce in the short run. In the long run, the firm should leave the industry.

    XYZ. Fact 1 means that $MR = MC$. Fact 2 means that the firm is making an economic loss and that it is not covering its variable (operating) costs—it should cease production in the short run. In the long run, the firm should leave the industry.

3. The first question to ask is: Am I maximizing profits? If the firm is not producing where $MR = MC$, then the situation might be completely turned around by adjusting output. If the firm is currently producing where $MR = MC$, then price is clearly less than short-run *ATC*. However, it is not clear whether an operating profit is being made. In Case A, the firm should shut down; in Case B, because it can cover its variable costs, it should not.

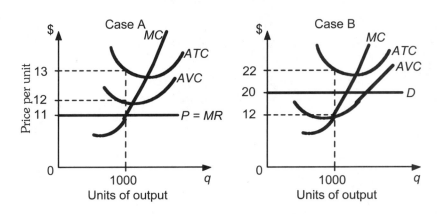

Regarding diminishing returns and increasing returns to scale, there is no inconsistency. The former is a short-run concept (and, in fact, applies for almost all producers) while the latter is a long-run concept.

4.   (a)   Refer to the following table.

q	ATC_{small}	ATC_{medium}	ATC_{large}
1	$5.00	$7.40	$12.00
2	$4.00	$5.20	$9.00
3	$3.20	$4.30	$7.00
4	$3.00	$3.75	$5.90
5	$3.20	$3.20	$5.00
6	$3.40	$2.80	$4.30
7	$4.00	$2.50	$3.81
8	$5.60	$2.25	$3.45
9	$7.60	$2.50	$3.19
10	$9.60	$3.00	$3.00
11	$11.60	$3.75	$2.85
12	$13.60	$4.75	$2.75
13	$15.60	$6.00	$2.80
14	$18.00	$8.00	$3.00

(b)   Refer to the following table.

q	MC_{small}	MC_{medium}	MC_{large}
1	$4.00	$4.00	$7.00
2	$3.00	$3.00	$6.00
3	$1.60	$2.50	$3.00
4	$2.40	$2.10	$2.60
5	$4.00	$1.00	$1.40
6	$4.40	$0.80	$0.80
7	$7.60	$0.70	$0.87
8	$16.80	$0.50	$0.93
9	$23.60	$4.50	$1.11
10	$27.60	$7.50	$1.29
11	$31.60	$11.25	$1.35
12	$35.60	$15.75	$1.65
13	$39.60	$21.00	$3.40
14	$49.20	$34.00	$5.60

(c)   The firm should not produce. Even in the case of the small plant, the firm will incur a loss because $2.40 × 4 is less than $12. If the firm had committed to the small plant, in the short run it should shut down because it cannot cover its variable costs. Note that total fixed costs are only $1.00, with variable costs accounting for the remainder.

(d)   The medium plant is best, with the lowest total costs. Neither of the two other plant sizes has an average cost as low as the price. Producing up to the output where price equals (or is greater than) marginal cost, DEF should produce 8 units of output. The firm's economic profit is ($2.40 − $2.25) × 8, or $1.20.

(e)   Refer to the following diagram.

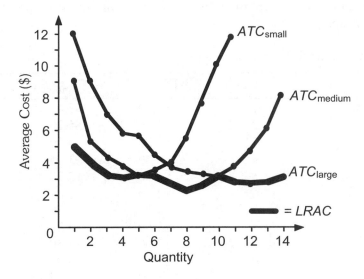

(f)   Internal economies of scale occur until the minimum point of the long-run average cost curve, i.e., at eight units, after which point diseconomies take over.

(g)   Because DEF is earning an economic profit, new firms will enter the industry. There are no external economies or diseconomies of scale, so the firm's long-run average cost curve will not change position. For the same reason, the long-run industry supply curve is horizontal. As new firms enter, market supply increases from S_1 to S_2 and the market price will decrease from $2.40 to $2.25 at which point the process will cease because the market price has reached the minimum long-run average cost. Economic profits have been competed away. Given DEF's marginal cost values, the firm's output will remain at eight units.

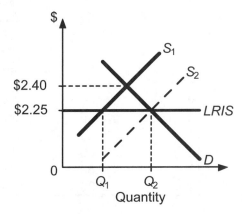

5.   The firm's demand curve graphs as a horizontal line. It is set at the industry level by the forces of demand and supply at a level of $6.

The market price is $6. The firm will make a short-run profit of $20 at an output level of 20 units. We would expect firms to enter this industry.

6.   Refer to the following diagram.

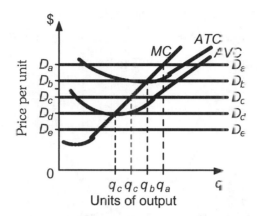

7.   (a)   This is a short-run diagram (because there are economic profits) for a perfectly competitive firm (because the demand curve is horizontal). Price is $10 and the profit-maximizing output level is output level C.

       (b)   The firm is earning normal profit at both Point A and Point D. Neither is a long-run equilibrium, however, because other firms can enter the market and make economic profits.

       (c)   Price will fall and the number of firms will increase.

8.   (a)   The firm is making normal profits ($P = ATC$), but is not maximizing profits because it is not producing where $MR = MC$.

       (b)   In the long run, because price is greater than the minimum $LRAC$ point, firms will enter the industry, forcing price to fall.

9.   (a)   Check that $P = MR = SRMC = SRAC = LRAC$.

       (b)   Average and marginal cost curves will rise.

       (c)   Short-run losses will be encountered.

       (d)   Some firms will shut down in the short run and supply will fall for the industry.

       (e)   Supply will decrease as firms exit the industry.

       (f)   Fall! As output rises for an increasing-cost industry, costs rise. Here output is shrinking, and costs would fall.

10.   (a)   Stay as it is, as it is already profit-maximizing.

       (b)   Price and quantity supplied increase in each case, and the number of firms is unchanged.

       (c) q_2; Q_2

       (d)   Yes in the short run; no in the long run.

       (e)   The profit-maximizing output level occurs where $MR = MC$.

       (f)   In the short run the firm is maximizing profits, but in the long run the economic profits will attract new competitions and a change in price will occur.

       (g)   Entering firms will push the supply curve to the right (to S_2), and price will decline. Price will fall back to its initial level because, at any other price, profits or losses will be made.

11. (a) Yes, each *ATC* is U-shaped.

(b) Method 1, which is cheapest until about 425 units

(c) Method 2 is cheapest from about 425 units until about 875.

(d) Method 3 is cheapest from about 875 units on.

(e)

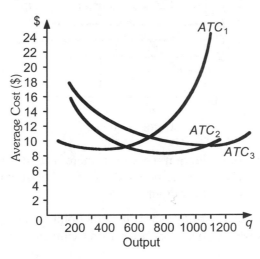

(f) *ATC* would rise to $17.00.

(g) Maintain Method 1 until production has grown to 425 units, then switch to Method 2. Maintain Method 2 until production has grown to 875 units, then switch to Method 3. In effect you are tracing out the *LRAC* for this firm.

(h) U-shaped, *in this case.*

(i) We release the fixed resource constraint as we move from one method of production to the next.

(j) The firm has increasing returns to scale (economies of scale).

12. (a) Refer to the following table.

Output	Total Cost	Total Variable Cost	Average Total Cost	Average Variable Cost	Marginal Cost
0	$10	$0	—	—	—
1	$22	$12	$22.00	$12.00	$12.00
2	$28	$18	$14.00	$9.00	$6.00
3	$38	$28	$12.67	$9.33	$10.00
4	$50	$40	$12.50	$10.00	$12.00
5	$64	$54	$12.80	$10.80	$14.00
6	$80	$70	$13.33	$11.67	$16.00
7	$100	$90	$14.29	$12.86	$20.00
8	$126	$116	$15.75	$14.50	$26.00

(b) The firm should produce four units of output, where *MR* = *MC*.

(c) The firm's total revenue is $48; the firm's total cost is $50. It will make an economic loss of $2.

(d)   Refer to the following table.

Output	Profit when Price = $6	Profit when Price = $10	Profit when Price = $16	Profit when Price = $20
0	−$10	−$10	−$10	−$10
1	−$16	−$12	−$6	−$2
2	−$16	−$8	$4	$12
3	−$20	−$8	$10	$22
4	−$26	−$10	$14	$30
5	−$34	−$14	$16	$36
6	−$44	−$20	$16	$40
7	−$58	−$30	$12	$40
8	−$78	−$46	$2	$34

(e)   Refer to the following table.

Price	Quantity Supplied	Case
$6	0	Shutdown
$10	3	Loss-minimization
$12	4	Profit-maximization
$16	6	Profit-maximization
$20	7	Profit-maximization

(f)   Refer to the following table. There are 100 identical firms. As price increases, output level increases as determined by the behavior of marginal cost.

Price	Quantity Supplied
$6	0
$10	300
$12	400
$16	600
$20	700

(g)   If the price is $12, economic profits are being earned by the typical firm. New firms will enter the industry, shifting the industry supply curve to the right. Consequently, the price will fall.

13.   (a)   Wilma will close down. Her loss will equal her total fixed costs of $30.

(b)   Wilma will produce as long as the price is $2.67 or more. $2.67 is the minimum average variable cost value.

(c)   At a price of $3.43, Wilma will produce 51 baskets and earn an economic profit of 93¢ ($174.93 − $174.00).

(d)   At a price of $3.00, Wilma will produce 44 baskets and make an economic loss of $18. If the typical firm in an industry is making an economic loss, firms will leave the industry in the long run in search of more attractive profits elsewhere.

(e)   As firms leave the industry, the industry supply curve will shift to the left and the market price will increase.

(f)   At a price of $6.00, Wilma will produce 60 baskets.

10

Input Demand: The Labor and Land Markets

Chapter Objectives

1. Explain why input demand is a "derived" demand.
2. Explain why inputs are simultaneously complements and substitutes.
3. Define and calculate marginal revenue product (*MRP*). Find the profit-maximizing hiring level for an input, given *MRP* and input price information. Explain why the *MRP* curve is identical to the input demand curve.
4. Identify the factors that affect the position of an input demand curve and explain how each factor shifts the curve.
5. In a world with more than one variable resource, derive and explain the factors influencing the demand curve for each input.
6. Explain what is meant by the term *pure rent* and explain why it arises.
7. In a world with more than one variable resource, state and interpret the conditions necessary for profit maximization.

Although there is much new material in this chapter, there is also a lot of familiar material, too. The discussion of the input markets reuses tools that you have already developed—e.g., profit maximization, marginal product, demand curves, and elasticity. Take this as a reminder that (for better or for worse) economics is a cumulative discipline—new material doesn't supplant earlier material, it builds upon it.

Keep in mind, too, that although the chapter talks mostly in terms of labor demand, the conclusions apply equally to other inputs, including capital.

BRAIN TEASER: "If employers hire only workers whose *MRP* is greater than or equal to the wage rate, society loses because the unemployed workers could still have produced some positive amount of production, which now is lost." What do you think of this statement? The concept of "consumer surplus" was discussed an earlier chapter. Apply this concept to the labor market, where the final worker hired earns the equivalent of his marginal revenue product. Who gets the "surplus" produced by earlier workers? Unemployed workers (whose marginal revenue product of labor is less than the wage) could still have produced some positive amount of production. Should we balance out the "surplus" and the "loss" and employ these workers? What do you think?

Objective 1

Explain why input demand is a "derived" demand.

When the management of the Miami Heat signs LeBron James to a contract, it does so because of the "output" (points and excitement) that James can produce for the team. The demand for his labor services is a demand *derived* from the demand for the team's output by its public. This specific conclusion is generally true for the demand for all types of input. (page 215)

LEARNING TIP: Review the introductory material on pp. 117-119. The underlying structure of Part II and the ongoing assumptions (perfect knowledge, perfect competition, homogeneous products) for this and subsequent chapters are set out there very clearly.◀

LEARNING TIP: This chapter's main theme is that the value of an input depends on society's valuation of the output produced by that input. Inputs will be hired as long as their contribution to the value of production exceeds their cost.◀

Practice

1.   Which of the following is a "derived demand"?
    (a)   The demand by your *Study Guide*'s author for a word processor
    (b)   The demand for Cracker Jacks at the ball game
    (c)   The demand for tax-free municipal bonds by a highly paid executive seeking to reduce her tax payments
    (d)   The demand for wood that would be used for the construction of new homes

    ANSWER: (d) This option is the only one involving the demand for an input by a producer. Cracker Jacks and bonds are not inputs. Wood, bought by a construction firm, is an input. ∎

Objective 2

Explain why inputs are simultaneously complements and substitutes.

Although fans of the L.A. Lakers might disagree (for them, the only valid product is a "W" in the win column), the product of the Lakers is "entertainment"—the Lakers compete with movies, rock concerts, and so on for the public's leisure dollars. The facilities in the Lakers' stadium add to the entire entertainment package (inputs are complements), but they may be seen as substitutes for Kobe Bryant (a team without a Bryant can attract fans by offering other facilities instead). At the team level, one player can assist (complement) the play of another and can also substitute for that player. (page 216)

ECONOMICS IN PRACTICE: The disruptive effects of the World Cup are mentioned on page 217. As a college student, what is your "production?" Can you think of comparable events during the semester that might diminish your productivity?
ANSWER: In some sense, your output is accumulated knowledge measured, in the first instance, by your grades. Colleges that have fraternity or sorority "rushes" may find student test scores declining during those times. Similarly, during basketball or football seasons, big games (or "March madness") might cause less scholastic effort as students camp out for tickets or travel to support their team. Preparation for Fall or Spring break might have diverted some students from academic concerns!

Practice

2.   Which of the following is true about input markets?
    (a)   Firms demand inputs in the labor market and supply inputs in the capital market.
    (b)   Firms supply inputs in the labor market and demand inputs in the capital market.
    (c)   Households supply inputs in the labor market and demand inputs in the capital market.
    (d)   Households supply inputs in the labor market and supply inputs in the capital market.

    ANSWER: (d) Households supply inputs to all resource markets; firms demand in all resource markets.

3.   To produce cloth, a mill owner must hire a weaver and a loom. The weaver and the loom are
        (a)   substitutable inputs.
        (b)   complementary inputs.
        (c)   both substitutable and complementary inputs.
        (d)   not inputs—they are factors of production.

        ANSWER: (b) To produce cloth, both inputs are required. Note: Factors of production are
                     inputs.

4.   To mine coal, a mine owner can use a robotic drill or a team of coal miners. The drill and the coal
        miners are
        (a)   substitutable inputs.
        (b)   complementary inputs.
        (c)   both substitutable and complementary inputs.
        (d)   unrelated inputs.

        ANSWER: (a) This is an either/or situation. The inputs are substitutes in this case.

5.   To mine coal, a mine owner can use a robotic drill or a team of coal miners. Within the group, the
        coal miners are
        (a)   substitutable inputs.
        (b)   complementary inputs.
        (c)   both substitutable and complementary inputs.
        (d)   unrelated inputs.

        ANSWER: (c) Each miner helps the others to produce coal (complements), and each can take
                     over from another worker (substitutes). Refer to page 216. ■

Objective 3

Define and calculate marginal revenue product (*MRP*). Find the profit-maximizing hiring level for
an input, given *MRP* and input price information. Explain why the *MRP* curve is identical to the
input demand curve.

Marginal revenue product (*MRP*)—the addition to total revenue attributable to the hiring of an additional
input—can be defined as the extra units of output (marginal product) times the price of the product.
Marginal revenue product of labor is the addition to revenue that occurs when an additional worker is
hired—it's the dollar value of the extra merchandise he produces (i.e., MP_L/P). In the short run, as extra
workers are hired, *MRP* falls because of diminishing marginal productivity. The *MRP* curve is typically
downward sloping. (page 217)

To maximize profits, the employer should hire each input up to the point at which *MRP* equals the
cost of hiring that input. For labor, wage will equal *MRP*. (page 219)

The *MRP* curve for a factor of production is identical with the demand curve for that factor. The
demand curve for labor is the marginal revenue product of labor curve. (page 219)

Profit Maximization and the Hiring Decision: Two rules from earlier chapters crop up in the "hiring
decision." The logic of profit maximization ($P = MC$) leads to Wage = MRP_L. No profit-maximizing
employer will hire a worker who doesn't pay his or her way.

Recall the rule developed to describe the consumer's utility-maximizing mix of purchases: the final
dollar spent on each good must provide the same utility. The same logic applies to profit maximization. It
shows up as: $MP_L/P_L = MP_K/P_K = MP_A/P_A$—the final dollar spent on each input must generate the same
amount of additional production.

Comment: Marginal productivity does not decline because the employer hires the "best" resources (workers, for example) first and then hires subsequent workers who are poorer in quality. While this pattern holds in the real world—the boss chooses the most able applicant first—it is not required. Even if all workers are equal in ability, diminishing returns will still set in just as, in Chapter 6, we consume equal additional cans of Coke, diminishing marginal utility will occur.

ECONOMICS IN PRACTICE: Just like Denzel Washington, mentioned on page 223, sports personalities such as Alex Rodriguez or LeBron James command huge salaries. Is the principle the same as in the case of Mr. Washington?

ANSWER: The principle is the same. The Yankees hire A-Rod ($112 million for five years) and the Miami Heat hire James ($110 million for six years) because the managements believe the increased ticket sales, merchandise sales, and advertising revenues will justify the outlay. Also, in sport, as in entertainment, it is important to win—a blockbuster movie is vastly more profitable than a flop. In the NBA, a scoreline of 100-99 is vastly different from a scoreline of 99-100. The contribution of a star, therefore, can be decisive.

ECONOMICS IN PRACTICE (CONTINUED): Another aspect of Denzel Washington's behavior should be considered. Working in theater represents a considerable cut in salary, relative to what he could earn in Hollywood. Why might he wish to accept the lower-paying job?

ANSWER: Denzel Washington may enjoy the variety he gets by mixing theater work and movie assignments and be willing to sacrifice some income. That variety may be worth more to him than a lucrative movie contract. Also, some acting aficionados see theater as "real" acting. By varying the types of assignments he accepts, Mr. Washington may be demonstrating his versatility and, therefore, increasing his market value.

Practice

Tom grows tomatoes, which sell for $1.20 per pound. His variable resource is labor, and he has recorded the productivity of his workers in the following table.

Number of Workers	Total Product	Marginal Product	Marginal Revenue Product
0	0	_____	_____
1	10	_____	_____
2	25	_____	_____
3	38	_____	_____
4	48	_____	_____
5	56	_____	_____

6. Fill in the marginal product and marginal revenue product columns.

ANSWER: Refer to the following table.

Number of Workers	Total Product	Marginal Product	Marginal Revenue Product
0	0		
1	10	10	$12.00
2	25	15	$18.00
3	38	13	$15.60
4	48	10	$12.00
5	56	8	$9.60

7. Graph the marginal product curve for the first five workers below.

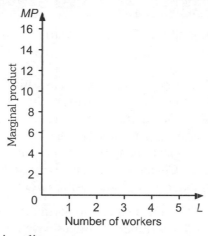

ANSWER: Refer to following diagram.

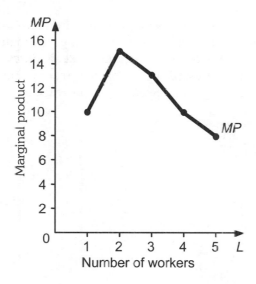

8.   If the wage is $12, Tom should hire
        (a)   two workers.
        (b)   three workers.
        (c)   four workers.
        (d)   five workers.

        ANSWER: (c) To maximize profits, Tom should not hire any worker whose *MRP* is less than $10. The *MRP* of the fifth worker is $9.60.

9.   The maximum wage that Tom would pay if he were to hire three workers is
        (a) $9.60.
        (b) $12.00.
        (c) $15.60.
        (d) $18.00.

        ANSWER: (c) To maximize profits, Tom should not hire the fourth worker (whose *MRP* is $12.00) at any wage above $12.00, but he would be willing to hire the third worker at $15.60. ■

Objective 4

Identify the factors that affect the position of an input demand curve and explain how each factor shifts the curve.

A profit-maximizing employer will hire any worker who pays his/her way. As the wage changes, the hiring level will change too, based on the *MRP* (demand for labor) schedule. Each point on the demand schedule equates input price and *MRP*. The equilibrium hiring condition is: $W = MRP$. It is equivalent to the $P = MC$ profit-maximization rule in output markets. The input demand curve will shift if marginal productivity changes (through technological change) or if the price of the product changes (through a change in the demand for the output). Changes in the quantity and price of other (complementary or substitutable) inputs are other factors that can shift the position of the input demand curve. (page 227)

ECONOMICS IN PRACTICE: On page 226, the textbook looks at the impact on land prices of the Europe's high-speed rail system. At the time of this writing, gas prices have recently crashed through the $4.00 per gallon barrier. What impact would you expect rising gasoline prices to have on prices in that housing market, and why?

ANSWER: With the cost of commuting increasing, distance from work (and from stores and schools) becomes a more important factor. Suburban houses, with long commutes, become less attractive than houses "closer in" (or closer to public transport or park-and-ride facilities) which become more desirable. Accordingly, prices in the already stressed U.S. housing market have reflected changing buyers' concerns. The value of land (and housing) is affected by the presence of nearby features.

Practice

10.   Given your MRP values from Question 6, graph the MRP curve below.

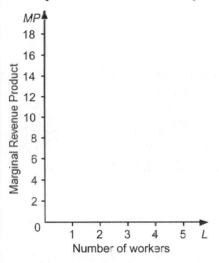

ANSWER: Refer to the following diagram.

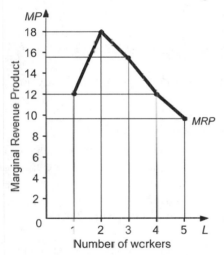

11.   If tomatoes sell for $1.20 a pound, Tom's demand for labor curve will have the same *shape* as the
       (a)   marginal product curve.
       (b)   total product curve.
       (c)   product demand curve.
       (d)   marginal cost curve.

ANSWER: (a) Check the diagram you've just drawn.

12.   Petra's Portland Cement is a perfectly competitive firm. Cement sells at $4 per bag. Petra
       employs 15 workers at a wage of $12 per hour. The marginal revenue product of the fifteenth
       worker is $8 per hour. To increase profits, Petra should
       (a)   increase employment until the *MRP* of labor equals $12.
       (b)   decrease employment until the *MRP* of labor equals $12.
       (c)   increase the price of cement to at least $8 per bag.
       (d)   increase the price of cement to at least $12 per bag.

ANSWER: (b) In a perfectly competitive industry, the producer has no control over price.
             Because wage exceeds *MRP*, Petra should reduce her labor force.

13. The supply of labor for the fishing industry falls. Which of the following events will occur? The wage rate will _____ and firms will _____ employment until *MRP* equals the new wage.
    (a) increase; increase
    (b) increase; decrease
    (c) decrease; increase
    (d) decrease; decrease

    ANSWER: (b) Refer to Figure 10.2 on page 219. A decrease in supply increases the price of labor (wage). To restore equality, *MRP* must increase. To accomplish this, fewer workers will be hired.

14. We saw in Chapter 8 (p. 172) that there is a link between marginal cost and marginal product of labor; in fact, $MC = W/MP_L$. We now know that $MRP_L = MP_L \cdot P$ If DoughCrust Bakery's marginal revenue product of labor is greater than the wage, it must be the case that
    (a) total revenues exceed total costs.
    (b) the wage is greater than the marginal cost.
    (c) DoughCrust's price exceeds its marginal cost.
    (d) DoughCrust's price is less than its marginal cost.

    ANSWER: (c) We know that $MRP_L = MP_L \cdot P$ and are told that $MRP_L > W$, so $MP_L \cdot P > W$. We know that $MC = W/MP_L$ so $MP_L \cdot MC = W$. If $MP_L \cdot P > W$ and $MP_L \cdot MC = W$ then $P > MC$. ■

Objective 5

In a world with more than one variable resource, derive and explain the factors influencing the demand curve for each input.

The same profit-maximizing principles apply with two variable factors of production as with one variable factor of production. However, when more than one factor is involved, an increase in the price of an input has a factor substitution effect and an output effect. These effects explain why, as wage increases, the quantity demanded of labor decreases. As the wage rises, capital is substituted for the now relatively more expensive labor—the factor substitution effect. Also, higher wages may mean higher production costs, lower production and less use of all inputs, including labor—the output effect. (page 222)

> **LEARNING TIP:** The factor substitution effect and the output effect are very closely related, conceptually, to the substitution effect and the income effect that you encountered in Chapter 6.◀
>
> **LEARNING TIP:** You can depict the factor substitution effect and the output effect on a diagram. Draw a labor demand curve. Suppose the price of robot car-machines decreases and that there is job loss on the assembly line. In the labor market, which factor is stronger, the factor substitution effect or the output effect?
>
> The lowered price of robots will increase management's desire to substitute capital for labor. The labor demand curve will decrease—this represents the factor substitution effect. Because production costs have fallen (cheaper robots), the company will wish to expand production because with lower costs and the same selling price, the company will earn higher profits. Expanding production means that the demand for labor will increase—this is the output effect. If labor demand fell, on balance, the factor substitution effect would be stronger.◀

The firm's input demand curve will shift position if demand for the firm's product changes (causing its price to change); if the amount, productivity, or price of other inputs change; or if the state of technology changes. Each of these changes will affect *MRP*—the dollar value of the extra merchandise produced by an additional unit of an input. (page 222)

Practice

15. The tendency of firms to move away from usage of a factor whose price has increased is called the
    (a) output substitution effect.
    (b) factor substitution effect.
    (c) complementarity effect.
    (d) income effect.

    ANSWER: (b) Refer to page 222 for a discussion of the factor substitution effect.

16. The output effect indicates that the quantity demanded of labor will
    (a) increase if the price of the final product increases.
    (b) decrease when the price of other factors increases.
    (c) increase if the price of labor increases.
    (d) increase if the price of labor decreases.

    ANSWER: (d) The output effect helps explain why the quantity of labor demanded increases as the price of labor decreases.

17. Labor is a normal input. If the price of labor increases, the factor substitution effect will cause the demand for labor to _____ and the output effect will cause the demand for labor to _____ .
    (a) increase; increase
    (b) increase; decrease
    (c) decrease; increase
    (d) decrease; decrease

    ANSWER: (d) Other resources will be used instead of the more expensive labor (factor substitution effect). Because costs of production have risen, less will be produced and less labor will be demanded (output effect).

18. The wage of workers (a variable resource) is increased. This will cause each of the following to occur EXCEPT the
    (a) firm's profit-maximizing output level will decrease.
    (b) firm will substitute away from labor to capital.
    (c) output effect will lead to a decrease in the demand for capital as well as labor.
    (d) *MRP* of the final worker hired will decrease.

    ANSWER: (d) Fewer workers are being hired. As extra workers are hired, *MRP* decreases; as fewer are hired, the *MRP* of the final worker increases.

19. The demand for labor will increase if
    (a) the wage paid to labor increases.
    (b) the wage paid to labor decreases.
    (c) there is an increase in the amount of capital used.
    (d) there is a decrease in the amount of capital used.

    ANSWER: (c) Additional capital (machinery) will let workers be more productive, thus affecting *MRP*.

20. A technological advance increases labor productivity. This will cause
    (a) an increase in the demand for labor.
    (b) an increase in the supply of labor.
    (c) a decrease in the demand for labor.
    (d) a decrease in the supply for labor.

    ANSWER: (a) MRP_L ($MP_L \cdot P$) has increased.

21. Mauro uses labor and capital to produce soccer balls. He finds that as the price of capital rises, he hires more workers and cuts back on the use of capital. This behavior is consistent with
    (a)   labor and capital being complementary inputs.
    (b)   the factor substitution effect.
    (c)   the increasing marginal productivity of labor.
    (d)   the dominance of the factor substitution effect over the output effect for capital.

    ANSWER: (b) Simply, Mauro is switching from one input to the other to reduce costs.

22. The demand for soccer balls decreases. This will cause Mauro to _____ his demand for labor and _____ his demand for capital.
    (a)   increase, increase.
    (b)   increase, decrease.
    (c)   decrease, increase.
    (d)   decrease, decrease.

    ANSWER: (d) Mauro will produce less because his costs have risen. He will need fewer workers and less capital. ■

Objective 6

Explain what is meant by the term *pure rent* and explain why it arises.

The market for land differs from the market for labor in one important respect: land prices are demand determined, due to the fact that land is strictly fixed in supply. The return to any factor of production in fixed supply is called a *pure rent*. Any site has a variety of uses and should be allocated to the user who is willing to pay the most. (page 224)

> **LEARNING TIP: Pure rent** emerges when *any* factor (not just land) is fixed in supply. Any payment greater than zero is a "bonus."
>
> Example: Suppose that Marlene has a PC she's willing to lend out (lease, if you want) to her suitemates, Charlene, Arlene, and Darlene. Each has a term paper due tomorrow morning and is willing to pay for the use of the PC (which is the only one available at such short notice). Marlene would take $6, but asks for bids. Charlene offers $7, Arlene, $8, and Darlene, $10. Darlene would have the use of the PC, and Marlene would receive a pure rent of $4.◀

Practice

23. The supply of land of a particular quality at a given location is
    (a)   perfectly elastic.
    (b)   perfectly inelastic.
    (c)   unitarily elastic.
    (d)   dependent on demand.

    ANSWER: (b) The supply of land isn't dependent on demand—the price is. The supply, however, is perfectly insensitive to changes in price.

24. A tax on landowners will _____ the quantity of land supplied and will _____ rents charged.
    (a)   decrease; decrease
    (b)   decrease; not affect
    (c)   not affect; decrease
    (d)   not affect; not affect

ANSWER: (d) The supply, however, is perfectly insensitive to changes in price or taxes. Because the rent charged is demand driven rents will not change. Economic rent will be reduced. ■

Objective 7

In a world with more than one variable resource, state and interpret the conditions necessary for profit maximization.

The profit-maximizing equilibrium is to "balance the margins" according to the following rule: $MRP_L/P_L = MRP_K/P_K = MRP_A/P_A = 1$ (the marginal revenue product/dollar of the final unit of each input should be equal and have a value of one). Put differently, using the least costly method of production, we have: $MP_L/P_L = MP_K/P_K = MP_A/P_A = 1$. (page 227)

Practice

25.   Sellco finds that its workers have an average revenue product of $20 (the final worker adding $10) and its machines have an average revenue product of $100 (the final machine adding $60). Workers earn $15 and machines cost $50. Assuming that Sellco is at the profit-maximizing output level, it should hire _____ workers and hire _____ machines.
(a)   more; more
(b)   more; fewer
(c)   fewer; more
(d)   fewer; fewer

ANSWER: (c) Compare MRP (not average revenue product) with the price of the input. MRP_L is less than P_L and MRP_K is greater than P_K.

By the conclusion of Chapter 10, Case, Fair and Oster have demonstrated how competitive firms decide how much of each resource to hire, how to combine those resources, and how much output to produce. As we shall see, the distribution of income is determined by the marginal revenue product of resources. ■

BRAIN TEASER SOLUTION: The initial statement is true, in that hiring extra workers whose marginal product is positive will make output increase. However, if the wage reflects opportunity cost, society would be gaining output at the cost of other (greater) output forgone. The surplus of workers becomes part of the profit of producers.

PRACTICE TEST

I. MULTIPLE-CHOICE QUESTIONS

Select the option that provides the single best answer.

_____ 1.   The firm has two inputs, capital and labor. Economic theory suggests that
(a)   these inputs are complementary but not substitutable.
(b)   these inputs are substitutable but not complementary.
(c)   these inputs are both complementary and substitutable.
(d)   labor is complementary, whereas capital is substitutable.

_____ 2. Labor demand is a "derived" demand because it
  (a) is derived from the demand for capital.
  (b) depends on the demand for outputs.
  (c) is derived from firms.
  (d) is derived from marginal revenue product.

_____ 3. The firm has one variable input—labor. The demand for labor is labor's
  (a) total product curve.
  (b) productivity times the wage rate.
  (c) marginal product curve.
  (d) marginal revenue product curve.

_____ 4. The firm is hiring labor and capital such that $MRP_L = P_L$ and $MRP_K < P_K$. The firm should certainly hire
  (a) more labor and more capital.
  (b) less capital.
  (c) less labor and less capital.
  (d) less labor and more capital.

_____ 5. You are told that $MP_L/P_L > MP_K/P_K$. Given a fixed amount of funds to produce more output, the firm should
  (a) shift dollars away from labor and toward capital.
  (b) shift dollars away from capital and toward labor.
  (c) hire more capital to increase MP_K.
  (d) hire more capital to decrease MP_K.

_____ 6. Downtown land is a normal input. If the price of downtown land decreases, then the factor substitution effect will _____ the quantity demanded and the output effect will _____ the quantity demanded.
  (a) increase; increase
  (b) increase; decrease
  (c) decrease; increase
  (d) decrease; decrease

_____ 7. The firm has two variable inputs—labor and capital. Suddenly the price of labor falls. The output effect indicates that
  (a) output will fall.
  (b) fewer of all factors will be demanded.
  (c) more labor will be demanded.
  (d) less labor will be demanded.

_____ 8. A firm has one variable input—labor. An increase in the price of the output will
  (a) increase the demand for labor.
  (b) decrease the demand for labor.
  (c) cause the factor substitution effect to outweigh the output effect.
  (d) cause the output effect to outweigh the factor substitution effect.

_____ 9.   The total product from three workers is 32 units and from four workers is 40 units. Output is selling at $2. What is the maximum the firm would be willing to pay the fourth worker?
   (a) $8
   (b) $10
   (c) $16
   (d) $20

_____ 10.   The firm has two variable inputs—labor and capital. Suddenly the price of labor rises. The factor substitution effect indicates that
   (a)   the marginal product of labor will fall.
   (b)   the marginal product of capital will fall.
   (c)   more labor will be demanded.
   (d)   less capital will be demanded.

_____ 11.   Tennis players earn more than economics professors. This is best explained by noting that
   (a)   consumers are willing to spend more to watch a tennis match than to listen to an economics professor.
   (b)   tennis players are more athletic.
   (c)   economics professors last longer—their income is spread out more.
   (d)   the demand for economics professors is more inelastic.

Use the following information to answer the next two questions.

There are five apartment buildings in town. Each year the nonland cost of Building #1 is $10,000; for Building #2, it's $20,000; for Building #3, it's $30,000; and so on.

_____ 12.   If each apartment building could generate $100,000 of revenues each year, how much is the pure economic rent of Building #1?
   (a) $100,000
   (b) $90,000
   (c) $50,000
   (d) $40,000

_____ 13.   If each apartment building could generate $40,000 in revenues each year, which building would earn zero pure economic rent?
   (a)   Building #4
   (b)   Building #3
   (c)   Building #5
   (d)   All plots will earn pure rents.

Use the following information to answer the next five questions.

Rhonda grows peaches, which she sells for $2 per pound. Her variable resource is labor, and she has recorded the productivity of her workers in the following table.

Number of Workers	Total Product	Marginal Product	Marginal Revenue Product
0	0	—	—
1	15		
2	40		
3	60		
4	75		
5	85		

_____ 14. The marginal product of the fifth worker is
   (a)   10.
   (b)   15.
   (c)   17.
   (d)   19.

_____ 15. The marginal revenue product of the second worker is
   (a) $25.
   (b) $30.
   (c) $40.
   (d) $50.

_____ 16. If the wage is $36, Rhonda should hire
   (a)   two workers.
   (b)   three workers.
   (c)   four workers.
   (d)   five workers.

_____ 17. The wage is $36. Currently, Rhonda is employing two workers. If she hires a third worker her profits would
   (a)   increase by $4.
   (b)   increase by $6.
   (c)   decrease by $4.
   (d)   decrease by $6.

_____ 18. The maximum wage that Rhonda would pay if she were to hire three workers is
   (a) $20.
   (b) $30.
   (c) $35.
   (d) $40.

_____ 19.   The price of labor decreases. The quantity demanded of labor will
      (a)   increase, because capital will be substituted for labor.
      (b)   increase, regardless of the relative strengths of the output effect and the factor substitution effect.
      (c)   be indeterminate—the factor substitution effect and the output effect work in opposite directions.
      (d)   decrease—if the output effect dominates the factor substitution effect.

Use the following diagram to answer the next four questions.

Drushka has a small firm that manufactures _matrushka_ dolls. His variable resource—labor—exhibits the marginal productivity behavior shown in the following diagram.

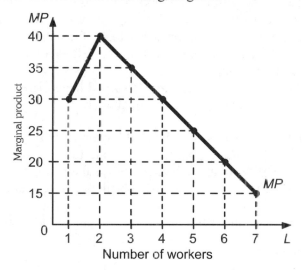

_____ 20.   Each _matrushka_ doll sells for 2 rubles. The marginal revenue product of the third worker is
      (a)   35 rubles.
      (b)   30 rubles.
      (c)   60 rubles.
      (d)   70 rubles.

_____ 21.   If the wage is 40 rubles, Drushka should hire
      (a)   three workers.
      (b)   four workers.
      (c)   five workers.
      (d)   six workers.

_____ 22.   The wage is 50 rubles. Currently, Drushka is employing five workers. If he hires a sixth worker his profits would
      (a)   increase by 5 rubles.
      (b)   increase by 10 rubles.
      (c)   decrease by 5 rubles.
      (d)   decrease by 10 rubles.

_____ 23.   The maximum wage that Drushka would pay if he were to hire four workers is
(a)   30 rubles.
(b)   40 rubles.
(c)   50 rubles.
(d)   60 rubles.

_____ 24.   Hitoshi, the owner of a Japanese restaurant, tells you that, because of an increase in the wage rate, he has sold the tables and chairs he used for outside seating and has reduced his hours of business. In economic terms, you could tell him each of the following EXCEPT that he
(a)   might have made a mistake. The factor substitution effect should have led him to substitute away from labor and to increase his capital.
(b)   has made a smart move. The wage hike has caused higher costs, which should lead him to cut production according to the output effect.
(c)   has made a smart move. The output effect of the wage hike has caused less demand for all inputs.
(d)   might have made a mistake. He should have increased output and hired more of all inputs to cover the increased labor costs.

_____ 25.   The price of labor increases. The demand for capital will
(a)   increase, because capital will be substituted for labor.
(b)   increase, if the output effect dominates the factor substitution effect.
(c)   be indeterminate—the factor substitution effect and the output effect work in opposite directions.
(d)   decrease—higher costs will reduce output and less capital will be needed.

II. APPLICATION QUESTIONS

1.   Palmer's flour mill operates in a perfectly competitive market and employs labor and capital. Labor costs $30 per day. Machines cost $36 per day. Currently, Palmer's has six machines and the marginal revenue product of capital is $30. Output sells at $5 per unit. Palmer's hires you as a consultant and provides you with the following production function.

Workers (days)	Total Output
1	9
2	17
3	24
4	30
5	35
6	39
7	42

(a)   In the short run, how many workers do you recommend Palmer's should hire per day to maximize profits?

(b)   Currently, is Palmer's maximizing profit? How can you tell?

(c)   In the short run, how can Palmer's improve its profitability?

(d)   In the long run, if Palmer's maintains its current output level, how can the firm improve its profitability?

(e) Given your answer to Part (d), explain how the marginal revenue product values of labor and capital will change.

(f) Explain to Dusty Palmer, the owner of the mill, why your answer to Part (d) is not the end of the analysis.

2. The number of haircuts given by Shear Delight each day is given by the equation $q = 10L - 0.5L^2$, where L is the number of hours of labor. MP_L is $10 - L$. The haircut industry is perfectly competitive with a price of $10 per haircut.

(a) What is the firm's demand for labor schedule?

(b) How many hours of labor will be hired at a wage of $20 per hour? A wage of $40 per hour?

(c) If the price of haircuts rose to $20 and the wage was $40 per hour, calculate the number of hours of labor hired and the number of haircuts provided.

(d) Given your answer to Part (c), calculate Shear Delight's daily profit.

3. The city of Greaseboro contains three firms, each of which operates in a perfectly competitive industry. The three firms are a fireworks factory, a poultry processing plant, and a textiles mill. Each firm employs unskilled workers who can move easily between firms.

The price of output is given in the following table.

Firm	Output Price
Fireworks factory	$8
Poultry plant	$1
Textiles mill	$2

Weekly marginal productivity information is given in the following table. Assume that marginal productivity diminishes at a constant rate between each set of data points.

Workers	Fireworks Factory	Poultry Plant	Textiles Mill
		Marginal Product per Worker	
0	—	—	—
100	100	1,200	500
200	90	1,000	450
300	80	800	400
400	70	600	350
500	60	500	300
600	50	400	250
700	40	300	200
800	30	200	150
900	20	100	100
1,000	10	0	50

(a)   Calculate the marginal revenue product values and include them in the following table.

	Marginal Product per Worker		
Workers	Fireworks Factory	Poultry Plant	Textiles Mill
100			
200			
300			
400			
500			
600			
700			
800			
900			
1,000			

(b)   Calculate the total demand for labor in Greaseboro at each of the weekly wage rates in the following table.

Wage	Fireworks Factory	Poultry Plant	Textiles Mill	Total Labor Demand
$800				
$700				
$600				
$500				
$400				
$300				
$200				

(c)

Wage	Total Labor Supply
$800	
$700	
$600	
$500	
$400	
$300	
$200	

As the wage level increases the quantity of labor supplied in Greaseboro increases, as shown in the equation, $Q = 1100 + 2W$, where W is the weekly wage. Complete the preceding table.

(d)   Graph the labor demand and labor supply curves in the following graph. Determine the equilibrium wage and level of employment.

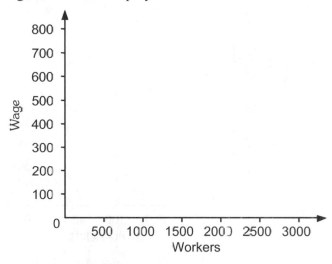

(e)   Calculate the level of employment in each industry.

Firm	Employment
Fireworks factory	_____
Poultry plant	_____
Textiles mill	_____

(f)   Verify that the profit-maximizing equilibrium conforms to the rule: $MRP_{ff}/P_{ff} = MRP_{pp}/P_{pp} = MRP_{tm}/P_{tm} = 1$.

4.   In a central area of the city of Fairview there are 300 vacant lots suitable for development. As the price per lot increases, the quantity demanded decreases, as indicated in the following table.

Price per Lot	Lots Demanded
$30,000	0
$25,000	100
$20,000	200
$15,000	300
$10,000	400
$5,000	500

(a)   Graph the market for vacant lots in Fairview. Show the equilibrium price.

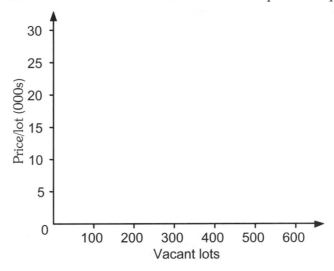

(b)   Suppose that the city government imposed a maximum price per lot of $10,000. What effect will this have on the number of lots available? What allocation problems will occur?

5.   Suppose that ABC Corporation sells audiocassettes in a perfectly competitive market at a price of $1 per unit and that the wage rate is $15.

Labor	MP	TP	TR	MRP
1	10			
2	20			
3	25			
4	23			
5	20			
6	18			
7	15			
8	12			

(a)   Calculate total product, total revenue, and *MRP*.

(b)   Draw the *MRP* schedule below and plot the wage too.

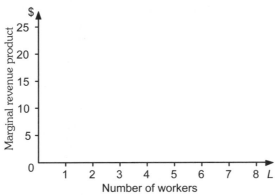

(c)   Note that *MRP rises* initially. Why?

(d)   Consider the first worker. Should she be hired, if the wage rate is $15?

(e)   Which is the first worker who won't be hired?

(f)   Make up a "hiring rule of thumb" for the profit-maximizing employer.

(g)   Confirm that *MRP* depicts the quantity of labor demanded at different wage levels.

6.   Examine the following production function for ABC Corporation, which sells audiocassettes in a perfectly competitive market at a price of $2 per unit. Labor is the only variable input. The wage rate of labor is $16.

Labor	MP	TP	TR	MRP
1	19	___	___	___
2	17	___	___	___
3	15	___	___	___
4	12	___	___	___
5	10	___	___	___
6	7	___	___	___
7	5	___	___	___

(a)   Calculate total product, total revenue, and *MRP*.

(b)   How many workers should be hired?

7.   Your firm is currently hiring labor and capital. The *MRP* of labor is $80 and that of capital is $120. Price of the final product is $2. The price of labor is $10 per unit and the price of capital is $20 per unit.

(a)   Is your firm maximizing profits? Explain.

(b)   Given your current budget, what should you do?

(c)   What will happen to the marginal productivity of capital? The marginal productivity of labor?

8.   Assume that shoes are produced with one variable factor of production—labor. Using the following production function, estimate the amount of labor that a competitive firm would hire, assuming that labor is available for $35 per day and that shoes sell for $10 per pair. (Hint: First determine the *MRP* schedule.)

Units of Labor (days)	Total Output (pairs of shoes)
1	5
2	9
3	12
4	14
5	15

9.   In the three preceding chapters we have visited Wilma's Wicker Baskets, a competitive firm that has the following production information. Suppose the price of a basket is $6.00.

(a)   Complete the following table.

Labor	Total Product	Marginal Product of Labor	Total Revenue	Marginal Revenue Product
0	0	—	0	—
1	5	5		
2	16	11		
3	27	11		
4	36	9		
5	44	8		
6	51	___		
7	56	___		
8	___	4		
9	63	3		
10	65	2		

(b)   If the wage per unit of labor is $24, determine how many workers the firm should hire. Why? How many baskets should be produced?

10.   During economic slowdowns (recessions), unemployment typically increases as employers cut back on production. However, during such recessionary episodes, economists have often observed that labor productivity has risen. Can you explain why we might expect this result?

11.   In 1811–1816, Ned Ludd and his followers (the "Luddites") smashed labor-saving knitting machines that had been installed in mills in England. They claimed the equipment had cost them their jobs. What assumption about the relationship between labor and capital were they using? Can you present a plausible counterargument against the Luddites?

Practice Test SOLUTIONS

I. SOLUTIONS TO MULTIPLE-CHOICE QUESTIONS

1.   (c)   Refer to page 216 for a discussion of this topic.

2.   (b)   Refer to page 215 for the definition of "derived demand.".

3.   (d)   The value of production by each additional worker determines how much (s)he will be paid.

4.   (b)   The marginal revenue product of the final machine is less than the cost of hiring it. The businessperson should cut back on capital usage.

5.   (b)   Per dollar, labor is contributing more than capital.

6.   (a)   When the price of a normal input decreases, the factor substitution effect and the output effect both increase the quantity demanded. Refer to page 222.

7.   (c)   Total cost of production is reduced because of the factor price decrease. More output is produced and more of all factors (including labor) is hired.

8.   (a)   An increase in the price of output will increase the MRP of the input. MRP is the demand for the input.

9.   (c)   Marginal product of the fourth worker is 8 units. $MRP = MP \times P = 8 \times \$2 = \$16$. This worker is worth as much as $16.

10. (b)   As less labor is hired, the marginal productivity of labor will increase. More of the relatively cheaper capital will be hired, resulting in a decrease in its marginal productivity.

11. (a)   Earnings depend on MRP. MRP depends on the selling price of output.

12. (b)   With a normal profit, Building #1 should earn $10,000. The additional $90,000 is economic rent.

13. (a)   With a normal profit, Building #4 should earn $40,000. If revenue is $40,000, this building earns zero economic rent.

14. (a)   Recall that MP is the change in total product ($85 - 75$) divided by the change in the number of workers (1).

15. (d) $MRP = MP \times$ wage. Refer to page 217 for the definition.

16. (b)   To maximize profits, Rhonda should not hire any worker whose MRP is less than $36. Point to ponder: What about the first worker?

17. (a)   The worker costs $36 and contributes $40, a gain of $4.

18. (d) The third worker's *MRP* is $40. To maximize profits, Rhonda should not hire the fourth worker (whose *MRP* is $30) at any wage above $30.

19. (b) Both effects work in the same direction.

20. (d) *MP* is 35. $MRP = MP \times P = 35 \times 2$ rubles = 70 rubles.

21. (d) *MRP* of the sixth worker is 40 rubles.

22. (d) The sixth worker's *MRP* is 40 rubles and (s)he would cost 50 rubles to hire. Drushka would lose 10 rubles.

23. (d) The fourth worker's *MRP* is 60 rubles.

24. (d) Both the factor substitution effect and the output effect indicate that the quantity of labor demanded should decrease as the wage increases.

25. (c) Demand for capital will tend to increase because labor is now more costly (factor substitution effect) *and* tend to decrease because the firm will want less of all inputs (output effect).

II. SOLUTIONS TO APPLICATION QUESTIONS

1. (a) Refer to the following table. Palmer's should hire until MRP_L = Wage, i.e., up to and including the fourth worker.

Workers (days)	Total Output	Marginal Product	*MRP*	Wage
1	9	9	$45	$30
2	17	8	$40	$30
3	24	7	$35	$30
4	30	6	$30	$30
5	35	5	$25	$30
6	39	4	$20	$30
7	42	3	$15	$30

(b) Palmer's is not maximizing profit. The profit-maximizing input combination follows the rule that the marginal revenue product/dollar of the final unit of each input should be equal. This is not so in this case because $MRP_L/P_L > MRP_K/P_K$.

(c) Palmer's can't improve its profitability in the short run—it's tied to the decisions it has made.

(d) Because $MRP_L/P_L > MRP_K/P_K$, Palmer's should reduce its capital. If the output level is maintained, and labor and capital as substitutes, more labor should be hired. The effect will be to reduce total cost and increase profit.

(e) *Ceteris paribus*, as additional workers are added, marginal revenue product of labor will decrease. *Ceteris paribus*, as fewer machines are hired, marginal revenue product of capital will increase. Both movements will help correct the imbalance between the ratios of *MRP* per dollar.

(f)   In Part (d) you note that, given the same output level, the firm should hire more workers and fewer machines and reduce total cost. Another way to look at this is to maintain the total cost and increase output. Output will increase because inputs are now being allocated more efficiently. However, with less than six machines, the marginal productivity of *labor* will fall, making the rise in labor less than that predicted by the answer to Part (d). Similarly, with more than four workers, the marginal productivity of *capital* will increase, making the decrease in capital less than that predicted by the answer to Part (d).

2.   (a) MP_L is $10 - L$, and $P = \$10$, then $MRP_L = \$10 \times [10 - L] = \$100 - \$10L$. The demand for labor schedule is given by $MRP_L = W$. Substituting W for MRP_L in the equation gives us the demand for labor schedule, $W = \$100 - \$10L$.

(b)   If $W = \$20$, then $\$20 = \$100 - \$10L$, therefore $L = 8$.
       If $W = \$40$, then $\$40 = \$100 - \$10L$, therefore $L = 6$.

(c)   If MP_L is $10 - L$, and $P = \$20$, then $MRP_L = \$20 \times [10 - L] = \$200 - \$20L$. The demand for labor schedule is given by $MRP_L = W$. Substituting W for MRP_L in the equation gives us the demand for labor schedule, $W = \$200 - \$20L$. If $W = \$40$, then $\$40 = \$200 - \$20L$, therefore $L = 8$. If $L = 8$, the equation $q = 10L - 0.5L^2$ gives $q = 80 - 32$, or 48 haircuts (i.e., 6 per hour).

(d)   Labor is the only input: total cost is $\$40 \times 8$, or $\$320$. Total revenue is $\$20 \times 48$, or $\$960$. Profit is $\$640$.

3.   (a)

| | Marginal Product per Worker | | |
Workers	Fireworks Factory	Poultry Plant	Textiles Mill
100	$800	$1,200	$1,000
200	$720	$1,000	$900
300	$640	$800	$800
400	$560	$600	$700
500	$480	$500	$600
600	$400	$400	$500
700	$320	$300	$400
800	$240	$200	$300
900	$160	$100	$200
1,000	$80	$0	$100

(b)

Wage	Fireworks Factory	Poultry Plant	Textiles Mill	Total Labor Demand
$800	100	300	300	700
$700	225	350	400	975
$600	350	400	500	1,250
$500	475	500	600	1,575
$400	600	600	700	1,900
$300	725	700	800	2,225
$200	850	800	900	2,550

(c)

Wage	Total Labor Supply
$800	2,700
$700	2,500
$600	2,300
$500	2,100
$400	1,900
$300	1,700
$200	1,500

(d)   Refer to the following diagram.

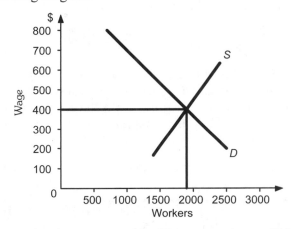

The equilibrium wage is $400 per week, and 1900 workers will be employed each week.

(e)

Firm	Employment
Fireworks factory	600
Poultry plant	600
Textiles mill	700

(f)   The profit-maximizing equilibrium rule is that the marginal product/dollar of the final unit of each input should be equal. In each case, *MRP* is $400 and the wage is $400.

4.   (a)   Refer to the following diagram. The equilibrium price is $15,000.

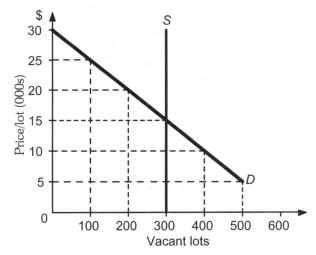

(b)   The number of lots available will remain at 300. However, because of the lower price, there has been an increase in quantity demanded to 400, and an excess demand exists. Because market price is no longer able to perform its rationing function, some other method of allocating lots to demanders will have to be found, e.g., first-come, first-served, special government permit, bribery, waiting lists, or a tedious application process.

5.   (a)   Refer to the following table.

Labor	MP	TP	TR	MRP
1	10	10	$10	$10
2	20	30	$30	$20
3	25	55	$55	$25
4	23	78	$78	$23
5	20	98	$98	$20
6	18	116	$116	$18
7	15	131	$131	$15
8	12	143	$143	$12

(b)   Refer to the following diagram. Note that marginal values are typically shown between units because they indicate change.

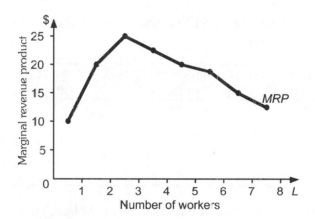

(c)   Increasing productivity.

(d)   Yes! Although ABC will take a loss because *MRP* is only $10, the first worker must be hired to hire subsequent "profitable" workers.

(e)   The eighth worker won't be hired.

(f)   Hire any input that at least pays its way.

(g)   Yes, it does. At a wage of $15, for example, seven workers are demanded; at $18, six workers are demanded.

6. (a)   Refer to the following table. For example, the total product of two workers is 36 units of output (19 + 17). Total revenue from 36 units of output is $72 (36 × $2). The second worker's *MRP* is $34 ($72 – $38).

Labor	*MP*	*TP*	*TR*	*MRP*
1	19	19	$38	$38
2	17	36	$72	$34
3	15	51	$102	$30
4	12	63	$126	$24
5	10	73	$146	$20
6	7	80	$160	$14
7	5	85	$170	$10

(b)   Five workers should be hired.

7. (a)   No. The final dollar spent on each input must generate the same additional production. We should hire such that $MP_L/P_L = MP_K/P_K$.

(b)   Cut back on capital and hire more workers.

(c)   Rise; fall.

8. If we assume that shoes sell for $10 per pair over and above the cost of leather and materials, we can derive the following table.

Units of Labor (days)	Total Output (pairs of shoes)	Marginal Product	*MRP*
1	5	5	50
2	9	4	40
3	12	3	30
4	14	2	20
5	15	1	10

The firm will hire two workers. A third worker would have an *MRP* of $30, which is less than the $35 wage rate.

(a)   Refer to the following table. For example, the sixth worker's marginal product is 7 units of output (51 – 44). Total revenue from 51 units of output is $306 (51 × $6). The sixth worker's *MRP* is $42 ($306 – $264).

Labor	Total Product	Marginal Product of Labor	Total Revenue	Marginal Revenue Product
0	0		0	
1	5	5	$30	$30
2	16	11	$96	$66
3	27	11	$162	$66
4	36	9	$216	$54
5	44	8	$264	$48
6	51	7	$306	$42
7	56	5	$336	$30
8	60	4	$378	$24
9	63	3	$378	$18
10	65	2	$390	$12

(b) If the wage per unit of labor is $24, Wilma should hire eight workers because the value of the marginal product of labor up to this point is equal to or greater than the marginal cost of hiring the workers. The firm should produce 60 baskets. Note that a wage of $24 per worker was established in Chapter 7. At a price of $6.00 per basket, we saw in Chapter 9 that the firm should produce 60 baskets. We have come full circle to the same conclusion by consideration of the input market.

10. One reason might be that during recessions workers afraid for their jobs, work harder . Even if that isn't the case, we'd still predict increasing productivity. Given the capital stock, with more workers marginal returns diminish so, with fewer workers marginal returns increase. As marginal productivity increases, average productivity should also increase.

11. The Luddites assumed that labor and capital were substitutes and that more productive machines had caused job loss. This is sometimes referred to as the "Luddite fallacy." Against this, the new machines increased labor productivity, reduced the price of output, and increased the size and competitiveness of the English woolen industry. This should have created new job opportunities.

11

Input Demand: The Capital Market and the Investment Decision

Chapter Objectives

1. Distinguish between tangible and intangible capital, investment, and depreciation. Define depreciation and identify two reasons why a capital asset depreciates.
2. Explain the role of interest and profit in capital accumulation.
3. Define the investment demand schedule and discuss the factors that influence its shape and position. Outline how changes in the market interest rate influence the investment decision.
4. Calculate and evaluate the present discounted value and the rate of return on a project. Explain how higher interest rates reduce present values.

In approaching this chapter, look for similarities between hiring decisions in the labor and land markets and those in the capital market. Capital may seem different because of the time dimension but businesspeople still weigh the benefits and the costs of employing new resources. Also, note that capital accumulation is not exclusive to the business community—households, the government, and you (human capital!) make capital-investment decisions.

BRAIN TEASER: Consider your college investment decision. Why are you in college? (Better jobs, more money in the future.) College has costs, and you could have started earning income immediately after high school. Is the outlay justified in terms of future earnings? Consider the concept of present value. College is an investment in human capital and can be analyzed using the same techniques as other potential capital investments.

What is the rate of return from investing in a college education? What annual income do you expect to make when you leave college? How much would you expect to make in an entry-level job without a college degree? Plug in your own numbers here, but I'll suppose that you answered $50,000 to the first question and $20,000 to the other. This is a difference of $30,000. In fact, average pay for a white high school graduate is $22,154, and for a black high school graduate it is $17,072. Will this differential increase or decrease as time goes by? (It should increase but, for the sake of simplicity, assume it remains constant.(

The explicit cost of four years at college is rising. Suppose that the average public college costs an average of $3,511 per year in tuition and fees. The average price tag for the private college is $12,994. Try to estimate the cost of your books and supplies.

For a student at the average public college, the total explicit cost of a degree is about $5,000 per year for four years. The opportunity cost is the $20,000 per year job that could not be taken. Total cost is about $25,000 per year for four years—$100,000.

Is the degree worth it? Assume the interest rate is 10 percent. Use the present value formula: $PV =$ Future Value $\div (1 + r)^t$ where t is years in the future.

The present value (*PV*) of the cost of the four years of college is:

$$\$25,000 + \$25,000/(1 + r)^1 + \$25,000/(1 + r)^2 + \$25,000/(1 + r)^3 = \$87,171.30$$

Calculate the present value of the difference in earnings, assuming that the current difference ($30,000) remains constant, and that you retire at the age of 50.

Can you calculate the rate of return on your investment?

Objective 1

Distinguish between tangible and intangible capital, investment, and depreciation. Define depreciation and identify two reasons why a capital asset depreciates.

Capital goods are those goods that can be used as inputs in the production process, both now and in the future. Capital may be *tangible* (machines, all construction, and inventories) or *intangible* (human capital, goodwill, and brand loyalty). Capital accumulation occurs not only in the business sector but also in the public sector (social capital, such as interstate highways) and in the households sector. (page 233)

Stocks are variables that are measured at a point in time (capital stock) whereas *flows* are measured over a period of time (earnings per month, investment per quarter, depreciation per year). *Investment* has a specific meaning for economists—investment is the creation of capital. It is *not* financial purchases, even the purchase of stock in a corporation.

Depreciation (a flow) is the decline in the economic value of an asset over time—think of it as an aging process. A unit of capital might depreciate simply because new technology renders it obsolete or because of wear and tear. (page 235)

> **LEARNING TIP:** It's easy to overlook the importance of **intangible capital**. Choose a business with which you are familiar and identify all the types of intangible capital in use—goodwill, name recognition, and the human capital of managers and employees. If, overnight, the firm's intangible capital evaporated, production and sales would shudder to a halt. Even with an excellent product, a salesperson who fails to "connect" with a customer will be ineffectual—trust is as important as it is intangible. ◀
>
> **Capital:** Because capital is so diverse, it is measured by its dollar value. Keep in mind at all times that capital should be thought of as a physical input and not as a monetary unit.

ECONOMICS IN PRACTICE: On page 235, the textbook looks at the 2010 IPO (initial public offering) of Tesla Motors, a new manufacturer of electric cars. The new stock sold for $17 per share. As of mid-August 2010, the price had risen to $19.10. Tesla is quoted on NASDAQ under the symbol TSLA. What is Tesla's stock price today? What may have caused the rise (or fall) of Tesla's stock since summer 2010? **ANSWER:** Stock prices are driven by expectations. In mid-2010, the economy was still languishing in the after-effects of the Great Recession. Furthermore, during that time, there were unanswered questions regarding government regulation and financial markets. By the time you read this these issues may have been resolved. More will be known about the effectiveness and acceptance of highway-worthy electric-car technology (affecting demand), and more rivals will be competing with Tesla.

Practice

1.   The construction of a new house is investment in
     (a)   social capital.
     (b)   a consumer durable good.
     (c)   tangible capital.
     (d)   human capital.

ANSWER: (c) All construction (including residential construction) is classified as capital. Social capital is usually provided by the state.

2.   HAL Corp. institutes a training program to introduce its employees to the new Orange computer. This should increase productivity. This is an investment in
(a)   tangible capital.
(b)   human capital.
(c)   social capital.
(d)   infrastructure capital.

ANSWER: (b) The quality of the labor force is being improved.

3.   Which of the following is not an example of capital?
(a)   An IBM warehouse
(b)   A Macintosh computer used by an IBM employee
(c)   A car used by an IBM service representative
(d)   The revenue earned by IBM this year

ANSWER: (d) Money is not capital! Refer to page 235 for a comment on this point.

4.   Capital is a _____ , investment is a _____ , and depreciation is a _____ .
(a)   stock; stock; stock
(b)   stock; flow; stock
(c)   flow; flow; stock
(d)   stock; flow; flow

ANSWER: (d) The capital *stock* is measured at a point in time. Investment takes place over time, as does depreciation.

5.   A columnist once argued that his educated brain cells were part of his _____ capital and that, as time passed, the rate at which they were being depleted should be counted as _____ (for tax purposes).
(a)   social; investment
(b)   depreciation; depreciation
(c)   human; investment
(d)   human; depreciation

ANSWER: (d) The quality of human resources counts as human capital. Wear and tear (and the death of brain cells through the passage of time) is depreciation. Note: The IRS is not convinced by this argument.

6.   Which of the following is **not** an act of investment?
(a)   A marketing firm buys a new automated mailing machine.
(b)   Pat Doyle's college education is paid for by his parents.
(c)   FedEx delivers the mail.
(d)   The Doyles build a new vacation home.

ANSWER: (c) Mail delivery is a productive activity, but FedEx is not increasing its productive capacity in the process. Note that a new vacation home is construction of a residential structure—its use is not considered. ∎

Objective 2

Explain the role of interest and profit in capital accumulation.

Ownership of capital generates *capital income* (usually profit and interest), which rewards households for postponing consumption and channeling resources into investment instead. Capital markets act as one method of channeling these funds to investment purposes. Capital income is the income flow paid to the owners of capital which induces them to supply funds. It also the spurs on that the process of capital allocation and accumulation. (page 236)

Funds for investment projects can be raised by a firm in a number of ways, such as business loans, venture capital, the firm's retained earnings, or issuing shares of stock. One particular financial market is the mortgage market. In the past, banks and savings and loans made mortgage loans to households (using the value of the property as collateral). More recently, it has been mortgage brokers or bankers who have written these types of loans and then sold them to a secondary market. In all cases, however, the pattern is similar—households are the ultimate lenders while firms decide which are the most attractive investments. Household saving limits how much investment can occur.

Interest encourages consumers to defer consumption. Interest and profit reward innovation and risk-taking—encouraging entrepreneurs to both develop new products and processes and to respond to changes in consumer preferences.

ECONOMICS IN PRACTICE: On page 241, the textbook examines who holds stock in Microsoft and Activision and notes that Microsoft has a much higher rate of institutional holdings (64.60 percent) than does Activision (36.40 percent). Why? In contrast, Activision insiders (those who work for the company), hold a much higher proportion of its stock (58.03 percent) than do Microsoft's insiders (12.25 percent). Again, why the difference? Are these differences to be expected?

ANSWER: Microsoft is one of the stock market's "blue-chip" companies. As such, it is believed to be a safe long-term investment and, therefore, is attractive to institutional investors. Activision, on the other hand, is a newer company with a shorter track record and operates in an industry with a greater deal of competition and volatility. It is also a smaller company than Microsoft so any market change (innovations by a rival, for instance) may have a larger impact on its share price, making it a riskier bet than Microsoft. With respect to insider holdings, new companies, still seeking to attract customers and profits, often "pay" employees with stock. In addition, ownership of the company may encourage employees to work harder toward the company's success.

ECONOMICS IN PRACTICE: On page 243, the textbook looks at flows of venture capital into wind-farm technology in China, a new "green" industry where both risks and rewards may be great. Such venture capital flows occur any time a significant shock shakes up the business world. Changes in regulations or political alignments, the emergence of a new technology such as the Internet all signal profit opportunities to the brave of heart. Can you think of other examples (either in the past or today) of a similar rush by risk-takers into a new frontier?

ANSWER: Nature abhors a vacuum. The discovery of gold in California in 1849 and the Homestead Act of 1862 are historical examples of entrepreneurs wagering on unproven hopes. The "Lost Colony" of Virginia is another poignant case. The growth of Silicon Valley in the late 1970s was driven by technological change. The opening up and subsequent explosive growth of the Chinese and Vietnamese economies are other examples where venture capital has responded to new opportunities.

Practice

7. The two most important types of capital income are
   (a) investment and saving.
   (b) profit and interest.
   (c) dividends and rents.
   (d) pure economic rent and disposable income.

   ANSWER: (b) Refer to the section in the textbook starting on page 237 for a discussion of capital income.

8. The ultimate suppliers of financial capital are
   (a) households.
   (b) the private banking sector.
   (c) the central bank (the "Fed").
   (d) businesses.

   ANSWER: (a) Ultimately, all income—and therefore all funds for investment purposes—derives from households.

9. Walt asks Virginia to lend him $3,000 for 12 months. Walt agrees to pay Virginia $3,150 at the end of that time. The interest rate that Virginia could have earned if she had not loaned to Walt is 6 percent. Virginia has earned an economic profit of
   (a) −$30.
   (b) $30.
   (c) $150.
   (d) −$9.

   ANSWER: (a) Virginia earned $150 in interest. She could have earned $180 ($3,000 × 1.06). The loan to Walt cost her $30.

Use the following information to answer the next three questions. Eight-year-old Josh has discovered that the price his friends can charge while selling lemonade on the sidewalk has doubled because of the hot summer weather. Lemonade selling is a perfectly competitive industry and previously the reward was not quite enough to encourage Josh to participate. Now, however, he rushes home to borrow ingredients from his parents, builds a lemonade stand, and writes out a price list.

10. Josh's ingredients are _____ capital, and his lemonade stand and price list are _____ .
    (a) inventory; durable equipment
    (b) inventory; nonresidential construction
    (c) intangible; durable equipment
    (d) intangible; nonresidential construction

    ANSWER: (a) Stocks of inputs or unsold output is inventory. The lemonade stand is durable.

11. Josh promises his parents, using his candy allowance as collateral, to repay the face value of his borrowed ingredients. He is financing his investment with
    (a) venture capital.
    (b) economic profits.
    (c) retained earnings.
    (d) a zero-interest direct loan.

    ANSWER: (d) If Josh repays the full value of the ingredients he pays no interest. This is the equivalent of a direct loan. If Josh writes out the promise to pay, he has issued a bond.

12. As a result of the existence of economic profits caused by increased demand, resources allocated to the lemonade industry have _____ . Lemonade prices will _____ .
    (a) increased; increase
    (b) increased; decrease
    (c) decreased; increase
    (d) decreased; decrease

    ANSWER: (b) More lemonade will be available, and consequently, prices and economic profit will decrease.

Use the following information to answer the next two questions. The health club industry is perfectly competitive and in long-run equilibrium. As the baby boomers age and sag, the demand for health clubs increases.

13.   Existing health clubs will earn _____ economic profits. We would predict _____ investment in the health club industry.
(a)   short-run; increased
(b)   short-run; decreased
(c)   long-run; increased
(d)   long-run; decreased

ANSWER: (a) Higher demand will lead to higher profits in the short run: recall that economic profits are zero in the long run for competitive firms. As existing firms expand and as firms enter the industry, capital accumulation will occur.

14.   Firms outside the health club industry (but using similar resources) will see their costs _____ and will _____ the quantity of resources they use.
(a)   increase; increase
(b)   increase; decrease
(c)   decrease; increase
(d)   decrease; decrease

ANSWER: (b) Recall that "costs" to an economist are opportunity costs—the value of the next-best alternative forgone. Cost depends on the reward that can be earned in an alternative activity, e.g., provision of health club services. As those earnings rise, costs increase for nonparticipants, profits decrease, and resources will be reallocated to the health club industry. ∎

Objective 3

Define the investment demand schedule and discuss the factors that influence its shape and position. Outline how changes in the market interest rate influence the investment decision.

The firm must form an expectation of both the future earnings and future costs of a project. The difference between expected future earnings and the costs of a project, expressed as a percentage of the project cost, is the *expected rate of return*. The investment decision hinges on how this rate compares against the cost (interest) of providing capital for investment. If the expected rate of return exceeds the interest rate, then the investment project should be undertaken. As the interest rate rises, profitable projects become unprofitable and the demand for funds is reduced.

By ranking the expected yield on projects, the investment demand schedule is developed. The shape and slope of the investment demand curve critically dependant on the expectations of those making investment decisions—anything that affects expectations may affect investment. (page 244)

The profit-maximizing firm will employ capital up to the point at which its marginal revenue product equals its price, i.e., it will invest whenever the expected rate of return exceeds the interest rate. (page 245)

LEARNING TIP: The logic behind the investment demand curve is identical to that of other demand curves. The interest rate is the "price" of investment, and the expected rate of return plays the role of "other factors" that influence investment. As before, the interest rate changes as you move along the curve; if at a given rate of interest, the expected rate of return changes, you shift the curve. ◀

LEARNING TIP: The investment decision involves a comparison of the project's expected future benefits and its opportunity cost. The opportunity cost is the market interest rate. If the expected future benefits are not at least equal to the interest rate, the project should not be undertaken. ◀

Practice

Use the following table for the next four questions. Sellco has the following list of investment projects to consider.

Project	Total Investment Amount	Expected Rate of Return (%)
A. New corporate headquarters	$300,000	20
B. Personal computers for sales force	$60,000	16
C. Training for employees	$140,000	10
D. Wellness program	$60,000	9
E. Employee leisure facility	$80,000	5
F. New canteen	$40,000	5

15. If the interest rate is 14 percent, Sellco would fund
    (a) only Project A.
    (b) Projects A and B.
    (c) Projects A, B, and C.
    (d) Projects D and E only.

    ANSWER: (b) Projects A and B have expected rates of return exceeding the interest rate—they are worthwhile.

16. If the interest rate is 21 percent, Sellco would fund
    (a) only Project A.
    (b) Projects B, D, and E only.
    (c) Projects B and E only.
    (d) None of the above are correct.

    ANSWER: (d) No project offers a high enough expected rate of return to justify the expense.

17. At an interest rate of 14 percent, Sellco's total investment would amount to
    (a) zero, as no project has a return equal to 14 percent.
    (b) $360,000.
    (c) $500,000.
    (d) $200,000.

    ANSWER: (b) $300,000 (Project A) + $60,000 (Project B).

18. If the interest rate is 5 percent, Sellco would fund
    (a) Project E only.
    (b) Project F only, because it is less expensive than Project E.
    (c) Projects E and F only, because their expected rate of return is equal to 5 percent.
    (d) all the projects.

    ANSWER: (d) The rule is that the firm should undertake any and all projects that have an expected rate of return equal to or greater than the interest rate.

19. The expected cost of an investment
    (a) depends on the interest rate.
    (b) is zero if the firm uses its own funds.
    (c) is zero if the investment is undertaken by the government.
    (d) is inversely related to its expected income stream.

    ANSWER: (a) Refer to the discussion on page 242.

20. An increase in the market interest rate will cause a
    (a) rightward shift in the investment demand curve.
    (b) leftward shift in the investment demand curve.
    (c) movement up the investment demand curve.
    (d) movement down the investment demand curve.

    ANSWER: (c) Refer to Figure 11.3 on page 244 for more on this point.

21. Firms become quite pessimistic because the government has announced higher business taxes. This will cause the investment demand curve to shift _____ and the level of investment to _____.
    (a) right; increase
    (b) right; decrease
    (c) left; increase
    (d) left; decrease

    ANSWER: (d) If expectations are reduced, investment demand will decrease. Refer to page 244.

22. Sellco is a perfectly competitive profit-maximizing firm. It will invest in new capital up to the point at which the
    (a) rate of return equals the expected interest rate.
    (b) expected rate of return equals the interest rate.
    (c) expected rate of return equals the expected interest rate.
    (d) rate of return equals the interest rate.

    ANSWER: (b) The interest rate is incurred today, at the time of the investment; the earnings will accrue in the future and, today, they are estimates.

23. Republican politicians often state a commitment to reduce corporate taxes. If business leaders believed this pledge then, *ceteris paribus*, it would most likely cause firms to plan to
    (a) increase investment because of the expectation that interest rates would be lower.
    (b) increase investment because of the expectation of higher after-tax benefits.
    (c) decrease investment because less effort would be needed to achieve a given level of after-tax income.
    (d) leave investment unchanged because business tax cuts would not affect the demand for their product and, ultimately, the demand for an input is a "derived" demand.

    ANSWER: (b) Lower taxes lead to higher after-tax profits and higher expected rates of return. ■

Objective 4 (Appendix)

Calculate and evaluate the present discounted value and the rate of return on a project. Explain how higher interest rates reduce present values.

When considering discounting and the role of *present (discounted) value* in evaluating investment projects, remember that a future dollar is worth less than a dollar in hand today, and should be discounted in value. Discounting puts dollars of all vintages on a common basis—present value. The discount rate is the interest rate and the formula used is:

$$PV = R \div (1 + r)^t$$

where R is the future value of payments, r is the interest rate, and t is the number of time periods. Invest if the present value of the expected stream of earnings exceeds the cost of the project. The rate of return and present value methods of evaluation give equivalent conclusions. (page 248)

Note: The formula tells us that, as interest rates rise, the present value of a project will fall and the project will be less likely to be undertaken—the same conclusion that we arrived at with the method using investment demand and the expected rate of return.

Present Value Example: What is the opportunity cost of removing $100 from your bank account for one year? The interest rate. If it is 10 percent, then the opportunity cost is $10.00. The $100 may be worth $110 at the end of the year if left in the bank. $100 today equals $110 in a year. Turn this the other way: $110 future dollars are worth $100 today, given the interest rate—that is, $110/(1 + 0.1) = $100.

What would that $100 be worth at the end of two years if it were left in the bank? $121.00 or $100 × 1.1 × 1.1. Or, $121 two years in the future is worth $100 today. Formally, this relationship is:

$$\text{Present Value} = \text{Future Value}/(1 + \text{interest rate})^t$$

A Present Value Table: Here is a table showing the present value of $100 payable at various dates and at various interest rates. Example: The promise of $100 two years from today has a present value of $90.00 if the interest rate is 6 percent.

Interest Rate (r)	1 Year	2 Years	3 Years	10 Years	20 Years
0.03	97.09	94.26	91.51	74.41	55.37
0.04	96.15	92.46	88.90	67.56	45.64
0.05	95.24	90.70	86.38	61.39	37.69
0.06	94.34	90.00	83.96	55.84	31.18
0.07	93.46	87.34	81.63	50.83	25.84
0.08	92.59	85.73	79.38	46.32	21.45

LEARNING TIP: Remember that future dollars are worth less—we *discount* their value.◀

Practice

24. The market interest rate is 25 percent. The present value of $500 to be delivered in one year is
    (a) $400.
    (b) $125.
    (c) $625.
    (d) $2,000.
    ANSWER: (a) $PV = R \div (1 + r)^t = \$500 \div 1.25^1 = \$400$.

25. Sellco should invest in a project if the present value of its income stream is greater than
    (a) the full cost of the project.
    (b) (or equal to) the full cost of the project.
    (c) the interest rate.
    (d) (or equal to) the interest rate.
    ANSWER: (b) If the value today of the project's earnings is greater than or at least equal to the cost of implementing the project, Sellco will make a profit. ∎

BRAIN TEASER SOLUTION: If the difference between the college wage and the noncollege wage remains the same ($30,000), and you retire at the age of 50, the present value of difference in earnings is about $204,591.18.

This gives a rate of return on investment in human capital of 234.7 percent ($204,591.18/$87,171.30). For most students, the full cost of four years of college is recouped within six years of graduation.

PRACTICE TEST

I. MULTIPLE-CHOICE QUESTIONS

Select the option that provides the single best answer.

_____ 1. Suppose the central bank (the "Fed") repeatedly hikes interest rates in order to dampen rising prices. Which of the following explanations best describes the Fed's view of the economy?
- (a) An increase in interest rates will reduce investment, which, in turn, will reduce production, making the economy's expansion less rapid. A less-rapid expansion will put less upward pressure on the national price level.
- (b) Higher interest rates lead to higher expectations about profits, which shifts the investment demand curve out.
- (c) Lower prices will lead to a lower marginal revenue product of capital, which will discourage investment. Because the demand for investment goods is part of national demand, national demand (and the national price level) will be lower than otherwise.
- (d) Higher interest rates make fewer investments profitable, and because the demand for investment goods is part of national demand, national demand (and the national price level) will be lower than otherwise.

_____ 2. A frequently heard argument is that government deficits cause higher interest rates. Assuming that this is so, then, *ceteris paribus*, reducing the government deficit should
- (a) increase investment and increase the marginal revenue product of capital.
- (b) increase investment and decrease the marginal revenue product of capital.
- (c) decrease investment and increase the marginal revenue product of capital.
- (d) decrease investment and decrease the marginal revenue product of capital.

_____ 3. Changes in the physical capital stock are caused by
- (a) investment and stock purchases.
- (b) investment and depreciation.
- (c) obsolescence and interest rate changes.
- (d) accumulation and discounting of value.

_____ 4. Which of the following is **not** an act of investment?
- (a) Paying for courses at a technical college
- (b) Construction of a bridge by the state government
- (c) The purchase of new solar technology by a business
- (d) Buying a government bond

_____ 5. Which of the following is **not** an example of capital?
- (a) An office block owned by IBM
- (b) Brand loyalty of consumers to IBM
- (c) A share of IBM stock
- (d) An IBM computer

_____ 6. In which case will investment be greatest?

	Market Interest Rate	Inflation Rate
(a)	8	7
(b)	9	0
(c)	6	2
(d)	7	3

_____ 7. A new machine will yield $500 a month in earnings for one year. The machine's maintenance is estimated to cost $2,000 a year. Its scrap value will be zero. If the current market interest rate is 8 percent, the firm would be willing to pay _____ to get the machine.
 (a) $62,500
 (b) $6,250
 (c) $50,000
 (d) $75,000

_____ 8. Billy Bob knows that he will buy a new car either this month or a year from now. The current price is $20,000, and next year he estimates that it will be $24,000. If his discount rate is 10 percent he should
 (a) not buy either this year or next.
 (b) buy now.
 (c) buy next year.
 (d) be indifferent, as both options have the same present value.

_____ 9. The expected rate of return on an investment depends on all of the following EXCEPT the
 (a) expected interest rate.
 (b) amount of revenue attributable each year to the project.
 (c) length of time that the project provides additional cost savings or revenue.
 (d) price of the investment.

_____ 10. Investment projects will be funded up to the point where the
 (a) interest rate and the expected rate of return are equal.
 (b) expected rate of return is zero.
 (c) rate of return is maximized.
 (d) expected rate of return is maximized.

_____ 11. A bond pays $1,000 in one year (and nothing else before or after). The interest rate is 20 percent. The most one should pay for this bond is
 (a) $1,200.
 (b) $800.
 (c) $909.09.
 (d) $833.33.

_____ 12. The expected cost of an investment is _____ if the funds are borrowed, and is _____ if the project is self-financed.
 (a) positive; positive
 (b) positive; zero
 (c) zero; positive
 (d) zero; zero

_____ 13. Goodwill _____ a form of capital, and inventory _____ a form of capital.
     (a)   is; is
     (b)   is; is not
     (c)   is not; is
     (d)   is not; is not

_____ 14. As the interest rate increases, the cost of new investment projects becomes _____ and the number of profitable investment projects becomes _____ .
     (a)   higher; higher
     (b)   higher; lower
     (c)   lower; higher
     (d)   lower; lower

_____ 15. When the interest rate increases, the expected rate of return of an investment _____ and the present value of the investment _____ .
     (a)   decreases; decreases
     (b)   decreases; does not change
     (c)   does not change; decreases
     (d)   does not change; does not change

II. APPLICATION QUESTIONS

1. Camille has an important career decision to make. She intends to retire in five years. If she stays in her present job, she expects to earn $44,000 per year for those five years. However, she has been offered the opportunity to take a two-year training program, after which she will earn $80,000 per year for the remaining three years of her work life. The training program is free, but Camille will be unable to work during the two-year period. She has sufficient savings to tide her over the two-year training period.

    (a)   Camille has asked her sister Clarissa which option she should take. Clarissa said that she should go for the training program because, after all, $44,000 times 5 is less than $80,000 times 3. Camille is still unconvinced and asks your opinion. What would you advise?

    (b)   Explain to Camille the problem with the basis of Clarissa's advice.

    (c)   Suppose the interest rate is 10 percent. Can you now offer Camille a definitive answer to her career choice?

    (d)   The training program is an investment in human capital as is a college education for high school graduates. If the government wished to encourage additional investment in human capital, should it increase or decrease the interest rate?

    (e)   Based on your answer to Part (d), should the government adopt a "high-interest rate" strategy or a "low-interest rate" strategy if it wished to encourage long-term rather than short-term investment projects?

2. Two of your assistants, Judy and Jody, have each devised an investment project costing $750 and earning a total income of $1,000. Judy's project will return a steady stream of income, $200 per year for five years. Jody's project starts more slowly, with $100 in each of the first three years, then $300 and $400 in the last two. The interest rate is 10 percent. How can you explain, nontechnically, to Jody why his project is unacceptable, although Judy's has been given the go-ahead? If he pressed you for proof, what would you do?

3. Every so often, excitement in the nation rises because the Powerball lottery prize reaches $100 million. The prize is disbursed to the winner at a rate of $5 million per year for 20 years. Given these numbers, does the winner really win $100 million?

4. Many alumni donate funds to their college or university.

   (a) G. P. A. Crammer has just pledged $500,000 payable on his retirement which will be in 20 years time. In present value terms, if the interest rate is 7 percent, how much did Crammer pledge? Use the present value table in the Objective 4 above.

   (b) If the interest rate falls to 3 percent, what is the present value of Crammer's pledge?

5. The Johnson family decides to have a house built that costs $500,000. This year the Johnsons have a disposable (after-tax) income of $200,000, of which $125,000 is spent on current consumption and the rest is used as a down payment on the house. The additional $375,000 is borrowed from aged Aunt Agatha who earns no income and currently lives off her wealth. Assume that Aunt Agatha sells some shares of stock to acquire the cash for the loan. Jack Diamond, who earned $1,000,000 last year (after tax), buys the stock from Aunt Agatha for $375,000 and spends the remaining $625,000 on current consumption.

   For each of the three parties, calculate:

   (a) The amount of saving during the period by
   the Johnsons   Aunt Agatha   Jack Diamond
   _____   _____   _____

   (b) The quantity of investment during the period by
   the Johnsons   Aunt Agatha   Jack Diamond
   _____   _____   _____

   (c) Any change in net worth for
   the Johnsons   Aunt Agatha   Jack Diamond
   _____   _____   _____

   (d) Any change in capital stock for
   the Johnsons   Aunt Agatha   Jack Diamond
   _____   _____   _____

6 Imagine a 10-year bond issued by ABC Corp. with a face value of $1,000 and an interest rate of 12 percent.

   (a) What is the annual interest payment?

   (b) How much would you pay for the bond if the bond had three years to maturity and the market interest rate is 12 percent?

   (c) If the market rate was ___, the bond would be less attractive, and its price would _____.

   (d) If the market rate changed to 8 percent, and the bond had three years to maturity, the value of the bond would _____ to _____.

   (e) When the market rate is below the interest rate of the bond, the market price of the bond will be _____ than its face value. When the market rate is above the interest rate of the bond, the market price of the bond will be _____ than its face value.

7. Consider the investment demand schedule. Indicate if investment would increase (I) or decrease (D) in the following cases.

   (a) An increase in interest rates

   (b) The development of a new technology

   (c) The expectation of new technological developments

   (d) The expectation of a corporate tax increase

   (e) The expectation of more generous tax write-offs for depreciation

   (f) A new product line is introduced

   (g) The industry is experiencing short-run economic losses

   (h) The industry is encountering diseconomies of scale

8. Judy and Jody each devise an investment project costing $900 and earning a total income of $1,200. Judy's project will return a steady stream of income, $300 per year, for four years. Jody's project starts more slowly, with $100 in each of the first three years, then $900 in the last year. The interest rate is 10 percent.

   Use present value to decide if either project should be undertaken.

9. A dollar today and a dollar next year have different values. Discounting puts dollars of all vintages on a common basis—present value. The following case exemplifies this and highlights the importance of the market interest rate.

   Here are two projects. Each has the same total cost and revenue.

	Project 1		Project 2	
Year	Costs	Revenues	Costs	Revenues
1	$700	$0	$300	$100
2	$100	$100	$300	$600
3	$0	$900	$200	$300
	$800	$1,000	$800	$1,000

   (a) Is the rate of return equal for both projects?

   (b) Intuitively, which project is the better investment?

   (c) Suppose the interest rate is 10 percent. Which project is the better investment?

   (d) What else is revealed?

10. Consider the investment demand schedule.
    (a) What economic variables does it relate?

    (b) What determines its slope and its position?

    (c) It is said that this investment is volatile. Do you think that this is reflected by the shape of the curve, by its position, or by both?

Explain how investment behavior would be affected by

(d)   A cut in interest rates

(e)   The development of a new technology

(f)   The expectation of new technological developments

(g)   The expectation of a corporate tax increase

11.   Relative to previous decades, the recent U.S. personal saving rate has been low. In the 1980s the saving rate was in excess of 10 percent while, presently, it typically hovers at 2 percent. At the same time, business investment in the United States has been running at over 15 percent. If savers are the ultimate financers of investment, how can this situation be possible?

Practice Test SOLUTIONS

I. SOLUTIONS TO MULTIPLE-CHOICE QUESTIONS

1. (d) Given the investment demand schedule, higher interest rates prompt less investment, lower demand in the economy, and prices that are lower than would otherwise be the case.

2. (b) Reducing the government deficit should decrease interest rates and increase investment. As investment increases, the marginal revenue product of capital will decrease because marginal productivity will decrease.

3. (b) The capital stock increases through investment and decreases through wear and tear (depreciation).

4. (d) Investment is the creation of new productive capacity. Option A represents an improvement in human capital. Option D is the transfer of a financial asset.

5. (c) A share of IBM stock is a financial asset. Brand loyalty is a type of "goodwill."

6. (a) Investment will be greatest when the real interest rate is lowest. The real interest rate is the market interest rate minus the inflation rate.

7. (c) Earnings are $6,000 per year and costs are $2,000. The expected profit is $4,000. Cost = expected profit divided by interest rate = $4,000/0.08 = $50,000.

8. (b) *PV* of purchase today = $20,000.
   PV of purchase next year = $24,000/1.1 = $21,818.18. Because the *PV* today is less, he should buy today.

9. (a) The current market interest rate is the key factor, not the expected interest rate.

10. (a) Investment projects will be funded if the expected rate of return exceeds or is equal to the interest rate. Refer to page 244.

11. (d) Price of bond = future value/(1 + r) = $1,000/1.2 = $833.33

12. (a) Even if a project is self-financed, there is an opportunity cost—the interest rate forgone. Refer to page 242 for more on this point.

13. (a) Goodwill is intangible capital; inventory is tangible capital. Refer to page 234.

14. (b) In general, the higher the interest rate, the cost of new investment projects will be higher and the number of profitable investment projects will be fewer. Note that the investment demand curve is downward sloping.

15. (c) Present value is affected by interest rate changes; expected rate of return is not.

II. SOLUTIONS TO APPLICATION QUESTIONS

1. (a) Clarissa's advice may be sound, but for the wrong reason. You really can't give Camille much help without knowing the interest rate.

   (b) Clarissa is assuming a dollar today and a dollar five years in the future are identical in value. She is ignoring present value (or assuming that the interest rate is 0 percent).

(c)   Camille should not accept the offer of the training program. The present value of $44,000 per year for five years is:
$44,000/(1.1) + \$44,000/(1.1^2) + \$44,000/(1.1^3) + \$44,000/(1.1^4) + \$44,000/(1.1^5) =$
$\$40,000.00 + \$36,363.63 + \$33,057.85 + \$30,052.59 + \$27,320.54 = \$166,794.61.$
The present value of $80,000 per year for the three final years is:
$80,000/(1.1^3) + 80,000/(1.1^4) + 80,000/(1.1^5) =$
$\$60,105.18 + \$54,641.08 + \$49,673.70 = \$164,419.97.$

        Because the present value of the current position exceeds that of the "training plus new position," Camille is better advised to retain her present position.

(d)   To encourage investment of any kind, the government should decrease the interest rate. At the extreme, using Clarissa's assumption of a 0 percent interest rate, the PV of the training program would exceed the PV of the five-year position ($240,000 exceeds $220,000).

(e)   A "low-interest rate" strategy will promote longer-term investments—the "discount" applied to future earnings is smaller. Lowering the interest rate makes the present value of all future income streams higher, but the effect is more pronounced over longer time periods.

2.   Although each project earns a total income of $1,000, the present value of Jody's project is lower. This is because each dollar earned five years from now is worth less than each dollar earned one year from now. Judy's project accumulates revenue faster.

    If Jody demanded proof, set up the following table calculating present values. Judy's project has a present value of $758.16, whereas Jody's trails at $701.96.

	Judy's Project		Jody's Project	
Year	Income	PV	Income	PV
1	$200	$181.82	$100	$90.91
2	$200	$165.29	$100	$82.64
3	$200	$150.26	$100	$75.13
4	$200	$136.60	$300	$204.90
5	$200	$124.18	$400	$248.37
	$1,000	$758.16	$1,000	$701.96

3.   No, winners don't really win $100 million in current dollars. If the interest rate is assumed to be 5 percent (for example), the final $5,000,000 would be worth only(!) $1,884,447 in present value terms $(5,000,000/1.05^{20})$.

4.   (a)   Given an interest rate of 7 percent, $100 would be worth $25.84. $500,000 would be worth $129,200

   (b)   Given an interest rate of 3 percent, $100 would be worth $55.37. $500,000 would be worth $276,850

5.

		Johnsons	Aunt Agatha	Jack Diamond
(a)	Saving	$75,000	can't tell	$375,000
(b)	Investment	$500,000	0	0
(c)	Change in net worth	$75,000	0	$375,000
(d)	Change in capital stock	$700,000	0	0

6. (a) $120

    (b) $120/(1.12^1) + $120/(1.12^2) + $120/(1.12^3) + $1,000/(1.12^3) =
          $107.14 + $95.66 + $85.41 + $711.78 = $1,000.00

    (c)   higher; fall

    (d)   rise;
          $120/(1.08^1) + $120/(1.08^2) + $120/(1.08^3) + $1,000/(1.08^3) =
          $111.11 + $102.88 + $95.26 + $793.83 = $1,103.08

    (e)   higher; lower

7. (a)   D   (b)   I   (c)   I or D   (d)   D
    (e)   I   (f)   I   (g)   D   (h)   D

8. Judy's project should be undertaken. Present value is $950.96, which is greater than the $900 cost, but Jody's project would bring in only $863.40 in present value.

9. (a)   No!

    (b)   Project 2

    (c)   Project 2 is clearly superior, once all the values have been converted to a common basis. Some calculation can be avoided by looking at the net cash flow (revenue – cost).

	Project 1			**Project 2**		
Year	**Cash Flow**	**÷ Conversion**	**PV**	**Cash Flow**	**÷ Conversion**	**PV**
1	–$700	1.100	–$636.36	–$200	1.100	–$181.82
2	0	1.210	0.00	$300	1.210	$247.93
3	$900	1.331	$676.18	$100	1.331	$75.13
			$39.82			$141.24

    (d)   Both projects are profitable, so the rate of return exceeds 10 percent.

10. (a)   Investment demand relates the market interest rate (the cost of borrowing funds) to the quantity of new capital (investment) demanded.

    (b)   The investment demand curve's slope and position are critically affected by the expectations of those making investment decisions. Expectations can be influenced by political events, circumstances abroad, or changes in the domestic economy.

    (c)   Volatility is reflected by both the shape and position of the curve. If demand is elastic, changes in the interest rate will provoke large changes in the level of investment. The curve will shift position, perhaps dramatically, as expectations change.

    (d)   When there is a cut in interest rates, the cost of financing a new project falls. Given that the revenue from the project remains unchanged, profits will rise. More projects will become profitable and more investment will occur.

    (e)   The development of a new technology may make the existing capital stock obsolete (or less competitive), forcing a wave of new investment.

    (f)   If new technological developments are expected, firms may delay investment, because they don't to be locked into an old technology. Investment will fall.

(g)   If there is an expectation that corporate taxes will increase, there is an expectation that after-tax profits will decrease. This is likely to dampen investment.

11.   First, there is a definitional issue. Some activities most of us would call "saving" are not defined that way, such as interest paid on home loans or contributions to retirement funds. Given that, the mismatch between U.S. saving and U.S. investment is most easily explained by the inflow of foreign funds. China, for example, has loaned U.S. businesses about $400 billion. Many U.S. industries are controlled by foreign owners. Sound recording industries have 97 percent foreign ownership, for instance.

12

General Equilibrium and the Efficiency of Perfect Competition

1. Define general equilibrium and distinguish it from partial equilibrium. Distinguish the effects on a general equilibrium of a given change in one market.
2. Define allocative, or Pareto, efficiency. Outline why we know that resources are allocated efficiently, outputs are distributed efficiently, and the correct output mix is achieved in a perfectly competitive economy.
3. List each of the conditions underpinning the perfectly competitive model and indicate how perfect competition results in efficient production.
4. Identify four causes of market failure and describe how they arise. Explain the results each market failure presents and suggest how each might be rectified.

This chapter plays three major roles and is both a beginning and an end. First, while presenting a general equilibrium model, it reviews all of the partial equilibrium material developed for the perfectly competitive model from Chapter 6 onwards. Second, it establishes an "efficiency" benchmark against which subsequent market structures (monopoly, etc.) and related topics will be measured. Last, Chapter 12 previews the sequence of upcoming chapters (13 through 19), in a sense providing a convenient "road map" for the remainder of your microeconomics principles course.

The first half of the chapter is essentially a review of previous material. Use it as such. The Amazon Kindle example gives you a chance to check up on your understanding of changes in demand, cost curves, consumer and producer surplus, the role of profit and loss, and long-run adjustments.

Although a formal proof of general equilibrium is mathematically complex, you can see the big picture if you use your intuition. When a system in equilibrium is shocked, all portions of it adjust until "balance" is restored.

BRAIN TEASER I: Suppose, back in Neanderthal days, food and hunting equipment were distributed according to strength. Compare this method of allocation with a system based on equity (fairness), and another based on efficiency. Recall that efficiency involves producing what people want at the lowest cost. How are the methods different, and how are they similar?

Now suppose that you are a severely physically handicapped individual in today's economy, unable to work and requiring costly medical supplies. Which of the three methods would *you* prefer?

BRAIN TEASER II: Lifeboat: Suppose there is just one place left in an eight-person lifeboat and still two persons in the water who wish to be saved. How should the seat be allocated, first in terms of efficiency and then in terms of equity? Should the "more valuable" person be saved? How would you measure this? Or the stronger person saved? Or, perhaps, the weaker? (The strong one might survive outside the boat.) Or should all *eight* seats be reallocated? Should there be some kind of bidding process, or should straws be drawn? Would there be any way to determine if Pareto-efficient changes were possible?

Objective 1

Define general equilibrium and distinguish it from partial equilibrium. Distinguish the effects on a general equilibrium of a given change in one market.

Firms and households make simultaneous decisions in output and input markets, trying to maximize profit and utility, respectively. A *partial equilibrium* approach looks at individual markets for specific goods, but some issues require a broader view—a *general equilibrium* perspective. Changes in one market affect other markets—products have substitutes and complements, for example. General equilibrium analysis examines this process. (page 254)

  If a hard frost damages the Florida orange crop, it is easy to go beyond partial equilibrium analysis (the price of oranges will increase), to conclude that the price of orange juice will decrease (if you can't figure out why, refer to Chapter 3), as will the price of substitutes such as grapefruit juice. In real life, we do this sort of analysis all the time, especially when moving from input markets to product markets. If there is another conflict in the Middle East, how will it affect the price of gasoline? The demand for electric cars? The more closely related two markets are, the more significant the effect on one if there is a change in the other.

> **LEARNING TIP:** Trace through the implications of the textbook's extended example on market adjustment to changes in demand (pp. 254–256). It is both a good review of partial equilibrium concepts and a good example of general equilibrium analysis.◀

Practice

1.   General equilibrium analysis ignores which of the following questions?
    (a)   Are equilibria in different markets compatible?
    (b)   Can all markets achieve equilibrium simultaneously?
    (c)   How will a change in demand in Market *A* affect circumstances in other markets?
    (d)   What are the equilibrium conditions for markets other than Market *A*?

    ANSWER: (d)   General equilibrium analysis is not concerned with single markets.

2.   General equilibrium exists whenever
    (a)   normal profits are being earned.
    (b)   total excess demand equals total excess supply.
    (c)   quantity demanded equals quantity supplied in each market.
    (d)   income is allocated equitably.

    ANSWER: (c)   Refer to page 254. All markets must be in equilibrium at the same time.

Use the following information for the next four questions: Arboc has only two products—ground nuts and goat cheese. These goods are substitutes and are produced by perfectly competitive firms. Initially, both markets are in long-run equilibrium. Now consumer preferences shift away from goat cheese and toward ground nuts.

3.   Given the preceding information, which of the following will **not** occur?
    (a)   In the short run, goat cheese producers will incur losses.
    (b)   In the short run, there will be an increase in the demand for ground nut workers.
    (c)   In the long run, more firms will enter the ground nut industry.
    (d)   More capital will flow into the production of goat cheese.

    ANSWER: (d)   Less capital will flow into the production of goat cheese.

4.   Given the preceding information, we would expect
        (a)   short-run profits in the ground nut industry.
        (b)   long-run losses in the goat cheese industry.
        (c)   long-run profits in the ground nut industry.
        (d)   short-run losses in the ground nut industry.

        ANSWER: (a)   You can't get long-run profits or losses.

5.   As a producer of goat cheese, your best short-run strategy is to
        (a)   leave the industry and enter the ground nut industry.
        (b)   switch over to ground nut production.
        (c)   set your output level to equalize marginal cost and the market price.
        (d)   cut your price to become more competitive and to increase your market share.

        ANSWER: (c)   To maximize profits, produce where $P = MC$. If you can't cover your operating costs, you'd be better off closing down.

6.   The demand for inputs used in goat cheese production will _____ and the demand for inputs used in ground nut production will _____ .
        (a)   increase; increase
        (b)   increase; decrease
        (c)   decrease; increase
        (d)   decrease; decrease

        ANSWER: (c)   Input demand, recall, is influenced by the price of the final product. As goat cheese producers scale back operations, they will cut their demand for inputs. Ground nut producers will increase their input demand. ∎

Objective 2

Define allocative, or Pareto, efficiency. Outline why we know that resources are allocated efficiently, outputs are distributed efficiently, and the correct output mix is achieved in a perfectly competitive economy.

Efficiency is one criterion for evaluating any given economic system or market, and for flagging potential problems in the perfect operation of the market system. An economy achieves allocative efficiency if it produces, as cheaply as possible, the commodities that consumers want. A change is *efficient* if at least one person is made better off and no person is made worse off as a result of that change. A Pareto-efficient economy is one in which all such changes have already been made. Even if a change "hurts" some individuals, it is still *potentially efficient* if the gains outweigh the losses. (Gainers could fully compensate losers and still come out ahead.) (page 256)

Efficiency: You may have some difficulty with the concept of efficiency. One way to assess an economy's performance is in terms of how well it meets the needs of its consumers. The efficiency concept captures this notion. The major point to take away from this chapter is that perfectly competitive markets result in maximum allocative efficiency—the "best" mix of outputs, produced as cheaply as possible. Any movement away from the perfectly competitive ideal (externalities, for example) leads to distortions—either too much or too little of a good is produced, or the price or cost is too high.

As mentioned in the textbook, we can look at efficiency graphically using demand and supply analysis, and the concepts of producer and consumer surplus. A market is as efficient as possible when the aggregate of producer surplus and consumer surplus is maximized. This occurs where the demand curve and supply curve intersect.

LEARNING TIP: By this point in your studies, you may be so used to thinking of equilibrium at that intersection that considering why is it "best" and what is happening at other output (non-equilibrium) levels may be a challenge. Try drawing a demand and supply diagram—extend the curves to the vertical axis. Put in the equilibrium price and quantity. First, shade in the area representing the combined consumer and producer surpluses (the area "between" the curves). Now choose any output level other than the equilibrium output level and consider what has happened to the combined area. (It will decrease.) The total "gain" to society is maximized at equilibrium. ◀

ECONOMICS IN PRACTICE: On page 257, there is an article that traces through the widespread impact of the increased popularity of ethanol. Because corn is used to produce ethanol, it has become more attractive for farmers to produce, leading them to produce less wheat. The price of wheat increased as a result. Now choose your own example—make it one that has had widespread impacts—and see how far you can make the ripple effects extend. If you're stuck, how about the effects of a removal of economic sanctions on Cuba? Or the impacts of global warming?

ANSWER: In 2008, Honda rolled out its hydrogen fuel cell vehicle, the FCX Clarity. If the demand for such vehicles blossoms (a change in consumer preferences), the demand for conventional gas-fueled cars would decrease. Profits for the less-favored cars would decline. As the same time, the demand for oil by drivers would decrease. This would decrease the price of oil, which would have additional impacts on both energy costs for businesses and heating oil for consumers. For extra credit, you should be able to draw demand and supply diagrams to help you describe the effects of your change. In the Clarity example, the demand for fuel cell cars increases, the demand for conventional cars and for oil decreases.

Practice

7.   Pareto optimality is present in Robinson Crusoe Land when
    (a)   any improvement in the welfare of Robinson reduces the welfare of Friday.
    (b)   the benefits from production are divided evenly.
    (c)   an improvement in the welfare of Robinson does not reduce the welfare of Friday.
    (d)   the benefits from production are divided according to effort.

    ANSWER: (a) Pareto optimality pertains to any situation where making one or more persons better off has an adverse impact on the welfare of another.

8.   On Milly's Milk Farm, overtime (which runs to 20 hours per week) has traditionally been awarded on the basis of seniority. Old Joshua Merriweather (who has been on the farm since he was a lad, 80 years ago) invariably does all the overtime himself. The four other farm workers (who want to work some overtime) propose a "fair shares for all" method of allocating overtime. We can conclude that
    (a)   the new method is certainly Pareto optimal.
    (b)   the traditional method is certainly Pareto optimal.
    (c)   both methods are certainly Pareto optimal.
    (d)   neither method is certainly Pareto optimal.

    ANSWER: (d) An increase in the welfare of the four workers will reduce Joshua's welfare. The traditional method is not certainly optimal because the four workers' loss in welfare may exceed Joshua's increase in welfare. It may be potentially efficient.

9.   You own a calculus book from a course you took last semester. You paid $40 for it as a used textbook at the college bookstore. You value it at $15, but its sell-back value at the bookstore is only $10. Is selling the book to the bookstore Pareto efficient?
    (a)   Yes, because $10 is better than nothing, and you could use the cash.
    (b)   Yes, because it is a voluntary exchange—no one is twisting your arm.
    (c)   No, because the market price of the book is $40.
    (d)   No, because the $10 is less than the $15 value you place on the book.

ANSWER: (d) Selling for $10 an item that you value at $15 results in a loss. If, as in Option (a), you could use the cash, this should have affected your valuation of the book.

10. You have a calculus book from a course you took last semester. You paid $40 for it as a used textbook at the college bookstore. Because its sell-back value is only $10 and you value it at $15, you have decided to keep it. Now Arnold (a math major, who values the book at $25) offers you $20. Is selling the book to Arnold Pareto efficient?

(a) Yes, because both you and Arnold have gained from the trade.
(b) Yes, because Arnold has compensated you for the loss imposed by the college bookstore sell-back policy.
(c) No, because you are still selling a book that costs $60 for $20.
(d) No, because you could have got $5 more—Arnold would have paid as much as $25.

ANSWER: (a) A voluntary exchange must make at least one of the participants better off. In this case, you dispose of a book worth $15 to you for $20 (gain) and Arnold receives a book worth $25 to him for $20 (gain). Given the decision not to sell to the bookstore, that transaction becomes irrelevant. ∎

Objective 3

List each of the conditions underpinning the perfectly competitive model and indicate how perfect competition results in efficient production.

The perfectly competitive model developed over the previous chapters leads to an efficient (optimal) allocation of resources. The system works because resources are allocated among firms efficiently, final products are allocated among households to maximize utility, and the system produces the mix of goods and services (including leisure) that society wants. (page 259)

Efficient Output Mix: $P = MC$: It's important to grasp that, by operating where $P = MC$, firms produce the most efficient combination of outputs. The logic is displayed graphically in Figure 12.2—get a good understanding of that diagram. You saw the right-hand side of the diagram in Chapter 6 and the left-hand side in Chapter 10. Go back now and review that material.

The price of a good reflects the good's value to the household—you won't pay more for a good than its value to you. Remember, too, that the marginal cost of Good X embodies the opportunity cost of the next most preferred alternative forgone, Good Y. If the price that consumers are willing to pay for Good X is less than that opportunity cost, i.e., the value of Good Y, then producing the extra unit of Good X must reduce their utility. If the marginal cost of producing Good X is lower than the price of Good X, then more of Good X should be produced.

Finally, don't forget that perfect competition extends to input markets—both workers and employers are price takers in the labor market, for instance. If the labor market equilibrium condition $W = MRP_L$ doesn't hold, inefficiency occurs.

Practice

11. If an economy has competitive input and output markets, and firms who maximize profits, the economy will

(a) achieve an efficient allocation of resources.
(b) achieve an equitable distribution of income.
(c) minimize differences between the marginal revenue products of different types of inputs.
(d) allow the marginal utility of consumers to be maximized.

ANSWER: (a) In the absence of "market failures" (discussed in the textbook on page 262), these economic conditions will result in an efficient allocation of resources.

12. The condition that ensures that consumers get the goods they want is
    (a) $MR = MC$.
    (b) $P = MC$.
    (c) $MR = P$.
    (d) $P = ATC$.

    ANSWER: (b) In this case, the marginal cost of a good for society is equal to the value placed on that good by society.

13. The price of a bag of jellybeans is $1.00. The total cost of producing 24 bags of jellybeans is $24.75. The total cost of producing 25 bags of jellybeans is $25.25. The total cost of producing 26 bags of jellybeans is $26.00. Currently, 25 bags of jellybeans are being produced. Society would benefit if
    (a) the twenty-sixth bag of jellybeans is produced.
    (b) production is kept at 25 bags.
    (c) the price of jellybeans is increased.
    (d) production is reduced to 24 bags of jellybeans.

    ANSWER: (a) *MC* of the 26th bag is 75¢. Because price exceeds *MC*, the 26th bag should be produced.

14. The social value of a bag of jellybeans is the
    (a) price of the bag of jellybeans.
    (b) marginal revenue of the bag of jellybeans.
    (c) marginal cost of the bag of jellybeans.
    (d) total cost of the bag of jellybeans.

    ANSWER: (a) Price reflects the value society puts on a good. Refer to page 261.

15. Marginal cost of a bag of jellybeans is a measure of
    (a) the value society places on a bag of jellybeans.
    (b) society's net gain when the bag of jellybeans is produced.
    (c) society's net loss when the bag of jellybeans is produced.
    (d) what society gives up to produce the bag of jellybeans.

    ANSWER: (d) Marginal cost measures the opportunity cost to society of the resources used in producing the jellybeans.

16. Dot and Ted Sfeir own a firm ("Dotted Spheres") that produces size 5 soccer balls in a perfectly competitive market. They produce 600 balls a week at a cost of $8 per ball, which is the lowest possible long-run average cost. The market price is $14. Which of the following is true?
    (a) Dotted Spheres' current output level is efficient because average cost is minimized.
    (b) Society would be better off if Dotted Spheres increased its current output level because price exceeds marginal cost.
    (c) Society would be better off if Dotted Spheres increased its current output level because price exceeds average cost.
    (d) Society would be better off if Dotted Spheres decreased its current output level because this will increase the firm's profits.

    ANSWER: (b) If average cost is minimized at $8, then marginal cost is also $8. (If you're uncertain on this, review Chapter 8.) Price, then, exceeds the cost of producing an extra ball, so more should be produced. ∎

Objective 4

Identify four causes of market failure and describe how they arise. Explain the results each market failure presents and suggest how each might be rectified.

In the real world, the stringent conditions of the perfectly competitive model might not be met. In such a situation a *market failure* occurs and inefficiencies creep into the system of unregulated markets. (page 262)

(a) *Imperfect competitive markets*, such as monopoly (where there is only one seller), arise when firms have some measure of control over price and/or competition. Economic profits may be maintained indefinitely if competitors can be barred from entry. The consequences are higher prices and more restricted production than would occur in a competitive environment—consumers lose.

(b) *Public goods* provide benefits even to those who do not pay for them. Because one can consume without having to pay, there is a powerful incentive not to pay, i.e., to be a free rider. Although private firms might be able to produce public goods, the problem is that they will not produce enough of them, because they cannot compel consumers to pay their fair share. By using tax dollars, the government can produce a sufficient quantity of public goods and improve efficiency.

(c) *Externalities* (costs or benefits encountered by a party outside a transaction) do not enter into the calculations of profit- and utility-maximizing firms and consumers. If externalities *are* a factor, the allocation of resources is likely to be suboptimal, even if the market is perfectly competitive.

(d) *Misinformation or poor information* affects the market participant's ability to make an informed choice. The less informed he or she is, the more likely a suboptimal outcome is.

Inefficient Output Mix: $P \neq MC$: Although in different ways, the efficient $P = MC$ condition is infringed in each of the four cases. Check how the condition fails in each of the preceding four cases. If, for a good, either the valuation of the benefit to society (price) or the opportunity cost to society (marginal cost) is incorrect, then a sub-optimal mix of output will occur.

ECONOMICS IN PRACTICE (SUPPLEMENTAL): Is ticket scalping efficient?
ANSWER: Ticket scalping is yet another example of the power of demand and supply. Tickets are allocated to the highest bidder—presumably those who value the tickets most highly.

ECONOMICS IN PRACTICE (CONTINUED): Before eBay (founded 1995), markets were significantly less efficient, especially with respect to used items—buyers and sellers couldn't find each other as easily. Is smuggling another example of market forces attempting to prevail despite government restrictions? How about sex tourism? Or underage drinking? How is your answer affected if such trades involve externalities?
ANSWER: Trade restrictions on imported goods reduce efficiency because they prevent buyers and sellers from legally indulging in voluntary exchange. Smuggling exists because customers are willing to pay the illegal price (which may include a substantial mark-up) to receive a good they want. Both the customer and the smuggler gain. Other options may be more practical if the ban is on a service. With sex tourism, for example, the buyer presumably finds the additional expense of traveling worthwhile in order to escape from domestic legal restrictions on prostitution. Underage drinking is illegal but, nevertheless, a fact of life. Additional resources (time or a fake ID, for instance) must be used to accomplish the exchange. The underlying point is that, in each of the cases discussed, both parties gain from the voluntary exchange. However, if the exchange involves externalities (transmission of disease, substance abuse, drunk driving) a case can be made that restrictions are corrective and can improve efficiency.

Practice

17. In the market for apples there is a consumer surplus, and a short-run economic profit is being made. This is conclusive evidence of
    (a) externalities.
    (b) market failure.
    (c) apples being a public good.
    (d) None of the above are correct.

    ANSWER: (d) Consumer surplus and short-run economic profits are possible in a perfectly competitive industry. Refer to page 89 in the textbook to review the concept of consumer surplus.

18. The firms in a perfectly competitive industry merge into one big firm and then impose barriers to entry into the industry. We can say that
    (a) we can expect that externalities will begin to appear.
    (b) the product of this industry is a public good.
    (c) the price of the product will be higher, and the output lower, than under perfect competition.
    (d) this firm will be unable to maximize profits.

    ANSWER: (c) Imperfect markets are a source of inefficiency. Refer to page 262.

19. The production of Good Z involves positive externalities. A perfectly competitive industry will _____ this good; a monopoly will _____ this good.
    (a) overproduce; overproduce
    (b) overproduce; underproduce
    (c) underproduce; overproduce
    (d) underproduce; underproduce

    ANSWER: (d) The presence of a positive externality means that the market does not capture the full benefits to society flowing from this good.

20. Public goods are a source of market failure because
    (a) they permit economic profits to occur in the long run.
    (b) they are provided by government agencies.
    (c) their benefits cannot be limited to the consumers who purchase them.
    (d) they can be produced more cheaply by private firms.

    ANSWER: (c) Because benefits cannot be limited to those who purchase them, the demand for public goods does not reflect their social value.

21. The production of Good Y imposes a cost on the purchaser. Good Y
    (a) has negative externalities.
    (b) has positive externalities.
    (c) is a public good.
    (d) is a typical good.

    ANSWER: (d) All goods involve costs (and benefits). Only those goods that pass costs (or benefits) on to third parties exhibit externalities.

22. The licensing of cosmetologists is an attempt to
    (a) control provision of a public good.
    (b) improve the imperfect information for buyers of this service.
    (c) impose externalities on potential competitors.
    (d) correct an imperfectly competitive market structure.

ANSWER: (b) Licensing offers buyers the benefit of knowing that practitioners have achieved a given quality of performance. It may also operate as a barrier to entry (not an externality).

23.   Ground nuts are sold by a monopoly and goat cheese is sold by perfectly competitive firms. When both markets are in equilibrium,
(a) $P > MC$ for both goods.
(b) $P = MC$ for both goods.
(c) $P = MC$ for ground nuts and $P > MC$ for goat cheese.
(d) $P > MC$ for ground nuts and $P = MC$ for goat cheese.

ANSWER: (d) In perfect competition, $MR = P = MC$. In monopoly, $P > MR = MC$.

24.   Levees (that prevent floods) along the Mississippi are a _____ . The free market will _____ them.
(a)   private good; overproduce
(b)   private good; underproduce
(c)   public good; overproduce
(d)   public good; underproduce

ANSWER: (d) Levees provide benefits for all residents. The free market will tend to build too few.

25.   A museum in Britain once exhibited a display of Roman coins. After some time, a small boy approached the curator and pointed out that one of the "coins" was, in fact, a dirty plastic bottle top! An economist would say that
(a)   society lost, because the value of the exhibit was reduced.
(b)   society lost, because, although the exhibit might never be sold, society now knew that the coin was a fake.
(c)   society gained, because better information about the exhibit was now available.
(d)   society gained, because now the remaining coins were even more rare.

ANSWER: (c) Refer to page 264. ■

BRAIN TEASER I SOLUTION: Equity would dictate fair shares to all. It may be wiser to make sure that the skilled hunters have enough food and supplies to continue to provide for the other tribe members. Some order of precedence (pecking order) may have survival value. This assumes, of course, that the strongest are also the most skilled in hunting, and this might be an invalid assumption. Allocation according to efficiency means that the Neanderthals should maximize social well-being. In the short term, this might be interpreted as fair shares for all—in the longer term, it might be interpreted as giving the hunters enough food and supplies to retain their effectiveness and then dividing up the remaining supplies according to need.

From the point of view of self-interest, the severely handicapped individual would presumably prefer the equitable allocation of resources. As a society, we continually address the question of "how much is too much?" in a given case.

BRAIN TEASER II SOLUTION: Lifeboat: In terms of efficiency, the single seat should be allocated to the person who "wants" it more. Clearly, it is in the interest of each individual to inflate the magnitude of his or her needs. From the point of view of society, the more valuable person should be saved. In terms of equity, a "fair" method might involve flipping a coin. Clearly, though, all seats should be reassigned. This will be strongly resisted by the occupants of the boat. Life, then, is unlikely to be either fair or efficient.

A LOOK AHEAD

The previous chapters have set up the perfectly competitive framework—the economist's version of the best of all possible worlds. If perfect competition can't be attained then neither can allocative efficiency. Imperfections—externalities, public goods, inadequate information, monopoly power—occur in the real world and mess things up. The conclusions reached in this and the preceding chapters will be used to assess the performance of markets where imperfections exist.

PRACTICE TEST

I. MULTIPLE-CHOICE QUESTIONS

Select the option that provides the single best answer.

_____ 1. Which of the following indicates that we have an efficient output market?
   (a) Wage equals the marginal revenue product of labor.
   (b) Price of the output equals the marginal cost of the output.
   (c) Price of the output equals the marginal revenue product.
   (d) Marginal utility is greater than the price of the output.

Use the following information to answer the next five questions. Chicken and beef are the only goods produced in the economy. Each is a constant-cost industry and each is currently in equilibrium. Suddenly there is a permanent shift in the preferences of consumers in favor of chicken and away from beef.

_____ 2. We would expect
   (a) short-run losses in the beef industry.
   (b) long-run losses in the beef industry.
   (c) short-run losses in the chicken industry.
   (d) long-run losses in the chicken industry.

_____ 3. Relative to the current price, the price of chicken would _____ in the short run and _____ in the long run.
   (a) rise; remain unchanged
   (b) fall; remain unchanged
   (c) rise; fall
   (d) fall; rise

_____ 4. As a beef producer, in the short run, your best strategy is to
   (a) shut down immediately.
   (b) keep operating as long as you can cover your fixed costs.
   (c) keep operating as long as you can cover your variable costs.
   (d) cut the price of your beef to win your customers back.

_____ 5. As a chicken producer, in the short run, your best strategy is to
   (a) increase your beef-producing facilities.
   (b) cut price to increase market share.
   (c) expand production until marginal cost is again equal to price.
   (d) buy more of every input to expand production.

_____ 6. As the economy moves from the initial long-run equilibrium to the final long-run equilibrium, with respect to inputs, we would expect that
   (a) each industry will continue to use the same amounts of inputs because these are constant-cost industries.
   (b) all input markets will be affected.
   (c) the labor market will not be affected.
   (d) only the labor and capital markets will be affected because land is fixed in supply.

_____ 7. Sellco introduces a new policy that reduces the cost of joining the company club but limits how frequently club members can use the facilities. As a result, some employees will lose and some will gain. On balance, the new plan bestows benefits of $1,000 at a cost of S300. The company's previous policy was _____ . The new policy is _____ .
  (a)   inefficient; potentially efficient
  (b)   Pareto optimal; potentially efficient
  (c)   efficient; Pareto optimal
  (d)   inefficient; Pareto optimal

_____ 8. Barriers to entry are most closely linked with
  (a)   externalities.
  (b)   public goods.
  (c)   monopolies.
  (d)   perfect competition.

_____ 9. Pollution is an example of
  (a)   a public good.
  (b)   an externality.
  (c)   imperfect competition.
  (d)   imperfect information.

_____ 10. The milk industry is perfectly competitive, selling its product at $3.00 per gallon. The marginal cost of milk at Dana's Dairy is $2.50. Dana should price her product at
  (a) $3.00.
  (b) $2.50.
  (c)   50¢.
  (d) $2.75.

_____ 11. Mike's Milkery is able to exclude other firms from entering its market. This is an example of
  (a)   an externality.
  (b)   external competition.
  (c)   a monopoly.
  (d)   a public good.

_____ 12. All of the following are sources of market inefficiency EXCEPT
  (a)   public goods.
  (b)   externalities.
  (c)   monopolistically competitive firms.
  (d)   lack of control by individual firms over price.

_____ 13. Relative to perfect competition, imperfect competition will produce
  (a)   lower prices and more output.
  (b)   lower prices and less output.
  (c)   higher prices and more output.
  (d)   higher prices and less output.

_____ 14. A market is Pareto efficient if
(a) any change that improves the welfare of one individual reduces the welfare of another.
(b) income is equally distributed.
(c) output is equally distributed.
(d) it produces any mix of output at the lowest cost.

_____ 15. Which of the following activities is least likely to generate an externality?
(a) Wearing perfume
(b) Smoking a cigarette
(c) Reading a comic book
(d) Plowing snow from a road

_____ 16. Ruth tithes (i.e., gives one-tenth of her income) to her church. Which of the following is true?
(a) This exchange is Pareto optimal, because Ruth can use this charitable contribution as a tax deduction.
(b) This exchange is Pareto optimal, otherwise the two parties would not voluntarily agree to the exchange.
(c) This exchange is not Pareto optimal because, as the church has no option but to accept the money, it is not a voluntary exchange.
(d) This exchange is not Pareto optimal, because Ruth does not necessarily receive any good or service in exchange.

_____ 17. The highly competitive hog industry is booming in the southeastern states. Opponents, however, point out the presence of negative externalities that firms ignore. When deciding how much to produce, the typical firm will produce
(a) more than the efficient output level.
(b) less than the efficient output level.
(c) the efficient output level because the firm is competitive.
(d) the efficient output level because the industry is competitive.

Use the following information for the next three questions. Tobacco Belt land can be used for the production of either tobacco or soybeans. The Surgeon General finds definitive evidence that cigarette smoking shortens a smoker's life. This leads to a shift in preferences away from tobacco products and towards soybean consumption.

_____ 18. As the Tobacco Belt economy moves from the initial equilibrium to the new equilibrium, we would predict that

(a) all input markets will be affected.
(b) all input markets, except land (which can be used for both tobacco and soybeans), will be affected.
(c) the land market will not be affected because tobacco and soybeans require different farming techniques.
(d) the labor market will not be affected because unskilled workers are employed in both types of product.

_____ 19. As the Tobacco Belt economy moves from the initial equilibrium to the new equilibrium, we would predict all of the following EXCEPT that
   (a)   farms producing tobacco will experience short-run losses.
   (b)   farms producing soybeans will experience short-run profits.
   (c)   more farmers will switch over to soybean production and away from tobacco production.
   (d)   additional capital will move into tobacco production to make up for the loss of land resources.

_____ 20. Minnie Cooper owns a soybean farm. Her best profit-maximizing strategy is to
   (a)   cut her prices to increase her market share of the expanding industry.
   (b)   plant tobacco because, as fewer farmers plant tobacco, its price will rise.
   (c)   increase soybean production to earn short-run economic profits.
   (d)   decrease soybean production to force the price higher.

II. APPLICATION QUESTIONS

1. Two refugees, Alex (who likes candy) and Branko (who likes to smoke), have found their way to a Red Cross camp in Eastern Europe. They each receive a Red Cross parcel containing 20 cigarettes and 20 pieces of candy.

	Alex		Branko	
	Cigarettes	**Candy**	**Cigarettes**	**Candy**
Red Cross	20	20	20	20
Experiment	12	30	24	10
Trade I				
Trade II (Pavel)				

You (an entrepreneur) are also in the refugee camp and you know the preferences of your two colleagues. As an "experiment," you ask Alex how many cigarettes he would trade in order to receive 10 more units of candy—Alex replies 8. You ask Branko how many cigarettes he would need to be induced to trade 10 units of candy—he replies 4.

   (a)   Suppose you act as a middleman and reallocate the candy and cigarettes between Alex and Branko according to the numbers provided by the experiment. Who gains? Does anyone lose? Is this a Pareto optimal action?

   (b)   Can you see any way of profiting from the present situation? If so, how? Write the results of the trade in the table above. You have provided a service. Assuming no half cigarettes or half pieces of candy, derive the maximum possible profit. Call this "Trade I." Who gains? Does anyone lose? Is this a Pareto optimal action?

   (c)   Suppose a rival trader (Pavel) observes the economic profits that you are earning and decides to undercut you when the next Red Cross parcels are distributed to Alex and Branko. Assuming no half cigarettes or half pieces of candy, derive the maximum possible profit for Pavel. Call this "Trade II."

   (d)   When will this process end and who are the major winners?

2. There is certainly a demand for, and supply of, hardwoods for construction. Suppose they are produced by a perfectly competitive industry. Evidence suggests that depletion of the rainforests may be responsible in part for increasing world temperatures, i.e., "the greenhouse effect." Does

the presence of this side effect pose any problems for our conclusion that perfect competition produces an efficient mix of goods?

3. The market for personal computers began booming in the 1990s. In what ways did that boom affect the labor market? What new skills were demanded? How were those skills produced? Suppose Andrea Hacker just bought a PC for $2,000. If PCs didn't exist, how might Andrea have spent the same $2,000? What happens to employment in the sectors where these items are produced?

4. If I buy a good—for example, a new DVD—and share it with my friend, allowing her to "rip" it, does my action improve or diminish the allocative efficiency of the economic system? Why? Suppose, instead, I resell the DVD to my friend. Does this affect your answer?

5. We have an economy that produces only two goods—guns and butter. Each industry is perfectly competitive and there are constant returns to scale. You have been appointed as assistant to the Assistant Secretary of Commerce. Because of a reduction in geopolitical tensions, the demand for guns is expected to decrease quite substantially in the near future, however, because of the peaceful climate, the demand for butter will increase. The Assistant Secretary has asked you to prepare a report on the full effects of this change.
    What will be the effect on:
    (a)   The price and quantity of guns?

    (b)   The price and quantity of butter?

6. Given the profit-maximizing output level, a firm will seek to minimize costs—you can't earn maximum profits if you allow a more costly than necessary method of production. The connection between utility maximization and profit maximization is less evident. The following example lets you work through the link between the maximizing behavior of households and of firms.
    (a)   What, in words, is the utility-maximizing rule? (Check back to Chapter 6 for the "household equilibrium condition" if you're not too sure.)

    (b)   With only two goods, A and B, what is the utility-maximizing formula?
    The ratio $MU_A/MU_B = P_A/P_B$ must be true for every pair of goods. If you want, put in numbers to confirm the ratios.
    (c)   What, in words, is the profit-maximization rule?

    (d)   Write down an interpretation of the meaning of MC.

    (e)   Now, write down the profit-maximizing formula. Does it hold for all profit maximizers?

    (f)   Let's generalize by noting that $P_A = MC_A$ and $P_B = MC_B$.
    Observe that the two results combined give: $MU_A/MU_B = MC_A/MC_B$. The perfectly competitive model results in the production of exactly those quantities of each of the goods requested by consumers, given their opportunity costs—i.e. the optimal output mix.
         Now, let's violate the equalities in this formula to check your understanding. Suppose, for example, that Good A is apples and Good B is butter, and the following is true: $MU_A = 50$, $MC_A = 40$ and $MU_B = 60$, $MC_B = 30$. Substitute these values into the formula. What does the inequality tell you?

    (g)   What should be the response?

    (h)   What will happen to each of the four values?

Here is evidence that profit maximizers will respond to consumer demands to produce the desired product mix.

7.   Match up the "market failure" with the infringed "perfectly competitive" assumption and the correct example.

	Market Failure	Assumption	Example
(a)	Externality		
(b)	Imperfect competition		
(c)	Public goods		
(d)	Partial information		

Assumptions
A.   All participants will be price takers.
B.   All costs and benefits will be borne by producers and consumers.
C.   Perfect knowledge.
D.   To benefit from consumption one must pay the supplier.

Examples
National defense
Monopoly
"Lemons" in the car market
Noise pollution

Practice Test SOLUTIONS

I. SOLUTIONS TO MULTIPLE-CHOICE QUESTIONS

1. (b) Refer page 261 for more on efficiency.

2. (a) A reduction in demand will reduce profits in the beef industry.

3. (a) The demand for chicken has increased. In the short run, this will result in higher prices and higher profits. In the long run, new firms will enter the industry, increasing supply and reducing price. Because the industry is constant-cost, price will return to the original level.

4. (c) In the short run you have fixed costs to consider. If you can cover your variable (operating) costs, you should produce.

5. (c) The profit-maximizing rule is to set production at the level where $P(MR) = MC$.

6. (b) One industry has expanded and the other has contracted, so they would not maintain the same usage of inputs. We should see all input markets being impacted by the change in demand for outputs.

7. (a) The previous plan was inefficient because the benefits of the new plan outstrip the costs. We can't say that the new plan is Pareto optimal because further changes might improve the welfare of employees still more.

8. (c) Refer to page 263 for more on externalities.

9. (b) Refer to page 263 for more on externalities.

10. (a) The profit-maximizing rule is to set production at the level where $P(MR) = MC$. Dana is a (perfectly competitive) price taker. She should increase production.

11. (c) If Mike can exclude others from his market, he has established a monopoly through the use of barriers to entry.

12. (d) Lack of control over price is a hallmark of perfect competition.

13. (d) Typically, imperfectly competitive producers will restrict output and charge higher prices.

14. (a) Refer to page 256 for more on Pareto efficiency.

15. (c) Refer to page 263 for more on externalities.

16. (b) Because the exchange takes place and is voluntary, neither party is hurt and at least one of the two parties must gain.

17. (a) Even if an industry is perfectly competitive, when the producer ignores the social cost of a negative externality, production will be too high.

18. (a)   Refer to page 254.

19. (d)   There should be a general decline in the quantity of all resources used in tobacco production.

20. (c)   As price rises, it will be greater than marginal cost at the initial output level, so Sarah should increase production until $P = MC$ once more. A perfectly competitive firm is a price taker.

II. SOLUTIONS TO APPLICATION QUESTIONS

1. (a)   If you merely replicate the experiment, no one gains! Alex and Branko get different, but no more satisfying, allocations. The experiment, recall, asked what an *equivalent* allocation would be. Because you have taken some trouble to effect the exchange, but have received no reward for your enterprise, you have lost. This exchange is not a Pareto optimal action.

	Alex		Branko	
	Cigarettes	Candy	Cigarettes	Candy
Red Cross	20	20	20	20
Experiment	12	30	24	10
Trade I	12	30	24	10
Trade II (Pavel)	13	30	24	10

(b)   In general, given identical initial parcels of goods, different preferences, and zero transactions costs, trade will *always* be beneficial. It's easy to forget that you, as facilitator, need a reward.
Trade I: "Borrow" 10 pieces of candy from Branko, promising him cigarettes in return. Give Alex the 10 pieces of candy and take 8 cigarettes in return—Alex has not lost. "Pay" Branko 4 cigarettes for the borrowed candy—Branko has not lost. You have gained 4 cigarettes. Because no one has lost and you have gained, this is a Pareto optimal action.

(c)   Trade II: Pavel "borrows" 10 pieces of candy from Branko, promising him cigarettes in return. Pavel gives Alex the 10 pieces of candy and generously takes 7, not 8, cigarettes in return—Alex has gained. "Pay" Branko 4 cigarettes for the borrowed candy—Branko has not lost. Pavel has gained 3 cigarettes. No one has lost and Pavel and Branko have gained, this is a Pareto optimal action. Note: You have not lost because you were not a participant in this round of trading.

(d)   The process ends when profits are pushed so low that they can be pushed no lower, i.e., normal profits are being earned. As the entrepreneurs take less of a cut, the consumers, Alex and Branko, keep more and therefore gain.

Note: Alex and Branko gain because of competition. You and Pavel have an incentive to collude and/or impose barriers to entry to reduce competition and keep profits high. Such action reduces market efficiency.

2.   The basic conclusion in this chapter is that perfect competition will provide the "best" allocation of resources. However, we should recall that the presence of externalities undermines this conclusion. Cutting down forests to produce hardwoods may, indeed, produce externalities that our perfectly competitive producers choose to ignore.

3. Demand for technically trained labor increased. Programmers, designers, systems analysts of all kinds, and skilled assembly workers experienced an increase in demand. Technical schools and major universities began training programs. Firms did on-the-job training. Andrea might have done any number of things, like buying a (used) car or some new clothes or traveling. Employment falls in those sectors.

4. Home recording of DVDs reduces economic efficiency. It represents an externality. The market demand for DVDs does not accurately represent the true demand for DVDs. Because the market for new DVDs is affected by the market for used DVDs, resale does not reduce efficiency.

5. (a) The demand for guns will shift to the left—the price and quantity traded will decrease in the short run. Firms will leave the industry because short-run economic losses are being made. This exodus of firms will make the market supply curve shift to the left. This movement will continue until normal profits are achieved. Given constant returns to scale, the long-run industry supply curve will be horizontal, and the initial price level will be restored. The quantity of resources allocated to this industry will be reduced.

    (b) The demand for butter will shift to the right—the price and quantity traded will increase in the short run. Firms will enter the industry because short-run economic profits are being made. The additional firms will make the market supply curve shift to the right. This movement will continue until normal profits are achieved. Given constant returns to scale, the long-run industry supply curve will be horizontal, and the initial price level will be restored. The quantity of resources allocated to this industry will be increased.

6. (a) The last dollar spent on each good should purchase an equal amount of marginal utility.

    (b) $MU_A/P_A = MU_B/P_B$.

    (c) Produce until the quantity is reached where marginal revenue is inadequate to cover marginal cost.

    (d) Marginal cost is the opportunity cost of the resources used to produce the final unit of output—the value of the other goods that we could have produced instead.

    (e) $P = MR = MC$. This is true for all profit maximizers in perfect competition.

    (f) The per-dollar cost of the last units of satisfaction from apples is relatively too high ($50/40 < 60/30$).

    (g) Spend less on apples and reallocate funds to butter.

    (h) Diminishing marginal utility will drive MU_A up and MU_B down. whereas decreasing marginal productivity will make MC_A fall and MC_B rise until a balance is struck.

7. (a) B Noise pollution

    (b) A Monopoly

    (c) D National defense

    (d) C "Lemons" in the car market

Comprehensive Review Test

The following questions provide a wide-ranging review of the material covered in Part II (Chapters 6-12) of the textbook. Each question deals with a topic or technique important for your understanding of economic principles. If you miss a question you should return to the relevant section of the chapter in the textbook and fine-tune your understanding.

I. MULTIPLE-CHOICE QUESTIONS

Select the option that provides the single best answer.

_____ 1. Denni has a straight, downward-sloping demand curve for cookies. A decrease in the price of cookies
  (a)   will make Denni's budget constraint swivel inwards.
  (b)   will result in an increase in the absolute value of Denni's price elasticity for cookies.
  (c)   shift Denni's demand curve for cookies to the right.
  (d)   will increase Denni's consumer surplus.

_____ 2. There is an increase in the interest rate. The operation of the substitution effect will _____ current saving. The operation of the income effect will _____ current saving.
  (a)   increase, increase
  (b)   increase, decrease
  (c)   decrease, increase
  (d)   decrease, decrease

Use the following information for the next two questions. Joe's recreation budget is $120 per month which he divides between attending movies (which cost $10) and buying CDs (which cost $15). Joe finds that the satisfaction derived from the final movie of the month is 50 units while the satisfaction from the final CD is 60 units. Assume diminishing marginal utility is present.

_____ 3. How should Joe adjust his spending pattern on movies and CDs?
  (a)   Joe should attend more movies and buy fewer CDs because the marginal utility of movies is more than that of CDs.
  (b)   Joe should attend more movies and buy fewer CDs because the marginal utility per dollar of movies is more than that of CDs.
  (c)   Joe should attend fewer movies and buy more CDs because the marginal utility of CDs is more than that of movies.
  (d)   Joe should attend fewer movies and buy more CDs because the marginal utility per dollar of CDs is more than that of movies.

_____ 4. As Joe adjusts his purchases of movies and CDs to achieve maximum satisfaction, the marginal utility of movies will
  (a)   increase because he is attending more movies.
  (b)   increase because he is attending fewer movies.
  (c)   decrease because he is attending more movies.
  (d)   decrease because he is attending fewer movies.

_____ 5. There is an increase in the interest rate. The operation of the income effect will _____ current saving because _____.
   (a) increase; at higher interest rates the individual earns more from previously saved income.
   (b) increase; the opportunity cost of each dollar spent has increased.
   (c) decrease; at higher interest rates the individual earns more from previously saved income.
   (d) decrease; the opportunity cost of each dollar spent has increased.

_____ 6. *To Air is Humane* is currently producing 5,000 units of output, using 25 units of labor and 20 units of capital. The marginal product of labor is 200, while the marginal product of capital is 100. The price of labor is $2, and the price of capital is $3. Given this information, which of the following is true?
   (a) The firm is currently using the optimal mix of labor and capital.
   (b) The firm should increase labor and reduce capital.
   (c) The firm should reduce labor and increase capital.
   (d) The firm should increase labor and increase capital.

_____ 7. In perfect competition, the industry's demand curve is _____; the firm's demand curve is _____.
   (a) horizontal; horizontal
   (b) horizontal; downward sloping
   (c) downward sloping; horizontal
   (d) downward sloping; downward sloping

_____ 8. The consumption level maximizing utility from goods A and B is indicated by the formula
   (a) $MR = MC$.
   (b) $P = MC$.
   (c) $P = ATC$ (min).
   (d) $MU_A/Price_A = MU_B/Price_B$.

_____ 9. DEF, Corp. is employing 100 units of labor and 50 units of capital to produce 2,000 widgets. Labor costs $10 per unit and capital costs $30 per unit. For the quantities of inputs employed, the marginal product of labor is 3 and the marginal product of capital is 10. Given the output level, the firm
   (a) is producing at the lowest possible cost.
   (b) could lower production costs by using more capital and less labor.
   (c) could increase its profit by using more labor and less capital.
   (d) could lower production costs by using more labor and less capital.

_____ 10. The total value Paul places on one apple a day is $2.00. The total value of two apples a day is $3.10; of three apples a day, $3.70; of four apples, $4.00; and of five apples, $4.20. Apples cost 50¢ each. To maximize his consumer surplus, how many should Paul buy?
   (a) At least five.
   (b) Five.
   (c) Four.
   (d) Three.

_____ 11. The income effect for normal Good *A* occurs when
    (a)   a decrease in income makes the consumer buy more of Good *A*.
    (b)   a decrease in income encourages consumers to buy more of substitute Good *B*, which is inferior.
    (c)   a decrease in the price of Good *A* makes consumers better off so that they can buy more of the Good *A*.
    (d)   an increase in the price of Good *A* encourages consumers to buy more of inferior Good *B*.

_____ 12. Labor is the variable resource in a factory that produces basketballs. At the point where diminishing returns are beginning to occur the
    (a)   average product of labor is maximized.
    (b)   average product of labor is minimized.
    (c)   long-run average cost curve is at its minimum.
    (d)   average product of labor is increasing.

_____ 13. A factory reorganizes production and finds that the marginal productivity of its variable resource (labor) has increased in the short run. We would expect that the factory's
    (a)   marginal cost has increased at each output level.
    (b)   marginal cost has decreased at each output level.
    (c)   average variable cost has increased at each output level.
    (d)   average total cost has increased at each output level.

_____ 14. Which of the following is the best explanation for the fact that the marginal revenue that perfectly competitive Farmer Gustafson receives from an additional bushel of wheat is constant and equal to its price?
    (a)   Gustafson supplies an insignificant fraction of the total market supply of wheat.
    (b)   The market demand curve for wheat is downward sloping.
    (c)   There are few good substitutes for wheat.
    (d)   In the short run no new firms can enter this industry.

_____ 15. Walt's Widgets is a profit-maximizing, perfectly competitive firm. In the long run, if Walt earns zero economic profit, he will
    (a)   shut down.
    (b)   decrease his output level but may not shut down.
    (c)   increase his output level to attract more business.
    (d)   remain at his current output level.

Use the following diagram to answer the next six questions.

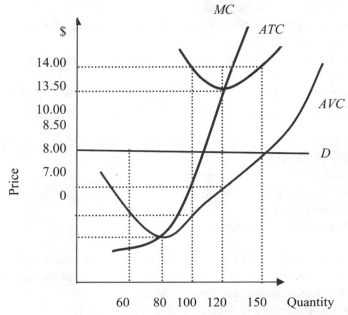

_____ 16. The short-run, profit-maximizing output level is
    (a) 80.
    (b) 100.
    (c) 120.
    (d) 150.

_____ 17. The short-run, profit-maximizing price is
    (a) $14.00.
    (b) $13.50.
    (c) $10.00.
    (d) $7.00.

_____ 18. In the short run, maximum economic profit is
    (a) −$420.
    (b) −$400.
    (c) $200.
    (d) $420.

_____ 19. Total fixed cost
    (a) is $600.
    (b) is $800.
    (c) is $1,400.
    (d) cannot be calculated from the information given.

_____ 20. At 120 units of output, marginal cost is _____ than marginal revenue. Economic profit can be increased by _____ output.
    (a) greater; increasing
    (b) greater; decreasing
    (c) less; increasing
    (d) less; decreasing

_____ 21. We would expect firms to
(a)   enter this industry in the short run.
(b)   enter this industry in the long run.
(c)   leave this industry in the short run.
(d)   leave this industry in the long run.

_____ 22. A perfectly competitive firm's short-run supply curve is that part of its marginal cost that is
(a)   upward sloping.
(b)   above the average total cost curve.
(c)   above the average variable cost curve.
(d)   above the average fixed cost curve.

_____ 23. In the short run, a perfectly competitive firm can earn economic profits if the market price is greater than
(a)   average total cost.
(b)   average fixed cost.
(c)   average variable cost.
(d)   marginal cost.

_____ 24. The government requires all the firms in the perfectly competitive widget industry to adopt antipollution equipment that increases production costs. We would expect
(a)   the market demand for widgets to decrease.
(b)   the market supply curve for widgets to shift left in the long run.
(c)   firms to leave the industry in the short run.
(d)   the long-run economic profits of the typical firm to be reduced.

_____ 25. The wheat industry is perfectly competitive and is in long-run equilibrium. Which statement best describes the short-run effects of a decrease in the demand for wheat? The price of wheat will _____; quantity traded will _____; the output of the typical farmer will _____.
(a)   increase; increase; increase
(b)   increase; increase; decrease
(c)   decrease; decrease; increase
(d)   decrease; decrease; decrease

_____ 26. When a firm experiences "economies of scale" _____ as output increases.
(a)   its fixed costs decrease
(b)   its average costs decrease
(c)   its total costs decrease
(d)   the marginal productivity of its fixed inputs increase

_____ 27. Which of the following indicates that we have an economically efficient market?
(a)   Wage equals marginal product of labor.
(b)   Price of the product equals the marginal cost of the product.
(c)   Price of the product equals the marginal revenue of the product.
(d)   Marginal utility of the product is greater than the price of the product.

_____ 28. Which of the following would *not* shift a competitive firm's labor demand curve to the right?
   (a)   An increase in the price of the firm's output
   (b)   A decrease in the wage rate
   (c)   An increase in the productivity of labor
   (d)   A decrease in the cost of other inputs complementary to labor

Use the following table to answer the next three questions. Widgetland can combine capital and labor in a variety of ways to produce each widget.

Technology	Units of Capital	Units of Labor
A	2	18
B	4	12
C	6	6
D	9	3

_____ 29. Which technology is the most capital-intensive?
   (a)   A
   (b)   B
   (c)   C
   (d)   D

_____ 30. The hourly wage is $10 and the hourly price of capital is $15, which technology should Widgetland select?
   (a)   A
   (b)   B
   (c)   C
   (d)   D

_____ 31. Widgetland is considering opening a plant in a country where the hourly wage is $4. The hourly price of capital remains at $15. Which technology should Widgetland select?
   (a)   A
   (b)   B
   (c)   C
   (d)   D

II. APPLICATION QUESTIONS

Here is some production information for the Smiley-Smile Mouthwash Company.

Number of Workers	Marginal Product	Total Product	Average Product
0	--		--
1	12		
2	14		
3	22		
4	12		
5	10		
6	8		
7	6		
8	4		
9	2		

1.   Complete the Total Product and Average Product columns.

2.   With which worker do diminishing returns begin to occur?

3.   When the marginal product of labor is positive and increasing, is total product rising or falling?
     When marginal product of labor is positive and decreasing, is total product rising or falling?

4.   If marginal product of labor became negative, what would happen to total product?

Each worker costs $10 to hire. In addition, Smiley-Smile has total fixed costs of $60.

5.   Use the information from the table above to help you complete the following table.

Total Product	Total Cost	ATC	AVC	AFC	MC
		--	--	--	--

6.   Make up a rule: "When marginal cost is rising, average total cost is RISING / FALLING / CAN'T TELL."

7.   Make up a rule: "When average variable cost is falling, average total cost is RISING / FALLING / CAN'T TELL."

8.   How can you tell that Smiley-Smile is operating in the short run?

Smiley-Smile is a perfectly competitive profit-maximizing firm.

9.   If the market price is $1.00 per unit, how many units of output (bottles of mouthwash) will the firm produce?

10.   At a price of $1.00, calculate the firm's total economic profit or loss.

11.   At a price of $1.00, should Smiley-Smile stay in business in the short run? Why?

12.   At a price of $1.00, what will happen in the long run to the number of firms, the position of the industry supply curve, and the market price?

13.   If the market price is $2.50 per unit, how many units of output (bottles of mouthwash) will the firm produce?

14.   At a price of $2.50, calculate the firm's total economic profit or loss.

15. You have the information to derive Smiley-Smile's supply schedule for the prices given the following.

Price/bottle	Smiley-Smile's SupplySchedule	MarketSupply
$3.50	_____	_____
$3.00	_____	_____
$2.50	_____	_____
$2.00	_____	_____
$1.50	_____	_____
$1.00	_____	_____

16. Suppose that there are 100 identical firms in the market. Calculate total market supply. Following is the market demand schedule in the mouthwash market.

Price/bottle	MarketDemand
$3.50	4,800
$3.00	6,800
$2.50	8,800
$2.00	10,800
$1.50	12,800
$1.00	14,800

17. Determine the short-run equilibrium price and equilibrium quantity traded.

18. Confirm that, when the market price is $2.50, the marginal revenue product of the last worker hired is equal to the wage.

Review Test SOLUTIONS

I. SOLUTIONS TO MULTIPLE-CHOICE QUESTIONS

1. (d) There is an increase in the difference between how much Denni would pay and how much she does pay for cookies (the triangular area between price and the demand curve). Answer C is a serious error. A change in price does not cause a shift in the position of a demand curve. Movement down a straight-line demand curve results in a less elastic demand.

2. (b) Refer to Chapter 6 (p. 135) for a discussion of this topic.

3. (b) Compare the marginal utility per dollar values. Movies offer more utility per dollar.

4. (c) As more of a good is purchased, the marginal utility of the last item consumed decreases.

5. (c) Higher interest rates will generate more interest on existing saved funds, so now less will need to be saved to achieve a given income level in the future.

6. (b) The optimal combination of resources equalizes the marginal product per dollar of each input. In the given situation the marginal product of labor per dollar was lower than that of capital.

7. (c) The industry demand curve is a normal downward-sloping curve—competition makes the demand curve facing each firm horizontal.

8. (d) To maximize utility, one should try to equalize the satisfaction per dollar from each good.

9. (b) The optimal combination of resources equalizes the marginal product per dollar of each input. In the given situation the marginal product of capital per dollar was lower than that of labor.

10. (d) Paul should buy up to the point where price equals marginal benefit. The marginal benefit of the third apple is 60¢ while the marginal benefit of the fourth apple is 30¢.

11. (c) The income effect occurs when, as price changes, spending power (income) changes, and the consumer's purchasing level is influenced.

12. (d) Marginal product of labor is at a maximum when diminishing returns are just beginning to emerge, so the average product of labor is still rising. Refer to Figure 7.4 on page 155.

13. (b) With one variable resource, when marginal product increases, marginal cost decreases—the denominator of the marginal cost formula has increased.

14. (a) Gustafson has no control over price.

15. (d) Although economic profit is zero, a normal rate of return is included in costs. In addition, in long-run equilibrium, economic profits *must* be zero.

16. (b) This is the output level at which marginal revenue equals marginal cost.

17. (c) $10.00 is the market price, based on the demand curve.

18. (b)   At the profit-maximizing output level, average total cost is $14, while the price is $10. There is a $4 loss on each of the 100 units produced.

19. (a)   When output is 100 units, average fixed cost is $6 ($ATC - AVC$).

20. (b)   Output should be reduced to 100 units, where marginal revenue equals marginal cost.

21. (d)   Firms cannot enter or leave in the short run. If this is a typical firm and it is making an economic loss, firms will leave the industry in the long run.

22. (c)   Refer to page 184 to see how this conclusion is reached.

23. (a)   Refer to page 180 for more on how to maximize profits.

24. (b)   Profitability has been reduced, resulting in some firms leaving the industry in the long run.

25. (d)   Draw a demand and supply diagram to verify this.

26. (b)   There are no fixed inputs in the long run! Economies of scale yield decreasing average costs.

27. (b)   Price represents the marginal benefit of the product. Economic inefficiency occurs if production is at any level other than where marginal benefit equals marginal cost.

28. (b)   A change in the wage rate will cause a movement along the labor demand curve.

29. (d)   Technology D has the greatest amount of capital per unit of output.

30. (c)   Total cost of production per hour is the least ($150) when Technology C is used.

31. (a)   Total cost of production per hour is the least ($102) when Technology A is used.

II. Solutions to Application Questions

1.   Refer to the following table.

Number of Workers	Marginal Product	Total Product	Average Product
0	--	0	--
1	12	12	12
2	14	26	13
3	22	48	16
4	12	60	15
5	10	70	14
6	8	78	13
7	6	84	12
8	4	88	11
9	2	90	10

2.   Diminishing returns begin with the fourth worker.

3. When marginal product is positive, total product will always increase.

4. If marginal product of labor became negative, total product would decrease.

5. Refer to the following table.

Total Product	Total Cost	ATC	AVC	AFC	MC
0	$ 60.00	--	--	--	--
12	$ 70.00	$5.83	$0.83	$5.00	$0.83
26	$ 80.00	$3.08	$0.77	$2.31	$0.71
48	$ 90.00	$1.88	$0.63	$1.25	$0.45
60	$100.00	$1.67	$0.67	$1.00	$0.83
70	$110.00	$1.57	$0.71	$0.86	$1.00
78	$120.00	$1.54	$0.77	$0.77	$1.25
84	$130.00	$1.55	$0.83	$0.71	$1.67
88	$140.00	$1.59	$0.91	$0.68	$2.50
90	$150.00	$1.67	$1.00	$0.67	$5.00

6. When marginal cost is rising, average total cost could be either rising or falling. "Can't tell" is the best answer.

7. "When average variable cost is falling, average total cost is falling."

8. Smiley-Smile has some fixed resources, which cannot occur in the long run when all resources are variable.

9. If the market price is $1.00 per unit, then marginal revenue is $1.00 per unit. To maximize profit the firm should produce where MR = MC, i.e., at an output level of 70.

10. At a price of $1.00, total revenue is $70 while total cost is $110. Smiley-Smile will make an economic loss of $40.

11. Smiley-Smile should stay in business in the short run, making a loss of $40 because, if it shut down it would make a loss of $60 (its fixed costs).

12. In the long run, firms will leave this industry, industry supply will decrease, and market price will increase.

13. If the market price is $2.50 per unit, then marginal revenue is $2.50 per unit. To maximize profit the firm should produce where MR = MC, i.e., at an output level of 88.

14. At a price of $2.50, total revenue is $220 while total cost is $140. Smiley-Smile will make an economic profit of $80.

15. Refer to the following table.

Price/bottle	Smiley-Smile's SupplySchedule	MarketSupply
$5.00	90	9,000
$2.50	88	8,800
$1.67	84	8,400
$1.25	78	7,800
$1.00	70	7,000

16. Refer to the preceding table.

17. The equilibrium price is $2.50 and equilibrium quantity traded is 8,800 bottles.

18. When the market price is $2.50, the marginal revenue product of the last worker hired (the eighth) is $2.50 × 4. This equals the wage, which is given as $10.00.

13

Monopoly and Antitrust Policy

Chapter Objectives

1. List the "perfectly competitive" assumptions that are not met by a monopolist and relate these to the features found in such a "single-seller" market.
2. Define marginal revenue and explain why the monopolist's marginal revenue decreases as output increases.
3. Draw and interpret a diagram representing both the price and output choices of a profit-maximizing monopolist.
4. Draw a diagram to compare a monopolist's performance relative to that of a perfectly competitive firm in terms of price, output, and the effect on income distribution.
5. Name five types of barriers to entry. Distinguish a natural monopoly from other monopolies.
6. Identify the welfare loss caused by the presence of a monopoly.
7. Explain what is meant by price discrimination and discuss its effects.
8. Identify the two major policy positions adopted by the government with respect to promoting/restricting competition within an industry exhibiting monopoly characteristics. Name the two government organizations charged with combating antitrust violations.

BRAIN TEASER: Suppose the monopolist's demand curve is *not* a straight line but a rectangular hyperbola—i.e., a line with the same area underneath it at all points.

(a)   What does this information tell you about total revenue ($P \times q$) as output increases?

(b)   What do you think the marginal revenue values will be? What will the *MR* curve look like?

(c)   What will the price elasticity be along this demand curve? Can you use the behavior of total revenue to help you predict elasticity?

(d)   Use the following table to confirm your predictions.

Price	Quantity	TR	MR
$24	1	_____	_____
$12	2	_____	_____
$8	3	_____	_____
$6	4	_____	_____
$4	6	_____	_____
$3	8	_____	_____
$2	12	_____	_____

(e)   Now graph demand and marginal revenue in the following diagram.

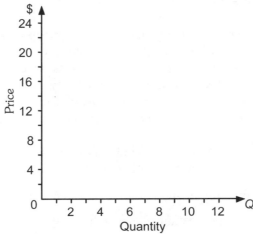

(f)   Define "marginal cost." Can *MC* ever be zero?

(g)   Now draw a "typical" marginal cost curve on your diagram. What will the profit-maximizing output level be?

Objective 1

List the "perfectly competitive" assumptions that are not met by a monopolist and relate these to the features found in such a "single-seller" market.

Travel to Europe and experience "Bed and Breakfast" in a private household offering cheap overnight accommodation to tourists. This feature of tourist travel is a reasonable approximation of a perfectly competitive market. The key elements include (1) many sellers and buyers; (2) fairly homogeneous products; and (3) ease of entry into the industry (all you need is a spare bedroom!). Private motels at the beach are a similar example in the United States. When these competitive elements are absent, imperfect competition (monopoly, oligopoly, or monopolistic competition) is present. Reduced competition bestows market power—the ability to adjust price while retaining customers. The perfectly competitive firm, in contrast, has no market power. (page 269)

The college dorm for a first-semester freshman is close to being a monopoly because (s)he may be required to reside in a dorm. A *pure monopoly* occurs when there is a single firm in an industry producing a product with no close substitutes (in this case, campus accommodation), and where there are significant barriers to the entry of competitors. Clearly, the trick is to define what is included in the market. How close do substitutes have to be for monopoly not to exist? Are, for instance, Macintosh and PCs part of a single market for computers?

Practice

1. A pure monopoly is an industry with a single firm that produces a product that has _____ close substitutes and in which there are _____ barriers to entry.
    (a)   many; significant
    (b)   many; no
    (c)   no; significant
    (d)   no; no

    ANSWER: (c) Refer to page 270 for the definition of monopoly.

2. Peter's Pan Pizzeria operates in an imperfectly competitive market. Which of the following statements does not apply to this firm?
    (a)   Peter's Pan Pizzeria has some control over the price it charges.
    (b)   Peter's Pan Pizzeria has a downward-sloping demand curve.
    (c)   Peter's Pan Pizzeria does not compete with the other pizzerias in town.
    (d)   Peter's Pan Pizzeria has some market power.

    ANSWER: (c) If other pizzerias produce close substitutes for Peter's pizza, Peter's is a monopolistically competitive firm and does compete.

3. When _____ substitutes are present, an imperfectly competitive firm has _____ power to raise price.
    (a)   more; more
    (b)   fewer; more
    (c)   fewer; less
    (d)   no; unlimited

    ANSWER: (b) The more close substitutes there are, the more difficult it is for a firm to persuade customers to buy if it raises its price. Option (d) looks like a logical extension of this but even a monopolist is governed by the Law of Demand.

4. The _____ broadly we define an industry, the _____ substitutes it has, and the _____ elastic the demand for its products.
    (a)   more; more; more
    (b)   more; fewer; less
    (c)   less; more; less
    (d)   less; fewer; less

    ANSWER: (b) The broader the definition of an industry, the more difficult it is to find a substitute and the less elastic the demand. It's easier to find a substitute for BP gasoline than it is to find a substitute for gasoline itself. ■

Objective 2

Define marginal revenue and explain why the monopolist's marginal revenue decreases as output increases.

In imperfect competition, *marginal revenue is less than price* because, to sell an extra unit, the firm must cut the price and that price cut applies to all units bought. The addition to revenue from selling the extra unit is less than the price charged. When few items are affected by the price cut, the increase in sales increases total revenue, and marginal revenue is positive. However, as progressively more items suffer a lower price, the increase in revenue from the new sales is offset by the decrease in revenue from existing sales, and total revenue decreases—marginal revenue becomes negative. (page 271)

LEARNING TIP: In order to understand what is happening to revenue as price and quantity change, examine the following diagram.

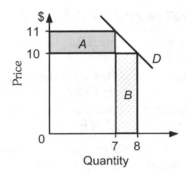

When price is $11 and $10, respectively, total revenue is $77 and $80, respectively. Marginal revenue is $3. Now consider area *A* and area *B*. Verify that they are $7 and $10 respectively. Area *A* represents the revenue lost because of the price change whereas Area *B* represents the revenue gained. Comparing the two, let us calculate *MR* visually. As price falls and output expands, the one-unit revenue increase dwindles in importance beside the multiunit revenue decrease—imagine the difference in areas if, rather than 7 and 8 units, the diagram showed 1007 and 1008 units.

Review Chapter 5's section on price elasticity and the total revenue test. Note that as price decreases, total revenue increases when demand is elastic (*MR* is positive), and that total revenue decreases when demand is inelastic (*MR* is negative). ◀

LEARNING TIP: You have already derived the cost curves for a perfectly competitive firm and industry. The cost curves used in this and subsequent chapters are the *same* as those that you've seen before—nothing new to learn! The economic forces that shaped them in previous chapters (diminishing returns in the short run and economies of scale in the long run) are just as valid for an imperfectly competitive firm. When drawing the diagram, most people find it easier to draw the "cost diagram" first and then put in the demand and marginal revenue curves afterwards. The **only** differences occur in the revenue parts of the diagram. Demand for the firm is the same as the market demand—there is only one firm. For a straight-line demand curve, the marginal revenue curve is a straight line whose slope is twice as steep as that of the demand curve. ◀

Practice

5.   In a monopoly,
      (a)   the market demand curve is above, and parallel to, the marginal revenue curve.
      (b)   the marginal revenue curve is downward sloping.
      (c)   increasing price will not result in a decrease in quantity demanded.
      (d)   we assume that the demand curve is unknown.

      ANSWER: (b) Refer to Figure 13.3 on page 274. Note: The market demand curve is above, but not parallel to, the marginal revenue curve.

Use the following table to answer the next four questions. The Uretown Yokels ice hockey team is the only live sports entertainment in Uretown. Here is some information about their ticket prices and attendance at their games.

Ticket Price	Total Attendance	Total Revenue	Marginal Revenue
$14	100	_____	_____
$12	200	_____	_____
$10	300	_____	_____
$8	400	_____	_____
$6	500	_____	_____
$4	600	_____	_____

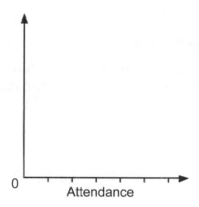

6.   Fill in the total revenue and marginal revenue columns in the preceding table, then graph the demand and marginal revenue curves.

ANSWER: See the following table.

Ticket Price	Total Attendance	Total Revenue	Marginal Revenue
$14	100	$1,400	
$12	200	$2,400	$10
$10	300	$3,000	$6
$8	400	$3,200	$2
$6	500	$3,000	-$2
$4	600	$2,400	-$6

Note: Recall that marginal revenue is found by dividing the change in total revenue by the change in quantity.

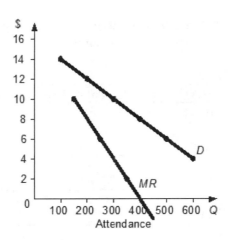

7. At a price of $12 per ticket, the Yokels attract 200 spectators. For the Yokels to attract 300 spectators, they would have to _____ price. Total revenue would _____ .
    (a) increase; increase
    (b) increase; decrease
    (c) decrease; increase
    (d) decrease; decrease

    ANSWER: (c) See the preceding table.

8. When the Yokels decrease the price from $12 to $10 to attract 300 spectators, total revenue increases, indicating that demand is _____ and that marginal revenue is _____ .
    (a) elastic; positive
    (b) elastic; negative
    (c) inelastic; positive
    (d) inelastic; negative

    ANSWER: (a) Refer to page 274 and Figure 13.3. Marginal revenue is positive when demand is elastic.

9. If the Yokels cut the price from $12 to $10 per ticket, each new customer will _____ and each regular customer will _____ .
    (a) increase total revenue by $10; increase total revenue by $2
    (b) increase total revenue by $10; decrease total revenue by $2
    (c) decrease total revenue by $10; increase total revenue by $2
    (d) decrease total revenue by $10; decrease total revenue by $2

    ANSWER: (b) The increase in total revenue is $600. *TR* increases by 100 × $10 (new customers) and decreases by 200 × $2 (regular customers). ∎

Objective 3

Draw and interpret a diagram representing the price and output choices of a profit-maximizing monopolist.

Monopolists (and other types of imperfectly competitive firms) must decide how much output to produce, how to produce it, and how much of each input to hire, just as a perfectly competitive firm must do. However, monopolists must also decide which price to set. This is determined by the "*MR = MC*" rule. The "demand side," then, limits the monopolist. The firm can't charge any price, because they are limited by the demand for their product. (page 274)

Marginal Revenue and the Profit-Maximizing Rule: $MR = MC$: Marginal revenue—the amount by which total revenue changes as output increases by one unit—is a key concept that you've seen before. Perfect competition is a special case, where $P = MR$. For any firm with a downward-sloping demand curve, price is greater than marginal revenue. *The profit-maximizing output level can always be found by equating marginal revenue and marginal cost (MR = MC).* The monopolist, therefore, doesn't charge the highest price to get the most profit—s/he takes both cost and revenue (demand) information into account.

Graphing Pointer: Having found where $MR = MC$, it is tempting to move immediately to the vertical axis and identify that value as the price, e.g., OF in the diagram in the following Practice Questions. This is a mistake! Always refer to the demand curve to determine the correct price. Draw a line up from the intersection of marginal revenue and marginal cost to the demand curve and then over to the vertical axis to get the correct price.

LEARNING TIP: This section is filled with opportunities for you to review your understanding. Verify what is depicted by the short-run "cost picture." Review the logic behind the "profit-maximization rule" and that the optimal output level occurs where $MR = MC$. Finally, check your understanding of the unique relationship between price and quantity supplied—the supply curve. Why is there no supply curve for the monopolist?◀

Practice

Use the following diagram to answer the next three questions.

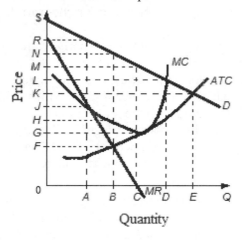

10. The profit-maximizing output level is
     (a) OA.
     (b) OB.
     (c) OD.
     (d) OE.

     ANSWER: (b) This is the output level where $MR = MC$.

11. The profit-maximizing price is
     (a) OF.
     (b) OG.
     (c) OH.
     (d) ON.

     ANSWER: (d) At output level OB, the demand curve shows that the price can be as high as ON.

12.   The firm's maximum economic profit is
      (a)   *OB* × *HN*.
      (b)   *OC* × *GM*.
      (c)   *OB* × *FN*.
      (d)   *OC* × *HN*.

      ANSWER: (a)   Total economic profit is (price − *ATC*) × *Q*, so (*ON* − *OH*) × *OB*.

13.   A monopolist, producing at the output level where marginal revenue and marginal cost are equal, is currently earning an economic loss. The firm is covering its variable costs. The firm should
      (a)   increase its price.
      (b)   decrease its output.
      (c)   increase its output.
      (d)   maintain its current output.

      ANSWER: (d)   The firm is at its profit-maximizing output level. Increasing price will move it away from that level. Because the firm is covering its variable costs, it should not shut down. ∎

Objective 4

Draw a diagram to compare a monopolist's performance relative to that of a perfectly competitive firm in terms of price, output, and the effect on income distribution.

In terms of welfare and efficiency, monopoly compares poorly with perfect competition. Assuming similar costs, the monopolist will overprice and underproduce. Monopoly is not efficient because output is not set where $P = MC$, the firm does not use the lowest-cost production method, and the distribution of income is altered (through the appropriation of consumer surplus, which is like a private tax).

   If a competitive industry were to become a monopoly, price would increase and quantity would decrease. Consumers would lose through the higher prices and reduced level of production—in general, society loses when a monopoly replaces perfect competition. There is a deadweight loss, as discussed in Chapter 4. Additionally, as we will see, the monopolist might indulge actions to prevent competition, i.e., rent-seeking behavior. (page 276)

   Comment: Remember the long-run perfectly competitive equilibrium result: $P = MC = LRAC(\text{minimum}) = SRAC(\text{minimum})$. First, in monopoly, the firm will not minimize average costs. Second, the monopolist will not produce the output that society considers to be optimal (where $P = MC$).

Practice

Use the following table which provides *long-run* information about the market for apples to answer the next four questions. Price is price per pound of apples.

Quantity (pounds)	Price per Pound	Marginal Revenue	Marginal Cost	Average Total Cost
100	$1.40	—	—	$2.00
200	$1.07	$0.74	$0.50	$1.50
300	$0.92	$0.62	$0.46	$0.75
400	$0.80	$0.44	$0.44	$0.70
500	$0.66	$0.10	$0.43	$0.65
600	$0.50	−$0.30	$0.50	$0.50
700	$0.30	−$0.80	$0.59	$1.00

14. Given the *cost* information above, a perfectly competitive industry would charge a price of _____ per pound and produce _____ pounds of apples.
    (a) 80¢; 400
    (b) 44¢; 400
    (c) 50¢; 600
    (d) 30¢; 600

    ANSWER: (c) The perfectly competitive industry will produce at the lowest point on its long-run average cost curve. Because price and marginal revenue are identical in perfect competition, and *MR* must equal *MC* to maximize profits, the price will also be 50¢.

15. Given the cost information above, a monopoly would charge a price of _____ per pound and produce _____ pounds of apples.
    (a) 80¢; 400
    (b) 44¢; 400
    (c) 50¢; 600
    (d) 30¢; 600

    ANSWER: (a) The monopolist will produce where *MR* = *MC*. Price is then determined.

16. Given the information above, a profit-maximizing monopoly would earn an economic profit of
    (a) $144.
    (b) $40.
    (c) zero.
    (d) –$104.

    ANSWER: (b) Economic profit is $(P - ATC) \times Q$. In this case, $(80¢ - 70¢) \times 400 = \$40$.

17. From the previous questions, we can formulate the following long-run rule: The monopolist will produce _____ and charge _____ than the perfectly competitive industry.
    (a) more; more
    (b) more; less
    (c) less; more
    (d) less; less

    ANSWER: (c) If this is still unclear, review the answers to the three previous questions and read pp. 276–267 in the textbook. ∎

Objective 5

Name five types of barriers to entry. Distinguish a natural monopoly from other monopolies.

Monopoly can only persist if barriers to entry are present. *Barriers to entry* are the reason that this situation can arise and endure. Different forms of barriers to entry are: economies of scale, legal barriers (patents, government rules), the exclusive ownership of a necessary input, and network effects. Government rules and economies of scale are typical reasons for the emergence of *natural* monopolies. Network effects can be felt every time you use e-mail or your cell phone—the more other users there are, the more recipients you can contact. (page 278)

> **Comment:** Note the term "externalities" in the discussion of network effects. This term first appeared in Chapter 12 and will crop up again, most notably in Chapter 16. In the present context, when new users join a network, existing users receive a benefit.

A *natural monopoly* occurs where average costs decrease as output levels rise because of long-lasting economies of scale. In such circumstances, a single-firm industry can be the most efficient way to organize production, better even than perfect competition. Here it would be undesirable to break up the monopoly, because economies of scale would be lost. Such an industry is usually regulated. (page 278)

ECONOMICS IN PRACTICE: On page 280, the textbook explores the cable TV industry. It is claimed that this is an example of a natural monopoly. What evidence is presented in support of this view? If cable TV is a natural monopoly, why is it beneficial to prevent competition in this case?

ANSWER: It is stated that there are high initial costs to set up the system but relatively low variable costs once the system is in operation. This implies that the average cost decreases as the number of subscribers increases—a hallmark of a natural monopoly. If more than one firm competed in a market, there would be wasteful duplication of service, and average costs of production would increase.

Practice

18. Your local electric company maintains its monopoly because of
    (a) a patent.
    (b) product differentiation.
    (c) advertising.
    (d) a government-bestowed franchise.

    ANSWER: (d) Cable TV and local telephone companies are other examples. Refer to page 278.

19. If a natural monopoly is split into a number of smaller competing firms, price will
    (a) increase, because smaller firms will have higher average costs.
    (b) increase, because each firm will experience diseconomies of scale.
    (c) decrease, because additional competition is taking place.
    (d) increase in the short run because of the disruption, but decrease in the long run because of the additional competition.

    ANSWER: (a) Each firm is driven up along the average cost curve as output level falls. The firms don't experience diseconomies of scale—they aren't large enough.

20. For the typical natural monopolist, in the short run fixed costs are relatively _____ and marginal costs are relatively _____ .
    (a) high; high
    (b) high; low
    (c) low; high
    (d) low; low

    ANSWER: (b) Refer to page 278. ∎

Objective 6

Identify the welfare loss caused by the presence of a monopoly.

With the exception of a natural monopoly, we would expect a monopoly to produce less and charge more than a perfectly competitive industry. In fact, the monopoly reduces the welfare of their customers and undermines the efficiency of the marketplace.

> **Comment:** Figure 13.8 on page 281 is *extremely important* for this and subsequent chapters. First, review your knowledge of profit maximization ($MR = MC$), the meaning of demand (marginal benefit), consumer surplus, and the essential meaning of marginal cost—the opportunity cost of production. Confirm that, in order to maximize society's welfare gain, the firm should produce at the output level where P (MB) = MC. Unfortunately, in the case of monopoly, it doesn't maximize society's welfare gain, but instead curtails output and raises prices. Conclusion: Society loses when it

encounters a monopoly. The finding of a net social loss (and higher prices and restricted output) is a theoretical basis for antitrust policies and regulation.

With economic profits present, there is an incentive to prevent a change in the *status quo*. Rent-seeking behavior refers to actions taken by firms to preserve economic profits. An industry might lobby heavily to prevent opening of markets, or might even attempt to "capture" government regulatory agencies—the consumer watchdog becomes the industry lapdog!

Practice

Use the following diagram, which shows the revenue and cost curves for coffee, to answer the both next three questions in this section, and Question 24 in the next section. Initially, this is a perfectly competitive industry.

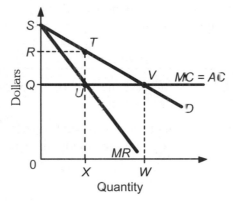

21.   If the coffee industry becomes a monopoly, the loss in social welfare is equal to _____ . The monopolist will be willing to spend an area equal to _____ to preserve the monopoly.
       (a)   *TUV*; *QRTV*
       (b)   *TUV*; *QRTU*
       (c)   *QRTU*; *TUV*
       (d)   *QRTV*; *TUV*

       ANSWER: (b)   The perfectly competitive firm would produce *W* units at a price of *Q* dollars. The monopolist will reduce output to *X* units and charge the higher price of *R* dollars. The welfare loss due to the decrease in output and the increase in price is *TUV*. The monopolist's profit [(price – average cost) × quantity], i.e., *QRTU*, is the amount (s)he is willing to spend to maintain the monopoly.

22.   If the coffee industry becomes a monopoly, the loss in consumer surplus will be
       (a)   *TUV*.
       (b)   *RST*.
       (c)   *QRTU*.
       (d)   *QRTV*.

       ANSWER: (d)   With perfect competition, the consumer surplus would be *QSV*. With monopoly, the consumer surplus shrinks to *RST*. *QRTV* represents the difference in consumer surplus. Refer to the textbook's page 89 to review this concept.

23.   If the coffee industry becomes a monopoly, the firm can indulge in rent-seeking behavior to the extent of
       (a)   *QSTU*.
       (b)   *TUV*.
       (c)   *QRTU*.
       (d)   *QRTV*.

ANSWER: (c) The firm will be willing to sacrifice all of its excess profits to fight off competition.

Objective 7

Explain what is meant by price discrimination and discuss its effects.

Imperfectly competitive firms, such as monopolies, may be able to practice price discrimination. By charging different customers different prices, profits can be boosted. Essentially, the seller must identify those buyers who are willing to pay more for a good and those who will pay less. The seller is appropriating a portion of the consumer surplus. With perfect price discrimination, because each successive unit is sold at the price indicated by the demand curve, price and marginal revenue are equal. Accordingly, the output level selected by the monopolist will be equal to the efficient output level, as production will continue until price equals marginal cost. (page 283)

Practice

Use the preceding diagram, which shows the revenue and cost curves for coffee, to answer the next question. Initially, this is a perfectly competitive industry.

24.   If the coffee industry becomes a monopoly that practices perfect price discrimination, the profit-maximizing output level will be _____ and the monopolist's economic profit will be _____ .
(a)   *0X; QSV*
(b)   *0X; QRTV*
(c)   *0W; QSV*
(d)   *0W; QRTV*

ANSWER: (c) The firm will produce where *MR = MC*. Recall that, with perfect price discrimination, the demand curve represents marginal revenue. The entire area between the demand curve and the average cost curve represents economic profit for the monopolist. ∎

Objective 8

Identify the two major policy positions adopted by the government with respect to promoting/restricting competition within an industry exhibiting monopoly characteristics. Name the two government organizations charged with combating antitrust violations.

When imperfect competition fails to produce the efficient level of output, the government may choose to intervene to improve the allocation of society's resources. There are two apparently conflicting government stances—first, promotion of competition and restriction of market power through *trust-busting legislation*, and second, restriction of competition by *regulation* of industries. Antitrust is meant to promote competition; regulation intends to restrict competition. Both policies are intended to promote economic efficiency. Regulation is dealt with in Chapter 14. (page 285)

   Antitrust legislation began in 1887 with the Sherman Act of 1890, which made monopoly and trade restraints illegal. The 1914 Clayton Act strengthened Sherman and made clear which forms of trade restraint were illegal. The Federal Trade Commission was also created at this time to investigate unfair competition. (page 285)

   Enforcement of antitrust laws is done by the FTC and the Antitrust Division of the Justice Department. Private citizens can also bring antitrust suits. The courts can impose civil and criminal penalties and can specifically forbid illegal actions in the future. (page 286)

ECONOMICS IN PRACTICE: On page 287, the textbook looks at a 2010 antitrust case based on the NFL's practice of negotiating as a single unit with various apparel companies seeking to market team logos. How did the court decide in this case, and what was the basis for the court's decision?

ANSWER: The NFL's position, that there was significant competition between NFL teams and between the NFL and other forms of entertainment, was rejected. The court found that team logos are not good substitutes for one another and that the NFL's exclusive licensing deal violated antitrust rules by having teams operate collectively with the consequence of driving up licensing revenues.

ECONOMICS IN PRACTICE (CONTINUED): Think about college sports, such as basketball and football, and the top-flight student-athletes who play them and earn significant revenues for their conferences. These sports are controlled by the NCAA, which is a non-profit organization. The colleges that comprise the NCAA have collectively agreed not to offer remuneration to athletes. To offer remuneration, it could be argued, might trigger a bidding war for top players and would shatter the appearance of amateurism among college athletes. Should college athletes be paid for their services? Do you think the NCAA's collective agreement not to pay infringes antitrust law?

ANSWER: Opinions will differ on this one! Clearly, student-athletes do receive scholarships and training. However, under the guise of the NCAA, the colleges are effectively operating collectively to drive down their expenses. Until fairly recently, when athletes began to move directly from high school, unsalaried college participation was the only avenue to professional sports.

Practice

25. The policy positions taken by the government with respect to imperfectly competitive industries are to _____ competition through antitrust legislation and to _____ competition through regulation.
    (a)   promote; promote
    (b)   promote; restrict
    (c)   restrict; promote
    (d)   restrict; restrict

    ANSWER: (b) Broadly, antitrust legislation breaks up large companies into smaller units or prevents mergers, whereas regulation establishes a single supplier of a product and then controls the firm's behavior.

26. Unfair methods of competition in commerce are prosecuted by the
    (a)   Federal Trade Commission.
    (b)   Federal Truth in Advertising Commission.
    (c)   Federal Drug Administration.
    (d)   Trade Section of the Justice Department.

    ANSWER: (a) Refer to page 286. ∎

BRAIN TEASER SOLUTION:

(a)   Total revenue is the same at all price levels.

(b)   Marginal revenue will be constant at zero. This would be shown as a horizontal line drawn *on* the quantity axis!

(c)   Because, as price rises, *TR* neither rises (inelastic demand) nor falls (elastic demand), demand is unitarily elastic at all points. If you're unsure how total revenue links with elasticity, review pp. 105–107.

(d)   See the following table.

Price	Quantity	*TR*	*MR*
$24	1	24	0
$12	2	24	0
$8	3	24	0
$6	4	24	0
$4	6	24	0
$3	8	24	0
$2	12	24	0

(e)   See the following diagram.

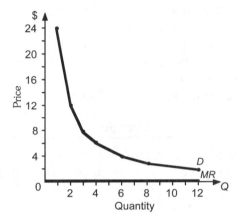

Demand has a regular shape (downward sloping) although it is a curving line instead of a straight line. Marginal revenue, though, is unusual—it graphs along the horizontal axis, because it is always zero.

(f)   Marginal cost is the additional cost caused by increasing output by one unit. It can't be zero (if, as is usually assumed, inputs are infinitely divisible).

(g)   Do you see a problem? In this unusual case, *MR* doesn't seem to equal *MC* at *any* level of output! The solution? The firm gets the same total revenue at each output level so to maximize profits it will produce one unit—enough to get the revenue, but where total costs are minimized. Think about it: *MR* for the first unit is $24, because *TR* must be zero when none are sold. (Notice we've broken the "rectangular hyperbola" assumption.) Rest assured that your "*MR* = *MC*" profit-maximization rule will work for all the ,cases you'll have to analyze. This example is merely to challenge your understanding.

PRACTICE TEST

I. MULTIPLE-CHOICE QUESTIONS

Select the option that provides the single best answer.

_____ 1.   A pure monopoly is best defined as a firm
        (a)   selling a product for which there are no close substitutes.
        (b)   making short-run economic profits.
        (c)   with a degree of market power.
        (d)   with a downward-sloping demand curve.

_____ 2.   Which of the following is not a barrier to entry?
(a)   Ownership of patent rights
(b)   Ownership of private property
(c)   The possession of a government franchise
(d)   Substantial economies of scale

_____ 3.   Monty the Monopolist is seeking to maximize profits. Currently, he is producing where marginal revenue is less than marginal cost. He should
(a)   increase production.
(b)   reduce price.
(c)   reduce production.
(d)   produce where price is equal to marginal cost.

_____ 4.   The profit-maximizing monopolist must decide all of the following EXCEPT
(a)   output level.
(b)   price level.
(c)   the wage level.
(d)   the combination of inputs.

_____ 5.   A monopolist is currently maximizing profits. We can conclude that
(a)   he is maximizing total revenue and minimizing total cost.
(b)   he has reduced the difference between marginal revenue and marginal cost to zero.
(c)   he is maximizing total revenue and marginal revenue.
(d)   he is producing where marginal revenue equals average cost.

_____ 6.   Manuel the Monopolist sells at a price of $4. His marginal cost is $3 and the price elasticity of demand is –0.6. We can conclude that Manuel
(a)   is maximizing profit.
(b)   should increase output.
(c)   should decrease output.
(d)   should decrease price.

_____ 7.   Mandy the Monopolist operates a firm that is not a natural monopoly. Relative to a perfectly competitive industry, we would expect Mandy to have
(a)   lower prices and lower output.
(b)   lower prices and higher output.
(c)   higher prices and higher output.
(d)   higher prices and lower output.

Use the following diagram to answer the next eight questions. The cost information and the industry demand curve apply in both perfect competition and monopoly. There is no price discrimination, unless mentioned explicitly.

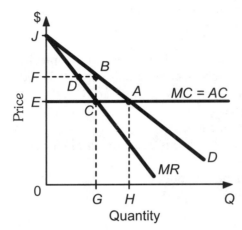

_____ 8. This perfectly competitive industry becomes a monopoly. Price will _____ , and quantity will _____ .
(a) fall to *E*; fall to *G*
(b) fall to *E*; rise to *H*
(c) rise to *F*; rise to *H*
(d) rise to *F*; fall to *G*

_____ 9. With a profit-maximizing monopolist, the net loss of social welfare is shown by area
(a) *FBCE.*
(b) *BAC.*
(c) *EABF.*
(d) *BCD.*

_____ 10. To preserve the monopoly, this firm would be willing to spend up to
(a) *FBCE.*
(b) *BAC.*
(c) *EABF.*
(d) *ABDC.*

_____ 11. If this industry were initially perfectly competitive and subsequently became a monopoly, then the amount of consumer surplus transferred to the monopolist is shown by the area
(a) *DBC.*
(b) *ABC.*
(c) *FBCE.*
(d) *FBAE.*

_____ 12. If this industry were perfectly competitive, consumer surplus would be shown by the area
(a) *ABC.*
(b) *JEA.*
(c) *FBCE.*
(d) *FBAE.*

_____ 13.   If this industry were a monopoly, consumer surplus would be shown by the area
   (a)   ABC.
   (b)   HEA.
   (c)   JFB.
   (d)   ECBH.

_____ 14.   If this industry were a monopoly practicing perfect price discrimination the firm's economic profit would be
   (a)   JEA.
   (b)   EFBC.
   (c)   EFBA.
   (d)   EJBC.

_____ 15.   If this industry were a monopoly practicing perfect price discrimination the deadweight loss, relative to perfect competition, is
   (a)   ABC.
   (b)   GBAH.
   (c)   FJB.
   (d)   zero.

_____ 16.   Mike the Monopolist produces where marginal revenue equals marginal cost equals average total cost. His economic profits will be
   (a)   positive.
   (b)   negative.
   (c)   zero.
   (d)   indeterminate—it depends on demand conditions too.
          (Try sketching this one.)

_____ 17.   A monopoly produces where marginal revenue exceeds marginal cost.
   (a)   The firm could increase profits by increasing output.
   (b)   The firm could increase profits by decreasing output.
   (c)   The firm is making an economic profit.
   (d)   The firm is earning a negative economic profit (loss).

_____ 18.   Use the following information for Firm A. Total revenue = $1,200. Total cost = $400. Price = $12. MR = $10. Total variable cost = $300. MC = $6. This is a _____ firm currently in a _____ situation.
   (a)   perfectly competitive; short-run
   (b)   monopolistic; short-run
   (c)   monopolistic; long-run
   (d)   perfectly competitive; long-run

_____ 19.   Molly the Monopolist faces an elastic demand curve. If she decreases price, marginal revenue will be _____ and total revenue will _____ .
   (a)   positive; rise
   (b)   positive; fall
   (c)   negative; rise
   (d)   negative; fall

_____ 20.   The long-run average cost curve of a natural monopoly is
   (a)   upward sloping at the output level where it crosses the market demand curve for the good.
   (b)   upward sloping at all levels of output.
   (c)   downward sloping at all levels of output.
   (d)   downward sloping at the output level where it crosses the market demand curve for the good.

II. APPLICATION QUESTIONS

1. In 2012, the U.S. airline industry is radically transformed. Following a vicious price war and a series of mergers, one company (Unison Airlines) has emerged as the sole survivor. Unison adopts a new slogan (*Fly in Unison—or Walk*) and hires you as a consultant on pricing policy. Unison offers a one-way trip from Atlanta to Washington. The marginal cost for each passenger is $40. Fixed cost is $500,000. Demand information is shown in the following table. Note: The demand and marginal revenue curves are linear.

Price of One-Way Trip Tickets	One-Way Trips Demanded per Year (thousands)	Marginal Revenue
_____	_____	_____
_____	_____	_____
_____	_____	_____
$140	6	
$130	8	_____
$120	10	_____
$110	12	_____
$100	14	_____
$90	16	_____
$80	18	_____
$70	20	_____

   (a)   Complete the table. Remember that demand is linear.

   (b)   Give the demand equation in the form $P = X - YQ_d$, where X and Y are numbers and Q_d is the quantity demanded.

   (c)   Calculate the quantity demanded when the price is zero.

   (d)   Give the marginal revenue equation in the form $MR = X - ZQ_d$, where X and Z are numbers.

   (e)   Calculate the quantity demanded when the marginal revenue is zero. Careful!

Suppose that Unison's corporate chiefs wish to charge a single, profit-maximizing ticket price for all their Atlanta-Washington customers.

   (f)   Which price will maximize profits?

(g)   Calculate Unison's total cost at the profit-maximizing output level.

(h)   Calculate Unison's economic profits.

(i)   Draw a diagram showing the demand, marginal revenue, and marginal cost curves.

(j)   Calculate the consumer surplus and interpret your finding for Unison's top brass.

(k)   Determine the efficient output level and price.

(l)   A noted economist, Dr. Faircase, who is opposed to Unison's monopoly position, has claimed that the loss in social welfare caused by Unison has a monetary value of $300,000. How would you advise Unison to reply?

(m)   Is it coincidental that the welfare loss and the consumer surplus values are identical?

(n)   A campaign is being waged to split up Unison into smaller independent units. The management wants to know the maximum amount they should allocate to a "war chest" to lobby and to buy political favors.

(o)   Calculate Unison's economic profits at the efficient output level.

(p)   If the government required that Unison price tickets at the efficient price, what would be Unison's long-run response?

(q)   Suppose the government requires that the price be set at the efficient level, but will offer Unison a subsidy to maintain the flight. How great a subsidy per passenger would the government have to offer Unison to induce them to keep the flight open?

(r)   The firm is able to practice perfect price discrimination. Determine the firm's total economic profit.

2.   Veterinary services can be provided at any level for an opportunity cost of $60,000 per vet. Yearly demand for veterinary services is given by $P = \$300,000 - 4Q_d$. ($P$ is the dollar price per vet.)

(a)   Calculate the marginal revenue equation.

(b)   In the space below, graph the demand, MR, MC, and AC curves for veterinary services. Put in numerical values where possible.

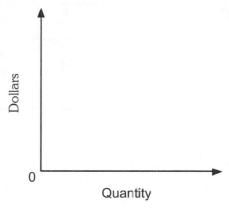

(c)   The American Veterinary Association operates as a profit-maximizing monopoly. Calculate the price and output level in this industry.

(d)   Calculate the total economic profit per vet.

(e)   If entry into this industry was unrestricted, state the price and output level that would emerge.

3.   You are a profit-maximization consultant specializing in monopolies. Three firms seek your advice, but, in each case, the information the firm can provide is incomplete. You will be able, however, to recommend one of the following **short-run** actions and write a justification of your proposal. To verify your answer and for some additional graphing practice, try sketching the diagram in each case.

Recommended actions
1.   Remain at current output level
2.   Increase output
3.   Decrease output
4.   Shut down
5.   Uncertain—the figures provided cannot possibly be correct.

Firm	Price	MR	TR	Q	TC	MC	ATC	AVC
A	6.40	3.10	____	1,000	6,400	3.00	____	3.24

Recommendation: _____
Justification:

Firm	Price	MR	TR	Q	TC	MC	ATC	AVC
B	12.80	____	____	2,000	____	12.80	12.00	9.24

Recommendation: _____
Justification:

Firm	Price	MR	TR	Q	TC	MC	ATC	AVC
C	5.00	4.00	30,000	____	____	4.00	5.10	5.05

Recommendation: _____
Justification:

4.   (a)   Fill in the blanks in the table that refer to a monopolist.

Price	Quantity	TR	MR
$8	2	____	____
$7	____	$21	____
$6	4	____	____
$5	____	____	$1
$4	6	____	____
$3	____	$21	____

(b)   Why, when price falls from $6 to $5, does total revenue increase by only $1?

5.   The food service at your university is run by a single firm (Food Service). The following table shows the monthly demand for meals and total costs.

(a)   Complete the table.

Sales (units)	Price (per meal)	Total Cost	MR	MC
4,000	$1.50	$6,100		
5,000	$1.40	$6,400		
6,000	$1.30	$6,800		
7,000	$1.20	$7,300		
8,000	$1.10	$8,000		
9,000	$1.00	$9,000		
10,000	$0.90	$10,200		

(b)   If Food Service tries to maximize profits, it will set the price per meal at _____ (of the choices given here).

(c)   Students form a committee to regulate the food service. They want to maximize consumers' welfare, given that total costs are covered. The price they set should be _____ .

(d)   Between which two price levels is the market demand curve unitarily elastic?

6.   **Graphing Pointer:** This diagram is meant to depict a monopoly in long-run equilibrium. P^* and Q^* are equilibrium quantity and price, respectively. However, if this is the situation that is meant to be shown, there are several errors in the graph. Indicate as many errors as possible and explain, based on your economic understanding, *why* they are errors.

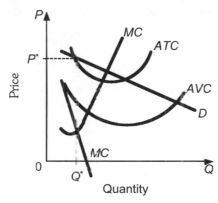

7.   The following example lets you use your intuition to construct a diagram for a monopoly.

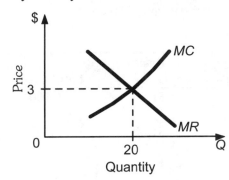

(a)   Where on the diagram will the firm maximize profits (or minimize losses)?

(b)   What is the price?

(c)   Draw your own demand curve on the diagram. Now work out price.

(d)   Finally, sketch in a short-run average total cost curve. Is this firm making a profit or a loss?

(e)   Are losses feasible in long-run equilibrium?

8.   Nowadays, if you change cell phone service providers, your phone number goes with you. This was not always true. Until 2003, a switch of provider meant a new number. Legislation to scrap this practice was consistently blocked by providers. Why? What has the present system meant in terms of monopoly power for companies that provide cell phone service? How does this relate to rent-seeking behavior?

9.   At first blush, most students dislike price discrimination, where different buyers are charged different prices for the same product. Consider prescription drug sales in the United States and Canada—one price in the United States, a different price in Canada. What permits different prices to occur and how have consumers responded?
        Now consider the provision of antiretrovirals (drugs that fight HIV/AIDS). Drug companies charge high prices for these drugs in the United States, but far lower prices in African countries where AIDS is rife. Is price discrimination beneficial in this case?

Practice Test SOLUTIONS

I. SOLUTIONS TO MULTIPLE-CHOICE QUESTIONS

1. (a) Monopoly means "single seller." Refer to page 270.

2. (b) There are no barriers to entry into a perfectly competitive industry, although the means of production may be privately owned.

3. (c) To maximize profits, the firm should produce where $MR = MC$. When marginal revenue is less than marginal cost, too much is being produced.

4. (c) The labor market determines the wage level, and this market may be perfectly competitive. The monopolist would be a wage taker with no control.

5. (b) To maximize profits, the firm must be producing where $MR = MC$.

6. (c) If MR is –0.6, demand is inelastic and MR is negative. If so, MC must exceed MR, and Manuel should reduce output.

7. (d) Refer to Figure 13.8 on page 281. Note: The natural monopolist is an exception to this rule.

8. (d) In the perfectly competitive industry, output is established where $P = MC$. In the monopoly, output is where $MR = MC$. Given the demand curve, price will rise.

9. (b) Refer to Figure 13.8 on page 281.

10. (a) The monopolist's economic profit is $(P - AC) \times Q$. (S)He would be willing to sacrifice all of this in order to maintain the monopoly.

11. (c) Refer to Figure 13.8 on page 281.

12. (b) Refer to page 281.

13. (c) Refer to page 281.

14. (a) With perfect price discrimination, the firm will produce up to the point where $P = MC$. Economic profit is the triangle between the demand curve and the average cost curve.

15. (d) With perfect price discrimination, the monopoly produces at the efficient output level and there is no loss in welfare.

16. (a) For the monopolist, the demand curve is above the MR curve. If $MR = ATC$, the price exceeds ATC and Mike is earning an economic profit.

17. (a) The firm should produce at the output level where $MR = MC$. Because we don't know anything about the relationship between price and ATC we can't say whether or not a profit is being made (Option (c)).

18. (b) Price is not equal to *MR*—Firm A is not perfectly competitive. Because total costs are greater than variable costs, there must be fixed costs—a short-run phenomenon.

19. (a) A decrease in price represents a movement down Molly's demand curve. When demand is elastic, marginal revenue (addition to total revenue) is positive and, given a decrease in price, total revenue will increase.

20. (d) The hallmark of a natural monopoly is that it experiences such substantial economies of scale that one firm can service market demand. Long-run average costs decrease when economies of scale are present.

II. SOLUTIONS TO APPLICATION QUESTIONS

1. (a) See the following table.

Price of One-Way Trip Tickets	One-Way Trips Demanded Per Year (thousands)	Marginal Revenue
$170	0	
$160	2	$160
$150	4	$140
$140	6	$120
$130	8	$100
$120	10	$80
$110	12	$60
$100	14	$40
$90	16	$20
$80	18	$0
$70	20	–$20

(b) $P = 170 - 5Q_d$. The slope is rise/run. As price falls by $10, quantity rises by 2—the slope is –5. The vertical intercept, i.e., when Q_d is zero, occurs when price is 170. We get the equation $P = 170 - 5Q_d$.

(c) Given $P = 170 - 5Q_d$, when $P = 0$, $170 = 5Q_d$, therefore $Q_d = 34$.

(d) $MR = 170 - 10Q_d$. Recall that the marginal revenue curve has the same vertical intercept as the demand curve, i.e., $170. The slope is twice as steep as that of the demand curve, i.e., –10.

(e) Given $MR = 170 - 10Q_d$, when $MR = 0$, $170 = 10Q_d$, therefore $Q_d = 17$. Comment: Note that the table seems to give the value as 18. This apparent discrepancy is because the table reports the marginal revenue in the range from 16 to 18. The table reports discrete values, whereas the formula is a continuous function.

(f) Set $MR = MC$, i.e., $170 - 10Q_d = 40$. $Q_d = 13$. When $Q_d = 13$, $P = 105.

(g) $TC = TFC + TVC$. *TFC* is given as $500,000. To get *TVC*, recall that *MC* is the addition to total cost as extra units are produced, i.e., variable cost. $TVC = $40 \times 13,000 = $520,000$. $TC = $500,000 + $520,000 = $1,020,000$.

(h)   Economic profits $TR = P \times Q = \$105 \times 13,000 = \$1,365,000$.
       $TC = \$1,020,000$. Economic profits = $345,000.

(i)   Refer to the following diagram.

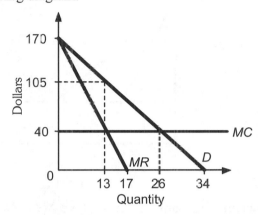

(j)   Consumer surplus is the area between price and the demand curve, i.e., $0.5(170 - 105) \times 13,000 = \$422,500$. Consumer surplus refers to difference between the value of the extra benefits derived by customers and the price they paid.

(k)   The efficient output level is where $P = MC$. Because MC is constant at $40, P must equal $40. Substituting that price into the demand equation, we get output to be 26.

(l)   The social loss is $0.5(\$105 - \$40) \times (26,000 - 13,000)$, or \$422,500. This, in fact, is greater than the value given by Faircase, so it's probably best to not comment. If comment is required, either Unison should not dispute Faircase's claim or, in an attempt to confuse the issue, mention the consumer surplus value, which exceeds $300,000. This, of course, is a complete red herring!

(m)   Given straight-line curves, it's not a coincidence. Because the MR curve is twice the slope of the demand curve, it bisects MC. From that point, geometry requires identical triangles for the two concepts. Other examples, and the real world, are not so clear cut.

(n)   Rent-seeking behavior tells us that the firm can allocate all of their economic profits ($345,000) to defeat the campaign.

(o)   Economic profits = $TR - TC$. $TR = P \times Q = \$40 \times 26,000 = \$1,040,000$.
       $TC = TFC + TVC$. $TFC = \$500,000$. $TVC = \$40 \times 26,000 = \$1,040,000$.
       $TC = \$500,000 + \$1,040,000 = \$1,540,000$. Economic profits = –$500,000.

(p)   Unison would stop offering this flight—no firm will make an economic loss indefinitely.

(q)   The economic loss is –$500,000 to fly 26,000 passengers. The subsidy would be $19.23 (approximately).

(r)   Given perfect price discrimination, the firm's economic profit is the triangular area between price and the demand curve, i.e., $0.5(170 - 105) \times 26,000 = \$845,000$.

2.   (a) $MR = \$300,000 - 8Q_d$. Recall that the marginal revenue curve has the same vertical intercept as the demand curve, i.e., $300,000. The slope is twice as steep as that of the demand curve, i.e., –8.

(b)   See the following diagram.

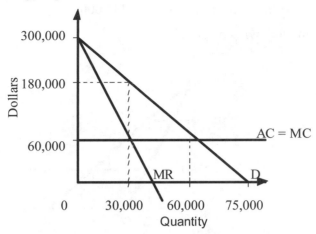

(c)   The profit-maximizing output level is where *MR* = *MC*, i.e., where *Q* = 30,000. When *Q* is 30,000, *P* is $180,000.

(d)   Total economic profit = *TR* = *TC*.
TR = *P* × *Q* = $180,000 × 30,000 = $5,400,000,000.
TC = *AC* × *Q* = $60,000 × 30,000 = $1,800,000,000.
Total economic profit equals $3,600,000,000. Per vet, this is $120,000.

(e)   In perfect competition, economic profits would be driven to zero. The price would be $60,000 (i.e., equal to marginal cost). When *P* = $60,000, quantity is 60,000.

3.   See each of the following cases.

Firm	Price	MR	TR	Q	TC	MC	ATC	AVC
A	6.40	3.10	6,400	1,000	6,400	3.00	6.40	3.24

Recommendation: 2
Justification: Firm A is earning a normal profit, even when not maximizing profit. Because *MR* > *MC*, the firm should expand production.

Firm	Price	MR	TR	Q	TC	MC	ATC	AVC
B	12.80	<12.80	25,600	2,000	24,000	12.80	12.00	9.24

Recommendation: 3
Justification: *MR* is less than price and therefore less than 12.80. *MR* < *MC*. The firm should reduce output. It should not close down because an economic profit can be earned.

Firm	Price	MR	TR	Q	TC	MC	ATC	AVC
C	5.00	4.00	30,000	6,000	30,600	4.00	5.10	5.05

Recommendation: 4
Justification: *MR* = *MC*. The firm should shut down because it is unable to cover its variable costs of production.

4. (a)   See the following table.

Price	Quantity	TR	MR
$8	2	$16	—
$7	3	$21	$5
$6	4	$24	$3
$5	5	$25	$1
$4	6	$24	−$1
$3	7	$21	−$3

(b)   Total revenue rises by only $1 ($MR = \$1$) because price had to fall to $5 to increase sales by one unit. $5 of extra revenue were generated by selling the extra unit. Unfortunately, though, the other four units, each of which could have been sold at $6, had to have $1 trimmed off their price tag. So the seller lost $4 on those units. Net gain was $1.

5. (a)   See the following table.

Sales (units)	Price (per meal)	Total Cost	MR	MC
4,000	$1.50	$6,100	—	—
5,000	$1.40	$6,400	$1.00	$0.30
6,000	$1.30	$6,800	$0.80	$0.40
7,000	$1.20	$7,300	$0.60	$0.50
8,000	$1.10	$8,000	$0.40	$0.70
9,000	$1.00	$9,000	$0.20	$1.00
10,000	$0.90	$10,200	$0.00	$1.20

(b) $1.20, where $MR < MC$ for the next step of 1000 units

(c) $1.00, where $P = MC$.

(d)   Between 90¢ and $1.00. The demand curve is unitarily elastic where MR is zero. Confirm this with the total revenue test—as price increases, total revenue remains constant in this price range.

6.   The cost diagram: MC doesn't intersect AVC or ATC at their minimum points. The diagram shows a short-run situation, because $ATC - AVC = AFC$. Fixed costs can show up only in the short run.
        The revenue diagram: The downward-sloping MC curve should be labeled MR. $MR = MC$ tells us that this firm is maximizing profits—as we'd expect. At that output level (Q^*), price equals average cost. Normal profits are being earned. However, a section of the demand curve lies above ATC, which must mean that economic profits are possible. Therefore, the demand and the marginal revenue curves don't agree.

7. (a)   Where $MR = MC$

(b)   It is unknown because there is no demand curve shown.

(c)   The demand curve is downward sloping and above the MR curve. (Note for perfectionists: With a straight-line demand curve, the slope of MR is twice as steep as that of the demand curve.) Remember that the quantity variable is *already determined*: only that knife-edge vertical line rising from the "20 units" output level is of any significance. Read off the price when output is 20 units.

(d) The final diagram may reveal normal *or* economic profits *or* losses being made—it depends on where you've positioned the demand curve and the *ATC* curve.

(e) No! The monopolist would leave the industry. Only two cases are possible, the one with economic profits being the typical representation of a monopolist.

8. Existing companies realized that changing your cell phone number was an inconvenience—notifying all your contacts of your new number could be time-consuming. Consumers, then, became less willing to switch and less price-sensitive. There was money to be made by imposing barriers. The new practice of transferability removed this barrier. Existing providers indulged in rent-seeking behavior (lobbying Congress) to prevent the change.

9. Re-importation of drugs into the United States is illegal—enforcement is by the Food and Drug Administration. Patent laws prevent competing companies from marketing name-brand drugs. Government rules, then, bestow a monopoly on U.S. drug companies. American consumers have been bypassing the law by using the Internet and mail order to buy drugs from Canada.

Clearly, using high prices in the United States to finance the provision of drugs in African countries is beneficial to the African recipients (especially if, as is likely, they could not otherwise afford the drugs). As long as the price charged to Africans exceeds the marginal cost, the drug companies also gain. In fact, if we have perfect price discrimination, the result mimics perfect competition.

14

Oligopoly

Chapter Objectives

1. Identify the features that characterize an oligopolistic firm and industry.
2. Outline the Five Forces Model and relate it to an oligopoly.
3. Identify and discuss the behavioral implications of the collusion model, the Cournot model, and the price-leadership model.
4. Use game theory to analyze the strategies available to rivals in a two-person game.
5. Describe ways in which an oligopolistic industry may be inefficient.
6. Explain what the Herfindahl-Hirschman Index is, how it is calculated, and how it is used in antitrust matters.

As you read through this chapter and the next, you will find it helpful to keep in mind the classifications made by **industrial organization** economists. They classify their investigations into an industry under three broad categories:

(a)   Market structure: How many firms are there? Are there economies of scale? How big are the four, or eight, largest firms?

(b)   Conduct: How do firms behave? How are prices set? Do firms advertise?

(c)   Performance: Is the industry efficient? Does it promote growth?

Pose questions such as these as you examine oligopoly in this chapter (and monopolistic competition, in Chapter 15).

BRAIN TEASER: Suppose you obtain a license to sell ice cream on the beach. There is only one other licensed seller of ice cream on the beach who has set up right in the middle of the beach. How would you respond to his/her presence? Where would you locate? How would you make your pricing decisions? Would you compete or collude?

Objective 1

Identify the features that characterize an oligopolistic firm and industry.

Oligopoly is the market structure with a "few" interdependent firms, each having market power and exerting strong barriers to entry. Products may be differentiated (cars) or standardized (oil). Firms may compete in terms of price or they may not. The behavior of one firm in an oligopolistic industry depends on the reactions of the others. Because the actions of each firm depend on the expected reactions of its rivals, this market structure is notoriously complex.

LEARNING TIP: As a rule of thumb, one fairly reliable way to identify an oligopolistic industry is to check which firms are advertising in national publications (like *Newsweek*), or on prime-time television, or are sponsoring large international events (such as the Olympics or the World Cup). Such firms are likely to be oligopolists. Why? A perfectly competitive firm has no differentiated product to advertise, a monopolist (which might sometimes advertise) already controls the industry and, as we will see in Chapter 15, a monopolistically competitive firm is likely to be too small to be able to advertise nationally. ◀

Practice

1. Which of the following industries is the best example of an oligopoly?
    (a)   Corn production
    (b)   Automobile production in the United States
    (c)   Pizzerias in New York City
    (d)   Production of t-shirts

    ANSWER: (b) There are a few large interdependent firms with significant economies of scale.

2. Which of the following features typically apply more to oligopoly than to monopoly or perfect competition?
    (a)   Product differentiation and many firms
    (b)   More than one firm in the market and interdependence between firms
    (c)   Negligible barriers to entry and easy entry into the market
    (d)   Significant barriers to entry and easy entry into the market

    ANSWER: (b) An oligopoly, unlike a monopoly, has more than one firm and, unlike perfect competition, the actions of one firm impact the revenues of others.

3. Perfectly competitive firms differ from oligopolists in that each perfectly competitive firm
    (a)   faces a downward-sloping demand curve, while an oligopolist does not.
    (b)   tries to differentiate its products from those of its rivals, while an oligopolist does not.
    (c)   competes with others on price, when an oligopolist never does.
    (d)   is small relative to the size of its industry; an oligopolist frequently is large relative to the size of its industry.

    ANSWER: (d) There are many firms in perfect competition, few in oligopoly. ∎

Objective 2

Outline the Five Forces model and relate it to an oligopoly.

The Five Forces model identifies the competitive forces that determine the level of competition and profitability in an industry. Central to this model is the rivalry among the existing firms in the industry. In oligopoly, there are a few firms, each watchful of the actions of its rivals. The number of firms, their size distribution (as measured by the concentration ratio), and the degree of product differentiation are important factors. The easier it is for new firms to enter, or the greater the availability of substitutes, the less able firms will be to sustain profits. Profitability is also influenced by conditions in both input markets and output markets. In each case, the stronger the oligopolist's relative bargaining position, the greater the firm's opportunity to increase its profits.

Contestable markets arise when the threat of entry by potential rivals is high. Often, this may be because the industry's capital stock is very mobile—the airline industry is the standard example. If profit opportunities emerge in one market—the route from Washington to New York, for instance—capital will flow there until the profits are competed away. Because there is easy entry into, and exit from, the industry, oligopolists in perfectly contestable markets behave like firms in a perfectly competitive industry, earning only normal profits in the long run.

LEARNING TIP: The Five Forces model (Figure 14.1) can be applied to any type of industry. Use it to review your understanding of perfect competition and monopoly as well as your grasp of the features of oligopoly. Apply it again, with monopolistic competition, in Chapter 15. ◀

ECONOMICS IN PRACTICE: On page 296, the textbook relates changes in the record industry (specifically, changes due to the Internet) to the Five Forces model. Newcomers (and established acts) can now gain widespread exposure cheaply through YouTube while music files can be shared and downloaded easily. Musicians can now connect directly with their listeners, making it more difficult for the music labels to earn profits. Considering the "five forces" in this market. Which have been changed most significantly by the presence of the Internet?

ANSWER: If we define the "industry" as only the major labels (Sony, EMI, etc.), the Internet has had an distinct impact on three of the forces. Established suppliers (Madonna) are able to thrive without a record contract (which strengthens their bargaining position), buyers no longer need to buy expensive CDs, and there are more (non-label) substitutes available. The effect on potential entrants (setting up as a new major label) and the effect on rivalry *within* the "industry" has been less.

If we broaden the field to consider the recorded "music industry" (not just the majors), the ability of uncontracted musicians to gain access has increased and, as a consequence, so has rivalry within the industry.

ECONOMICS IN PRACTICE (CONTINUED): Can you think of other industries that have been significantly affected by the growth of the Internet? If so, apply the Five Forces model to those situations.

ANSWER: One example is news publishing. The traditional newspaper, like the traditional record label, is in serious decline. Suppliers of news can reach their audience (buyers) directly (perhaps through YouTube or a blog). Entry is low-cost and there is a profusion of substitutes. Or encyclopedias. For many users, the traditional set of encyclopedias has been superseded by Wikipedia. And so on.

Practice

4. The widget industry contains ten equally sized firms. However, firms pair off and merge, leaving five equally sized firms. Initially, the four-firm concentration ratio is _____ ; subsequently the four-firm concentration ratio is _____ .
   (a) 10 percent; 5 percent
   (b) 10 percent; 20 percent
   (c) 40 percent; 20 percent
   (d) 40 percent; 80 percent

   ANSWER: (d) Initially, each of the ten firms has 10 percent of the market; subsequently, each firm has 20 percent of the market.

5. According to the Five Forces model, which of the following changes should make industry profits increase?
   (a) An increase in the ability of potential rivals to enter the industry
   (b) An increase in the number of firms in the industry
   (c) An increase in the availability of substitute products
   (d) An increase in the relative strength of suppliers of inputs

   ANSWER: (d) If there is a relative strengthening in the bargaining position of input suppliers, such as workers, firms in the industry would expect to see costs increase.

6. Of the following, which is most likely to have contestable markets?
   (a) Nuclear power generation
   (b) Trucking
   (c) Dentistry
   (d) Automobile manufacturing

   ANSWER: (b) It is fairly cheap to enter and leave the trucking industry.

7.   Using to the Five Forces model, which force is critical when contestable markets emerge?
        (a)   Availability of substitute products
        (b)   Threat of potential entry
        (c)   Relatively weak buyers
        (d)   Relatively weak suppliers

        ANSWER: (b) Because entry barriers are low in contestable markets, firms are forced to behave
                like firms in perfect competition. ∎

Objective 3

Identify and discuss the behavioral implications of the collusion model, the Cournot model, and
the price-leadership model.

Models, such as the collusion model, the Cournot model, and the price leadership model, have been
devised to display how firms might react to the interdependence that is characteristic of oligopolistic
markets.

Collusion, either explicitly (through the formation of a cartel) or implicitly, occurs when firms act in
such a way that prices are fixed. Several conditions are necessary for collusion to work well: ideally, there
should be only a few firms selling similar products to buyers with an inelastic demand, who do not have
close substitutes available. If these conditions prevail in a cartel, the cartel operates in exactly the same
fashion as a single-firm monopoly. Each firm, though, has strong incentives to "cheat" on the agreement.
OPEC, the oil-producing cartel, is an example of collusion.

The price-leadership model assumes one large firm and a cluster of smaller, competitive firms. The
dominant firm maximizes profits subject to both market demand and the behavior of the other firms. The
smaller firms produce as much as they wish at the price set by the leader, and then that firm services the
remaining customers.

Collusion and price leadership can be attractive strategies to avoid price competition and to maintain
profits. Not surprisingly, real-world examples of collusion and price leadership continue to emerge. A few
years ago, several Ivy League universities were accused of price-fixing—agreeing not to compete on
offers of financial aid to qualified students. Does this practice produce a social benefit (students choose
the college that best fits their intellectual needs (the colleges' argument) or does it suppress competition?

In New York, milk and Italian bread have been examples of collusion, with a few powerful firms
conspiring to keep prices high. Following the demise of the New York milk cartel, which had survived for
50 years, a gallon of milk tumbled in price by 30 percent.

Cournot's model is of a duopoly—the industry has only two firms selling identical products—and,
although it is quite mechanistic, it can still offer insights into behavior in an oligopolistic market. Each
firm maximizes profits and takes the output of the other as given. The more one rival produces, the less
market is left for the other firm. Given market demand, each firm subtracts what it expects the rival firm
to produce, and chooses its output to maximize its profits based on the market that is left. Eventually, the
firms split the market and charge the same price. Expectations of future behavior don't enter into the
Cournot model. The output level arrived at by the firms lies somewhere between the perfectly competitive
outcome and that for a monopoly. With more than two firms, the result moves closer to the perfectly
competitive result.

LEARNING TIP: Some textbooks present diagrams for each of the three models (and other
oligopoly models). However, whether presented in words or in diagrams, remember the main
message—in each case, a behavioral assumption is included. The oligopolist must remain aware
that his actions may provoke a response from his rivals.◀

Practice

8. If profit-maximizing oligopolists collude, the result is the same as if the industry were
    (a) monopolistically competitive.
    (b) perfectly competitive.
    (c) a monopoly.
    (d) using price leadership.

    ANSWER: (c) Several profit-maximizing oligopolists operating together are the equivalent of a monopolist. Refer to page 297 for more about cartels.

9. For a cartel to operate successfully,
    (a) the members must be producing a homogeneous (standard) product.
    (b) demand for the cartel's product must be elastic.
    (c) demand for the cartel's product must be inelastic.
    (d) there must be a single dominant firm.

    ANSWER: (c) If many substitutes are available, customers can go elsewhere when there is a price hike.

10. The demand faced by the dominant firm in the price-leadership model is
    (a) established first, then the demand for other firms is determined based on total market demand.
    (b) equal to the sum of the demand curves of the smaller firms.
    (c) determined by subtracting the supply of the smaller firms from the market demand curve.
    (d) determined by subtracting the demand of the smaller firms from the market supply curve.

    ANSWER: (c) The smaller firms are allowed to satisfy part of market demand—the dominant firm handles the rest. Refer to page 298.

11. In the Cournot model of duopoly, the new firm is assumed to believe that its demand is equal
    (a) the amount sold by the existing firm.
    (b) to the market demand, less the amount sold by the existing firm.
    (c) to half of the market demand.
    (d) to half the amount sold by the existing firm.

    ANSWER: (b) The new firm assumes that the more its rival sells, the less market will be left for it to service. ■

Objective 4

Use game theory to analyze the strategies available to rivals in a two-person game.

Game theory analyzes oligopoly as a series of strategic moves and countermoves—how players might react to the actions of their opponents, given the rules of the game and potential payoffs. A payoff matrix sets out the results of these moves. Because the behavior of one player affects the fortunes of the other this context applies easily to oligopoly. In some situations a dominant strategy will emerge—a move that yields a player the best outcome regardless of his opponent's actions. A Nash equilibrium occurs if a player employs his best strategy, given the actions of the rival.

The "prisoners' dilemma" is a familiar game, one in which players must decide, without cooperation, on a course of action—should each prisoner confess or stonewall, given the payoff matrix in Figure 14.4? In this case, the dominant strategy (the one that is best for him, regardless of what the other player does), is for each player is to confess. Clearly, though, it would be better for both Rocky and Ginger if they could collude and agree to stonewall. The application to the business world is obvious. Equally true, it would be in the best interest of, say, Rocky to agree with Ginger to stonewall, but then confess and go free. However, while this strategy might work for a single game, it would fail over repeated games— Ginger would "learn" not to trust Rocky.

LEARNING TIP: In game theory, when considering a payoff matrix for a player such as Ginger, (Figure 14.4), begin with action of the *other* player. If Rocky doesn't confess, Ginger is better off to confess (going free instead of spending 1 year in jail). If Rocky does confess, Ginger is still better off to confess (spending 5 years in jail instead of 7 years). Ginger has a dominant strategy— confess. The Nash equilibrium in this example is for both to confess. ◀

In the business world, many games are repeated and learning may take place. Without explicitly colluding, firms may be able to signal intentions. In a single game, a firm cutting price may gain many customers and hurt its rival. However, if this strategy were repeated and the firms indulged in a mutually destructive price war, each may prefer to signal that they will not compete in terms of price. In general, in repeated games, players have the capacity to learn from the past. Will a rival agree to observe a price agreement but then cheat by cutting price? Has she done this in the past? A ***tit-for-tat*** strategy is one that signals that a company will follow its competitor's lead. Note that the criminal world's solution to the prisoners' dilemma is summed up by the phrase "honor among thieves" (no confessing), enforced by penalizing "squealers"—the payoff matrix, in fact, may not include all of the costs or benefits of confessing.

ECONOMICS IN PRACTICE: On page 306, the textbook examines whether firms in the music industry are guilty of price fixing with respect to digital downloads. What are the salient facts in this case? Do you think a similar situation exists with respect to printed textbooks and e-books?
ANSWER: The court found evidence of collusion by focusing on the fact that, although the cost of producing and distributing downloads is substantially lower than for physical CDs, the price of downloads remained comparable. Had the market been competitive, reduced costs should have driven down prices.
In the textbook market, it does seem that competitive forces do prevail, with e-books being cheaper than traditional textbooks.

ECONOMICS IN PRACTICE (CONTINUED): Clearly, oligopolists may be unwilling to cut prices because rivals might interpret this as aggressive behavior and then retaliate. But what about situations where firms might feel the need to raise price? The fast food and automobile industries have built a trap for themselves. No fast-food firm has been able to break away from the popular "99¢ menu," despite rising costs. Similarly, automobile firms find it difficult to move away from low interest-rate financing. Apart from advertising, what other ways might rivals choose to enhance profits without raising their price? Can you think of some examples?
ANSWER: In each of following examples, firms are reluctant to raise their price because they might lose their competitive edge. Many consumers are quite sensitive to price differences, but are less aware of additional charges that might be imposed. Accordingly, the airline industry has progressively reduced in-flight services to avoid raising ticket prices, and many firms began charging additional fees for checked baggage. Beginning with market leader Bank of America, banks began charging fees for withdrawals at ATMs. As in the case of breakfast cereals, firms may reduce the size of a portion but keep the packaging and price unchanged.

ECONOMICS IN PRACTICE (CONTINUED): In the 1960s and 1970s, oligopolistic tobacco companies advertised cigarettes on television. However, the American Cancer Society argued successfully that it should be permitted to follow such advertisements with anti-smoking messages. These messages reduced the demand for cigarettes but no individual firm wanted to withdraw its ads. How do you think the tobacco industry responded (since they couldn't prevent the ads from being run)?
ANSWER: No single firm wanted to stop its advertising because it would lose its marketing edge relative to its rivals. However, if all firms agreed to stop advertising voluntarily, there was an incentive to cheat.

In fact, the tobacco industry lobbied Congress and led the fight to impose a ban on cigarette advertising on television.

Practice

Use the following information and payoff matrix to answer the two questions. Lewis and Clark each run a cement business. Demand is not strong enough to justify raising price, so each is limited to maintaining the current price or reducing it. The following table gives the payoff matrix.

		Clark's Action	
		Cut Price	**Maintain Price**
Lewis's Action	**Cut Price**	Lewis's profit $25,000 Clark's profit $25,000	Lewis's profit $45,000 Clark's profit $20,000
	Maintain Price	Lewis's profit $20,000 Clark's profit $45,000	Lewis's profit $30,000 Clark's profit $30,000

12. Lewis's dominant strategy is
   (a)   to wait and see what Clark does.
   (b)   to maintain her price.
   (c)   to cut her price.
   (d)   unknown, because it depends on her risk preference.

   ANSWER: (c) If Lewis maintains her price, her profit may be as low as $20,000. If she cuts her price, the lowest profit she should get is $25,000. Clark's position is identical. We are looking at a potential price war.

13. If Lewis and Clark agree to collude to improve each firm's payoff, the best short-run profit-maximizing strategy for Lewis is to agree that
   (a)   neither firm will cut price and then to honor the agreement.
   (b)   neither firm will cut price and then to cut price anyway.
   (c)   both firms will cut price and to honor the agreement.
   (d)   both firms will cut price and then to maintain her price anyway.

   ANSWER: (b) If Clark maintains his price and Lewis cheats, Lewis gains. If Clark cheats (and maintains his price), then Lewis's lowering of her price is still the optimal choice for her. (Note: In the long run, with repeated games, Lewis and Clark would be better advised to honor their collusive agreement.) ∎

Objective 5

Describe ways in which an oligopolistic industry may be inefficient.

There is some debate regarding the efficiency of oligopolists. Oligopoly is inefficient because output is restricted to less than that which society would prefer ($P > MC$). Firms may end up in wasteful deadlocks. Product differentiation and advertising may also be wasteful. Although they may reap economies of scale and foster technological improvements, the balance of opinion is that oligopolies allocate resources inefficiently. (page 306)

Practice

14. In oligopoly, an inefficient output level will occur EXCEPT in the
    (a) cartel model.
    (b) contestable market model.
    (c) Cournot model.
    (d) price-leadership model.

    ANSWER: (b) Because it is easy to enter and leave the industry, the threat of competition forces oligopolists to behave efficiently. Refer to page 306.

15. In the Cournot duopoly model, the oligopolists are
    (a) efficient, because they jointly maintain a stable price once equilibrium is reached.
    (b) efficient, because they jointly maintain a stable output level once equilibrium is reached.
    (c) inefficient, because they fail to produce the output level at which society's welfare is maximized.
    (d) inefficient, because changes in demand are not reflected by changes in price and output level.

    ANSWER: (c) The greater the number of firms in the Cournot model, the more closely they approach the perfectly competitive price and output result. ∎

Objective 6

Explain what the Herfindahl-Hirschman Index is, how it is calculated, and how it is used in antitrust matters.

The *Herfindahl-Hirschman Index* (HHI) is a measure of competition and market structure and is used as a guide to decide whether mergers are permitted. The percentage market share of each firm is squared, and the values totaled. In general, the higher the score, the greater the degree of concentration. If the score is less than 1,000, the industry is thought of as unconcentrated—mergers would go unopposed. In the range 1,000 to 1,800, any proposed merger that would increase the index by 100 or more would be challenged. In an industry with an HHI of greater than 1,800 (a concentrated industry), any merger pushing the index up by 50 points or more would be challenged. (page 308)

   Example: Industry A has 100 firms, each having a 1 percent share. The HHI is 100 and a merger between any two firms would be unopposed. Industry B has 100 firms, with 99 each having a 0.5 percent share and the other having a 50.5 percent share. The HHI would be 2575. A merger between the big firm and any one other firm would be challenged because it would increase the index by 50.5.

Practice

16. The Herfindahl-Hirschman Index for refrigerators is 2253 whereas that for women's dresses is 20. A merger between refrigerator producers would _____ be challenged. A merger between producers of women's dresses would _____ be challenged.
    (a) certainly; certainly
    (b) certainly; not
    (c) not; certainly
    (d) not; not

    ANSWER: (b) If the HHI exceeds 1,800, a merger is automatically challenged. If the HHI is less than 1,000, the merger will be unopposed.

17. Leonard, Adolph, Julius, Herbert, and Milton each run one of the five firms in Industry A. The firms have equal market shares. The Herfindahl-Hirschman Index is
    (a) 25.
    (b) 100.
    (c) 500.
    (d) 2,000.

    ANSWER: (d) $20^2 \times 5 = 2,000$.

18. Leonard, Adolph, Julius, Herbert, and Milton each run one of the five firms in Industry A. The firms have equal market shares. A merger between Julius and Milton would be
    (a) automatically challenged by the Justice Department.
    (b) challenged by the Justice Department if the HHI rose by more than 100.
    (c) challenged by the Justice Department if the HHI rose by more than 200.
    (d) unopposed.

    ANSWER: (a) Because the HHI is greater than 1,800, the merger would be challenged automatically. ■

BRAIN TEASER SOLUTION: If you believe your ice cream is as good as, or better than, that of your competitor, you should locate in the middle of the beach. This should be the most convenient spot for your customers and should not give your rival an overall advantage. You should get a 50 percent share of the customers. Any other location will bring you fewer customers and less revenue. If you fear you might lose in a price war with your rival, a quiet piece of negotiation might produce a cartel from which both sellers would gain.

PRACTICE TEST

I. MULTIPLE-CHOICE QUESTIONS

Select the option that provides the single best answer.

_____ 1. The Five Forces model explains
    (a) the number of firms in an oligopoly.
    (b) why oligopolists usually produce differentiated products.
    (c) why an oligopolist will match a competitor's price increase.
    (d) the relative profitability of an industry and identifies in which area firm rivalry is likely to be most intense.

_____ 2. Industrial organization economists analyze industries by considering three broad categories. Which of the following is not one of those categories?
    (a) Behavior
    (b) Market structure
    (c) Performance
    (d) Efficiency

_____ 3. The special kind of oligopoly that has only two firms is known as
    (a) a bi-lateral monopoly.
    (b) a duopoly.
    (c) a prisoner's dilemma.
    (d) the price leadership model.

_____ 4. XM Satellite and Sirius Satellite are the only two supplies in the satellite radio industry. The four-firm concentration ratio in this industry is
    (a)   2 percent.
    (b)   25 percent.
    (c)   50 percent.
    (d)   100 percent.

Bonnie and Clyde are caught robbing a store. They may be charged with armed robbery—a more serious crime. The police can't prove armed robbery unless one of the pair confesses to it. The following table gives the "punishment matrix."

		Clyde's Action	
		Don't Confess	**Confess**
Bonnie's Action	**Don't Confess**	Both get 2 years in jail	Clyde gets 6 months Bonnie gets 10 years
	Confess	Clyde gets 10 years Bonnie gets 6 months	Both get 6 years in jail

_____ 5. If both Bonnie and Clyde adopt the strategies that minimize the damage that the other can do, then
    (a)   neither will confess.
    (b)   both will confess.
    (c)   only Clyde will confess.
    (d)   only Bonnie will confess.

_____ 6. Price leadership
    (a)   makes tacit collusion difficult to detect.
    (b)   is a strategy used in monopolistic competition.
    (c)   is possible only when homogeneous goods are marketed.
    (d)   is possible only when differentiated goods are marketed.

_____ 7. A cartel
    (a)   encourages price competition among members.
    (b)   should make prices more stable.
    (c)   is present only in the case of firms selling an identical product.
    (d)   is present only in the case of two firms—a duopoly.

_____ 8. All oligopolistic industries
    (a)   have significant barriers to entry.
    (b)   practice product differentiation.
    (c)   have fewer than 16 firms.
    (d)   have firms large enough to exercise some control over the market price.

_____ 9. A group of firms that get together to set price and output jointly is called
    (a)   an oligopoly.
    (b)   a duopoly.
    (c)   a cartel.
    (d)   a price-leadership industry.

_____ 10. An oligopoly in which entry or exit is costless fits which model best?
  (a)   The price-leadership model
  (b)   The contestable market
  (c)   Game theory
  (d)   Collusion

_____ 11. For a cartel to operate, which of the following conditions need not be present?
  (a)   The members must comply with the cartel's rules.
  (b)   The members must be firms of similar size.
  (c)   Demand must be inelastic.
  (d)   There must be few substitutes for the cartel's product.

_____ 12. The Cournot model assumes all of the following EXCEPT that
  (a)   each firm anticipates the price movements of the other.
  (b)   there are only two firms in the industry.
  (c)   both firms maximize profits.
  (d)   each firm takes the output of the other as given.

_____ 13. A market is contestable if
  (a)   it contains many firms, each with a standardized product.
  (b)   entry to and exit from the industry are costless.
  (c)   each firm has a small share of the market and only normal profits are earned in long-run equilibrium.
  (d)   only normal profits are earned in the short run and in long-run equilibrium.

Use the following information and payoff matrix to answer the following question. Glaxo and Pfizer are the two firms in the pharmaceuticals industry. Each company markets a medicine for hypertension. Each firm must decide whether to conduct additional research to improve their medicine or to abandon research. If only Glaxo improves its drug, it will attract customers away from Pfizer, and vice versa. If both conduct successful research, demand will remain unchanged, but profits will decrease because of the costly research program. The following table gives the payoff matrix.

		Glaxo	
		Abandon Research	**Conduct Research**
	Abandon Research	Pfizer's profit $10 million	Pfizer's profit $0
Pfizer		Glaxo's profit $10 million	Glaxo's profit $18 million
	Conduct Research	Pfizer's profit $18 million	Pfizer's profit $9 million
		Glaxo's profit $0	Glaxo's profit $9 million

_____ 14. From the payoff matrix we can conclude that
  (a)   Glaxo does not have a dominant strategy.
  (b)   Glaxo's dominant strategy is to conduct research.
  (c)   Glaxo's dominant strategy is to abandon research.
  (d)   Glaxo's dominant strategy is to conduct research, but only if Pfizer does not.

_____ 15. If the two firms collude to improve their profits, the best short-run profit-maximizing strategy for Glaxo is to agree to
   (a) conduct research and then to honor the agreement.
   (b) conduct research and then to abandon research.
   (c) abandon research and then to honor the agreement.
   (d) abandon research and then to conduct research anyway.

_____ 16. The only oligopoly model in which price equals marginal cost in the long run is the
   (a) Cournot model.
   (b) contestable markets model.
   (c) price-leadership model
   (d) collusion model.

_____ 17. A firm that makes decisions according to the maximin criterion chooses the strategy that gives the
   (a) highest possible maximum loss to the firm.
   (b) highest possible minimum payoff to the firm.
   (c) lowest possible maximum loss to the firm.
   (d) lowest possible minimum payoff to the firm.

_____ 18. A Herfindahl-Hirschman Index of 900 would classify an industry as
   (a) unconcentrated.
   (b) mildly concentrated.
   (c) moderately concentrated.
   (d) concentrated.

_____ 19. An industry has a Herfindahl-Hirschman Index of 1,600. A merger would be
   (a) unopposed.
   (b) opposed, if it raised the index by more than 50.
   (c) opposed, if it raised the index by more than 100.
   (d) opposed in all circumstances.

_____ 20. In an industry where one firm has a 40 percent market share and two others each have a 30 percent market share, the Herfindahl-Hirschman Index is
   (a) 300.
   (b) 2,500.
   (c) 3,400.
   (d) 5,200.

II. APPLICATION QUESTIONS

1. Here is a list of the major companies in the fast-food industry:
   (a) McDonald's
   (b) Burger King
   (c) Wendy's
   (d) KFC
   (e) Hardee's

   Here is a list of characteristics for each fast-food restaurant chain:
   U. The restaurant with the best breakfasts
   W. The place to get chicken
   X. The fast-food place that kids love; the number one fast-food restaurant
   Y. The fast-food restaurant for those without children looking for good values

Z.   The other big fast-food restaurant

Note that the list of characteristics does not include advertising slogans, names of products, or corporate symbols. Despite that, match up the restaurant chain with its description.

2.   Industry A has 100 firms; 99 of the firms have a 0.5 percent share of the market each, and the other, Red Inc., has a 50.5 percent share.

(a)   Red Inc. proposes a horizontal merger with one of the other firms. Would the Justice Department challenge the merger? Explain.

(b)   Suppose, instead, that seven of the small firms propose a merger. Would this be opposed?

Industry B has two firms, with a 20 percent market share each, three firms with 10 percent each, and six firms with 5 percent each.

(c)   Calculate the Herfindahl-Hirschman Index for Industry B.

(d)   Now two of the firms controlling 10 percent of the market propose a merger. Calculate the HHI if the merger took place.

(e)   Why or why not would the merger be opposed?

3.   Firm A and Firm B must each decide an advertising strategy. If both firms advertise, each will earn $6 million. If neither firm advertises, Firm A's profits will be $2 million and Firm B's profits will be $5 million. If only Firm A advertises, it will earn $10 million and Firm B will earn $2 million. If only Firm B advertises, Firm A will earn $3 million and Firm B will earn $4 million.

(a)   Complete the following payoff matrix.

		Firm B's Action	
		Advertise	**Don't Advertise**
Firm A's Action	**Advertise**	A's profit: B's profit:	A's profit: B's profit:
	Don't Advertise	A's profit: B's profit:	A's profit: B's profit:

(b)   Does Firm A have a dominant strategy? If so, what is it?

(c)   Does Firm B have a dominant strategy? If so, what is it?

(d)   You are the manager for Firm B and you must take one action or the other. Which action would you choose if you follow a maximin strategy?

4.   List the "five forces" featured in the Five Forces model. Choose an industry that you feel represents oligopoly. How would each of these forces have to change in order to reduce industry profits?

5.   Is each of the following statements true or false? Explain.

(a)   For a cartel to be effective, product demand must be inelastic.

(b)   In game theory, a Nash equilibrium requires that each player has a dominant strategy.

(c)   The perfectly contestable markets model of oligopoly gives an outcome with respect to profitability that is similar to that of perfect competition.

6. L-tryptophan is a naturally occurring amino acid found in food (such as turkey and milk). For years it was manufactured for use in the treatment of chronic insomnia. One foreign supplier devised a new fermentation process. Unfortunately, the L-tryptophan produced was found to cause a rare disease (EMS), and all L-tryptophan was banned by the Food and Drug Administration (FDA) until its use could be proved to be safe and effective. A market existed for L-tryptophan and it met a need. However, a pharmaceutical company might have had to spend millions of dollars on research to convince the FDA that the drug is both safe and effective. Note that, because L-tryptophan occurs in nature, it cannot be patented. The producer would not have a monopoly.

   You may have noticed L-tryptophan on sale at your local WalMart. Do some research on this issue. Did one firm undertake the research needed to prove L-tryptophan safe? Which oligopoly model most closely approximates this market, and why?

7. Which industries do you think are the most concentrated? You'll need to guess here. Rank the following eight *alphabetized* industries, ("1" being the most concentrated and "8" being the least concentrated), then check the *Practice Test Solutions* section to see if your intuition is correct. Just as a guide, the actual four-firm concentration ratio for the eight industries is included *in ascending order* in the third column. It is not meant to suggest that beer's ratio is 98 percent, for instance.

Industry	Ranking	Four-firm Concentration Ratio
Beer	_____	98 percent
Bottled Water	_____	93 percent
Cheese	_____	85 percent
Dog and Cat Food	_____	64 percent
Paper	_____	52 percent
Video Game Consoles	_____	34 percent
Soft Drinks	_____	26 percent
Women's and Girls' Apparel	_____	12 percent

8. Watch 10 ads on TV; listen to 10 on the radio; read 10 in a weekly magazine, and read another 10 in the daily newspaper. Does the amount of *information* in each differ? Which medium seems to contain the most information? Which the least? Do the different media attract a similar mix of monopolistically competitive and oligopolistic firms? In which medium is oligopoly most prominent? In which are monopolistically competitive firms most important? Why do you think these differences occur?

9.   Refer to Application Question 2 in Chapter 13 and to the following diagram. Initially, veterinary services are provided by the American Veterinary Association and can be provided at any level for an opportunity cost of $60,000 per vet. The yearly demand, marginal revenue, and marginal cost curves for veterinary services are shown below (P is the dollar price per vet.) The profit-maximizing output level (Q) was shown to be 30,000. When Q is 30,000, the profit-maximizing price is $180,000 and the industry's total economic profit equals $3,600,000,000.

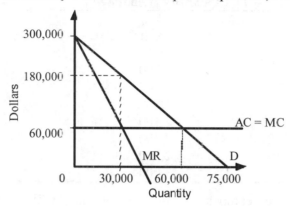

Initially, the AVA is a monopolist. Now a breakaway organization (the American Pets Association) enters the market selling identical veterinary services. A Cournot duopoly is formed.

(a)   Draw the reaction function for each firm in the following diagram. Include the numerical values for the endpoints of the functions. Determine the intersection point of the reaction functions.

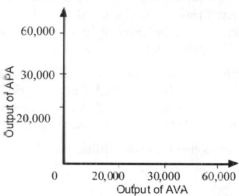

(b)   Relative to the monopoly, what has happened to the industry's output level?

(c)   Relative to the monopoly, what must have happened to the industry's price level?

10. Use the following demand schedule to answer the questions. Initially, this is a perfectly competitive market. For simplicity, assume that the marginal cost of producing additional units is zero. Any increase in total revenue, therefore, represents an increase in total profit.

(b) Complete the total revenue column in the table.

Price	Quantity Demanded	Total Revenue
$9	300	_____
$8	600	_____
$7	900	_____
$6	1,200	_____
$5	1,500	_____
$4	1,800	_____
$3	2,100	_____
$2	2,400	_____
$1	2,700	_____
$0	3,000	

(b) Under perfect competition, how many units will be produced? What will be the equilibrium price?

(c) The firms form a profit-maximizing monopoly. How many units will be produced by the monopoly and what will be the equilibrium price? (Think about the relationship between total revenue and total cost!)

(d) At this point, half of the original firms break away and set up a separate company. However the two new firms (ABC Corp. and CBA Corp.) form a cartel to establish the price that will yield the greatest level of joint profits. How many units will each firm produce and what will be the equilibrium price?

(e) CBA cheats on the price-fixing agreement and the cartel breaks up—the industry becomes a Cournot duopoly. Initially, each firm sets price and output at the level chosen by the cartel—$5 and 750 units. Suppose that CBA increases production from 750 to 900. What will happen the CBA's total revenue and to ABC's total revenue?

(f) Draw the reaction functions for the two firms. Include as much detail as possible.

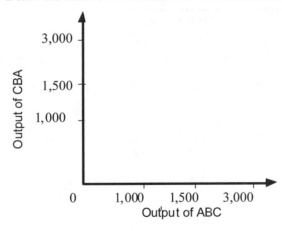

(g) Fill in the following matrix. Each firm can choose to increase output from 750 to 900 or maintain output at 750.

		CBA'sAction	
		Output = 900	**Output = 750**
ABC's	**Output = 900**	CBA's change in revenue: ABC's change in revenue:	CBA's change in revenue: ABC's change in revenue:
Action	**Output = 750**	CBA's change in revenue: ABC's change in revenue:	CBA's change in revenue: ABC's change in revenue:

(h) What is CBA's dominant strategy (if any)?

(i) Can you determine the equilibrium market price and market quantity after repeated games (assuming no collusion)?

Practice Test SOLUTIONS

I.   SOLUTIONS TO MULTIPLE-CHOICE QUESTIONS

1.   (d)   The Five Forces model identifies the competitive forces that shape the level of competition and the relative profitability of an industry.

2.   (d)   Efficiency is a yardstick of performance, rather than an organizational classification.

3.   (b)   A duopoly is an oligopoly that has only two firms. The Cournot model is an example of a duopoly.

4.   (d)   If there are only two firms, then they must account for 100 percent of the market.

5.   (b)   If Bonnie confesses, Clyde would minimize the damage by having confessed too. Six years is better than 10. Bonnie would argue similarly.

6.   (a)   Refer to page 298 for more on price leadership.

7.   (b)   Cartels are set up to control prices. Having identical products makes it easier for firms to form a cartel, but it is not essential.

8.   (d)   Influence over market price is a common feature. Many oligopolistic models assume high barriers to entry—the perfectly contestable markets model does not.

9.   (c)   Refer to page 297. See OPEC!

10.   (b)   In the contestable markets model, firms must have mobile and transferable resources that can be switched from one use—and one industry—to another. Refer to page 295.

11.   (b)   In OPEC (a very successful and long-lasting cartel), some member countries, such as Saudi Arabia, are very large oil producers whereas others, such as Gabon and Ecuador, are comparatively small.

12.   (a)   In the Cournot model, output is given. The two firms in the duopoly do not guess each other's price movements.

13.   (b)   The main point about contestable markets is that it is easy to get into them and to get out of them.

14.   (b)   Whether or not Pfizer chooses to do research, Glaxo preferred strategy is to do research. A dominant strategy (by definition) does not depend on the rival's choice.

15.   (b)   If Glaxo and Pfizer both agree to abandon research, and then Glaxo cheats, it can boost its profits.

16.   (b)   If economic profit exists, competition from new entrants will drive down the price until it equals marginal cost. Refer to page 306.

17.   (b)   Refer to page 303 for more on the maximin strategy.

18.   (a)   Refer to Figure 14.7 on page 308.

19.   (c)   An HHI of 1,600 lies in the middle region. It would be opposed if the index were raised "too much," i.e., by more than 100. Refer to Figure 14.7 on page 308.

20.   (c)   The industry has only three firms, because 40 percent + 30 percent + 30 percent = 100 percent. $HHI = 40^2 + 30^2 + 30^2 = 3,400$.

II. SOLUTIONS TO APPLICATION QUESTIONS

1.   Here is my list, based on my perceptions.
    (a) X.   (b) Z.   (c) Y.   (d) W.   (e) U.

Even if your selections differ from those given here, it is of interest that you could distinguish among restaurant chains. What differences do you perceive and *where* do you think these differing perceptions have come from? They have probably been guided by effective Madison Avenue advertising campaigns. Burger King's apparent lack of image may pose a problem to the company.

2.   (a)   The Justice Department would challenge the merger of Red Inc. and another firm, as the HHI is over 1,800 (a concentrated industry) and would rise by more than 50.
        HHI (before merger) = $50.5^2 + [(0.5^2) \times 99] = 2,575$
        HHI (after merger) = $51.0^2 + [(0.5^2) \times 98] = 2,625.5$ (assuming the merged firms retained their market shares)

    (b)   HHI (before merger) = $50.5^2 + [(0.5^2) \times 99] = 2,575$
        HHI (after merger) = $50.5^2 + 3.5^2 + [(0.5^2) \times 92] = 2,585.5$
        The HHI would rise by less than 50; the merger would not be opposed.

    (c)   The HHI = $20^2 + 20^2 + [(10^2) \times 3] + [(5^2) \times 6] = 1,250$

    (d)   HHI (after merger) = $[20^2 \times 3] + 10^2 + [(5^2) \times 6] = 1,450$

    (e)   The HHI would rise by more than 100; the merger would be opposed.

3.   (a)   Refer to the following payoff matrix.

		Firm B's Action	
		Advertise	**Don't Advertise**
Firm A's	**Advertise**	A's profit: $6 million B's profit: $6 million	A's profit: $10 million B's profit: $2 million
Action	**Don't Advertise**	A's profit: $3 million B's profit: $4 million	A's profit: $2 million B's profit: $5 million

    (b)   Firm A should advertise. If B advertises, A's position is better if it also advertises ($6 million instead of $3 million). If B does not advertise, A gains more by advertising ($10 million instead of $2 million).

    (c)   Firm B does not have a dominant strategy. If A advertises, B's position is better if it also advertises ($6 million instead of $2 million). If A does not advertise, B gains more by not advertising ($5 million instead of $4 million).

     (d)   You should advertise. The maximin strategy seeks to maximize the gain in the worst-case scenario. If A advertises, the worst possibility for B is to not advertise ($2 million profit, instead of $6 million). If A does not advertise, the worst possibility for B is to advertise ($4 million profit, instead of $5 million). Advertising earns the greatest payoff in this case ($4 million).

4.   The five forces are: potential entrants, substitute products, suppliers (of inputs), buyers (of output), and the degree of rivalry among existing firms. Consider the pharmaceutical industry as an example. If rivalry between existing firms becomes more intense, perhaps through advertising, profitability should decrease for the industry. According to the model, if the threat of potential entrants increases (perhaps because of technological or legal changes), or more and closer substitutes become available (Canadian medications or generics), or if the strength of suppliers (union growth) and buyers (AARP or medical insurance companies) increases relative to the industry, then the lower pharmaceutical industry profits should be.

5.   Identify whether each of the following statements is true or false. Explain.
     (a)   True. If the cartel's members try to increase price and demand is elastic, the cartel's revenues will decrease as consumers move to substitutes.

     (b)   False. A dominant strategy is best, regardless of the behavior of other players. It is not dependent on the actions of others. A Nash equilibrium, on the other hand, has each player choosing his best strategy *given* the behavior of the other players.

     (c)   True. Because entry is costless in contestable markets, even large oligopolistic firms end up acting like perfectly competitive firms.

6.   No single producer was willing to undertake the expense of proving L-tryptophan safe because no patent could be earned. Research was reviewed by the FDA itself. Indeed, because drug companies could transfer production facilities between different uses, the market would have become close to a perfectly contestable market. Eventually, the FDA approved L-tryptophan for production and several brands are currently available.

7.   Refer to the following table. The industries are ranked from most concentrated (1) to least concentrated (8). Note that, as a rough rule of thumb, an industry having a concentration ratio in excess of 40 percent is thought of as oligopolistic.

Industry	Ranking	Four-firm Concentration Ratio
Beer	3	85 percent
Bottled Water	4	52 percent
Cheese	6	34 percent
Dog and Cat Food	5	64 percent
Paper	7	26 percent
Video Game Consoles	1	98 percent
Soft Drinks	2	93 percent
Women's and Girls' Apparel	8	12 percent

8.   You should find that different companies and different types of companies use different media. National oligopolies (Coke, Exxon, Procter & Gamble) use TV and magazines, for instance. Radio and newspapers tend to attract more local and more monopolistically competitive advertisers. Advertising represents a barrier to entry; by advertising lavishly, perhaps oligopolies prevent the entrance of credible rivals.

9.   (a)   See the following diagram.

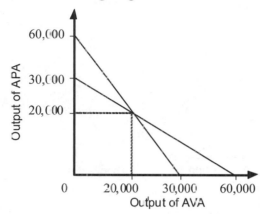

(j)   Output level has increased from 30,000 to a total of 40,000.

(k)   Given the demand curve, price must have decreased from $180,000 to $140,000.

10.   (a)   See the following table.

Price	Quantity Demanded	Total Revenue
$9	300	$2,700
$8	600	$4,800
$7	900	$6,300
$6	1,200	$7,200
$5	1,500	$7,500
$4	1,800	$7,200
$3	2,100	$6,300
$2	2,400	$4,800
$1	2,700	$2,700
$0	3,000	0

(b)   Under perfect competition, firms would produce until $P = MC$. Because MC is zero, the industry's output would be 3,000 units and the price would be zero.

(c)   If marginal cost is zero, the monopolist will maximize profits by producing where total revenue is maximized. The monopolist will charge a price of $5 and sell 1,500 units.

(d)   The cartel will operate exactly like a monopoly, fixing the price at $5. Each firm will produce 750 units.

(e)   CBA's revenue (and profit) will increase by $750 (150 × $5) while ABC's will shrink by the same amount. Individually, each firm has an incentive to expand output.

(f)   See the following diagram.

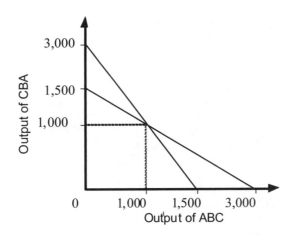

(g) See the following payoff matrix.

		CBA's Action	
		Output = 900	**Output = 750**
ABC's Action	**Output = 900**	CBA's change in revenue: –$150 ABC's change in revenue: –$150	CBA's change in revenue: –$750 ABC's change in revenue: +$750
	Output = 750	CBA's change in revenue: +$750 ABC's change in revenue: –$750	CBA's change in revenue: 0 ABC's change in revenue: 0

(h)   CBA's dominant strategy is to increased output, as is ABC's.

(i)   The firms will each continue to expand output (and be forced to reduce price) until each firm produces 1,000 units and sells at a price of $2.67 per unit.

15

Monopolistic Competition

Chapter Objectives

1. Identify the features that characterize a monopolistically competitive firm and industry.
2. Define product differentiation and explain why it occurs.
3. Explain the arguments for and against advertising.
4. Interpret the graph of a profit-maximizing, monopolistically competitive firm, indicating the profit-maximizing output level and price. Explain why the monopolistically competitive firm will make only normal profits in long-run equilibrium.
5. Identify and analyze the factors in monopolistic competition that cause inefficiency and resource misallocation.

BRAIN TEASER: Select four local restaurants. In which ways have these restaurants successfully differentiated their product from one another and from their competitors? What *is* their "product"? How significant a role does advertising play in product differentiation ? Is it equivalent in volume for all four restaurants? Do they use the same advertising media or appeal to the same clientele? Do you feel that their advertising is mainly "informative" or "persuasive?"

If you were planning to establish a restaurant in your town, with which factors would you be most concerned? How would you attempt to cultivate a clientele? How would you respond to your competitors? Which do you feel is the more accurate representation of the restaurant business in your town, the monopolistically competitive model or the oligopolistic model? Why?

Objective 1

Identify the features that characterize a monopolistically competitive firm and industry.

Monopolistic competition is characterized by a large number of small firms, none of which can control market price, but that produce slightly differentiated products. There are few barriers to entry in monopolistic competition. Restaurants are an excellent example.

LEARNING TIP: Monopoly has *one* firm, oligopoly a *few*, perfect competition and monopolistic competition *many*. The distinguishing characteristic of monopolistic competition is **product differentiation**. Except for the downward-sloping demand and marginal revenue curves the perfectly and monopolistically competitive short- and long-run stories are very similar. Monopolistic competition differs from monopoly and oligopoly in that firms in these industries can't affect the market price by virtue of their size. The oligopolist may or may not differentiate its product—as with most things in oligopoly, it depends.

It will help you to keep in mind clear examples of each market structure:

(a) Perfect competition: the stock market (unless there is insider trading), word processing

(b) Monopolistic competition: your local restaurant scene

(c) Oligopoly: DeBeers, the diamond cartel that functions almost like a monopoly; OPEC, the cartel with a fairly homogeneous product (oil); the U.S. car industry, which tries to differentiate

(d) Pure monopoly: Glaxo, the developers of AZT, the first anti-AIDS drug, or Pfizer, the originator of Viagra

---

Now go and find your own examples!

Figure 15.1 summarizes the characteristics that distinguish each market structure. ◀

Practice

1. Each of the following is a characteristic of monopolistic competition EXCEPT
   (a) many firms.
   (b) product differentiation.
   (c) few barriers to entry.
   (d) mutual interdependence.

   ANSWER: (d) Refer to p 314. Mutual interdependence characterizes oligopoly. There are barriers to entry but they are insubstantial.

2. In monopolistic competition, firms achieve some market power
   (a) by growing larger.
   (b) by merging with other firms into a cartel.
   (c) by establishing barriers to exit from the industry.
   (d) through product differentiation.

   ANSWER: (d) Refer to page 314. ∎

Objective 2

Define product differentiation and explain why it occurs.

Product differentiation occurs when a product is distinguished in the minds of consumers from alternatives in some positive way. Product differentiation may be affected by differences in tastes, coordination needs, or economies of scale. Proponents of product differentiation believe that consumers' tastes differ and that they prefer variety over sameness—evidence from behavioral economics suggests that this can be taken too far, however. (page 315)

Firms may indulge in *horizontal* differentiation (where products are adapted in ways that make them more desirable to some consumers and less desirable to others) or *vertical* differentiation (where a product is perceived as more desirable by all consumers than other alternatives).

Product Differentiation and Advertising: Advertising and expectations play a powerful role in product differentiation, as the following (true) story shows. Various regulars in a bar were firm supporters of one or the other of two brands of cheap Scotch. Sometimes, the bar would run out of the favorite brand of one faction and its patrons would grudgingly have to consume the other brand. Invariably, expressing dissatisfaction, they swore that they could tell the difference. The point is that they drank with their eyes: both bottles contained the *same* brand of Scotch. The barman topped them up before opening time—using a third, even cheaper, brand!

Product Differentiation and Consumer Tastes: Local radio is a good example of monopolistic competition—the airwaves are abuzz with radio stations claiming that they're the answer to your listening requirements. In the mid-1990s, KLAX in Los Angeles was languishing at the lower end of the top 40 stations with a playlist that was indistinguishable from that of its competitors. Changing formats, KLAX zoomed to be the city's premier station within three months, claiming the loyalty of one million listeners. KLAX found a "new" product—*ranchera* and *banda* (Mexican country music). As we would expect, because barriers to switching formats in the radio industry are low, other stations challenged for a share of this market, which is estimated at between three and five million listeners.

Similarly, between 1995 and 2005, the Hispanic population in the state of North Carolina increased fivefold. Inevitably, Spanish language radio stations and groceries emerged to meet the needs of these new consumers.

ECONOMICS IN PRACTICE: On page 318, the textbook looks at Honest Tea's Green Dragon brand and how it has differentiated its product from those of competitors such as Snapple and SoBe. Based on the information given in the text, how has the firm set its product apart? Is this horizontal differentiation or vertical differentiation?

ANSWER: Price is one aspect of differentiation—higher price brands suggest higher quality. Doubtless packaging plays a part—"Green Dragon" suggests green tea from China. For consumers shopping for "honest" tea, health issues may be a factor—green tea is supposedly healthier because it contains antioxidants and less caffeine than coffee. Finally, there is some emphasis in the diagram on reduced sugar, which might be an attraction for diabetics or calorie-counters. This is an example of horizontal differentiation—Snapple buyers may not appreciate the lower sugar content and higher price.

Practice

3.   Recent research in behavioral economics suggests that
      (a)   a great many choices makes product selection easier for consumers.
      (b)   consumers may be attracted by many choices but may avoid having to make decisions.
      (c)   consumers will buy more of a product when there are many varieties.
      (d)   a limited range of choices makes product selection more difficult for consumers.

      ANSWER: (b) Refer to page 317. Consumers may be overwhelmed by a proliferation of product choices.

4.   In well-working markets, the degree of product variety reflects each of the following EXCEPT
      (a)   the number of firms in the market.
      (b)   differences in consumer tastes.
      (c)   any gains from coordination.
      (d)   cost economies from standardization.

      ANSWER: (a) Refer to page 316. Perfect competition and monopolistic competition both have many firms but, in one case, an entirely standardized product and, in the other, product differentiation.

5.   Which of the following is an example of vertical differentiation?
      (a)   A new Chinese restaurant opens up in a town with many such restaurants.
      (b)   A Chinese restaurant offers a new takeout service like its rivals.
      (c)   A Chinese restaurant extends its hours of operation over the weekend.
      (d)   A Chinese restaurant changes to a takeout only operation—the first in town.

      ANSWER: (c) Longer hours of operation will improve overall quality of service for all customers. Option (d) may be better for some consumers, but less appealing to others. ∎

Objective 3

Explain the arguments for and against advertising.

Product differentiation (making one's product appear unique) is important in monopolistic competition, and advertising can be an important aid in making the firm's or industry's demand curve less elastic (sensitive to price). (page 315)

    Supporters of advertising argue that the firm must make consumers aware of its products and differentiate them from those of its competitors. In addition, higher quality (or more efficiently produced) goods should prevail over inferior rivals, resulting in greater efficiency in the use of scarce resources. However, consumers need to know about the choices open to them, so advertising is necessary. (page 320)

Opponents of advertising argue that it contains little information and squanders resources while highlighting small or nonexistent distinctions between brands. Advertising distorts consumer preferences and may reduce the buyer's ability to choose rationally. In addition, the high level of costly and distracting promotions—billboards, junk mail, radio and TV jingles—that consumers must endure, and ultimately pay for, may represent a barrier to entry that reduces competition. There is no clear answer one way or the other. (page 320)

Right Answers in Economics: President Truman once wished for a "one-handed economist." On all issues his economic experts invariably told him "on one hand, this, and on the other hand, that." Economics often gives "maybe" answers—in the current chapter, for example, advertising has both benefits *and* costs.

ECONOMICS IN PRACTICE (SUPPLEMENTAL): There is a current (2010) proposal to label the nutritional value of restaurant meals with the aim of reducing unhealthy food choices, and thus reducing obesity. Opponents argue that customers might go "elsewhere," but where could that be? In addition, assuming that patrons do have some inkling that steak with a side order of cheese fries, followed by a chocolate cake, and washed down with a double Scotch might be unhealthy, how effective would such labeling be? What is the evidence, according to the article? Finally, what might be the impact of a "fat" tax on restaurant meals?

ANSWER: Customers could abstain from high-calorie meals (or restaurants) and order more healthy meals. Alternatively, they could prepare more meals at home. To the extent that restaurant meals offer "convenience," the effect of the legislation might be to encourage additional recourse to the unhealthy frozen foods discussed in Chapter 2. Regarding the effectiveness of labeling, this is clearly an open question—after all, the frozen foods just referred to are labeled but widely used. The article suggests that, currently, few patrons bother with or care about the calorie information. If a tax were imposed on the fat content of meals, it should increase the prices of less healthy choices relative to more healthy ones. To the extent that obesity places demands on the nation's (tax-funded) Medicaid system, negative externalities are imposed on society. We deal with externalities in the following chapter.

Practice

6. Which one of the following is least likely to be offered as an argument by proponents of advertising?
   (a) Advertising can promote competition.
   (b) Advertising encourages product innovation which, in turn, benefits consumers.
   (c) Advertising helps consumers to make rational, informed choices.
   (d) Advertising presents entirely factual information to consumers.

   ANSWER: (d) While much advertising may be informational, some elements (such as paid celebrity endorsements) are not.

7. Monopolistic competition differs from perfect competition because in monopolistic competition
   (a) there are few firms.
   (b) entry into the industry is difficult.
   (c) there are many firms.
   (d) firms can differentiate their products.

   ANSWER: (d) Refer to the list of characteristics on page 314. ■

Objective 4

Interpret the graph of a profit-maximizing, monopolistically competitive firm, indicating the profit-maximizing output level and price. Explain why the monopolistically competitive firm will make only normal profits in long-run equilibrium.

Graphically, monopolistic competition is similar to Chapter 13's monopoly picture while conceptually quite different on the demand side—the demand curve in the monopoly diagram shows the entire market demand. Demand is downward sloping, as in monopoly, but is more elastic because of the many close substitutes for the monopolistic competitor's product. Unlike perfect competition, the demand faced by the firm is not perfectly elastic, because of the presence of product differentiation. Profit maximization occurs at the production level where marginal revenue is equal to marginal cost—as with monopoly. Short-run profits or losses are possible—as with monopoly. In long-run equilibrium, *unlike* monopoly, only *normal* profits must prevail due to easy entry into, and exit from, the industry. Economic profits attract new firms which in turn, lessen the demand for each firm's product, driving the demand curve leftward towards the average cost curve and normal profits. (page 322)

LEARNING TIP: The "cost diagram" for monopolistic competition is the same as that for perfect competition and monopoly—it's the demand side that's different. Draw the cost curves first, then fit in the demand and marginal revenue curves to suit your needs. ◀

Graphing Pointer: In monopolistic competition, the long-run equilibrium graph *must* have the demand curve just touching the average cost curve. This is the profit-maximizing output level so, to be consistent, *MR* must equal *MC* at that same output level, too! If you can't work out why this must be true, go back to Chapter 8 now and review profit maximization.

Practice

8. Monopolistic competition differs from perfect competition because, unlike the perfect competitor, the monopolistically competitive firm
    (a)   faces a perfectly inelastic demand curve.
    (b)   can earn positive economic profit in the short run and in the long run.
    (c)   cannot earn positive economic profit even in the short run.
    (d)   does not have the same marginal revenue at every output level.

    ANSWER: (d)   Because demand is downward sloping for the monopolistically competitive firm, marginal revenue will lie below it.

9. When profits are being maximized, the monopolistically competitive firm's price
    (a)   equals its marginal revenue.
    (b)   exceeds its marginal cost.
    (c)   is less than its marginal revenue.
    (d)   equals its marginal cost.

    ANSWER: (b)   To maximize profits, the firm will produce where *MR* = *MC*. Because price exceeds *MR*, price must therefore also exceed *MC*.

10. The monopolistically competitive firm's demand curve will be _____ elastic than that of the perfectly competitive firm. The monopolistically competitive market demand curve will be downward sloping, _____ the market demand curve in perfect competition.
    (a)   more; like
    (b)   more; unlike
    (c)   less; like
    (d)   less; unlike

ANSWER: (c) Given product differentiation, the degree of substitutability will be less than it is in perfect competition. The market demand curve is downward sloping in both market structures. The *firm's* demand curve is horizontal in perfect competition.

Use the following diagram to answer the next eight questions. This diagram depicts Salon Dion, a firm in the monopolistically competitive beauty parlor industry.

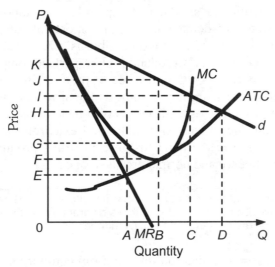

11.   Salon Dion's profit-maximizing output level is
(a)   *OA*.
(b)   *OB*.
(c)   *OC*.
(d)   *OD*.

ANSWER: (a) This is the output level where *MR* = *MC*.

12.   The profit-maximizing price is
(a)   *OE*.
(b)   *OF*.
(c)   *OG*.
(d)   *OK*.

ANSWER: (d) Use the demand curve to determine price.

13.   In the short run, Salon Dion will earn a total economic profit of
(a)   *OA* × *OG*.
(b)   *OA* × *OK*.
(c)   *OA* × *GK*.
(d)   *OA* × *EK*.

ANSWER: (c) Total economic profit equals $(P - ATC) \times q$.

14.   This diagram depicts a monopolistic competitor in the
(a)   short run, because marginal cost is less than average total cost at the profit-maximizing output level.
(b)   short run, because economic profits are being earned.
(c)   long run, because no fixed costs are shown.
(d)   long run, because the firm is maximizing its profits.

ANSWER: (b) As shown in the preceding question, Salon Dion is earning an economic profit. Because of easy entry into the industry, such a circumstance cannot be maintained in the long run.

15.   In the long run, firms will _____ this industry and, for the typical firm, such as Salon Dion, quantity demanded will equal _____ .
(a)   enter; marginal cost
(b)   enter; average total cost
(c)   exit; marginal cost
(d)   exit; average total cost
ANSWER: (b) Firms enter, attracted by short-run economic profits. Refer to page 324.

16.   In the long run, Salon Dion's demand curve will shift to the _____ and become more _____ .
(a)   right; inelastic
(b)   right; elastic
(c)   left; inelastic
(d)   left; elastic
ANSWER: (d) Each firm will lose some of its market share as firms enter the industry. Demand will become more elastic because of the larger number of substitutes.

17.   In the long run, Salon Dion's marginal revenue curve will shift to the _____ and become more

_____ .
(a)   right; inelastic
(b)   right; elastic
(c)   left; inelastic
(d)   left; elastic
ANSWER: (d) Refer to the answer to the preceding question. Demand and marginal revenue are linked. If you can't see why this is true, review pp. 271–274 in Chapter 13.

18.   Assuming that the cost curves of this typical firm remain unchanged, in the long run there will be _____ firms in this industry, each producing _____ output.
(a)   more; more
(b)   more; less
(c)   fewer; more
(d)   fewer; less
ANSWER: (b) Given short-run profits, more firms will enter the industry. If *MR* shifts left and *MC* remains unchanged, Salon Dion's profit-maximizing output level will decrease. ∎

Objective 5

Identify and analyze the factors in monopolistic competition that cause inefficiency and resource misallocation.

The presence of monopolistic competition has some welfare consequences. Because the firm produces where *MR* = *MC* and, because price is greater than *MR*, price is greater than marginal cost at the profit-maximizing output level. This is inefficient because society wants production to occur up to the point where *P* = *MC*. In the long run, because demand is downward sloping, average cost is not minimized or, to put it another way, resources are not used to their maximum efficiency—there is excess plant capacity. Note, though, that despite the inefficiencies generated by this market structure, there are benefits springing from an extensive menu of choices. (page 326)

Practice

19. Peter's Pan Pizzeria is a monopolistically competitive firm. In the short run, Peter is earning a positive economic profit by producing at the output that minimizes his long-run average cost. In the long run, Peter will _____ production and average cost will _____ (assuming constant returns to scale in the pizza industry).
    (a) increase; increase
    (b) increase; remain unchanged
    (c) decrease; increase
    (d) decrease; remain unchanged

    ANSWER: (c) Try drawing this. Peter must be earning economic profits. Reasoning: Where *ATC* is minimized, *MC* equals *ATC*. To maximize profits, Peter must equalize *MR* and *MC*, *MR* also equals *ATC*. Given a downward-sloping demand curve, price must exceed *MR* and, therefore, price must exceed *ATC*, and a profit will be earned. Other firms will enter the industry and, as Peter's market share contracts, his average costs will increase.

20. Monopolistic competition is
    (a) efficient because entry is unrestricted and only normal profits can be earned in long-run equilibrium.
    (b) efficient because society receives as much of the good as is demanded.
    (c) not efficient because too little output is produced at too high a cost.
    (d) not efficient because there are too many small firms, each involved with a small share of the entire market.

    ANSWER: (c) In long-run equilibrium, the typical firm does not operate where its costs per unit are minimized. Also, the profit-maximizing output level results in too little of the good being produced. Options (a) and (d) also describe perfect competition. ∎

BRAIN TEASER SOLUTION: This is an opinion question. Note that the product of a restaurant is not just food—it is the entire "dining experience" that includes location, decor, service, and so on.

PRACTICE TEST

I. MULTIPLE-CHOICE QUESTIONS

Select the option that provides the single best answer.

_____ 1. In the long run, economic profits earned in a monopolistically competitive industry will cause _____ the industry and a _____ shift of the typical firm's demand curve.
    (a) entry into; rightward
    (b) entry into; leftward
    (c) exit from; rightward
    (d) exit from; leftward

_____ 2. Each of the following is a characteristic of monopolistic competition EXCEPT
    (a) products are differentiated.
    (b) there is a large number of sellers.
    (c) firms will charge the same price.
    (d) each firm has some degree of market power.

_____ 3. Each of the following is an example of product differentiation EXCEPT
   (a)   advertising.
   (b)   after-sales service.
   (c)   development of "new and improved" products.
   (d)   producing where marginal revenue equals marginal cost.

_____ 4. In monopolistic competition
   (a)   firms can be either large or small relative to the entire market.
   (b)   all firms must be small relative to the entire market.
   (c)   there are substantial economies of scale present for each firm.
   (d)   all firms are price takers.

_____ 5. *Ground Zero* is a profit-maximizing coffee shop in a monopolistically competitive market. The owner, Mr. Bean, increases his prices by 10 percent. No other coffee shop follows suit. We would predict that
   (a)   *Ground Zero* will lose all of its customers.
   (b)   *Ground Zero's* profits will increase.
   (c)   *Ground Zero's* profits will decrease.
   (d)   *Ground Zero* will attract more customers.

_____ 6. *Ground Zero* is a profit-maximizing coffee shop in a monopolistically competitive market. We know that, in the short run,
   (a)   price equals average total cost.
   (b)   price equals average variable cost.
   (c)   price equals marginal revenue.
   (d)   marginal revenue equals marginal cost.

_____ 7. For the monopolistically competitive firm in long-run equilibrium, its price
   (a)   exceeds its marginal cost.
   (b)   exceeds its average cost.
   (c)   equals its marginal cost.
   (d)   is less than its marginal cost.

_____ 8. Unlike a monopolist, a monopolistically competitive firm
   (a)   can earn positive economic profit in the short run but not in the long run.
   (b)   has a downward-sloping marginal revenue curve.
   (c)   can never cover its minimum average cost in the long run.
   (d)   may sell to many buyers.

_____ 9. In monopolistically competitive markets, the high degree of product variety reflects
   (a)   modest cost economies from standardization and few differences in consumer tastes.
   (b)   modest cost economies from standardization and wide differences in consumer tastes.
   (c)   substantial cost economies from standardization and few gains from coordination.
   (d)   substantial cost economies from standardization and many gains from coordination.

_____ 10.   Which statement is **false?** For the monopolistically competitive firm, economic profits
      (a)   will never occur, because it is easy for firms to enter the industry.
      (b)   attract new firms, causing each existing firm's demand curve to shift left.
      (c)   attract new firms, causing each existing firm's demand curve become more elastic.
      (d)   will be zero in long-run equilibrium.

The following diagram is for a typical firm in a monopolistically competitive industry. Use it to answer the next six questions.

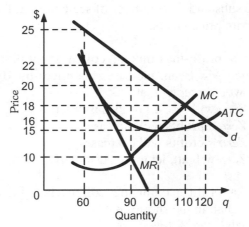

_____ 11.   The profit-maximizing price is
      (a) $10.
      (b) $15.
      (c) $18.
      (d) $22.

_____ 12.   The equilibrium output for this firm is
      (a)   60.
      (b)   90.
      (c)   100.
      (d)   110.

_____ 13.   This firm is making an economic profit of
      (a) $540.
      (b) $1,040.
      (c) $420.
      (d) $630.

_____ 14.   In the long run, we would expect to see the
      (a)   demand curve shift to the right and the average total cost curve shift down.
      (b)   demand curve shift to the left and the marginal cost curve shift up.
      (c)   marginal revenue curve shift to the left and the average total cost curve shift up.
      (d)   marginal revenue curve shift to the left and the demand curve shift to the left.

_____ 15.   The efficient output level (the one that would maximize consumer welfare) is
      (a)   60 units.
      (b)   90 units.
      (c)   100 units.
      (d)   110 units.

_____ 16.   In long-run equilibrium the firm produces an output of 70 units. Assuming no change in the position of the cost curves, the firm's excess capacity is
(a)   10 units.
(b)   20 units.
(c)   30 units.
(d)   40 units.

_____ 17.   Advertising should make the monopolistically competitive firm's demand curve _____ and marginal revenue curve _____ .
(a)   flatter; flatter
(b)   flatter; steeper
(c)   steeper; flatter
(d)   steeper; steeper

_____ 18.   You are the manager of a monopolistically competitive office-cleaning firm. The firm is in long-run equilibrium. In an effort to boost sales and to distinguish your firm from its rivals, you launch an advertising campaign. What will be the effects of the advertising campaign (assuming that it is successful) as the firm moves to a new long-run equilibrium?
(a)   Average cost will increase; demand and marginal revenue curves will shift right and become more elastic; price will increase.
(b)   Average cost will increase; demand and marginal revenue curves will shift right and become less elastic; price will increase.
(c)   Marginal cost will shift to the right; demand and marginal revenue curves will shift right and become more elastic; price will increase.
(d)   Marginal cost will shift to the right; demand and marginal revenue curves will shift right and become less elastic; price will increase.

Use the following information to answer the next two questions. The Upper Crust Bakery Company, a monopolistically competitive firm, produces 10,000 loaves per day at a price of $2.00 per loaf. Marginal revenue and marginal cost are each $1.70. At that production level, total cost is $30,000, and total fixed cost is $7,500.

_____ 19.   In the short run, Upper Crust should
(a)   maintain the current output level, making short-run economic profits.
(b)   maintain the current output level, despite making short-run economic losses.
(c)   increase output level to the point where price equals marginal cost.
(d)   shut down.

_____ 20.   Relative to the individual firm's demand curve in the short run, we would predict that in the long run the surviving bakeries will face demand curves that are further to the
(a)   right and more elastic.
(b)   right and less elastic.
(c)   left and more elastic.
(d)   left and less elastic.

II. APPLICATION QUESTIONS

1.   Often, economists don't have complete demand schedules and cost curves—they must make do with a few numbers. Suppose that you have the following numbers for Rose's Tea Shop, a firm in a monopolistically competitive industry.

| Total Revenue = $1,200 | Total Cost = $700 | Price = $12 |
| Marginal Revenue = $10 | Total Variable Cost = $300 | $MC = \$6$ |

Explain how you know that:

(a)   This firm is imperfectly competitive.

(b)   This firm is not maximizing profit.

(c)   This firm is operating in the short run.

(d)   The demand curve is further right than it will be in the long run.

(e)   There is excess capacity.

(f)   Sketch the diagram for this firm based on your information and your economic knowledge of cost and revenue curves. Put in numerical values where you can.

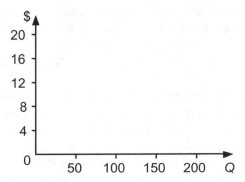

2.   Suppose that you have the following table of numbers for a firm. You know that the firm is operating in a monopolistically competitive industry.

Output	Total Cost	Marginal Cost	Quantity Demanded	Price	Marginal Revenue
0	$28	_____	0	$30	_____
1	$40	_____	1	$28	_____
2	$50	_____	2	$26	_____
3	$58	_____	3	$24	_____
4	$68	_____	4	$22	_____
5	$80	_____	5	$20	_____
6	$94	_____	6	$18	_____
7	$110	_____	7	$16	_____
8	$130	_____	8	$14	_____
9	$160		9	$12	

(a)   Calculate the marginal cost and marginal revenue values at each output level and enter them in the table.

(b)   Determine the profit-maximizing price and output level.

(c)   Calculate total economic profit.

(d)   Describe what will happen to the number of firms in this industry in the long run, and explain why.

(e)   Describe what will happen to this firm's demand curve in the long run, and explain why.

3.   Lou and Howard own a small monopolistically competitive pizza parlor—The Nice Slice. Because of declining sales, they have hired you as a consultant to examine their pricing and advertising strategy. You are provided with some information regarding daily demand at The Nice Slice under three conditions—when there is no advertising (which is the current situation); when only The Nice Slice advertises; when all pizzerias advertise. You are also told that when The Nice Slice advertises, it costs a flat fee of $20 per day

Price/ Pizza	No Advertising		Nice Slice Advertises		All Pizzerias Advertise	
	Quantity Demanded	Marginal Revenue	Quantity Demanded	Marginal Revenue	Quantity Demanded	Marginal Revenue
$16	3	_____	7	_____	5	_____
$15	4	_____	8	_____	6	_____
$14	5	_____	9	_____	7	_____
$13	6	_____	10	_____	8	_____
$12	7	_____	11	_____	9	_____
$11	8	_____	12	_____	10	_____
$10	9		13		11	

(a)   Complete the table.
        Now that you have the revenue information, you ask Lou and Howard about their costs. Howard tells you that each pizza costs a constant $4 to make. Advertising costs are not included.

(b)   Determine the profit-maximizing daily output level and price for The Nice Slice under each of the three advertising conditions.

Condition	Price	Output
No advertising	_____	_____
Nice Slice advertises	_____	_____
All pizzerias advertise	_____	_____

(c) Calculate economic profit of The Nice Slice under each of the three conditions.

Condition	Total Revenue	Total Cost	Profit
No advertising	_____	_____	_____
Nice Slice advertises	_____	_____	_____
All pizzerias advertise	_____	_____	_____

(d) Complete your assignment by writing a brief report to Lou and Howard advising them on the best advertising strategy to adopt.

4. Examine the following graph, which depicts a monopolistically competitive firm.

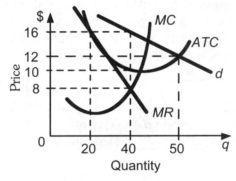

The profit-maximizing output level is _____ . The price is $_____ . Marginal revenue is $_____ . Total revenue is $_____ . Total cost is $_____ . Total profit is $_____ .

5. The firm represented by the following diagram is either monopolistically competitive or a monopoly. The firm is currently producing at output level A.

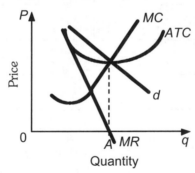

(a) At output level A, is the firm maximizing profits?

(b) What price is this firm charging currently? (Sketch your answer on the graph and label the price P_1.)

(c) If different from P_1, sketch in the profit-maximizing price as P_2.

(d) Is this a short- or long-run situation, or can't you tell?

(e) This is an *imperfectly* competitive firm. How do you know?

(f) If this is the long run, what kind of imperfectly competitive industry is this, or can't you tell?

(g)   If the firm raises production above level *A*, what will happen to total revenue?

6.   This exercise is a check on your understanding of graphs, the concept of the long run, and of monopolistic competition.

The following diagram is meant to depict a monopolistically competitive firm in long-run equilibrium (i.e., when $MR = MC$, $ATC = P$) with $P*$ and $Q*$ being the equilibrium quantity and price respectively. However, if this is the situation that is meant to be shown, there are several errors. Find as many as possible and explain, based on your economic understanding, why they are errors.

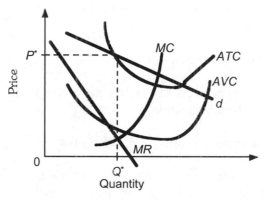

7.   In recent years, Spanish-language radio stations have been springing up across the country. Are these stations examples of perfect competition, monopolistic competition, or oligopoly?

Practice Test SOLUTIONS

I. SOLUTIONS TO MULTIPLE-CHOICE QUESTIONS

1. (b) Economic profits attract new firms. Each firm will have a smaller market share, depicted by a leftward shift of the demand curve.

2. (c) Typically, monopolistic firms, e.g., restaurants, do not charge the same price.

3. (d) Producing where $MR = MC$ is a guide to maximizing profits. It has nothing to do with product differentiation.

4. (b) Refer to the list of characteristics on page 314.

5. (c) If the firm is already at its profit-maximizing output level, then raising its price will move it away from profit-maximization.

6. (d) If the firm is maximizing profits, it must hold that marginal revenue equals marginal cost.

7. (a) Price exceeds marginal revenue and when maximizing profit, marginal revenue equals marginal cost. Therefore, price must exceed marginal cost.

8. (a) Easy entry into the market will compete away any short-run economic profits.

9. (b) Monopolistically competitive industries have wide differences in consumer tastes, few gains from coordination, and modest cost economies from standardization.

10. (a) It is easy for firms to enter a monopolistically competitive industry—but only in the long run. Economic profits can be earned in the short run.

11. (d) Profits are maximized where $MR = MC$. Given the output level, the equilibrium price, based on the position of the demand curve, will be $22.

12. (b) Profits are maximized at the output level where $MR = MC$.

13. (a) Economic profit $= (P - ATC) \times q = (\$22 - \$16) \times 90 = \$540$.

14. (d) The typical firm is earning an economic profit in the short run. The presence of economic profits will attract new firms, resulting in a reduction in each firm's market share. This change will affect demand and marginal revenue. Refer to page 324.

15. (d) Consumer welfare is maximized at the output level where $P = MC$.

16. (c) Average costs are minimized at an output level of 100 units. If, in the long run, the firm produces only 70 units, it has an excess capacity of 30.

17. (d) Advertising is intended to make consumers more interested in purchasing a product and in making other rivals appear less attractive. At a given output level, demand should become less elastic (steeper curve), and this will have a similar effect on marginal revenue.

18.   (b)   Average cost will increase; demand and marginal revenue curves will shift right and become less elastic as the firm becomes more "different" from its rivals; price will increase (because costs have risen).

19.   (d) $TVC = TC - TFC = \$30,000 - \$7,500 = \$22,500$. $AVC = TVC/q = \$22,500/10,000 = \$2.25$. Because P is less than AVC, the firm should shut down.

20.   (b)   As firms, such as Upper Crust, leave the industry, the market will be divided among a smaller number of firms, each with fewer substitutes.

II. SOLUTIONS TO APPLICATION QUESTIONS

1.

Total Revenue = $1,200	Total Cost = $700	Price = $12
Marginal Revenue = $10	Total Variable Cost = $300	MC = $6

(a)   This firm is imperfectly competitive because the demand curve is downward sloping. ($P > MR$).

(b)   This firm is not maximizing profit because $MR \neq MC$. (Because MR is greater than MC, the firm should expand production.)

(c)   We know that this firm is operating in the short run for two reasons. First, there are fixed costs (which can occur only in the short run) because $TC > TVC$. Second, this monopolistically competitive firm is making economic profits, which can only happen in the short run.

(d)   The demand curve is further right than it will be in the long run because as new firms, attracted by the economic profits, enter, the firm's market share will erode.

(e)   There is excess capacity because the firm is not producing where average cost is minimized. If $P = \$12$ and $TR = \$1,200$, the firm must be selling 100 units. If $TC = \$700$, average total cost must be $7, which is higher than MC. If the extra cost is less than the average cost, then the average cost must be falling and, therefore, not being minimized.

(f)   Refer to the following diagram.

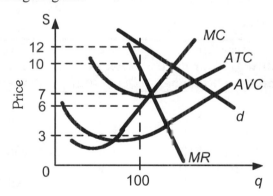

2. (a) Refer to the following table. Marginal cost is "change in total cost" ÷ "change in quantity" and marginal revenue is "change in total revenue" ÷ "change in quantity."

Output	Total Cost	Marginal Cost	Quantity Demanded	Price	Marginal Revenue
0	$28		0	$30	
		$12			$28
1	40		1	28	
		$10			$24
2	50		2	26	
		$8			$20
3	58		3	24	
		$10			$16
4	68		4	22	
		$12			$12
5	80		5	20	
		$14			$8
6	94		6	18	
		$16			$4
7	110		7	16	
		$20			$0
8	130		8	14	
		$30			−$4
9	160		9	12	

(b) 5; 20

(c) $20 ($100 − $80)

(d) In the long run, firms will enter this industry, attracted by the higher-than-normal profits.

(e) The demand curve will shift to the left and become less inelastic because of the presence of more (and closer) substitutes. This move will continue until the demand curve is just tangential to the average total cost curve and the firm is earning normal profits.

3. (a) Refer to the following table.

Price/ Pizza	No Advertising Quantity Demanded	No Advertising Marginal Revenue	Nice Slice Advertises Quantity Demanded	Nice Slice Advertises Marginal Revenue	All Pizzerias Advertise Quantity Demanded	All Pizzerias Advertise Marginal Revenue
$16	3		7		5	
		$12		$8		$10
$15	4		8		6	
		$10		$6		$8
$14	5		9		7	
		$8		$4		$6
$13	6		10		8	
		$6		$2		$4
$12	7		11		9	
		$4		$0		$2
$11	8		12		10	
		$2		−$2		$0
$10	9		13		11	

(b)   Refer to the following table. Values are derived by setting $MR = MC = \$4$.

Condition	Price	Output
No advertising	$11	8
Nice Slice advertises	$13	10
All pizzerias advertise	$12	9

(c)   Refer to the following table.

Condition	Total Revenue	Total Cost	Profit
No advertising	$88	$32	$56
Nice Slice advertises	$130	$40 + $20	$70
All pizzerias advertise	$108	$36 + $20	$52

(d)   If The Nice Slice chooses to advertise, its short-run profits will be $70 per day, up from the current level of $56 per day. However, this is based on the assumption that the rival pizzerias do not retaliate by advertising too. If they do retaliate, The Nice Slice will end up with an economic profit of $52 per day, *less* than the current level of $56 per day. Because the downside loss is slight ($4 per day) and the gain substantial ($14 per day), advertising is a good strategy. The less probable it is that rivals will retaliate, the more advisable it is to advertise.

4. $q^* = 40$. $p^* = \$16$. $MR = \$8$. $TR = P \times q = \$16 \times 40 = \$640$.
$TC = ATC \times q = \$10 \times 40 = \$400$.
Economic profit $= TR - TC = \$640 - \$400 = \$240$.

5.   (a)   No ($MR \neq MC$)

       (b)   Refer to the following diagram.

       (c)   Refer to the following diagram.

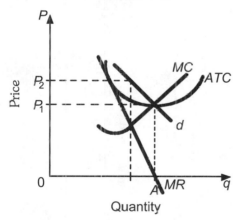

       (d)   We can't tell yet if it's a long- or short-run situation. Refer to answer (f) following.

       (e)   The demand curve is downward sloping, so it can't be perfectly competitive.

       (f)   It must be a monopoly. Monopolistically competitive firms make only normal profits in long-run equilibrium.

       (g)   Total revenue will fall because marginal revenue is negative.

6.   Error 1: The *MC* curve should intersect both the *ATC* and the *AVC* curves at their minimum points. The "average-marginal" rule determines this.

Error 2: The profit-maximizing output level (q^*, not Q^*) occurs, as shown, where $MR = MC$, but the demand and *ATC* intersection is inconsistent. At higher output levels, demand exceeds *ATC*, indicating economic profits whereas, at "Q^*," only normal profits occur.

Error 3: The existence of economic profits indicates that this is not a long-run situation. The existence of fixed costs ($ATC - AVC$) also reveals this to be a short-run diagram. There is also no long-run average cost curve depicted.

Note: If you had trouble with this problem, review Application 5 in Chapter 13.

7.   Because Spanish-language radio stations, as a group and individually, offer product differentiation, they cannot be perfectly competitive. Because there are many firms and fairly easy entry they are monopolistically competitive rather than oligopolistic.

16

Externalities, Public Goods, and Social Choice

Chapter Objectives

1. List two sources of market failure.
2. Define externality and explain why externalities are a source of market failure. Explain the terms marginal damage cost, marginal social cost, and marginal private cost. Explain why social costs and private costs may differ, and give examples.
3. Draw a graph depicting a negative externality. Explain why the presence of a negative (positive) externality will lead to an overproduction (underproduction) of the good. Evaluate five different methods of internalizing an externality.
4. Identify the two critical characteristics of public goods. Explain why a free market would underproduce public goods and identify the two "problems" associated with the production of public goods.
5. Outline the Samuelson-Musgrave theory of the optimal provision of public goods. Describe why government provision of public goods is likely to lead to dissatisfaction.
6. Outline the issues involved in social choice.
7. Identify potential sources of government inefficiency.

Keep in mind that this chapter examines examples of market failure. The past two chapters have looked at only one aspect—imperfect competition. The causes of market failure discussed in the present chapter and the one following can occur even in perfectly competitive industries. In Chapter 12, review Figure 12.3—note how externalities upset the scales in this diagram. The benefits of perfect competition ensue only if the equilibrium output level is also the efficient output level. The firm maximizes profits in response to private marginal costs and benefits; if society's marginal costs and benefits are otherwise, inefficiency results.

BRAIN TEASER: What would be the implications if Joe Pacifist were allowed to refuse to pay taxes earmarked for the defense budget? Should Joe be permitted a free ride on a bus that is obliged to run in any case? Are the two cases the same? Should we have compulsory taxation to pay for defense? What other options might be feasible?

Objective 1

List two sources of market failure.

Externalities and public goods are major sources of *market failure*—that is, a situation when the perfectly competitive market is unable to reach an allocatively efficient competitive equilibrium. One other source of failure, imperfect information, is covered in Chapter 17, while the present chapter also examines government failure. (page 329)

Practice

1. In perfect competition, a market failure occurs when, in the long run, the industry
    (a)   produces so much that average costs are minimized.
    (b)   produces so much that total profits are maximized.
    (c)   produces so much that the marginal benefit of the last unit produced exceeds its marginal cost.
    (d)   increases production past the output level where price is first equal to marginal revenue.

    ANSWER: (c)   The industry should produce until marginal benefit equals marginal cost. If marginal benefit does not equal marginal cost, a market failure has occurred. All other options refer to long-run equilibrium conditions in perfect competition. ∎

Objective 2

Define externality and explain why externalities are a source of market failure. Explain the terms marginal damage cost, marginal social cost, and marginal private cost. Explain why social costs and private costs may differ, and give examples.

Externalities occur when the actions or decisions of one agent impose a cost (a negative externality), or bestow a benefit (a positive externality), on second or third parties. There is no incentive to figure these costs (or benefits) into the decision to act. With a negative externality a wedge is driven between marginal cost, as faced by producers or consumers, and price. Producers look only at *marginal private cost*. A broader view would encompass all extra costs of production—*marginal social costs*. The difference between the two (*marginal damage cost*) is due to the presence of an externality. When we fail to consider these additional costs (or benefits) to society, inefficient outcomes emerge—even in perfect competition. When external costs are present, more production occurs than society would prefer. When external benefits are present, the market, on its own, will produce less than society would like. Pollution is the "classic" example of an external cost. (page 329)

LEARNING TIP: Keep in mind one example of a good having an external cost (a paper mill producing effluent) and one example of a good having an external benefit (the CD you borrow from a friend and then duplicate). Plug in your own example when working through the consequences of externalities. ◀

LEARNING TIP: Keep in mind that negative externalities generate "spillover costs" while positive externalities bestow "spillover benefits." An externality exists whenever marginal social benefit differs from marginal private benefit, or marginal social cost differs from marginal private cost. Externalities may occur during the production of a good or during its consumption.

The concept of externalities is easy to grasp—pollution, for instance, is all around us. Think of some topical and local examples of your own. Don't forget externalities providing benefits! Many goods provide both external costs and benefits. The classic example is the beekeeper and his neighbor, the apple-grower—the bees sting the workers in the orchard, yet pollinate the apple trees, and the beekeeper receives "free" honey.

What is less obvious is that the quantification of externalities (and so, claims for compensation) is extremely difficult—almost any position can be plausibly defended. Take the local examples you've thought of, and look for the counterargument (the "silver lining" to a negative externality). ◀

Practice

2.   Assume there are no externalities. If price exceeds marginal cost, the benefits to consumers are _____ than the cost of resources needed to produce the good. _____ should be produced.
   (a)   greater; More
   (b)   greater; Less
   (c)   less; More
   (d)   less; Less

   ANSWER: (a) If the price exceeds the cost of the final unit produced, society is deriving extra benefits. Production should increase until $P = MC$.

3.   _____ is the sum of the marginal costs of producing a good and the correctly measured damage costs involved in the process of production.
   (a)   Marginal damage cost
   (b)   Marginal social cost
   (c)   Marginal private cost
   (d)   Marginal external cost

   ANSWER: (b) MSC (marginal social cost) includes both the internal and external costs of production. Refer to page 330.

4.   When marginal social cost exceeds the firm's marginal private cost, the industry's supply curve is too far to the _____ and _____ is being produced.
   (a)   right; too much
   (b)   right; too little
   (c)   left; too much
   (d)   left; too little

   ANSWER: (a) Marginal cost is underestimating the true cost to society. Recall that the firm's (and the industry's) supply curve is based on MC.

5.   As production increases, marginal damage costs are likely to
   (a)   remain constant.
   (b)   increase.
   (c)   decrease.
   (d)   become negative.

   ANSWER: (b) Refer to page 333 and particularly Figure 16.2 in the textbook.

6.   An individual will continue an activity until marginal
   (a)   benefit equals marginal social cost.
   (b)   benefit equals marginal damage cost.
   (c)   social cost equals marginal private cost.
   (d)   benefit equals marginal private cost.

   ANSWER: (d) The individual will compare the marginal benefit with the extra privately borne cost. ■

Objective 3

Draw a graph depicting a negative externality. Explain why the presence of a negative (positive) externality will lead to an overproduction (underproduction) of the good. Evaluate five different methods of internalizing an externality.

When there are no externalities, (with marginal damage cost being zero) marginal private cost and marginal social cost will be equal. Graphically, marginal damage cost acts as a wedge between marginal private cost and marginal social cost. The externality increases the marginal cost for society. With increasing costs, society would prefer that less of the good be provided than will be chosen by the private individual. In the face of a negative externality, the market produces more than society would consider efficient. (page 334)

Externalities may be controlled in a variety of ways, although no one way works in all circumstances. Five remedies for the problem of externalities are possible. These are:

(a)   Government-imposed taxes (negative externalities) and subsidies (positive externalities)
(b)   Private bargaining and negotiation (the Coase Theorem)
(c)   Legal rules and procedures (such as injunctive relief and liability rules)
(d)   The sale or auctioning of rights to impose externalities (such as pollution credits)
(e)   Direct government regulation (page 334)

ECONOMICS IN PRACTICE: On page 338, the textbook examines the fraught issue of babies and externalities. Can you think of other examples where babies impose externalities on others? The problem is what can be done in such situations. Clearly, one solution does not fit all situations. Consider a restaurant, where a crying baby may reduce the enjoyment of other diners. What measures might reduce externalities in such a setting?

ANSWER: Babies impose negative externalities in most public places—in movie theaters, restaurants, parks, and on airplane flights, to name a few situations. In the case of a restaurant, a "brat tax" has been suggested—with children paying more, instead of less, than adults. The advantage could be that the revenue received could be used to subsidize the meals of other diners, compensating them for any inconvenience. Or there could be "child-free" nights, "child-free" areas in restaurants, or even age restrictions.

LEARNING TIP: Think of the Coase Theorem as another application of the idea of "balancing the margins." In this case, once the property rights to a good are defined and the true marginal benefit and marginal cost determined, an efficient equilibrium can be established. ◀

Practice

Use the following diagram which depicts information for the chemical producer, Tox Inc., for the next five questions.

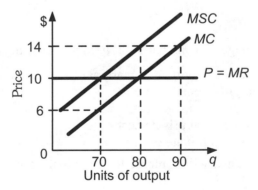

7.   The firm depicted in the diagram is operating in a(n) _____ competitive industry. External _____ are present.
     (a)   perfectly; benefits
     (b)   perfectly; costs
     (c)   imperfectly; benefits
     (d)   imperfectly; costs

     ANSWER: (b) Demand is horizontal—perfect competition. *MSC* is higher than *MC*—marginal damage costs are present.

8. The profit-maximizing firm will produce
    (a)   60 units of output.
    (b)   70 units of output.
    (c)   80 units of output.
    (d)   90 units of output.

    ANSWER: (c) The firm will produce where $P(MR) = MC$.

9. The efficient output level is
    (a)   60 units of output.
    (b)   70 units of output.
    (c)   80 units of output.
    (d)   90 units of output.

    ANSWER: (b) The efficient output level is where $MSC = MB$ (as represented by price).

10. The marginal damage cost imposed by this firm is
    (a) $4 per unit of output.
    (b) $6 per unit of output.
    (c) $10 per unit of output.
    (d) $14 per unit of output.

    ANSWER: (a) Marginal damage cost is the difference between the marginal social cost and the marginal cost. In the diagram, at 80 units of output, MSC is $14 and MC is $10.

11. To achieve an efficient output level, the government could impose a tax of
    (a) $4 per unit.
    (b) $6 per unit.
    (c) $10 per unit.
    (d) $14 per unit.

    ANSWER: (a) This tax will increase the (private) production costs and make them the same as the marginal social costs

12. Bees yield positive externalities (through pollination activities). The government could increase market efficiency by
    (a)   taxing beekeepers to reduce the number of hives.
    (b)   subsidizing beekeepers to increase the number of hives.
    (c)   requiring beekeepers to buy licenses for their hives.
    (d)   regulating beekeepers to cap the number of hives per beekeeper.

    ANSWER: (b) With a positive externality, the goal is to increase the provision of the good or service.

13. Mr. Lyons, who is a beekeeper, moves into the house next to Ms. Samson, who is severely allergic to bee stings. In fact, she values the risk and inconvenience involved at $200 per month. Houses in a bee-free neighborhood rent for $300 per month more than her current payment. Ms. Samson's best option is to
    (a)   move to the bee-free neighborhood.
    (b)   request compensation from Mr Lyons for $300, the difference between the rents.
    (c)   request compensation from Mr Lyons for $200, the value of the inconvenience.
    (d)   request compensation from Mr Lyons for $100, the difference between the rents.

    ANSWER: (c) Presumably Ms. Samson had already figured in the rental difference when making her original housing choice. Her "loss" in welfare is the $200. ∎

Objective 4

Identify the two critical characteristics of public goods. Explain why a free market would underproduce public goods and identify the two "problems" associated with the production of public goods.

Public goods are goods whose benefits are received collectively by all members of society (nonrival) and/or whose benefits can be denied to no one (nonexcludable), even if they refuse to pay. Because of these characteristics, public goods will either be underproduced or not produced at all if the private sector is made responsible for their provision. Two problems of public goods are the free-rider problem and the drop-in-the-bucket problem. (page 341)

The legal system is a classic example of a public good. What would society be like without known and enforced laws? Much of the framework of the market economy would collapse. Property rights and possessions would be endangered. There would be an unwillingness to trade by mail, to accept checks, or to offer trade credit. We derive benefits from law enforcement, but what choices do we have as individuals? We could each hire our own law enforcer in the "law market," but that wouldn't entirely solve the problem because enforcement would be neither uniform nor just. In addition, there would still be no mechanism for establishing laws, except by precedent and tradition.

The only effective solution is for society to act as a unit, levying taxes to pay for a system of justice. This publicly provided good does not erode the free-market system; rather, it *enhances* it. The justice system is nonexcludable and nonrival in consumption (unless there is a sudden crime wave). Also, note that the "drop-in-the-bucket" and "free-rider" problems are present. A town that is crime-free when a new resident moves into it doesn't experience extra costs from his relocation. His tax dollars will make no great difference in the fight against crime, and if he avoids payment he will still receive protection.

Not all goods provided by the government are pure public goods. Elementary education, where individuals may be excluded, but where society in general gains from their inclusion, is usually provided by the state. The heart of the public goods issue is that the market fails to provide an adequate amount of such goods because there is neither an incentive to buy, nor to sell, privately. Consumers can "free ride," and the provision of a unit of the good, given nonrivalry in consumption, will service purchasers and free riders alike.

LEARNING TIP: Keep in mind a clear example of a public good (a lighthouse or, better still, national defense). Confirm that, for a good to be a public good, consumption is nonrival and consumers can't be excluded from the benefits provided. ◀

ECONOMICS IN PRACTICE: On page 341, the textbook looks at the "hot" issue of global warming and the growing hopes that in 2010 a stronger international commitment could be achieved. The United States has persistently refused to sign the Kyoto Protocol, which was hammered out in 1997. Accepting, for the sake of argument, that carbon emissions do cause global warming and that the United States is a significant emitter of greenhouse gases, what economic reasons might be behind the refusal of the United States to sign on to the Kyoto Treaty? You can use both externalities and public goods in your answer.

ANSWER: First, pollution is a negative externality and, by acting to reduce emissions, the United States would incur additional costs to producers and consumers. Because the United States is such a significant polluter, these costs would be significant. Other countries, which pollute less, would be less disadvantaged. In fact, so the argument goes, the ability of the U.S. to compete in global markets would be impaired while others would gain. Ultimately, the largest polluter cannot sign on to Kyoto *because* it's the largest polluter! Climate control is also a public good (nonrival, nonexcludable). The drop-in-the-bucket argument is implausible in the case of the United States, but the free-rider argument is tempting. The United States can enjoy the all benefits of emission controls without paying for them. Note that widespread trade sanctions by foreigners would be more difficult to coordinate against a major international player than against a comparatively small nation.

ECONOMICS IN PRACTICE (CONTINUED): The United States and China are at different points in their growth trajectory. Do you feel that the same emission standards should be applied to both countries? And what should be done for small developing countries, including those whose main resource might be rainforests? Again, externalities and public goods may figure in your answer. Are you in favor of "bribing" nations with subsidies or aid packages?

ANSWER: Clearly, opinions will (and do) differ! One side would argue that pollution is pollution, regardless of its source. In this case, there may be an argument for international compensation for countries that curtail their greenhouse gases for the good of the global economy. On the other hand, an argument is made that developed countries have benefited from decades of environmental abuse (for which all are now suffering) and, therefore a different standard ought to be applied.

Practice

---

14.   Public goods are _____ in consumption and nonpurchasers _____ be excluded from their benefits.
   (a)   rival; can
   (b)   rival; cannot
   (c)   nonrival; can
   (d)   nonrival; cannot

   ANSWER: (d)   These are the two characteristics of public goods. Plug in an example (national defense) to see how they relate. Refer to page 341 for a discussion of these characteristics.

15.   Because public goods are nonexcludable, individuals are usually unwilling to pay for them. This characteristic is known as the
   (a)   drop-in-the-bucket problem.
   (b)   impossibility theorem.
   (c)   Coase Theorem.
   (d)   free-rider problem.

   ANSWER: (d)   If the consumer can receive a good free of charge, there is a strong temptation not to pay.

16.   As the number of recipients of a public good increases, the number of free riders will tend to
   (a)   increase because, as the size of the group increases, it is more difficult to detect free riders.
   (b)   increase because, as the size of the group increases, individuals become rivals for the benefits of the good.
   (c)   decrease because, as the size of the group increases, the per person payment will decrease.
   (d)   decrease because, as the size of the group increases, it is easier to exclude noncontributors.

   ANSWER: (a)   Refer to page 342 for a more complete discussion of this issue. ∎

Objective 5

Outline the Samuelson-Musgrave theory of the optimal provision of public goods. Describe why government provision of public goods is likely to lead to dissatisfaction.

To determine the optimal (most efficient) level of provision, Samuelson devised the demand curve for public goods. The price each consumer is willing to pay is summed at each output level. An efficient provision of public goods will still leave many consumers dissatisfied, however, because some will prefer more and others less. To ensure an efficient level of provision, the preferences of each consumer would have to be revealed, which is possible only in theory because of the incentive not to reveal one's preferences. In practice, imperfect social choice mechanisms, such as majority rule, are used.

The Tiebout hypothesis offers the possibility that an efficient mix of public goods may be produced if consumers make their preferences known by changing location in response to government-offered goods. (page 343)

Practice

17. The optimal level of provision of a public good occurs when society's _____ is equal to the _____ of the good.
    (a)   total willingness to pay; total cost
    (b)   total willingness to pay; marginal cost
    (c)   marginal willingness to pay; total cost
    (d)   marginal willingness to pay; marginal cost

    ANSWER: (b) The demand curve totals the willingness to pay and this is equated with the marginal (social) cost to determine the optimal output level.

Use the following table for the next three questions. Society consists of two persons—Robinson and Friday. The table shows the quantity demanded by each of units of a public good—defense. Assume that each person's demand curve is a straight line.

Price	Robinson's Quantity Demanded	Friday's Quantity Demanded
$3.00	3	1
$2.00	5	2
$1.00	7	3

18. Each of the following is a point on society's demand curve for defense EXCEPT
    (a)   one unit at a price of $7.00.
    (b)   three units at a price of $4.00.
    (c)   five units at a price of $2.00.
    (d)   seven units at a price of $2.00.

    ANSWER: (d) The demand curve must be summed vertically, i.e., at each output level. Example: Friday will pay $3.00 to receive one unit and Robinson will pay $4.00 to receive one unit (Robinson's demand curve is a straight line). One unit, not two, is produced to be shared.

19. Complete the following demand schedule.

Society's Quantity Demanded	Price
7	_____
6	_____
5	_____
4	_____
3	_____
2	_____
1	_____

ANSWER: Refer to the following demand schedule.

Society's Quantity Demanded	Price	Robinson	Friday
7	$1.00	$1.00	—
6	$1.50	$1.50	—
5	$2.00	$2.00	—
4	$2.50	$2.50	—
3	$4.00	$3.00	$1.00
2	$5.50	$3.50	$2.00
1	$7.00	$4.00	$3.00

20. The marginal cost of each unit of defense is $4.00. What is the optimal number of units of defense that should be provided?
    (a) Two units
    (b) Three units
    (c) Four units
    (d) Five units

    ANSWER: (b) Society should produce until $P = MC$. ∎

Objective 6

Outline the issues involved in social choice.

Arrow's impossibility theorem illustrates the difficulty of establishing a consistent consensus given a lack of unanimity. The impossibility theorem proves that it can't be done. The voting paradox is an example of this theorem. Due to a lack of incentives to take on tough choices, government may be inefficient. However, the ultimate question remains *how much* government involvement is required, not *whether* it is required. (page 346)

Practice

21. The demonstration that majority-rule voting can produce contradictory and inconsistent results is known as
    (a) the impossibility theorem.
    (b) the voting paradox.
    (c) adverse selection.
    (d) moral hazard.

    ANSWER: (b) The voting paradox exemplifies the impossibility theorem.

Use the following information to answer the next two questions. Axl, Brigitta, and Carl have to choose one of four options (A, B, C, D). Individual preferences, from highest to lowest, are shown. Majority voting will be used by pairing options, the loser being excluded from further consideration.

Axl	Brigitta	Carl
A	B	C
B	C	A
C	A	D
D	D	B

22.   If A is first paired against B, the option finally selected will be
(a)   A.
(b)   B.
(c)   C.
(d)   D.

ANSWER: (c) Carl will vote for A over B. Pairing A and C, Brigitta will cast the swing vote for C. Everyone prefers C over D.

23.   If B is first paired against C, the option finally selected will be
(a)   A.
(b)   B.
(c)   C.
(d)   D.

ANSWER: (a) Axl will vote for B over C. Pairing A and B, Carl will cast the swing vote for A. Everyone prefers A over D. ∎

Objective 7

Identify potential sources of government inefficiency.

Recent work suggests that government officials may seek to maximize their own utility, rather than that of the society they serve. Incentives to be efficient might be inadequate. Furthermore, whereas an inefficient private firm faces the discipline of market forces and may be driven out of business, that is not necessarily the case for those in the public sector. (page 348)

Special-interest groups may use resources to sway the government's decision-making process in their direction through rent-seeking behavior. Even if the government can determine what the optimal level is for the provision of public goods, there is no guarantee that that level will be forthcoming.

ENDPOINT: INTERVENTION OR NOT?

Be aware that, during the last several chapters, a battle has been raging between those who believe that the free market works efficiently and those who believe that more structured control is required. You might pigeonhole the two camps as the "Small Government" and "Big Government" schools of public policy.

In this chapter, "Big Government" is drawing attention to ways in which the free market fails if left uncorrected. For externalities, "Small Government" retaliates with the Coase Theorem and the private sale or auction of externality rights. For public goods, the debate tends to center on the question of which goods are clearly public goods. The "Small Government" school also retaliates with such concepts as "the voting paradox" and "the impossibility theorem"—hoping to undermine the belief that the government allocates efficiently.

The battle continues in the following chapters.

BRAIN TEASER SOLUTION: If Joe can refuse to pay taxes earmarked for defense, so can we all. If Joe rides the bus free, then other (paying) passengers would see an incentive to do the same. Revenues would decrease, and the bus service might cease. The two cases, though, are not the same. In the former case, Joe is trying to opt out; in the latter, he is trying to opt in. The traditional response to financing defense expenditures has been taxation and, because voluntary taxes are unlikely to raise sufficient revenue, they must be compulsory. It's difficult to imagine other options for funding this public good.

PRACTICE TEST

I. MULTIPLE-CHOICE QUESTIONS

Select the option that provides the single best answer.

_____ 1.   Which of the following is not a good example of an externality?
  (a)   A hamburger
  (b)   Noise pollution
  (c)   Jack's cigarette smoke for Jill, who also smokes
  (d)   Jack's cigarette smoke for Jane, who doesn't smoke

_____ 2.   For the Coase Theorem to work, all of the following must be true EXCEPT
  (a)   the basic rights at issue must be understood.
  (b)   the majority of concerned individuals participate.
  (c)   there must be no impediments to bargaining.
  (d)   only a few people can be involved.

_____ 3.   Which of the following is not advanced as a method of remedying an externality?
  (a)   Government subsidies
  (b)   Private taxation
  (c)   Private bargaining
  (d)   Direct government regulation

_____ 4.   Firm A is producing at an output level where the marginal benefits to consumers are less than the marginal cost. Assuming no externalities, the price
  (a)   equals marginal cost.
  (b)   is less than marginal cost.
  (c)   is greater than marginal cost.
  (d)   is less than marginal damage cost.

_____ 5.   When the marginal social cost of a good exceeds its marginal private cost,
  (a)   too many units will be produced by the market.
  (b)   the market price will be too high.
  (c)   it is an example of a beneficial externality.
  (d)   too few resources will be allocated to its production.

_____ 6.   The production of a good imposes external costs on society. If these costs are not internalized then, from society's point of view, the firm is likely to
  (a)   underproduce.
  (b)   allocate too many resources to the production of the good.
  (c)   charge too high a price.
  (d)   make economic profits in the long run.

_____ 7.   Your campus radio station is best described as an example of a(n)
    (a)   external cost.
    (b)   good that is nonrival in consumption but that generates benefits that are excludable.
    (c)   good that is nonrival in consumption and that generates benefits that are nonexcludable.
    (d)   public good plagued by the easy-rider problem.

_____ 8.   Which of the following is the best example of a public good?
    (a)   A hamburger
    (b)   A high school
    (c)   Police protection
    (d)   A toll bridge

_____ 9.   All of the following are true about the voting paradox EXCEPT that
    (a)   it is an example of the impossibility theorem.
    (b)   it demonstrates the power wielded by the one who sets the voting agenda.
    (c)   it shows that, when preferences for public goods differ, any attempt to add the preferences can lead to inconsistencies.
    (d)   with majority rule, logrolling is necessary to get things done.

Use the following information to answer the next two questions. Arboc is an economy comprised of three individuals: Ed, Ted, and Ned. The table shows the maximum price that each will pay for various quantities of a good.

Quantity	Ed	Ted	Ned
1	$7	$10	$17
2	$5	$9	$15
3	$4	$7	$11
4	$3	$4	$10

_____ 10.   The maximum price that the private market would pay for the third unit is
    (a) $4.
    (b) $7.
    (c) $11.
    (d) $22.

_____ 11.   Now suppose that the good is a *public* good. The maximum price that society would pay for the third unit is
    (a) $7.
    (b) $7.33 (approximately).
    (c) $11.
    (d) $22.

_____ 12.   If there are external costs and these are not considered by perfectly competitive firms then, at the equilibrium output level,
    (a) $P = MC$ and $P = MSC$.
    (b) $P = MC$ and $P < MSC$.
    (c) $P < MC$ and $P = MSC$.
    (d) $P < MC$ and $P < MSC$.

_____ 13.   The two problems in the provision of public goods are
    (a)   nonrivalry in consumption and the drop-in-the-bucket problem.
    (b)   externalities and nonexcludability.
    (c)   nonexcludability and moral hazard.
    (d)   free riders and the drop-in-the-bucket problem.

_____ 14.   To derive the market demand for a public good, we sum the
    (a)   quantity demanded by each consumer at each possible price level.
    (b)   demand curve of each consumer horizontally.
    (c)   amounts that each consumer is willing to pay at each level of output.
    (d)   marginal social cost curve of each producer vertically.

_____ 15.   There are external costs, and these are not considered by perfectly competitive firms. The government imposes a tax so that the market is producing at the efficient output level. We can say that
    (a) $P = MSC$ and $MDC = 0$.
    (b) $P = MSC$ and $MDC > 0$.
    (c) $P < MSC$ and $MDC = 0$.
    (d) $P < MSC$ and $MDC > 0$.

_____ 16.   Your local public television station is having a fund drive. Public TV is the only TV station you watch. You rationalize your failure to contribute by telling yourself that your pledge would make no difference one way or the other. This is an example of the _____ problem. Because you will still be able to tune in whether you pledge or not, you are a(n) _____ .
    (a)   free-rider; free rider
    (b)   free-rider; externality
    (c)   drop-in-the-bucket; free rider
    (d)   drop-in-the-bucket; externality

_____ 17.   Majority voting as a mechanism for public choice involves each of the following problems EXCEPT
    (a)   When preferences are identical, inconsistent results can occur.
    (b)   Voters who select representatives vote infrequently.
    (c)   Choices are almost always limited to bundles of publicly provided goods.
    (d)   Voters have little incentive to be well informed about public choices.

Use the following information to answer the next three questions. Research has shown that Hayley Mills Incorp., a firm in the perfectly competitive paper industry, also produces pollution in the nearby Chicken River. The following table has been compiled showing the marginal cost (*MC*) and marginal social cost (*MSC*) of paper production. The market price of paper is $600 per ton.

Tons of Paper	*MC*	*MSC*
1	$400	$500
2	$500	$600
3	$600	$800
4	$700	$1,100

_____ 18. The marginal damage cost borne by society from the production of four tons of paper is
    (a) $1,100 per ton.
    (b) $275 per ton.
    (c) $400 per ton.
    (d) $100 per ton.

_____ 19. Hayley is able to ignore the damage costs. The firm will produce _____ tons of paper; the efficient output level is _____ tons.
    (a)   2; 2
    (b)   3; 2
    (c)   3; 3
    (d)   4; 3

_____ 20. To force this firm to produce at the efficient level, the government should
    (a)   impose a tax of $100 per ton.
    (b)   impose a tax of $200 per ton.
    (c)   grant a subsidy of $100 per ton.
    (d)   grant a subsidy of $200 per ton.

II. APPLICATION QUESTIONS

1. From the rubble of disowned economic dogmas and disenchanted citizens, a new state has been built in Eastern Europe—Freedonia. The newly elected Freedonian government is, naturally, keen to avoid the pitfalls of its predecessors, but it does realize that some (public) goods and services should be provided by the state. Jan Lipska, the Minister for Public Goods, has devised the following matrix, using the characteristics of public goods that she has read about in an economics textbook by Case, Fair and Oster.

	Public/Private Good Matrix	
	Rival	**Nonrival**
Excludable	I	II
Nonexcludable	III	IV

The Minister now calls in a top Western economic adviser (you!) to interpret the matrix.
    (a)   Ms. Lipska asks you what sort of good would be included in Category I, asks for examples, and asks how the government should treat these goods.

    (b)   Ms. Lipska now asks about the kind of good that should be included in Category IV, asks for examples, and asks how the government should treat these goods.

(c)   Ms. Lipska now asks about the kind of good that should be included in Categories II and III, asks for examples, and asks how the government should treat these goods.

(d)   The Minister considers Category I (pure private goods) and focuses on a particular industry—steel. She points out that steel is traditionally a polluter of the environment. Assuming that the government should do "something" about this issue on behalf of injured citizens, what might that "something" be?

(e)   Some goods, the Minister muses, can generate undesirable side effects at the consumption stage—a car, for example, can pollute. You see the way the Minister's mind is working. You set up a matrix for externalities.

	Externality Matrix	
	Production	Consumption
Negative Externality	I	II
Positive Externality	III	IV

Interpret the matrix for the Minister.

(f)   Ms. Lipska asks what actions the government might take in each of these categories. How would you reply?

2.   The inhabitants of the city of Croatoan, Virginia, have been coping with a transportation problem for years. The city is on an isthmus, and to connect it to the rest of civilization, there is one rocky, treacherous road that is almost invariably closed during the winter months. The proposed solution is to build a bridge to link Croatoan to the "mainland" more directly. John White, the city manager, has hired you to conduct an analysis of the costs and benefits of this project. He points out that the project is all-or-nothing—you can't build half a bridge. Having taken an introductory economics course in college, he agrees with you when you suggest that the community's consumer surplus of the bridge should be figured into the calculations.

After some work, you have estimated the demand schedule below.

Toll Fee	Usage per Year	Annual Revenues	Consumer Surplus	Total Annual Benefits
$1.00	0	_____	_____	_____
$0.80	20,000	_____	_____	_____
$0.60	40,000	_____	_____	_____
$0.40	60,000	_____	_____	_____
$0.20	80,000	_____	_____	_____
$0.10	90,000	_____	_____	_____
$0.00	100,000	_____	_____	_____

(a)   Complete the table.

The city manager now tells you that the building and maintenance of the bridge can be financed through a loan that will cost $40,000 per year, regardless of the amount of traffic. (Ignore present value considerations.)

(b)   Left to a free market and the demand curve above, would the bridge be built? Why?

(c)   Comparing the total annual benefit and the total annual cost, do you recommend that Croatoan go ahead with the project?

(d)   If White's objective is to maximize social welfare, should he impose a toll fee? If so, how much? Why?

(e)   If White wishes to offset as much of the cost as possible through toll revenues, which toll level should he set?

(f)   The strategies developed in Part (d) and Part (e) still leave Croatoan with an unpaid bill for the bridge. Recommend a method of deriving funds.

(g)   White, who is familiar with Freedonian politics (refer to Application Question 1), asks where the Croatoan bridge would fit into the "public/private goods matrix." How would you reply?

There remains an unresolved issue. The bay and the land surrounding it, over which the bridge is to be built, is owned by five families. The right to build the bridge must be bought from them. The bridge will certainly reduce the amenity of the exceptionally fine shoreline. $10,000 per year, to be divided equally, has been budgeted as compensation for the five families.

Each family places a monetary value on the amenity of the bay. Four different possible sets of values (A–D) are given in the following table. The higher the monetary value, the greater the amenity and the greater the loss of amenity if the bridge is built.

The amenity of the bay is a public good for the five families (none can be excluded, and the scenery is nonrival), so the compensation should be accepted only if the value of the compensation exceeds the value of the bay.

| Family | Distributions | | | |
	A	B	C	D
Dare	$1,500	$3,000	$5,000	$2,500
Howe	$1,500	$3,000	$3,000	$2,500
Archard	$1,500	$3,000	$1,000	$2,500
Harvie	$1,500	$3,000	$1,000	$500
Viccars	$1,500	$1,000	$1,000	$500

(h)   In which of the four cases should the compensation be accepted by the five families, allowing Croatoan's bridge project to go forward?

The families get together and, in true Croatoan fashion, decide to abide by majority rule.

(i)   Using majority rule, in which of the four cases will the compensation be accepted by the five families?

(j)   In which cases will the compensation be accepted even though its benefits do not adequately compensate the five families?

(k)   Majority rule may result in inefficient choices. In some sense, an enforced decision that affects one party adversely is like a negative externality—the actions of others adversely affect the individual. Referring to your answer to Part (i) and to the Coase Theorem, how and with what result might the families negotiate among themselves regarding the offered compensation?

3.   We can move from the textbook discussion of externalities to a graphical presentation. Recall the concepts of marginal social cost and marginal (private) cost—*MSC* and *MPC*, respectively. Similarly, define marginal social benefit and marginal private benefit—*MSB* and *MPB*, respectively. *MPC* and *MPB* are the same as the supply and demand curves with which you're familiar.

In the graph below, without externalities, $MSC = MPC$ and $MSB = MPB$. P_1 and Q_1 indicate the price and quantity of widgets traded in a free market. Because all costs and benefits are internalized, there is no market failure.

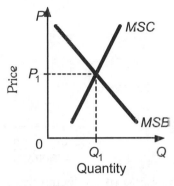

(a)   Negative externalities in production: What will happen if some of the costs are passed on to a third party? Draw the MPC curve. What effect have the spillover costs had? Can you think of an example of this situation?

(b)   Negative externalities in consumption: Return to the original diagram. Suppose that the consumption of widgets reduces the well-being of others. Why might this occur? Where will the MPB curve be, in relation to MSB, and what is the effect on resource allocation?

(c)   Positive externalities in consumption. Return to the original diagram. Suppose that the benefits from widgets accrue to persons other than the purchasers. What will happen to the diagram? What will be the effect on price and resource allocation? Can you think of any examples?

(d)   Positive externalities in production. Return to the original diagram. Suppose that the firm pays the cost of resources from which it derives no use. Can you think of an example? What will be the relationship between MSC and MPC?

4.   We have a society with three individuals—Ted, Ned, and Fred. The following table lists the maximum price each will pay for various quantities of a public good.

Quantity	Ted's Price	Ned's Price	Fred's Price
1	$9	$12	$16
2	$7	$10	$12
3	$5	$6	$9
4	$3	$4	$6
5	$1	$2	$3

(a)   How much will society pay for the second unit of the good?

(b)   Graph society's demand curve for this public good.

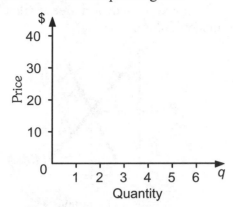

(c)   Suppose that the marginal cost of producing this good is $14 for each additional unit of output. What is the efficient level of provision?

(d)   Graph marginal cost to confirm your result.

(e)   If each person is charged an equal amount to cover the cost of provision, will any of them be happy with the situation?

5.   What do you think is the best way to deal with the following situations? Choose one of the following options.

Situations
(a)   A smoky factory
(b)   Noise pollution from a recently built airport
(c)   Pornographic magazines
(d)   Noise from car exhaust systems
(e)   Unsightly billboards
(f)   Noise pollution from a building site
(g)   Your roommate always parties on the night before your exams

Options
(a)   Tax or subsidy
(b)   Bargaining and negotiation
(c)   Legal rules
(d)   Direct regulation

6.   Jilly, Lilly, and Billie are roommates. Each likes a different kind of music. Jilly loves jazz, tolerates loud rock, and hates bluegrass. Lilly loves loud rock, is impartial to bluegrass, but loathes jazz. Billie adores bluegrass, can live with jazz, and despises loud rock. Their apartment has one (communally owned) radio. Billie asks your advice—how can she guarantee that only bluegrass will be played?

7.   We have a society with two consumers—Liz and Boris. The following table lists how much each will demand of a good at various prices.

Price	Liz's Quantity	Boris's Quantity
$10	0	0
$8	2	0
$6	4	0
$4	6	4
$2	8	8
$0	10	12

(a)   If this good is marketed as a private good, complete the following table.

Price	Total Quantity
$10	_____
$8	_____
$6	_____
$4	_____
$2	_____
$0	_____

(b)   If the marginal cost of this good is constant at $4, how much will be traded?

(c)   If this good is marketed as a public good, complete the following table.

Price	Quantity
$16	_____
$13	_____
$10	_____
$7	_____
$4	_____
$1	_____
$0	_____

(d)   If the marginal cost of this good is constant at $4, how much will be traded?

8.   The following table shows the costs associated with reducing pollution for two firms. Initially, each firm emits 6 units of pollution.

(a)   Complete the following table.

Firm A Reduction of Pollution (in units of pollution)	Firm A Marginal Cost of Reducing Pollution ($)	Firm A Total Cost of Reducing Pollution ($)	Firm B Reduction of Pollution (in units of pollution)	Firm B Marginal Cost of Reducing Pollution ($)	Firm B Total Cost of Reducing Pollution ($)
1	6	6	1	1	1
2	10	_____	2	3	_____
3	15	_____	3	6	_____
4	22	_____	4	_____	19
5	30	_____	5	_____	33
6	_____	123	6	20	53

Now the government, which wishes to reduce the overall level of pollution to 6 units, caps each firm's allowed pollution level at 3 units. Each firm must cut its pollution by 3 units.

(b)   By how many units must each firm reduce its pollution?

(c)   For Firm A, what is cost of reducing pollution by 3 units?

(d)   For Firm B, what is cost of reducing pollution by 3 units?

(e)   Having reduced pollution by the required amount, is there an opportunity for the two firms to trade one pollution permit? Which firm should buy and which should sell? Explain your answer.

(f)   Will the firms trade any further pollution permits? Explain your answer.

Practice Test SOLUTIONS

I. SOLUTIONS TO MULTIPLE-CHOICE QUESTIONS

1. (a) There is no external cost or external benefit attached to the production and/or consumption of a hamburger.

2. (b) Refer to page 334 for a discussion of the three requirements.

3. (b) Refer to page 334 for a summary of the methods of remedying an externality.

4. (b) Refer to page 330.

5. (a) The additional (external) costs reduce society's welfare, indicating that too much is being produced.

6. (b) If production decisions are based solely on marginal private cost, price will be artificially low, encouraging additional consumption and production.

7. (c) Your consumption of the radio station does not reduce its availability for others, nor can the radio station exclude any listeners.

8. (c) Public goods are nonrival and nonexcludable. Police protection is a communitywide service that is available to all.

9. (d) In the voting paradox example, things get done but outcomes needn't be consistent.

10. (c) In the private market, sum the demands vertically at each output level. Ned would be willing to pay $11 to buy the third unit.

11. (d) Sum the demand information vertically at each output level for a publicly provided good. Price will be $22 ($4 + $7 + $11).

12. (b) In perfect competition, the firm will set $P(MR) = MC$ to maximize profits. If there are external costs, MC will be less than MSC, therefore $P < MSC$.

13. (d) Nonrivalry and nonexcludability are characteristics of public goods, not problems.

14. (c) To derive the market demand for a private good, sum horizontally. For a public good, sum vertically. This technique measures the extra benefit received by society at each additional level of (nonexcludable) public good provision. Refer to page 344.

15. (b) If there are externalities, MDC is positive. The profit-maximizing firm produces where $P = MC$, which, with the tax, is equal to MSC.

16. (c) If a good or service has a large budget, the consumer may feel that her contribution is insignificant. Free riders get a good or service without paying for it.

17. (a) When preferences are identical, all parties will seek the same result.

18. (c) Marginal damage cost is marginal social cost minus marginal cost. Refer to page 333.

19. (b) The firm will produce where $P = MC$ whereas the efficient output level is where $P = MSC$.

20. (a) At the efficient output level of two tons, the government must increase the firm's private cost from $500 to $600.

II. SOLUTIONS TO APPLICATION QUESTIONS

1. (a) Category I includes pure private goods—goods that are rival in consumption and excludable. Freedonian sausage, clothing, and private cars would be examples. The government should leave well enough alone and let market forces provide this type of good.

    (b) Category IV includes pure public goods—goods that are nonrival in consumption and nonexcludable. Clean air, national defense, police protection, the legal system, public health, and fire protection would be examples. The government should provide this type of good.

    (c) Categories II and III are where the government needs to be careful because they include goods possessing one or other of the characteristics of public goods. The private sector can produce those goods in Category II because free riders can be excluded, but the private sector might underproduce, i.e., exclude those who are unwilling to pay even though their inclusion is virtually costless. Examples include the post office, public transport, and cable television. The private sector is unable to produce goods in Category III because free riders cannot be excluded. There is rivalry, so public provision might best have a user fee included. National parks during peak season or highways at rush hour are examples.

    (d) Given a negative externality in production, the offending firm will tend to overproduce. The government could impose a quota on production, or set a tax that would equate the marginal (private) cost and the marginal social cost.

    (e) Category I includes firms that impose spillover costs, such as the polluting steel industry.
    Category II includes those goods that impose spillover costs when used by consumers—Ms. Lipska's car, or noise pollution from a loud radio.
    Category III includes firms that provide spillover benefits: a beekeeper's bees provide pollination services; a new tourist attraction will draw visitors who spend money at restaurants and other local businesses; the training of entry-level employees who might be "pirated" by other firms/industries/regions.
    Category IV includes consumption that provides beneficial side effects. Examples may be less obvious for this case. Higher education, which might make students more responsible citizens, is an example. The purchase of medical injections for an infectious disease, careful tending of the weeds in your garden, or allowing someone to listen to or tape your CDs are other examples.

    (f) In the presence of negative externalities, the typical government policy is to tax to the extent of the marginal damage cost. Example: a high sales tax might be imposed on noisy boom boxes. In the presence of beneficial externalities, the government might provide a subsidy to stimulate production. Example: grants, or low-interest loans, for higher education.

2. (a) Refer to the following table.

Toll Fee	Usage per Year	Annual Revenues	Consumer Surplus	Total Annual Benefits
$1.00	0	$0	—	—
$0.80	20,000	$16,000	$2,000	$18,000
$0.60	40,000	$24,000	$8,000	$32,000
$0.40	60,000	$24,000	$18,000	$42,000
$0.20	80,000	$16,000	$32,000	$48,000
$0.10	90,000	$9,000	$40,500	$49,500
$0.00	100,000	$0	$50,000	$50,000

Example of consumer surplus calculation: When the fee is $0.40, the consumer surplus is $0.5(\$1.00 - \$0.40) \times 60,000$, or $18,000. Refer to the definition of consumer surplus on page 89 in Chapter 4.

(b) The bridge would not be built. The maximum possible revenue that can be obtained is $25,000, with a toll of 50¢. Because the cost is $40,000, a private firm would make an economic loss of at least $15,000.

(c) Croatoan should proceed because the total benefit exceeds the total cost.

(d) The city manager should not impose a toll fee. Any fee will reduce the total benefits from its maximum of $50,000. Suppose the toll were $1.00—no revenue would be raised. No benefits would accrue to Croatoan. By paying the bridge bill, the city would simply have lost $40,000. If, however, the toll were $0.00, no revenue would be raised, but $50,000 in consumer surplus would accrue. By paying the bridge bill, the city would gain $10,000.

(e) If a fee were to be charged, a toll of 50¢ would be preferred because revenues would be maximized at $25,000.

(f) Using the answer to Part (d), where no toll is charged, Croatoan will need to raise $40,000. Increasing taxes by $40,000 within the community would achieve the result. Note: issuing bonds within the community is preferred because individuals can choose whether or not to buy the bonds.

(g) A bridge is not a pure public good because, although it is nonrival (public), it is excludable (private)—Croatoan can charge a toll and exclude free riders, for example. It should be located in Category II.

(h) Compensation will be accepted with Distribution A and, if negotiation and trade between families is allowed, Distribution D. Refer to the following table. The total value of the bay's amenity is less than $10,000 in each of these cases.

Family	Distributions			
	A	B	C	D
Dare	$1,500	$3,000	$5,000	$2,500
Howe	$1,500	$3,000	$3,000	$2,500
Archard	$1,500	$3,000	$1,000	$2,500
Harvie	$1,500	$3,000	$1,000	$500
Viccars	$1,500	$1,000	$1,000	$500

Total Value of Amenity	$7,500	$13,000	$11,000	$8,500
Voting to Accept	Yes 5/No 0	Yes 1/No 4	Yes 3/No 2	Yes 2/No 3
Decision	Accept	Reject	Accept	Reject
Efficient Choice	Efficient	Efficient	Inefficient	Inefficient

(i)   The compensation will be accepted with Distributions A and C. Refer to the preceding table.

(j)   Distribution C. Refer to the preceding table.

(k)   With Distribution C, the families would accept compensation of $10,000, although the loss of amenity is valued at $11,000—a bad choice, especially for Dare and Howe. Coase's Theorem suggests that these two families could bribe one other (e.g., Archard) to vote with them. If Archard were given $1,000, his would become the swing vote. Even if Harvie and Viccars retaliated, the higher values placed on amenity by Dare and Howe would reverse the decision. The bridge project would not go through.

3.   (a)   The *MSC* curve will no longer represent all the costs borne by the firm. *MPC* will be lower. Lower price, more resources allocated to widget production. Pollution.

(b)   Noise pollution from a loud radio, air pollution from cars. *MSB* will be lower than *MPB*. Price will be higher, and more resources than the optimal amount will be allocated to widgets.

(c)   *MSB* will be higher than *MPB*. Prices will be lower, and less than what is socially optimal will be allocated.

Purchase of medical injections for an infectious disease, careful tending of the weeds in your garden, or allowing someone to listen to or tape your CDs

(d)   Training entry-level employees who are subsequently "attracted away" by other firms/industries/regions
MPC will be higher, and production will be less than the socially optimal level.

4.   (a) $29. Add Ted, Ned, and Fred's price together for the second unit of the good.

(b)   Refer to the following diagram.

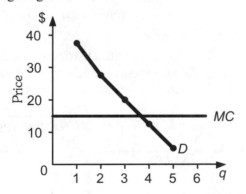

(c)   three units

(d)   Refer to the preceding diagram.

(e)   No one will be really happy. Each consumer would prefer to have more of the good produced, given its current price and their revealed preferences.

5.   (a)   D or A (regulation or taxation)

      (b)   D (regulation of flight patterns and jet engines and damages)

      (c)   D (regulation)

      (d)   D (regulation about mufflers)

      (e)   A (license fee—i.e., a tax)

      (f)   C (injunction)

      (g)   B (bargaining)

Most of these have several possible remedies. If your answers differ from these, reassess the pros and cons of each option.

6. First off, it's unlikely that Billie will prevent the others from having some say in what's played. She might, however, offer to buy them off, essentially renting the radio for her own use. The cost will depend on the preferences of her roommates.

      Perhaps you could suggest a cheaper alternative. Billie could request a round-table discussion and vote on the single kind of music acceptable to all. She should rig the voting sequence so that the first vote is jazz vs. loud rock. Jazz would win—Jilly and Billie vs. Lilly. The second vote should be between jazz and bluegrass. Bluegrass will win. Billie should then promptly adjourn the meeting before the others have time to think about the guile of their manipulative roommate.

7.   (a)   Refer to the following table.

Price	Total Quantity
$10	0
$8	2
$6	4
$4	10
$2	16
$0	22

      (b)   ten units

      (c)   Refer to the following table.

Price	Quantity
$16	0
$13 (8 + 5)	2
$10 (6 + 4)	4
$7 (4 + 3)	6
$4 (2 + 2)	8
$1 (0 + 1)	10
$0	12

      (d)   eight units

8.   (a)   See the following table. Of you had difficulty with this, review the material on the relationship between total and marginal values in Chapter 6.

Firm A Reduction of Pollution (in units of pollution)	Firm A Marginal Cost of Reducing Pollution ($)	Firm A Total Cost of Reducing Pollution ($)	Firm B Reduction of Pollution (in units of pollution)	Firm B Marginal Cost of Reducing Pollution ($)	Firm B Total Cost of Reducing Pollution ($)
1	6	6	1	1	1
2	10	16	2	3	4
3	15	31	3	6	10
4	22	53	4	9	19
5	30	83	5	14	33
6	40	123	6	20	53

(b)   Each firm must reduce pollution by 3 units.

(c)   For Firm A, the cost of reducing pollution by 3 units is $31 ($6 for the first unit, $10 for the second, and $15 for the third).

(d)   For Firm B, the cost of reducing pollution by 3 units is $10 ($1 for the first unit, $3 for the second, and $6 for the third).

(e)   The marginal cost of the third unit of pollution abatement for Firm A is $15. Firm B could cut its pollution by a fourth unit (from 3 units of pollution to 2 units) at a marginal cost of $9. Firm B should sell its third permit to Firm A. The price will be somewhere between $9 and $15 for both traders to gain.

(f)   Firm B will not sell its second permit because its value to B is $14, while Firm A would be willing to pay $10.

17

Uncertainty and Asymmetric Information

Chapter Objectives

1. Define expected value and, given the possible outcomes, calculate expected value.
2. Use the utility function to explain why individuals who are risk averse, risk neutral, or risk loving make the choices they make
3. Describe adverse selection and moral hazard and indicate how asymmetric information may interfere with market efficiency.
4. Identify potential remedies for problems caused by asymmetric information.

In previous chapters, it was assumed that decision makers had perfect information about products, prices, and other relevant factors. However, consumers and firms may very well have to make decisions under conditions of asymmetric information, where one side has superior information. In fact, there may be a strong incentive for one party to deceive the other, as when a used car is being traded or when health insurance is being sought. Uncertainty and asymmetric information are common in the real world. This chapter explores the economic implications of a world of uncertainty and asymmetric information.

The first part of the chapter reviews and extends some of concepts developed in Chapter 6 (utility); the second part traces out some of the consequences of asymmetric information in the real world.

BRAIN TEASER: Four-wheel drive (4WD) vehicles are generally reckoned to be safer than conventional two-wheel drive vehicles. However, evidence suggests that drivers of such vehicles are more likely to be involved in an accident. Assuming this evidence is accurate, why do you think this might be?

Objective 1

Define expected value and, given the possible outcomes, calculate expected value.

Faced with uncertainty and more than one possible outcome, individuals must predict the expected value of a situation in order to determine whether to proceed. *Expected value* (EV) is the sum of the payoffs (rewards) associated with each possible outcome weighted by the probability that that outcome will occur. A fair game occurs when the expected value of the game equals zero (the expected gains equal the expected costs). (page 354)

> **LEARNING TIP:** Keep in mind some examples of risk-averse behavior, such as buying fire insurance for your home even though the likelihood of loss is so small that the value of the premiums you pay exceeds the expected value of any insurance payout. ◀

Practice

1. You have a fair six-sided die, with sides numbered from one to six. When you roll the die, what is the probability of rolling either a 1 or a 2?
   (a) one chance in six (one sixth).
   (b) two chances in six (one third).
   (c) three chances in six (one half).
   (d) Impossible to determine because the outcome is uncertain.

   ANSWER: (b)

2. You have a fair six-sided die, with sides numbered from one to six. When you roll the die, what is the expected value of the result?
   (a) 1/6.
   (b) 1.
   (c) 3.
   (d) 3.5.

   ANSWER: (d)   Each side has an equal probability (1/6). EV = 1/6(1) + 1/6(2) + 1/6(3) + 1/6(4) + 1/6(5) + 1/6(6) = 3.5.

Note: If you experienced problems with the math content of the two preceding questions, you should review the probability chapter in an introductory statistics textbook in your campus library.

3. You are considering an investment project that has three possible outcomes. There is a 10 percent chance that you will lose $100, a 50 percent chance that you will gain $100, and a 40 percent chance that you will gain $200. What is the expected value of the project?
   (a) $100.
   (b) $120.
   (c) $140.
   (d) $200.

   ANSWER: (b)   EV = 0.1(–$100) + 0.5($100) + 0.4($200) = $120.

4. Jack charges Jill $10 to play a card game. If Jill cuts a deck of cards and finds a "spade," she wins $60, otherwise, she wins nothing. The probability of a spade is 0.25. Is this a fair game?
   (a) Yes, because Jill knows the odds of winning.
   (b) Yes, because the expected value of the reward exceeds the cost of playing.
   (c) No, because the expected value of the reward exceeds the cost of playing.
   (d) No, because the expected value of the reward is less than the cost of playing.

   ANSWER: (c)   A fair game is one whose expected value (expected benefits minus expected costs) is zero. The expected value of the reward is $15 (0.75($0) + 0.25($60)) while the cost is $10. ∎

Objective 2

Use the utility function to explain why individuals who are risk averse, risk neutral, or risk loving make the choices they make.

Typically, given two options with the same expected value, where one is certain and the other is uncertain, individuals will choose the certain deal—they are risk averse. A risk-loving individual, in contrast, would prefer the deal that is uncertain, even although the expected values are identical. The law of diminishing marginal utility, first discussed in Chapter 6, offers an explanation. If the marginal utility of income diminishes, gaining an extra dollar does not increase total utility as much as losing an extra dollar decreases total utility. On balance, the change in expected utility from a fair bet is negative in such a situation.

If an individual is willing to take a fair bet (one whose expected value is zero), he is risk neutral, but, if he requires the expected value to be positive before proceeding, he is risk averse, while a risk lover will proceed when the expected value is negative. (page 356)

In the presence of risk, a risk averse person will be willing to pay to reduce the consequences of that risk. The risk premium is the maximum price that a risk averse individual will be willing to pay to avoid taking a risk.

LEARNING TIP: The shape of the utility function for income reveals whether an individual is risk averse, risk neutral, or risk loving. The utility function for a risk-neutral individual is a straight upward-sloping line—each dollar offers the same utility as any other. For a risk-averse individual, the utility function increases at a decreasing rate while, for a risk lover, the function gets progressively steeper—extra dollars bestow more marginal utility than previous dollars.◀

Practice

Complete and use the following table for the next five questions. Note: If you have trouble completing the table, refer to Chapter 6.

Jill's Income	Total Utility	Marginal Utility
$0	0	
$20,000	30	
$40,000	50	_____
$60,000	_____	15
$80,000	75	
$100,000	80	_____

5. Based on the table, we can conclude that Jill is
   (a) risk loving because total utility is increasing at an increasing rate.
   (b) risk loving because total utility is increasing at a decreasing rate.
   (c) risk averse because total utility is increasing at an increasing rate.
   (d) risk averse because total utility is increasing at a decreasing rate.

   ANSWER: (d) An individual with diminishing marginal utility is risk-averse..

6. Currently, Jill earns $40,000. Her brother Jack offers to double her salary if she works for him. Jill believes that Jack's firm has an even chance of going bankrupt. If so, she will be paid nothing. This deal is
   (a) risk neutral.
   (b) risk averse.
   (c) a fair bet.
   (d) an unfair bet.

   ANSWER: (c) The expected value of the offer is $40,000 and the cost (the salary from the current job) is $40,000.

7. Jill's expected utility if she takes Jack's offer is _____ and her utility if she does not is _____ .
   (a) 50; 50
   (b) 50; 30
   (c) 75; 50
   (d) 0; 30

   ANSWER: (a) The expected value of the offer and her current salary are each $40,000.

8.   Will Jill accept Jack's job offer?
(a)   Yes, because the expected value of the offer and her current salary are each $40,000.
(b)   Perhaps. Because the expected value of the offer and her current salary are equal, she is indifferent.
(c)   No. The expected value of the offer and her current salary are each $40,000 and Jill is risk averse.
(d)   It is impossible to tell from the given information.
ANSWER: (c)   Jill is risk averse. The current (certain) $40,000 will be preferred to an uncertain offer with an expected value of $40,000.

9.   Jill's occupation is one in which the risk of becoming disabled in any given year is very high—50 percent, in fact. If Jill is not disabled, she earns her regular salary of $40,000. If she is disabled, she earns no income. She can buy disability insurance that will pay her full salary if she becomes disabled. The risk premium Jill would be willing to pay for such an insurance policy is
(a) $40,000.
(b) $20,000.
(c)   between $20,000 and $40,000.
(d)   less than $20,000.
ANSWER: (d)   Because Jill is risk averse, the total utility from $20,000 is more than half of the utility of $40,000. ■

Objective 3

Describe adverse selection and moral hazard and indicate how asymmetric information may interfere with market efficiency.

Asymmetric information is present when one party to a transaction has relevant information that the other party does not have. In the real world, this is a frequent situation. In a voluntary exchange with asymmetric information, trade becomes inefficient. Adverse selection can occur if a buyer or seller with incomplete or inaccurate information enters into an exchange with another party who has better information, the consequence being more poor quality goods ("lemons") and fewer high quality goods ("peaches") being exchanged than is desired. Buying a used car is often a painfully good example. (page 357)

The problems caused by adverse selection can be reduced through market signaling, where buyers and sellers communicate the quality of the product. Dealers willing to offer warranties, sellers with good reputations, or impartial inspections of goods by a third party may add information that can help to distinguish a lemon from a peach. In the used car market, all states have lemon laws that allow buyers to return an unsatisfactory car for a full refund.

Moral hazard arises when one party to a contract passes on the cost of his behavior to the other party. Behavior in the insurance market is an example. Do we expend as much effort to protect our property from damage or theft if it is insured? If not, others bear the cost of our actions. By reducing the personal cost of one's undesirable behavior, insurance may encourage such irresponsibility. (page 362)

> **LEARNING TIP:** Although both spring from the presence of asymmetric information, adverse selection and moral hazard are separate problems for efficient markets. Adverse selection occurs prior to a transaction while moral hazard is due to behavior following a transaction.◀

ECONOMICS IN PRACTICE: On page 360, the textbook looks at the issue of adverse selection in health care. Following full implementation of 2010's Patient Protection and Affordable Care Act, the Congressional Budget Office estimates that some 23 million residents will remain uninsured. These individuals include illegal immigrants and those who will opt to pay the annual penalty instead of buying insurance. This latter group is likely to be younger, single, citizens for whom the penalty is less expensive than the insurance. Is there any evidence of adverse selection in this information?

ANSWER: There is some suggestion of adverse selection. Presumably, the young citizens who choose not to buy health insurance will be healthier than the general purchaser. In some sense, less-healthy citizens are being covered. The illegal immigrants who are excluded, however, are not an example of adverse selection.

ECONOMICS IN PRACTICE (CONTINUED): Adverse selection was first discussed with reference to the used car market ("lemons"). Asymmetric information can cut both ways, however, in negotiations for a used car. What strategies might you adopt, as a potential buyer of a used car, to drive down the price?

ANSWER: Your goal is to get the car you want at the lowest price possible. Assuming you've found the car of your dreams (and haven't told the seller!), you should have gathered general information about prices of similar cars in the local market (substitutes) and had the car checked by a good mechanic. (The seller, of course, will tell you his car is quite exceptional, with low mileage, one careful owner, careful maintenance, and so on). Appearing keen to buy, being ill-informed, or well-dressed are signals the buyer should avoid. Conveying the message that there is no urgent need to buy shows that you can be price-sensitive and willing to walk away. Discount reasons for selling the car that are unrelated to the car itself. Be prepared to walk away from any transaction where the seller will not offer (or sell) a warranty.

ECONOMICS IN PRACTICE: On page 361, the textbook looks at the issue of items omitted from advertisements and reading between the lines. Buyers of used cars on eBay and other auction sites similarly face the problem of asymmetric information. What are some of the strategies used by sellers to encourage potential buyers to bid?

ANSWER: Typically, sellers display many photographs of the car they wish to sell and long lists of repairs or improvements that have been made. If the VIN (Vehicle Identification Number) is listed, the seller may offer a free report on the history of the vehicle through Carfax. Sellers may draw attention to their "feedback" (an indication of soundness and good reputation). Often, a seller may emphasize that the need to sell is for personal or financial reasons ("We have a baby and need a bigger car"), perhaps to signal that the listing is not a "lemon."

Practice

---

10.   Asymmetric information can cause _____ before a transaction and _____ after it.
        (a)   adverse selection; adverse selection
        (b)   adverse selection; moral hazard
        (c)   moral hazard ; adverse selection
        (d)   moral hazard; moral hazard

        ANSWER: (b) Poor information causes poor choices before a transaction (adverse selection). If, during a transaction, future behavior is not predictable, one party may be able to pass on the cost of his behavior to the other.

11.   Jack: "A universal health care system will lead to abuses by patients."
        Jill: "My private health-care plan has so many hidden conditions it's not much of a deal."
        Jack's statement focuses on _____: Jill's statement focuses on _____.
        (a)   adverse selection; adverse selection
        (b)   adverse selection; moral hazard
        (c)   moral hazard ; adverse selection
        (d)   moral hazard; moral hazard

        ANSWER: (c) Jack feels that patients will use the "free" system more than is necessary (moral hazard) while Jill feels that she has less complete information than the seller of health care.

12. Without market signals to indicate the quality of used cars, which of the following is most likely to occur?
    (a) Only peaches will be sold.
    (b) Only lemons will be sold.
    (c) The market will split into a market for peaches and a separate market for lemons.
    (d) Different prices will prevail for peaches and lemons.

    ANSWER: (b) With no way to distinguish between a peach and a lemon, only lemons will be sold.

13. Which of the following is the market in which asymmetric information is most likely to be present?
    (a) The market for new cars
    (b) The market for experienced architects
    (c) The market for breakfast cereal
    (d) The market for new college graduates

    ANSWER: (d) In each of the other cases, quality controls and/or previous history will be a useful guide for market participants.

14. Assume that there are two classes of individual—the healthy and the unhealthy. If adverse selection exists in the health insurance market, this will result in
    (a) more healthy individuals and more unhealthy individuals being insured.
    (b) more healthy individuals and fewer unhealthy individuals being insured.
    (c) fewer healthy individuals and more unhealthy individuals being insured.
    (d) fewer healthy individuals and fewer unhealthy individuals being insured.

    ANSWER: (c) Unhealthy clients will seek insurance, driving up costs and reducing the incentives for healthy people to seek insurance.

15. Universal health coverage will
    (a) reduce adverse selection and moral hazard.
    (b) reduce adverse selection but not moral hazard.
    (c) reduce moral hazard but not adverse selection.
    (d) increase adverse selection and moral hazard.

    ANSWER: (b) Without universal health coverage, there is an incentive for unhealthy individuals to seek coverage—adverse selection. Universal coverage would include all individuals, whether healthy or unhealthy.

16. In the used car market, there are lemons and peaches and, although buyers cannot distinguish between them, sellers can. We would expect _____ lemons to enter the market and _____ peaches to enter the market.
    (a) too many; too many
    (b) too many; too few
    (c) too few; too many
    (d) too few; too few

    ANSWER: (b) Refer to page 358 for a discussion of this example.

17. In the job market, which of the following is the job applicant's weakest market signal?
    (a) The fact that the applicant has a college degree
    (b) The reputation of the college from which the degree was received
    (c) Information about the graduate's GPA while in college
    (d) The major of the applicant

    ANSWER: (a) The quality of the degree is more significant than the fact that it has been received. ∎

Objective 4

Identify potential remedies for problems caused by asymmetric information.

With asymmetric information, individuals may have the wrong incentives when making decisions. In fact, many incentives (piece rates, commissions, or no-claims bonuses, for example) arise precisely because of uncertainty.

Mechanism design explores how contracts or transactions can be constructed in order to reward proper behavior in self-interested individuals, even in the face of asymmetric information. Piece rates and commissions, for instance, reward workers who are more productive and may well screen out workers who know that they are less productive. A less-productive worker will favor a fixed salary. Firms have an incentive to offer wellness programs—healthier employees are less likely to impose expensive health care claims. Co-payment requirements are intended to give clients an incentive to monitor health-care costs.

Practice

18. Because insured individuals _____ for medical services that they receive, they may _____ those services.
     (a) pay the full price; overuse
     (b) pay the full price; underuse
     (c) do not pay the full price; overuse
     (d) do not pay the full price; underuse

     ANSWER: (c) Moral hazard suggests that clients have an incentive to overuse medical services.

19. A health insurance co-pay is a form of
     (a) mechanism design that reduces adverse selection.
     (b) mechanism design that reduces moral hazard.
     (c) incentive contract that reduces adverse selection.
     (d) incentive contract that reduces moral hazard.

     ANSWER: (d) Refer to page 362 for more on moral hazard.

20. Labor contracts often include remuneration that is tied to worker performance for each of the following reasons EXCEPT
     (a) experience reveals that most workers are risk neutral and appreciate a challenge.
     (b) rewards linked to performance act as an incentive to work hard.
     (c) such a contract tends to discourage low-quality workers from applying.
     (d) such a contract tends to encourage high-quality workers to apply.

     ANSWER: (a) Research indicates that most individuals tend to be risk averse. ∎

BRAIN TEASER SOLUTION: There may be two reasons for the greater incidence of accidents in 4WD vehicles—adverse selection and moral hazard. Perhaps those who frequent roads with more dangerous surfaces or who drive in more dangerous conditions (snow, ice, or rain) tend to buy 4WD vehicles. In other words, 4WD users are a different population of drivers who are at higher risk of accidents. However, at least one study reports that, when other factors are held constant, 4WD vehicles are still more likely to be involved in accidents due to moral hazard. Users of 4WD vehicles may be less cautious because, paradoxically, they feel safer. Other road users may choose either to drive cautiously or to stay home when snow appears while owners of 4WDs may venture out without realizing the limitations of their skill or their vehicle.

PRACTICE TEST

I. MULTIPLE-CHOICE QUESTIONS

Select the option that provides the single best answer.

Use the following information for the next two questions. Consider the following game. You cut a deck of cards. If you get a diamond (which should happen a quarter of the time), you receive $10. If you don't, you pay $2.

_____ 1.   What is the expected value of the game?
   (a) $10.00.
   (b) $2.50.
   (c) $1.00.
   (d) $0.50.

_____ 2.   If Bill is risk averse, will he play the game?
   (a)   Yes, because the expected value is positive.
   (b)   No, because he only has one chance in four of winning.
   (c)   No—a risk-averse person will only play a fair game.
   (d)   Perhaps—it depends on how risk averse he is.

_____ 3.   As an individual's income increases, total utility
   (a)   increases at an increasing rate.
   (b)   increases at a decreasing rate.
   (c)   decreases at an increasing rate.
   (d)   decreases at a decreasing rate.

_____ 4.   The sum of the utilities coming from all outcomes of a deal, weighted by the probability of each outcome occurring is known as
   (a)   total utility.
   (b)   expected value.
   (c)   expected utility.
   (d)   expected marginal utility.

Use the following table for the next four questions. Emily, a recent college graduate, has two job offers. The jobs are identical (a one-year contract) except for how Emily is paid. In Job A, she will receive a fixed salary of $40,000 for the year. In Job B, she will receive a base salary of $20,000 and a bonus of $60,000 if she completes her project within a specified period. Emily believes she has an even chance of early completion.

Emily's Income	Total Utility
$0	0
$20,000	9
$40,000	16
$50,000	20
$60,000	23
$80,000	25
$100,000	26

_____ 5.   Based on the table, Emily is
(a)   risk neutral.
(b)   risk averse.
(c)   risk loving.
(d)   risk seeking.

_____ 6.   The expected value of Emily's income for each job offer is
(a) $40,000 for Job A and $80,000 for Job B.
(b) $40,000 for Job A and $50,000 for Job B.
(c) $20,000 for Job A and $80,000 for Job B.
(d) $20,000 for Job A and $50,000 for Job B.

_____ 7.   The expected utility of Emily's income for each job offer is
(a)   20 for Job A and 25 for Job B.
(b)   20 for Job A and 20 for Job B.
(c)   16 for Job A and 25 for Job B.
(d)   16 for Job A and 20 for Job B.

_____ 8.   Emily is risk averse. She is now offered a signing bonus of $10,000 if she accepts Job A. Which job should she accept and why?
(a)   Job A because, although Job B's expected value is higher, Job A's income is guaranteed.
(b)   Job A, because Job A's expected value is higher than Job B's.
(c)   Job B, because Job B's expected value is higher than Job A's.
(d)   Emily is indifferent between the two offers—the expected values are equal.

_____ 9.   The maximum price a risk-averse person will pay to avoid taking a risk is known as the
(a)   risk aversion price.
(b)   risk premium.
(c)   risk discount.
(d)   risk cost factor.

Complete and use the following table for the next question.

Income	Fred's Utility	Wilma's Utility
$0	0	0
$20,000	30	20
$40,000	50	40
$60,000	50	60
$80,000	75	80
$100,000	80	100

_____ 10.   From the table, we can conclude that Fred is _____ and Wilma is _____ .
(a)   risk averse; risk averse
(b)   risk averse; risk loving
(c)   risk loving; risk averse
(d)   risk averse; risk neutral

_____ 11. Red Cross health insurance company requires all prospective policy holders to undergo a medical examination before writing the policy to reduce _____ and to submit to annual health checks afterwards to reduce _____ .
(a)   adverse selection; adverse selection
(b)   adverse selection; moral hazard
(c)   moral hazard ; adverse selection
(d)   moral hazard; moral hazard

_____ 12. Warranties, good driving records, and performance in college are all examples of
(a)   adverse selection.
(b)   expected utility.
(c)   expected value.
(d)   market signals.

_____ 13. Robert is risk neutral. As a lumberjack, he has a 20 percent probability of receiving an injury that will disable him for a year. His salary is $30,000. What is the expected value of the insurance? What is the most would Robert be willing to spend on disability insurance that would pay his full salary if he became disabled?
(a) $6,000; $6,000
(b) $6,000; less than $6,000
(c)   More than $6,000; more than $6,000
(d) $6,000; less than $6,000

_____ 14. A risk-averse individual experiences _____ marginal utility from income; a risk-loving individual experiences _____ marginal utility from income.
(a)   increasing; increasing
(b)   increasing; decreasing
(c)   decreasing; increasing
(d)   decreasing; decreasing

Use the following information for the next two questions. In the market for a used 2006 Ford Escort, 60 percent of the vehicles offered for sale are peaches and 40 percent are lemons. There is no way for the buyer to distinguish between peaches and lemons before the transaction. Brian would pay $6,000 for a peach but only $2,000 for a lemon. Sellers of peaches are willing to sell for no less than $5,000 and sellers of lemons are willing to sell for no less than $1,000.

_____ 15. What is the expected value of a used 2006 Escort?
(a) $6,000
(b) $5,200
(c) $4,400
(d) $4,000

_____ 16. Over time the price in the market for 2006 Escorts will be between _____ and _____ will be traded.
(a) $2,000 and $5,000; both lemon and peaches
(b) $2,000 and $5,000; only peaches
(c) $1,000 and $5,000; both peaches and lemons
(d) $1,000 and $2,000; only lemons

_____ 17. Each of the following has been advanced as a possible effect of tying bonuses for public school teachers to the performance of their students on standardized tests EXCEPT
  (a)   teachers will tend to "teach to the test."
  (b)   incentive pay may screen out committed teachers.
  (c)   teachers are already highly motivated and monetary compensation will have little impact on the quality of teaching.
  (d)   incentive pay may attract poorly-motivated individuals to become teachers.

_____ 18. For a market signal to be effective in reducing _____ , it must be _____ for the high-quality seller to obtain.
  (a)   moral hazard; more costly
  (b)   moral hazard; less costly
  (c)   adverse selection; more costly
  (d)   adverse selection; less costly

_____ 19. Adverse selection and moral hazard are examples of
  (a)   expected utility.
  (b)   expected value.
  (c)   market signaling.
  (d)   asymmetric information problems.

_____ 20. Hugo is selling his very old Yugo on eBay, a market with asymmetric information. The going price for a Yugo is $100, and this is Hugo's asking price. Sadly, Hugo knows his Yugo is a "lemon." If price is used by buyers as a signal of quality in this market, Hugo should
  (a)   keep his asking price at $100.
  (b)   raise his asking price above $100.
  (c)   lower his asking price below $100.
  (d)   withdraw his car from the market.

II. APPLICATION QUESTIONS

1. One market signal is to offer to replace defective goods. Why does this distinguish between superior products and inferior products?

2. Pyro recently purchased fire insurance for his home. Because fire insurance reduces his risk of loss due to fire, it may also discourage him from making the effort to prevent fires. What is this the name of this problem? What might the insurance company do to reduce the problem? What effect does a deductible have on adverse selection or moral hazard?

3. Do you think that the problem of moral hazard is similar in degree for car insurance, health insurance, and life insurance? Why might it be different in the three cases?

4. Honest Orville and Shady Sam own used car dealerships opposite each other on Main Street. Orville's Autos always sells high-quality cars (peaches) while Sam's Sports and Saloons always sells low-quality cars (lemons). Unfortunately, buyers are not aware of this discrepancy in the conduct of the two firms. They would pay $12,000 for a peach but only $5,000 for a lemon. It costs Orville $10,000 to buy, inspect and scrupulously service each car he sells. Sam's offerings are merely cleaned and polished to a showroom sheen but are mechanically substandard. Each car costs Sam $4,000 to get ready for the showroom.

(a)   Assuming an even chance of getting a peach or a lemon, what is the expected value of a used car in this market?

(b)   What is Orville's profit? Sam's?

(c)   Predict what will happen over time to the proportion of peaches sold. Why will this happen?

(d)   Predict what will happen over time to the price of cars sold in this market? Why will this happen?

Now Orville decides to offer a warranty for his car—$6,000 per car for defective parts or bad workmanship. Because his cars are all peaches, he calculates that he will not have to pay for this signal of high quality.

(e)   If buyers believe that Orville's warranty does signal that he sells high-quality cars, what will happen to his profit?

(f)   If buyers believe that Orville's warranty signals that he sells high-quality cars and that Sam doesn't, what will happen to Sam's profit?

(g)   What will happen if Sam follows Orville's lead and offers a similar warranty?

(h)   Does it make sense for Orville and Sam to offer warranties?

(i)   Is there any moral hazard in this situation for Orville?

Practice Test SOLUTIONS

I.   SOLUTIONS TO MULTIPLE-CHOICE QUESTIONS

1.   (c)   Each of the four suits has an equal probability (1/4). EV = 1/4($10) + 3/4(–$2) = $1.00.

2.   (d)   Risk-averse Bill will only play if the expected value is positive. However, this game may still not offer enough of an incentive to play.

3.   (b)   As income increases, the marginal utility of each additional dollar decreases but is still positive, so total utility increases at a decreasing rate.

4.   (c)   Refer to the definition on page 355.

5.   (b)   The table shows that Emily's total utility from income is increasing at a decreasing rate. Because she benefits less from gaining a dollar than she gives up from losing a dollar she will be averse to a fair game.

6.   (c)   Emily is guaranteed $40,000 for Job A. The expected value of Job B is $50,000 ($20,000 + [1/2($40,000) + 1/2(0)]).

7.   (d)   Job A's $40,000 has an expected utility of 16 while Job B's expected value of $50,000 has an expected utility of 25.

8.   (b)   The extra $10,000 of guaranteed income makes the expected values equal. For risk-averse Emily, Job A, with its guaranteed income, is preferred.

9.   (b)   Refer to page 356 for more about risk premium.

10.   (d)   As income increases, Fred's marginal utility diminishes while Wilma's marginal utility is constant.

11.   (b)   Red Cross is trying to improve its information before the transaction to reduce adverse selection and to reduce subsequent unhealthy behavior by the policy holder (moral hazard).

12.   (d)   Warranties, good driving records, and performance in college help to communicate quality in a world of uncertainty.

13.   (a)   A risk-neutral individual receives the equal utility from each dollar received. The expected value of the insurance is $6,000.

14.   (c)   In each case the utility function slopes upwards but for the risk-averse individual the slope decreases, while, for the risk lover the slope increases.

15.   (c)   The expected value of a used Escort is $4,400 or [0.6($6,000) + 0.4($2,000)].

16. (d) Buyers will be unwilling to pay more than $4,400, leading sellers of peaches to withdraw their cars from the market.. This increases the probability of a lemon and the market price will decrease.

17. (d) Refer to page 363 for the discussion on this topic.

18. (d) Market signals act as a screen to reduce adverse selection. Refer to page 360.

19. (d) Adverse selection and moral hazard are examples of problems caused by asymmetric information.

20. (b) If Hugo raises his asking price, he is signaling to gullible buyers that his car is not a "lemon."

II. SOLUTIONS TO APPLICATION QUESTIONS

1. Sellers of superior goods will seldom have to meet the obligations of their guarantee. However, sellers of goods that are frequently likely to fail will find that the cost of the warranty will be high. If customers are willing to pay a premium for goods that have a warranty that is greater than the cost of satisfying that warranty, then warranties will only be offered by sellers of superior goods.

2. This is an example of moral hazard. To reduce moral hazard, the insurance company could require Pyro to install and maintain smoke detectors. Damage caused by negligence or intentional behavior could be excluded from the contract. A deductible does not affect moral hazard, because the cost of irresponsible behavior would be borne by Pyro. Adverse selection, however, would be reduced.

3. Moral hazard occurs when behavior changes in response to a contract. With the exception of suicides, life insurance is least likely to be affected by moral hazard. It is unlikely that ownership of a life insurance policy will make many individuals engage in life-threatening activities that they would not have engaged in anyway. With car insurance, drivers may become more reckless or less concerned about the security of their vehicles. To compensate for this, insurance companies may have no-claims bonuses, or clauses that limit liability if the policyholder is responsible for an accident. Similarly, the health insurance industry suffers from moral hazard if policyholders seek unnecessary procedures.

4. (a) EV = 1/2($12,000) + 1/2($5,000) = $8,500.

   (b) Orville will lose $1,500 ($8,500 – $10,000) on each car. Sam will gain $4,500 ($8,500 – $4,000) on each car.

   (c) Fewer and fewer peaches will be sold.

   (d) As the proportion of lemons increases relative to peaches, the expected value of a car will decrease until, when only lemons are sold, the price will be $5,000.

   (e) Orville's profit will increase to $2,000 ($12,000 – $10,000) as buyers become willing to pay for a high-quality car. His costs won't increase because the warranty won't be required.

   (f) If buyers suppose that a lack of warranty signals a low-quality car, the price of Sam's cars will decrease to $5,000. Sam's profit will shrink to $1,000 ($5,000 – $4,000).

(g)   Assuming buyers think that Sam's market signal indicates that he sells peaches, he will be able to sell his cars at $12,000. However, when customers return to enforce the warranty, his costs will increase by $6,000 to $10,000 and his profits will increase to $2,000.

(h)   It makes sense for both sellers to offer a warranty.

(i)   Orville's customers may be less careful about regular maintenance (oil changes, for instance), knowing that if their car develops a fault it may be covered by the warranty.

18

Income Distribution and Poverty

Chapter Objectives

1. Identify the three sources of household income and outline the factors that cause differences in that income.
2. Present the theoretical case for and against the minimum wage and summarize the evidence.
3. Describe the current pattern of income distribution. Identify the information provided by the Lorenz curve and the Gini coefficient.
4. Describe the trend in income inequality globally and identify possible causes.
5. Give the official definition of poverty. Describe the trend in poverty in the United States over the past four decades and distinguish between the poverty rates of different groups within the economy.
6. State the arguments for and against redistribution of income. Summarize the theories underlying these arguments.
7. Describe the two major government redistribution programs and the groups that they seek to reach.

Much of the material in this chapter is descriptive rather than theoretical. Aim to have a general idea about the sources of income in the economy, the trend in poverty, the major income-redistribution programs, and the arguments for and against each program.

LEARNING TIP: The entire chapter deals with the question of equity, rather than with the efficiency criterion that has dominated the previous chapters. The introductory section distinguishes between the equity (or fairness) criterion and the efficiency criterion for income distribution, and draws attention to three questions:

(a) What causes inequality?

(b) How can it be measured?

(c) What is the appropriate role for the government?

Use this three-part scheme to make sense of the material being presented in this chapter

Do not equate equity or fairness with equality—they are distinctly different concepts. It may be very equal if your professor gives everyone the same grade on your next exam, but it's unlikely to be fair or equitable!◀

BRAIN TEASER: This chapter looks at how income is distributed across households. Do you think that the distribution of income has become more or less equal since the mid-1960s? Wealth is also distributed across households. Is the distribution of wealth more equally or less equally distributed than income?

Objective 1

Identify the three sources of household income and outline the factors that cause differences in that income.

Households derive their income from three sources: (1) labor income, mainly wages and salaries (about 64 percent of personal income); (2) property, such as capital and land (about 22 percent of personal income); and (3) government transfer payments (about 14 percent of personal income).

Several factors may produce inequalities in income distribution. Wage and salary differences may arise because of the nature (quality) of the workers—skills, level of education or training, physical ability—or from the nature of the job—degree of risk, difficulty, or glamour. The distribution of unemployment and the number of wage earners in the family will also have an effect. Property income and transfer payments are also unevenly distributed, with wealthier families tending to have more income-earning property than do poorer families. The concept of human capital is important—we can "invest" in job skills and education. (page 368)

Certainly, accidents of birth may affect income distribution because property (and property income) can be passed on from one generation to the next. Socialist or Marxist economies, in particular, levy high "death duties" or estate taxes to reduce this source of inequality. An interesting example of this issue emerged in Britain when Queen Elizabeth (reputedly one of the world's richest women) "volunteered" to pay income taxes for the first time. The repeal of death taxes became a hot topic of debate during the 2004 presidential election campaign.

Practice

1. Patrick earns a degree in electrical engineering. This is an example of
   (a) investment in human capital.
   (b) wealth accumulation.
   (c) income redistribution.
   (d) a compensating differential.

   ANSWER: (a) The degree improves Patrick's knowledge and skills.

2. The major source of household income is
   (a) wages and salaries.
   (b) government payments.
   (c) property income.
   (d) inheritances and bequests.

   ANSWER: (a) Refer to page 367. More than half of personal income is received in the form of wages and salaries. Wage supplements raise this number to over 60 percent.

3. In some jobs, workers earn "danger money." Danger money is an example of
   (a) payment for human capital.
   (b) a compensating differential.
   (c) an equity differential.
   (d) a bonus.

   ANSWER: (b) Compensating differentials are paid to reward workers who undertake dangerous or unpleasant jobs.

4. Compensating differentials are best described as
   (a) government transfer payments to poor families to increase their standard of living.
   (b) wage differences caused by differences in human capital.
   (c) wage differences caused by differences in working conditions.
   (d) wage differences caused by differences in worker productivity.

   ANSWER: (c) Refer to the definition on page 368.

5. _____ comprise property income.
   (a) Economic profits and economic rents
   (b) Profits, rents, interest earnings, and dividends
   (c) Profits and dividends
   (d) Unearned interest payments and dividends

   ANSWER: (b) Refer to the definition on page 369.

6. Which of the following statements is false?
   (a) Transfer payments reduce income inequality.
   (b) Transfer payments are payments to individuals or households who provide no good or service in exchange.
   (c) Transfer payments are used by the government to alleviate poverty.
   (d) Eligibility for transfer payments is restricted to those in poverty.

   ANSWER: (d) Almost all workers are eligible for Social Security.

7. Congress passes a $6 billion flood-relief package for Midwest families affected by flooding of the Mississippi. This is
   (a) a compensating differential.
   (b) a transfer payment.
   (c) property income (rent).
   (d) sweat equity.

   ANSWER: (b) No good or service is required in return for the benefits received. ■

Objective 2

Present the theoretical case for and against the minimum wage and summarize the evidence.

The minimum wage has been used as a way to boost the incomes of low-wage workers. As a result of the minimum wage, those who work receive higher wages than would otherwise be the case while those who lose their jobs (as bosses try to economize) are worse off. The more elastic the demand for labor, the greater the job loss will be. Evidence is mixed, some indicating that a 10 percent increase in the minimum wage will result in a 1 percent decrease in employment, while other studies find minimal job loss. There is more on this topic in Chapter 10. (page 368)

Practice

Use the following labor market diagram to answer the next two questions.

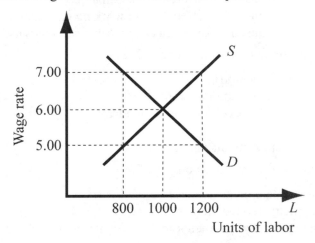

8. Refer to the preceding diagram. If a minimum wage of $7.00 were imposed, there would be an _____ workers and the wage rate would _____ .
    (a)   excess demand for; increase
    (b)   excess demand for; decrease
    (c)   excess supply of; increase
    (d)   excess supply of; decrease

    ANSWER: (c) The equilibrium wage is $6.00. The minimum wage imposition sets up a disequilibrium, forcing the wage rate higher and creating an excess supply of 400 workers.

9. Refer to the preceding diagram. If the minimum wage is set below the equilibrium wage, at $5.00,
    (a)   there will be an excess demand for labor of 400.
    (b)   there will be an excess supply labor of 400.
    (c)   the equilibrium wage rate will move from $6.
    (d)   there will be no effect on the labor market.

    ANSWER: (d) A minimum wage places a lower limit on the wage rate. In this market, given demand and supply conditions, the lowest the wage will go is $6.00. ■

Objective 3

Describe the current pattern of income distribution. Identify the information provided by the Lorenz curve and the Gini coefficient.

Economic income includes wages, salaries, dividends, interest received, proprietors' income, government transfer, rent, and so on. Capital gains are also included. Money income excludes government payments-in-kind (such as Medicare and Medicaid), and items such as capital gains, noncash gifts, and noncash inheritances. Money income is less inclusive and more evenly distributed than economic income.

   The distribution of income in the United States has remained quite stable for several decades. The *Lorenz curve* is a graphical device for describing the distribution of income in an economy. The *Gini coefficient* is a numerical measure of income inequality. A Gini coefficient of zero indicates a perfectly equal income distribution whereas the maximum score (one) indicates perfect inequality. If income were distributed equally, the Lorenz curve would be a 45° line. The more unequal distribution is, the more the curve bends below the 45° line, and the greater the Gini coefficient will be. U.S. income distribution is affected by race and size of household. (page 370)

ECONOMICS IN PRACTICE: On page 373, the textbook considers the increase in income inequality over the past thirty years. First, what does the reported study by Piketty and Saez suggest is the new major source of inequality in income? What was the major cause of income inequality in the past?
ANSWER: The researchers claim that, nowadays, the bulk of income inequality is due to inequality in returns to the workforce whereas previously inequality had been due largely to differences in the ownership of capital.

ECONOMICS IN PRACTICE (CONTINUED): One aspect of inequality that has attracted attention, as reported by Frydman, is the rapid growth in executive compensation. Four factors are briefly offered regarding this modern burgeoning of executive compensation. What are these four factors?
ANSWER: First, it must be observed that there is a great deal of debate on this topic. However, among possible factors are growth of the average size of the firm, the increased valuation of scarce human capital, changes in corporate governance, and changes in social norms.

ECONOMICS IN PRACTICE (CONTINUED): After the financial bailout in 2009, President Obama imposed pay restrictions on the executives of firms who had received federal assistance. What is your opinion of this regulation of the market for managerial skills? Do you think such a restriction will be successful in limiting salaries?
ANSWER: Opinions will differ regarding the desirability of the 2009 restriction. Evidence suggests, however, that businesses tend to find inventive ways to circumvent such restrictions. A widespread freeze on salaries and prices in the 1970s, for instance, was sidestepped by having employees receive "promotions," which justified higher compensation. In the 1990s, stock options became popular following a limitation on CEO salary tax deductability. Generous perks and severance packages were due to the same restriction.

Practice

10. The amount of money a household can spend without changing its net assets is called its
    (a) money income.
    (b) net property income.
    (c) economic income.
    (d) after-tax (disposable) income.
    ANSWER: (c) Refer to the definition on page 370.

11. According to the textbook, in 2006 the top 20 percent of households earned about _____ times as much total income as the bottom 20 percent.
    (a) three
    (b) four.
    (c) seven.
    (d) fourteen.
    ANSWER: (d) Refer to page 370 and Table 18.1. 47.5 percent/3.4 percent = 14.0.

12. A Gini coefficient of one means that
    (a) income is distributed equally.
    (b) all income is earned by one individual.
    (c) 50 percent of income is earned by the poorest 50 percent of the population.
    (d) 20 percent of income is earned by the richest 20 percent (quintile) of the population.
    ANSWER: (b) If the Gini coefficient is one, one individual earns all the income. The Lorenz curve would lie along the horizontal axis until 100 percent.

13.   In the bottom 10 percent of families, transfers account for more than _____ of income.
      (a)   20 percent
      (b)   50 percent
      (c)   75 percent
      (d)   80 percent
      ANSWER: (d)   Refer to the discussion on page 370.

14.   The Gini coefficient indicates the
      (a)   percentage of households below the poverty line.
      (b)   extent of income inequality in the economy.
      (c)   proportion of households with below-average earnings.
      (d)   proportion of money income that is in the form of transfer payments.
      ANSWER: (b)   The Gini coefficient is a measure of income inequality. ∎

Objective 4

Describe the trend in income inequality globally and identify possible causes.

Globally, 15 percent of the world's population lives in low-income countries, with an average annual per capita income of $650 in 2008. In both the advanced and developing countries, income distribution has shown a trend towards greater inequality. The reasons for this trend is the subject of debate, with possible sources being free trade, immigration, globalization (weakening the middle-income workers), technological change (strengthening the well-educated), or deregulation and declines in union power. While evidence on the impact of immigration is mixed, the role of technological change in increasing disparity seems clear. Inequality has been reduced somewhat by trade liberalization. (page 372)

Practice

15.   In general, over the past several decades, income inequality has been _____ in the advanced countries and _____ in the developing countries.
      (a)   increasing; increasing
      (b)   increasing; decreasing
      (c)   decreasing; increasing
      (d)   decreasing; decreasing
      ANSWER: (a)   Refer to page 373.

16.   Studies suggest that technological change has _____ income inequality and trade liberalization has _____ income inequality.
      (a)   increased; increased
      (b)   increased; decreased
      (c)   decreased; increased
      (d)   decreased; decreased
      ANSWER: (b)   Refer to page 373. ∎

Objective 5

Give the official definition of poverty. Describe the trend in poverty in the United States over the past four decades and distinguish between the poverty rates of different groups within the economy.

Poverty may be measured in either absolute or relative terms. The official U.S. poverty line is three times the cost of a nutritionally sound minimum "bundle" of food. A total of 36.5 million persons (14.3 percent of the population) were below the poverty line in 2009, compared with 22 percent in 1960 and 12.8 percent in the late 1980s. The poverty rate is higher among African-Americans and Hispanics than among whites, and women without husbands form the group with the highest poverty rate. (page 375)

Poverty: As you read through the statistics and assess the effectiveness of the income-redistribution programs outlined in this chapter, bear in mind the following: the poor are most often the children of the poor and the rich are most often the children of the rich. Poverty is strongly linked to family background. Additionally, most of those in poverty have failed to complete 10 years of schooling. What should this tell you about the importance of *human capital?*

Keep in mind the *underclass*, the group that even the statistics fail to measure, or programs help, simply because they have dropped out of the system. Do our poverty and income distribution figures record people such as teenage runaways, the rural unemployed, undocumented aliens, deinstitutionalized mental patients, or drug addicts? Are these groups part of the poverty problem?

Practice

17. Of the following groups, the one with the highest poverty rate is
    (a) Hispanics.
    (b) women living in households with no husband present.
    (c) children.
    (d) senior citizens.

    ANSWER: (b) Refer to Table 18.5 on page 376.

18. If the Department of Agriculture determines that the cost of a minimum food bundle is $5,000 per year, the poverty line is established at
    (a) $5,000 per year.
    (b) $10,000 per year.
    (c) $15,000 per year.
    (d) $20,000 per year.

    ANSWER: (c) The official poverty line is determined by multiplying the cost of the food bundle by three. Refer to the definition on page 375. ∎

Objective 6

State the arguments for and against redistribution of income. Summarize the theories underlying these arguments.

The main argument *against income redistribution* is that one should be allowed to retain one's earnings— for Angela to receive extra income, for example, Bill must lose some of his. A disincentive to work may exist both for the individual who loses income *and* for the transfer's recipient. It is argued that the U.S. economic system is based on private property ownership and freedom of contract. Redistribution might undermine the system and reduce incentives to improve oneself. (page 377)

The main argument *in support of income distribution* is a moral appeal—the rich should help those less fortunate than themselves enjoy the necessities of life. The utilitarians, Rawls, and Marx have all constructed quite sophisticated philosophical formulations in support of this view. (page 378)

In practice, most countries undertake some redistribution of income and wealth. Usually this is done through a progressive income tax system—where progressively higher tax rates are applied to the incomes of individuals with higher incomes—and through government payments (transfers). In the United States the overall tax system is only mildly progressive, but the transfer programs—including, among others, Social Security, "welfare," unemployment compensation, Medicare, and Medicaid—do pay most benefits to those in lower income brackets.

ECONOMICS IN PRACTICE: On page 384, the textbook looks at the issue of charitable giving and the "price of giving." It can be argued that, if the tax rate is increased, taxable dollars become worth less to taxpayers and donations to charity will increase. Clearly, individuals derive satisfaction from giving—Americans donate over $250 billion per year and respond to disasters like Hurricane Katrina with generous gifts of cash, goods, and time. However, in 2008, the American Red Cross reported that they were running out of funds for emergencies—private donations were not enough. Why does the government have to "subsidize" private charities by reducing the tax liabilities of contributors?

ANSWER: Although high-profile disasters (Hurricane Katrina or a tsunami) provoke high volumes of donations, privately funded efforts to care for communities in crisis and to alleviate poverty, hunger, and disease, are undersubscribed because their objective is a public good. If others in society voluntarily contribute and reduce poverty, slums, and street crime, I will benefit without having to make a contribution—the "free-rider" problem. In addition, any contribution I make will be an insignificant part of the total effort so self-interest dictates that I do not contribute—the "drop in the bucket" problem. Private charities will then have inadequate resources, requiring the government to become involved.

Practice

19. "A dollar is worth less to a rich person than to a poor person." This is a basic belief of
    (a) utilitarian justice.
    (b) Rawlsian justice.
    (c) Marxian justice.
    (d) social justice.

    ANSWER: (a) Utilitarians would argue that redistribution from rich to poor increases society's total utility. Refer to page 379.

20. _____ is a theory of income distribution that claims that the social contract emerging from the original position would maximize the well-being of the _____ .
    (a) Utilitarian justice; most typical member of society
    (b) Utilitarian justice; worst-off member of society
    (c) Rawlsian justice; most typical member of society
    (d) Rawlsian justice; worst-off member of society

    ANSWER: (d) In the original position, each member of society, according to Rawls, will be concerned about the position of the least fortunate.

21. Each of the following is an assumption in Rawls's theory except that
    (a) individuals are risk averse.
    (b) individuals may become rich.
    (c) individuals may become poor.
    (d) individuals may opt out of the social contract.

    ANSWER: (d) Bargaining will continue until all members of society agree on a contract.

22.   Marx argued that _____ value derives from labor and that profits were _____ .
        (a)   all; a necessary return for ownership of resources and risk-taking
        (b)   all; an expropriation of surplus value
        (c)   some; a necessary return for ownership of resources and risk-taking
        (d)   some; an expropriation of surplus value

        ANSWER: (b) According to Marx, the value of production depends solely on the amount of labor required to produce it. ■

Objective 7

Describe the two major government redistribution programs and the groups that they seek to reach.

The government has used two broad sets of programs to affect the distribution of income—taxes and expenditure programs. (page 380)

(a) *The tax system.* The progressivity of the income tax system is set against evidence that the U.S. tax system overall is almost proportional—each taxpayer, regardless of income, pays pretty much the same percentage of her or his income to the government. Conclusion: There's little income distribution being caused by the tax system.

(b) *Transfer and other expenditure programs.* Despite the purpose and scope of government expenditure programs, poverty has increased in recent years. Whether this is due to inadequate economic growth or inadequate redistribution programs remains an open question.

Welfare has been under increasing attack in recent years. The system may reduce incentives to work, be unfair to those who do work but receive low pay, and it may undermine "family values." Opponents also contend that welfare has failed in its goal—the number of households in poverty is higher than ever. Finally, if poverty is relative (refer to page 375), it may make more sense to dismantle the single national system and place responsibility at the state/local level.

Welfare Cadillacs: Abuses exist in government transfer programs—we are tempted to believe that "welfare" recipients are spongers. Despite this stereotype, a recent report indicated that 41.7 percent of poor people had a job and that only one-third of poor people received welfare. The same report indicated that 20 million Americans suffered from hunger each month.

Practice

23.   _____ is the transfer program given the credit for significantly reducing poverty among senior citizens.
        (a)   Medicare
        (b)   Social Security
        (c)   Food Stamps
        (d)   Temporary Assistance for Needy Families

        ANSWER: (b) Refer to page 381 for a description of the program and its effects.

24.   The Social Security system includes all of the following programs EXCEPT
        (a)   unemployment compensation.
        (b)   disability insurance program.
        (c)   health insurance program.
        (d)   OASI.

        ANSWER: (a) Refer to page 382. Unemployment compensation is part of the public assistance (welfare) program. ■

CONCLUSION

The chapter ends by pulling together some of the themes developed during earlier chapters. A market system operating with complete efficiency may still not be considered fair because some people—through handicap or inborn talent, luck, lack of education, or unemployment—will have more or less than others. In theory, efforts at redistribution should be aimed at redistributing well-being or *utility* which (unfortunately) is neither observable nor measurable. Income and wealth are substitute measures of utility. The government's income-redistribution program itself is an imperfect instrument, and the debate continues as to the appropriate extent of government intervention in the economy.

BRAIN TEASER SOLUTION: Since 1967, income distribution has remained remarkably constant with some slight movement towards greater inequality. Refer to Table 18.2 in the textbook for details. Wealth is less evenly distributed than income, being more concentrated in fewer families. One estimate by the Federal Reserve System reports that the richest 1 percent of households owned 38 percent of the nation's total net worth while our textbook notes that 70 percent of net worth is owned by the richest 10 percent while the lowest 40 percent holds only 2.6 percent.

PRACTICE TEST

I. MULTIPLE-CHOICE QUESTIONS

Select the option that provides the single best answer.

_____ 1. Inefficiency is shown in a utility possibilities frontier diagram by
    (a) a point inside the curve.
    (b) a point outside the curve.
    (c) the point where the curve reaches the vertical axis.
    (d) any point not on the curve.

_____ 2. If the Gini coefficient is equal to zero, all of the following certainly are true EXCEPT
    (a) the Lorenz curve graphs as a straight line.
    (b) income is equally distributed.
    (c) the lowest quintile of the population will receive as many dollars as the highest quintile.
    (d) we have an efficient distribution of income.

_____ 3. Society consists of two individuals, Richie Rich, (a millionaire who is so obsessed with money that his marginal utility of income increases with each extra dollar he gets) and Kermit the Hermit (a recluse who has rejected money and other earthly goods and finds that his marginal utility of income decreases with each extra dollar he gets). If income is transferred from the rich to the poor, we can say that society's
    (a) total utility will increase.
    (b) total utility will decrease.
    (c) total utility will remain unchanged.
    (d) total utility will change, but the net effect is uncertain.

_____ 4. Government retraining programs can be viewed as
    (a) an inefficient method of income redistribution.
    (b) an investment in human capital.
    (c) a movement away from the utility possibilities frontier.
    (d) regressive programs.

_____ 5. Which of the following is not a reason for variations in income from wages and salaries?
 (a) Ownership of differing amounts of human capital
 (b) Compensating differentials
 (c) Unemployment
 (d) Ownership of differing amounts of real capital

_____ 6. A politician promising to support greater equality of property income on one hand, and a more efficient allocation of resources on the other, may well be committed to two
 (a) conflicting objectives. The more efficient and rewarding the property market is, the more participants there will be.
 (b) conflicting objectives. To achieve efficiency it may be necessary to let investors earn large rewards from their investment.
 (c) complementary objectives. Efficiency and equality must go hand in hand in a growing market economy.
 (d) complementary objectives. The more efficient and rewarding the property market is, the more participants there will be.

_____ 7. If the resource markets work correctly, then rewards are based on productivity. Therefore,
 (a) because capital adds to the productivity of labor, owners of capital should earn a higher return.
 (b) because labor is essential to all production processes, labor should be paid a higher rate of return.
 (c) wages and salaries should be paid in accordance with the marginal productivity of workers.
 (d) because there are more workers than machines, labor should be cheaper to hire and so earn less.

_____ 8. Income redistribution is considered a public good. Which of the following is a problem for implementing income redistribution as it relates to public goods?
 (a) People see no point in contributing voluntarily because their contribution will be insignificant.
 (b) People deserve to retain the fruits of their labors.
 (c) Giving people handouts may reduce their incentives to work and save.
 (d) The poor are often "free riders" living on welfare.

_____ 9. The income tax system is "progressive." This means that
 (a) progressively more persons are taxed each year.
 (b) those with higher income pay a higher percentage of it in taxes.
 (c) if a person earning $10,000 pays $3,000 in taxes, a person earning $20,000 would pay twice as much ($6,000) in taxes.
 (d) the more you earn, the more you pay.

_____ 10. Which of the following is an argument for income redistribution?
 (a) Everyone is entitled to keep the fruits of his or her own efforts.
 (b) There is freedom of contract.
 (c) Society has a moral obligation to provide for the basic needs of all citizens.
 (d) Redistribution reduces incentives to work, save, and invest.

_____ 11. In successive decades, Country A records a Gini coefficient of 0.3 (1980s), 0.7 (1990s), and 1.0 (2000s). Population has remained stable throughout the time period. We can state that
   (a) Country A's income distribution has become more equal as time has passed.
   (b) Country A had fewer poor people in the 2000s than in the 1980s.
   (c) the top 20 percent of income was earned by a smaller number of families in the 2000s than in the 1980s.
   (d) the gap between Country A's Lorenz curve and the 45° line has decreased as time has passed.

_____ 12. Jackie Blue is a police officer who patrols a dangerous high-crime neighborhood. Jackie earns more than officers who work in low-crime neighborhoods. This is an example of a
   (a) return on human capital.
   (b) compensating differential.
   (c) productivity differential.
   (d) compensating productivity differential.

_____ 13. If we plot a Lorenz curve for U.S. income and another for U.S. wealth, the Lorenz curve for income will be _____ bowed; its Gini coefficient will be _____ .
   (a) more; larger
   (b) more; smaller
   (c) less; larger
   (d) less; smaller

_____ 14. The U.S. government could probably reduce the Gini coefficient by
   (a) reducing government spending on welfare programs.
   (b) eliminating student loan programs.
   (c) increasing taxes on inherited wealth.
   (d) cutting the capital gains tax rates.

_____ 15. If the area between the Lorenz curve and the line of perfect equality became larger, we could conclude that the distribution of income had become
   (a) more unequal.
   (b) less unequal.
   (c) more inefficient.
   (d) less inefficient.

_____ 16. According to Marx, the major source of inequality in the distribution of income is
   (a) property income.
   (b) labor income.
   (c) human capitalism.
   (d) social contracts.

_____ 17.   Alice and Betty have trained as nurses in Memphis. Alice moves to New York to work in a private hospital and earns $30,000. Betty moves to New Orleans to work as a community health nurse and earns $15,000. The cost of living is about 15 percent higher in New York than in New Orleans. Which of the following is true?
(a)   Alice is better off than Betty, because she earns $15,000 more.
(b)   Betty must be better off, because she did not need to take the job for $30,000.
(c)   Alice must be better off, because her earnings are double those of Betty but the cost of living in New York is less than double that in New Orleans.
(d)   We cannot determine who is better off, because income is an imperfect measure of utility.

Use the following utility possibilities frontier to answer the next question.

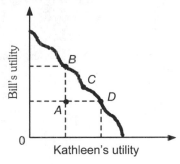

_____ 18.   Which of the following moves is (are) efficient?
(a)   *A* to *B*
(b)   *A* to *C*
(c)   *A* to *D*
(d)   All of the above moves are efficient.

Use the following Lorenz curve for the nation of Arboc to answer the next two questions.

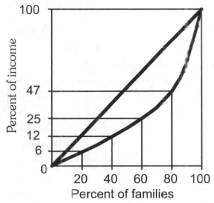

_____ 19.   The top fifth of Arbocali families earn _____ percent of income.
(a)   20
(b)   47
(c)   53
(d)   80

_____ 20. The third fifth of families earn _____ percent of income.
    (a)   6
    (b)   12
    (c)   13
    (d)   25

II. APPLICATION QUESTIONS

1. Use the following income distribution for the nation of Arboc.

Personal Income Class	Percent of All Families In This Class	Percent of Total Income Received By This Class	Percent of All Families In This and All Lower Classes	Percent of Total Income Received by This and All Lower Classes
Under $5,000	20	2	20	2
5,000–9,999	10	5	30	7
10,000–14,999	12	10	____	____
15,000–19,999	15	15	____	____
20,000–24,999	20	16	____	____
25,000–49,999	13	22	____	____
50,000 and over	10	30	100	100

    (a) Complete the preceding table.

    (b) Households earning less than $10,000 make up the lowest _____ percent of the population and receive _____ percent of the income, whereas those earning $25,000 or more make up _____ percent of the population and receive _____ percent of the income.

    (c) Use the information in the table to plot a Lorenz curve in the space below. Remember to plot the zero-zero point and to draw as smooth a curve as possible. Shade in the area on the graph that indicates inequality in income.

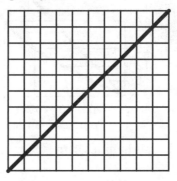

2. A tax is progressive (refer to page 380) if those with higher incomes pay a higher percentage of their income in tax. The opposite is called a regressive tax, i.e., those with higher incomes pay a lower percentage of their income in tax.
    (a) A progressive tax will make income distribution _____ (more/less) equal.

Three sales tax proposals have come before your state government. In each case, identify whether the tax will be progressive or regressive and its effect on the distribution of income.

(b)   A 20 percent sales tax on fur coats

(c)   A 12 percent sales tax on groceries

(d)   A general sales tax of 6 percent on all goods

3.   The Department of Agriculture has determined that a nutritionally sound minimum food bundle costs $23 per week per person.

(a)   Calculate the poverty line for a family of four.

The U.S. Bureau of the Census provides the following information for four-person families. There are 14,556,000 four-person families in the United States.

Income	Percentage of Families	Percentage of Income (Cumulative)
$75,000 and over	15.3	100.0
$50,000–$74,999	22.5	37.5
$35,000–$49,999	22.9	25.0
$25,000–$34,999	14.9	17.5
$15,000–$24,999	12.4	12.5
$10,000–$14,999	4.8	7.5
$5,000–$9,999	4.6	5.0
Under $5,000	2.7	2.5

(b)   Using the data points you have, plot a Lorenz curve for four-person families.

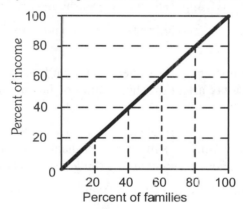

(c)   Draw a line (AB) perpendicular to the 45° line to the lower right-hand corner of the Lorenz curve diagram. The portion of this line between the Lorenz curve and the 45° line (AC), when divided by AB, gives an approximate estimate of the Gini coefficient. Estimate the Gini coefficient for this economy.

(d)   Given the income distribution above, calculate the poverty rate for four-person families. The poverty rate is the percentage of four-person families with incomes below the poverty line.

Mona Gregson is a twenty-five-year-old single mother with three children, Rachel, 8, Peter, 7, and Michael, 2. Mona dropped out of high school when she became pregnant with Rachel and never graduated. She has no marketable job skills and has never had a job. Each month, Mona receives $800 in Temporary Assistance for Needy Families and $300 in food stamps. She has applied for a housing subsidy but has been rejected. The family is eligible for Medicaid. Assume that she pays no taxes.

(e)   What is the Gregsons' money income? In the income distribution above, where does Mona's family fit? Are they poor?

(f)   What is Mona's annual economic income?

(g)   Mona's food stamp allowance is increased to $400 per month. How does this affect her economic income? Her money income? Her position in the income distribution?

The state government has instituted a 15-week vocational training program. The participant's welfare benefits are maintained and (s)he receives a modest travel allowance. Day care facilities are available during the program and for the first year after the trainee begins to work.

On completion of the program, the graduate will receive a $7.25 per hour clerical job with the state government. Monthly income is $1,200. However, 7.65 percent will go to FICA (Federal social security payroll tax) and 1.35 percent will go to state payroll tax. Annual Federal and state income tax payments will be $660. Commuting/parking fees amount to $25 per month.

(h)   If Mona completes the program and gets the promised clerical job, will the Gregsons still be below the poverty line?

(i)   Are the Gregsons better off with Mona employed or on welfare?

(j)   Calculate the "tax" imposed on Mona as she moves from welfare to work.

(k)   If Mona wishes to maximize her net income, should she stay on welfare or enter the training program?

The state government implements a 15 percent tax on food items.

(l) How will this new tax affect the distribution of income in Mona's state? How will the Gini coefficient change?

You decide to contribute $100 to help alleviate poverty. Family A and Family B are identical in all respects except that Family A is much poorer than Family B.

(m)   Would you be happier seeing your $100 go to Family A or to Family B?

(n)   Would you be happy if you kept your money and someone else contributed $100 to Family A?

Case, Fair and Oster suggest that income redistribution is a public good (refer to page 380). My increased happiness (from reduced income inequality) does not interfere with your happiness—nonrivalry. If income distribution becomes more equal, I cannot be excluded from the benefits—nonexcludability.

Two points arise: Contributions provide (some) satisfaction for the donor but, acting independently, the donor's benefits will probably be less than the costs. As the income level of the recipient rises, the marginal benefit derived *by the donor* from extra contributions decreases. The *MB* (marginal benefit) curve in the following diagram below reflects these conclusions. The marginal cost of a dollar donated is a dollar for the contributor. The *MC private* curve reflects this conclusion.

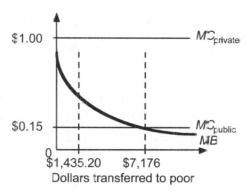

The poverty line is drawn at $14,352, and about 12 percent of families are "poor." Suppose that the average income of "poor" households is $14,352/2, or $7,176. The distribution above shows that 60 percent of families (the "well-off") earn $35,000 or more.

(o)   Each poor family requires how much, on average, to reach the poverty line? Ignore taxes and so on.

(p)   If each "well-off" family contributes an equal amount, how much would they have to contribute to alleviate poverty?

(q)   Explain why each well-off family, acting independently, will not contribute the amount you determined in Part (p). Use the preceding diagram.

(r)   The well-off families get together and sign a binding contract to contribute $1,435.20 each to help alleviate poverty. Explain why each well-off family will find it worthwhile to contribute.

(s)   Explain why such a contract is unlikely to be enacted.

4.   Imagine that, today, you lose your job (either real or imagined). You still have whatever savings and other assets you previously had, but you have no other immediate source of income, including welfare checks or parents. You still have any financial commitments previously contracted. How would you react to this financial crisis? As the days pass, you may begin to see the real distress concealed behind unemployment and poverty statistics and the genuine relief offered by government programs.

5.   To get a feel for poverty, volunteer at a local soup kitchen.

6.   Suppose that, in a two-person economy, there exists the following utility possibilities frontier.

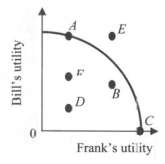

(a)   Which of the points is currently unattainable?

(b)   Which point would Bill prefer, *B* or *F*?

(c)   Which points represent maximum efficiency?

(d)   Why would Bill and Frank welcome a move from Point *D* to Point *B* on the curve?

(e)   Why would there be opposition to a move from *D* to *C*, but no opposition to a move from *D* to *A?*

7.   What is the meaning of equity and why might economists study it? Why might it be difficult to study? Is a more equal distribution of income also more equitable? Do you think that there might be a trade-off between equality and equity? If so, given your knowledge of the present distribution of income in the United States, would you favor more equality or more equity?

Practice Test SOLUTIONS

I. SOLUTIONS TO MULTIPLE-CHOICE QUESTIONS

1. (a)   A point inside the curve indicates that individual I or J, or both, could increase satisfaction without the other individual losing anything.

2. (d)   The income distribution is certainly equal, but it doesn't follow that it is efficient.

3. (b)   This is the opposite case to the one suggested by the utilitarians. Redistributing income from Richie to Kermit would reduce the total utility of each. To increase total utility, the redistribution should be reversed.

4. (b)   Training or retraining programs develop the talents and improve the skills of the labor force—i.e., they are an investment in human capital.

5. (d)   Ownership of real capital will result in nonwage income.

6. (b)   The politician is dealing with the arguments for and against redistribution (pp. 377-380). One argument against redistribution is that it reduces incentives to work and, therefore, reduces efficiency.

7. (c)   Note, though, that this is not the Marxian view.

8. (a)   This is the "drop-in-the-bucket" problem. Refer to page 380. For a more complete discussion of the characteristics and problems of public goods, return to pp. 341-343.

9. (b)   With a progressive tax system, extra earnings are taxed at higher rates. Option (d) is true whenever the marginal tax rate is positive, even if the tax system is not progressive.

10. (c)   Option (c) is an argument often used by those who favor income redistribution. The other options are cases made against income redistribution.

11. (c)   As the Gini coefficient increases, income inequality increases.

12. (b)   Because Jackie has a more dangerous, less attractive "beat," the extra payment she receives is a compensating differential. Refer to page 368.

13. (d)   U.S. income is more evenly distributed than U.S. wealth, so the Lorenz curve for income will be less bowed. The gap between the 45° line and the Lorenz curve (the Gini coefficient) will be smaller.

14. (c)   Taxing inheritances would reduce property income for subsequent generations.

15. (a)   The greater the gap, the greater the inequality.

16. (a)   For a summary of Marx's views, refer to page 379.

17. (d)   "It is important that you remember throughout this chapter that income and wealth are imperfect measures of well-being." Refer to page 377.

18. (d) A move is efficient if the utility of one individual increases without a decrease in the utility of the other.

19. (c) 80 percent of families earn 47 percent of the income; the remaining 53 percent of income is earned by the top 20 percent.

20. (c) The lowest 40 percent earn 12 percent of income. The lowest 60 percent earn 25 percent. By subtraction, the third fifth of families earns 13 percent.

II. SOLUTIONS TO APPLICATION QUESTIONS

1. (a) Refer to the following table.

Personal Income Class	Percent of All Families In This Class	Percent of Total Income Received By This Class	Percent of All Families In This and All Lower Classes	Percent Total Income Received By This and All Lower Classes
Under $5,000	20	2	20	2
5,000–9,999	10	5	30	7
10,000–14,999	12	10	42	17
15,000–19,999	15	15	57	32
20,000–24,999	20	16	77	48
25,000–49,999	13	22	90	70
50,000 and over	10	30	100	100

(b) 30; 7; 23; 52.

(c) Refer to the following diagram.

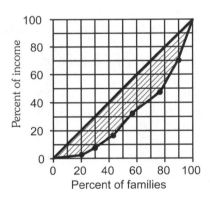

2. (a) more

(b) Progressive. Fur coats are bought predominantly by rich individuals, so poor families will be unaffected and rich purchasers will pay the tax.

(c) Regressive. A 6 percent sales tax on groceries must be paid by all households, but the poor spend a relatively larger proportion of their income of groceries so their tax payment will be relatively greater.

(d)   Regressive. A general sales tax is more broadly based than a food tax but, because poor households spend most or all of their income whereas rich households do not, the relative tax payment of the poor will be greater.

3.   (a) $23 × 4 × 52 × 3 = $14,352

        (b)   Refer to the following diagram.

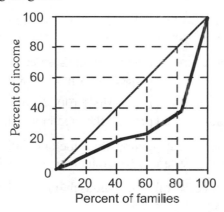

        (c)   The Gini coefficient = AC/AB = 11/28 = 0.39. Refer to the following diagram.

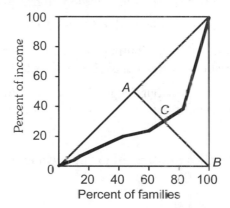

        (d) $14,352 is about 87 percent of the way through the third class. Correspondingly, 4.18 percent is about 87 percent of 4.8 percent. 2.7 percent + 4.6 percent + 4.18 percent = 11.48 percent of four-person families are in poverty. This amounts to 1,671,029 four-person families in poverty.

        (e)   The Gregsons are below the poverty line. Their yearly income is $800 × 12, or $9,600. Food Stamps, which are in-kind transfers, are not figured in. In the table, the Gregsons would be in the third-lowest category.

        (f)   Economic income would include both the cash and in-kind payments. The Gregsons' annual economic income would be ($800 + $300) × 12 = $13,200.

        (g)   Mona's economic income will rise by $100 per month. Annual economic income is $14,400. Her money income and her position in the income distribution are unchanged.

        (h)   Mona's gross annual income will be $1,200 × 12 = $14,400. This is (just) above the poverty line of $14,352.

        (i)   The Gregsons are worse off. Their gross income is $14,400. Deductions include payroll taxes of (0.0765 + 0.0135) × $14,400, or $1,296, income taxes of $660, and commuting/parking fees of $300. Total deductions are $2,256. The Gregsons' income, after deductions, is $12,144 which is less than her economic income from welfare ($14,400).

(j)   Taxes while on welfare = $0. Taxes while working = $1,956. Change = $1,956. Welfare income = $14,400. Work income: $14,400. Change = $0. Mona's income didn't change, but her tax liability increased by $1,956. This is a clear disincentive to work. Note that she also loses Medicaid benefits.

(k)   Unless she wishes to feel self-supporting, or she believes that the starting-level job will lead to higher wage positions, Mona should stay on welfare.

(l)   The distribution of income will become less equal. Refer to the answer to Part (c). The Gini coefficient will move closer to a value of 1.00.

(m)   Most persons would agree that the $100 would be worth more to Family *A* and that helping that family would provide the greater satisfaction.

(n)   Most persons derive satisfaction from the alleviation of poverty, especially if they don't have to pay for it. We cannot be excluded from this benefit if we refuse to contribute.

(o)   If the average income of "poor" households is $7,176, each family needs an additional $7,176 on average.

(p)   (12 percent/60 percent) × $7,176 = $1,435.20 per "well-off" household.

(q)   The marginal benefit of transferring $1,435.20 is less than the private marginal cost.

(r)   The families will find contributing $1,435.20 worthwhile because, by acting as a group, the marginal cost of transferring $7,176 dollars has been reduced for each family.

(s)   Poverty alleviation is a public good. If every other well-off family contributes and I don't, I get the benefits without the cost. If each family follows the same logic, no one will sign.

4–5.   The answers to these Applications are left to your own initiative.

6.   (a)   *E*

    (b)   *F*

    (c)   *A* and *C*. Any point on the frontier is a point of maximum efficiency.

    (d)   There would be an increase in utility for each.

    (e)   A move from *D* to *C* would reduce Bill's utility—he would certainly oppose this. However, a move from *D* to *A* would increase Bill's utility without reducing Frank's. (In terms of efficiency, what does this mean?)

19

Public Finance:
The Economics of Taxation

Chapter Objectives

1. Distinguish between the tax base and the tax rate structure. Distinguish among progressive, proportional, and regressive taxes.
2. Distinguish between the benefits-received principle and the ability-to-pay principle of taxation.
3. Evaluate the merit of consumption, expenditures, income and wealth as candidates for the "best" tax base.
4. Explain why households are the ultimate payers of all taxes—i.e., bear the incidence of the tax. Comment on the factors affecting the incidence of a particular tax, such as a payroll tax or corporation profits tax.
5. Define and measure excess burden and explain the principle of tax neutrality.
6. Demonstrate graphically the presence of the excess burden following the imposition of a tax, linking the resulting distortion to the relative elasticity of demand.
7. Describe the principle of second best.

There are many previously developed concepts at work in this chapter—demand and supply, consumer surplus, elasticity, income and substitution effects, marginal thinking, opportunity costs, etc. With respect to increasing the incentive to save, by cutting the marginal tax rate, the opportunity cost of a dollar spent is increased, so fewer dollars will be spent and more will be saved.

BRAIN TEASER: A progressive income tax system takes a larger fraction of income from a high-income taxpayer than from a low-income taxpayer, while a regressive tax system takes a smaller fraction of income from a high-income taxpayer. As a taxpayer, which tax system would you prefer?

Objective 1

Distinguish between the tax base and the tax rate structure. Distinguish among progressive, proportional, and regressive taxes.

Ultimately all taxes are paid by households. Each tax has two components: a *base*—the value on which the tax is levied—and a *rate structure*. The tax base of an income tax is income. Three candidates for the "best" tax base are consumption, income, and wealth. A given tax may be progressive, proportional, or regressive. A *progressive* (*regressive*) tax takes a larger (smaller) fraction of income from a high-income person than from a low-income person. A *proportional* tax takes the same fraction of income from everyone, regardless of income. With progressive taxes, the marginal tax rate is higher than the average tax rate. With regressive taxes, the marginal tax rate is lower than the average tax rate. (page 389)

> **LEARNING TIP:** Perhaps the single most important paragraph in Chapter 19 occurs on page 391, where marginal and average tax rates are distinguished. Keep in mind that it's the *marginal* tax rate that influences an individual's behavior—his or her outlook or working, saving, or investing a bit more or a bit less. ◀

ECONOMICS IN PRACTICE: On page 392 the textbook examines the structure of income tax rates in the United States. A common perception amongst taxpayers is that U.S. taxes are relatively high. But is this perception correct? The 1966 Beatles' song "Taxman" contains the line "It's one for you, nineteen for me" which refers to a supertax of 95 percent that was imposed on high income earners at the time by the British government. What is the average personal income tax rate paid by American taxpayers? How does this compare to other the G-7 countries (Japan, Canada, United Kingdom, Italy, France, Germany)?

ANSWER: In the United States, the average personal income tax rate is 28 percent. Relatively, this is quite low. In fact, only Japan (26 percent) has a lower personal tax rate while the rates in the other countries range from 32 percent (Canada) to 50 percent (France) and 53 percent (Germany).

Practice

1.   The measure or value on which a tax is levied is called the
        (a)   tax burden.
        (b)   tax structure.
        (c)   tax base.
        (d)   tax incidence.
        ANSWER: (c)   Refer to the definition on page 389.

2.   A regressive income tax has a(n) _____ marginal tax rate and a(n) _____ average tax rate.
        (a)   increasing; increasing
        (b)   increasing; decreasing
        (c)   decreasing; increasing
        (d)   decreasing; decreasing
        ANSWER: (d)   As income increases, more taxes must be paid, but a relatively smaller fraction of income is taxed away.

3.   We have a progressive income tax system. Jack earns $20,000 and pays $6,000 in taxes. Jill earns $40,000. She could pay _____ in taxes.
        (a) $6,000
        (b) $9,000
        (c) $12,000
        (d) $14,000
        ANSWER: (d)   Jill's income is double Jack's. In a progressive tax system, her tax liability will be more than double that of Jack.

Use the following information for the next four questions.

Income	TotalTaxes
$10,000	$1,000
$20,000	$4,000
$30,000	$7,000
$40,000	$12,000

4.   As income increases from $20,000 to $30,000, the marginal tax rate is
        (a)   10 percent.
        (b)   20 percent.
        (c)   25 percent.
        (d)   30 percent.
        ANSWER: (d)   Marginal tax rate is the change in total tax divided by the change in income. $(7,000 - 4,000)/(30,000 - 20,000) = 30$ percent.

5.   As income increases from $20,000 to $40,000, the marginal tax rate is
   (a)   20 percent.
   (b)   25 percent.
   (c)   30 percent.
   (d)   40 percent.

   ANSWER: (d)   Marginal tax rate is the change in total tax divided by the change in income.
         (12,000 – 4,000)/(40,000 – 20,000) = 40 percent.

6.   When the income level is $20,000, the average tax rate is
   (a)   10 percent.
   (b)   20 percent.
   (c)   25 percent.
   (d)   30 percent.

   ANSWER: (b)   Average tax rate is total tax/income. $4,000/$20,000 = 20 percent.

7.   The tax structure in this example is
   (a)   progressive.
   (b)   proportional.
   (c)   regressive.
   (d)   progressive at first, then regressive.

   ANSWER: (a)   Average tax rates increase as income level increases. ∎

Objective 2

Distinguish between the benefits-received principle and the ability-to-pay principle of taxation.

Two principles are used to judge whether a tax is "fair":
a.   the ability-to-pay principle suggests that those who are more able to pay should pay more.
b.   the benefits-received principle suggests that those who receive the benefits of the expenditures financed by a tax should be the ones to pay. (page 393)

   If the ability to pay principle is preferred, two additional principles—horizontal equity and vertical equity—follow. Those with equal abilities to pay should bear equal burdens (horizontal equity) while those who can pay more should pay more. This raises the issue of the "best" tax base (consumption, income, or wealth) and the degree of difference in contributions.

> **LEARNING TIP:** Make up a list of taxes and try to determine which principle is present. You should find that the ability-to-pay principle is favored in the United States.
>
> Note the disincentives that can occur with the ability-to-pay principle—the harder you work, the more you earn, and the more you pay! On the other hand, the "benefits-received" option implies that the poor and/or unemployed should be the ones to pay for their own income-support programs. ❨

Practice

8.   A _____ is the tax most likely to ensure vertical equity.
   (a)   progressive income tax
   (b)   regressive income tax
   (c)   sales tax on alcohol
   (d)   head tax of $100 per citizen

   ANSWER: (a)   Vertical equity is related to the ability-to-pay principle.

9.   Which of the following taxes is based on the benefits-received principle?
   (a)   A progressive property tax if the revenue is used to finance public education.
   (b)   A regressive property tax if the revenue is used to finance public education.
   (c)   A progressive property tax if the revenue is used to finance national defense.
   (d)   A flat-rate tax on car owners used to maintain and improve roads.

   ANSWER: (d) Those who pay the tax are the ones who derive the benefit in terms of improved driving conditions. ∎

Objective 3

Evaluate the merit of consumption, expenditures, income and wealth as candidates for the "best" tax base.

Three candidates for the most appropriate tax base are consumption, economic income, and wealth. The arguments for and against each are presented in the textbook.
(a) Consumption: Because the taxpayer's standard of living depends on spending, not income, consumption should be the favored tax base. Also, a tax on income discourages saving through double-taxation of saving. Such a distortionary tax imposes an excess burden. Sales and excise taxes are examples of consumption taxes.
(b) Economic Income: An income tax focuses on the individual's ability to pay. Proponents contend interest income from savings is just as much income as any other form of earnings and should therefore be subject to the same tax standards.
(c) Wealth: If the main concern is to tax those who can control economic resources, it is argued that wealth should be the preferred tax base. Wealth represents the accumulation, over the years, of stored spending power. The Federal Gift and Estate Tax and local property taxes are examples of wealth taxes.

Clearly, there is no single, simple answer to this debate and, in practice, most economies have evolved tax systems that use all three tax bases.
   Note that the effect of a tax on savings is an important element in this discussion. A consumption tax, such as a national sales tax, would tax savings only once while an income tax affects savings twice. (page 393)

> **LEARNING TIP:** Avoid the temptation to declare all taxes to be bad. Read through this section of the textbook critically. Which tax system would be least burdensome for you, personally, at the present time? Which would be least burdensome after you graduate? How does each system affect you as a senior citizen? Lastly, are your needs and society's needs unchanged in each case?◀

ECONOMICS IN PRACTICE: On page 396, the textbook looks at the issue of the Gift and Estate Tax that was phased out in 2010 for one year. This tax had been under attack for many years and was often referred to by opponents as the "death tax" because it was a tax on the estates of those who had died. The top tax rate in 2009 was 45 percent. What was the tax base in this case? What impact might this tax have had on the behavior of those who might have expected to pay it?
ANSWER: Wealth was the tax base. With a high marginal tax rate, individuals would have a strong incentive to reduce their holdings of wealth. Transferring wealth as gifts, however, was not a satisfactory option because of the gift component of the tax. Buying assets was also unattractive because that merely changed the form in which the wealth was held. However, individuals may have preferred to enjoy services—tourism, golf or cosmetic surgery—or to contribute to philanthropic activities or political campaigns. There was a clear incentive for older wealthy citizens to indulge in the purchase of expensive life-extending medical services, primarily because it reduced wealth, but also because it delayed the payment of the tax!

ECONOMICS IN PRACTICE (CONTINUED): George Steinbrenner, billionaire owner of the New York Yankees, died during 2010 when the tax was not in effect. How much did he save his heirs by dying in 2010?

ANSWER: According to the article, if Steinbrenner had died in 2009 (when the top tax rate was 45 percent) the estate tax bill would have been around half a billion dollars. If he had died in 2011 (with a top rate of 55 percent) then the tax bill would have been $600 million.

ECONOMICS IN PRACTICE (CONTINUED): In 2005, an Advisory Panel advocated a much simplified tax system. One frequently suggested proposal, a national sales tax, was rejected as impractical, although it had many supporters. Nine states, such as Tennessee, have virtually no income taxes, preferring to finance their expenditures with sales taxes. Which tax system is likely to be more regressive—an income tax or a sales tax? Relative to an income tax, what effect will a sales tax have on saving? What is the likelihood of tax shifting under the two schemes?

ANSWER: A consumption tax is likely to be more regressive—poorer people spend the bulk of their income and are, therefore, subject to the tax. Because it increases prices, a sales tax tends to discourage consumption, and increase saving. Finally, households may be able to shift a sales tax by buying items in neighboring states. Note that this option becomes less feasible with a national sales tax.

Practice

Use the following information to answer the next two questions. Brenda, an unmarried banker, rents her apartment and earned $40,000 last year. Her firm paid her medical insurance worth $5,000 and contributed $4,000 to her retirement plan. Brenda's rich aunt sent a check for $5,000 for her birthday. Brenda's hobbies include gardening—last year she grew $100 of produce. She has no time to do anything with her stock market portfolio and its value fell from $8,000 to $6,000 last year.

10.   Which of the following items would not be included in Brenda's economic income?
   (a)   The $8,000 in her stock market portfolio
   (b)   The unearned gift of $5,000 from her uncle
   (c)   The $100 of produce that never reached a market
   (d)   The decrease of $2,000 in the value of Brenda's stock portfolio

   ANSWER: (a)   This is wealth, not income.

11.   The best estimate of Brenda's economic income is
   (a) $46,100.
   (b) $52,100.
   (c) $54,100.
   (d) $60,100.

   ANSWER: (b)   Each item above should be included. The change in the value of the stock portfolio must be subtracted. ■

Objective 4

Explain why households are the ultimate payers of all taxes—i.e., bear the incidence of the tax. Comment on the factors affecting the incidence of a particular tax, such as a payroll tax or corporate profits tax.

The ultimate distribution of a tax is called the *tax incidence*. Often, taxes can be passed on (shifted) to other individuals—this is **tax shifting**. Taxes can distort economic decisions and change behavior. Demand and supply can both be affected by the presence of a tax, as can prices. Payroll taxes are largely shifted to workers and are regressive. Corporate tax seems to be borne by the owners of companies, with only slight impact on workers—tax shifting is less successful in this case. State and local taxes are mildly regressive, but federal taxes are mildly progressive. The U.S. tax system is proportional or very mildly progressive. (page 396)

Because the elasticity of labor supply is generally quite close to zero (workers must work, regardless), employers are able to shift most of the burden of the payroll tax to their workers.

LEARNING TIP: Case, Fair and Oster go through an extensive example while looking at the incidence of the payroll tax, first when labor supply is elastic, and then when it is inelastic. This is a good opportunity to review both the elasticity material in Chapter 5 and labor market material in Chapter 10.◀

The notion that households ultimately bear the burden of all taxes may seem difficult to grasp. The burden from sales taxes, property taxes, and personal income taxes is fairly easy to see. Capital gains taxes or corporate profit taxes, though, are also borne by households—households, in the final analysis, own the firms. Broad-based direct taxes, such as income tax, are difficult to shift while indirect taxes with a narrower base, such as the corporate tax, are easier to pass along.

LEARNING TIP: Check your own list of taxes to see in which cases tax shifting is possible. Remember that taxes change behavior and that eventually (even if you can shift a tax) the tax burden is borne by households.◀

Practice

12. The incidence of a tax refers to
    (a) the structure of the tax.
    (b) how frequently the tax is collected.
    (c) who bears the economic burden of the tax.
    (d) the impact of the tax on prices or wages.

    ANSWER: (c) Refer to page 396 for the definition.

13. The government imposes a tax on oranges. Most households reduce their purchases of oranges and buy other fruits instead. Their behavior is an example of tax
    (a) incidence.
    (b) shifting.
    (c) restructuring.
    (d) evasion.

    ANSWER: (b) Tax shifting occurs when a taxpayer changes her/his behavior to avoid a tax.

14. Of the following, a _____ would be the easiest to shift.
    (a) $100 tax per citizen
    (b) 10 percent excise tax on oranges
    (c) proportional income tax
    (d) 5 percent consumption tax

    ANSWER: (b) It would be fairly easy to avoid the tax by not purchasing oranges.

Use the following diagram to answer the next three questions. The diagram shows the demand (D) and supply (S) curves in the labor market. A payroll tax of $1.00 is imposed.

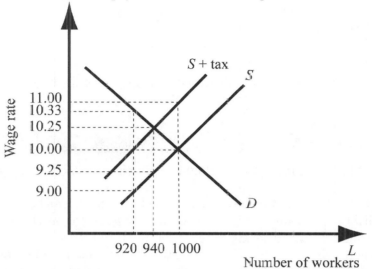

15.   Before the imposition of the payroll tax, the equilibrium wage rate was _____ and the equilibrium level of employment was _____ .
(a) $10.00; 1,000
(b) $10.00; 940
(c) $10.25; 1,000
(d) $10.25; 940

ANSWER: (a) This is where the labor demand curve and the original labor supply curve intersect.

16.   After the tax is imposed, _____ workers will each take home _____ per hour.
(a)   1,000; $10.00
(b)   1,000; $11.00
(c)   940; $10.25
(d)   940; $9.25

ANSWER: (d) Equilibrium hiring level is 940. At this level, firms will pay no more than $9.25 per worker.

17.   The workers' share of the tax burden is _____; the employer's share is _____ .
(a) $235; $235
(b) $235; $705
(c) $705; $235
(d) $705; $705

ANSWER: (c) Tax revenues are $940. Each worker lost 75¢ in wages; each employer has to pay 25¢.

18.   The imposition of a corporate income tax will _____ profits in the corporate sector and _____ profits in the noncorporate sector.
(a)   increase; increase
(b)   increase; decrease
(c)   decrease; increase
(d)   decrease; decrease

ANSWER: (d) Competitive forces will equalize profits throughout the economy. Higher taxes will reduce profits in all sectors.

19.   The _____ labor supply is, the _____ the proportion of a payroll tax will be borne by employees.
      (a)   more elastic; greater
      (b)   less elastic; less
      (c)   more inelastic; greater
      (d)   more inelastic; less

      ANSWER: (c)   In the extreme case, when labor supply is perfectly inelastic, all of a payroll tax will be borne by the workers. ■

Objective 5

Define and measure excess burden and explain the principle of tax neutrality.

The total burden of a tax is the sum of the revenue collected from the tax and any additional costs created because the tax has distorted economic choices. The *excess burden* (or *deadweight loss*) of a tax is the amount by which the total burden of a tax exceeds the total revenue collected. Given two taxes, the preferred tax is the one that imposes the smaller excess burden. Excess burdens are a form of waste, or lost value, therefore tax policy should be written with a view to minimizing them. *Neutral taxes*—which are most likely to be broad based—are preferred on the grounds that they do not hurt efficiency. (page 402)

> **LEARNING TIP:** Note also that when Case, Fair and Oster look at the size of excess burdens the logic they use is the same as that you encountered in Chapter 13 when looking at the welfare loss from monopoly. ◀

Practice

Use the following information to answer the next three questions. In the production of sweatbands, the current lowest-cost mix of labor and capital costs $6.00 per 10 sweatbands. A 50¢ tax is imposed per unit of labor. Producers react by switching to a different input mix, using only 5 units of labor to produce 10 sweatbands. The new input mix increases the cost of producing 10 sweatbands to $9.00.

20.   If 1,000 sweatbands are sold, the total tax revenue collected is
      (a) $30.00.
      (b) $25.00.
      (c) $250.00.
      (d) $300.00.

      ANSWER: (c)   Total tax on 10 sweatbands = 5 × 50¢ = $2.50. Total tax on 1,000 sweatbands = $2.50 × 100 = $250.

21.   If 1,000 sweatbands are sold, the total tax burden is
      (a) $30.00.
      (b) $45.00.
      (c) $300.00.
      (d) $450.00.

      ANSWER: (c)   Total tax burden = ($9.00 – $6.00) × 100 = $300.

22.   If 1,000 sweatbands are sold, the excess burden of the tax is
      (a) $30.00.
      (b) $50.00.
      (c) $250.00.
      (d) $300.00.

ANSWER: (b) The excess burden = the total tax burden – tax revenue = $300 – $250. ∎

Objective 6

Demonstrate graphically the presence of the excess burden following the imposition of a tax, linking the resulting distortion to the relative elasticity of demand.

The shifting of taxation can impose an excess burden (over and above the revenues collected) on society. The size of the burden depends on how much decisions change in response to the tax. In general, the greater responsiveness of buyers and sellers, as measured by price or income elasticity, the greater the excess burden. As an example, to the extent that land is very highly inelastic in supply, a uniform tax on all land would be less distortionary than taxes levied on other, more variable, resources. (page 404)

> **LEARNING TIP:** You'll get more out of the section on tax neutrality if you reread Chapter 12 first. Many of the concepts developed there (efficiency, consumer surplus, producer surplus, and so on) are reused in this section. ◀

Practice

23. A broad-based tax, such as a general energy tax, tends to distort choices _____ and impose _____ excess burdens than a specific tax (i.e., a gasoline tax).
    (a) more; higher
    (b) more; lower
    (c) fewer; higher
    (d) fewer; lower

    ANSWER: (d) The specific tax is more shiftable, leading to more distortions and greater excess burdens.

24. The total burden of a tax can be described as the
    (a) tax revenue minus the after-tax consumer surplus.
    (b) before-tax consumer surplus minus the after-tax consumer surplus.
    (c) tax revenue minus the excess burden.
    (d) excess burden minus the tax revenue.

    ANSWER: (b) The total burden is measured by how much consumer welfare has been reduced.

25. In two communities, Balado and Clathy, the level of demand for gasoline is identical but it is more elastic in Balado. Marginal cost is assumed to be constant. The imposition of a gasoline tax will cause a greater decrease in consumption in _____ and a greater excess burden in _____ .
    (a) Balado; Balado
    (b) Balado; Clathy
    (c) Clathy; Balado
    (d) Clathy; Clathy

    ANSWER: (a) As demand is more elastic in Balado, the tax-induced price hike will result in a larger decrease in consumption. ∎

Objective 7

Describe the principle of second best.

The *principle of second best* refers to the fact that a tax may distort an economic decision but need not always impose an excess burden. Sometimes—as in the case of an externality or in the presence of another distortionary tax—a new tax can correct the existing distortion, reduce the excess burden, and improve efficiency. (page 405)

Practice
---

26.   We would most likely wish to impose a nonneutral tax if _____ are present.
        (a)   externalities and public goods
        (b)   inelastic demand and other distortionary taxes
        (c)   externalities and other distortionary taxes
        (d)   inelastic demand and public goods

        ANSWER: (c) The adverse effects of both externalities and other distortionary taxes can be offset by nonneutral taxes.

27.   The principle of the second best states that
        (a)   taxes should be neutral.
        (b)   excess burdens will be minimized if demand is perfectly inelastic.
        (c)   a distortionary tax can improve economic efficiency if imposed in a situation where previous distortions were present.
        (d)   a broad-based tax is preferable to a tax on a specific product.

        ANSWER: (c) The principle of the second best is based on the argument that distortion may be corrected by the imposition of offsetting distortions. ∎

BRAIN TEASER SOLUTION: You would prefer a progressive system if your income is relatively low—richer taxpayers will bear the major burden of taxation. If you are relatively well off, you should prefer a regressive system.

PRACTICE TEST

I.   MULTIPLE-CHOICE QUESTIONS

Select the option that provides the single best answer.
_____   1.   The government imposes a new tax on Savings and Loans. Economic theory suggests that, ultimately, the tax will be paid by
               (a)   the owners of the Savings and Loans.
               (b)   the employees of the Savings and Loans.
               (c)   the banking sector.
               (d)   households, some of whom may not even have S&L deposits.

Use the following information to answer the next three questions. An economy has two sectors, agricultural and manufacturing, made up of farms and firms, respectively. In each sector capital earns a normal rate of return equal to 10 percent. The government imposes a 50 percent surtax on accounting profits in the manufacturing sector.

_____   2.   After the economy has fully adjusted to the new tax, who is the least likely to bear any of the tax burden?
               (a)   Owners of firms
               (b)   Owners of farms
               (c)   Consumers who buy mainly agricultural goods
               (d)   Consumers who buy mainly manufactured goods

_____ 3.   After the economy has fully adjusted, we would expect
   (a)   after-tax return to capital to be greater for firms than for farms
   (b)   after-tax return to capital to be greater for farms than for firms
   (c)   after-tax return to capital to be the same for both firms and farms.
   (d)   before-tax return to capital to be greater for farms than for firms.

_____ 4.   If the demand for manufactured goods is very inelastic, the increase in tax rate will be paid
   (a)   equally by firms and their customers.
   (b)   equally by farms and firms.
   (c)   mainly by firms.
   (d)   mainly by buyers of manufactured goods.

_____ 5.   The "excess burden" of a tax
   (a)   is equal to the tax revenues collected by it.
   (b)   occurs whenever the imposition of a tax distorts economic behavior.
   (c)   is equal to the consumer surplus.
   (d)   is equal to the increase in price caused by the tax increase.

_____ 6.   In the United States, most of the payroll tax is borne by workers because the elasticity of labor
   (a)   demand is close to zero.
   (b)   demand is close to one.
   (c)   supply is close to zero.
   (d)   supply is close to one.

_____ 7.   The cardinal principle of tax analysis is that
   (a)   the burden of a tax is borne by individuals or households.
   (b)   institutions are the final payers of taxes.
   (c)   wage earners are the final source of taxes.
   (d)   the incidence of a tax cannot be shifted.

_____ 8.   A new labor tax is levied on employers—the tax is $1 per unit of labor. The wage rate falls by 30¢. We can conclude that
   (a)   the income effect is stronger than the substitution effect.
   (b)   employees pay the bulk of the tax.
   (c)   the amount of labor used by firms has increased.
   (d)   the result would have been the same if the tax had been imposed on the workers, not the employers.

Use the following diagram to answer the next four questions. The diagram shows the demand (*D*) and supply (*S₁*) curves for ball bearings that are produced in a perfectly competitive industry.

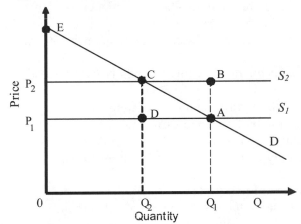

_____ 9.   The price of ball bearings is P_1. Which area represents the consumer surplus?
(a) P_1AE.
(b)   ACD.
(c) P_1P_2CD.
(d) P_2EC.

_____ 10.   Now a tax of $T is imposed that raises the price to P_2. Which area represents the tax revenue?
(a) $0\,P_1DQ_2$.
(b) P_1P_2CD.
(c) Q_1Q_2AC.
(d)   ABCD.

_____ 11.   Which area represents the excess burden of the tax to the consumer?
(a)   ABC.
(b)   CDA.
(c) Q_1Q_2AC.
(d) Q_1Q_2AD.

_____ 12.   The total burden of the tax is
(a) Q_2CAQ_1.
(b) Q_2CBQ_1.
(c) P_2CAP_1.
(d) P_1ABP_2.

_____ 13.   An income tax that "double taxes" saving tends to _____ the proportion of income consumed and _____ the proportion saved.
(a)   increase; increase
(b)   increase; decrease
(c)   decrease; increase
(d)   decrease; decrease

_____ 14. Most of a payroll tax is borne by _____ because labor supply is quite _____ .
  (a) employers; elastic
  (b) employers; inelastic
  (c) employees; elastic
  (d) employees; inelastic

_____ 15. Your boss explains that she will have to cut your wages by 10 percent because the local government has hiked her property taxes by 20 percent. This is an example of
  (a) tax shifting.
  (b) a regressive taxation.
  (c) a progressive taxation.
  (d) tax evasion.

_____ 16. Which of the following is a tax levied on a flow?
  (a) A tax on interest earned on savings in your bank account
  (b) A property tax
  (c) A tax on the savings in your bank account
  (d) A tax on the value of the stocks you own

Use the following information to answer the next four questions. A basketball, which is produced in a perfectly competitive industry, can be produced using either of two processes as summarized in the table. Currently, the price of a unit of labor is $2 and the price of a unit of capital is $2. Demand is perfectly inelastic at a quantity of 100 basketballs. Assume that costs are constant.

	Units of Capital	**Units of Labor**
Process A	5	4
Process B	2	8

_____ 17. The long-run market price of a basketball is
  (a) $12.
  (b) $18.
  (c) $22.
  (d) $24.

_____ 18. Now the government imposes a $1 per unit tax on each unit of capital used. The long-run market price of a basketball will be
  (a) $16.
  (b) $22.
  (c) $23.
  (d) $24.

_____ 19. The government imposes a $1 per unit tax on each unit of capital used. The government's tax revenue is
  (a) $4.
  (b) $100.
  (c) $200.
  (d) $400.

_____ 20. The government imposes a $1 per unit tax on each unit of capital used. The excess burden of the tax is
(a) $100.
(b) $200.
(c) $300.
(d) $400.

II. APPLICATION QUESTIONS

1. Jack and Jill are twins. They have identical salaries and each was given a $100,000 bond at birth (which would pay $10,000 each year) by Dame Dobb. Jack lives in a condominium with a rent of $10,000 each year. He uses the interest from the bond to pay his rent. Jill lives in an identical condo next door but she sold the bond, bought the condo, and pays no rent. In terms of income taxes, which twin is the better off?

2. In terms of personal income tax, the phenomenon of "bracket creep" has become less important because of the reduction in the number of tax brackets. It is still present for other tax bases , the effect being to increase the fraction of the tax base claimed by the government as inflation occurs. A numerical example will quickly clarify this issue. Suppose that the marginal tax rate (MTR) is 30 percent on all income up to $30,000, and 50 percent on all income above that. Initially, Fred Fiscal earns $30,000.
   (a) How much does he pay in taxes?

   Now suppose that there is a sudden doubling of all values denominated in dollars.
   (b) Will there be any distributional effects?

   (c) Calculate Fred's new tax liability.

   Note that prices have doubled but that Fred's take-home pay has failed to keep pace: spending power has been redistributed from Fred to Washington.

3. A successful computer consultant, Mike Macintosh, charges a fee of $120 per hour. The personal income tax system has very progressive marginal tax rates. The rate Mike faces is 75 percent.
   (a) How much does he earn per hour after tax?

   Mike's house needs some work. In addition to the materials, the painter, Peter, will charge for labor at a rate of $30 per hour.
   (b) Should Mike hire Peter or should he paint the house himself?

   (c) Mike discovers that Peter's marginal tax rate is 25 percent. How might Mike and Peter attempt to circumvent the tax system?

   (d) What other possibilities exist in this situation?

   (e) Mike and Peter agree to barter services. Painting the house takes 4 hours while the computer services take 2 hours. How is this beneficial for both?

4. A hearing aid can be produced in one of two ways, as shown in the table. Assume that the marginal cost of additional hearing aids is constant.

	Units of Capital	**Units of Labor**
Process A	6	3
Process B	4	6

The price of capital is $1 and the price of labor is $1. Demand is perfectly inelastic at a level of 100 units.

(a)   The long-run price in this unregulated competitive industry will be $_____, and Process _____ will be chosen.

(b)   Now the government imposes a $1 tax per unit of capital used. Price now would be $_____ using the original process, and $_____ using Process _____. The preferred process will be Process _____.

(c)   Tax revenue will be $_____. The excess burden of the tax will be $_____. The total burden of the tax is $_____.

5.   The following graph gives the labor demand and supply curves before and after the imposition of a $1.00 payroll tax.

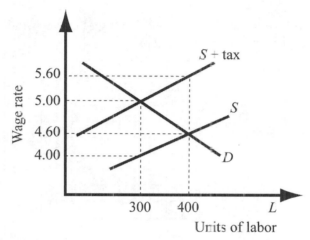

What was the original equilibrium wage rate and employment level? After the tax is imposed, the equilibrium wage and hiring level are $_____ and _____ jobs. Total tax revenue is $_____. The share of the tax paid by employees is $_____ and that paid by employers is $_____.

6.   Sketch a Lorenz curve showing some income inequality in each of the three diagrams following. (If necessary, check back to Chapter 18 to review the Lorenz curve.)

(a)   In the following diagram, show how the curve would change if the government introduced a more progressive tax system.

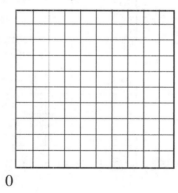

0

(b)   In the following diagram, show how the curve would change if the government introduced a more regressive tax system.

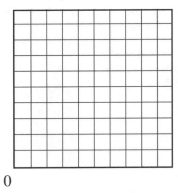

0

(c)   In the following diagram, show how the curve would change if the government introduced a proportional tax system.

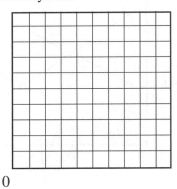

0

7.   Following is a tax table, showing average and marginal tax rates. However, there are some blanks.

(a)   Use your economic knowledge to complete the table.

Total Income	Total Taxes	Average Tax Rate	Marginal Tax Rate
$5,000	$750	_____	_____
$10,000	_____	_____	0.090
$15,000	_____	0.100	_____
$20,000	$1,600	_____	_____
$25,000	_____	_____	0.130
$30,000	_____	0.110	_____

(b)   Is this system progressive, regressive, or proportional?

Practice Test SOLUTIONS

I. SOLUTIONS TO MULTIPLE-CHOICE QUESTIONS

1. (d) Ultimately, all taxes are paid by individuals or households. Refer to page 396.

2. (c) Certainly firms and their customers will lose. Farms will lose because manufactured goods are part of their inputs. Farm customers will be most insulated from the new tax. Note that the less elastic the demand for farm products, the more of the tax will be borne by farm customers.

3. (c) Competitive forces will equalize the after-tax returns in the two sectors.

4. (d) Because the purchase of manufactured goods is difficult to avoid, manufacturers will be able to pass on the tax to their customers will little decrease in sales.

5. (b) For the definition of an excess burden, refer to page 402.

6. (c) The elasticity of labor supply is close to zero, meaning that the labor is fairly insensitive to decreases in wage caused by the imposition of the payroll tax.

7. (a) Ultimately, all taxes are paid by individuals or households. Refer to page 396.

8. (d) Refer to pp. 397-398 for a discussion of this issue.

9. (a) Consumer surplus is the (triangular) area between the price and the demand curve.

10. (b) Tax revenue depends on the tax rate (the distance P_1P_2) and the quantity sold.

11. (b) Total revenue collected is P_1P_2CB. The loss in consumer surplus is P_1P_2CA. The difference is the excess burden of the tax.

12. (c) The total burden is the tax burden (P_1P_2CD) plus the excess burden (CDA), or, looked at another way, the decrease in consumer surplus.

13. (b) Because the benefits from saving are reduced, taxpayers will tend to consume more and save less of their income.

14. (d) When labor supply is inelastic, employers are more able to pass on the burden of the payroll tax to employees. Refer to page 399.

15. (a) Tax shifting occurs when a tax is avoided, perhaps (as in this case), by passing on the burden to another party.

16. (a) Interest is earned during a period of time, i.e., it is a flow variable. Each of the other tax bases is a stock measured at a point in time.

17. (b) The lower-cost input mix (A) will be chosen. The cost of production is ($2 × 5) + ($2 × 4) = $18.

18. (b) Process A now costs $23 per ball while Process B costs only $22 per ball.

19.   (c)   Total tax = 100 (basketballs) × 2 (units of capital) × $1 = $200.

20.   (b)   Excess burden = total burden – tax revenues collected. Total burden = tax-induced increase in price × quantity sold = ($22 – $18) × 100 = $400. Taxes collected = $200.

II. SOLUTIONS TO APPLICATION QUESTIONS

1.   Jill has made the wiser move, at least in terms of income taxes. Jack earns $10,000 more income than Jill and he will be taxed on this. If, however, property taxes are present, the situation changes, and Jack may be relatively better off than Jill.

2.   (a) $9,000.

     (b)   Yes! Refer to the following table.

Pre-tax Income	MTR	Tax liability	After-tax income
$30,000	30 percent	$ 9,000	$21,000
$60,000	50 percent	$24,000	$36,000

     (c) $24,000 = $9,000 + ($30,000 × 0.5).

3.   (a) $12.50.

     (b)   Mike should paint his house himself—this is an example of a tax distortion! His after-tax income is $12.50 per hour; he is better employed in an activity that saves him $30 per hour. (The price system is signaling that Mike's efforts are worth $50 per hour, yet he is rational in allocating time to an activity saving him $30 per hour.)

     (c)   Mike could offer Peter a "cash basis" transaction. If Peter's marginal tax rate is 25 percent, the $30 pre-tax income is the equivalent of $22.50 after tax. Peter gains if he negotiates an "off-the-books" price of $25, and Mike's bill is lower.

     (d)   One possibility is that Mike and Peter can barter services although this is unlikely given Mike's occupation, which is not easy to barter. Perhaps Mike can computerize Peter's billing and accounting system in exchange for the painting services.

     (e)   Painting the house takes 4 hours and the computer services take 2 hours. Mike has saved 4 hours ($12.50 × 4 = $50) at the cost of 2 hours (worth $25.00). Similarly, Peter has worked 4 hours for a reward of $30 × 4 × 0.75 = $90 but received services that would have cost him $100 on the open market. Mike can gain, as can Peter, who can also avoid tax payments. The "underground economy" is created, in part, by a desire to avoid taxes.

4.   (a) $9. Average cost and marginal cost will both be $9. In perfect competition, $P = MR$, and to maximize profits, $MR = MC$. Therefore, $P = MC = 9. Process A is cheaper, given the price of labor and capital.

     (b) $15, because 6 units of capital are used. The entire tax hike will be passed on to the consumer because demand is perfectly inelastic. $14, ($10 + $4), will be the price using Process B. Process B is cheaper.

     (c)   Tax revenue = $4 × 100 units = $400. The excess burden of the tax = tax burden – revenues = $500 – $400 = $100. The total burden of the tax = (new price – initial price) × 100 = ($14 – $9) × 100 = $500.

5.   Original equilibrium wage is $4.60 with 400 jobs. The new equilibrium wage is $4.00 with 300 jobs. Total tax revenue is $300. The share of the tax paid by employees is $180 and that paid by employers is $120.

6.   Refer to the following diagrams.

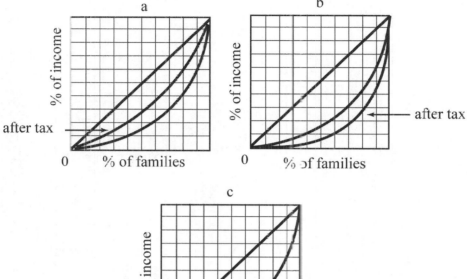

7.   (a)   Refer to the following table.

Total Income	Total Taxes	Average Tax Rate	Marginal Tax Rate
$5,000	$750	0.150	0.150
$10,000	$1,200	0.120	0.090
$15,000	$1,500	0.100	0.060
$20,000	$1,600	0.080	0.020
$25,000	$2,250	0.090	0.130
$30,000	$3,300	0.110	0.210

        (b)   This system is regressive until one's income reaches $20,000, after which it becomes progressive.

Comprehensive Review Test

The following questions provide a wide-ranging review of the material covered in Part III (Chapters 13-19) of the textbook. Each question deals with a topic or technique important for your understanding of economic principles. If you miss a question you should return to the relevant section of the chapter in the textbook and fine-tune your understanding.

I. MULTIPLE-CHOICE QUESTIONS

Select the option that provides the single best answer.

_____ 1. Monty the Monopolist is seeking to maximize profits. Currently he is producing where marginal revenue is more than marginal cost. He should
    (a)   increase production.
    (b)   increase price.
    (c)   reduce production.
    (d)   produce where price is equal to marginal cost.

Use the following information to answer the next three questions. Marcel the Monopolist has a constant marginal cost of $3. Fixed costs are $4.

Price	Quantity Demanded
$10	0
$9	1
$8	2
$7	3
$6	4
S5	5
S4	6
$3	7

_____ 2. Given the demand schedule and cost information, Marcel will maximize profits by setting a price of
    (a) $8.
    (b) $7.
    (c) $6.
    (d) $5.

_____ 3.   At the profit-maximizing output level, Marcel's economic profit will be
(a) $12.
(b) $10.
(c) $8.
(d) $6.

_____ 4.   Currently Marcel is producing at the output level where price equals marginal cost. Which of the following strategies will increase Marcel's profits?
(a)   Maintain price and output—Marcel is already maximizing profit.
(b)   Increase price and decrease output
(c)   Decrease price and increase output
(d)   Decrease price and decrease output

_____ 5.   The total cost to Walt's Widget Works of producing one widget is $24. The total cost of producing two widgets is $36. The total cost of producing three widgets is $50. Currently, $MR = MC$ at two widgets. Which of the following is certainly true when two widgets are produced?
(a)   The demand for Walt's widgets is elastic.
(b)   Walt is making an economic profit.
(c)   Walt is making an economic loss but should produce.
(d)   Walt is making an economic loss and should shut down.

_____ 6.   Many poor Arbocalis skimp on health care, become sick, and infect those who do buy health insurance. This represents
(a)   a positive externality.
(b)   a negative externality.
(c)   a public good.
(d)   defensive medicine.

_____ 7.   The "excess burden" of a tax
(a)   is equal to the tax revenues collected by it.
(b)   occurs whenever the imposition of a tax distorts economic behavior.
(c)   is equal to the consumer surplus.
(d)   is equal to the increase in price caused by the tax increase.

_____ 8.   The essence of the utilitarian argument in favor of income redistribution is that a dollar transferred from a rich person to a poor person will increase total utility because the marginal utility of a poor person
(a)   increases faster than that of a rich person.
(b)   increases more slowly than that of a rich person.
(c)   is higher than that of a rich person.
(d)   is lower than that of a rich person.

Use the following diagram, which depicts a monopolistically competitive firm, to answer the next four questions.

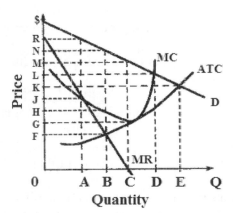

_____ 9. The profit-maximizing output level is
   (a) *OA*.
   (b) *OB*.
   (c) *OD*.
   (d) *OE*.

_____ 10. The profit-maximizing price is
   (a) *OF*.
   (b) *OG*.
   (c) *OH*.
   (d) *ON*.

_____ 11. The firm's maximum short-run profit is
   (a) *OB* × *HN*.
   (b) *OC* × *GM*.
   (c) *OB* × *FN*.
   (d) *OC* × *HN*.

_____ 12. In the short run, firms will _____ this industry. In the long run, firms _____ this industry.
   (a) enter; enter
   (b) enter; not enter
   (c) not enter; enter
   (d) not enter; not enter

_____ 13. Price exceeds marginal revenue for Mose the Monopolist because
   (a) Mose's firm faces a perfectly elastic demand curve.
   (b) Mose must reduce price on all units if he wants to attract more customers.
   (c) the demand exceeds average total cost at the profit-maximizing output level.
   (d) of economies of scale.

_____ 14. Wallace Gromits Incorporated is a natural monopoly if
  (a)   the firm holds patents that protect it from potential rivals.
  (b)   the government has issued Wallace an exclusive license to produce gromits.
  (c)   Wallace has sole ownership of toastite, an essential mineral in the production of gromits.
  (d)   economies of scale permit Wallace to produce gromits at a lower average cost than potential rivals.

_____ 15. Monopolistically competitive firms differ from oligopolists in that each monopolistically competitive firm
  (a)   faces a downward-sloping demand curve, but an oligopolist does not.
  (b)   tries to differentiate its products from those of its rivals, but an oligopolist does not.
  (c)   may compete with others on price, but an oligopolist never does.
  (d)   is small relative to the size of its industry; an oligopolist frequently is large relative to the size of its industry.

_____ 16. In long-run equilibrium, monopolistic competition is
  (a)   efficient because easy entry and exit eliminate economic profit.
  (b)   efficient because firms produce where marginal revenue and long-run average cost are equal and where average revenue and long-run average cost are equal.
  (c)   not efficient because too little output is produced—marginal cost is less than demand and average cost is not minimized.
  (d)   not efficient because too little output is produced—marginal cost is still increasing.

_____ 17. Mando the Monopolist is producing where demand is inelastic. An increase in price will
  (a)   increase total revenue, increase total cost and increase profit.
  (b)   increase total revenue, decrease total cost and increase profit.
  (c)   decrease total revenue, increase total cost and decrease profit.
  (d)   decrease total revenue, decrease total cost and increase profit.

_____ 18. "Many sellers each offering a somewhat differentiated product" is a description of
  (a)   perfect competition.
  (b)   monopoly.
  (c)   monopolistic competition.
  (d)   oligopoly.

_____ 19. A perfectly competitive firm maximizes profit by producing where _____ ; an imperfectly competitive firm maximizes profit by producing where _____ .
  (a) $P = MC$; $P + MC$
  (b) $P = MC$; $P > MC$
  (c) $MR = MC$; $P < MC$
  (d) $MR = MC$; $P = MC$

_____ 20. A market is contestable if entry
  (a)   and exit are costless.
  (b)   is easy but exit is restricted.
  (c)   is restricted but exit is easy.
  (d)   and exit are restricted.

_____ 21. To achieve the efficient output level, we must equate marginal benefit with marginal
(a)   damage cost.
(b)   social cost.
(c)   private cost.
(d)   external cost.

_____ 23. Papyrus Paper Mill is producing where its marginal revenue equals its marginal private cost. Marginal social cost exceeds Papyrus' marginal private cost. Papyrus is an example of
(a)   an externality.
(b)   a monopoly.
(c)   a public good.
(d)   regulated monopoly.

_____ 24. Country A has a Gini coefficient of 0.3 whereas Country B has a Gini coefficient of 0.7. We can now state that Country A has
(a)   more poor people than Country B.
(b)   fewer poor people than Country B.
(c)   a more equal distribution of income than Country B.
(d)   a less equal distribution of income than Country B.

Use the following diagram to answer the next five questions.

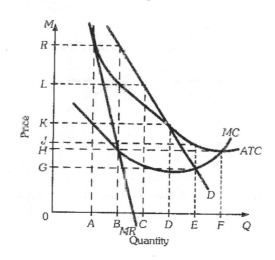

_____ 25. The type of industry depicted in the preceding diagram is best described as
(a)   a pure monopoly.
(b)   a natural monopoly.
(c)   imperfectly competitive.
(d)   an artificial monopoly.

_____ 26. At the most efficient output level, this firm would earn an economic
(a)   profit of $OB \times HR$.
(b)   profit of $OE \times GJ$.
(c)   loss of $OB \times HR$.
(d)   loss of $OE \times GJ$.

_____   27.   If Max, the owner of this firm, could choose his own output and price levels, he would
choose an output of _____ and a price of _____ .
(a)   *OB; OR*
(b)   *OD; OK*
(c)   *OE; OG*
(d)   *OF; OH*

_____   28.   If a price ceiling were imposed at *OG*, Max would
(a)   still produce *OB* units because this is where *MR = MC*.
(b)   have to receive a subsidy of *HL* dollars per unit.
(c)   have to receive a subsidy of *GJ* dollars per unit.
(d)   earn an economic profit of *OE × GJ*.

_____   29.   If a price were imposed at *OK*,
(a)   Max would earn an economic profit of *OD × GJ*.
(b)   the government would have to subsidize Max to the tune of *KG* dollars per unit.
(c)   Max would produce *OB* units because this is where *MR = MC*.
(d)   Max would make a normal profit and remain in the industry.

Use the following diagram to answer the next four questions. The diagram shows the demand (*D*) and
supply (*S*₁) curves for ball bearings, which are produced in a perfectly competitive industry.

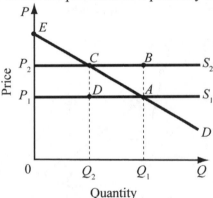

_____   30.   Their price is P_1. Which area represents the consumer surplus?
(a) P_1AE
(b)   *ADC*
(c) $P_1 P_2CD$
(d) P_2EC

_____   31.   Now a tax of *$T* is imposed that raises the price to P_2. Which area represents the tax
revenue?
(a) OP_1DQ_2
(b) P_1P_2CD
(c) Q_1Q_2AC
(d)   *ABCD*

_____   32.   Which area represents the excess burden of the tax to the consumer?
(a)   *ABC*
(b)   *CDA*
(c) Q_1Q_2CD
(d) Q_1Q_2AD

_____ 33.   The total burden of the tax is _____ .
   (a) Q_2CAQ_1
   (b) Q_2CBQ_1
   (c) P_2CAP_1
   (d) P_1ABP_2

II. APPLICATION QUESTIONS

Here is some information on the Hour Time Together Clock Company. HTT is a firm in an industry with no external economies or diseconomies of scale.

1.   Complete the following table.

Number of Workers	Marginal Product	Total Product	Product Price	Total Revenue	Marginal Revenue
0		0	--	$0	
	20				
1		_____	$30.00	_____	_____
	30				
2		_____	$29.00	$1,450	_____
	28				
3	_____	78	$28.00	_____	_____
4	_____	104	$27.00	_____	_____
5		125	$26.00	_____	_____
	19				
6		_____	$25.00	_____	_____
	10				
7		_____	$24.00	_____	_____
	8				
8	_____	_____	$23.00	_____	_____
9		168	$22.00	_____	_____
	2				
10		170	$21.00	_____	

2.   In the $27 – $28 price range, estimate the price elasticity of demand. Is it elastic, inelastic, unitary elastic, or can't you tell?

3.   Is this firm perfectly competitive or imperfectly competitive? How can you tell?

Hour Time Together has total fixed costs of $2,100. The wage of each (variable) worker is $120. Let us now suppose that Hour Time Together is a firm in a monopolistically competitive industry.

4.   Complete the following table.

Number of Workers	Marginal Product	Total Cost	Average Total Cost	Average Variable Cost	Marginal Cost
0		_____	--	$0	_____
	20				
1		_____	_____	_____	_____
	30				
2		_____	$46.80	_____	_____
	28				
3		$2,460	_____	_____	_____
	_____				
4		_____	_____	_____	_____
	_____				
5		_____	_____	_____	_____
	19				
6		_____	_____	_____	_____
	10				
7		_____	_____	_____	_____
	8				
8		_____	_____	$5.93	_____
	_____				
9		_____	_____	_____	_____
	2				
10		_____	_____		

5.   Find the profit-maximizing output level (of the output levels given).

6.   What price should be charged to maximize economic profit? What will be the maximum economic profit?

7.   Predict what will happen to the number of firms in this industry in the short run.

8.   Predict what will happen to the number of firms in this industry in the long run. Explain your answer.

Assume that the minimum short-run average cost (in the table) is also its minimum average cost in the long run.

9.   Describe what will happen to the position of its demand curve in the long run.

10.   Describe what will happen to the elasticity of its demand curve in the long run.

11.   Of the output levels given, what would be the price and output level of a perfectly competitive firm in the long run?

12.   Explain why (or why not) the firm's marginal cost curve will be steeper in the long run than in the short run.

Review Test SOLUTIONS

I.   SOLUTIONS TO MULTIPLE-CHOICE QUESTIONS

1. (a) If marginal revenue is more than marginal cost, Money should increase production until marginal revenue equals marginal cost.

2. (c) Marginal revenue is $3 and equal to marginal cost at 4 units of output. Refer to the following table.

Price	Quantity Demanded	Total Revenue	Marginal Revenue	Total Cost	Marginal Cost
$10	0	$0		$4	
			$9		$3
$9	1	$9		$7	
			$7		$3
$8	2	$16		$10	
			$5		$3
$7	3	$21		$13	
			$3		$3
$6	4	$24		$16	
			$1		$3
$5	5	$25		$19	
			-$1		$3
$4	6	$24		$22	
			-$3		$3
$3	7	$21		$25	

3. (c) At 4 units of output, total revenue is $24 and total cost is $16.

4. (b) Price equals marginal cost at 7 units. Because marginal revenue is less than marginal cost, Marcel should cut production. He is then able to increase the price he charges.

5. (a) The marginal cost of the second widget is $12. Marginal revenue is therefore $12. When marginal revenue is positive, the firm is operating in the elastic portion of its demand curve. If you missed this, review price elasticity of demand in Chapter 5.

6. (b) There is a spillover effect that reduces the welfare of the insurance purchasers.

7. (b) See page 402 to review the concept of the excess burden of a tax.

8. (c) Marginal utility decreases. The core of the utilitarian argument is that the marginal utility of a dollar given to a poor person is higher than the marginal utility of that dollar to a rich person.

9. (b) OB is the output level at which $MR = MC$.

10. (d) At output level OB, the firm's demand curve allows it to charge a price of ON.

11. (a) Maximum short-run profit is the output level (OB) times the difference between the price and average total cost (HN).

12. (c) Firms attracted by economic profit cannot enter an industry in the short run, but can do so in the long run.

13. (b) Demand is downward sloping for the firm. Consequently, additional units sold bring in less total revenue—marginal revenue decreases.

14. (d) The distinguishing feature of natural monopolies is long-lasting economies of scale that serve as a barrier against competition.

15. (d) There are many firms in monopolistic competition, few in oligopoly.

16. (c) Monopolistically competitive firms are inefficient because they underproduce and produce at too high an average cost.

17. (b) If demand is inelastic, then marginal revenue is negative. Therefore, marginal cost just exceed marginal revenue. An increase in price will reduce output towards the profit maximizing ($MR = MC$) output level.

18. (c) Neither monopoly nor oligopoly have many sellers. Perfect competition has a standardized product.

19. (b) Profit maximization involves producing where $MR = MC$. In perfect competition $P = MR$ whereas in imperfect competition $P > MR$.

20. (a) See page 295 for a discussion of contestable markets.

21. (b) Marginal social cost shows the true internal and external costs to society.

22. (d) See Figure 16.2 on p.333 in the textbook.

23. (a) Papyrus is generating externalities. The difference between marginal social cost and marginal private cost is marginal damage cost.

24. (c) Country A has a more equal distribution of income, but that doesn't mean that it has fewer poor people. A hypothetical Third World nation might have a Gini coefficient of zero (perfectly equal), but all of its inhabitants might live at subsistence level.

25. (b) For all relevant levels of demand, the long-run average cost curve slopes downward.

26. (d) The most efficient output level is where $P = MC$. At that level (OE), price is less than average cost—the firm will make a loss.

27. (a) Max will produce where $MR = MC$.

28. (c) The price ceiling establishes a price that is less than the average cost of production.

29. (d) At *OK* the rice and average cost are equal.

30. (a) Consumer surplus is the (triangular) area between the price and the demand curve.

31. (b) Tax revenue depends on the tax rate (the distance P_1P_2) and the quantity sold.

32. (b) Tax revenue is the area (the distance P_1P_2CB. The loss in consumer surplus is P_1P_2CA. The difference is the excess burden of the tax.

33. (c) The total burden is the tax burden (P_1P_2CD) plus the excess burden (CDA), looked at another way, the decrease in consumer surplus.

II. SOLUTIONS TO APPLICATION QUESTIONS

1. See the following table.

Number of Workers	Marginal Product	Product Price	Total Revenue	Marginal Revenue	Marginal Cost
0		0	--	$0	
	20				$30.00
1		20	$30.00	$600	
	30				$28.33
2		50	$29.00	$1,450	
	28				$26.21
3		78	$28.00	$2,184	
	26				$24.00
4		104	$27.00	$2,808	
	21				$21.05
5		125	$26.00	$3,250	
	19				$18.42
6		144	$25.00	$3,600	
	10				$9.60
7		154	$24.00	$3,696	
	8				$3.75
8		162	$23.00	$3,726	
	6				-$3.75
9		168	$22.00	$3,696	
	2				-$61.00
10		170	$21.00	$3,570	

2. As the price increases from $27 to $28, total revenue decreases. This relationship indicates that demand is elastic. If you are unsure why this is the case, check pp. 105–107 in the textbook.

3. This is an imperfectly competitive firm. It has a downward-sloping demand curve or, alternatively, price is not equal to marginal revenue (as would be the case for a perfectly competitive firm).

4.   Refer to the following table.

Number of Workers	Marginal Product	Total Cost	Average Total Cost	Average Variable Cost	Marginal Cost
0		$2,100	--	--	
	20				$6.00
1		$2,220	$111.60	$6.00	
	30				$4.00
2		$2,340	$46.80	$4.80	
	28				$4.29
3		$2,460	$31.54	$4.62	
	26				$4.62
4		$2,580	$24.81	$4.62	
	21				$5.71
5		$2,700	$21.60	$4.80	
	19				$6.32
6		$2,820	$19.58	$5.00	
	10				$12.00
7		$2,940	$19.09	$5.43	
	8				$15.00
8		$3,060	$18.89	$5.93	
	6				$20.00
9		$3,180	$18.93	$6.43	
	2				$60.00
10		$3,300	$19.41	$7.06	

5.   Ideally, the firm should produce where marginal revenue equals marginal cost. In this case, the best the firm can do, of the options available, is to produce 144 units. Any greater level of output would make marginal cost exceed marginal revenue.

Number of Workers	Total Product	Total Cost	Marginal Cost	Marginal Revenue
0	0	$2,100		
			$6.00	$30.00
1	20	$2,220		
			$4.00	$28.33
2	50	$2,340		
			$4.29	$26.21
3	78	$2,460		
			$4.62	$24.00
4	104	$2,580		
			$5.71	$21.05
5	125	$2,700		
			$6.32	$18.42
6	144	$2,820		
			$12.00	$9.60
7	154	$2,940		
			$15.00	$3.75
8	162	$3,060		
			$20.00	-$3.75
9	168	$3,180		
			$60.00	-$61.00
10	170	$3,300		

6. Maximum economic profit is $780, which is achieved at a price of $25.

7. The number of firms will remain unchanged. Firms can neither enter nor leave an industry in the short run!

8. The number of firms will increase because new firms will enter the industry attracted by economic profits.

9. New firms will enter the industry, reducing Hour Time Together's market share and shifting its demand curve to the left until it is tangent with the long-run average cost curve.

10. There will be more substitutes in the long run. Hour Time Together's demand will become more elastic.

11. The perfectly competitive firm is forced to produce at its minimum average cost output level. In our example this occurs at an output level of 162 units. Price will be $18.89.

12. The firm's marginal cost curve will be steeper—there are fewer constraints in the long run for any given change in output level.

20 [34]

International Trade, Comparative Advantage, and Protectionism

Chapter Objectives

1. Distinguish between an open and a closed economy. Distinguish between a trade surplus and a trade deficit.
2. Distinguish between absolute advantage and comparative advantage and explain the logic behind the theory of comparative advantage. Given a particular two-country, two-good situation, calculate which country will trade which good and indicate the feasible range for the terms of trade.
3. Calculate the limiting values of the exchange rate in a given example and relate the exchange rate to the notion of comparative advantage. Describe how changes in the exchange rate can affect trade flows.
4. Provide an intuitive explanation of the Heckscher-Ohlin theorem.
5. Define a tariff, an export subsidy, and a quota. Outline, using a demand and supply analysis, the costs involved in the imposition of a tariff.
6. Give the arguments for and against protection. Describe the costs involved in permitting free trade.

BRAIN TEASER: Choose some locally produced goods or, if nothing appropriate is available, beer, cigarettes, paper clips, or chewing gum. Suppose that the government has announced that it will protect only goods that are essential for national defense. What arguments can you come up with that would support each industry's claim for protection? Be creative! Remember that arguments that sound plausible may be difficult to refute.

Objective 1

Distinguish between an open and a closed economy. Distinguish between a trade surplus and a trade deficit.

In open economies such as the United States, aggregate expenditures are affected by the presence of exports and imports. We have seen international trade steadily increase in importance throughout the last several decades, as goods and services have moved across borders. If exports exceed imports, the country runs a *trade surplus*. In the oil-expensive years of the 1970s and 1980s, the value of imports into the United States swelled to over 12 percent of GDP (gross domestic product), and the United States began to experience *trade deficits*—that is, its imports exceeded its exports. Deficits have been recorded annually ever since. (page 410 [664])

LEARNING TIP: Learn the difference between exports and imports. Imports are foreign-produced goods consumed here. Exports are domestically produced goods sold to customers overseas. Imports and exports are not opposites; they are determined by different factors.◀

Comment: The two terms, "balance of payments" and "balance of trade," are not synonymous. The balance of trade refers only to exports and imports of goods, while the balance of payments includes all international transactions.

Practice

1.   If the value of U.S. exports exceeds the value of U.S. imports, the United States has a
     (a)   balance of trade surplus.
     (b)   balance of trade deficit.
     (c)   balance of payments surplus.
     (d)   balance of payments deficit.

     ANSWER: (a)   There may be a balance of payments surplus or deficit—it depends on U.S. performance on all of its international transactions. ■

Objective 2

Distinguish between absolute advantage and comparative advantage and explain the logic behind the theory of comparative advantage. Given a particular two-country, two-good situation, calculate which country will trade which good and indicate the feasible range for the terms of trade.

The *theory of comparative advantage* provides the rationale for free trade. Given a two-country, two-good world, and assuming that the countries have relative cost advantages in the production of different goods, Ricardo showed that both trading partners could benefit from specialization in the production of the good in which they have the comparative advantage. Each country should specialize in the production of that good in which it has a comparative advantage and trade its surplus for the good that it is weaker at producing. Production and welfare will be maximized. Country A is said to have an *absolute advantage* if it can produce a unit of output with fewer resources than Country B. Comparative advantage, though, is a relative concept. Country A will have a *comparative advantage* in whichever good it can produce comparatively cheaper. Specialization and trade allow a country to consume more of a good than it can produce by itself. (page 411 [665])

> **LEARNING TIP:** If you're like most individuals, you'll need several numerical examples to strengthen your grasp of pure trade theory. The Applications below take you through all the steps included in the text.
>   Comparative advantage hinges on the concept of *opportunity cost*. (Take a little time to go back and review the material you learned in Chapter 2, especially Application questions 2, 7, and 10 of this Guide. They will lead you through the opportunity cost concept that underlies the theory of comparative advantage.) The producer (person, firm, or country) with the lower opportunity cost will hold the comparative advantage in that product. Don't be misled—absolute advantage is irrelevant.
>   Using the production possibility frontier (ppf) diagram, trade will be advantageous if the production possibility frontiers have differing slopes. The slope depicts opportunity cost. Differing slopes means that a comparative advantage exists—i.e., that the relative costs of production differ. Even though Country A may be more efficient in producing both goods—an absolute advantage—it is the *comparative* advantage of Country A that will establish the preferred pattern of specialization and trade. The country with the flatter production possibility frontier has an advantage in the good on the horizontal axis.◀

Given that specialization occurs, the *terms of trade* (the "price" at which one good trades for the other) must be negotiated. For trade to be beneficial for the exporter, the "price" of the exported good (in terms of the imported good) must be greater than its cost of production. A range of potential terms of trade will exist. The deal cut within this range will depend on the relative negotiating strengths of the two partners. (page 415 [669])

Practice

Refer to the following table to answer the next four questions. The table shows the possible output levels from one day of labor input.

	Arbez	Arboc
Wheat	12 bushels	6 bushels
Cloth	12 yards	12 yards

2.   Arbez
     (a)   has an absolute advantage in the production of cloth.
     (b)   has an absolute advantage in the production of wheat.
     (c)   has a comparative advantage in the production of cloth.
     (d)   should export cloth to Arboc.

     ANSWER: (b) Arbez can produce absolutely more wheat per worker than Arboc can.

3.   The opportunity cost of one bushel of wheat in Arboc is
     (a)   1/2 yard of cloth.
     (b)   2 yards of cloth.
     (c)   6 yards of cloth.
     (d)   12 yards of cloth.

     ANSWER: (b) Six bushels take the inputs that could have produced 12 yards of cloth, therefore 1 bushel costs 2 yards of cloth.

4.   Which of the following statements is false?
     (a)   Arboc has an absolute advantage in the production of wheat.
     (b)   Arbez should export wheat to Arboc and import cloth from Arboc.
     (c)   The opportunity cost of wheat is twice as high in Arboc as in Arbez.
     (d)   The opportunity cost of a yard of cloth in Arbez is one bushel of wheat.

     ANSWER: (a) Arboc is half as productive per worker as Arbez in wheat production.

5.   Arboc and Arbez decide to specialize according to the law of comparative advantage and trade with one another. We would expect that
     (a)   the trade agreement will be somewhere between 1 bushel of wheat for 1 yard of cloth and 1 bushel of wheat for 2 yards of cloth.
     (b)   the trade agreement will be somewhere between 1/2 bushel of wheat for 1 yard of cloth and 2 bushels of wheat for 1 yard of cloth.
     (c)   Arboc will benefit from trading with Arbez, but Arbez will not benefit from trading with Arboc.
     (d)   Arboc will specialize in the production of wheat and Arbez will specialize in the production of cloth.

     ANSWER: (a) The Arbezani opportunity cost of 1 bushel of wheat is 1 yard of cloth. Arboc's opportunity cost of 1 bushel of wheat is 2 yards of cloth.

6.   The ratio at which exports are traded for imports is known as the
        (a)   exchange rate.
        (b)   trade balance.
        (c)   balance of exchange.
        (d)   terms of trade.
        ANSWER: (d)   Refer to page 415 [669] for the definition.

Use the following diagrams, which show the production possibility frontiers (ppf's) for Malaysia and Sri Lanka, to answer the next nine questions. Each country has an equal quantity of resources.

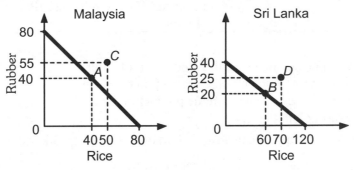

7.   Which of the following statements is true?
        (a)   Malaysia has an absolute advantage in the production of rubber; Sri Lanka has an absolute advantage in the production of rice.
        (b)   Sri Lanka has an absolute advantage in the production of rubber; Malaysia has an absolute advantage in the production of rice.
        (c)   Malaysia has an absolute advantage in the production of both goods.
        (d)   Sri Lanka has an absolute advantage in the production of both goods.
        ANSWER: (a)   Refer to page 411 [665] for the definition of absolute advantage.

8.   Which statement is false?
        (a)   In Malaysia, the opportunity cost of one unit of rubber is one unit of rice.
        (b)   In Malaysia, the opportunity cost of one unit of rice is one unit of rubber.
        (c)   In Sri Lanka, the opportunity cost of one unit of rubber is three units of rice.
        (d)   In Sri Lanka, the opportunity cost of one unit of rice is three units of rubber.
        ANSWER: (d)   The Sri Lankan opportunity cost of one unit of rice is a third of a unit of rubber.

9.   Which of the following statements is true?
        (a)   Malaysia has a comparative advantage in the production of rubber; Sri Lanka has a comparative advantage in the production of rice.
        (b)   Sri Lanka has a comparative advantage in the production of rubber; Malaysia has a comparative advantage in the production of rice.
        (c)   Malaysia has a comparative advantage in both goods.
        (d)   Sri Lanka has a comparative advantage in both goods.
        ANSWER: (a)   Refer to page 414 [668]. A country can *never* have a comparative advantage in both goods.

10. Given that Malaysia and Sri Lanka decide to trade,
    (a) Malaysia should specialize in the production of rubber; Sri Lanka should specialize in the production of rice.
    (b) Malaysia should specialize in the production of rice; Sri Lanka should specialize in the production of rubber.
    (c) Malaysia and Sri Lanka should each devote half their resources to the production of each commodity.
    (d) Malaysia should specialize in the production of rubber; Sri Lanka should produce some rice but continue to produce some rubber.

    ANSWER: (a) Malaysia's comparative advantage lies in rubber production; Sri Lanka's lies in rice. Each should play to their strength and specialize.

11. Before trade, Malaysia produced at Point *A* on its production possibility frontier and Sri Lanka produced at Point *B*. Given complete specialization based on comparative advantage, total rubber production has risen by _____ and total rice production has risen by _____ .
    (a) 80; 120
    (b) 120; 80
    (c) 40; 60
    (d) 20; 20

    ANSWER: (d) Total rubber production was 60 (40 + 20); now it is 80. Total rice production was 100 (40 + 60); now it is 120.

12. After trade, Malaysia is consuming at Point *C* and Sri Lanka is consuming at Point *D*. Malaysia is exporting _____ units of rubber and Sri Lanka is exporting _____ units of rice.
    (a) 80; 100
    (b) 55; 70
    (c) 25; 50
    (d) 15; 10

    ANSWER: (c) Malaysian rubber production is 80, and domestic consumption is 55, leaving 25 for export. Sri Lankan rice production is 120, and domestic consumption is 70, leaving 50 for export.

13. After trade, Malaysia is consuming at Point *C* and Sri Lanka is consuming at Point *D*. Malaysia is importing _____ units of rice and Sri Lanka is importing _____ units of rubber.
    (a) 80; 100
    (b) 50; 25
    (c) 25; 50
    (d) 15; 10

    ANSWER: (b) Refer to the answer to the previous question. In a two-country world, Country A's exports are Country B's imports.

14. Which statement is true?
    (a) Only Sri Lanka will benefit if the terms of trade are set at 1:2, rubber to rice.
    (b) Only Malaysia will benefit if the terms of trade are set at 1:2, rubber to rice.
    (c) Both countries will gain if the terms of trade lie between 3:1 and 1:1, rubber to rice.
    (d) Both countries will gain if the terms of trade lie between 1:1 and 1:3, rubber to rice.

    ANSWER: (d) Check these values against the opportunity cost values you calculated in Question 8. Also note the correct value of the rubber : rice ratio in Question 12.

15.   Which statement is false? If the terms of trade are set at
       (a)   1:1, rubber to rice, only Sri Lanka will gain.
       (b)   1:2, rubber to rice, both countries will gain.
       (c)   1:3, rubber to rice, only Malaysia will gain.
       (d)   1:4, rubber to rice, both countries will wish to produce rice.

       ANSWER: (d) If the terms of trade are set at 1:4, rubber to rice, then rubber is relatively valuable and can cover its opportunity cost in both countries. Both will wish to produce rubber. ■

Objective 3

Calculate the limiting values of the exchange rate in a given example and relate the exchange rate to the notion of comparative advantage. Describe how changes in the exchange rate can affect trade flows.

Trade flows are affected by comparative advantage but also by the exchange rate (the "price" of the domestic currency in terms of a foreign currency). There will be some range of exchange rates that will permit mutually beneficial specialization and trade. (page 416 [670])

   The distribution of benefits from trade depends on the exchange rate. To buy foreign goods one must hold foreign currency, which is bought and sold in the foreign exchange market. If the value of the dollar changes, the relative attractiveness of the foreign goods will be affected. A strengthening dollar will decrease the price tag of an imported Toyota for a U.S. buyer, but the price tag of the domestically produced Ford will not change—the relative attractiveness of the Toyota will increase. Tourists watch exchange rates keenly—a stronger dollar is good news because each dollar will buy more foreign currency and, therefore, more foreign goods and services (which have, in that sense, become cheaper).

   The previous comparative advantage material (in Chapter 2) was based on production capabilities only—supply is important; demand is absent. By incorporating prices, the demand side of the market can be represented.

> **LEARNING TIP:** An increase in the value of the dollar means that foreign goods cost U.S. citizens less (imports increase), but U.S. goods cost foreigners more (exports fall). Choose a foreign country and currency and make up your own example. ◀

Practice

16.   The exchange rate is one British pound equals $1.75. If the exchange rate changes to one British pound equals $1.50, we can conclude that, for a British buyer, a pair of American-made moccasins have become _____ expensive and, for a U.S. buyer, a British cashmere sweater has become _____ expensive.
       (a)   more; more
       (b)   more; less
       (c)   less; more
       (d)   less; less

       ANSWER: (b) Each pound is worth less U.S. currency—British buyers are becoming poorer. The opposite is true for U.S. buyers of British goods.

17.   As the exchange rate changes from one British pound equals $1.50 to one British pound equals $2.00, British traders will gain _____ from trade with the United States, and American traders will gain _____ from trade with the United Kingdom.
        (a)   more; more
        (b)   more; less
        (c)   less; more
        (d)   less; less
        ANSWER: (b) Each pound is worth more U.S. currency. British producers, selling the same amount of exports, will be able to claim more U.S. goods than before.

Use the following table, which shows the domestic prices per unit of steel and corn in Arboc and Arbez, to answer the next three questions.

	Arboc	Arbez
Steel	20 opek	48 bandu
Corn	30 opek	87 bandu

18.   If the exchange rate is 1 opek = 1 bandu, then
        (a)   Arboc will import both steel and corn.
        (b)   Arbez will import both steel and corn.
        (c)   Arboc will import steel and Arbez will import corn.
        (d)   Arboc will import corn and Arbez will import steel.
        ANSWER: (b) In Arbez, the domestic prices of steel and corn are 48 bandu and 87 bandu, respectively. The imported prices are 20 bandu and 30 bandu, respectively.

19.   If the exchange rate is 1 opek = 3 bandu, then
        (a)   Arboc will import both steel and corn.
        (b)   Arbez will import both steel and corn.
        (c)   Arboc will import steel and Arbez will import corn.
        (d)   Arboc will import corn and Arbez will import steel.
        ANSWER: (a) In Arboc, the domestic prices of steel and corn are 20 opeks and 30 opeks, respectively. The imported prices are 16 opeks and 29 opeks, respectively.

20.   Two-way trade will occur only if the price of the opek is between
        (a)   1.0 bandu and 3.0 bandu.
        (b)   1.5 bandu and 2.4 bandu.
        (c)   2.4 bandu and 2.9 bandu.
        (d)   1.5 bandu and 3.0 bandu.
        ANSWER: (c) If the exchange rate is 1 opek = 2.4 bandu, no trade in steel will occur. If the exchange rate is 1 opek = 2.9 bandu, no trade in corn will occur. Between these rates, Arboc will import steel and Arbez will import corn. ∎

Objective 4

Provide an intuitive explanation of the Heckscher-Ohlin theorem.

The *Heckscher-Ohlin theorem* builds on the theory of comparative advantage by focusing on the differing factor endowments of countries. Some countries seem more labor-abundant (India, China) whereas others are more capital abundant (United States, Japan). The Heckscher-Ohlin theorem states that a country will specialize in and export that good whose production calls for a relatively intensive use of the input that the country has in abundance. If India has an abundance of labor and little capital then India should export labor-intensive goods and import capital-intensive goods, for example. (page 418 [672])

The assembly of T-shirts requires a large stock of semiskilled cheap labor with little capital. This favors Indonesia. Research into the capabilities of fiber optics requires a large stock of expensive capital. This favors the United States. The production of timber requires an abundant stock of forest land—a requirement that Canada meets.

In practice, the United States exports Californian wine and imports Italian wine. Germany ships BMWs to Sweden and imports Volvos. There is product differentiation and a range of consumer preferences. Foreign goods may be more exclusive or thought of as "better."

Practice

21. The Heckscher-Ohlin theorem explains that a country's comparative advantage stems from
    (a) acquired comparative advantage
    (b) relative factor endowments
    (c) product differentiation
    (d) differences in consumer preferences

    ANSWER: (b) The Heckscher-Ohlin theorem explains the presence of a country's comparative advantage by its relative factor endowments. A country with an abundance of labor will specialize in goods requiring labor-intensive production.

22. We observe that Arbez produces wooden ornaments (a labor-intensive activity), and that Arboc produces plastic containers (a capital-intensive activity). Which of the following statements is true?
    (a) Arbez has more labor than Arboc; Arboc has more capital than Arbez.
    (b) Arboc has more labor than Arbez; Arbez has more capital than Arboc.
    (c) Labor is relatively abundant in Arbez.
    (d) Labor is relatively abundant in Arboc.

    ANSWER: (c) Assuming that the two countries are being rational, Arbez is producing the good in which it has a comparative advantage. ■

Objective 5

Define a tariff, an export subsidy, and a quota. Outline, using a demand and supply analysis, the costs involved in the imposition of a tariff.

Tariffs, export subsidies, and quotas are examples of trade barriers. *Tariffs* are taxes on imports (usually), designed to force up their price; *export subsidies* are government payments to U.S. exporters, intended to make them more competitive overseas; *quotas* are limits on the quantity of imports. *Dumping* is meant to price competitors out of the market; having achieved market domination, the firm can then raise prices. (page 419[673])

ECONOMICS IN PRACTICE: On page 422 [676], the textbook reports that, during the recent recession, there was increased political pressure to impose greater trade restrictions. One case was that of European Union tariffs on Chinese shoes. China was accused of "dumping" (selling at below cost) by the Europeans. Dumping is a convenient charge as it may not be easy to disprove. Why would a country wish to sell its products at lower than its cost of production?
ANSWER: One aspect of dumping is that it is intended to undermine the domestic industry—in the present example, the Italian shoe industry. Having weakened or destroyed the local competition, the dumper may then be able to increase the price charged for its exports. A second reason for dumping is that the producer may prefer to sell at a loss by maintaining employment levels in an ailing industry.

ECONOMICS IN PRACTICE (CONTINUED): What is an export tariff and why would a country impose such a tariff?

ANSWER: An export tariff is a tax on a country's exports (rather than on its imports). It seems counterintuitive for a nation *not* to want to export but that is the effect of such a tariff. There are several possible reasons for the imposition of an export tax. In Argentina, for instance, in 2008, the government hiked the tax on beef exports from 5 percent to 15 percent in order to reduce export profitability, increase domestic supplies and reduce inflation. During the Cold War, export tariffs were imposed by the West in order to discourage exports to Soviet bloc nations.

Practice

Use the following diagram to answer the next three questions. The diagram shows the American demand for and supply of T-shirts. The world price is $8 per shirt.

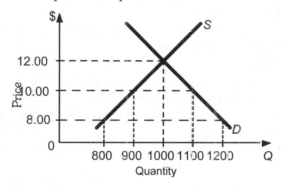

23.   In an unrestricted open market, the U.S. will
(a)   export 400 T-shirts.
(b)   export 200 T-shirts.
(c)   import 400 T-shirts.
(d)   import 200 T-shirts.

ANSWER: (c)   At a price of $8, there is an excess U.S. demand of 400.

24.   The garment industry successfully lobbies Congress to impose a $2 per shirt tax on imports. Now the U.S. will
(a)   export 400 T-shirts.
(b)   export 200 T-shirts.
(c)   import 400 T-shirts.
(d)   import 200 T-shirts.

ANSWER: (d)   An excess demand remains that must be met from overseas.

25.   The government will collect _____ in tariff revenues.
(a) $100
(b) $200
(c) $400
(d) $800

ANSWER: (c)   The government collects $2 per shirt on each of the 200 imported shirts. ∎

Objective 6

Give the arguments advanced for and against protection. Describe the costs involved in permitting free trade.

Historically, the United States has imposed high tariffs, particularly during the Great Depression of the 1930s. After the Second World War, there was increased pressure to liberalize trade, leading to the General Agreement on Trade and Tariffs (GATT) in 1947. In 1995, the World Trade Organization (WTO) was established and has grown to be the main organization for promoting and facilitating freer trade among nations. (page 422 [676])

There have been ongoing moves towards economic integration, with what is now known as the European Union forming the world's largest free-trade area in 1991. NAFTA (a free-trade agreement involving the United States, Canada, and Mexico) went into effect in 1994.

The case for free trade is based on the theory of comparative advantage. Voluntary trade benefits the participants. Welfare increases if trade flows are allowed to follow their "natural" pattern; obstacles, such as tariffs and quotas, reduce that efficiency and result in a deadweight loss of welfare. Higher-cost production results. (page 422 [676])

The argument in favor of protection is based on the observation that efficient foreign competition will result in job loss for domestic workers and lost production. Individual arguments for protection from foreign competition may include claims that cheap foreign labor is "unfair," that national security must be protected, that trade encourages dependency on foreigners, that trade may encourage environmentally unsound production, and that we need to let infant industries develop. Some of these arguments are simply false, and others are misused. (page 424 [678])

Whatever the merits of the debate, most economists favor free trade and, increasingly, evidence shows that governments across the world have been reducing tariffs.

LEARNING TIP: When trying to make sense of Figure 20.4 (34.4) and the effects of a tariff, recall that the concept of deadweight loss is dealt with in Chapter 4. ◖

ECONOMICS IN PRACTICE: On page 425 [679], the textbook reproduces "A Petition," a famous article from the nineteenth century French satirist Frederic Bastiat. Bastiat, it should be noted, favored an import quota over a tariff. Now consider the case of softwood imports from Canada into the United States. From 2002 until 2006, the United States imposed an average tariff of 29 percent on Canadian softwoods harvested in forests owned by the provinces (in response to alleged dumping). Privately-owned Canadian lumber was not subject to the tariff. First, what do you think happened to the balance of production in Canada between privately and publicly owned lumber? More importantly, from the U.S. point of view, can you predict what happened to the relative efficiency of U.S. and Canadian lumber mills and to the size of the U.S. lumber industry? Why would a quota have been a better option from the point of view of the U.S. lumber industry?

ANSWER: The production of privately owned lumber grew while publicly-owned timber production slumped. There was also a geographical shift in production—because the maritime provinces (Nova Scotia, New Brunswick) feature private ownership, they were big gainers from the U.S. measure. British Columbia's lumber industry lost 15,000 jobs. Protected American mills remained relatively high cost while Canadian mills were forced to become more efficient. In fact, many American mills closed down. A quota, rather than a tax, would have preserved a portion of the market for less efficient U.S. mills—a market that was eroded by Canadian competitiveness even in the face of a tariff. As a footnote, after the tariff had been scrapped, the WTO found the U.S. position on dumping "inconsistent."

Practice

26.   Which of the following is not an argument used by protectionists?
(a)   Infant industries need support until they are strong enough to compete.
(b)   Restricting trade builds up dependency on other counties.
(c)   Protection is needed in the light of unfair foreign practices, in order to ensure a level playing field.
(d)   Cheap foreign labor makes competition unfair.

ANSWER: (b)   Refer to page 368xx [678] for more on protectionist views. ∎

BRAIN TEASER SOLUTION: Almost any appeal can be made if one is sufficiently creative! Refer to Bastiat's "Petition" on page 425 [679].

PRACTICE TEST

I.   MULTIPLE-CHOICE QUESTIONS

Select the option that provides the single best answer.

_____   1.   According to the textbook, imports accounted for about _____ of the GDP of the United States in 1970 and about _____ of GDP today.
(a)   2 percent; 10 percent
(b)   7 percent; 17 percent
(c)   17 percent; 31 percent
(d)   53 percent; 70 percent

_____   2.   A country imports less than it exports. It has
(a)   an export subsidy.
(b)   a tariff quota.
(c)   a trade surplus.
(d)   a trade deficit.

_____   3.   Relative to Arboc, Arbez has a comparative advantage in the production of goat milk. We can say that Arbez
(a)   uses fewer resources to produce goat milk than does Arboc.
(b)   must also have an absolute advantage in the production of goat milk.
(c)   is the producer with the lower opportunity cost of producing goat milk.
(d)   should diversify into other products rather than trade with the high-cost, inefficient Arbocalis.

_____   4.   In trade between Arboc and Arbez, an increase in the exchange rate of the Arbezani currency (the bandu) relative to that of the Arbocali currency (the opek) means that
(a)   Arbezani goods will appear to be relatively cheaper to the Arbocalis.
(b)   Arbocali goods will appear to be relatively cheaper to the Arbezanis.
(c)   Arbez will lose any comparative advantage that it had.
(d)   Arbez will experience a decreasing trade deficit.

_____   5.   The Heckscher-Ohlin theorem states that Arbez will have a(n) _____ advantage in the production of a good that uses its relatively _____ .
(a)   absolute; scarce input intensively
(b)   absolute; abundant input intensively
(c)   comparative; abundant input intensively
(d)   comparative; scarce input intensively

_____ 6.   Two goods are produced, pins and needles. Jill has a comparative advantage in the production of pins. Relative to Jack, and with the same resources, Jill
(a)   is better at producing pins than at producing needles.
(b)   is better at producing both pins and needles.
(c)   can produce pins more efficiently than Jack.
(d)   can produce more pins than Jack.

_____ 7.   Jill chooses to trade pins for needles with Jack. It is likely that
(a)   Jill's gains equal Jack's losses.
(b)   pins are more expensive than needles.
(c)   each trader receives goods that he or she values more highly than those he or she gives up.
(d)   neither trader can gain more than the other.

For questions 8–10, assume that Arbez and Arboc have the same amount of resources and similar preferences for goat milk and bananas. The table shows the number of labor hours needed to produce 1 liter of goat milk and 1 kilo of bananas.

	Arbez	Arboc
Goat Milk	0.3	0.6
Bananas	0.5	0.2

_____ 8.   According to the preceding table,
(a)   Arbez has a comparative advantage in the production of both goods.
(b)   Arbez has a comparative advantage in the production of bananas, and Arboc has a comparative advantage in the production of goat milk.
(c)   Arbez has a comparative advantage in the production of goat milk, and Arboc has a comparative advantage in the production of bananas.
(d)   Arboc has a comparative advantage in the production of both goods.

_____ 9.   According to the table, one hour of labor produces
(a)   3 liters of goat milk in Arbez and 6 liters in Arboc.
(b)   5 kilos of bananas in Arbez and 2 kilos in Arboc.
(c)   2 kilos of bananas in Arbez and 5 kilos in Arboc.
(d)   6 liters of goat milk in Arboc and 2 kilos of bananas in Arboc.

_____ 10.   For trade to occur, the terms of trade might be
(a)   2 liters of goat milk for 1 kilo of bananas.
(b)   1 liter of goat milk for 4 kilos of bananas.
(c)   1 liter of goat milk for 0.7 of a kilo of bananas.
(d)   3 liters of goat milk for 1 kilo of bananas.

_____ 11.   Tariffs and quotas are economically inefficient because
(a)   the government does not collect any revenues under a tariff.
(b)   imports rise and this reduces the welfare of consumers.
(c)   producers are saved from the pressure of foreign competition.
(d)   domestic prices must be reduced.

_____ 12.   Which of the following is an argument in favor of increased protection?
     (a)   U.S. consumers have become too dependent on foreign countries for their luxury goods.
     (b)   National defense can be jeopardized if strategic supplies are produced by foreigners.
     (c)   Running a persistent trade deficit is unhealthy and must be avoided.
     (d)   Higher tariffs increase the welfare of U.S. consumers.

_____ 13.   Each of the following is a trade barrier EXCEPT
     (a)   a flexible exchange rate.
     (b)   a quota.
     (c)   an export subsidy.
     (d)   a tariff.

_____ 14.   Statement 1: A country with an absolute advantage in the production of a good will also have a comparative advantage.
Statement 2: A country with a comparative advantage in the production of a good will also have an absolute advantage.
Statement 1 is _____ ; Statement 2 is _____ .
     (a)   true; true
     (b)   true; false
     (c)   false; true
     (d)   false; false

_____ 15.   A tariff _____ increase the government's tax receipts; a quota _____ increase the government's tax receipts.
     (a)   does; does
     (b)   does; does not
     (c)   does not; does
     (d)   does not; does not

_____ 16.   In Tokyo, a Big Mac sells for 500 yen. The dollar : yen exchange rate is one dollar per 125 yen. The price of the Big Mac in dollars is
     (a) $500.00.
     (b) $0.25.
     (c) $4.00.
     (d) $5.00.

_____ 17.   In Tokyo, a Big Mac sells for 500 yen. The exchange rate changes from one dollar for 125 yen, to one dollar for 250 yen. The price of the Big Mac in dollars
     (a)   has increased.
     (b)   has decreased.
     (c)   has not changed.
     (d)   has doubled.

_____ 18.   The Heckscher-Ohlin theorem explains the pattern of trade by focusing on
     (a)   comparative advantage.
     (b)   absolute advantage.
     (c)   relative factor endowments.
     (d)   exchange rate variations.

_____ 19.   As the exchange rate changes from one British pound equals $1.50 to one British pound equals $1.00, the terms of trade shift _____ the United States. American traders will gain _____ from trade with the United Kingdom.
  (a)   in favor of; more
  (b)   in favor of; less
  (c)   against; more
  (d)   against; less

_____ 20.   We would expect a tariff imposed on an import to _____ the price of the import and to _____ the price of domestic substitutes for the import.
  (a)   increase; increase
  (b)   increase; not affect
  (c)   decrease; decrease
  (d)   decrease; not affect

II. APPLICATION QUESTIONS

1.   The Arbezani Minister of Trade, a firm believer in the Heckscher-Ohlin theorem, asks your advice regarding some recent changes within the Arbezani economy. In each of the following cases, he wishes to know whether or not the Heckscher-Ohlin explanation of trade flows will be strengthened. Arbez has established a free-trade region with its sole trading partner, Arboc.

  (a)   Arbezani unions in a substantial number of industries lobby successfully for increased restrictions on movement between industries, e.g., longer apprenticeships, work permits, drug testing of new entrants into an industry.

  (b)   It has been discovered that Arbez and its trading partner, Arboc, have identical endowments of all resources.

  (c)   Nationalistic Arbezani politicians, concerned about the loss of sovereignty caused by a free-trade area, have successfully passed restrictions on the flow of labor and other inputs between Arbez and Arboc.

2.   The nations of Noil and Regit produce loaves and fish. The labor supply is 12,000 labor units per year in Noil, whereas in Regit, the labor supply is 72,000 labor units per year. Assume that labor is the only input and that costs are constant within each economy.
  The costs of producing loaves and fish, in labor units, are given in the following table.

Units of Labor Supply Needed to Produce 1 Unit of:	Noil	Regit
Loaves	2	3
Fish	1	3

  (a)   Calculate the maximum output levels of loaves and fish for each economy and enter your results in the following table.

Maximum Units Produced:	Noil	Regit
Loaves	_____	_____
Fish	_____	_____

(b)   Draw the production possibility frontiers for each nation.

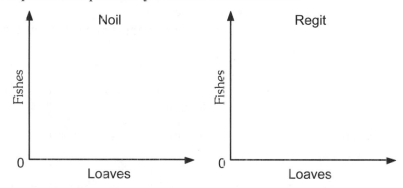

(c)   When questioned about the possibility of establishing trade between the two nations, the Regitani Minister of Trade states his government's official line—the proposal is ludicrous because Regit has an advantage in the production of each good. Is the Regitani view correct?

In both nations, the custom is to consume two loaves with each fish.

(d)   Assume that no trade takes place. Calculate the annual production of loaves and fish that will most satisfactorily meet demand in each country separately. Also determine the total production of loaves and fish for the two countries without trade.

Maximum Units Produced:	Noil	Regit	Total
Loaves	_____	_____	_____
Fish	_____	_____	_____

(e)   Yielding to pressure, the Regitani government opens its borders to trade with Noil. Based on comparative advantage, which good should Noil specialize in producing? Explain.

(f)   Assuming that specialization and trade flows are dictated by comparative advantage, determine the quantity of loaves and fish that can be produced.

(g)   Suppose that the terms of trade are established at 1 fish = 2 loaves. Determine the consumption of loaves and fish in each country.

Units Consumed:	Noil	Regit
Loaves	_____	_____
Fish	_____	_____

(h)   Has trade been mutually beneficial in this case?

(i)   Suppose that the terms of trade are established at 1 fish = 1 loaf. Determine the consumption of loaves and fish in each country.

Units Consumed:	Noil	Regit
Loaves	_____	_____
Fish	_____	_____

(j)   Has trade been mutually beneficial in this case?

(k)   Suppose that the terms of trade are established at 2 fish = 1 loaf. Determine the consumption of loaves and fish in each country.

Units Consumed:	Noil	Regit
Loaves	_____	_____
Fish	_____	_____

(l)   Has trade been mutually beneficial in this case?

(m)   Determine the "price" of a loaf (in terms of fish) necessary to have mutually beneficial two-way trade.

3.   The domestic price of Arbocali cloth is 4 opeks per yard. The domestic price of Arbezani leather is 12 bandu per hide. Arboc sells cloth to Arbez and Arbez sells hides to Arboc. The opek : bandu exchange rate is 2 opeks per bandu. The exchange rate is flexible.

      Ignoring transportation and other such costs, calculate the price in Arbez of a yard of imported Arbocali cloth and the price in Arboc of an imported Arbezani hide.

4.   Use the diagrams below to answer this question.

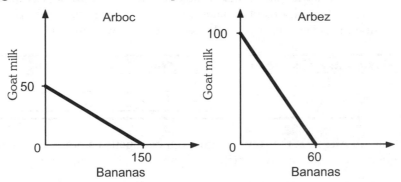

(a)   What is the opportunity cost of 1 kilo of bananas in Arboc?

(b)   What is the opportunity cost of 1 kilo of bananas in Arbez?

(c)   Which country has a comparative advantage in the production of bananas?

(d)   What is the opportunity cost of 1 liter of goat milk in Arboc?

(e)   What is the opportunity cost of 1 liter of goat milk in Arbez?

(f)   Which country has a comparative advantage in the production of goat milk?

(g)   If the terms of trade were 1 liter of goat milk/kilo of bananas, which country would want to export goat milk?

(h)   If the terms of trade were 3 liters of goat milk/kilo of bananas, Arboc should produce _____ and Arbez should produce _____ .

(i)   Suppose that the terms of trade were 1 kilo of bananas/1.5 liters of goat milk. _____ would export bananas and _____ would export goat milk.

5. Arboc and Arbez produce wine and cheese, and each has constant costs of production. The domestic prices for the two goods are given in the following table. At the moment 1 Arbocali opek is traded for 1 Arbezani bandu.

	Arboc	Arbez
Wine	40 opeks	120 bandu
Cheese	20 opeks	30 bandu

(a) Which country has a comparative advantage in cheese production?

(b) Which country has a comparative advantage in wine production?

(c) At the present exchange rate (1 opek = 1 bandu), will two-way trade occur? Explain.

(d) Which country will have a balance of trade deficit?

(e) What should happen to the value of the opek, relative to the bandu?

(f) If the exchange rate is 1 opek = 2 bandu, what would happen to trade?

(g) Cheese making is capital intensive, and wine making is labor intensive. Which country should have the relatively abundant supplies of labor, if the Heckscher-Ohlin theory is correct?

(h) If the exchange rate is 1 opek = 4 bandu, what would happen to trade?

6. Here are the domestic demand and supply schedules for diapers.

Price	Quantity Demanded	Quantity Supplied
$6	800	1,100
$5	1,000	1,000
$4	1,200	900
$3	1,400	800
$2	1,600	700

(a) Graph the demand and supply curves.

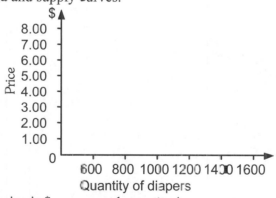

(b) The equilibrium price is $_____ and quantity is _____ .

(c) The world price for diapers is $3. Show this on the diagram as *Pw*. What will be the levels of domestic consumption and domestic production?

In order to preserve employment, diaper manufacturers contend successfully that theirs is an "infant industry" and should be protected.

(d)   A tariff is imposed that raises the price of imported diapers to $4. Show this on the diagram as *Pt*.

(e)   The tariff causes an increase in price and an increase in domestic production of _____ units. Consumption will fall to _____ units.

(f)   Imports will be _____ units. The tariff will yield $_____ in tax revenues.

(g)   Shade in the areas representing the net welfare loss caused by the tariff.

(h)   The loss in welfare is $_____.

Practice Test SOLUTIONS

I.   SOLUTIONS TO MULTIPLE-CHOICE QUESTIONS

1.   (b)   Refer to page 409 [663] for this information.

2.   (c)   Refer to page 410 [664] for the definition.

3.   (c)   Arbez might be relatively inefficient in producing both goods but relatively less inefficient in producing goat milk. Because Arbez has a comparative advantage in producing goat milk, its opportunity cost of producing goat milk must be less.

4.   (b)   As the Arbezani currency becomes more powerful, Arbocali goods will become cheaper when calculated in terms of the Arbezani currency.

5.   (c)   Refer to page 419 [673] for a statement of the Heckscher-Ohlin theorem.

6.   (a)   Remember that comparative advantage is a relative concept. It requires that we compare two producers and two goods.

7.   (c)   In voluntary trade, we expect each trader to gain something more than (s)he traded.

8.   (c)   Goat milk is relatively cheap to produce in Arbez and bananas require relatively few resources in Arboc. In a two-good, two-country situation, one party can never have a comparative advantage in both goods.

9.   (c)   0.5 labor hour gives 1 kilo of bananas in Arbez—1 hour gives 2 kilos. 0.2 labor hour gives 1 liter of milk in Arboc—1 hour gives 5 liters.

10.   (c)   The terms of trade must lie in the range from 1 liter of goat milk : 3/5 kilo of bananas to 1 liter of goat milk : 3 kilos of bananas. If Arbez has 6 hours of labor, it could produce 20 liters of goat milk or 12 kilos of bananas—a ratio of 1: 3/5. If Arboc has 6 hours of labor, it could produce 10 liters of goat milk or 30 kilos of bananas—a ratio of 1:3.

11.   (c)   Tariffs impose welfare losses in two ways. Consumers pay a higher price and, as mentioned in this question, marginal producers are allowed to survive. Option (b) is incorrect—imports don't increase, they decrease. Refer to page 423 [677].

12.   (b)   The national security argument is persistent.

13.   (a)   Refer to page 419 [673] for a discussion of trade barriers.

14.   (d)   A country may have an absolute advantage in the production of Good A and Good B; it may have a comparative advantage in the production of Good A and, therefore, a comparative disadvantage in Good B. Similarly, a country with a comparative advantage in the production of Good A might be less efficient than its partner in producing either good.

15.   (b)   A tariff is a tax that provides revenues; a quota merely restricts the number of units that may be imported.

16. (c) 125 yen equal $1.00, therefore, 500 yen equal $4.00

17. (b) 125 yen equal $1.00, therefore 500 yen equal $4.00; 250 yen equal $1.00; 500 yen equal $2.00.

18. (c) Refer to page 419 [673] for more on the Heckscher-Ohlin Theorem.

19. (a) Dollars are becoming relatively more valuable.

20. (a) A tariff will drive up the price of the import, increasing demand for domestic substitutes whose price will then increase.

II. SOLUTIONS TO APPLICATION QUESTIONS

1. (a) Heckscher-Ohlin assumes that inputs are mobile within an economy. Such restrictions will work against Heckscher-Ohlin because, as an economy begins to specialize and trade, it will wish to reallocate inputs.

   (b) According to Heckscher-Ohlin, comparative advantage is dependent on differences in factor endowments. No differences in factor endowments, no comparative advantage: no comparative advantage, no trade. Arbez and Arboc should have no basis for trade.

   (c) The new restrictions should not affect the pattern of trade. The Heckscher-Ohlin theorem assumes that inputs are not mobile between countries.

2. (a) Refer to the following table.

Maximum Units Produced:	Noil	Regit
Loaves	6,000	24,000
Fish	12,000	24,000

   (b) Refer to the following diagrams.

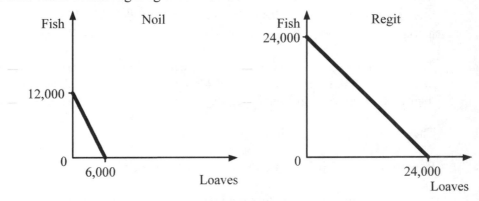

   (c) The Regitani view is mainly incorrect. Regit does have an absolute advantage in the production of both loaves and fish, but it does not have a comparative advantage in both, and it is comparative advantage that determines whether or not trade is advantageous.

(d)   Refer to the following table.

Maximum Units Produced:	Noil	Regit	Total
Loaves	4,800	16,000	20,800
Fish	2,400	8,000	10,400

Draw a line from the origin with a slope of 1/2 (corresponding to one fish for every two loaves). The solution is where the line intersects the production possibility frontier.

(e)   Noil should produce fish. In Noil, the cost of producing 1 loaf is 2 fish whereas the cost of producing 1 loaf in Regit is 1 fish. Loaves are less costly in Regit. Regit has a comparative advantage in loaves; Noil has a comparative advantage in fish.

(f)   Noil can produce 12,000 fish and Regit can produce 24,000 loaves.

(g)   Refer to the following table.

Units Consumed:	Noil	Regit
Loaves	12,000	12,000
Fish	6,000	6,000

Noil can produce 12,000 fish and export 6,000, earning 12,000 loaves in return. Regit can produce 24,000 loaves and export 12,000, earning 6,000 fish in return.

(h)   Trade has benefited Noil, but Regit has a lower standard of living than it had before trade!

(i)   Refer to the following table.

Units Consumed:	Noil	Regit
Loaves	8,000	16,000
Fish	4,000	8,000

Noil can produce 12,000 fish and export 8,000, earning 8,000 loaves in return. Regit can produce 24,000 loaves and export 8,000, earning 8,000 fish in return.

(j)   Trade has benefited Noil, but Regit's standard of living is unchanged.

(k)   Refer to the following table.

Units Consumed:	Noil	Regit
Loaves	4,800	16,000
Fish	2,400	8,000

Noil can produce 12,000 fish and export 9,600, earning 4,800 loaves in return. Regit can produce 24,000 loaves and export 4,800, earning 9,600 fish in return.

(l)   Trade has benefited Regit, but Noil's standard of living is unchanged.

(m)   The terms of trade need to be between 1 loaf = 1 fish and 1 loaf = 2 fish.

3.   A yard of imported Arbocali cloth will cost 2 bandu in Arbez. An imported Arbezani hide will cost 24 opeks in Arboc.

4.   (a)   1/3 of a liter of goat milk

       (b)   5/3 liters of goat milk

(c)   Arboc

(d)   3 kilos of bananas

(e)   6/10 of a kilo of bananas

(f)   Arbez

(g)   Arbez, because it can produce a liter of goat milk at a cost of less than one kilo of bananas and, therefore, can gain through this specialization.

(h)   bananas; bananas. One kilo of bananas can be sold for 2 liters of goat milk. Both Arboc and Arbez can produce bananas more cheaply than this (1/3 of a liter of goat milk and 5/3 liters of goat milk, respectively).

(i)   Arboc; Arbez. One kilo of bananas can be sold for 1.5 liters of goat milk. Arboc can produce bananas more cheaply than this (1/3 of a liter of goat milk) and so will produce bananas. One liter of goat milk can be sold for 2/3 kilo of bananas. Arbez can produce goat milk more cheaply than this (6/10 of a kilo of bananas) and so will produce goat milk.

5.   (a)   Arbez. Wine is four times as expensive as cheese in Arbez, but only twice as expensive in Arboc.

       (b)   Arboc. Each country must have a comparative advantage in one of the goods.

       (c)   No. Because Arboc can produce both goods more cheaply, the Arbezanis will import both. The Arbocalis will not wish to buy either Arbezani product.

       (d)   Arbez, because it has some imports and zero exports.

       (e)   The Arbocali currency (the opek) should be heavily demanded (by Arbezanis seeking to buy Arbocali goods). The demand for the bandu will be low. The opek will rise in value; the bandu will fall in value.

       (f)   At a price of 30 bandu (15 opeks), Arbezani cheese will now be cheaper than Arbocali cheese (at a price of 20 opeks). Arboc will import cheese. Arbez will continue to import Arbocali wine. At a price of 40 opeks (80 bandu), Arbocali wine is still cheaper than that produced in Arbez (at a price of 120 bandu).

       (g)   Arboc

       (h)   At a price of 30 bandu (7.50 opeks), Arbezani cheese will be cheaper than Arbocali cheese (at a price of 20 opeks). Arboc will import cheese.
At a price of 40 opeks (160 bandu), Arbocali wine will be more expensive than that produced in Arbez (at a price of 120 bandu). Arboc will import wine.
Arboc will have a trade deficit and Arbez a surplus.

6. (a)   Refer to the following diagram.

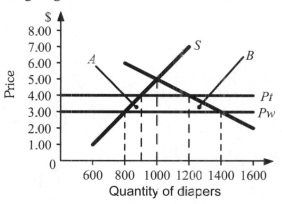

    (b) $5; 1,000.

    (c)   Refer to the preceding diagram; 1,400, 800.

    (d)   Refer to the preceding diagram.

    (e)   100; 1,200

    (f)   300; $300

    (g)   Refer to the preceding diagram. The net welfare loss is shown by triangular areas A and B.

    (h) $(50 + 100)

21 [36]
Economic Growth in Developing and Transitional Economies

Chapter Objectives

1. Describe the relationship between economic development and economic growth. Distinguish among conditions in the so-called First, Second, Third, and Fourth World countries.
2. List the factors that influence economic development. Explain why capital infrastructure is important for economic development.
3. Describe four strategic options affecting economic development.
4. Distinguish between economic growth and economic development. Discuss experiments conducted to assess programs related to education, health and population growth.
5. Summarize the economic measures taken by former planned economies to transform themselves into viable market-based economies.

BRAIN TEASER: During the Soviet era, almost all agricultural land was collectively owned. However, peasants were permitted to own small plots that amounted to about 1 percent of the total acreage under cultivation. Economist Milton Friedman pointed out that this small portion of land was responsible for about 33 percent of the total value of agricultural production in the Soviet Union. Can you explain this situation?

Objective 1

Describe the relationship between economic development and economic growth. Distinguish among conditions in the so-called First, Second, Third, and Fourth World countries.

In the past, the nations of the world have been roughly divided into three groups: the First World (Western, industrialized), the Second World (ex-Socialist, whose future is now uncertain), and the Third World (poor, largely agricultural). Nowadays, though, things are less clear cut. There is more mobility— China and India are almost in a class by themselves while others, such as Argentina and Korea, are breaking away from the Third World category and are being termed "newly industrialized countries." A number of nations are lagging so far behind that they have been called the "Fourth World" group. The main characteristic of a Third World country is that the great majority of its inhabitants are poor. Other dimensions that distinguish the "haves" from the "have nots" are health care, educational facilities, and the percentage of the population engaged in agriculture. (page 433 [713])

> **Comment:** There's no single unambiguous term that distinguishes the "developing nations" as the textbook deals with them. After all, in one sense, the United States is a developing economy too. "Third World" tends to have some political undertones. Remember that these nations are a pretty varied group, including South American, Asian, and African countries as diverse as Mexico and Mali, Taiwan, and Togo. Don't allow yourself to overgeneralize!

Practice

---

1. The poorest of the developing nations are sometimes known as the
    (a)   First World.
    (b)   Second World.
    (c)   Third World.
    (d)   Fourth World.

    ANSWER: (d) Refer to page 434 [714].

2. Most of the Fourth World nations are to be found in
    (a)   Latin America.
    (b)   sub-Saharan Africa.
    (c)   Southeast Asia.
    (d)   the former republics of the Soviet Union and its satellites.

    ANSWER: (b) Most of the very poorest nations are found to the south of the Sahara desert in
    Africa.

3. Per capita Gross Domestic Income (GDI) is _____ in developed countries, and infant mortality
    is _____ than in other countries.
    (a)   higher; higher
    (b)   higher; lower
    (c)   lower; higher
    (d)   lower; lower

    ANSWER: (b) Refer to Table 21.1 (36.1) in the textbook for this information. ∎

Objective 2

List the factors that influence economic development. Explain why capital infrastructure is
important for economic development.

No single theory has emerged to explain the development process, but various factors have been
identified as potential constraints on development. These include a low rate of accumulation of physical
capital, a lack of human capital, a lack of social overhead capital (infrastructure), and a lack of
entrepreneurial ability. These factors limit productivity and economic growth. Also, a lack of basic
infrastructure (access to water, electricity, health services, and education facilities, for instance) can
diminish the quality of life. (page 435 [715])

> **LEARNING TIP:** Pay attention to what is happening in your own state and locality. Many of the
> sources and strategies discussed in this chapter are not limited to poor foreign regions. Debates on
> economic development are also frequent at the state and local government level.◀

ECONOMICS IN PRACTICE: On page 438 [718], the textbook looks at the extent of corruption and how it
might retard economic development. Government agencies and red tape may impede entrepreneurs.
Consider the potential problems involved in getting permission to open a small business given the
presence of corrupt officials. What options might you explore and what might be the effects on the
optimal allocation of resources?
ANSWER: In one study on the effects of corruption on economic activity, researchers in Peru, paying
bribes only when essential, reportedly took the best part of a year to open a small factory. In such a
situation, entrepreneurs may give up, pay bribes or, perhaps, choose to operate as part of the
"underground economy," i.e., businesses that are not officially recognized. In the first case, the result is a
less efficient allocation of resources. If bribes are paid, there is a redistribution of income. If the business

goes underground, the state may lose tax revenues, health and safety regulations may be ignored, and workers may be exploited. Finally, when corruption is present, international funds that are intended for development projects may be siphoned off for private gain rather than public benefit.

Practice

4.   The brain drain refers to
       (a)   the movement of talented personnel from a developing country to a developed country.
       (b)   the absence of skilled entrepreneurs in the developing countries.
       (c)   declining literacy rates.
       (d)   the loss of human capital through the ravages of malnutrition.

       ANSWER: (a) Refer to page 437 [717] for the definition.

5.   Each of the following has been advanced as a plausible constraint on development EXCEPT the quantity of
       (a)   available capital.
       (b)   available labor.
       (c)   infrastructure.
       (d)   entrepreneurial ability.

       ANSWER: (b) The typical developing country has adequate numbers of workers, although specific skills may be limited.

6.   Capital shortages are a typical problem for developing countries. Each of the following is a plausible cause of capital shortages EXCEPT
       (a)   a lack of incentives leading to low saving rates.
       (b)   the inherent riskiness of investment in a developing nation.
       (c)   government policies, such as price ceilings and appropriation of private property.
       (d)   widespread poverty resulting in little surplus after consumption needs are met.

       ANSWER: (d) The vicious-circle-of-poverty hypothesis fails to account for the success of previously poor nations like Japan. Refer to page 436 [716]. ∎

Objective 3

Describe four strategic options affecting economic development.

Many, often conflicting, development strategies have been attempted over the years.

(a) Government control or private enterprise? The economy must choose the appropriate balance between free markets and centralized planning. Industrial planning permits coordination of economic activities that private individuals or firms might not undertake (disease and pest control, or literacy training, for instance), and the channeling of funds into efficient projects or sectors from which development might spring, but such planning would be difficult for a Third World nation to administer.

(b) Agriculture or industrialization? Development used to be equated with industrialization; many Third World nations sought to move away from agriculture and toward industrial production. However, merely trying to replicate the structure of the developed nations does not guarantee development. Opinion now favors a balanced growth in both agricultural and industrial sectors—"walking on two legs."

(c) Export promotion or import substitution? Import substitution calls for the encouragement of homegrown substitutes for imported goods. This strategy has failed in almost every case; it results in high-cost production protected by trade barriers. Export promotion calls for producing goods for the export market and has seen some measure of success, although it depends on the willingness of the developed nations to import Third-World production. China and, earlier, Japan, have made successful use of export-led development.

(d) Microfinance is a comparatively recent innovation. Borrowers receive small loans with no collateral required. The loans are financed with very small savings deposits. Such funding of emerging businesses is impractical for large financial institutions but community-based financing has had considerable success because it relies heavily on local interpersonal knowledge and peer lending. (page 439 [719])

Following the Second World War, the initial emphasis was largely on rapid growth. The 1970s, however, saw increasing concern about how the benefits of growth were (or were not) being distributed. Despite growth, poverty persisted for a large percentage of those living in developing countries, and aid was often tied to programs to satisfy basic needs. More recently, income redistribution has lost its prominence to market efficiency.

Despite differences, China and India are good examples of rapid economic development accomplished by differing strategies. China's growth has been led by the manufacturing sector while India's is driven by a flourishing service sector. Both economies, however, share an emphasis on adopting free market economics.

ECONOMICS IN PRACTICE: On page 442 [722], the textbook examines how an innovation—cell phones—has improved the efficiency of fish markets in India, increasing profits and reducing waste. The cell phones improved information about market conditions and allowed a better matching-up of buyers and sellers. Internet sales operate on a similar principle—reducing transactions costs through the application of a new technology. Your textbook refers to another example of the same principle—microfinancing, on pages 441–442 [721–722]. Review that material and confirm that a similar process—reducing the cost of information—is present and that growth possibilities are being enhanced by its application.

ANSWER: Peer lending solves many of the problems associated with conventional financing in developing countries. Most projects are too small for mainstream banks to justify the expense of information collecting. By simplifying the loan process and by incentivizing the community's collection of information about creditworthiness (who gets loans first), funds are allocated more efficiently. This innovation, like the use of cell phones by the fishermen, reduces waste and fosters a better climate that permits development opportunities to be exploited.

Practice

7.   Experience suggests that, of the following, the development approach most likely to succeed is
   (a)   rapid industrial mechanization coupled with labor migration to the industrial centers.
   (b)   intensive training of human capital to occupy technologically advanced positions in import-substitution industries.
   (c)   a balanced promotion of both the agricultural sector and the manufacturing sector.
   (d)   slow, careful industrial growth combined with rapid expansion in food provision to improve human capital.

   ANSWER: (c) This is the "walking on two legs" strategy. Refer to page 440 [720].

8. Noil is a small sub-Saharan nation with few sophisticated resources. However, it constructs an airport and hotel with lavish Western facilities and offers safari trips into its beautiful mountain ranges to groups from developed countries. Noil is best described as having opted for a(n) _____ development strategy.
   (a) import substitution
   (b) export promotion
   (c) rural exploitation
   (d) balanced growth

   ANSWER: (b) Tourism is an export.

9. Microfinance uses peer lending to avoid the problem of
   (a) imperfect information.
   (b) minimal entrepreneurship.
   (c) nonrepayment of loans.
   (d) high interest rates.

   ANSWER: (a) Local, small-group microfinance gives reliable borrowers a strong incentive to ensure that only other reliable borrowers will be selected to enter the scheme.

10. Relative to traditional bank loans, most microfinance loans are to _____ and repayment begins _____.
    (a) men; quickly
    (b) men; slowly
    (c) women; quickly
    (d) women; slowly

    ANSWER: (c) The great majority of microfinance loans are received by women and repayment of the loan typically begins quickly.

11. Generally, import substitution policies have
    (a) failed in almost every case.
    (b) succeeded, but only while the cost of imported oil was held down.
    (c) not been an unqualified success, but have had a better track record than export promotion policies.
    (d) succeeded in Latin America, but failed in Africa and had mixed results in Asia.

    ANSWER: (a) Import substitution policies reduce exports and foster inefficient, inappropriate (i.e., capital-intensive) production methods. ∎

Objective 4

Distinguish between economic growth and economic development. Discuss experiments conducted to assess programs related to education, health and population growth.

Economic growth and economic development should be treated as separate processes. Economic growth, as measured by higher levels of per capita income, may be taking place although indicators of economic development, such as nutrition, health, and education, may not be changing. Growth may occur without development. Whereas the World Bank had initially emphasized policies that would foster general economic growth, since the 1990s the focus has reversed to stress narrower, microeconomically oriented programs that bestow benefits on the most needy. (page 443 [723])

Three major areas that contribute to individual poverty—education, health and population—have received much attention. Are there simple ways to make programs more effective in these areas? Typically, as economies expand, the rewards from additional education also increase. Given limited resources, decisions must be made in order to maximize pay-offs from educational investments. One area of concern is absenteeism among not only students but also teachers. It has been found that modest compensation for attendance can have a significant beneficial impact.

Many inhabitants of developing countries suffer from poor health that traps them in poverty, despite the availability of cheap effective treatments. Potential solutions include more health education and improved delivery systems for public health programs. Experiments have shown, however, that the beneficial effects of health education are minimal, and that even small user fees for medical services can dramatically slash treatment rates.

The Third World death rate has tumbled sharply because of better medical treatment, but the birthrate has declined much more slowly. Although large families may provide a cheap labor pool today and support in old age tomorrow, rapid expansion in the population places burdens on public services and may be undesirable from the viewpoint of society.

Over two hundred years ago, Malthus predicted increasing impoverishment unless population growth was reduced. However, Malthus failed to foresee the dramatic increases in agricultural productivity that have occurred over the years. In addition, there has been a trend towards reduced family size. In some nations, economic incentives have been applied successfully to encourage smaller families. (page 446 [726])

Practice

12. Usually, as economies grow, the returns to education _____ and more parents in the developing world have _____ their family size.
    (a)   increase; increased
    (b)   increase; decreased
    (c)   decrease; increased
    (d)   decrease; decreased

    ANSWER: (b) With more complex societies, education becomes more beneficial. With limited resources, it makes sense for families to "train" fewer children more intensively.

13. In a study on the treatment of intestinal worms, Kremer and Miquel found that modest user fees _____ treatment rates.
    (a)   greatly increased
    (b)   greatly decreased
    (c)   slightly increased
    (d)   slightly decreased

    ANSWER: (b) Refer to page 445 [725] for more information about this study.

14. In a study on the treatment of intestinal worms, Kremer and Miquel found that health education _____ very effective and that individuals _____ sensitive to cost and benefit considerations.
    (a)   was; were
    (b)   was; were not
    (c)   was not; were
    (d)   was not; were not

    ANSWER: (c) Refer to page 445 [725] for more information about this study.

15. Malthus predicted that the world population would grow at a(n) _____ growth rate, and the production of food would increase more _____ .
    (a)   increasing; rapidly
    (b)   increasing; slowly
    (c)   constant; rapidly
    (d)   constant; slowly

ANSWER: (d) Refer to page 446 [726]. Note that a constant rate of growth means rapid absolute growth in the population—10 percent of 100 is only 10; 10 percent of 10,000 is 1,000.

16. Schultz argued that technical progress has _____ returns to education. This, in turn, has encouraged a(n) _____ in family size.
(a) increased; expansion
(b) increased; reduction
(c) decreased; expansion
(d) decreased; reduction

ANSWER: (b) By reducing family size, children can achieve a higher level of education. (substituting quality for quantity)

17. High fertility rates may cause all of the following EXCEPT
(a) falling saving rates.
(b) reduced availability of social programs for each individual.
(c) labor shortages.
(d) food shortages.

ANSWER: (c) As the population expands, there should be no labor constraint. ∎

Objective 5

Summarize the economic measures taken by former planned economies to transform themselves into viable market-based economies.

Beginning in the 1990s, the centrally economies of the former Soviet bloc began moves towards liberalization of markets. There were increased incentives, and the removal of price controls, with countries moving at different rates. There has been much debate whether the reform requirements should be introduced rapidly by "shock therapy" or phased in gradually. In fact, in the Russian case, due to the crippled state of the state-owned enterprises, shock therapy was not a feasible option, even if it had been the preferred alternative. Poland's shock therapy, on the other hand, was a success. China, India, and Vietnam are notable additions to the list of economies seeking to inject more competition into their economic practices. (page 447 [727])

Six requirements for a successful transition from a planned economy to a market-based one have been identified:
1. Macroeconomic stabilization
2. Deregulation of prices and trade liberalization
3. Privatization of the means of production
4. The establishment of a "support system" for the market
5. A social safety net to lessen the distress of unemployment and poverty
6. External assistance

Comment: The economic reforms within the former Soviet republics, China, India and other states are ongoing. You should be able to flesh out the material in this chapter by keeping your ears and eyes open to the news reports. Have the economic reforms been identical in each country? How much success/resistance are they experiencing? From the mid-1990s, Cuba began shifting position on economic matters and more so in the past few years. The Vietnamese (and Vietnamese businesspersons in the United States) argued successfully for the relaxation of U.S.-imposed commercial barriers. Both of these economies are well worth watching.

Tragedy of Commons: Usually, property owned communally, such as the bison, the dodo, or the grasslands of sub-Saharan Africa, is rapidly depleted. Taking the example of common grazing land, there is little incentive for the individual farmer to conserve pasture, and indeed the opposite may be true. Self-interest dictates that one would make the most of the "free" resources, although such thinking by each farmer would lead to a depletion of those resources. At this point you might note the old saying that "Good fences make good neighbors." Capitalism, then, relies on the emergence of self-interest and the rewards of private property because the former without the latter would result in the tragedy of commons.

Practice

18.   Each of the following is seen as a requirement for a successful transition from socialism to a market-based economy EXCEPT
      (a)   price regulation.
      (b)   provision of a commercial infrastructure—i.e., market-supporting institutions.
      (c)   removal of trade barriers.
      (d)   a freely operating labor market.

      ANSWER: (a)   To ration scarce resources efficiently, prices should be free to adjust.

19.   The notion that collective ownership of resources may be inefficient because individuals do not bear the full cost of their own decisions is called
      (a)   exploitation.
      (b)   the tragedy of commons.
      (c)   surplus value.
      (d)   the externality effect.

      ANSWER: (b)   Refer to page 449 [729] for a discussion of this topic.

20.   Each of the following is an example of the tragedy of commons EXCEPT
      (a)   pollution in the Great Lakes.
      (b)   overgrazing of shared tribal land.
      (c)   the decimation of the American bison by nineteenth-century settlers.
      (d)   the slaughtering of his entire herd by a Texan rancher.

      ANSWER: (d)   The herd is private property. ∎

BRAIN TEASER SOLUTION: Peasants had more incentive to work their own plots intensively—anything they produced, they could keep or sell. On the collective land, there were far fewer incentives for the individual to work hard because output was owned by the state. In addition, peasants often "borrowed" state resources to help them with their private plots. Furthermore, peasants were motivated to produce desirable produce that they could trade.

PRACTICE TEST

I.   MULTIPLE-CHOICE QUESTIONS

Select the option that provides the single best answer.

_____   1.   Which of the following are characteristics of the average developing country?
             (a)   Large populations and high savings rates
             (b)   Low levels of human capital and low per capita GDP
             (c)   High infant mortality and high pollution indexes
             (d)   Low health standards and high literacy rates

_____ 2. Import substitution occurs when a country
- (a) becomes developed.
- (b) erects trade barriers.
- (c) no longer has sufficient foreign exchange to buy imports.
- (d) strives to produce goods that were previously imported.

_____ 3. Economic development occurs when there is an increase in the
- (a) per capita nominal GDP.
- (b) per capita real GDP.
- (c) material well-being of the nation's citizens.
- (d) labor force.

_____ 4. Lack of economic development might be caused by
- (a) a low marginal propensity to consume.
- (b) an excess supply of private overhead capital.
- (c) a high literacy rate.
- (d) inadequate amounts of social overhead capital.

_____ 5. Which of the following is an example of an improvement in social overhead capital?
- (a) A multinational corporation opens a new plant.
- (b) The workers at the local textile mill establish a credit union.
- (c) There is an increase in the rate of growth of per capita real GDP.
- (d) A national adult literacy program is established by the government.

_____ 6. Labor is relatively abundant in Arboc. Arboc might best be able to develop by
- (a) using production techniques that are capital intensive.
- (b) using production techniques that employ labor and capital in fixed and equal proportions.
- (c) specializing in the production of labor-intensive commodities that should be relatively cheaper to produce.
- (d) specializing in the production of capital-intensive commodities, which should be marketable at relatively higher prices.

_____ 7. Local firms in Arboc are unlikely to undertake large investment projects such as highway construction because
- (a) the government is unlikely to share the cost.
- (b) interest rates are higher for the borrowed funds necessary for such projects.
- (c) the benefits from such projects cannot be easily bought or sold.
- (d) international agencies such as the World Bank and the IMF prefer short-term projects.

_____ 8. Adopting the strategy of "walking on two legs" means that
- (a) men and women should be treated equally in the workplace.
- (b) import substitution and export promotion should be attempted simultaneously.
- (c) attention must be paid to developing both the industrial sector and the agricultural sector.
- (d) the dependent links with old colonial nations should be severed.

_____ 9.   Import substitution might fail to promote economic development if
   (a)   producers use domestic inputs that are lower in cost than imported inputs.
   (b)   firms make use of capital-intensive production methods that fail to reduce unemployment.
   (c)   such goods require labor-intensive methods of production.
   (d)   after establishment, these industries are subsidized by the state.

_____ 10.   The "export promotion" strategy calls for
   (a)   the running of a balance of trade deficit.
   (b)   the production of goods that are demanded by consumers in the developed countries.
   (c)   the production of export goods for domestic consumers.
   (d)   the domestic production of goods that previously had been imported.

_____ 11.   Sending savings from the Third World nation of Arboc to the United States _____ to growth in Arboc's physical capital. New Arbocali import controls will tend to _____ investment in Arboc.
   (a)   leads; increase
   (b)   leads; decrease
   (c)   does not lead; increase
   (d)   does not lead; decrease

_____ 12.   Deregulating prices is likely to cause _____ ; removing subsidies will cause _____ in the short term.
   (a)   higher prices for staple items; unemployment
   (b)   higher prices for staple items; increased employment
   (c)   lower prices for staple items; unemployment
   (d)   lower prices for staple items; increased employment

_____ 13.   China's recent economic growth has been led by the _____ sector; India's has been led by the _____ sector.
   (a)   export; manufacturing
   (b)   manufacturing; service
   (c)   service; manufacturing
   (d)   export; export

_____ 14.   In Arboc, the state provides goods such as education, national defense, universal health care, and roads. Other industries, which are privately owned, face government regulations on pollution and worker safety. Minimum wage legislation is present and wage earners are taxed on their income. Arboc is best described as
   (a)   socialist.
   (b)   communist.
   (c)   capitalist.
   (d)   totalitarian.

_____ 15.   "Shock therapy" refers to
   (a)   the sudden change experienced by the Soviet Union following Gorbachev's economic reforms.
   (b)   the overthrow of the Soviet Union's economic system.
   (c)   Stalin's goal of electrification of collective farms.
   (d)   rapid deregulation of prices, liberalization of trade, and privatization.

_____ 16.   _____ Poland, China has favored a _____ approach to development.
    (a)   Like; rapid
    (b)   Like; gradual
    (c)   Unlike; rapid
    (d)   Unlike; gradual

_____ 17.   All of the following discourage Third World development EXCEPT
    (a)   the lack of skilled entrepreneurs.
    (b)   insufficient social overhead capital.
    (c)   insufficient labor-saving technological innovation.
    (d)   inadequate amounts of human capital.

_____ 18.   _____ is a development strategy that is designed to encourage sales abroad.
    (a)   Import substitution
    (b)   Export promotion
    (c)   "Walking on two legs"
    (d)   Dependency

_____ 19.   Rapid population growth rates may cause all of the following EXCEPT
    (a)   an eventual increase in the proportion of working-age adults in the population.
    (b)   an increase in the number of dependents.
    (c)   decreases in the rate of capital formation.
    (d)   decreases in saving rates.

_____ 20.   The "tragedy of commons" exemplifies the problem of _____ in the case of resources that are owned _____ .
    (a)   inefficiency; privately
    (b)   inequity; privately
    (c)   inefficiency; publicly
    (d)   inequity; publicly

_____ 21.   In a study on the treatment of intestinal worms, Kremer and Miquel found that self-sustaining medical programs funded by modest user fees would be likely to have
    (a)   large positive effects
    (b)   large negative effects
    (c)   small positive effects
    (d)   small negative effects

II. APPLICATION QUESTIONS

1.   Compare and contrast the economic conditions in the "First World" and the Third World. Take a "typical" country from each group, for example, France and Peru. Examine such issues as life expectancy, number of doctors per thousand persons, educational level, rate of inflation, unemployment, and so forth. (A good source is the _World Development Report_, published annually by the World Bank—it will be in your library. The Bank's website is at www.worldbank.org.) Compare the figures for an NIC (newly industrialized country), such as Taiwan or Korea with those of a sub-Saharan African nation. Is there really such a thing as a "typical" Third World nation?

2.   Suppose that 10 units of food are required per person per year in the developing nation of Arboc. Due to improved crops and farming techniques, food production will increase by a fixed amount every 10 years—suppose this amount is 1,000 units of food so that, in 2010, food production is

11,000 units. Arboc currently exports its surplus food production. Imports run at a constant 2,000 units. Because of high birth rates and decreasing death rates, Arboc's population increases by 50 percent every 10 years.

(a)   Given the conditions specified, complete the following table.

Year	Food Production	Population	Food Requirements	Food Surplus/Deficit
2000	10,000	400	4,000	+6,000
2010	11,000	_____	_____	_____
2020	_____	_____	_____	_____
2030	_____	_____	_____	_____
2040	_____	_____	_____	_____

(b)   What happens in or about the year 2030?

(c)   Other things unchanged, what will happen to Arboc's balance of trade?

(d)   Given the situation in 2040, what do you think will happen to Arboc?

3.   Choose any developing country for comparison against the United States. Profile your country by doing research into the following characteristics. You can do this by reading, for example, the World Bank's most recent annual *World Development Indicators* or by visiting its website www.worldbank.org.

   The characteristics you collect will require numbers. The numbers in parentheses are the values for the United States from the 2009 Report.

(a)   Life expectancy at birth   _____   (77.4 years)

(b)   Adult illiteracy rate   _____   (1 percent)

(c)   Population with access to safe water (percent)   _____   (100 percent)

(d)   GNI per capita   _____   ($41,400)

(e)   Agriculture as percentage of output   _____   (2 percent)

(f)   Infant mortality rate (per 1,000 live births)   _____   (6.43)

(g)   Percentage of population living on less than $1 per day   _____   (0 percent)

4.   List the following countries from most market based to least market based: Russia, United States, France, Cuba, Japan, China.

5.   Underline the correct answer found in parenthesis.
   Russia's economic reform package included:
(a)   price controls: (increased/decreased/removed)

(b)   market-supporting institutions: (increased/decreased/ removed)

(c)   ownership of resources: more (centralized/privatized)

(d)   external aid: (increased/decreased/removed)

(e)   job security: (increased/decreased/removed)

(f)   trade: (restricted/liberalized)

(g)   money supply growth: (increased/curtailed)

6.   Why do birth rates tend to decrease as economies develop?

7.   Considering a treatment program for intestinal worms, Kremer and Miquel found that there was a dramatic 80 percent decline in treatment rates in the presence of even a small user fee. We are told that this is very much in keeping with economic principles. What do these results suggest to you about the perceived effectiveness of the treatments?

Practice Test SOLUTIONS

I. SOLUTIONS TO MULTIPLE-CHOICE QUESTIONS

1. (b) Refer to page 434 [714] for a full discussion of the characteristics of developing nations.

2. (d) Import substitution is a strategy that attempts to establish a domestic industry that can provide goods to replace imports. Refer to page 440 [720].

3. (c) Improvements in per capita GDP do not guarantee development.

4. (d) To grow, an economy needs an adequate quantity and quality of resources, including socially provided resources.

5. (d) Social overhead capital includes projects that cannot be undertaken privately.

6. (c) This is an application of the Heckscher-Ohlin theorem from Chapter 19 (34).

7. (c) If the good is a "public good" a private firm may find it difficult to derive revenues from it. A fee or tax, however, might be imposed by the government.

8. (c) The Chinese phrase "walking on two legs" describes the need to have both agricultural and industrial sectors developing together.

9. (b) To be effective, the strategy must play to the strengths of its own economy—typically labor-intensive production.

10. (b) Refer to page 441 [721] for a discussion of this development strategy.

11. (d) Refer to the discussion of capital flight on page 436 [716].

12. (a) Staple items were underpriced; inefficient firms will be driven out of business without subsidies.

13. (b) Manufacturing has been most important in China whereas the service sector has fueled India's expansion.

14. (c) With the exception of the health care, Arboc is quite like the United States.

15. (d) Refer to page 451 [731].

16. (d) China's approach to development (*moshi guohe*) has been gradual whereas Poland successfully employed "shock therapy."

17. (c) The quantity of labor is not a significant constraint in the Third World. Labor-saving technology, then, is not critical to successful development.

18. (b) Refer to page 441 [721] for a discussion of this development strategy.

19. (a) As more children are born, even as the population ages, the proportion of adults will decrease.

20.   (c)   "Commons" are commonly owned land. Typically, this resource is treated inefficiently.

21.   (b)   Kremer and Miquel found that there was a dramatic decline in treatment rates in the presence of even a small user fee.

II. SOLUTIONS TO APPLICATION QUESTIONS

1.   Although there is no single model for a developing nation, certain common characteristics emerge—high birthrates, improving life expectancy, improvements in literacy rates, better/more nutrition and shelter, and so on.

2.   (a)   Refer to the following table.

Year	Food Production	Population	Food Requirements	Food Surplus/Deficit
2000	10,000	400	4,000	+6,000
2010	11,000	600	6,000	+5,000
2020	12,000	900	9,000	+3,000
2030	13,000	1,350	13,500	−500
2040	14,000	2,025	20,250	−6,250

(b)   Food requirements outstrip food production.

(c)   As the food surplus decreases, less will be available for export and the balance of trade will become less favorable. Somewhere around 2028, the trade surplus in food will become a deficit.

(d)   This is an open question. Arboc will be heavily in debt and will need to import food to feed its population. Imports of industrial goods would slacken. Reduced health care (per person) might cause famine and disease, reducing the population. Arboc might borrow to finance its overseas spending and might have to receive ongoing foreign aid. Population control policies would have to be considered or individuals might emigrate.

3.   Answers will depend on the country chosen.

4.   There can be some dispute here—systems evolve and emphases change—but a plausible ranking would be: Japan, United States, France, Russia, China, Cuba.

5.   removed; increased; privatized; increased; decreased; liberalized; curtailed

6.   Birth rates may decrease for several reasons in the face of economic development. Development usually involves a movement away from agriculture, where large families provide a valuable labor force. With the growth of government agencies, there is diminished need for an extended family to provide support. With women entering the labor force, the opportunity cost of child-bearing increases.

7.   Applying cost and benefit principles, we must conclude that there is a low private valuation placed on deworming. The study cited in fact states that individuals felt that the treatment was not effective. In that case, any fee would be a disincentive to treatment.

Comprehensive Review Test

The following questions provide a wide-ranging review of the material covered in Part IV (Chapters 20 and 21 (34 and 36)) of the textbook. Each question deals with a topic or technique important for your understanding of economic principles. If you miss a question you should return to the relevant section of the chapter in the textbook and fine tune your understanding.

I. MULTIPLE-CHOICE QUESTIONS

Select the option that provides the single best answer.

_____ 1. A tariff imposed on imported French wine will cause the U.S. price of French wine to _____ and U.S. production of wine to _____.
    (a) increase; increase
    (b) increase; decrease
    (c) decrease; increase
    (d) decrease; decrease

_____ 2. Trade barriers _____ welfare. Trade barriers _____ domestic employment in industries that lack a comparative advantage.
    (a) increase; increase
    (b) increase; decrease
    (c) decrease; increase
    (d) decrease; decrease

_____ 3. A U.S. tariff imposed on goods that can be produced more cheaply overseas would tend to
    (a) benefit American consumers by making these goods cheaper.
    (b) make the goods more expensive in other (overseas) markets.
    (c) equalize the costs of production between U.S. producers and foreign producers.
    (d) make U.S. producers artificially more competitive relative to foreigners.

Refer to the following table to answer the next nine questions.

	England	Portugal
Wine	9 bottles	6 bottles
Cloth	18 yards	9 yards

_____ 4. England has an absolute advantage in the production of
    (a) cloth
    (b) wine.
    (c) both goods.
    (d) neither good.

_____ 5.   The opportunity cost of one bottle of wine in Portugal is
    (a)   2/3 of a yard of cloth.
    (b)   1⅓ yards of cloth.
    (c)   1½ yards of cloth.
    (d)   9 yards of cloth.

_____ 6.   England and Portugal decide to specialize according to the law of comparative advantage and begin trading with one another. We would expect that the terms of trade will be somewhere between
    (a)   1 bottle of wine for 1 yard of cloth and 1/2 of a bottle of wine for 1 yard of cloth.
    (b)   2/3 of a bottle of wine for 1 yard of cloth and 1½ bottles of wine for 1 yard of cloth.
    (c)   1/2 of a bottle of wine for 1 yard of cloth and 1½ bottles of wine for 1 yard of cloth.
    (d)   1/2 of a bottle of wine for 1 yard of cloth and 2/3 of a bottle of wine for 1 yard of cloth.

_____ 7.   Which of the following statements is true?
    (a)   England has a comparative advantage in the production of wine; Portugal has a comparative advantage in the production of cloth.
    (b)   England has a comparative advantage in the production of cloth; Portugal has a comparative advantage in the production of wine.
    (c)   England has a comparative advantage in both goods.
    (d)   Portugal has a comparative advantage in both goods.

_____ 8.   Suppose the terms of trade are that 1 bottle of wine trades for 1 yard of cloth. England should specialize in _____ production; Portugal should specialize in _____ production.
    (a)   cloth; cloth
    (b)   cloth; wine
    (c)   wine; cloth
    (d)   wine; wine

_____ 9.   Suppose the terms of trade are that 1 bottle of wine trades for 1¾ yard of cloth. England should specialize in _____ production; Portugal should specialize in _____ production.
    (a)   cloth; cloth
    (b)   cloth; wine
    (c)   wine; cloth
    (d)   wine; wine

_____ 10.   According to the theory of comparative advantage trade between the two countries will
    (a)   equalize their consumption levels.
    (b)   benefit all industries in each country.
    (c)   permit each partner to use its resources in the most efficient way.
    (d)   permit each partner to achieve a consumption mix at some point on its production possibility frontier.

_____ 11. In terms of production possibility frontiers, if England's maximum production of cloth is 1,800 yards, its maximum production of wine is _____ bottles. If Portugal's maximum production of wine is 1,200 bottles, its maximum production of cloth is _____ yards.
  (a)   0; 0
  (b)   900; 900
  (c)   900; 1,800
  (d)   1,800; 900

_____ 12. Based on the information in the previous question, we should now conclude that
  (a)   England has an absolute advantage in the production of both goods.
  (b)   England has an absolute advantage in the production of cloth only.
  (c)   Portugal has an absolute advantage in the production of wine.
  (d)   England has an absolute advantage in the production of neither good.

_____ 13. The United States and the United Kingdom both produce cashmere sweaters and leather vests. In the United States, sweaters sell for $150 and vests sell for $150. In the United Kingdom, sweaters sell for £60 and vests sell for £100. Suppose the pound/dollar exchange rate is £1 = $2.
  (a)   The United States will import both sweaters and vests from the United Kingdom.
  (b)   The United States will import sweaters from the United Kingdom; the United Kingdom will import vests from the United States.
  (c)   The United States will import sweaters from the United Kingdom; the United Kingdom will import sweaters from the United States.
  (d)   The United Kingdom will import both sweaters and vest from the United States.

_____ 14. The small Asian nation of Regit chooses to follow an import substitution strategy and builds a fertilizer plant to serve its rice farmers. Based on similar experiments elsewhere, we would expect to see all of the following EXCEPT
  (a)   high fertilizer production costs.
  (b)   the imposition of tariffs to protect domestic fertilizer production.
  (c)   capital-intensive fertilizer production techniques.
  (d)   a rise in the international competitiveness of the nation's rice farmers.

_____ 15. Each of the following is a tactic typical of the export promotion strategy EXCEPT
  (a)   reducing the value of the domestic currency relative to other currencies.
  (b)   increasing the nation's ability to compete domestically with the exports of other nations.
  (c)   the provision of subsidies to exporters.
  (d)   the provision of preferential investment tax breaks to exporting firms.

_____ 16. Each of the following is a basic requirement for a successful transition from socialism to a market-based economy EXCEPT
  (a)   a social safety net to deal with unemployment and poverty.
  (b)   free and fair democratic elections.
  (c)   deregulation of prices and liberalization of trade.
  (d)   macroeconomic stabilization.

_____   17.   Capitalism and socialism are distinguished primarily by the
    (a)   ownership of labor.
    (b)   number of political parties.
    (c)   ownership of capital.
    (d)   distribution of income throughout society.

_____   18.   The Russian transition to a market economy required all of the following EXCEPT
    (a)   deregulation of prices.
    (b)   privatization of the means of production.
    (c)   the institution of controls over wages.
    (d)   the removal of trade barriers.

_____   19.   In the early transitional phase to a free labor market and liberalization of prices we would most likely see all of the following EXCEPT
    (a)   increased risk of unemployment.
    (b)   increased instability in prices.
    (c)   increased instability in wages.
    (d)   reduced incentives to work.

_____   20.   Each of the following is seen as a requirement for a successful transition from socialism to a market-based economy EXCEPT
    (a)   macroeconomic stabilization.
    (b)   privatization.
    (c)   price regulation.
    (d)   a freely operating labor market.

II. APPLICATION QUESTIONS

The nations of Arboc and Arbez each produce shirts (S) and potatoes (P). The production possibility frontier for Arboc is described by the equation $S = 60 - 2P$. The production possibility frontier for Arbez is described by the equation $S = 60 - 4P$.

1.   Draw a production possibility frontier graph that shows all the points that are feasible for Arboc. Put "shirts" on the vertical axis and "potatoes" on the horizontal axis. Draw a separate ppf diagram for Arbez. Include the values at the end points of the ppf in each case.

2.   Arboc has a constant-cost production possibility frontier. How do you know?

3.   Is the product mix of 20 shirts and 20 units of potatoes on Arboc's production possibility frontier? If not, is it a feasible output mix?

4.   On the Arbocali production possibility frontier, what is the opportunity cost of each unit of potatoes?

5.   On the Arbezani production possibility frontier, what is the opportunity cost of each unit of potatoes?

6.   Which country has a comparative advantage in the production of shirts? Which country has a comparative advantage in the production of potatoes?

7.   If the terms of trade were one unit of potatoes traded for one shirt, what would be the pattern of trade?

8. If the terms of trade were one unit of potatoes traded for three shirts, what would be the pattern of trade?

9. Now assume Arboc becomes more efficient and can double its output of both shirts and potatoes. Which good(s) should Arboc now produce and trade? Explain your answer.

10. Explain what will happen to the opportunity cost of shirts in Arbez if a new high-yielding hybrid potato is introduced into Arbez.

Review Test SOLUTIONS

I. SOLUTIONS TO MULTIPLE-CHOICE QUESTIONS

1. (a) The tax will push up the price of the import. This will increase the demand for substitutes.

2. (c) Refer to pages 422-424 [676-678] for the statement of the case for free trade.

3. (d) Typically, tariffs are for the protection of producers, not for the benefit of consumers. A tariff doesn't increase costs of production, as such, for a foreign producer, but rather increases the costs of marketing the good.

4. (c) England can produce absolutely more cloth and more wine per worker than Portugal can.

5. (c) Six bottles take the inputs that could have produced 9 yards of cloth, therefore 1 bottle costs 1½ yard of cloth.

6. (d) The English opportunity cost of 1 bottle of wine is 2 yards of cloth. Portugal's opportunity cost of 1 bottle of wine is 1½ yards of cloth.

7. (b) The English opportunity cost of 1 bottle of wine is 2 yards of cloth. Portugal's opportunity cost of 1 bottle of wine is 1½ yards of cloth.

8. (a) The English opportunity cost of 1 bottle of wine is 2 yards of cloth—it doesn't pay to produce wine. Similarly for Portugal, because 1 bottle of wine costs 1½ yards of cloth.

9. (b) The English opportunity cost of 1 bottle of wine is 2 yards of cloth—it pays to produce cloth and trade it for wine. For Portugal, because 1 bottle of wine costs 1½ yards of cloth, it pays to produce wine and trade it for cloth.

10. (c) Each country will beable to consume a combination of goods beyond its production possibility frontier and use its resources in the least costly (more efficient) manner.

11. (c) England can produce twice as many units of cloth as units of wine. Portugal can produce 3 units of cloth for every 2 units of wine.

12. (a) The maximum production levels for cloth are equal, and wine production is greater in Portugal, but those considerations do not get to the heart of absolute advantage. England uses fewer resources per yard of cloth and per bottle of wine—just as we concluded in Question 4.

13. (b) In Britain, imported sweaters cost $120 and vests cost $200—sweaters are cheaper in Britain; vests are cheaper in the United States.

14. (d) High-cost fertilizer will reduce the ability of the rice farmers to compete with foreign rice.

15. (b) This is typical of import substitution.

16. (b) Free and fair democratic elections (a political issue) are not part of the list of basic requirements.

17. (c) In a capitalist system, ownership of the means of production (capital and land) is in the hands of capitalists and in the hands of the state under a communist system.

18. (c) For the market economy to function correctly, both wages and prices must be free to adjust.

19. (d) The move from a planned economy to a market economy involves risk.

20. (c) To achieve efficiency, prices must be permitted to adjust to changes in demand and supply.

II. SOLUTIONS TO APPLICATION QUESTIONS

1. Refer to the following diagram.

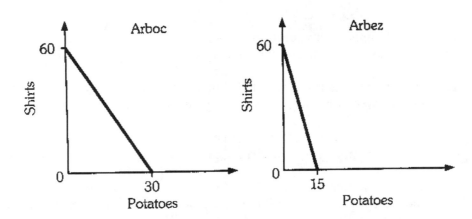

2. Arboc's production possibility frontier graphs as a straight line—the trade-off resources are switched between goods.

3. The product mix of 20 shirts and 20 units of potatoes is feasible and on the production possibility frontier. If 20 shirts are produced (using one-third of Arboc's resources), the other two-thirds can be employed producing potatoes.

4. In Arboc, each unit of potatoes costs 2 shirts.

5. In Arbez, each unit of potatoes costs 4 shirts.

6. Arbez has a comparative advantage in the production of shirts whereas Arboc country has a comparative advantage in the production of potatoes.

7. If the terms of trade were one unit of potatoes traded for one shirt, both countries would wish to produce and trade shirts.

8. If the terms of trade were one unit of potatoes traded for three shirts, Arboc would gain by producing potatoes and Arbez would gain by specializing in shirt production.

9. The opportunity cost of shirts and potatoes has not changed in Arboc, therefore Arbez retains its comparative advantage in the production of shirts.